CONTINUITY AND CHANGE
IN EU LAW

Continuity and Change in EU Law

Essays in Honour of Sir Francis Jacobs

Edited by
ANTHONY ARNULL
PIET EECKHOUT
and
TAKIS TRIDIMAS

Foreword by
Lord Bingham of Cornhill

UNIVERSITY PRESS

OXFORD
UNIVERSITY PRESS

Great Clarendon Street, Oxford OX2 6DP

Oxford University Press is a department of the University of Oxford.
It furthers the University's objective of excellence in research, scholarship,
and education by publishing worldwide in

Oxford   New York

Auckland Cape Town Dar es Salaam Hong Kong Karachi
Kuala Lumpur Madrid Melbourne Mexico City Nairobi
New Delhi Shanghai Taipei Toronto

With offices in

Argentina Austria Brazil Chile Czech Republic France Greece
Guatemala Hungary Italy Japan Poland Portugal Singapore
South Korea Switzerland Thailand Turkey Ukraine Vietnam

Oxford is a registered trade mark of Oxford University Press
in the UK and in certain other countries

Published in the United States
by Oxford University Press Inc., New York

© The Several Contributors, 2008

The moral rights of the authors have been asserted

Crown copyright material is reproduced under Class Licence
Number C01P0000148 with the permission of OPSI
and the Queen's Printer for Scotland

Database right Oxford University Press (maker)

First published 2008

All rights reserved. No part of this publication may be reproduced,
stored in a retrieval system, or transmitted, in any form or by any means,
without the prior permission in writing of Oxford University Press,
or as expressly permitted by law, or under terms agreed with the appropriate
reprographics rights organization. Enquiries concerning reproduction
outside the scope of the above should be sent to the Rights Department,
Oxford University Press, at the address above

You must not circulate this book in any other binding or cover
and you must impose the same condition on any acquirer

British Library Cataloguing in Publication Data

Data available

Library of Congress Cataloging in Publication Data

Data available

Typeset by Newgen Imaging Systems (P) Ltd., Chennai, India
Printed in Great Britain
on acid-free paper by
Biddles Ltd., King's Lynn

ISBN 978–0–19–921903–2

1 3 5 7 9 10 8 6 4 2

Foreword

It was not until 1972, with enactment of the European Communities Act 1972 and the entry of the UK into the Common Market, that British lawyers generally had occasion to look in any serious way at the European Court of Justice, the central legal institution of this (to us) novel regime. On doing so, they found several unfamiliar features. None, perhaps, was more unfamiliar than the office of Advocate General. Was he, as the job title suggested, a super-advocate, a permanent *amicus curiae,* enjoying special advocacy rights like the Attorney General in England and Wales in former days? Or was he in effect, despite his job title, a judge of first instance, giving his own judgment on the issues to be decided and the result to be achieved, so as to guide but not bind the Court, the Advocate General himself being a member of the Court and not in essence an advocate, and certainly not a partisan advocate?

This second description was plainly nearer the mark, and the UK recognized the importance of the office from the outset by sending its brightest and best to fill the UK's Advocate General slot at Luxembourg. Jean-Pierre Warner, Advocate General from 1973–81, filled the office with notable distinction, as did Gordon Slynn from 1981–8. But none has filled it with greater distinction than Francis Jacobs, to whose manifold achievements this wide-ranging book is powerful testimony.

Francis's career can be seen in retrospect to be the product of intelligent design. For having garnered a rich harvest of academic laurels, he spent two years at the European Commission of Human Rights at Strasbourg and then, in the very early days of British membership, two years as a legal secretary at the ECJ in Luxembourg. Thus armed, he became Professor of European Law at King's College London, a chair which he held from 1974 until his appointment as Advocate General in 1988. But Francis was no study-bound stay-at-home academic. He combined his professorial duties with an active European practice, making frequent appearances in the ECJ and making his invaluable expertise available to a number of leading counsel less well versed than he in the niceties of Community law, until he himself took silk in 1984.

Francis does not, apparently, hold the record for length of service in the Court at Luxembourg. But his almost record-breaking term of 18 years as Advocate General, from 1988 to 2006, a period of dramatic change, has served to highlight how important the role of Advocate General is in the European firmament, but also (in one sense at least) how enviable. For European practice requires the judges to speak with a single voice, the voice of a committee. No doubt there are occasions when a judge produces an immaculate draft judgment to which all members enthusiastically assent with minimal amendment. But anecdote suggests that this is not the invariable, or even the common, course of events, a fact which will not surprise those with experience of sitting in multi-judge courts where dissents are permitted. And so the judges must struggle to find words which will satisfy the majority, perhaps reflecting the doubts of some and the reservations of others. The eventual text may represent a triumph of judicial diplomacy, but may also betray an element of opacity and obscurity to which even judicial diplomats may on occasion have recourse.

The Advocates General are subject to no such inhibitions. They speak with their own voices, not through the medium of a committee. Thus while the voice of the individual judge can scarcely be heard in the judgment of the Court (and is not intended to be so), and the contribution of individual judges to the jurisprudence of the Court is ordinarily hard to assess, the views of the Advocate General are, for better or worse, like those of the first instance judge, fully exposed to public, professional and judicial scrutiny.

Of course, the Advocate General has no licence to behave irresponsibly. He or she is bound to respect the existing case law of the Court and will be slow to suggest departures from existing authority or radical changes of direction. But the opportunity exists to nudge the Court towards new conclusions, to raise new ideas, to throw doubt on accepted orthodoxy, to bring a single judgment, coherent and informed, to bear on the complex and various problems which confront the Court.

This is an opportunity of which Francis has taken full advantage, very much to the benefit of the law, the ECJ and those (which is all of us) whose lives are touched by the decisions made in Luxembourg. The contributions to this book contain numerous references to cases in which the observations of Advocate General Jacobs, usually but not invariably followed by the Court, have illuminated the topic under discussion.

This is a very interesting collection of essays. It is also a fitting tribute to one of the most illustrious and influential figures in the history of the ECJ.

Tom Bingham

House of Lords
15 October 2007

Preface

This collection of essays commemorates the work of Professor Sir Francis Jacobs, KCMG, QC, one of Europe's most distinguished scholars and practitioners of European Union law. Francis Jacobs began his academic career in 1963, when he took up a post as Lecturer in Jurisprudence at the University of Glasgow. Two years later, he moved to the London School of Economics, where he remained for four years. There then followed an interlude which set the tone for the rest of his career. From 1969–72, he worked in Strasbourg in the Secretariat of the European Commission of Human Rights and the Legal Directorate of the Council of Europe. On the accession of the United Kingdom to the European Communities, he moved to Luxembourg as référendaire to the first British Advocate General at the European Court of Justice, J-P Warner. During this time, he completed work on the first edition of his classic work, *The European Convention on Human Rights*, published by Oxford University Press in 1975. Francis's duties as a référendaire were more varied than those of some of his successors and included the purchase of furniture for Advocate General Warner's chambers. It included a table his family insisted was necessary 'to put things on'. The table was still there when Francis moved into the same chambers as a member of the Court some 15 years later, though he rarely put anything on it.

In 1974, Francis left the Court to take up a Chair in European Law at King's College London, where he remained until 1988. During that period, he was enormously productive. In the year following his arrival, he published (with Andrew Durand) *References to the European Court: Practice and Procedure* (1975), a revised reprint from *Atkin's Court Forms*, and in 1976 an important edited collection entitled *European Law and the Individual* (1976). It was while he was at King's that he and Neville Brown (who somehow persuaded him to become a supporter of Wolverhampton Wanderers Football Club) wrote their seminal book, *The Court of Justice of the European Communities*, the first edition of which was published in 1977. Francis's time at King's also saw the launch, under his editorship, of the *Yearbook of European Law* in 1981 and the Oxford European Community Law Series (now the Oxford EC Law Library) in 1986.

Alongside his flourishing career as an academic, Francis began in 1974 to develop a highly successful practice at the English Bar, taking silk in 1984. Anyone discussing with him in the late 1980s important decisions of the English courts on points of Community law, or cases in Luxembourg in which the United Kingdom had been involved, was likely to find that he had acted for one or other of the parties. He was made a Bencher of the Middle Temple in 1990.

Francis's achievements as a scholar and a barrister had made him a well-known figure among both academic and practising lawyers, but it was the activity to which he was to devote the next period of his professional life that enabled him to make such a profound and durable contribution to the development of the law in Europe. In 1988, Lord Mackenzie Stuart, the first British Judge at the Court of Justice and its President since 1984, retired and was succeeded by Sir Gordon Slynn, until then the British Advocate General. On 7 October 1988, Francis was sworn in as Sir Gordon Slynn's successor and went on to serve as Advocate General at the Court until 10 January 2006, making him the second longest serving Advocate General (after Advocate General Roemer) in the history of the institution and one of its longest serving members.

The role of an Advocate General, in cases to which he or she is assigned, is normally to give an independent opinion on the issues raised by the case and to recommend an outcome to the Judges, with whom Advocates General enjoy equal status. As the work of a single author, the opinion of the Advocate General often provides a richer analysis of a case than the judgment, whose collegiate character tends to make it terser and more formal. Opinions of Advocates General may be cited in future cases before the Community Courts and the national courts and are frequently the subject of analysis by academic commentators. Francis's opinions were characterized by their intellectual rigour, clarity and inventiveness. Hardly any aspect of the Court's case law was untouched by their influence, although it has perhaps been especially marked in the areas of judicial review, fundamental rights, freedom of movement and intellectual property. His willingness to tackle directly many of the conundrums which so perplex commentators and practitioners was widely admired and his opinions are frequently discussed in the academic literature.

Francis's retirement as Advocate General in 2006 (and return to academic life as Professor of Law at King's College London) makes the publication of a collection of essays in his honour appropriate and timely. The theme of this collection is continuity and change in EU law over broadly the period during which Francis served as Advocate General. That period saw momentous changes in the character of the Union. It encompassed the Treaty of Maastricht, which superimposed the Union on the pre-existing European Community, as well as the Treaties of Amsterdam and Nice; the proclamation of the Union's Charter of Fundamental Rights; the drafting of the Treaty establishing a Constitution for Europe; the creation of the Court of First Instance and the Civil Service Tribunal; the completion of the single market, and the enlargement of the Union to 15 Member States in 1995 and 25 Member States in 2004. It also witnessed a profound change in the nature of much academic scholarship on the law of the Union. At the same time, the Court continues in the 21st century to grapple with issues which preoccupied it in the 1980s, such as the effect of directives, the circumstances in which individuals should be permitted to seek the annulment of measures adopted by the Union's institutions and the scope of the Treaty rules on freedom of movement.

Some of these issues are discussed in this collection. It is divided into five parts examining respectively: institutional questions; fundamental rights; the internal market and economic and monetary union; external relations; and general issues. The contributors are drawn from a variety of constituencies, including the national and European judiciaries, legal practice and the academic world. We hope that the variety of the contributors' backgrounds and the topicality of the general theme will appeal to both academic and practising lawyers throughout Europe and beyond with an interest in the European Union and its legal system.

We all at different periods served as référendaires in Francis's chambers at the Court of Justice. Like his other référendaires, we found working there fascinating and immensely rewarding. Francis was an ideal boss, always courteous, always patient, always willing to discuss the law (and other matters), always willing to read and comment on our draft publications notwithstanding the many other demands on his time. His own first book, *Criminal Responsibility* (1971), was not concerned with European law at all. According to the introduction, its object was 'to examine the concept of responsibility in the light of the modern development of the criminal law'. A preface by the great HLA Hart (Francis's DPhil supervisor at Oxford in the early 1960s) commented on 'Dr Jacobs's rare combination of legal scholarship and philosophical acumen'. By the time he had become an Advocate General, he had added to those qualities an encyclopaedic understanding of European law and the incisiveness of a top QC. It was a pleasure and a privilege to work for him.

AA
PE
TT

September 2007

Contents

Table of Cases — xv
Table of Treaties and Legislation — li
List of Abbreviations — lxi
List of Contributors — lxv

I. INSTITUTIONAL QUESTIONS

1. The Functioning of the Court of Justice in an Enlarged Union and the Future of the Court — 3
   Konrad Schiemann

2. The Changing Role of the Advocate General — 20
   Eleanor Sharpston

3. The Court of First Instance, its Development, and Future Role in the Legal Architecture of the European Union — 34
   Nicholas Forwood

4. Litigating in Luxembourg and the Role of the Advocate at the Court of Justice — 48
   David Vaughan and Margaret Gray

5. *Locus Standi* of Individuals under Article 230(4): The Return of Euridice? — 70
   Takis Tridimas and Sara Poli

6. The EFTA Court, the ECJ, and the Latter's Advocates General – a Tale of Judicial Dialogue — 90
   Carl Baudenbacher

II. FUNDAMENTAL RIGHTS

7. The Role of the ECJ in the Protection of Fundamental Rights — 125
   Antonio Tizzano

8. The Strasbourg Perspective and its Effect on the Court of Justice: Is Mutual Respect Enough? — 139
   Robin CA White

9. The EU Charter of Fundamental Rights, Not Binding but Influential: the Example of Good Administration — 157
   Jacqueline Dutheil de la Rochère

10. Administrative Justice and Standards of Substantive
    Judicial Review   172
    Jeffrey Jowell

III. INTERNAL MARKET AND ECONOMIC AND MONETARY UNION

11. The Definition of Measures Having Equivalent Effect   189
    Laurence W Gormley
12. The Concept of Abuse in the Freedom of Establishment of
    Companies: a Case of Double Standards?   205
    Vanessa Edwards and Paul Farmer
13. Recurring Cycles in the Internal Market: Some Reflections
    on the Free Movement of Services   228
    Andrea Biondi
14. Continuity and Change in the Law Relating to Services   243
    David Edward and Niamh Nic Shuibhne
15. The Financial Services Single Market and the Interface between
    Community Law and Domestic Law   260
    Eva Lomnicka
16. Equal Before the Law? Not if You Want to Register a Trade Mark   283
    David T Keeling
17. The Evolution of Economic and Monetary Union – Some
    Legal Issues   297
    JA Usher

IV. EXTERNAL RELATIONS

18. A Panorama of Two Decades of EU External Relations Law   323
    Piet Eeckhout
19. Multilevel Constitutionalism and Judicial Protection of Freedom
    and Justice in the International Economic Law of the EC   338
    Ernst-Ulrich Petersmann
20. Dual-use Goods: (Mis)Understanding *Werner* and *Leifer*   354
    Alan Dashwood
21. Direct Effect of Treaties in the US and the EU, the Case of the
    WTO: Some Perceptions and Proposals   361
    John H Jackson

V. GENERAL ISSUES

22. The European Court, the Brussels Convention/Regulation and the Establishment of an Efficient System for International Litigation in Europe 385
 Trevor C Hartley

23. About Rules and Principles, Codification and Legislation, Harmonization and Convergence, and Education in the Area of Contract Law 400
 Walter van Gerven

24. The Americanization of EU Law Scholarship 415
 Anthony Arnull

25. The Effect of EU Law on the Italian Courts 432
 Giuseppe Tesauro

26. The Effect of European Community Law on Irish Law and the Irish Constitution 446
 Nial Fennelly

Index 463

Table of Cases

European Court of Justice and Court of First Instance—A-Z order

A-Punkt Schmuckhandels GmbH v Schmidt, Case C-444/04 [2006] ECR I-nyr
 (23 February 2006) 201
Abertal and Others v Council, Case C-264/91 [1993] ECR I-3265 74
Abler, Case C-340/01 [2003] ECR I-14023 119
Agip Petroli, Case C-456/04 [2006] ECR I-3395 207
Ahokainen & Leppik v Virallinen syyttäjä, Case C-434/04 [2006] ECR I-nyr
 (28 September 2006) 97, 101, 193, 198
Åklagaren v Mickelsson & Roos, Case C-142/05 (pending, opinion of
 14 December 2006) 202
Akrich, Case C-109/01 [2003] ECR I-9607 .... 142, 206, 212, 227
Aktien-Zukerfabrik Schöppenstedt v Council, Case 5/71 [1971] ECR 975 190
Alabaster, Case C-147/02 [2004] ECR I-3101 26
Albany, Case C-67/96 [1999] ECR I-5751 117
Alfa Vita Vassilopoulos AE et al v Elliniko Dimosio, Nommarkhiaki Aftodiikisi Ioanninon,
 Joined Cases C-158 and 159/04 [2006] ECR I-nyr (14 September 2006) 190, 193, 198
Algera et al v Common Assembly, Joined Cases 7/56 and 3–7/57 [1957–58] ECR 39 190
Alpharma v Council, Case T-70/99 [2002] ECR II-3495 .... 84, 85, 95, 106
Alpine Investments BV v Minister van Financiën, Case C-384/93 [1995]
 ECR I-1141 .... 199, 231, 232, 238, 244, 248,
 253, 255, 256, 267, 272
Altmark Trans, Case C-280/00 [2003] ECR I-7747 98
AM & S Europe Ltd v Commission, Case 155/79 [1982] ECR 1575 .... 66, 190
Amministrazione Finanze dello Stato v Simmenthal, Case 106/77 [1978] ECR 629 .... 437, 440
Amurta, Case C-379/05 110
ANAV, C-410/04 [2005] ECR I-3303 234
Andersson, Case C-321/97 [1999] ECR I-3551 .... 101, 102
Angonese v Cassa di Risparmio di Bolzano, Case C-281/98 [2000] ECR I-4139 248
Anomar and Others, Case C-6/01 [2003] ECR I-8621 229
Aragonesa de Publicidad Exterior SA et al v Departamento de Sanidad y Seguridad
 Social de la Generalitat de Cataluña, Cases C-1/90 and C-176/90 [1991]
 ECR I-4151 .... 193, 194, 197, 198
Arblade and Others, criminal proceedings against, Case 369/96 [1999] ECR I-8453 247
ARE Case see Commission v Germany
Area Cova and others v Council, Cases C-300/99 P and C-388/99 P [2001] ECR I-983 78
Armement Coopératif Artisanal Vendéen (ACAV), Case T-138/98 [2000] II-341 78
Arnaud and Others v Council, Case C-131/92 [1993] ECR I-2573 74
Asia Motor France, Case T-28/90 [1992] ECR II-2285 33
Association des Centres Distributeurs Edouard Leclerc v Au Blé Vert Sàrl,
 Case 229/83 [1985] ECR 1 .... 191, 206, 209, 217
Associazione Industrie Siderurgique Italiane (ASSIDER) v High Authority,
 Case 3/54 [1954–56] ECR 63 190
Atochem, Case T-3/89 [1991] ECR II-1177 33
Austria v Commission, Case C-99/98 [2001] ECR I-1101 115
Automec, T-24/90 [1992] ECR II-2223 33

xvi   *Table of Cases*

Bacardi France v Télévision française 1 SA (TF1), Groupe Jean-Claude Darmon SA and
    Girosport SARL, Case C-429/02 [2004] ECR I-6613........................ 257
Bactria Industriehygiene-Service Verwaltungs GmbH v Commission Case T-339/00
    [2002] ECR II-2287... 78, 85
Badeck, Case C-158/97 [2000] ECR I-1875...................................... 116
Banca popolare di Cremona, Case C-475/03 [2006] ECR I-9373.................... 61
Banchero, Case C-387/93 [1995] ECR I-4663.................................... 198
Barber v Guardian Royal Exchange, Case C-262/88 [1990] ECR I-1889............. 65
BASF AG v Präsident des Deutschen Patentamts, Case C-44/98 [1999] ECR I-6269 203
BASF, Case T-4/89 [1991] ECR II-1523.. 33
BECTU, Case C-178/99 [2001] ECR I-4881...................................... 164
Béguelin Import, Case 22/71 [1971] ECR 949................................... 237
Belgium v Humbel, Case 263/86 [1988] ECR 5365............................... 251
Belgium v Spain, Case C-388/95 [2000] ECR I-3123....................... 193, 203
Bellio Fratelli v Prefettura di Treviso, Case C-286/02 [2004]
    ECR I-3465..................................... 91, 95, 104, 106, 107, 108, 119
Berthu v Commission, Case T-175/96 [1997] ECR II-811......................... 309
BEUC v Commission, Case T-256/97 [2000] ECR II-101.......................... 331
Bickel and Franz, criminal proceedings against, Case C-274/96 [1998] ECR I-7637 253
Bidar v London Borough of Ealing; Secretary of State for Education and Skills,
    Case C-209/03 [2005] ECR I-2119............................. 165, 244, 251, 252
Blesgen, Case 75/81 [1982] ECR 1211.................................. 193, 195, 203
Bluhme, criminal proceedings against, Case C-67/97 [1998] ECR I-8033......... 256
Boehringer, Case C-143/00 [2002] ECR I-3759................................. 110
Boehringer Ingelheim II, Case C-348/04, judgment of 26 April 2007......... 97, 100, 110
Bond van Adverteerders v Netherlands, Case 352/85 [1988] ECR 2085............. 251
Booker Aquaculture and Hydro Seafood, Joined Cases C-20/00 and C-64/00 [2003]
    ECR I-7411... 165
Bosphorus Hava Yollari Turuzm v Minister for Transport, Case C-84/95 [1996]
    ECR I-3953... 27, 459, 460
Bouchoucha, Case C-61/89 [1990] ECR I-3551...................... 206, 207, 209, 217
Brasserie du Pêcheur/Factortame III, Joined Cases C-46 and C-48/93 [1996]
    ECR I-1029... 52, 443, 456
Brentjens, Joined Cases C-115/97, C-116/97 and C-117/97 [1999] ECR I-6025..... 117
Briheche (Serge) v Ministère de l'intérieur, de la sécurité intérieure et des libertés locales,
    Case 319/03 [2004] ECR I-8807....................................... 103
Brzeziński, Maciej, Case C-313/05 [2007] ECR I-0000.......................... 240
Buet & Educational Business Services (EBS) SARL v Ministère public, Case 382/87
    [1989] ECR 1235.. 194, 197, 198
Bulk Oil v Sun International, Case 174/84 [1986] ECR 559..................... 355
Bundesverband der Nahrungsmittel, Case T-391/02, Order of 10 May 2004
    [2004] ECR II-1447... 84
BUPA Hospitals, Case C-419/02 [2006] ECR I-1685........................ 207, 212
Buralux v Council, Case C-209/94 P [1996] ECR I-615................ 73, 74, 75, 81
Burmanjer, Criminal proceedings against, Case C-20/03 [2005]
    ECR I-4133.. 201, 246, 250, 256
Cadbury Schweppes, Case C-196/04 [2006] ECR I-7995 .... 213, 214, 217, 218, 219, 220,
                                                              221, 222, 224, 225, 226
Caixa-Bank France v Ministère de l'Économie, Case C-442/02 [2004] ECR I-8961........ 267
Calfa, Case C-348/96 [1999] ECR I-11... 236
Calpak v Commission, Joined Cases 789 and 790/79 [1980] ECR 1949.............. 72
Campo Ebro v Council, Case T-472/93 [1995] ECR II-421..................... 73, 74

Table of Cases

Campus Oil and Others v Minister for Industry and Energy, Case 72/83 [1984]
ECR 2727 356
Canal Satélite Digital v Adminstración General del Estado, and Distribuidora de
Televisión Digital SA (DTS), Case C-390/99 [2002] ECR I-607 246
Candolin, Case C-537/03 [2005] ECR I-5745 .... 99–100, 109, 121, 122
Carbonati Apuani, Case 72/03 [2004] ECR I-8027 26
Carpenter v Secretary of State for the Home Department, Case 60/00 [2002]
ECR I-6279 .... 229, 252
Cassa Nazionale di Previdenza ed Assistenza a favore degli avvocati e dei Procuratori v
Council, Case 87/95P [1996] ECR I-2003 78
Cassis de Dijon *see* Rewe-Zentral AG v Bundesmonopolverwaltung für Branntwein,
Case 120/78
Casteels v Commission, Case 40/84 [1985] ECR 667 86
Centro Servizi Spediporto Srl v Spedizione Marittima del Golfo Srl, Case C-96/94
[1995] ECR I-2883 .... 203, 240
Centro-Con *see* Queen, *ex parte* Centro-Com v HM Treasury and Bank of England,
Case C-124/95
Centros, Case C-212/97 [1999] ECR I-2357 .... 210, 211, 215, 216, 218, 219,
220, 221, 222, 224, 225, 247
Chemie Linz, Case T-15/89 [1992] ECR II-1275 33
Chemische Afvalstoffen Dusseldorp BV et al v Minister van Volkshuisvesting, Ruimtelijke
Ordening en Milieubeheer, Case C-203/96 [1988] ECR I-4075 191
Chen *see* Zhu and Chen v Secretary of State for the Home Department, Case C-200/02
Chenobyl case *see* Parliament v Council (Chernobyl case)
Chiquita, Case T-19/01 [2005] ECR II-315 .... 334, 336
Christel Schmidt, Case C-392/92 [1994] ECR I-1311 107
CILFIT v Ministry of Health, Case 283/81 [1982] ECR 3415 5
Cinéthèque SA v Federation Nationale des Cinémas Français, Joined Cases 60 and
61/84 [1985] ECR 2605 127
Cipolla and Others, Cases C-94/04 and C-202/04 [2006] ECR I-11421 229
CIRFS and Others v Commission, Cases C-313/90 [1993] ECR I-1125 88
CMC Motorradcenter GmbH v Baskiciogullari, Case C-93/9 [1993]
ECR I-5009 .... 203, 256
CNL v HAG GF, Case C-10/89 [1990] ECR I-3711 .... 27, 65, 70, 190
Coca Cola Company, Case R 1206/2006–2, 22 December 2006 295
Coditel and others v Cine-Vog Films and Others, Case 262/81 [1982] ECR 3381 268
Codorniu v Council Case C-309/89 [1994] ECR I-1853 .... 72, 73, 77, 80, 84, 85, 89
Cofaz and Others v Commission, Case 169/84 [1986] ECR 391 .... 87, 88
Coillte Teoranta, Case T-244/00 [2001] ECR II-1275 79
Colim, Case C-33/97 [1999] ECR I-3175 199
Comafrica SpA and Dole Fresh Fruit Europe Ltd & Co v Commission, Joined
Cases T-198/95, T-171/96, T-230/97, T-174/98 and T-225/99 [2001] II-1975 78
Commission v Anic Partecipazioni, Case C-49/92 P [1999] ECR I-4125 309
Commission v Austria, Case C-147/03 [2005] ECR I-5969 .... 206, 212, 252
Commission v Belgium, Case C-2/90 (Walloon waste case) [1992] ECR I-4431
(Walloon waste) 191, 193
Commission v Belgium, Case C-211/91 [1992] ECR I-6757 224
Commission v Council, Case 22/70 (ERTA Case) [1971] ECR 263 76
Commission v Council, Case C-25/94 [1996] ECR I-1469 159
Commission v Council, Case C-176/03 [2005] ECR I-7879 .... 165, 329
Commission v Council, Case C-27/04, 13 July 2004 318
Commission v Council, Case C-91/05 (pending) 328

xviii *Table of Cases*

Commission v Denmark, Case C-47/88 [1990] ECR I-4509 240
Commission v Denmark, Case C-192/01 [2003] ECR I-9693 .... 94, 96, 99, 106, 107, 113, 119, 193
Commission v Denmark, Case C-464/02 [2005] ECR I-7929 224
Commission v ECB, Case C-11/00, 10 July 2003 312
Commission v Finland, Case C-54/05 [2007] ECR I-nyr (15 March 2007) 193
Commission v France [1998] I-5325 116
Commission v France, Case 173/83 [1985] ECR 491 203
Commission v France, Case 252/83 [1986] ECR 3663 267
Commission v France, Case 269/83 [1985] ECR 837 202
Commission v France, Case 188/84 [1986] ECR 419 203
Commission v France, Case C-381/93 [1994] ECR I-5145 235
Commission v France, Case C-265/95 [1997] ECR I-6959 .... 202, 248
Commission v France, Case C-184/96 [1998] ECR I-6197 203
Commission v France, Case C-24/00 [2004] ECR I-1277 .... 96, 119, 203
Commission v Germany, Case C-205/84 [1986] ECR 3755 267
Commission v Germany, Case C-61/94 [1996] ECR I-3989 330
Commission v Germany, Case C-78/03 P (ARE Case), judgment of
  13 December 2005 .... 71, 82, 87, 88
Commission v Greece, Case C-391/92 [1995] ECR I-1621 .... 197, 198, 199
Commission v Greece, Case C-120/94 [1996] ECR I-1513 .... 27, 327–328
Commission v Greece, Case C-375/95 [1997] ECR I-5981 240
Commission v Greece, Case C-82/05 [2006] ECRI-nyr (14 September 2006) 199
Commission v Greece, Case C-178/05, judgment of 7 June 2007 207
Commission v Ireland, Case 13/80 [1981] ECR 1625 191
Commission v Italy, Case 103/84 [1986] ECR 1759 202
Commission v Italy, Case C-101/94 [1996] ECR I-2691 267
Commission v Italy, Case C-35/96 [1998] ECR I-3851; TAR Lazio, Section I,
  27 March 1996, n 476 442
Commission v Italy, Case C-49/00 [2001] ECR I-8575 165
Commission v Italy, Case C-421/01 [2003] ECR I-6445 193
Commission v Jégo-Quéré, Case C-263/02 P [2004] ECR I-3425, Opinion of
  10 July 2003 .... 136, 164
Commission v Netherlands, Case C-41/02 [2004] ECR I-11375 .... 95, 99, 119
Commission v Portugal, Case C-171/02 [2004] ECR I-5645 .... 212, 217
Commission v Portugal, Case C-345/05, judgment of 26 October 2006 .... 104, 119
Commission v Spain, Case C-12/00 [2003] ECR I-459 199
Commission v Sweden, Case C-104/06, judgment of 18 January 2007 nyr 119
Commission v Sytraval and Brink's France, Case C-367/95 P [1998] ECR I-1719 88
Commission v T-Mobile Austria GmbH, Case C-141/02 P, judgment
  of 22 February 2005 [2005] ECR I-1283 82
Commission v United Kingdom, Case 165/82 [1983] ECR 3431 129
Commission v United Kingdom, Case 207/83 (Origin marking case) [1985] ECR 1205 191
Commission v United Kingdom, Case C-246/89 R [1989] ECR 3125; [1991]
  REC I-4585 .... 52, 219, 226
Commission v United Kingdom, Case C-222/94 [1996] ECR I-4025 102
Commission v United Kingdom, Case C-466/98 [2002] ECR I-9427 61
Coname, Case C-231/03 [2005] ECR I-7287 234
Consorzio del Prosciutto di Parma and and Salumificio S Rita v Asda Stores Ltd and
  Hygrade Foods Ltd, Case C-108/01 [2003] ECR I-5121 248
Consorzio Industrie Fiammiferi v Autorità Garante Concorrenza e Mercato,
  Case C-198/01 [2003] ECR I-8055 440

Table of Cases   xix

Cook v Commission, Case C-198/91 [1993] ECR I-2487 88
Corsica Ferries France SA v Gruppo Antichi Ormeggiatori del Porto di Genova Coop.
  Arl et al (Corsica Ferries III), Case C-266 [1998] ECR I-3949 . . . . 203, 240
Corsten, Case C-58/98 [2000] ECR I-7919 . . . . .231, 247
Costa v Enel, Case 6/64 [1964] ECR 585. . . . . 127, 435, 440, 451
Cotter and McDermott v Minister for Social Welfare, Case C-377/89 [1991]
  ECR I-1155 455
Council of the City of Stoke-on-Trent et al v B & Q plc, Case C-169/91 [1992]
  ECR I-6635. . . . . .194, 197
Courage v Crehan, Case C-453/99 [2001] ECR I-6297. . . . . 58, 403
Cowan v Trésor Public, case 186/87 [1989] ECR 195. . . . . 236, 253
Cremer, Case 125/76 [1977] ECR 1593 207
Criminal proceedings against Arblade and Others, Case 369/96 [1999] ECR I-8453 247
Criminal proceedings against Bickel and Franz, Case C-274/96 [1998] ECR I-7637. 253
Criminal Proceedings against Bluhme, Case C-67/97 [1998] ECR I-8033 256
Criminal proceedings against Burmanjer, Case C-20/03 [2005] ECR I-4133 . . . . . 246, 250, 256
Criminal proceedings against Harry Franzén, C-189/95 [1997] ECR I-05909 . . . . . 102, 114, 119
Criminal proceedings against Jan-Erik Anders Ahokainen and Mati Leppik,
  Case C-434/04, judgment of 28 September 2006 . . . . 97, 101, 193, 198
Daily Mail, Case 81/87 [1988] ECR 5500 . . . . .219, 220, 226
Danish Beekeeping Case *see* Criminal Proceedings against Bluhme, Case C-67/97 [1998]
  ECR I-8033
De Coster, Case C-17/00 [2001] ECR I-9445. 232
De Danske Bilimportører, Case C-383/01 [2003] ECR I-6065 240
de Lasteyrie du Saillant, Case C-9/02 [2004] ECR I-2409. 213
Decker, Case C-120/95 [1998] ECR I-1831 . . . . 232, 233
Delattre, Case C-369/88 [1991] ECR I-1487 . . . . .194, 198
Deliège, Christelle, Cases C-51/96 and C-191/97 [2000] ECR I-2549. . . . . .239, 240, 256
Denkavit International BV Denkavit France SARL v Ministre de l'Economie, des
  Finances and de l'Industrie, Case C-170/05, 27 April 2006 nyr. 11, 113, 114, 119
Deutscher Apothekerverbund eV v 0800 Doc Morris NV et al, Case C-222/01 [2003]
  ECR I-14887 . . . . 200, 238
Deutz and Geldermann v Council, Case 26/86 [1987] ECR 941 . . . . 72, 74
D'Hoop v Office national de l'emploi, Case 224/98 [2002] ECR I-619 251
Diamantis, C-373/97 [2000] ECR I-1705 207
DIP SpA et al v Commune di Bassano di Grappa et al, Case-140/94 [1995]
  ECR I-3257 203
Donckerwolcke v Procureur de la République, Case 41/76 [1976] ECR 1921. . . . . 326, 355
DOW AgroSciences BV, Case T-45/02 [2003] ECR II-1973 84
Drijvende Bokken, case C-219/97 [1999] ECR I-6121 117
DSM, Case T-8/89 [1991] ECR II-1833 33
Du Pont de Nemours Italiana SpA v Unità Sanitaria Locale no. 2 di Carrara,
  Case C-21/88 [1990] ECR I-889 193
Dürbeck, Case 112/80 [1981] ECR 1095 352
Ebony Maritime SA and Loten Navigation Co Ltd v Prefetto della Provincia di
  Brindisi and others, Case C-177/95 [1996] ECR I-1111 125
Eichsfelder Schlachtbetrieb, C-515/03 [2005] ECR I-7355 207
Einfuhr- und Vorratsstelle für Getreide und Futtermittel v Köster, Case 25/70 [1970]
  ECR 1161. 127
Elsevier Inc ('BUILDING INSIGHTS. BREAKING BOUNDARIES'),
  Case R 407/2004–2 26 November 2004 . . . . 292, 293, 294
Emesa Sugar (Free Zone) NV v Aruba, Case 17/98 [2000] ECR I-665. . . . . 16, 143

Emmott v Minister for Social Welfare, Case C-208/90 [1991] ECR I-4269 455
Emsland-Stärke, Case C-110/99 [2000] I-11569 . . . . 207, 208, 212, 214, 223, 227
Enichem Anic, Case T-6/89 [1991] ECR II-1623 33
ERTA Case *see* Commission v Council (ERTA Case)
Esso Española SA v Comunidad Autonoma de Canarias, Case C-134/94 [1995]
 ECR I-4223. 203
Établissements Biret v Council, Case C-94/02 P [2003] ECR I-10565. 334
Établissements Toulorge, Case T-167/02 [2003] ECR II-1111 84
Éts Delhaize Frères et Compagnie Le Lion SA v Promalvin SA et al,
 Case C-47/90 [1992] ECR I-3669 (Rioja) 193, 203
European Federation for Cosmetic Ingredients, Case T-196/03 [2004]
 ECR II-4263 84
European Parliament *see* Parliament
Extramet Industrie v Council, Case C-356/89 [1991] ECR I-2501. . . . . 71, 72, 77, 80, 81
Factortame, *ex p*, Case C-213/89 [1990] ECR I-2433. . . . . 52, 56, 58, 76, 446, 452
Factortame II, C-221/89 [1991] ECR I-3905 . . . . .219, 226
Factortame III *see* Brasserie du Pêcheur/Factortame III, Joined Cases C-46/93 and
 C-48/93 [1996] ECR I-1029
Fédération Charbonnière de Belgique v High Authority, Case 8/55 [1954–56]
 ECR 245 189–190
Federatión de Cofradías de Pescadores de Guipúzcoa P-R, Case C-300/00 [2000]
 ECR I-8797 75
Federazione Nazionale del Commercio Oleario (Federolio), Case T-122/96 [1997]
 ECR II-1559. 78
Fediol v Commission, Case 70/87 [1989] ECR 1781 331
Ferreira, Case C-348/98 [2000] ECR I-6711 . . . . .108, 119
Ferrero oHG mbH v Duplo Corporation ('DUPLO/DUPLO'), Case R 802/1999–1
 5 June 2000 287
Ferring, Case C-53/00 [2001] ECR I-9067 98
Festersen, Case C-370/05, judgment of 25 January 2007. 130
Fidium Finanz AG v Bundesanstalt für Finanzdienstleistungsaufsicht,
 Case C-452/04 judgment of 3 October 2006. . . . . 96, 105, 302
Finanzamt Hamburg-Am Tierpark v Burda Verlagsbeteiligungen GmbH,
 Case C-284/06 (pending) 111
FKP Scorpio Konzertproduktionen GmbH v Finanzamt Hamburg-Eimsbüttel,
 Case C-290/04 [2006] ECR I-9461. . . . . 244, 246, 247, 257, 302
Fost Plus VZW, Case T-142/03, Order of 16 February 2005 [2005] ECR I-589. 84
France v High Authority, Case 1/54 [1954–56] ECR 1 . . . . 20, 21
Francesco Atzori, Giuseppe Atzeni, Giuseppe Ignazio Boi, Joint Cased C-346/03 and
 C-529/03 [2003] ECR II-6037 84
Francovich and Bonifaci v Italy, Cases C-6/90 and C-9/90 [1991]
 ECR I-5537 . . . . 440, 443, 444, 446, 455
Fratelli Costanzo v Comune di Milano, Case 103/88 [1989] ECR 1839. 440
Fruit Company v Commission, Joined Cases 41–44/70 [1971] ECR 411 72
Gambelli, Case c-243/01 [2003] ECR I-13031; Court of Cassation, United Criminal
 Sections 26 April 2004 n 23271. . . . . 236, 443
Gasser v MISRAT Case C-116/02, 9 December 2003 . . . . 389–390, 397
GB-INNO-BM v Confédération du commerce luxembourgeois, Case C-362/88
 [1990] ECR I-667 . . . . 194, 195, 198, 250
Gebhard v Consiglio dell' Ordine degli Avvocati e Procuratori di Milano,
 Case C-55/94 [1995] ECR I-4165 . . . . .249, 257, 344

Table of Cases

Geitling Ruhrkohlen-Verkaufsgesellschaft and Others v ECSC High Authority,
   Case 2/56 [1957] ECR 9. 126
Geitling v High Authority, Joined Cases 36–38/59 and 40/59 [1960] ECR 857. 126
GEMO, Case C-126/01 [2003] ECR I-13769 .... 98, 134
General Milk Products, Case C-8/92 [1993] ECR I-779 .... 207, 217
General Union of Personnel of European Organizations v Commission, Case 18/74
   [1974] ECR 933. 129
Germany v Parliament and Council, Case 376/98 [2000] ECR I-8419 242
Gilli & Andres, Case 788/79 [1980] ECR 2071 190
Gonnelli, Case T-231/02, Order of 2 April 2004 [2004] ECR II-1051 84
Gottrup-Klim, Case 250/92 [1994] ECR I-5641 239
Graf v Filmoser Maschinenbau GmbH, Case C-190/98 [2000] ECR I-493. 256
Graffione, Case C-313/94 [1996] I-2727 287
Grand Duchy of Luxembourg v European Parliament, Case 230/81 [1983] ECR 255 53
Grant v South-West Trains, Case C-249/96 [1998] ECR I-621 23
Greenham and Abel, C-95/01 [2004] ECR I-1333. .... 99, 113, 119, 203
Greenpeace, Council and Others v Commission, Case C-321/95 P [1998]
   ECR I-1651 .... 75, 78, 81
Groener v Minister for Education et al, Case C-379/89 [1989] ECR 3967 193
Groenveld (PB) BV v Produktschap voor Vee en Vlees, Case 15/79 [1979]
   ECR 3409 .... 202, 203, 248
Groupement des Industries Sidérugiques Luxembourgeoises v High Authority,
   Joined Cases 7 and 9/54 [1954–56] ECR 175 190
Groupement National des Négociants en Pommes de Terre (Belgapom) v ITM
   Belgium SA et al, Case C-63/94 [1995] ECR I-2467 .... 193, 198
Gruppo La Perla SpA v OHIM ('NIMEI LA PERLA MODERN CLASSIC/LA
   PERLA'), Case T-137/05, judgment of 16 May 2007 288
Grzelczyk v Centre public d'aide sociale d'Ottignies-Louvain-la-Neuve,
   Case C-184/99 [2001] ECR I-6193 251
Guimont, Case C-448/98 [2000] ECR I-10663 .... 203, 229
Güney-Görres, Joined Cases C-232/04 and C-233/04 [2005] ECR I-11237 .... 99, 119
HAG II, Case C-10/89 [1990] ECR I-3711 .... 27, 65, 70, 190
Halifax, Case C-255/02 [2006] ECR I-1609 .... 205, 206, 212, 214, 222, 223, 227
Hamburger Hafen- und Lagerhaus Aktiengesellschaft, Case T-69/96 [2001]
   ECR II-1037 78
Harry Franzén, criminal proceedings against, C-189/95 [1997] ECR I-05909 ..... 102, 114, 119
Hauptzollamt Mainz v Kupferberg, Case 104/81 [1982] ECR 3641. 330
Hautala, Case C-359/99 [2001] ECR I-9565 164
Her Majesty's Customs and Excise v Schindler, Case C-275/92 [1994] ECR I-1039 246
Hercules Chemicals v Commission, Case c-1/92 [1999] ECR I-4235 442
Hoechst AG v Commission, Joined Cases 46/87 and 227/88 [1989] ECR 2859. 142
Hoechst, Case T-10/89 [1992] ECR II-629 33
Houtwipper, Case C-293/93 [1994] ECR I-4249. 203
Hüls, Case T-9/89 [1992] ECR II-499 33
Hünermund et al v Landesapothekerkammer Baden-Württemberg,
   Case C-292/92 [1993] ECR I-6787 .... 190, 195, 198, 200, 202, 232, 258
Ikea Wholesale v Commissioners of Customs and Excise, Case C-351/04,
   opinion of 6 April 2006, para 87, judgment pending 335
Imperial Chemical Industries, Case C-264/96 [1998] ECR I-4695 .... 213, 214, 225
Imperial Chemical Industries, Case T-13/89 [1992] ECR II-1021 33
Ingmar GB Ltd v Eaton Leonard Technologies Inc, Case C-381/98 [2000] ECR I-9305 278

Inspire Art, Case C-167/01 [2003] ECR I-10155 .... 211, 216, 217, 218, 221, 223, 225, 226
Inter-Environnement Wallonie v Région Wallonne, Case C-129/96 [1997] ECR I-7411 27
International Business Machines Corporation v Commission, Case 60/81 [1981]
  ECR 2639 190
International Fruit Company v Produktschap voor Groenten en Fruit,
  Joined Cases 21–24/72 [1972] ECR 1219 330
International Transport Workers' Federation and the Finnish Seamen's Union v
  Viking Line ABP and Oü Viking Line Eesti, Case C-438/05, nyr 117
Internationale Handelsgesellschaft mbH v Einfuhr- und Vorratsstelle für Getreide und
  Futtermittel, Case 11/70 [1970] ECR 1125 .... 127, 129
Jan-Erik Anders Ahokainen and Mati Leppik, Case C-434.04, judgment of
  28 September 2006 .... 97, 101
JCB Services v Commission, Case C-167/04 P, judgment of 21 September 2006 125
Jebarah Kenneth trading as Screw You ('SCREW YOU'), Case R 495/2005–4G,
  6 July 2006 .... 287, 290
Jégo-Quéré v Commission, Case T-177/01 [2002] ECR II-2365 .... 77, 78, 79, 80–84, 89,
                                                                      134, 136, 164
Jersey Potato, Case C-293/02 [2005] ECR I-9543 229
JFE Engineering Corp v Commission, Joined Cases T-67/00, T-68/00, T-71/00 and
  T-78/00 [2004] ECR II-1575 163
Johnston (Marguerite) v Chief Constable of the Royal Ulster Constabulary,
  Case 222/84 [1986] ECR 1651 .... 76, 128, 142
Kaba v SSHD, Case C-466/00 [2003] ECR I-2219 .... 16, 18
Kadi v Council and Commission, Case T-315/01 [2005] ECR II-3649 ... 328, 333, 334, 336, 343
Kahn Scheppvaart BV v Commission, Case T-398/94 [1996] ECR II-447 80
Kalanke, Case C-450/93 [1996] ECR I-3051 116
Kapniki A Michailidis AE, Case T-100/94 [1998] ECR II-3115 78
Karner Industrie-Auktionen GmbH v Troostwijk GmbH, Case C-71/02 [2004]
  ECR I-3025 246
KB v The National Health Service Pensions Agency and the Secretary of State for
  Health, Case C-11701 [2004] ECR I-541 .... 23, 167
Keck & Mithouard, Joined Cases C-267/91 and 268/91 [1993] ECR I-6097 ...... 190, 195–198,
                                                                      199, 201, 202, 203, 204, 228,
                                                                      237, 238, 240, 241, 244,
                                                                      254, 255, 256, 259
Kefalas, Case C-367/96 [1998] ECR I-2843 .... 206, 207
Keller Holding, Case C-471/04, judgment of 23 February 2006 .... 104, 119
Kesko Oy v Commission, Case T-22/97 [1999] ECR II-3775 53
Kledingverkoopbedrijf de Geus en Uitdenbogerd v Robert Bosch GmbH et al,
  Case 13/61 [1962] ECR 45 189
Knoors, Case 115/78 [1979] ECR 399 .... 206, 207, 215, 217
Koch v Union Cycliste Internationale, Case 36/78 [1974] ECR 1405 248
Kofoed, Case C-321/05, judgment of 5 July 2007 207
Kohll, Case C-158/96 [1998] ECR I-1931 .... 232, 233
Koninklijke Scholten Honig, Case 101/76 [1979] ECR 797 72
Konstantinidis, Case C-168/91 [1993] ECR I-1191 .... 27, 61, 71
Konsumentombudsmannen (KO) v De Agiostini (Svenska) Förlag AB,
  Cases C-34–36/95 [1997] ECR I-3843 .... 92, 98, 112, 198, 200, 231, 238
Konsumentombudsmannen (KO) v Gourmet International Products AB (GIP),
  Case C-405/98 [2001] ECR I-1795 .... 198, 200, 238, 253, 256
Konsumentombudsmannen v TV-shop i Sverige AB, Cases C-35/95 and C-36/95
  [1997] ECR I-3843 .... 92, 98, 112, 200

Table of Cases xxiii

Krantz (H) GmbH & Co v Ontvanger der Directe Belastingen et al,
  Case C-69/88 [1990] ECR I-583 .... 203, 256
Kraus, Case C-19/92 [1993] ECR I-1663 206
Lair, Case 39/86 [1988] ECR 3161 .... 206, 209, 215, 217
Lankhorst-Hohorst, Case C-324/00 [2002] ECR I-11779 .... 213, 214
Leclerc [1985] see Association des Centres Distributeurs Edouard Leclerc v Au Blé Vert Sàrl,
  Case 229/83 [1985] ECR 1
Leclerc-Siplec v TF1 Publicité and M6 Publicité Case C-412/93 [1995]
  ECR I-179 .... 102, 190, 197, 198, 200, 202, 237
Leifer and Others, Case C-83/94 [1995] ECR I-3231. .... 326, 354, 355, 357, 358, 360
Ligur Carni Srl et al v Unità Sanitaria Locale no XV di Genova et al,
  Cases C-277, 318 and 319/91 [1993] ECR I-6621............................. 197
Lindorfer v Council, Case C-227/04 P opinion of 27 October 2005 134
Luisi and Carbone v Ministero del Tesoro, Joined cases 286/82 and 26/83 [1984]
  ECR 377 .... 245, 252
Lutz Herrera v Commission, Cases T-219/02 and T-337/02 [2004] ECR II-1407 164
McDermott and Cotter v Minister for Social Welfare, Case 286/85 [1987] ECR 1453....... 455
Manninen, Case C-319/02. 113
Marchandise et al, Case C-332/89 [1991] ECR I-1027........................... 194, 197
Marks & Spencer, Case c-446/03 [2005] ECR I-10837 213
Marleasing SA v La Commerciale Internacionale de Alimentacion SA,
  Case C-106/89 [1990] ECR I-4135 .... 433, 441
Martínez Sala v Freistaat Bayern, Case C-85/96 [1998] ECR I-2691 .... 244, 253
Matra v Commission, Case C-225/91 [1993] ECR I-3203. 88
max.mobil Telekommunikation, Case T-54/99 [2002] ECR II-313. .... 82, 163
Meca-Medina, David, case C-519/04 P [2006] ECR I-0000 239
Meilicke, Case C-292/04 (6 March 2007)... 302
Metro I, Case 26/76 [1977] ECR 1875.. 239
Milk Marque and National Farmers' Union, Case C-137/00 [2003] ECR I-7975 207
Ministère de l'Economie, des Finances et de l'Industrie v GEMO SA, Case C-126/01
  [2003] ECR I-13769 .... 98, 134
Mobistar and Belgacom Mobile, Joined Cases C-544/03 and C-545/03 [2005]
  ECR I-7723... 240
Mobistar v Commune de Fléron, Joined Cases C-544/03 and C-545/03 [2005]
  ECR I-7723... 256
Monsanto Agricoltura Italia, Case C-236/01 [2003] ECR I-8105 .... 95, 99, 106
Montedipe, Case T-14/89 [1992] ECR II-1155...................................... 33
Monteil & Samanni, Case 60/89 [1991] ECR I-1547............................ 194, 198
Morellato v Comune di Padova, Case C-416/00 [2003] ECR I-9343..................... 199
Morgan and Bucher, Joined Cases C-11/06 and C-12/06, judgment of 23 October 2007 252
Müller-Fauré, Case C-385/99 [2003] ECR I-4509................................... 233
Nadin and Nadin-Lux, C-151/04 [2005] ECR I-11203 224
Nakajima v Council, Case C-69/89 [1991] ECR I-2069............................. 331
Nardone v Commission, Case C-181/03 P [2005] ECR I-199 165
Nederlandse Antillen v Commission, Case T-32/98 [2000] ECR II-201 rvrsd
  C-142/00 [2003] ECR I-3483 82
Netherlands v Parliament and Council, Case C-377/98 [2001]
  ECR I-7079... 27, 125, 134, 166, 331, 338
Nippon Seiko KK and others v Commission, Case 119/77 [1979] ECR 1303............. 53
NMB v Commission, Case 188/88 [1992] ECR I-1689 65
Nold v Commission, Case 4.73 [1974] ECR 491 .... 127, 128, 129
NTN Toyo Bearing Co Ltd et al v Council, Case 113/79 [1979] ECR 1185 190

Table of Cases

Nuove Industrie Molisane v Commission, Case T-212/00 [2002] ECR I-347 78
Oebel, Case 155/80 [1981] ECR 1993 .... 194, 202
Officier van Justitie v de Peijper, Case 75/104 [1976] ECR 613. 193
Officier van Justitie v van Haaster, Case 190/73 [1974] ECR 1123 193
Omega Spielhallen- und Automatenaufstellungs-GmbH v Oberbürgermeisterin
    der Bundesstadt Bonn, Case C-36/02 [ECR] I-9609 .... 130, 166, 232, 237
Oosthoek's Uitgeversmaatschappij BV, Case C-286/81 [1982] ECR 4575 .... 194, 198
Opel Austria GmbH v Council of the European Union, Case T-115/94 [1997]
    ECR II-39 .... 103, 104, 120, 331
Ospelt and Schlössle Weissenberg, Case C-452/01 [2003] ECR I-9763 ..... 91, 99, 104, 105, 116
Österreichischer Gewerkschaftsbund, Case C-220/02 [2004] ECR I-5907 165
Oude Littikhuis and Others, Case C-399/93 [1995] ECR I-4515. 237
Oversea-Chinese Banking Corporation Limited ('EASI-CASH' and 'EASI-CARD'),
    Cases R 96/1998–1 and R 99/1998–1, 20 November 1998 .... 291, 292
Owusu v Jackson Case C-281/02 [2005] QB 801. .... 393–394, 395
Oy AA, Case C-213/05, judgment of 18 July 2007. 213
Oy Liikenne, Case C-172/00 [2001] ECR I-745. 93
P&O European Ferries, Joined Cases T-116/01 and T-118/01 [2003] ECR II-2957 163
P v S, Case C-13/94 [1996] ECR I-2143. .... 23, 142
Paletta, Case C-45/90 [1992] ECR I-3423. 206
Paletta II, Case C-206/94 [1996] ECR I-2357 207
Parking Brixen, Case C-458/03 [2005] ECR I-8612 234
Parliament v Council, Case 13/83 [1985] ECR 1513 53
Parliament v Council, Case 302/87 [1988] ECR 5615 159
Parliament v Council, Case C-70/88 (Chernobyl case) [1990] ECR I-2041 .... 76, 190
Parliament v Council, Case C-436/03 [2006] ECR I-3733 52
Parliament v Council, Case C-540/03 [2006] ECR I-5769 .... 135, 148, 168
Parliament v Council, Case C-317/04 [2006] ECR I-4721 165
Part Service, Case C-425/06 (pending) 212
Partie Ecologiste 'Les Verts' v European Parliament, Case 294/83 [1986] ECR 1339. 76
Paul Vannieuwenhuyze-Morin, Case T-321/02 [2003] ECR II-1997. 84
Pavlov, Joined Cases C-180/98 to C-184/98 [2000] ECR I-645. 117
Peralta, Case C-379/92 [1994] ECR I-3453. .... 203, 240
Pesca Valentia, Case 223/86 [1988] ECR 83. 452
Petrofina, Case T-2/89 [1991] ECR II-1087 33
Pfizer Animal Health v Council, Case T-13/99 [2002] ECR II-3305 .... 84, 85, 95, 99, 106
Philip Morris International v Commission, Joined Cases T-377/00, T-379/00, T-380/00,
    T-260/01 and T-272/01 [2003] ECR II-1............................. 163
Phillips-Van Heusen Corp v OHIM ('BASS/PASH'), Case T-292/01 [2003]
    ECR II-4335 287
Pigs and Bacon Commission v McCarren & Company, Case 177/78 [1979]
    ECR 2161 .... 451, 453
Piraiki-Patraiki v Commission, Case 11/82 [1985] ECR 207 77
Pistre et al, Cases C-321–324/94 [1997] ECR I-2343. 203
Placanica and others, Cases C-338, 359 and 360/04 [2007] ECR I-1891 .... 236, 443
Plaumann, Case 25/62 [1963] ECR 95. .... 71, 73, 76, 77, 79, 80, 81, 84,
  88, 89, 118
Polydor v Harlequin, Case 270/80 [1982] ECR 379. 301
Portugal v Council, Case C-149/96 [1999] ECR I-8395; 3 JIEL (2000) 441 .... 330, 335
Prais v Council, Case 130/75 [1976] ECR 1589. .... 53, 129
Prantl, Case 16/83 [1984] ECR 1299. 202

Table of Cases

Procter & Gamble v OHIM, Case C-383/99 P [2001] ECR I-6251 287
Procter & Gamble v OHIM, Case T-163/98 [1999] ECR II-2383 287
Procter & Gamble ('BABY-DRY'), Case R 35/1998–1, 31 July 1998 295
Procter & Gamble ('DEVICE OF BACKGROUNDS WITH COLOURED
  GRANULES [FIG. MARK]'), Case R 962/2004–2 17 December 2004. 292
Procureur du Roi v Dassonville et al, Case 8/74 [1974] ECR 837 .... 192, 193, 194, 197,
  202, 203, 204, 228, 230, 233,
  236, 254, 255, 256, 259
Punto Casa SpA et al v Sindaco del Commune di Capena et al, Cases C-69 and 258/93
  [1994] ECR I-2355. .... 194, 198
Pyres v Commission, Case T-256/01 [2005] ECR II-25 164
Queen, *ex parte* Centro-Com v HM Treasury and Bank of England, Case C-124/95
  [1997] ECR I-81 .... 327, 354, 355, 357, 358, 359, 360
Queen v Secretary of State for Health *ex parte* British American Tobacco Ltd,
  Case C-491/01, judgment of 10 December 2002 83
Queen v Secretary of State for Transport, *ex parte* Factortame Ltd, case c-213/89 [1990]
  ECR I-2433 .... 219, 226, 446, 452
Quietlynn & Richards v Southend Borough Council, Case C-23/89 [1990]
  ECR I-3059. .... 194, 195, 197, 203
Quinn v Ireland and AG and anor, Tector v Ireland and AG and anor, Quinn v Ireland
  and AG and anor (No 2), 30 March 2007 449
R v Thompson, Case 7/78 [1978] ECR 2247 311
Racke v Hauptzollamt Mainz, Case C-162/96 [1998] ECR I-3655 .... 328, 332
Racke v HZA Mainz, Case 136/77 [1978] ECR 1245 184
Radlberger Getränkegesellschaft mbH & Co KG, S Spitz KG v Land Baden-Württemberg,
  C-309/02 [2004] ECR I-nyr (14 December 2004). 201
Reading Borough Council v Payless DIY Ltd et al, Case C-304/90 [1992] ECR I-6493. . .194, 197
Rechberger, Case C-140/97 [1999] ECR I-3499. .... 101, 102, 106
Regina v Kent Kirk, Case 63/83 [1984] ECR 2689. 129
Rewe-Zentral AG v Bundesmonopolverwaltung für Branntwein, Case 120/78 [1979]
  ECR 649 .... 193, 196, 203, 228, 232, 233, 254, 268
Rhône-Poulenc, Case T-1/89 [1991] ECR II-867 33
RIchards (Sarah Margaret) v Secretary of State for Work and Pensions,
  Case C-423/04 [2006] ECR-3585. 23
Richardt and 'Les Accessoires Scientifiques Case C-367/89 [1991] ECR I-4621..... .326, 354, 355
Rochdale Borough Council v Anders, Case C-306/88 [1992] ECR I-6457 .... 194, 197
Roquette Frères v Council, Case 138/79 [1980] ECR 3333 72
Roquette Frères v Directeur général de la concurrenceé de la consommation et de la
  répression des fraudes, Case C-94/00 [2002] ECR 9011 .... 129, 142
Rosengren (Klas) and Others v Rikåsklagaren, Case C-170/04, opinion of AG
  Mengozzi 30 November 2006, nyr. 114, 115
Royal Scholten-Honig v Intervention Board for Agricultural Produce, Joined
  cases 103 and 145/77 [1978] ECR 2037 .... 290, 292
Ruckdeschel v Hauptzollamt Hamburg–St Annen, Joined Cases 117/76 and 16/77
  [1977] ECR 1753 .... 283, 288
Ruiz Bernáldez, Case C-129/94 [1996] ECR I-1829 .... 100, 108
Rutili (Roland) contre Ministre de l'intérieur, Case 36/75 [1975] ECR 1219. .... 128, 142
SA CNL-SUCAL NV v HAG GF AG, Case C-10/89 [1990] ECR I-3711 .... 27, 65, 70, 190
SA Hercules Chemicals, Case T-7/89 [1991] ECR II-1711 33
SA Musique Diffusion Française and Others v Commission, Joined cases 100–103/80
  [1983] ECR 1825 140

Säger v Dennemeyer, Case C-76/90 [1991] ECR I-4221 . . . . 27, 230, 236, 249, 256, 268
Saint Gobain, Case C-307/97 [1999] ECR I-6161 219
Salamander and others v Parliament/Council case, Case T-172/98 [2000] ECR II-2487 . . . 78, 79
Salt Union Ltd v Commission, Case T-330/94 [1996] ECR II-1475. 79
Salzgitter AG v Commission, Case T-308/00 [2004] ECR II-1933 97
Sandoz, Case 174/82 [1983] ECR 2445 . . . . 96, 107
Sanz de Lera, Cases C-163, 165 and 250/94 [1995] ECR I-4821 301
SAT.1 Satellitenfernsehen GmbH v OHIM ('SAT.2'), Case C-329/02 P [2004] ECR I-8317 . . . 290
SAT.1 v OHIM, Case T-323/00 [2002] ECR II-2839 290
Schmidberger (Eugen) Internationale Transporte und Planzüge v Republik Österreich,
    Case C-112/00 [2003] ECR I-5659 . . . . 71, 128, 130, 134, 142, 202, 248
Schmidt (Christel), Case C-392/92 [1994] ECR I-1311 107
Schnitzer, Case C-215/01 [2003] ECR I-14847 . . . . .247, 249
Schutzverband gegen Unlauteren Wettbewerb v TK Heimdienst Sass GmbH,
    Case C-254/98 [2000] ECR I-151 . . . . .198, 199, 256
Schutzverband gegen unwesen in der Wirtschaft e V v Yves Rocher GmbH,
    Case C-126/91 [1993] ECR I-2361 . . . . 194, 197, 198
Schutzverband gegen Unwesen in der Wirtschaft v Weinvertriebs GmbH,
    Case 59/82 [1983] ECR 1217. 190
SCP Bosscher, Studer & Fromentin v SA British Motors Wright et al, Case C-239/90
    [1991] ECR I-2023. . . . . .194, 198
Segers, Case 79/85 [1986] ECR 2375. . . . . 209, 212, 216, 217, 218, 222
Semeraro Casa Uno Srl et al v Sindaco del Commune di Erbusco et al,
    Cases C-418–421/93 [1996] ECR I-2975 . . . . .194, 198, 199
Senator Lines, Joined Cases T-191/98, T-212/98, T-213/98 and T-214/98 [1999]
    ECR II-2531 143
Sgarlata v Commission, Case 40/64 [1965] ECR 279. 126
Shell International Chemical Company, Case T-11/89 [1992] ECR II-757 33
Sheptonhurst Ltd v Newham Borough Council, Case C-350/89 [1991]
    ECR I-2387. . . . . 194, 195, 197, 203
Shevill v Presse Alliance SA, Case C-68/93 [1995] ECR I-415; [1995] 2 AC 18; [1995] 2
    WLR 499; [1995] All ER (EC). 391
Signal Communications v OHIM ('TELEYE'), Case T-128/99 [2001] ECR II-3273 287
Silhouette, Case C-355/96 [1998] ECR I-4799 . . . . 27, 112, 113, 119
Simet and Others v ECSC High Authority, Joined Cases 36–41/58 [1959] ECR 331. 126
Simmenthal SpA v Amministrazione delle finanze dello Stato, Case 70/77 [1978]
    ECR 1453 55
Singh, Case C-370/90 [1992] ECR I-4265. 206
Smits & Peerbooms, Case C-157/99 [2001] ECR I-5473 . . . . 233, 234
SNF SA v Commission, Case T-213/02 [2004] ECR II-3047. 84
Sniace SA, Case T-141/03, Judgment of 14 April 2005 [2005] ECR I-1197 84
Société Civil Immobolière Parodi v Banque H Albert de Bary et Cie, Case C-222/95
    [1997] ECR I-3899 267
Société d'importation Edouard Leclerc v TFI Publicité SA et al, Case C-412/93
    [1995] ECR I-179. . . . . 102, 190, 197, 198, 200, 202, 237
Society for the Protection of Unborn Children (Ireland) Ltd v Grogan and others,
    Case C-159/90 [1991] ECR I-4685. . . . . 193, 244, 250, 251, 256, 459
Sodemare and Others v Regione Lombardia, Case C-70/95 [1997] ECR I-3395 253
Sofivo v Council, Cases T-14/97 and T-15/97 [1998] ECR II-4191. 78
Solange II judgment 1986 137
Solvay & Cie, Case T-12/89 [1992] ECR II-907. 33

Table of Cases

Sony Computer Entertainment Ltd v Commission, Case T-243/01 [2003]
    ECR II-4189 .... 84, 86
Sotgiu v Deutsche Bundespost, Case C-152/73 [1974] ECR 153 230
Spain v Eurojust, C-160/03 [2005] ECR I-2077 165
Spain v United Kingdom, Case C-145/04 judgment of 12 September 2006
    [2006] ECR I-7917 52
SPUC v Grogan, Case C-159/90 [1991] ECR I-4685 .... 193, 244, 250, 251, 256, 459
Stahlwerke Peine-Salzgitter, Case T-120/89 [1992] ECR II-279. 33
Stauder (Erich) v City of Ulm – Sozialamt, Case 29/69 [1969] ECR 419 .... 127, 129
Stichting Collectieve Antennevoorziening Gouda and Others v Commissariaat voor
    de Media, Case C-288/89 [1991] ECR I-4007 129
Stichting Greenpeace, Case C-321/95 P [1998] ECR I-1651 .... 75, 78, 81
Stork v High Authority, Case 1/58 [1959] ECR 17 126
Streamserve Inc v OHIM ('STREAMSERVE'), Case T-106/00 [2002]
    ECR II-723 .... 284, 285, 294
Surinder Corp v OHMI, Case T-242/02 [2005] ECR II-2793 163
Süzen, Case C-13/95 [1997] ECR I-1259 .... 93, 106, 107, 119
Sveriges Betodlares [Centralförening] and Henrikson v Commission,
    Case C-406/96 P [1997] ECR I-7531 .... 87, 88
Tankstation't Heuske vof & Boermans, Cases C-401 and 402/92 [1994] ECR I-2199 .... 194, 198
Templeman, joined cases C-96/03 and C-97/03 [2005] ECR I-1895 52
Test Claimants in Class IV of the ACT Group Litigation, Case C-374/04
    23 February 2006 nyr 113, 114, 119
Test Claimants in the Thin Cap Group Litigation, Case C-524/04, judgment of
    13 March 2007 ('Thin Cap') [2007] ECR I-2107................... 213, 214, 222, 225
Tetra Pak, T-51/89 [1990] ECR II-309. 33
Theodor Kohl KG v Ringelhan and Rennett SA, Case 177/83 [1984] ECR 3651 191
Thieffry v Conseil de l'Ordre des avocats à la cour de Paris, Case 71/76 [1977] ECR 765 254
TNT Traco SpA, Case C-340/99 [2001] ECR I-4109 165
Tokyo Electric Company Ltd (TEC) and others v Council, Joined Cases 260/85 and
    106/86 [1988] ECR 5855 53
Torfaen Borough Council v B & Q plc, Case 145/88 [1989] ECR 3851 .... 194, 195, 240
Traghetti del Mediterraneo, Case C-173/03 [2006] ECR I-5177 440
Trasporti Castelletti v Hugo Trumpy Case C-159/97 [1999] ECR I-1597 388
Trummer and Meyer, Case C-222/97 [1999] ECR I-1661 302
Tulliasiamies and Siilin, Case C-101/00 [2002] ECR I-7487 240
Tunnel Refineries Limited v Council, Case 114/81 [1982] ECR 3189. 53
Turner v Grovit, Case C-159/02 27 April 2004 [2005] 1 AC 101 .... 391–393, 397
TV10, Case C-23/93 TV10 [1994] ECR I-4795 .... 206, 212, 215, 217
Überseering, Case C-208/00 [2002] ECR I-9919 165
UEAPME v Council, Case C-321/95 [1998] ECR II-2335. 80
Unectef v Heylens, Case C-222/86 [1987] ECR-4097 .... 170, 344
Unibet v Justitiekanslern, Case C-432/02 judgment of 13 March 2007 135
Unilever Bestfoods (Ireland) Ltd, formerly Van den Bergh Foods Ltd v Commission,
    Case C-552/03 P [2006] ECR I-9091 453
Unión de Pequenos Agricultores *see* UPA
Union départementale des syndicates CGT de l'Aisne v SIDEF Conforama et al,
    case C-312/89 [1991] ECR I-997 194
Union Royale Belge des Sociétés de Football Association ASBL et al v Bosman et al,
    Case C-415/93 [1995] ECR I-4921 .... 199, 201
United Kingdom v Commission, Case 84/85 [1987] ECR 3765. 53

xxviii *Table of Cases*

United Kingdom v European Parliament and Council, Case C-217/04 [2006] ECR I-3771 ... 52
University of Huddersfield Higher Education Corporation, Case C-223/03 [2006]
  ECR I-1751 ....207, 212
UPA, Case C-50/00 P [2002] ECR I-6677...................... 26, 27, 71, 74, 75, 76, 77, 78,
  79, 80, 81, 82, 84, 88, 89, 118,
  135, 136, 164
UPA v Council, Case T-173/98 [1999] ECR II-3357 74
USA Detergents Inc, Case R 20/1997–1 XTRA.............................289, 290, 291
Van Binsbergen, Case 33/74 [1974] ECR 1299...................206, 215, 217, 224, 230, 232,
  233, 236, 254, 259
Van de Bijl, Case 130/88 [1989] ECR 3039 ....206, 207, 217
Van de Haar, Cases 177/82 and 178/82 [1984] ECR 1797 202
Van den Bergh Foods formerly HB Ice Cream Ltd v Commission, Case T-65/98 [2003]
  ECR II-4653 453
Van der Kooy and Others v Commission, Joined Cases 67/85, 68/85 and 70/85 [1988]
  ECR 219 88
Van der Woude, Case 222/98 [2000] ECR I-7111 117
Van Gend en Loos v Nederlandse Administratie der Belastingen, Case 26/62
  [1963] ECR 1...324, 329, 432, 438
Van Parys, Case C-377/02 [2005] ECR I-1465 .... 334, 336
Van Zuylen v HAG, Case 192/73 [1974] ECR 731.................................. 65
Vanbraekel, Case C-368/98 [2001] ECR I-5363 233
Verband Sozialer Wettbewerb e V v Clinique Laboratoires SNC et al, Case C-315/92
  [1994] ECR I-317... 197
Verein gegen Unwesen in Handel und Gewerbe Köln e V v Mars GmbH,
  Case C-370/93 [1995] ECR I-1923 ....197, 198
Vereinigte Familiapress Zeitungsverlags-und vertriebs GmbH v Heinrich Bauer Verlag,
  Case c-368/95 [1997] ECR I-3689....................................... 198
Vergani, Case C-207/04 [2005] ECR I-7453 162
Verholen, Joined Cases C-87/90, C-88/90 and C-89/90 [1991] ECR I-3757 76
Veronica, Case C-148/91 [1993] ECR I-487 ....206, 212, 215, 217
Viacom Outdoor (Viacom II), Case C-134/03 [2005] ECR I-1167 .... 239, 240
Viking Line Abp v The International Transport Workers' Federation and the Finnish
  Seamen's Union, Case C-438/05 (pending)................................. 242
Villiger, Case T-154/02 [2003] ECR II-1921 84
Vivien Prais v Council, Case 1130/75 [1976] ECR 1589 .... 53, 129
Volcano Corporation ('VIRTUAL HISTOLOGY'), Case R 1029/2004–27
  December 2005... 294, 295
Vonier v Commission, Case T-165/03 [2004] ECR II-1575 163
Vonk, Case C-279/05, judgment of 11 January 2007 [2007] ECR I-239 207
Wachauf v Bundesamt für Ernährung und Forstwirtschaft, Case 5/88 [1989]
  ECR 2609 .... 125, 129
Walter Rau Lebensmittelwerke v De Smedt PvbA, Case 251/82 [1982] ECR 3961.......... 190
Watts v Bedford Primary Care Trust and Secretary of State for Health,
  Case C-372/04 [2006] ECR I-4325....................................233, 251
Webb, Case 279/80 [1981] ECR 3305 230
Weber, Case C-328/00 [2002] ECR I-1461 79
Weber v Commission, Case T-482/93 [1996] ECR II-609........................... 79
Werhof, Case C-499/04 [2006] ECR I-2397..................................... 165
Werner v Germany, Case C-70/94 [1995] ECR I-3189 .... 326, 354, 355, 356, 357, 358, 360
Westzucker v EVS Zucker, Case 57/72 [1973] ECR 321............................ 184

'WHITENING MULTI-ACTION' case, Case R 118/2003–2, 22 June 2004 290
Wiener, Case C-338/95 [1997] ECR I-6495. 23
Williams v Court of Auditors, Case 134/84 [1985] ECR 2225 .... 286, 292
Witte v Parliament, Case 188/83 [1984] ECR 3465 286
Wouters, Case C-309/99 [2002] ECR I-1577. 239
Wünsche Handelsgesellschaft [1987] 3 CMLR 2225 137
XTRA USA Detergents Inc Case R 20/1997–1 .... 289, 290, 291
Yamaha Kabushiki Kaisha ('JUNIOR KIT'), Case R 22/2003–2, 4 July 2005 296
Yusuf v Council and Commission, Case T-306/01 [2005] ECR II-3353 .... 328, 333, 334,
336, 343
Z v European Parliament, case C-270/99 [2001] ECR I-9197 134
Z v Parliament, Case C-270/99 [2001] ECR I-9197 171
Zhu and Chen v Secretary of State for the Home Department, Case C-200/02 [2004]
ECR I-9925 244

European Court of Justice and Court of First Instance—numerical order

Court of Justice

Case 1/54 France v High Authority [1954–56] ECR 1 .... 20, 21
Case 3/54 Associazione Industrie Siderurgique Italiane (ASSIDER) v High
Authority [1954–56] ECR 63 190
Joined Cases 7 & 9/54 Groupement des Industries Sidérugiques Luxembourgeoises v
High Authority [1954–56] ECR 175 190
Case 8/55 Fédération Charbonnière de Belgique v High Authority [1954–56]
ECR 245 189–190
Case 2/56 Geitling Ruhrkohlen-Verkaufsgesellschaft and Others v ECSC High
Authority [1957] ECR 9. 126
Joined Cases 7/56 & 3–7/57 Algera et al v Common Assembly [1957–58] ECR 39 190
Case 1/58 Stork v High Authority [1959] ECR 17 126
Joined Cases 36-41/58 Simet and Others v ECSC High Authority [1959] ECR 331 126
Joined Cases 36-38/59 and 40/59 Geitling v High Authority [1960] ECR 857. 126
Case 13/61 Kledingverkoopbedrijf de Geus en Uitdenbogerd v Robert Bosch
GmbH et al [1962] ECR 45 189
Case 25/62 Plaumann [1963] ECR 95 .... 71, 73, 76, 77, 79, 80, 81,
84, 88, 89, 118
Case 6/64 Costa v Enel [1964] ECR 585 .... 127, 435, 440, 451
Case 40/64 Sgarlata v Commission [1965] ECR 279 126
Case 29/69 Stauder (Erich) v City of Ulm – Sozialamt [1969] ECR 419. .... 127, 129
Case 11/70 Internationale Handelsgesellschaft mbH v Einfuhr- und Vorratsstelle
für Getreide und Futtermittel [1970] ECR 1125 .... 127, 129
Case 22/70 Commission v Council (ERTA case) [1971] ECR 263 76
Case 25/70 Einfuhr- und Vorratsstelle für Getreide und Futtermittel v Köster [1970]
ECR 1161. 127
Joined Cases 41-44/70 Fruit Company v Commission [1971] ECR 411 72
Case 5/71 Aktien-Zukerfabrik Schöppenstedt v Council [1971] ECR 975 190
Case 22/71 Béguelin Import [1971] ECR 949 237
Joined Cases 21–24/72 International Fruit Company v Produktschap voor Groenten
en Fruit [1972] ECR 1219 330
Case 57/72 Westzucker v EVS Zucker [1973] ECR 321 184
Case 4/73 Nold v Commission [1974] ECR 491. .... 127, 128, 129
Case C-152/73 Sotgiu v Deutsche Bundespost [1974] ECR 153. 230
Case 190/73 Officier van Justitie v van Haaster [1974] ECR 1123 193

Case 192/73 Van Zuylen v HAG [1974] ECR 731 65
Case 8/74 Procureur du Roi v Dassonville et al [1974] ECR 837 .... 192, 193, 194, 197,
  202, 203, 204, 228, 230,
  233, 236, 254, 255, 256, 259
Case 18/74 General Union of Personnel of European Organizations v Commission
  [1974] ECR 933 129
Case 33/74 Van Binsbergen [1974] ECR 1299 .... 206, 215, 217, 224, 230,
  232, 233, 236, 254, 259
Case 36/74 Walrave and Koch v Union Cycliste Internationale [1974] ECR 1405 248
Case 36/75 Rutili (Roland) contre Ministre de l'intérieur [1975] ECR 1219 .... 128, 142
Case 104/75 Officier van Justitie v de Peijper [1976] ECR 613 193
Case 130/75 Prais (Vivien) v Council [1976] ECR 1589 .... 53, 129
Case 26/76 Metro I [1977] ECR 1875 239
Case 41/76 Donckerwolcke v Procureur de la République [1976] ECR 1921 .... 326, 355
Case 71/76 Thieffry v Conseil de l'Ordre des avocats à la cour de Paris [1977] ECR 765...... 254
Case 101/76 Koninklijke Scholten Honig [1979] ECR 797 72
Cases 117/76 and 16/77 Ruckdeschel v Hauptzollamt Hamburg–St Annen [1977]
  ECR 1753 .... 283, 288
Case 125/76 Cremer [1977] ECR 1593... 207
Cases 117/76 and 16/77 Ruckdeschel v Hauptzollamt Hamburg–St Annen [1977]
  ECR 1753 .... 283, 288
Case 70/77 Simmenthal SpA v Amministrazione delle finanze dello Stato [1978]
  ECR 1453 55
Joined Cases 103 and 145/77 Royal Scholten-Honig v Intervention Board for
  Agricultural Produce [1978] ECR 2037................................. 290, 292
Case 106/77 Amministrazione Finanze dello Stato v Simmenthal [1978] ECR 629..... 437, 440
Case 119/77 Nippon Seiko KK and others v Commission [1979] ECR 1303 53
Case 136/77 Racke v HZA Mainz [1978] ECR 1245 184
Joined Cases 103 and 145/77 Royal Scholten-Honig v Intervention Board for
  Agricultural Produce [1978] ECR 2037................................. 290, 292
Case 7/78 R v Thompson [1978] ECR 2247....................................... 311
Case 115/78 Knoors [1979] ECR 399......................................206, 207, 215, 217
Case 120/78 Rewe-Zentral AG v Bundesmonopolverwaltung für Branntwein
  [1979] ECR 649 .... 193, 196, 203, 228, 232,
  233, 254, 268
Case 177/78 Pigs and Bacon Commission v McCarren & Company [1979] ECR 2161 ...451, 453
Case 15/79 Groenveld (PB) BV v Produktschap voor Vee en Vlees [1979]
  ECR 3409 .... 202, 203, 248
Case 113/79 NTN Toyo Bearing Co Ltd et al v Council [1979] ECR 1185 190
Case 138/79 Roquette Frères v Council [1980] ECR 3333............................ 72
Case 155/79 AM & S Europe Ltd v Commission [1982] ECR 1575 .... 66, 190
Case 788/79 Gilli & Andres [1980] ECR 2071 190
Joined Cases 789 and 790/79 Calpak v Commission [1980] ECR 1949.................. 72
Case 13/80 Commission v Ireland [1981] ECR 1625 191
Joined Cases 100–103/80 SA Musique Diffusion Française and Others v Commission
  [1983] ECR 1825 140
Case 112/80 Dürbeck [1981] ECR 1095.. 352
Case 155/80 Oebel [1981] ECR 1993 .... 194, 202
Case 270/80 Polydor v Harlequin [1982] ECR 379 301
Case 279/80 Webb [1981] ECR 3305.. 230
Case 60/81 International Business Machines Corporation v Commission [1981] ECR 2639.... 190

Table of Cases

Case 75/81 Blesgen [1982] ECR 1211.................................193, 195, 203
Case 104/81 Hauptzollamt Mainz v Kupferberg [1982] ECR 3641....................330
Case 114/81 Tunnel Refineries Limited v Council [1982] ECR 3189....................53
Case 230/81 Grand Duchy of Luxembourg v European Parliament [1983] ECR 255..........53
Case 262/81 Coditel and others v Cine-Vog Films and Others [1982] ECR 3381..........268
Case 283/81 CILFIT v Ministry of Health [1982] ECR 3415...........................5
Case 286/81 Oosthoek's Uitgeversmaatschappij BV [1982] ECR 4575................194, 198
Case 11/82 Piraiki-Patraiki v Commission [1985] ECR 207..........................77
Case 59/82 Schutzverband gegen Unwesen in der Wirtschaft v Weinvertriebs GmbH
   [1983] ECR 1217...190
Case 165/82 Commission v UK [1983] ECR 3431..................................129
Case 174/82 Sandoz [1983] ECR 2445..96, 107
Cases 177/82 and 178/82 Van de Haar [1984] ECR 1797...........................202
Case 251/82 Walter Rau Lebensmittelwerke v De Smedt PvbA [1982] ECR 3961..........190
Joined Cases 286/82 and 26/83 Luisi and Carbone v Ministero del Tesoro [1984]
   ECR 377..245, 252
Case 13/83 Parliament v Council [1985] ECR 1513..............................53
Case 16/83 Prantl [1984] ECR 1299..202
Joined Cases 286/82 and 26/83 Luisi and Carbone v Ministero del Tesoro
   [1984] ECR 377...245, 252
Case 63/83 Regina v Kent Kirk [1984] ECR 2689................................129
Case 72/83 Campus Oil and Others v Minister for Industry and Energy [1984]
   ECR 2727...356
Case 173/83 Commission v France [1985] ECR 491.............................203
Case 177/83 Theodor Kohl KG v Ringelhan and Rennett SA [1984] ECR 3651..........191
Case 188/83 Witte v Parliament [1984] ECR 3465..............................286
Case 207/83 Commission v United Kingdom [1985] ECR 1205......................191
Case 229/83 Association des Centres Distributeurs Edouard Leclerc v Au Blé Vert Sàrl
   [1985] ECR 1...191, 206, 209, 217
Case 252/83 Commission v France [1986] ECR 3663............................267
Case 269/83 Commission v France [1985] ECR 837.............................202
Case 294/83 Partie Ecologiste 'Les Verts' v European Parliament [1986] ECR 1339.........76
Case 40/84 Casteels v Commission [1985] ECR 667............................86
Joined Cases 60 and 61/84 Cinéthèque SA v Federation Nationale des Cinémas Français
   [1985] ECR 2605..127
Case 103/84 Commission v Italy [1986] ECR 1759..............................202
Case 134/84 Williams v Court of Auditors [1985] ECR 2225....................286, 292
Case 169/84 Cofaz and Others v Commission [1986] ECR 391.....................87, 88
Case 174/84 Bulk Oil v Sun International [1986] ECR 559.......................355
Case 188/84 Commission v France [1986] ECR 419..............................203
Case 205/84 Commission v Germany [1986] ECR 3755............................267
Case 222/84 Johnston (Marguerite) v Chief Constable of the Royal Ulster
   Constabulary [1986] ECR 1651......................................76, 128, 142
Joined Cases 67/85, 68/85 and 70/85 Van der Kooy and Others v Commission
   [1988] ECR 219..88
Case 79/85 Segers [1986] ECR 2375..........................209, 212, 216, 217, 218, 222
Case 84/85 United Kingdom v Commission [1987] ECR 3765.......................53
Joined Cases 260/85 and 106/86 Tokyo Electric Company Ltd (TEC) and others v
   Council [1988] ECR 5855...53
Case 286/85 McDermott and Cotter v Minister for Social Welfare [1987] ECR 1453.......455
Case 352/85 Bond van Adverteerders v Netherlands [1988] ECR 2085................251

Case 26/86 Deutz and Geldermann v Council [1987] ECR 941......................72, 74
Case 39/86 Lair [1988] ECR 3161 ....206, 209, 215, 217
Joined Cases 260/85 and 106/86 Tokyo Electric Company Ltd (TEC) and others v
    Council [1988] ECR 5855..53
Case 222/86 Unectef v Heylens [1987] ECR-4097............................170, 344
Case 223/86 Pesca Valentia [1988] ECR 83..452
Case 263/86 Belgium v Humbel [1988] ECR 5365................................251
Joined Cases 46/87 and 227/88 Hoechst AG v Commission [1989] ECR 2859............142
Case 70/87 Fediol v Commission [1989] ECR 1781................................331
Case 81/87 Daily Mail [1988] ECR 5500....................................219, 220, 226
Case 186/87 Cowan v Trésor Public [1989] ECR 195............................236, 253
Case 302/87 Parliament v Council [1988] ECR 5615................................159
Case 382/87 Buet & Educational Business Services (EBS) SARL v Ministère public
    [1989] ECR 1235...194, 197, 198
Case 5/88 Wachauf v Bundesamt für Ernährung und Forstwirtschaft [1989]
    ECR 2609...125, 129
Case C-21/88 Du Pont de Nemours Italiana SpA v Unità Sanitaria Locale no. 2
    di Carrara [1990] ECR I-889..193
Case C-47/88 Commission v Denmark [1990] ECR I-4509..........................240
Case C-69/88 Krantz (H) GmbH & Co v Ontvanger der Directe Belastingen et al
    [1990] ECR I-583...203, 256
Case C-70/88 Parliament v Council (Chernobyl case) [1990] ECR I-2041..............76, 190
Case 103/88 Fratelli Costanzo v Comune di Milano [1989] ECR 1839..................440
Case 130/88 Van de Bijl [1989] ECR 3039....................................206, 207, 217
Case C-145/88 Torfaen Borough Council v B & Q plc [1989] ECR 3851..........194, 195, 240
Case C-188/88 NMB v Commission [1992] ECR I-1689................................65
Joined Cases 46/87 and 227/88 Hoechst AG v Commission [1989] ECR 2859............142
Case C-262/88 Barber v Guardian Royal Exchange [1990] ECR I-1889..................65
Case C-306/88 Rochdale Borough Council v Anders [1992] ECR I-6457............194, 197
Case C-362/88 GB-INNO-BM v Confédération du commerce luxembourgeois
    [1990] ECR I-667...194, 195, 198, 250
Case C-369/88 Delattre [1991] ECR I-1487....................................194, 198
Case C-10/89 CNL-SUCAL NV v HAG GF AG (HAG II) [1990] ECR I-3711...27, 65, 70, 190
Case C-23/89 Quietlynn & Richards v Southend Borough Council [1990]
    ECR I-3059...194, 195, 197, 203
Case C-60/89 Monteil & Samanni [1991] ECR I-1547............................194, 198
Case C-61/89 Bouchoucha [1990] ECR I-3551......................206, 207, 209, 217
Case C-69/89 Nakajima v Council [1991] ECR I-2069................................331
Case C-106/89 Marleasing SA v La Commerciale Internacionale de Alimentacion
    SA [1990] ECR I-4135...433, 441
Case C-213/89 The Queen v Secretary of State for Transport, ex parte
    Factortame Ltd [1990] ECR I-2433......................52, 56, 58, 76, 446, 452
Case C-221/89 Factortame [1991] ECR I-3905 (Factortame II)....................219, 226
Case C-246/89 R Commission v United Kingdom [1989] ECR 3125; [1991]
    ECR I-4585...52, 219, 226
Case C-288/89 Stichting Collectieve Antennevoorziening Gouda and Others v
    Commissariaat voor de Media [1991] ECR I-4007..............................129
Case C-309/89 Codorniu v Council [1994] ECR I-1853............72, 73, 77, 80, 84, 85, 89
Case C-312/89 Union départementale des syndicates CGT de l'Aisne v SIDEF
    Conforama et al [1991] ECR I-997...194
Case C-332/89 Marchandise et al [1991] ECR I-1027............................194, 197

Table of Cases

Case C-350/89 Sheptonhurst Ltd v Newham Borough Council [1991]
 ECR I-2387.. 194, 195, 197, 203
Case C-358/89 Extramet Industrie v Council [1991] ECR I-2501 .... 71, 72, 77, 80, 81
Case C-367/89 Richardt and 'Les Accessoires Scientifiques' [1991] ECR I-4621 ... .326, 354, 355
Case C-377/89 Cotter and McDermott v Minister for Social Welfare [1991] ECR I-1155 455
Case C-379/89 Groener v Minister for Education et al [1989] ECR 3967 193
Cases C-1 & 176/90 Aragonesa de Publicidad Exterior SA et al v Departamento de Sanidad y
 Seguridad Social de la Generalitat de Cataluña [1991] ECR I-4151 ...... 193, 194, 197, 198
Case C-2/90 Commission v Belgium (Walloon waste case) [1992] ECR I-4431 .... 191, 193
Cases C-6/90 and C-9/90 Francovich and Bonifaci v Italy [1991]
 ECR I-5237.. 440, 443, 444, 446, 455
Case C-45/90 Paletta [1992] ECR I-3423 206
Case C-47/90 Éts Delhaize Frères et Compagnie Le Lion SA v Promalvin SA et al
 [1992] ECR I-3669 (Rioja)... 193, 203
Case C-76/90 Säger v Dennemeyer [1991] ECR I-4221 .... 27, 230, 236, 249, 256, 268
Joined Cases C-87/90, C-88/90 and C-89/90 Verholen [1991] ECR I-3757................ 76
Case C-159/90 Society for the Protection of Unborn Children (Ireland) Ltd
 (SPUC) v Grogan and others [1991] ECR I-4685............ 193, 244, 250, 251, 256, 459
Cases C-1 & 176/90 Aragonesa de Publicidad Exterior SA et al v Departamento
 de Sanidad y Seguridad Social de la Generalitat de Cataluña [1991]
 ECR I-4151 .... 193, 194, 197, 198
Case C-208/90 Emmott v Minister for Social Welfare [1991] ECR I-4269 455
Case C-239/90 SCP Bosscher, Studer & Fromentin v SA British Motors Wright et al
 [1991] ECR I-2023...194, 198
Case C-304/90 Reading Borough Council v Payless DIY Ltd et al [1992] ECR I-6493 ...194, 197
Case C-313/90 CIRFS and Others v Commission [1993] ECR I-1125................... 88
Case C-370/90 Singh [1992] ECR I-4265 206
Case C-126/91 Schutzverband gegen unwesen in der Wirtschaft e V v Yves Rocher
 GmbH [1993] ECR I-2361..194, 197, 198
Case C-148/91 Veronica [1993] ECR I-487............................206, 212, 215, 217
Case C-168/91 Konstantinidis [1993] ECR I-1191..............................27, 61, 72
Case C-169/91 Council of the City of Stoke-on-Trent et al v B & Q plc [1992]
 ECR I-6635...194, 197
Case C-198/91 Cook v Commission [1993] ECR I-2487............................... 88
Case C-211/91 Commission v Belgium [1992] ECR I-6757........................... 224
Case C-225/91 Matra v Commission [1993] ECR I-3203 88
Case C-264/91 Abertal and Others v Council [1993] ECR I-3265...................... 74
Joined Cases C-267 and 268/91 Keck and Mithouard [1993] ECR I-6097 .... 190, 195–198,
                                                                                199, 201, 202, 203, 204, 228,
                                                                                237, 238, 240, 241, 244,
                                                                                254, 255, 256, 259
Cases C-277, 318 and 319/91 Ligur Carni Srl et al v Unità Sanitaria Locale
 no XV di Genova et al [1993] ECR I-6621...................................... 197
Case C-1/92 Hercules Chemicals v Commission [1999] ECR I-4235 442
Case C-8/92 General Milk Products [1993] ECR I-779..........................207, 217
Case C-19/92 Kraus [1993] ECR I-1663 206
Case C-26/92 Van Gend en Loos v Nederlandse Administratie der Belastingen
 [1963] ECR 1...324, 329, 432, 438
Case C-49/92P Commission v Anic Partecipazioni [1999] ECR I-4125................... 309
Case C-93/92 CMC Motorradcenter GmbH v Baskiciogullari [1993] ECR I-5009..... 203, 256
Case C-131/92 Arnaud and Others v Council [1993] ECR I-2573..................... 74

Case C-250/92 Gottrup-Klim [1994] ECR I-5641 239
Case C-275/92 Her Majesty's Customs and Excise v Schindler [1994] ECR I-1039 246
Case C-292/92 Hünermund et al v Landesapothekerkammer
  Baden-Württemberg [1993] ECR I-6787 .... 190, 195, 198, 200, 202, 232, 258
Case C-315/92 Verband Sozialer Wettbewerb e V v Clinique Laboratoires SNC et al
  [1994] ECR I-317 197
Case C-379/92 Peralta [1994] ECR I-3453 .... 203, 240
Case C-391/92 Commission v Greece [1995] ECR I-1621 .... 197, 198, 199
Case C-392/92 Christel Schmidt [1994] ECR I-1311 107
Joined Cases C-401 & 402/92 Tankstation't Heuske vof & Boermans [1994]
  ECR I-2199 .... 194, 198
Case C-13/95 Süzen [1997] ECR I-1259 .... 93, 106, 107, 119
Case C-23/93 TV10 [1994] ECR I-4795 ....206, 212, 215, 217
Joined Cases C-46/93 and C-48/93 Brasserie du Pêcheur/Factortame III [1996]
  ECR I-1029 .... 52, 443, 456
Case C-68/93 Shevill v Presse Alliance SA [1995] ECR I-415; [1995] 2 AC 18;
  [1995] 2 WLR 499; [1995] All ER (EC) 391
Cases C-69 and 258/93 Punto Casa SpA et al v Sindaco del Commune di
  Capena et al [1994] ECR I-2355 ....194, 198
Case C-293/93 Houtwipper [1994] ECR I-4249 203
Case C-370/93 Verein gegen Unwesen in Handel und Gewerbe Köln e V v
  Mars GmbH [1995] ECR I-1923 ....197, 198
Case C-381/93 Commission v France [1994] ECR I-5145 235
Case C-384/93 Alpine Investments BV v Minister van Financiën
  [1995] ECR I-1141 .... 199, 231, 232, 238, 244, 248,
                                                     253, 255, 256, 267, 272
Case C-387/93 Banchero [1995] ECR I-4663 198
Case C-399/93 Oude Littikhuis and Others [1995] ECR I-4515 237
Case C-412/93 Leclerc-Siplec v TF1 Publicité and M6 Publicité [1995]
  ECR I-179 .... 102, 190, 197, 198, 200, 202, 237
Case C-412/93 Société d'importation Edouard Leclerc v TFI Publicité SA et al
  [1995] ECR I-179 .... 102, 190, 197, 198, 200, 202
Case C-415/93 Union Royale Belge des Sociétés de Football Association ASBL et al v
  Bosman et al [1995] ECR I-4921 ....199, 201
Cases C-418/93-421/93 Semeraro Casa Uno Srl et al v Sindaco del Commune di
  Erbusco et al [1996] ECR I-2975 ....194, 198, 199
Case C-450/93 Kalanke [1996] ECR I-3051 116
Case C-13/94 P v S [1996] ECR I-2143 .... 23, 143
Case C-25/94 Commission v Council [1996] ECR I-1469 159
Case C-55/94 Gebhard v Consiglio dell' Ordine degli Avvocati e Procuratori
  di Milano [1995] ECR I-4165 ....249, 257, 344
Case C-61/94 Commission v Germany [1996] ECR I-3989 330
Case C-63/94 Groupement National des Négociants en Pommes de Terre (Belgapom) v
  ITM Belgium SA et al [1995] ECR I-2467 ....193, 198
Case C-70/94 Werner v Germany [1995] ECR I-3189 .... 326, 354, 355, 356, 357, 358, 360
Case C-83/94 Leifer and Others [1995] ECR I-3231 .... 326, 354, 355, 357, 358, 360
Case C-96/94 Centro Servizi Spediporto Srl v Spedizione Marittima del Golfo Srl
  [1995] ECR I-2883 .... 203, 240
Case C-101/94 Commission v Italy [1996] ECR I-2691 267
Case C-120/94 Commission v Greece [1996] ECR I-1513 .... 27, 327–328
Case C-129/94 Ruiz Bernáldez [1996] ECR I-1829 .... 100, 108

Table of Cases

Case C-134/94 Esso Española SA v Comunidad Autonoma de Canarias [1995]
ECR I-4223. 203
Case C-140/94 DIP SpA et al v Commune di Bassano di Grappa et al [1995]
ECR I-3257. 203
Cases C-163, 165 and 250/94 Sanz de Lera [1995] ECR I-4821. 301
Case C-206/94 Paletta II [1996] ECR I-2357. 207
Case C-209/94 P Buralux v Council [1996] ECR I-615 . . . . 73, 74, 75, 81
C-222/94 Commission of the European Communities v United Kingdom of
Great Britain and Northern Ireland [1996] ECR I-4025 102
Cases C-163, 165 and 250/94 Sanz de Lera [1995] ECR I-4821. 301
Case C-313/94 Graffione [1996] I-2727. 287
Cases C-321–324/94 Pistre et al [1997] ECR I-2343 203
Cases C-34–36/95 Konsumentenombudsmannen (KO) v De Agiostini (Svenska)
Förlag AB et al [1997] ECR I-3843 . . . . 92, 98, 112, 198, 200, 231, 238
Cases C-35/95 and C-36/95 Konsumentombudsmannen v TV-shop i Sverige AB
[1997] ECR I-3843 . . . . 92, 98, 112, 200
Case C-70/95 Sodemare and Others v Regione Lombardia [1997] ECR I-3395. 253
Case C-84/95 Bosphorus Hava Yollari Turuzm v Minister for Transport [1996]
ECR I-3953. . . . . 27, 144, 459, 460
Case 87/95 P Cassa Nazionale di Previdenza ed Assistenza a favore degli avvocati
e dei Procuratori v Council [1996] ECR I-2003 78
Case C-120/95 Decker [1998] ECR I-1831 . . . . 232, 233
Case C-124/95 The Queen, *ex parte* Centro-Com v HM Treasury and Bank of
England [1997] ECR I-81 . . . . 327, 354, 355, 357, 358, 359, 360
Case C-177/95 Ebony Maritime SA and Loten Navigation Co Ltd v Prefetto della
Provincia di Brindisi and others [1996] ECR I-1111 125
Case C-189/95 Criminal proceedings against Harry Franzén [1997]
ECR I-05909. . . . . 102, 114, 119
Case C-222/95 Société Civil Immobolière Parodi v Banque H Albert de
Bary et Cie [1997] ECR I-3899 267
Case C-265/95 Commission v France [1997] ECR I-6959 . . . . 202, 248
Case C-321/95 P Greenpeace, Council and Others v Commission [1998] ECR I-1651. . . . . 75, 78, 81
Case C-321/95 UEAPME v Council [1998] ECR II-2335 80
Case C-338/95 Wiener [1997] ECR I-6495. 23
Case C-367/95 P Commission v Sytraval and Brink's France [1998] ECR I-1719. 88
Case C-368/95 Vereinigte Familiapress Zeitungsverlags-und vertriebs GmbH v
Heinrich Bauer Verlag [1997] ECR I-3689. 198
Case C-375/95 Commission v Greece [1997] ECR I-5981 240
Case C-388/95 Belgium v Spain [2000] ECR I-3123. . . . . 193, 203
Case C-35/96 Commission v Italy [1998] ECR I-3851; TAR Lazio Section I
27 March 1996, n 476 442
Cases C-51/96 and C-191/97 Christelle Deliège [2000] ECR I-2549. . . . . 156, 239, 240
Case C-67/96 Albany [1999] ECR I-5751 117
Case C-85/96 Martínez Sala v Freistaat Bayern [1998] ECR I-2691. . . . . 244, 253
Case C-129/96 Inter-Environnement Wallonie v Région Wallonne [1997] ECR I-7411. 27
Case C-149/96 Portugal v Council [1999] ECR I-8395; 3 JIEL (2000) 441 . . . . 330, 335
Case C-158/96 Kohll [1998] ECR I-1931. . . . . 232, 233
Case C-162/96 Racke v Hauptzollamt Mainz [1998] ECR I-3655 . . . . 328, 332
Case C-184/96 Commission v France [1998] ECR I-6197 203
Case C-203/96 Chemische Afvalstoffen Dusseldorp BV et al v Minister van
Volkshuisvesting, Ruimtelijke Ordening en Milieubeheer [1988] ECR I-4075 191

Case C-249/96 Grant v South-West Trains [1998] ECR I-621 23
Case C-264/96 Imperial Chemical Industries [1998] ECR I-4695 .... 213, 214, 225
Case C-266/96 Corsica Ferries France SA v Gruppo Antichi Ormeggiatori del
 Porto di Genova Coop. Arl et al (Corsica Ferries III) [1998] ECR I-3949 .... 203, 240
Case C-274/96 Criminal proceedings against Bickel and Franz [1998] ECR I-7637 253
Case C-348/96 Calfa [1999] ECR I-11 236
Case C-355/96 Silhouette [1998] ECR I-4799 .... 27, 112, 113, 119
Case C-367/96 Kefalas [1998] ECR I-2843 .... 206, 207
Case 369/96 Criminal proceedings against Arblade and Others [1999] ECR I-8453 247
Case C-406/96 P Sveriges Betodlares [Centralförening] and Henrikson v
 Commission [1997] ECR I-7531 .... 87, 88
Case C-33/97 Colim [1999] ECR I-3175 199
Case C-35/97 Commission v France, Case C-35/97 [1998] I-5235 116
Case C-67/97 Criminal Proceedings against Bluhme [1998] ECR I-8033 256
Joined Cases C-115/97, C-116/97 and C-117/97 Brentjens [1999] ECR I-6025 117
Case C-140/97 Rechberger [1999] ECR I-3499 .... 101, 102, 106
Case C-158/97 Badeck [2000] ECR I-1875 116
Case C-159/97 Trasporti Castelletti v Hugo Trumpy Case [1999] ECR I-1597 388
Cases C-51/96 and C-191/97 Christelle Deliège [2000] ECR I-2549 .... 239, 240, 256
Case C-212/97 Centros [1999] ECR I-2357 .... 210, 211, 215, 216, 218,
 219, 220, 221, 222, 224,
 225, 247
Case C-219/97 Drijvende Bokken [1999] ECR I-6121 117
Case C-222/97 Trummer and Meyer [1999] ECR I-1661 302
Case C-307/97 Saint Gobain [1999] ECR I-6161 219
Case C-321/97 Andersson [1999] ECR I-3551 .... 101, 102
Case C-373/97 Diamantis [2000] ECR I-1705 207
Case 17/98 Emesa Sugar (Free Zone) NV v Aruba [2000] ECR I-665 .... 16, 143
Case C-44/98 BASF AG v Präsident des Deutschen Patentamts [1999] ECR I-6269 203
Case C-58/98 Corsten [2000] ECR I-7919 .... 231, 247
Case C-99/98 Austria v Commission [2001] ECR I-1101 115
Joined Cases C-180/98 to C-184/98 Pavlov [2000] ECR I-645 117
Case C-190/98 Graf v Filmoser Maschinenbau GmbH [2000] ECR I-493 256
Case C-222/98 Van der Woude [2000] ECR I-7111 117
Case C-224/98 D'Hoop v Office national de l'emploi [2002] ECR I-619 251
Case C-254/98 Schutzverband gegen Unlauteren Wettbewerb v TK Heimdienst
 Sass GmbH [2000] ECR I-151 .... 198, 199, 256
Case C-281/98 Angonese v Cassa di Risparmio di Bolzano [2000] ECR I-4139 248
Case C-348/98 Ferreira [2000] ECR I-6711 .... 108, 119
Case C-368/98 Vanbraekel [2001] ECR I-5363 233
Case C-376/98 Germany v Parliament and Council [2000] ECR I-8419 242
Case C-377/98 Netherlands v European Parliament and Council [2001]
 ECR I-7079 .... 27, 125, 134, 166, 331, 338
Case C-381/98 Ingmar GB Ltd v Eaton Leonard Technologies Inc [2000]
 ECR I-9305 278
Case C-405/98 Konsumentombudsmannen (KO) v Gourmet International
 Products AB (GIP) [2001] ECR I-1795 .... 198, 200, 238, 253, 256
Case C-448/98 Guimont [2000] ECR I-10663 .... 203, 229
Case C-466/98 Commission v United Kingdom [2002] ECR I-9427 61
Case C-110/99 Emsland-Stärke [2000] I-11569 .... 207, 208, 212, 214, 223, 227
Case C-157/99 Smits & Peerbooms [2001] ECR I-5473 .... 233, 234

Table of Cases

Case C-178/99 BECTU [2001] ECR I-4881 164
Case C-184/99 Grzelczyk v Centre public d'aide sociale d'Ottignies-Louvain-la-Neuve
    [2001] ECR I-6193.. 251
Case C-270/99 P, Z v Parliament [2001] ECR I-9197............................ 134, 171
Joined Cases C-300/99 P and C-388/99 P Area Cova and others v Council [2001]
    ECR I-983... 78
Case C-309/99 Wouters [2002] ECR I-1577 239
Case C-340/99 TNT Traco SpA [2001] ECR I-4109................................ 165
Case C-359/99 Hautala [2001] ECR I-9565.. 164
Case C-383/99 P Procter & Gamble v OHIM [2001] ECR I-6251 287
Case C-385/99 Müller-Fauré [2003] ECR I-4509 233
Joined Cases C-300/99 P and C-388/99 P Area Cova and others v Council [2001]
    ECR I-983... 78
Case C-390/99 Canal Satélite Digital v Adminstración General del Estado, and
    Distribuidora de Televisión Digital SA (DTS) [2002] ECR I-607 246
Case C-453/99 Courage v Crehan [2001] ECR I-6297 .... 58, 403
Case C-11/00 Commission v ECB 10 July 2003 312
Case C-12/00 Commission v Spain [2003] ECR I-459 199
Case C-17/00 De Coster [2001] ECR I-9445... 232
Joined Cases C-20/00 and C-64/00 Booker Aquaculture and Hydro Seafood [2003]
    ECR I-7411... 165
Case C-24/00 Commission v France [2004] ECR I-1277 .... 96, 119, 203
Case C-49/00 Commission v Italy [2001] ECR I-8575 165
Case C-50/00 P UPA [2002] ECR I-6677 .... 26, 27, 71, 74, 75, 76, 77, 78,
                                                 79, 80, 81, 82, 84, 88, 89,
                                                 118, 135, 136, 164
Case C-53/00 Ferring [2001] ECR I-9067... 98
Case C-60/00 Carpenter v Secretary of State for the Home Department [2002]
    ECR I-6279... 229, 252
Joined Cases C-20/00 and C-64/00 Booker Aquaculture and Hydro Seafood [2003]
    ECR I-7411... 165
Case C-94/00 Roquette Frères v Directeur général de la concurrenceé de la
    consommation et de la répression des fraudes [2002] ECR 9011 .... 129, 142
Case C-101/00 Tulliasiamies and Siilin [2002] ECR I-7487 240
Case C-112/00 Schmidberger (Eugen) Internationale Transporte und Planzüge v
    Republik Österreich [2003] ECR I-5659 .... 71, 128, 130, 134, 142, 202, 248
Case C-137/00 Milk Marque and National Farmers' Union [2003] ECR I-7975 207
Case C-143/00 Boehringer [2002] ECR I-3759..................................... 110
Case C-172/00 Oy Liikenne [2001] ECR I-745 93
Case C-208/00 Überseering [2002] ECR I-9919 165
Case T-212/00 Nuove Industrie Molisane v Commission [2002] ECR I-347............... 78
Case T-244/00 Coillte Teoranta [2001] ECR II-1275 79
Case C-280/00 Altmark Trans [2003] ECR I-7747 98
Case C-300/00 Federación de Cofradías de Pescadores de Guipúzcoa P-R [2000]
    ECR I-8797... 75
Case T-308/00 Salzgitter AG v Commission [2004] ECR II-1933.......... 97
Case C-324/00 Lankhorst-Hohorst [2002] ECR I-11779 .... 213, 214
Case C-328/00 Weber [2002] ECR I-1461.. 79
Joined Cases T-377/00, T-379/00, T-380/00, T-260/01 and T-272/01 Philip Morris
    International v Commission [2003] ECR II-1 163
Case C-416/00 Morellato v Comune di Padova [2003] ECR I-9343 199

Case C-466/00 Kaba v SSHD [2003] ECR I-2219. 16
Case C-6/01 Anomar and Others [2003] ECR I-8621 229
Case C-95/01 Greenham and Abel [2004] ECR I-1333 . . . . 99, 113, 119, 203
Case C-108/01 Consorzio del Prosciutto di Parma and and Salumificio S Rita v
   Asda Stores Ltd and Hygrade Foods Ltd [2003] ECR I-5121 248
Case C-109/01 Akrich [2003] ECR I-9607 . . . . 142, 206, 212, 227
Case C-117/01 KB v The National Health Service Pensions Agency and the Secretary
   of State for Health [2004] ECR I-541 . . . . 23, 167
Case C-126/01 Ministère de l'Economie, des Finances et de l'Industrie v GEMO SA
   [2003] ECR I-13769 . . . . 98, 134
Case C-167/01 Inspire Art [2003] ECR I-10155 . . . . 211, 216, 217, 218, 221,
   223, 225, 226
Case C-192/01 Commission v Denmark [2003] ECR I-9693 . . . . .94, 96, 99, 106, 107, 113,
   119, 193
Case C-198/01 Consorzio Industrie Fiammiferi v Autorità Garante Concorrenza e
   Mercato [2003] ECR I-8055 440
Case C-215/01 Schnitzer [2003] ECR I-14847. . . . . .247, 249
Case C-222/01 Deutscher Apotherkerverbund eV v 0800 Doc Morris NV et al [2003]
   ECR I-14887 . . . . 200, 238
Case C-236/01 Monsanto Agricoltura Italia [2003] ECR I-8105 . . . . .95, 99, 106
Case C-243/01 Gambelli [2003] ECR I-13031; Court of Cassation, United Criminal
   Sections 26 April 2004 n 23271. . . . . 236, 443
Case C-340/01 Abler [2003] ECR I-14023 119
Case C-383/01 De Danske Bilimportører [2003] ECR I-6065 240
Case C-420/01 Commission v Italy [2003] ECR I-6445 193
Case C-452/01 Ospelt and Schlössle Weissenberg [2003] ECR I-9743 . . . . . 91, 99, 104, 105, 116
Case C-491/01 The Queen v Secretary of State for Health *ex parte* British American
   Tobacco Ltd, judgment of 10 December 2002 83
Case C-9/02 de Lasteyrie du Saillant [2004] ECR I-2409 213
Case C-36/02 Omega Spielhallen- und Automatenaufstellungs-GmbH v
   Oberbürgermeisterin der Bundesstadt Bonn [ECR] I-9609. . . . . .130, 166, 232, 237
Case C-41/02 Commission v Netherlands [2004] ECR I-11375 . . . . .95, 99, 119
Case C-71/02 Karner Industrie-Auktionen GmbH v Troostwijk GmbH [2004]
   ECR I-3025. 246
Case C-94/02 P Etablissements Biret v Council [2003] ECR I-10565 334
Case C-116/02 Gasser v MISRAT 9 December 2003. . . . . 389–390, 397
Case C-141/02 P Commission v T-Mobile Austria GmbH [2005] ECR I-1283 82
Case C-147/02 Alabaster [2004] ECR I-3101. 26
Case C-159/02 Turner v Grovit 27 April 2004 [2005] 1 AC 101. . . . . .391–393, 397
Case C-171/02 Commission v Portugal [2004] ECR I-5645 . . . . .212, 217
Case C-200/02 Zhu and Chen v Secretary of State for the Home Department [2004]
   ECR I-9925. 244
Case C-220/02 Österreichischer Gewerkschaftsbund [2004] ECR I-5907 165
Case C-255/02 Halifax [2006] ECR I-1609. . . . . .205, 206, 212, 214, 222, 223, 227
Case C-263/02 P Commission v Jégo-Quéré [2004] ECR I-3425, Opinion of
   10 July 2003. . . . . 136, 164
Case C-281/02 Owusu v Jackson [2005] QB 801. . . . . 393–394, 395
Case C-286/02 Bellio Fratelli v Prefettura di Treviso [2004] ECR I-3465 . . . . . . 91, 95, 104, 106,
   107, 108, 119
Case C-293/02 Jersey Potato [2005] ECR I-9543. 229

Table of Cases xxxix

Case C-309/02 Radlberger Getränkegesellschaft mbH & Co KG, S Spitz KG v
 Land Baden-Württemberg [2004] ECR I-nyr (14 December 2004)................. 201
Case C-319/02 Manninen 113
Case C-329/02 P SAT.1 Satellitenfernsehen GmbH v OHIM ('SAT.2') [2004]
 ECR I-8317 290
Case C-377/02 Van Parys [2005] ECR I-1465 .... 334, 336
Case C-419/02 BUPA Hospitals [2006] ECR I-1685 ....207, 212
Case C-429/02 Bacardi France v Télévision française 1 SA (TF1), Groupe Jean-Claude
 Darmon SA and Girosport SARL [2004] ECR I-6613. 257
Case C-432/02 Unibet v Justitiekanslern, judgment of 13 March 2007. 135
Case C-442/02 Caixa-Bank France v Ministère de l' Économie [2004] ECR I-8961 267
Case C-464/02 Commission v Denmark [2005] ECR I-7929 224
Case C-20/03 Criminal proceedings against Burmanjer [2005] ECR I-4133. . .201, 246, 250, 256
Case C-72/03 Carbonati Apuani [2004] ECR I-8027 26
Case C-78/03 P Commission v Germany (ARE case), judgment of
 13 December 2005..71, 82, 87, 88
Joined Cases C-96/03 and C-97/03 Templeman [2005] ECR I-1895..................... 52
Case C-134/03 Viacom Outdoor (Viacom II) [2005] ECR I-1167................... 239, 240
Case C-147/03 Commission v Austria [2005] ECR I-5969 .... 206, 212, 252
Case C-160/03 Spain v Eurojust [2005] ECR I-2077................................ 165
Case C-173/03 Traghetti del Mediterraneo [2006] ECR I-5177....................... 440
Case C-176/03 Commission v Council [2005] ECR I-7879........................165, 329
Case C-181/03 P Nardone v Commission [2005] ECR I-199......................... 165
Case C-209/03 Bidar v London Borough of Ealing; Secretary of State for Education
 and Skills [2005] ECR I-2119. .... 165, 244, 251, 252
Case C-223/03 University of Huddersfield Higher Education Corporation [2006]
 ECR I-1751 ....207, 212
Case C-231/03 Coname [2005] ECR I-7287 234
Case 319/03 Briheche (Serge) v Ministère de l'intérieur de la sécurité intérieure et
 des libertés locales [2004] ECR I-8807 103
Case C-320/03 Commission v Austria [2005] ECR I-nyr (15 November 2005)............ 201
Joint Cases C-346/03 and C-529/03 Francesco Atzori, Giuseppe Atzeni, Giuseppe
 Ignazio Boi [2003] ECR II-6037... 84
Case C-436/03 Parliament v Council [2006] ECR I-3733........................... 52
Case C-446/03 Marks & Spencer [2005] ECR I-10837.............................. 213
Case C-458/03 Parking Brixen [2005] ECR I-8612................................ 234
Case C-475/03 Banca popolare di Cremona [2006] ECR I-9373........................ 61
Case C-515/03 Eichsfelder Schlachtbetrieb [2005] ECR I-7355....................... 207
Joined Cases C-346/03 and C-529/03 Francesco Atzori, Giuseppe Atzeni, Giuseppe
 Ignazio Boi [2003] ECR II-6037... 84
Case C-537/03 Candolin [2005] ECR I-5745.......................99–100, 109, 121, 122
Case C-540/03 Parliament v Council [2006] ECR I-5769..................... 135, 148, 168
Joined Cases C-544/03 and C-545/03 Mobistar and Belgacom Mobile [2005]
 ECR I-7723... 240
Joined Cases C-544/03 and C-545/03 Mobistar v Commune de Fléron [2005]
 ECR I-7723... 256
Case C-552/03 P Unilever Bestfoods (Ireland) Ltd, formerly Van den Bergh
 Foods Ltd v Commission [2006] ECR I-9091 453
Case C-27/04 Commission v Council 13 July 2004................................ 318
Case C-145/04 Spain v United Kingdom [2006] ECR I-7917......................... 52

Table of Cases

Case C-151/04 Nadin and Nadin-Lux [2005] ECR I-11203 224
Joined Cases C-158 and 159/04 Alfa Vita Vassilopoulos AE et al v Elliniko Dimosio,
  Nommarkhiaki Aftodiikisi Ioanninon [2006] ECR I-nyr (14 September 2006) 193, 198
Joined Cases C-158 & 159/04 Alfa Vita Vassilopoulos AE et al v Elliniko Dimosio
  [2006] ECRI-nyr (14 September 2006) 190, 198
Case C-167/04 P JCB Services v Commission judgment of 21 September 2006............ 125
Case C-170/04 Klas Rosengren and Others v Rikåsklagaren, opinion of AG Mengozzi
  30 November 2006, nyr..114, 115
Case C-196/04 Cadbury Schweppes [2006] ECR I-7995.............. 213, 214, 217, 218, 219,
  220, 221, 222, 224, 225, 226
Joined Cases C-94/04 and C-202/04 Cipolla and Others [2006] ECR I-11421............ 229
Case C-207/04 Vergani [2005] ECR I-7453...................................... 162
Case C-217/04 United Kingdom v European Parliament and Council [2006] ECR I-3771.... 52
Case C-227/04 P Lindorfer v Council, opinion of 27 October 2005 134
Joined Cases C-232/04 and C-233/04 Güney-Görres [2005] ECR I-11237..............99, 119
Case C-290/04 FKP Scorpio Konzertproduktionen GmbH v Finanzamt
  Hamburg-Eimsbüttel [2006] ECR I-9461..................... 244, 246, 247, 257, 302
Case C-292/04 Meilicke (6 March 2007)... 302
Case C-317/04 Parliament v Council [2006] ECR I-4721 165
Cases C-338, 359 and 360/04 Placanica and others, judgment of 6 March 2007 .... 236, 443
Case C-348/04 Boehringer Ingelheim II, judgment of 26 April 2007 ....97, 100, 110
Case C-351/04 Ikea Wholesale v Commissioners of Customs and Excise, opinion of
  6 April 2006, para 87, judgment pending.................................... 335
Cases C-338, 359 and 360/04 Placanica and others [2007] ECR I-1891 .... 236, 443
Case C-372/04 Watts v Bedford Primary Care Trust and Secretary of State for
  Health [2006] ECR I-4325..233, 251
Case C-374/04 Test Claimants in Class IV of the ACT Group Litigation
  23 February 2006 nyr 113, 114, 119
Case C-410/04 ANAV [2005] ECR I-3303 234
Case C-423/04 Sarah Margaret Richards v Secretary of State for Work and Pensions
  [2006] ECR-3585 23
Case C-434/04 Criminal proceedings against Jan-Erik Anders Ahokainen and
  Mati Leppik, judgment of 28 September 2006 .... 97, 101, 193, 198
Case C-444/04 A-Punkt Schmuckhandels GmbH v Schmidt [2006] ECR I-nyr
  (23 February 2006) 201
Case C-452/04 Fidium Finanz AG v Bundesanstalt für Finanzdienstleistungsaufsicht
  judgment of 3 October 2006 .... 96, 105, 302
Case C-456/04 Agip Petroli [2006] ECR I-3395 207
Case C-471/04 Keller Holding, judgment of 23 February 2006 ....104, 119
Case C-499/04 Werhof [2006] ECR I-2397 165
Case C-519/04 P David Meca-Medina [2006] ECR I-0000 239
Case C-524/04 Test Claimants in the Thin Cap Group Litigation judgment of
  13 March 2007 ('Thin Cap') [2007] ECR I-2107....................213, 214, 222, 225
Case C-54/05 Commission v Finland [2007] ECR I-nyr (15 March 2007) 193
Case C-82/05 Commission v Greece [2006] ECRI-nyr (14 September 2006)............. 199
Commission v Council, Case C-91/05 (pending) 328
Case C-142/05 Åklagaren v Mickelsson & Roos (pending, opinion of
  14 December 2006)... 202
Case C-170/05 Denkavit International BV Denkavit France SARL v Ministre
  de l'Economie, des Finances and de l'Industrie, 27 April 2006 nyr 113, 114, 119
Case C-178/05 Commission v Greece, judgment of 7 June 2007...................... 207
Case C-231/05 Oy AA, judgment of 18 July 2007 213

Table of Cases

Case C-279/05 Vonk [2007] ECR I-239 207
Case C-313/05 Brzeziński, Maciej [2007] ECR I-0000 240
Case C-321/05 Kofoed, judgment of 5 July 2007 207
Case C-345/05 Commission v Portugal, judgment of 26 October 2006 .... 104, 119
Case C-370/05 Festersen, judgment of 25 January 2007 130
Case C-379/05 Amurta 110
Case C-438/05 International Transport Workers' Federation and the Finnish
    Seamen's Union v Viking Line ABP and Oü Viking Line Eesti, nyr 117
Case C-438/05 Viking Line Abp v The International Transport Workers' Federation and the
    Finnish Seamen's Union (pending) 242
Joined Cases C-11/06 and C-12/06 Morgan and Bucher, judgment of 23 October 2007 252
Case C-104/06 Commission v Sweden, judgment of 18 January 2007 nyr 119
Case C-284/06 Finanzamt Hamburg-Am Tierpark v Burda Verlagsbeteiligungen
    GmbH (pending) 111
Case C-425/06 Part Service (pending) 212

European Court of Justice—Opinions

Opinion 1/75 [1975] ECR 1355 325
Opinion 1/91 [1991] ECR I-6079 .... 120, 121
Opinion 2/94 [1996] ECR I-1759 147

Court of First Instance

Case T-137/05 Gruppo La Perla SpA v OHIM ('NIMEI LA PERLA MODERN
    CLASSIC/LA PERLA'), judgment of 16 May 2007 288
Case T-1/89 Rhône-Poulenc [1991] ECR II-867 33
Case T-2/89 Petrofina [1991] ECR II-1087 33
Case T-3/89 Atochem [1991] ECR II-1177 33
Case T-4/89 BASF [1991] ECR II-1523 33
Case T-6/89 Enichem Anic [1991] ECR II-1623 33
Case T-7/89 SA Hercules Chemicals [1991] ECR II-1711 33
Case T-8/89 DSM [1991] ECR II-1833 33
Case T-9/89 Hüls [1992] ECR II-499 33
Case T-10/89 Hoechst [1992] ECR II-629 33
Case T-11/89 Shell International Chemical Company [1992] ECR II-757 33
Case T-12/89 Solvay & Cie [1992] ECR II-907 33
Case T-13/89 Imperial Chemical Industries [1992] ECR II-1021 33
Case T-14/89 Montedipe [1992] ECR II-1155 33
Case T-15/89 Chemie Linz [1992] ECR II-1275 33
Case T-51/89 Tetra Pak [1990] ECR II-309 33
Case T-120/89 Stahlwerke Peine-Salzgitter [1992] ECR II-279 33
Case T-24/90 Automec [1992] ECR II-2223 33
Case T-28/90 Asia Motor France [1992] ECR II-2285 33
Case T-472/93 Campo Ebro v Council [1995] ECR II-421 .... 73, 74
Case T-482/93 Weber v Commission [1996] ECR II-609 79
Case T-100/94 Kapniki A Michailidis AE [1998] ECR II-3115 78
Case T-115/94 Opel Austria v Council [1997] ECR II-39 .... 103, 104, 120, 331
Case T-330/94 Salt Union Ltd v Commission [1996] ECR II-1475 79
Case T-398/94 Kahn Scheppvaart BV v Commission [1996] ECR II-447 80
Joined Cases T-198/95, T-171/96, T-230/97, T-174/98 and T-225/99 Comafrica
    SpA and Dole Fresh Fruit Europe Ltd & Co v Commission [2001] II-1975 78
Case T-69/96 Hamburger Hafen- und Lagerhaus Aktiengesellschaft [2001]
    ECR II-1037 78

Case T-122/96 Federazione Nazionale del Commercio Oleario (Federolio) [1997]
ECR II-1559. 78
Joined Cases T-198/95, T-171/96, T-230/97, T-174/98 and T-225/99 Comafrica
SpA and Dole Fresh Fruit Europe Ltd & Co. v Commission [2001] II-1975. 78
Case T-175/96 Berthu v Commission [1997] ECR II-811 309
Cases T-14/97 and T-15/97 Sofivo v Council [1998] ECR II-4191 78
Case T-22/97 Kesko Oy v Commission [1999] ECR II-3775. 53
Joined Cases T-198/95, T-171/96, T-230/97, T-174/98 and T-225/99 Comafrica
SpA and Dole Fresh Fruit Europe Ltd & Co v Commission [2001] II-1975 78
Case T-256/97 BEUC v Commission [2000] ECR II-101 331
Case T-32/98 Nederlandse Antillen v Commission [2000] ECR II-201 rvrsd C-142/00
[2003] ECR I-3483 82
Case T-65/98 Van den Bergh Foods formerly HB Ice Cream Ltd v Commission [2003]
ECR II-4653 453
Case T-138/98 Armement Coopératif Artisanal Vendéen (ACAV) [2000] II-341 78
Case T-163/98 Procter & Gamble v OHIM [1999] ECR II-2383. 287
Case T-172/98 Salamander and others v Parliament/Council case [2000] ECR II-2487 . . . 78, 79
Case T-173/98 UPA v Council [1999] ECR II-3357 74
Joined Cases T-198/95, T-171/96, T-230/97, T-174/98 and T-225/99 Comafrica
SpA and Dole Fresh Fruit Europe Ltd & Co v Commission [2001] II-1975 78
Joined Cases T-191/98 T-212/98, T-213/98 and T-214/98 Senator Lines [1999]
ECR II-2531 143
Case T-13/99 Pfizer Animal Health v Council [2002] ECR II-3305 . . . . 84, 85, 95, 99, 106
Case T-54/99 Max.mobil Telekommunikation [2002] ECR II-313 . . . . 82, 163
Case T-70/99 Alpharma v Council [2002] ECR II-3495 . . . . 84, 85, 95, 106
Case T-128/99 Signal Communications v OHIM ('TELEYE') [2001] ECR II-3273. 287
Joined Cases T-198/95, T-171/96, T-230/97, T-174/98 and T-225/99 Comafrica
SpA and Dole Fresh Fruit Europe Ltd & Co v Commission [2001] II-1975 78
Joined Cases T-67/00, T-68/00, T-71/00 and T-78/00 JFE Engineering Corp v Commission
[2004] ECR II-1575. 163
Case T-32/98 Nederlandse Antillen v Commission [2000] ECR II-201 rvrsd C-142/00 [2003]
ECR I-3483. 82
Case T-106/00 Streamserve Inc v OHIM ('STREAMSERVE') [2002]
ECR II-723. . . . . 284, 285, 294
Case T-323/00 SAT.1 v OHIM [2002] ECR II-2839 290
Case T-339/00 Bactria Industriehygiene-Service Verwaltungs GmbH [2002]
ECR II-2287 . . . . 78, 85
Case T-19/01 Chiquita [2005] ECR II-315. . . . . 334, 336
Joined Cases T-116/01 and T-118/01 P&O European Ferries [2003] ECR II-2957 163
Case T-177/01 Jégo-Quéré v Commission [2002] ECR II-2365. . . . . 77, 78, 79, 80–84,
89, 134, 137, 164
Case T-243/01 Sony Computer Entertainment Ltd v Commission [2003] ECR II-4189 . . . 84, 86
Case T-256/01 Pyres v Commission [2005] ECR II-25 164
Joined Cases T-377/00, T-379/00, T-380/00, T-260/01 and T-272/01 Philip Morris
International v Commission [2003] ECR II-1 163
Case T-292/01 Phillips-Van Heusen Corp v OHIM ('BASS/PASH') [2003]
ECR II-4335 287
Case T-306/01 Yusuf v Council and Commission [2005] ECR II-3353. . . . 328, 333, 334, 336, 343
Case T-315/01 Kadi v Council and Commission [2005] ECR II-3649. . . . 328, 333, 334, 336, 343
Case T-45/02 DOW AgroSciences BV [2003] ECR II-1973 84
Case T-154/02 Villiger [2003] ECR II-1921. 84

Table of Cases   xliii

Case T-167/02 Etablissements Toulorge [2003] ECR II-1111 84
Case T-213/02 SNF SA v Commission [2004] ECR II-3047 84
Case T-219/02 and T-337/02 Lutz Herrera v Commission [2004] ECR II-1407 164
Case T-231/02 Gonnelli, Order of 2 April 2004 [2004] ECR II-1051 84
case T-242/02 Surinder Corp v OHMI [2005] ECR II-2793 163
Case T-321/02 Paul Vannieuwenhuyze-Morin [2003] ECR II-1997 84
Case T-219/02 and T-337/02 Lutz Herrera v Commission [2004] ECR II-1407 164
Case T-391/02 Bundesverband der Nahrungsmittel, Order of 10 May 2004
    [2004] ECR II-1447 84
Case T-141/03 Sniace SA, Judgment of 14 April 2005 [2005] ECR I-1197 84
Case T-142/03 Fost Plus VZW, Order of 16 February 2005 [2005] ECR I-589 84
Case T-165/03 Vonier v Commission [2004] ECR II-1575 163
Case T-196/03 European Federation for Cosmetic Ingredients [2004] ECR II-4263 84

European Court of Human Rights

Banković and Others v Belgium and 16 other Contracting States, App No 52207/99,
    admissibility decision of 12 December 2001 140
Bosphorus Hava Yollari Turizm Ve Ticaret Anonim Sirketi v Ireland,
    App No 45036/98 (2006) 42 EHRR 1 .... 23, 137, 167, 342
CFDT v European Communities, App No 8030/77, decision of 10 July 1978
    (1978) 13 DR 231 139
Cyprus v Turkey App No 25781/94, judgment of 10 May 2001 (2001) 35 EHRR 731 140
D v European Communities, App No 13539/88, decision of 19 January 1989 139
Emesa Sugar BV v Netherlands, App No 62023/00, decision of 13 January 2005 143
Ferrari v Italy, 28 July 1999 389
Fretté v France, App No 36515/97, judgment of 26 February 2002 167
Goodwin v United Kingdom, App No 28957/95 (2002) 35 EHRR 18 .... 135, 167
Heinze v Contracting Parties who are also Parties to the European Patent Convention,
    App No 12090/92, decision of 10 January 1994 (1994) 76A DR 125; (1994)
    18 EHRR Ch168 141
Hess (Ilse) v United Kingdom, App No 6231/73, decision of 28 May 1975 (1975) 2 DR 72 ... 139
I v United Kingdom, App No25680/98, judgment of 11 July 2002 167
Kress v France, App No 39594/98, judgment of 7 June 2001, Reports of Judgments
    and decisions 2001-VI 16
Lawless v Ireland, App No 332/57 1961, Series A, No 3 447
Loizidou v Cyprus (Preliminary Objections), App No 15319/89, judgment of
    3 March 1995 (1995) 20 EHRR 99 .... 140, 149
Loizidou v Turkey (Preliminary Objections), judgment of 23 March 1995, Series
    A no 310 .... 145, 350
M & Co v Federal Republic of Germany, App No 13258/87, decision of
    9 February 1990 (1990) 64 DR 138 140
Matthews v United Kingdom, App No 24833/94, judgment of 18 February 1999
    (1999) 29 EHRR 361 .... 142, 146
Parfits v Greece, App No 20323/92 (1999) 27 EHRR 566 142
Pretty v United Kingdom, Rep 2002-III 340
Senator Lines v the Fifteen Member States of the European Union,
    App No 56672/00, (2004) 39 EHRR SE3 143
Smith and Grady v UK (1999) 29 ECHR 493 182
SW v United Kingdom and CR v United Kingdom Rep 1995, 363 340
Vo v France, App 53924/00 (2005) 40 EHRR 12 .... 135, 342
Waite and Kennedy app no 26083/94, [1999] RJD 393 343

EFTA Court—A-Z order

Ask v ABB and Aker, Case E-2/96, Efta Court Report [1995–96] 65 93
Bankers' and Securities' Dealers Association of Iceland v EFTA Surveillance
    Authority (HFF), Efta Court Report, Case E-9/04 [2006] 42 99
Bellona *see* Technologien Bau- und Wirtschaftsberatung GmbH and Bellona
    Foundation v EFTA Surveillance Authority, Case E-2/02
EFTA Surveillance Authority v Norway ('Finnmark'), Case E-3/05, Efta Court
    Report [2006] 101 115
EFTA Surveillance Authority v Norway (Kellogg), Case E-3/00, Efta Court
    Report [2001–2002] 73 .... 94, 95, 96, 99, 106, 107, 108
EFTA v University of Oslo, Case E-1/02, Efta Court Report [2003] 1 ....103, 116
Eidesund (Eilert) v Stavanger Catering A/S, Case E-2/95, Efta Court Report [1995–96] 1 93
ESA v Iceland, Case E-1/03, Efta Court Report [2003] 143 ....104, 119
Fesil and Finnfjord and Others v EFTA Surveillance Authority, Joined Cases
    E-5/04, E-6/04 and E-7/04, Efta Court Report [2005] 117 115
Finanger *see* Storebrand Skadeforsikring AS v Veronika Finanger, Case E-1/99
Fokus Bank ASA v Norwegian State, Caw E-1/04 [2004], Efta Court Report 11.... 91, 104, 105,
    111, 114, 116, 119
Forbrukerombudet v Mattel Scandinavia and Lego Norge, Joined Cases E-8/94
    and E-9/94, Efta Court Report [1994–1995] 113............................. 102
HOB-vín v The Icelandic State and Afengis- og tóbaksverslun ríkisins (The State
    Alcohol and Tobacco Company of Iceland), Case E-4/05, Efta Court
    Report [2006] 3..114, 115
Husbanken II, Case E-4/97, Efta Court Report [1999] 1............................. 98
Karlsson, Case E-4/01, Efta Court Report [2002] 155......................106, 120, 121
Kellogg's judgment *see* EFTA Surveillance Authority v Norway (Kellogg), Case E-3/00
Konsumentombudsmannen v De Agostini (Svenska) Förlag AB, Case E-4/94,
    Efta Court Report [1994–95] 89 92
Konsumentombudsmannen v TV-shop i Sverige AB, Case E-5/94, Efta Court
    Report [1994–95] 93 92
LO, Case E-8/0, Efta Court Report [2002] 114.................................... 117
Maglite, Case E-2/97, Efta Court Report [1997] 127......................... 112, 113, 119
Mattel Scandinavia and Lego Norge, Joined Cases E-8/94 and E-9/94, judgment
    of 16 June 1995 ....92, 98, 102, 112
Merck v Paranova, case E-3/02, Efta Court Report [2003] 101 .... 97, 100, 109, 110
Norway v EFTA Surveillance Authority, Case E-6/98, Efta Court Report [1999] 74......... 97
Norwegian Bankers' Association v EFTA Surveillance Authority, Case E-7/97,
    Efta Court Report [1999] 1 98
Norwegian Federation of Trade Unions and Others v Norwegian Association of Local and
    Regional Authorities and Others, Case E-8/00, Efta Court Report [2002] 114 116
Paranova v Merck, case E-3/02, Efta Court Report [2003] 101 .... 97, 100, 109, 110
Pedicel A/S v Sosial- og helsedirektoratet (Directorate for Health and Social Affairs),
    Case E-4/04, Efta Court Report [2005] 1 106
Rasmussen, Case E-2/04, Efta Court Report [2004] 57............................. 99
Restamark, Case E-1/94, Efta Court Report [1994–1995] 15 .... 97, 101, 102, 103, 104, 120
Scottish Salmon Growers Association Limited v EFTA Surveillance Authority,
    Case E-2/94 [1994-1995], Efta Court Report 59 ....91, 104
State Debt Management Agency v Islandsbanki-FBA, Case E-1/00, Efta Court
    Report [2000–2001] 8..96, 99, 105
Storebrand Skadeforsikring AS v Veronika Finanger, Efta Court Report,
    Case E-1/99 [1999] 119 .... 100, 108, 109, 119, 121, 122

Table of Cases

Sveinbjörnsdóttir, Case E-9/97, Efta Court Report [1998] 95 ...... 101, 102, 103, 106, 120, 122
Technologien Bau- und Wirtschaftsberatung GmbH and Bellona Foundation v
   EFTA Surveillance Authority, Case E-2/02 [2003], Efta Court Report 52...... 91, 117, 118
Tore Wilhelmsen AS v Oslo kommuneé, Case E-6/96, Efta Court Report [1997] 53......... 119
Transportbedriftenes Landsforening and Nor-Way Bussekspress AS v EFTA
   Surveillance Authority, Case E-3/03, Efta Court Report [2004] 1.................... 98
Ulstein and Røiseng, Case E-2/96, Efta Court Report [1995–96] 65............... 92–93, 106

EFTA Court—numerical order

Case E-1/94 Restamark, Efta Court Report [1994–1995] 15......... 97, 101, 102, 103, 104, 120
Cases E-2/94 Scottish Salmon Growers Association Limited v EFTA Surveillance
   Authority [1994-1995], Efta Court Report 59............................... 91, 104
Case E-4/94 Konsumentombudsmannen v De Agostini (Svenska) Förlag AB, Efta
   Court Report [1994–95] 89.. 92
Case E-5/94 Konsumentombudsmannen v TV-shop i Sverige AB, Efta Court Report
   [1994–95] 93... 92
Joined Cases E-8/94 and E-9/94 Forbrukerombudet v Mattel Scandinavia and
   Lego Norge, Efta Court Report [1994–1995] 113...................... 92, 98, 102, 112
Case E-2/95 Eidesund (Eilert) v Stavanger Catering A/S, Efta Court Report [1995–96] 1..... 93
Case E-2/96 Ask v ABB and Aker, Efta Court Report [1995–96] 65..................... 93
Case E-2/96 Ulstein and Røiseng, Efta Court Report [1995–96] 65............... 92–93, 106
Case E-6/96 Tore Wilhelmsen AS v Oslo kommuneé, Efta Court Report [1997] 53......... 119
Case E-2/97 Maglite, Efta Court Report [1997] 127........................ 112, 113, 119
Case E-4/97 Husbanken II, Efta Court Report [1999] 1............................... 98
Case E-7/97 Norwegian Bankers' Association v EFTA Surveillance Authority, Efta
   Court Report [1999] 1.. 98
Case E-9/97 Sveinbjörnsdóttir, Efta Court Report [1998] 95............... 101, 102, 103, 106,
                                                                                   120, 122
Case E-6/98 Norway v EFTA Surveillance Authority, Efta Court Report [1999] 74......... 97
Case E-1/99 Storebrand Skadeforsikring AS v Veronika Finanger, Efta Court Report
   [1999] 119.. 100, 108, 109, 119, 121, 122
Case E-1/00 State Debt Management Agency v Islandsbanki-FBA, Efta Court
   Report [2000–2001] 8.. 96, 99, 105
Case E-3/00 EFTA Surveillance Authority v Norway (Kellogg judgment),
   Efta Court Report [2001–2002] 73...................... 94, 95, 96, 99, 106, 107, 108
Case E-8/00 Norwegian Federation of Trade Unions and Others v Norwegian
   Association of Local and Regional Authorities and Others, Efta Court
   Report [2002] 114.. 116, 117
Case E-4/01 Karlsson, Efta Court Report [2002] 155..................... 106, 120, 121
Case E-1/02 EFTA v University of Oslo, Efta Court Report [2003] 1 .... 103, 116
Case E-2/02 Technologien Bau- und Wirtschaftsberatung GmbH and Bellona
   Foundation v EFTA Surveillance Authority [2003], Efta Court Report 52..... 91, 117, 118
Case E-3/02 Paranova v Merck, Efta Court Report [2003] 101.............. 97, 100, 109, 110
Case E-1/03 ESA v Iceland, Efta Court Report [2003] 143...................... 104, 119
Case E-3/03 Transportbedriftenes Landsforening and Nor-Way Bussekspress
   AS v EFTA Surveillance Authority, Efta Court Report [2004] 1.................... 98
Case E-1/04 Fokus Bank ASA v Norwegian State [2004], Efta Court Report 11 .... 91, 104, 105,
                                                                          111, 114, 116, 119
Case E-2/04 Rasmussen, Efta Court Report [2004] 57......................... 99
Case E-4/04 Pedicel A/S v Sosial- og helsedirektoratet (Directorate for Health and
   Social Affairs), Efta Court Report [2005] 1.................................... 106

Joined Cases E-5/04, E-6/04 and E-7/04 Fesil and Finnfjord and Others v EFTA
  Surveillance Authority, Efta Court Report [2005] 117............................115
Case E-9/04 Bankers' and Securities' Dealers Association of Iceland v EFTA
  Surveillance Authority (HFF), Efta Court Report [2006] 42......................99
Case E-3/05 EFTA Surveillance Authority v Norway ('Finnmark'), Efta Court
  Report [2006] 101 115
Case E-4/05 HOB-vín v The Icelandic State and Afengis- og tóbaksverslun ríkisins (The
  State Alcohol and Tobacco Company of Iceland), Efta Court Report [2006] 3 ..... 114, 115

OHIM Boards of Appeal
Case R 20/1997–1 XTRA USA Detergents Inc 289, 290, 291
Case R 35/1998–1 Procter & Gamble ('BABY-DRY'), 31 July 1998.....................295
Cases R 96/1998–1 and R 99/1998–1 Oversea-Chinese Banking Corporation Limited
  ('EASI-CASH' and 'EASI-CARD'), 20 November 1998...............291, 292, 291, 292
Case R 312/1999–2, 2 August 2000...290
Case R 802/1999–1 Ferrero oHG mbH v Duplo Corporation ('DUPLO/DUPLO'),
  5 June 2000 287
Case R 407/2004–2 Elsevier Inc ('BUILDING INSIGHTS. BREAKING
  BOUNDARIES') 26 November 2004..292, 293
Case R 22/2003–2 Yamaha Kabushiki Kaisha ('JUNIOR KIT'), 4 July 2005.............296
Case R 118/2003–2 ('WHITENING MULTI-ACTION'), 22 June 2004 290
Case R 862/2004–2 Procter & Gamble ('DEVICE OF BACKGROUNDSWITH
  COLOURED GRANULES [FIG. MARK]'), 17 December 2004....................292
Case R 1029/2004–2 Volcano Corporation ('VIRTUAL HISTOLOGY'),
  7 December 2005 ....294, 295
Case R 495/2005–4 G Jebarah Kenneth trading as Screw You ('SCREW YOU'),
  6 July 2006 ....287, 290
Case R 1206/2006–2 The Coca Cola Company, 22 December 2006...................295

Canada
R v Chaulk [1990] 3 SCR 1303 180
R v Oakes [1986] 1 SCR 103 180

Estonia
Eesti Vabariigi Riigikohus, judgment No 3 of the Constitutional Review Chamber of the
  Supreme Court 21 January 2004 135

France
Case No 287110, Société Arcelor Atlantique etorraine et autres, judgment of
  8 February 2007 137

Ireland
Attorney General v X [1992] 1 IR 1 459
Byrne v Ireland [1972] IR 241 454
Campus Oil v Minister for Industry [1983] IR 82 454
Cityview Press Ltd v An Comhairle Oiliúna and others [1980] 1 IR 381 458
Conway v INTO [1991] 2 IR 305..454
Crotty v An Taoiseach and others [1987] IR 713 ....447, 450, 451
Crowley v Ireland [1980] IR 102 454
D v Health Service Executive (HC) decision 9 May 2007 (unreported)...............459
Emerald Meats v Minister for Agriculture [1997] 1 IR 1 454–455

Greene v Minister for Agriculture [1990] 2 IR 17.................................... 457
HB Ice Cream Ltd v Masterfoods [1990] 2 IR 463................................ 453
Lawlor v Minister for Agriculture [1990] 1 IR 356................................ 456
McBride v Galway Corporation [1998] 1 IR 485 453
Maher v Minister for Agriculture and Rural Development [2001] 2 IR 139............ 457, 461
Masterfoods v HB Ice Cream Ltd [1993] ILRM 145 .... 453, 454
Maxwell v Minister for Agriculture [1999] 2 IR 474................................ 455
Meagher v Minister for Agriculture, Ireland and the Attorney General [1994]
  1 IR 329.. 457, 461
O'Laighléis and in the matter of the Constitution, In re Gearóid [1960] IR 93 447
Pesca Valentia v Minister for Fisheries and others [1985] IR 193 451
Pigs and Bacon Commission v McCarre, High Court (unreported) 30 June 1978.......... 451
SIAC v Mayo County Council [2002] 3 IR 148................................... 453
Society for the Protection of Unborn Children (Ireland) Limited v Grogan [1989] IR 753.... 458
Tate v Minister for Social Welfare [1995] 1 IR 418................................ 455

Italy

Acciaierie San Michele, Corte Costituzionale, 27 December 1965, n 98 .... 435, 437
Corte Costituzionale, judgment No 135 of 11-24 April 2002........................ 135
Costa v ENEL, Corte Costituzionale, 7 March 1964, n 14 435
Fragd, Corte Costituzionale, 21 April 1989 n 232/1989............................ 438
Frontini, Corte Costituzionale, 27 December 1973, n 183.......................... 436, 437
Giampaoli, Corte Costituzionale, 18 April 1991 n 168 438
Granital, Corte Costituzionale, 8 June 1984, n 170............................... 437, 438
Industrie Chimiche IC, Corte Costituzionale, 30 October 1975, n 232............... 436, 437
Messaggero Servizi, Corte Costituzionale, 15 December 1995 n 536................. 438, 439

Norway

Storebrand Skadeforsikring AS v Veronika Finanger 16.11.2000, Sivilsak
  Nr 55/1999, Inr 49B/2000.. 121–122
Veronika Finanger v The State, 28 October 2005, HR-2005-0169 – P, Case No 2005/412 ... 122

Spain

Tribunal Constitucional de España judgment No 292/2000 of 30 November 2000 135

United Kingdom

A v Secretary of State for the Home Department [2004] UKHL 56 (the Belmarsh case) 185
Associated Provincial Picture Houses v Wednesbury Corporation [1948]
  KB 223 ....172, 176, 177, 180, 181, 182, 186
Attorney General v Arthur Andersen, *The Times*, 13 October 1987 395
Backhouse v Lambeth London Borough Council, *The Times*, 14 October 1972............ 177
Belmarsh case *see* A v Secretary of State for the Home Department
Boehringer [2004] EWCA (Civ) 129.. 110
Brown v Stott [2003] 1 AC 681 176
Buchanan (James) & Co Ltd v Babco Forwarding & Shipping (UK) Ltd [1977]
  QB 208, CA.. 205
Bugdaycay v Home Secretary [1987] AC 514 182
Bulmer v Bollinger [1974] Ch 401 .... 67, 420
City of Bradford Metropolitan Council v Secretary of State for the Environment
  [1986] JPL 598.. 178
Coote v Granada Hospitality Ltd (No 2) [1999] 3 CMLR 334........................ 420

Table of Cases

Council of Civil Service Unions v Minister for the Civil Service [1985] AC 374............ 181
Countryside Alliance and Others and the Secretary of State for Environment
    [2006] EWHC 817, CA.. 241
Daly *see* R (Daly) v Secretary of State for the Home Department
de Freitas v Permanent Secretary of Ministry of Agriculture Fisheries Land and
    Housing [1999] 1 AC 69 180
E v Secretary of State for the Home Department [2004] EWCA Civ 49;
    [2004] QB 1044... 183
EMI v CBS [1976] RPC 1 67
ex parte Omega Air [2000] EuLR 254 67
Factortame [1991] 1 AC 603.. 58
GCHQ Case *see* Council of Civil Service Unions v Minister for the Civil Service
Grampian Regional Council v Aberdeen City Council (1984) 47 P and CR 633, HL 178
Hall & Co Ltd v Shoreham-by-Sea Urban District Council [1964] 1 WLR 240 178
Huang (FC) v Secretary of State for the Home Department [2007] UKHL 11 185
Kay v Lambeth London Borough Council [2006] UKHL 10 185
Michalak v Wandsworth London Borough Council [2003] 1 WLR 617 184
N (Kenya) v Secretary of State for the Home Department [2004] EWCA Civ 1094........ 179
Pulhofer v Hillingdon London Borough Council [1986] AC 484 .... 181, 184
R (Alconbury) v Secretary of State for the Environment and the Regions [2001]
    2 WLR 1389 184
R (Association of British Civilian Internees: Far East Region) v Secretary of
    State for Defence [2003] QB 1397.....................................180, 181
R (Daly) v Home Secretary [2001] 2 AC 532; [2001] UKHL 26................. 176, 180, 181
R (Farrakhan) v Secretary of State for the Home Department [2002] QB 1319 184
R (Harris) v Secretary of State for the Home Department [2001] INLR 584 179
R (Hindawi) v Secretary of State for the Home Department [2004] EWHC 78............. 186
R (Hooper) v Secretary of State for Work and Pensions [2003] 1 WLR 2623............... 184
R (Khatun) v Newham London Borough Council [2004] EWCA Civ 55; [2005] QB 37 178
R (Mount Cook Land Ltd) v Westminster City Council [2003] EWCA Civ 1346.......... 179
R (on the application of Pro-Life Alliance) v BBC [2003] 2 WLR 1403 182
R (W) v Thetford Youth Justices [2002] EWHC 1252................................ 184
R (X) v Chief Constable of Midlands Police [2004] 1 WLR 1518 186
R v Barnsley Metropolitan Borough Council, *ex p* Hook [1976] 1 WLR 1052............. 177
R v Brent London Borough Council, *ex p* Assegai (1987) 151 LGR 891 178
R v Chief Constable of the Merseyside Police, *ex p* Calveley [1986] 1 QB 424 184
R v Chief Constable of Sussex, *ex p* International Trader's Ferry [1997] 3 WLR 132 179
R v Flintshire County Licensing Committee, *ex p* Barrett [1957] 1 QB 350............... 179
R v Henn and Darby [1981] AC 850, 905C 64
R v Hillingdon London Borough Council, *ex p* Royco Homes Ltd [1974] 1 QB 720 178
R v Home Secretary, *ex p* Swati [1986] 1 WLR 477 184
R v Lord Chancellor, *ex p* Maxwell [1997] 1 LR 104............................... 172
R v Ministry of Agriculture, Fisheries and Food, *ex p* Astonquest [2000] EuLR 371 184
R v Ministry of Defence, *ex p* Smith [1996] QB 517................................ 182
R v Ministry of Defence, *ex p* Walker [2000] 1 WLR 806 180
R v North and East Devon Health Authority, *ex p* Coughlan [2000] QB 213 183
R v Secretary of State for Education and Employment, *ex p* Begbie [2000] 1 WLR 1115 184
R v Secretary of State for the Environment, *ex p* Notts County Council [1986] AC 240...... 181
R v Secretary of State for the Home Department, *ex p* Benwell [1984] ICR 723............ 177
R v Secretary of State for the Home Department, *ex p* Brind [1991] 1 AC 696 ...... 177, 182, 183

Table of Cases

R v Home Secretary, *ex p* Daly [2001] 2 AC 532; [2001] UKHL 26 . . . . 176, 180, 181
R v Secretary of State for the Home Department, *ex p* Leech (No 2) [1994] 2 QB 198 182
R v Secretary of State for the Home Department, *ex p* Pierson [1998] AC 539 183
R v Secretary of State for the Home Department, *ex p* Simms 183
R v Secretary of State for the Home Department, *ex p* Turgut [2001] 1 All ER 719 184
R v Secretary of State for the Home Department, *ex p* Witham [1997] 1 WLR 104 183
R v Secretary of State for Social Services, *ex p* Stitt [1990] COD 288 184
R v Secretary of State for Transport, *ex p* Pegasus Holidays (London) Ltd and
 Airbro (UK) Ltd [1988] 1 WLR 990 178
Raji v General Medical Council [2003] UKPC 24 176
Rhys-Harper v Relaxion Group [2001] 2 CMLR 1115 (CA) 420
Rhys-Harper v Relaxion Group [2003] 2 CMLR 44 (HL). 420
Rondel v Worsley [1967] 1 QB 443 48
Rooke's case (1598) 5 Co Rep 99b 177
Secretary of State for Trade and Industry, *ex p* BT3G Ltd [2001] EWCA Civ 1448;
 [2001] EuLR 325 179
Turner v Grovit [1999] 3 WLR 794 (CA). 393
Wilson v First County Trust Ltd [2003] UKHL 40 184

United States of America

'Charming Betsy' case 366, 367
Chevron case 367

Table of Treaties and Legislation

TREATIES AND CONVENTIONS

Accession Treaty (United Kingdom) 142
Agreement between the EFTA States on the establishment of a Surveillance Authority and a Court of Justice (SCA)
   Art 3(1) 118
   Art 3(2) 91
Bretton-Woods Agreements 344
Brussels Convention *see* Convention on Jurisdiction and the Enforcement of Judgments in Civil and Commercial Matters, Brussels 1968
Constitution Establishing the International Labor Organization (1919) 341
Constitutional Treaty . . . . viii, 36, 39, 40, 83, 133, 136, 148, 149, 241, 246, 299, 316, 325, 326, 329, 336, 339, 415, 430
   Preamble 430
   Art I-2 149
   Art I-3 . . . . 340, 352
   Art I-9 167
   Art I-9(2) 148
   Art I-11 326
   Art I-12(5) 407
   Art I-17 407
   Art I-25(1) 316
   Art I-29 40
   Art I-44 316
   Part II 148, 158, 430
   Arts II-11–II-114 158
   Art II-111 159
   Art II-112
      paras 4–6 158
   Art II-194 316
   Art III-355 13
   Art III-356 40
   Art III-357 13
   Art III-359 36
   Art III-365 136
   Art III-365(4) 83
   Arts 61–110 339
   Protocol on the Euro Group 306
      Art 1 307
      Art 2 307

Convention for the Protection of Individuals with regard to Automatic Processing of Personal Data 155
Convention on Jurisdiction and the Enforcement of Judgments in Civil and Commercial Matters, Brussels 1968 . . . . 264, 385, 386, 390, 394
   Title II 386
   Art 2 395
   Art 4(2) 388
   Art 5(1) 392
   Art 5(5) 392
   Art 16 387
   Art 17 . . . . 387, 388
   Art 21 . . . . 387, 390, 391
   Art 22 387
   Art 23 387
   Art 23(1) 397
   Art 27 397
   Art 28 . . . . 386, 387, 397
   Art 53 392
   Art 55 386
EC Treaty 91, 266–267, 297, 329, 350, 376
   Preamble 359–360, 430
   Title IV 146
   Art 3(1)(c) 244
   Art 3g 350
   Art 4 350
   Art 4(1) 310
   Art 4(2) 308
   Art 4(4) 309
   Art 6 . . . . 344, 350
   Art 10 . . . . 82, 144, 159, 202, 441
   Art 12 248
   Art 13 . . . . 162, 164
   Art 16 134
   Art 18 253
   Art 21(3) 169
   Art 28 (ex Art 30) . . . 97, 101, 102, 107, 114, 119, 190, 191, 192, 193, 195, 197, 202, 203, 232, 233, 248, 250
   Art 29 . . . . 193, 202, 248, 457

Art 30 (ex Art 36)... 96, 107, 190, 191, 192, 193, 196, 355, 356, 454	Art 104(7)–(10) 315
Art 31. . . . . 102, 114, 119	Art 104(11) 318
Art 40(3) 455	Art 104(12) 317
Art 43 .... 111, 206, 210, 211, 212, 214, 216, 217, 218, 219, 226, 267	Art 105. 298, 350
	Art 105(1) 313
	Art 105(2) 299
Art 45. 245	Art 106 311
Art 46 .... 232, 245	Art 106(1)–(2) 311
Art 47 .... 235, 245	Art 107(6) 307, 309
Art 48 .... 206, 210, 211, 212, 216, 217, 219, 245, 246, 257	Art 108 312
	Art 109. 312
Art 49 ...... 96, 206, 209, 215, 229, 230, 231, 232, 233, 234, 235, 236, 239, 240, 245, 250, 253, 254, 256	Art 110(3) 307
	Art 111. . . . . 298, 313
	Art 111(1)–(3) 313
	Art 113. 359
	Art 116(1). 300
Art 49 (ex 59). 267	Art 116(4) 300, 314
Art 50 .... 209, 230, 231, 245, 246, 247, 251, 302	Art 117. 300
	Art 117(1). 300
Art 51. 245	Art 121. . . . . 300, 314
Art 52. 235	Art 121(1). 304
Art 55. 245	Art 121(3) 307
Art 56 .... 96, 110, 111	Art 122 303
Art 56 (ex Art 73b). 104–105	Art 122(2) 304
paras 1–2 301	Art 122(3) 307, 313, 315
Art 56(1) 105	Art 122(4) 313
Art 57 301	Art 122(5) 316
Art 58 .... 111, 301	Art 123 .... 307, 310
Art 59 301	Art 123(2) 300
Art 60 .... 249, 301, 359	Art 123(4) 306, 308, 310, 312
Art 60(1) 325, 328	Art 133. . . . . 327, 355, 358
Art 68 25	Art 141. 23, 162
Art 81. . . . . 44, 68, 441, 454	Art 141(4) 103
Art 81(1) (ex 85(1)) 117	Art 149(2) 412
Art 82 .... 44, 68, 441, 442, 454	Art 149(4) 407
Art 86 441	Art 150(4) 407
Art 88(2) 87, 88	Art 151. 409
Art 88(3) 87, 88, 89	Art 151(4). 407
Art 93 .... 115, 407	Art 152(4) 407
Art 94 407	Art 205(2) 316
Art 95 407	Art 205(4) 316
Art 95(1) 407	Art 213(2) 312
Art 95(4)–(5) 407	Art 220 .... 40, 259
Art 96 407	Art 220(1) 20
Art 97 407	Art 220(2) 26
Art 98 350	Art 221 .... 3, 11
Art 99 306	Art 221(1). 31
Art 104 .... 299, 300	Art 222 (ex Art 166). 11, 12, 14, 18, 24, 26, 453
Art 104(2) 314, 318	
Art 104(2)(a)–(b). 314	Art 222(1) 20
Art 104(6) 314, 315	Art 222(2) 70, 98

Table of Treaties and Legislation

Art 223 15
Art 225 33
Art 225(2) 24, 27, 45
Art 225(3) 24, 27
Art 225a 36, 40
Art 226 . . . . 50, 315
Art 227 . . . . 50, 52, 315
Art 228 202
Art 229a 45
Art 230 . . . . 50, 75, 135, 163
Art 230(4) (ex Art 173(2)) 71, 72, 73,
74, 76, 79, 81, 84,
86, 89, 118,
135, 136
Art 234 . . . . 23, 32, 50, 54, 78, 79, 109,
144, 201, 259, 434,
438, 439, 440, 454
Art 235 . . . . 76, 78, 79, 147
Art 249 . . . . 407, 457
Art 252 311
Art 253 169
Art 288 . . . . 76, 169, 352
Art 288(2) 79, 400, 401, 402
Art 293 386
Art 296 358
Art 297 . . . . 328, 358
Art 300 . . . . 146, 313, 340
Art 301 . . . . 325, 328, 356, 359
Art 307 340
Art 308 . . . . 162, 309, 319
Danish Protocol
  para 2 315
Protocol on the Excessive Deficit
  Procedure 314
Protocol 5 25
UK Protocol
  Art 5 . . . . 312, 313
  Art 8 313
  para 5 315
EEC Treaty 126, 141, 216
Art 36 454
Art 59 230
Art 73b 105
Art 99 407
Art 100 407
Art 100a 407
Art 119 65
Art 166 24
Art 168a 36, 38, 46
Art 173(2) 72
Art 177 . . . . 21, 61, 142, 454

EEC-Yugoslavia cooperation
  agreement 332
Euratom Treaty 36
European Coal and Steel Community
  Treaty 36
European Convention on Human
  Rights (1950) 126, 128, 131, 139,
149, 150, 151, 152, 155,
157, 158, 167, 171, 172,
183, 184, 340, 341,
350, 369
Art 2 342
Art 5 . . . . 175, 447
Art 6 . . . . 78, 79, 135,
136, 140, 141, 143,
152, 389, 390
Art 6(1) 16, 169
Art 8 . . . . 142, 148, 168
Art 8(1) 129
Art 12 . . . . 147, 167
Art 13 . . . . 78, 79, 135, 136
Art 14 . . . . 148, 164, 175
Art 33 151
Art 59 148
Protocol 1
  Art 1 145
  Art 3 142
Protocol 4
  Art 2(1) 130
Protocol 7
  Art 2 37
Protocol 11 152
Protocol 14 . . . . 152, 153, 154
  Art 17 . . . . 148, 151
European Economic Area
  Agreement (1992) 90, 332
Art 3(1)–(2) 91
Art 3(4)–(5) 91
Art 6 91
Art 11 . . . . 94, 103
Art 13 96
Art 16 103
Art 36(2) 118
Art 40 . . . . 99, 105, 111
Arts 41–67 99
Art 59(2) 98, 99
Art 61(1) 98
Art 97 91
Annex XII 105
European Patent Convention 45, 141
European Social Charter 1961 . . . . . . 128, 155

General Agreement on Tariffs and
    Trade (GATT) 1947 ...... 330, 341,
        347, 362, 373, 375, 377
Hague Convention on Choice of Court
    Agreements 2005 385
    Art 5(2) 397
International Court of Justice
    Statute
    Art 38 349
International Covenant on Civil and
    Political Rights 1966 128
International Labor Organization
    Constitution
    Preamble 344
Kyoto Protocol 137
Lugano Convention 264
Maastricht Treaty see Treaty on
    European Union (Maastricht)
Marrakesh Agreement Establishing
    the World Trade Organization
    15 April 1994 363
Reform Treaty (draft) 336
Rome Convention [1980]
    OJ L226/1 .... 260, 263, 264,
        265, 266, 272, 276,
        277, 280
    Art 3 265
    Art 3(3) 265
    Art 4(2) 265
    Art 5(2) 265, 278
    Art 5(3) 265, 266
    Art 5(4)(b) 265
    Art 6(1) 265, 274
    Art 7(1) 265
    Art 7(2) 265, 266
    Art 16 265
    Art 20 .... 266, 272
Single European Act 1986 .... 36, 37, 38, 131,
        167, 244, 324, 359, 407, 448, 450
    Title III 359
    Part III 447, 450
    Art 3(1) 118
Treaty of Amsterdam ...... viii, 105, 131, 167,
        309, 311, 448, 450
Treaty establishing a Constitution for
    Europe see Constitutional Treaty
Treaty on European Union
    (Maastricht) .... viii, 39, 104, 131,
        167, 297, 300, 308, 324,
        326, 329, 415, 448, 450
    Preamble 430

Title V 360
Title VI 29
Art 1 430
Art 3 328
Art 6 .... 131, 403
Art 6(1) 132
Art 6(2) 131, 157, 333
Art 7 .... 132, 162, 403
Art 11(1) 358
Art 46 333
Art 46(d) 132
Art 47 329
Art 49 131
Art J.3 357
Protocol 4 25
Treaty of Nice .... viii, 24, 26, 36, 39–41,
        45, 46, 131, 132, 133,
        448, 451
    Declaration No 3 159
Treaty of Rome 1957 .... 263, 432, 435
    Art 189 437
United Nations Charter 333, 334, 340
    Preamble 349
    Art 1 349
    Arts 55–56 349
    Art 103 343
Universal Declaration of Human Rights
    Art 1 339
    Art 23 339
Uruguay Round treaties 363, 377
Vienna Convention on Human
    Rights and Application of
    Biology and Medicine 155
Vienna Convention on the Law of
    Treaties 350, 367
    Preamble 351
    Art 18 .... 331, 332
World Trade Organization
    Agreement 330
    Preamble 351
    Art 7.1 351
    Art 9 351
    Agreement on Trade-related
        aspects of Intellectual
        Property Rights (TRIPS) 331
    Preamble 351
    Art 8 351
    Art 62.4 351
    Charter
    Art XVI:1 371
    Art XVI:4 371

Table of Treaties and Legislation

Art XX 352
Constitution 346
Dispute Settlement Understanding . . . 335, 336, 352
   Art 3 352
   Art 3.2 351
   Art 21.6 335
   Art 22.8 335
Marrakesh Agreement Establishing the World Trade Organization 15 April 1994 363
Technical Barriers to Trade Agreement . . . 331
Treaty 362, 363, 372, 377, 378
TRIPS *see* Agreement on Trade-related aspects of Intellectual Property Rights
Uruguay Round Agreement 377

EU LEGISLATION

Regulations
Regulation 17/62 [1962] OJ Eng Sp Ed 87
   Art 14(3) 66
Regulation 1612/68 [1968] OJ L257/2 115, 160
Regulation 2603/69 354
   Art 1 . . . . 355, 356
   Art 11 . . . . 355, 356
Regulation 1408/71 [1971]
   OJ L149/2 . . . . 115, 233
   Art 73 115
Regulation 2730/79 [1979] OJ L317/1 207
Regulation 1371/84 [1984] OJ L132/11 . . . 456
Regulation 568/85 [1985] OJ L65/5 207
Regulation 3889/89 [1989]
   OJ L378/16 455
Regulation 4024/89
   Art 1(1) 455
Regulation 4064/89 [1990] OJ L257/13 . . 441
Regulation 1432/92 [1992] OJ L151/4 356
   Preamble 360
Regulation 3950/92 458
Regulation 253/93 73
   Art 4(3)(i)(a) 73, 74
Regulation 990/93/EEC [1993]
   OJ L102/14 . . . . 144, 459
   Art 8 459
Regulation 40/94 [1994] OJ L11/1 . . . . 45, 285
   Art 7 . . . . 290, 291, 292
   Art 7(1)(b)-(c) 285, 289
   Art 51(1)(a) 292
   Art 131 296
Regulation 3381/94 [1994] OJ L367/1 357

Art 3(1) 357
Art 19(5) 357
Annex II 357
Annex III 357
Regulation 118/97 [1997] OJ L28/1 233
Regulation 258/97
   Art 12 95
Regulation 950/97 [1997] OJ L142/1 87
Regulation 1103/97 [1997] OJ L162/1 309
   Art 2 309
Regulation 1466/97 [1997] OJ L209/1 . . . 314
Regulation 1467/97 [1997]
   OJ L209/6 . . . . 314, 318, 319
   Art 2(2) 318, 319
   Art 2(5) 319
   Art 2(7) 319
   Art 11 318
Regulation 974/98 [1998]
   OJ L139/1 . . . . 309, 310
   Art 1(a) 311
   Art 1(h) 311
   Art 2 . . . . 309, 310
   Art 3 310
   Art 4 310
   Art 6 310
   Art 6(2) 310
   Art 7 311
   Art 9 310
   Art 10 . . . . 310, 311
   Art 15 311
   Art 16 311
Regulation 975/98 [1998]
   OJ L139/6 311–312
Regulation 2532/98 [1998] OJ L318/4 307
Regulation 2821/98 84
Regulation 2866/98 [1998] OJ L359/1 312
Regulation 659/99 115
Regulation 1073/99 312
Regulation 1256/99 [1999] OJ L160/73 . . . 458
Regulation 1334/2000 [2000]
   OJ L159/1 325
   Annex I 357, 360
   Annex II 357, 360
Regulation 44/2001 [2001] OJ L12/1 . . . 264, 265, 277, 280, 385, 386
   Title II 386
   Art 4(2) 388
   Art 7(2) 265
   Art 16(2) 265, 273
   Art 22 387

Art 23 387
Art 23(1) 387
Art 26 264
Art 27 .... 264, 387, 397
Art 28 .... 264, 387, 397
Art 29 ....264, 387
Art 30 387
Art 35(1) 386, 387
Regulation 1049/2001 [2001]
    OJ L145/43 160
Regulation 1338/2001 [2001]
    OJ L181/6 306
Regulation 1339/2001................306
Regulation 1/2003 [2003] OJ L1/1 68
Regulation 261/2004 [2004] OJ L46/1 ...248
Regulation 1056/2005 [2005]
    OJ L174/5 319
Regulation 1297/2006.................270
Regulation 162/2007 [2007] OJ L53/1 ...162
Regulation 168/2007..................134
Regulation 717/2007 [2007]
    OJ L171/32 248
Regulation approving the WTO Treaty...377

Directives

Directive 64/221/EEC [1964]
    OJ Spec. Ed 117...............161
Directive 64/427/EEC.................209
Directive 68/360/EEC [1968]
    OJ Spec. Ed 485...............161
Directive 70/524/EEC OJ [1998] L 351/4 ..84
Directive 72/194/EEC.................161
Directive 73/148/EEC [1973]
    OJ L172/14 .... 161, 245
Directive 73/239/EEC............221, 268
    Art 6 269
    Art 7 269
Directive 75/34/EEC [1975]
    OJ L14/10 161
Directive 75/35/EEC.................161
Directive 76/207/EEC [1976]
    OJ L39/40 .... 103, 160
Directive 77/187/EEC [1977]
    OJ L61/26 .... 93, 119
Directive 77/780 [1977]
    OJ L322/30 .... 221, 268
Directive 79/7/EEC [1979] OJ L6/24 455
Directive 79/267/EEC.................221
Directive 84/450/EEC............. 92, 112
Directive 85/611/EEC [1985]
    OJ L375/3 .... 221, 268

Directive 88/357/EEC [1988] OJ L172 ...268
    Art 7 263
Directive 88/361 [1988] OJ L178/5 299
Directive 88/361/EEC [1988] OJ L178/5 ...301
    Art 1 105
    Annex 302
Directive 89/102/EEC
    Art 7(1) 112
    Art 7(2) 100
Directive 89/104/EEC [1989]
    OJ L40/1 .... 46, 110
Directive 89/391/EEC
    Art 16(1) 161
Directive 89/552/EEC................112
    Art 2(2) 92, 98
    Art 16.........................92
Directive 89/646/EEC [1989]
    OJ L386/1 .... 220–221, 268, 269
Directive 90/232/EEC.............99–100
Directive 90/364/EEC [1990]
    OJ L180/26 161
Directive 90/365/EEC [1990]
    OJ L180/28 161
Directive 90/434/EEC [1990] O L225/1
    Art 11(1)(a).....................225
Directive 92/49/EEC [1992] OJ L228 ... 221,
                                263, 268
    Art 1(c)........................269
    Art 4 269
    Art 5 269
Directive 92/50/EEC [1992]
    OJ L209/1 234
Directive 92/96/EEC.................221
Directive 93/6/EEC..................221
Directive 93/22/EEC [1993]
    OJ L141/27 .... 221, 268
Directive 93/38/EEC.................234
Directive 93/96/EEC [1993]
    OJ L317/59 161
Directive 95/26/EC..................221
Directive 98/8/EC....................85
Directive 98/44/EC [1998] OJ L213/13...166
Directive 2000/12/EC [2000]
    OJ L126/1 .... 221, 268
Directive 2000/31/EC [2001]
    OJ L178/1 ....268, 270–276
    Recital 5............ 271, 274, 275, 276
    Recital 21......................270
    Recital 22.....................274, 275
    Recital 23......................274
    Recital 55.....................273, 274

Table of Treaties and Legislation

Art 1(4) 274, 275
Art 2(c) 271, 274
Art 2(h) 270
Art 3 272
Art 3(1) 271, 272, 274
Art 3(2) 271, 272, 274, 275, 276
Art 3(3) 271, 273
Art 3(4)–(6).....................271
Arts 4–15........................270
Directive 2001/107/EC [2002]
    OJ L41/20 221
Directive 2002/14/EC [2002]
    OJ L80/29 161
Directive 2002/65/EC [2002]
    OJ L271/16 .... 268, 276–281
Preamble 280
Recital 4....................277, 279
Recital 6....................277, 279
Recital 7............... 277, 279, 280
Recital 8....................277, 280
Recital 13.......................276
Recital 28...................277, 279
Art 2(a) 277
Art 3 277
Art 3.1(1)(a) 277, 279
Art 3.1(1)(e)–(f) 277
Art 3.1(3)(f) 278
Art 4 277
Art 4(2) 276
Art 5 277
Art 5(2)–(3) 278, 280, 281
Art 6 277
Art 6.3..........................278
Art 7 277
Art 11...........................278
Art 12.2.........................277
Art 13 278
Art 16.......................278, 280
Directive 2002/73/EC [2002]
    OJ L269/15 160
Directive 2002/83/EC [2002]
    OJ L345.....................268
Art 1.1(e) 269
Arts 32–36......................263
Directive 2002/93/EC
Art 4 269
Art 5.1.........................269
Directive 2003/86/EC [2003]
    OJ L251/12 .... 148, 160, 168
Preamble 168
Directive 2003/88/EC [2003]
    OJ L299/9 161

Directive 2003/109/EC [2004]
    OJ L16/44 160
Directive 2004/18/EC [2004]
    OJ L134/114 234
Directive 2004/38/EC [2004]
    OJ L158/77 160–161
Directive 2004/39/EC [2004]
    OJ L145/1 .... 221, 268
Art 4.1(20)–(21).................269
Art 5(1) 269
Art 13(1) 269
Art 13(9) 269
Art 16...........................269
Art 19...........................269
Art 21...........................269
Art 22 269
Art 22(7) 270
Art 25 269
Art 27 .... 269, 270
Art 28 .... 269, 270
Art 31...........................269
Art 31(1)........................270
Art 32 269
Art 32(1) 270
Art 32(7) 269, 270
Art 61.2.........................270
Directive 2004/40/EC [2004]
    OJ L159/1 161
Directive 2004/113/EC [2004]
    OJ L373/37 161
Directive 2006/48/EC [2006]
    OJ L177/1 ....220, 268
Recital 10.......................269
Art 4.1(7).......................269
Art 4.1(8).......................269
Art 22 269
Art 23 269
Art 40 269
Directive 2006/73/EC.............270
Directive 2006/123/EC [2006]
    OJ L376/36 .... 234, 241, 243,
                  248, 249, 256, 259
Preamble
    Recital 34......................251
Art 1 235
Art 2 235
Art 16...........................235
Art 20 248

Decisions

Decision 74/120 [1974] OJ L63/16.......299
Decision 76/787 [1976] IJ L278/5 142

Decision 90/141 [1990] OJ L78/23 . . 299, 301
Decision 90/142 [1990] OJ L78/25 300
Decision 93/350 [1993] OJ L144/21. 38
Decision 94/149 [1994] OJ L66/29 38
Decision 94/942/CFSP of
    19 December 1994. 357
Decision 98/317 [1998] OJ L139/30. 303
Decision 98/345 [1998] OJ L154/33. 307
Decision 1988 creating a Court of First
    Instance. 36, 37
    Art 3(3) 38
Decision 1999/268. 87
Decision 2000/427 [2000]
    OJ L167/19. . . . . .304, 305
Decision 2001/462/EC-ECSC. 170
Decision 2003/861 [2003] L325/44. 306
Decision 2003/862 [2003] L325/45. 306
Decision 2004-505DC,
    19 November 2004 158
Decision 2004/11 [2004]
    OJ L230/56 313
Decision 2004/407 of 26 April 2004,
    OJ 2004 L132/5. . . . . .40, 41
Decision 2004/752/EC, Euratom of 2
    November 2004. 41
Decision 2005/696/EC [2005] OJ
    L266/60–61 41
Decision 2006/495/EC [2006]
    OJ L195/25 304
Decision 2006/849/EC [2006]
    OJ L330/28 306
Decision 2006/850/EC [2006]
    OJ L330/30 306

RESOLUTIONS

Council Resolution 1466/97 [1997]
    OJ L209/1 317
Council Resolution 1467/97 [1997]
    OJ L209/6. 317
Council Resolution 1055/2005 [2005]
    OJ L174/1 317
Council Resolution 1056/2005 [2005]
    OJ L174/5 . . . . 317, 319
Council Resolution 2169/2005 [2005]
    OJ L346/1 311
    Recital 6. 311
    Art 1(2) 311
Council Resolution of 5 December 1978
    Art 3 303
Council Resolution of 16 June 1997. 304

    para 1.6 . . . . .303, 305
Council Resolution of 7 July 1997
    [1997] OJ C236/7 310
Council Resolution of
    3 May 1998 310
Council Resolution on the Stability
    and Growth Pact [1997]
    C236/1 . . . . . . 314, 315, 317, 318, 319

EUROPEAN COURT OF JUSTICE

Practice Directions relating to direct
    actions and appeals,
    OJ 2004 L 361, 15 . . . . .58, 59
Rules of Procedure. 15, 16, 49, 54, 55
    Art 16. 15
    Art 27(2)–(4) .9
    Art 29 . . . . 6, 7, 56
    Art 29(2) 28
    Art 30 56
    Art 42(2) 28
    Art 44(2) 5
    Art 61. 17
    Art 63 9
    Art 94(1) 54
    Art 94(3)–(4) 54
    Art 104(1) 6
    Art 104(3) 29
    Art 104a. 29, 30
    Art 104b 30
Statute of the Court 15, 49, 54
    Art 2 9
    Art 14.2 313
    Art 17. 31
    Art 20 . . . . 15, 56
        para 2. 56
    Art 20(5) 14, 24, 26, 56
    Art 23 . . . . 8, 427
    Art 35. 9
    Art 37 16
    Art 40 . . . . 5, 427
    Art 53. 427
    Art 56 427
    Art 62 24
    Annex
        Art 3 13

EEA DIRECTIVE

Motor Vehicles Insurance
    Directives. 108, 119, 121

EFTA COURT

Rules of Procedure
  Art 97 106
Statute of the Court
  Art 20 106

MISCELLANEOUS ACTS

Charter of Fundamental
  Rights 132–135, 147,
                      148, 150, 151, 152, 155,
                      157–158, 159, 162, 165,
                      167, 168, 174, 175
  Preamble 339
  Title IV 161
  Title V 169
  Chp V 174
  Art 1 .... 166, 338, 339
  Art 3(2) 134
  Art 9 .... 147, 167
  Art 15(1) 258
  Art 21 .... 160, 161, 164
  Arts 22–24 161
  Art 27 161
  Art 31 161
  Art 36 134
  Art 41 .... 163, 168, 169, 170, 171, 174
  Art 41(1) 171
  Art 47 .... 78, 79, 136, 163
  Art 51 158
  Art 51.1 159
  Arts 52–54 158
European Code of Good Administrative
  Behaviour 133–134
Joint Declaration of the European
  Parliament, the Council and the
  Commission of 5 April 1977
  [1977] OJ C103/1 .... 131, 146
Laeken Declaration 157

NATIONAL LEGISLATION

Belgium
Accountability Law 1975 405
Bankruptcy Law 1997 405
Commercial Code 1807 404
Financial Institutions Law 1999 405

Canada
Charter of Rights and Freedoms 180

France
Civil Code
  Art 14 388
Commercial Code 1807 404
Constitution 137

Germany
Compensation Act 87
Fundamental Law 126

Ireland
Constitution 1937 .... 448, 459, 460
  Art 3.1 447
  Art 4 447
  Art 5 446
  Art 6 446
  Art 15.1.2 446
  Art 15.4.1 447
  Art 28 446
  Art 29.4.3 .... 448, 450, 452
  Arts 29.4.4–29.4.7 448
  Art 29.4.10 448
  Art 29.6 447
  Art 34 446
  Art 34.3.2 447
Constitution of the Irish Free State 1922 .. 447
European Communities Act 1972 450
  s 2 449
  s 3 .... 449, 457
  s 3(2) 457
  s 4 449
  s 4(3)–(5) 457
European Communities (Amendment) Act
  1973 450
  s 4 449

Ireland secondary legislation
European Communities (Milk Levy)
  Regulations 1985 456
European Communities (Milk Quota)
  Regulations 2000 458

Italy
Civil Code 441
  Art 2043 444
Constitution 439, 440
  Art 11 .... 436, 437

Namibia
Constitution
  Art 18 173

Netherlands

Civil Code 404, 406

Norway

Automobile Liability Act 121
Corporate Tax Act 111

Portugal

Civil Code 108

South Africa

Constitution 174
   s 33 . . . . 173, 174
   s 33(3)(c) 174
Interim Constitution 1994
   s 24 173
Promotion of Administrative Justice
   Act 2002 174

Sweden

Alcohol Law. 114

Switzerland

Civil Code 1907. 404

United Kingdom

Civil Jurisdiction and Judgments Act 1982
   s 42 392
Human Rights Act 1998 . . . . 152, 185
Magna Carta, Art 20 177
Merchant Shipping Act 1988
   ss 13–14. 52
Town and Country Planning
   Act 1990
   s 70(1) 178
Trade Marks Act 1938
   s 17(2) 190

UK Secondary legislation

Civil Procedure Rules 1998
   (SI 1998/3032)
   r 6.20(3). 394
Financial Services (Distance
   Marketing) Regulations 2004
   (SI 2004/2095) 280

United States of America

Constitution
   Art VI 362, 374, 375
Trade Agreement Act of 1979,
   19 USC 2504 373
Uruguay Round Agreement Act of
   1994, Sec.102. 374

List of Abbreviations

AC	Appeal Cases
AG	Advocate General
AJIL	American Journal of International Law
All ER	All England Law Reports
Art	Article
CA	Court of Appeal
CCBE	Conseil des Barreaux de l'Union Européenne/Council of the Bars and Law Societies of the European Union
CDE	Cahiers de Droit Européen
CFI	Court of First Instance of the European Communities
CFSP	Common Foreign and Security Policy
ChD	Chancery Division
CLJ	Cambridge Law Journal
CMLR	Common Market Law Reports
CML Rev	Common Market Law Review
COM	Communication
CT	Constitutional Treaty (Treaty establishing a Constitution for Europe)
CYELS	Cambridge Yearbook of European Legal Studies
DCT	Draft Constitutional Treaty
Dec	Decision
Dir	Directive
EAEC	European Atomic Energy Community ('Euratom')
EBLR	European Business Law Review
EC	European Community; also EC Treaty
ECB	European Central Bank
ECHR	European Convention on Human Rights
ECJ	European Court of Justice (the Court of Justice of the European Communities)
ECLR	European Competition Law Review
ECR	European Court Reports

ECSC	European Coal and Steel Community
ECtHR	European Court of Human Rights
EEA	European Economic Area
EEC	European Economic Community
EFTA	European Free Trade Association
EHRLR	European Human Rights Law Review
EHRR	European Human Rights Reports
EJIL	European Journal of International Law
ELJ	European Law Journal
ELR	European Law Review
EPL	European Public Law
EU	European Union
FSR	Fleet Street Reports
GATT	General Agreement on Tariffs and Trade
HL	House of Lords
ICLQ	International and Comparative Law Quarterly
IGC	Intergovernmental conference
ILJ	Industrial Law Journal
IJEL	Irish Journal of European Law
JCMS	Journal of Common Market Studies
JEPP	Journal of European Public Policy
JSPTL	Journal of the Society of Public Teachers of Law
LQR	Law Quarterly Review
LS	Legal Studies
MCA	Monetary compensatory amount
MEE	Measures having equivalent effect
MJ	Maastricht Journal of European and Comparative Law
MLR	Modern Law Review
OECD	Organisation for Economic Cooperation and Development
OHIM	Office for Harmonization in the Internal Market (Trade Marks and Designs)
OJ	Official Journal of the European Union

OJLS	Oxford Journal of Legal Studies
PL	Public Law
QB	Queen's Bench
QBD	Queen's Bench Division
QR	Quantitative restriction (on imports)
Rec	Recueil de la Jurisprudence de la Cour de justice et du Tribunal de première instance
Reg	Regulation
RPC	Reports of Patent, Design and Trade Mark Cases
RTDE	Revue Trimestrielle de Droit Européen
SEA	Single European Act
STC	Simon's Tax Cases
TEU	Treaty on European Union (Maastricht Treaty)
VAT	Value added tax
WLR	Weekly Law Reports
WTO	World Trade Organization
YEL	Yearbook of European Law

List of Contributors

Anthony Arnull is Professor of European Law and Head of the Birmingham Law School, University of Birmingham. He is Consultant Editor of the *European Law Review*, having been its Co-Editor from 1996–2007. He served as a référendaire in the chambers of Advocate General Jacobs from 1989–92.

Prof Dr Carl Baudenbacher is President of the EFTA Court and Director of the Institute of European and International Law at the University of St Gallen.

Andrea Biondi is Professor of European Law and Co-Director, Centre of European Law, King's College London. He is a member of the Bar of Florence and an Academic Member of Francis Taylor Buildings Chambers in London. He is General Editor of the Kluwer European Law Collection.

Alan Dashwood is Professor of European Law at Cambridge and a Fellow of Sidney Sussex College. He is also a Barrister and was formerly a Director in the Legal Service of the EU Council of Ministers.

Jacqueline Dutheil de la Rochère is Professor of European Law, Jean Monnet Chair, at the University of Paris II, and Director of its Centre de droit Européen. She is a former President of her University, and served as a Deputy Representative of the French Government on the Convention which drafted the EU Charter of Fundamental Rights.

Sir David Edward is a member of the Privy Council and sits part-time as a Judge in the Inner House of the Court of Session. He was a Judge of the European Court of Justice (1992–2004) and the first British Judge of the European Court of First Instance (1989–92). He was the Salvesen Professor of European Institutions and Director of the Europa Institute at the University of Edinburgh (1985–9).

Vanessa Edwards has served as a référendaire of Advocate General Jacobs and is currently a référendaire of Advocate General Eleanor Sharpston. She was previously a practising solicitor with Linklaters and a lawyer-linguist at the Court of Justice. She is the author of *EC Company Law* (1999).

Piet Eeckhout is Professor of European Law and Director of the Centre of European Law, King's College London. He is Co-Editor of the *Yearbook of European Law*, and served in Advocate General Jacobs's chambers from 1994–8. He is an associate academic member of Matrix Chambers.

Paul Farmer is Head of the EU Law Practice Group in the London office of Dorsey & Whitney. He previously held the posts of référendaire in the chambers of Advocate General Jacobs and Head of the Tax Policy Department in the Taxation and Customs Directorate General of the European Commission in addition to spending a number of years in independent practice at the Bar at Pump Court Tax Chambers.

List of Contributors

Nial Fennelly is a Judge of the Supreme Court of Ireland. He was Advocate General at the Court of Justice from 1995–2000, the only Irish lawyer to have held that post.

Nicholas Forwood was called to the Bar in 1970 and appointed Queen's Counsel in 1987. From 1995–9, he served as Chair of the CCBE's Permanent Delegation to the European Court of Justice. He has been a Judge of the Court of First Instance of the European Communities since December 1999.

Laurence W Gormley is Professor of European Law and Jean Monnet Professor, University of Groningen (Jean Monnet Centre of Excellence), Professor at the College of Europe, Bruges, and a barrister.

Margaret Gray is a barrister at Brick Court Chambers, London, and the Law Library, Dublin. She was formerly référendaire to Judges Macken and Ó Caoimh at the Court of Justice of the European Communities.

Trevor Hartley is a Professor Emeritus of Law at the London School of Economics, where he has been teaching law since 1969. He is the author of various books on EC law and conflict of laws, including *The Foundations of European Community Law* (6th edn, 2007) and *International Commercial Transactions and Litigation: Text, Cases and Materials on Private International Law* (forthcoming).

John H Jackson is University Professor and Director of the Institute of International Economic Law at the Georgetown University Law Center, Washington DC. He was previously Hessel E Yntema Professor of Law at the University of Michigan and served as General Counsel for the Office of the President's Special Representative for Trade. He is founding Editor and Editor-in-Chief of the *Journal of International Economic Law*.

Jeffrey Jowell QC is Professor of Law at University College London and a practising barrister. He is the UK's member on the Venice Commission (the Council of Europe's Commission for Democracy through Law) and a member of the Royal Commission on Environmental Pollution.

David T Keeling is a Member of the Boards of Appeal of the Office for Harmonization in the Internal Market (Trade Marks and Designs). He served as référendaire for Advocate General Jacobs. He is the author of *Intellectual Property Rights in EU Law Volume I, Free Movement and Competition Law* (2004).

Eva Lomnicka is Professor of Law at King's College London and a practising barrister with an advisory practice, mainly in consumer credit and financial service regulation. Her research interests centre on the regulation of financial services.

Ernst-Ulrich Petersmann is Head of the Law Department in the European University Institute at Florence, Italy, former Professor at the University of Geneva and its Graduate Institute of International Studies, and legal advisor in GATT and the WTO (1981–2006). He has been secretary, member or chairman of numerous GATT and WTO dispute settlement panels, and was Chairman of the International Trade Law Committee of the International Law Association.

Sara Poli is a lecturer (ricercatrice) in European Law at the University of Rome Tor Vergata. She has also taught at the universities of Trieste and Southampton, and has been a Jean Monnet fellow at the European University Institute.

Sir Konrad Schiemann has been a Judge of the Court of Justice since 2004. He practised at the English Bar from 1964–86 and served as a High Court Judge from 1986–95 and a Lord Justice of Appeal from 1995–2003.

Eleanor Sharpston has been an Advocate General at the Court of Justice since January 2006, when she succeeded Advocate General Jacobs. She had previously combined private practice at the Bar (in Brussels and then London, taking silk in 1999) with an academic career at UCL and then Cambridge, where she remains a Fellow of King's College. She served as a référendaire at the Court with Lord Slynn from 1987–90.

Niamh Nic Shuibhne is Reader in EC Law at the University of Edinburgh, where she is also an Associate Director of the Europa Institute. Her research interests span various aspects of European Community law. At present, she is working primarily on internal market and free movement law with particular focus on EU citizenship and the free movement of persons.

Giuseppe Tesauro is a Judge of the Italian Constitutional Court. He served as Advocate General at the Court of Justice from 1988–98 and was Professor of European Community Law at the University of Naples.

Antonio Tizzano is a Judge at the European Court of Justice. He previously served there as Advocate General (2000–6). He is Professor of European Law at the University of Rome, and practised at the Italian Bar.

Takis Tridimas is the Sir John Lubbock Professor of Banking Law and the Deputy Director of the Centre for Commercial Law Studies at Queen Mary College, University of London. He is also Professor at the Dickinson School of Law, Pennsylvania State University. He served as Chairman of the Committee set up by the EU Council of Ministers to draft the Treaty of Accession of 2003 and as a référendaire in the chambers of Advocate General Jacobs from 1992–5. He is an academic member of Matrix Chambers.

John Usher is Professor of European Law and Head of the School of Law, University of Exeter. He was référendaire to Advocate General Warner at the European Court of Justice from 1974–8. More recently, he held the Salvesen Chair of European Institutions at the University of Edinburgh (1995–2004). He has been a Visiting Professor at the College of Europe in Bruges since 1986, an Honorary Bencher of Lincoln's Inn since 1993 and a Fellow of the Royal Society of Edinburgh since 1998, and was awarded a Jean Monnet Chair *ad personam* in 1997.

Walter van Gerven is Emeritus Professor of Law at the universities of Leuven and Maastricht; distinguished Visiting Professor at the University of Tilburg; former Advocate General at the ECJ; a member of the Committee of Independent Experts set up by the European Parliament to investigate fraud, mismanagement and nepotism in the EU Commission and, more recently, of the Independent Panel reviewing the World Bank's Department of Institutional Integrity. He has served as the President of the Belgian Banking Commission. He has also taught at the University of Chicago, Stanford University and the University of Michigan, amongst others. Professor van Gerven is the founder and General Editor of the series of casebooks on the common law of Europe.

David Vaughan CBE, QC is a barrister. He is a Deputy High Court Judge and a Judge at the Court of Appeal of Jersey and Guernsey. He is Honorary Professor of European

Law at Durham University, a member of the Advisory Board of the Centre for European Legal Studies of Cambridge University, and the Chairman of the Editorial Board of the *European Law Reports*. He was the joint founder of the Bar European Group in 1970 and is currently its honorary Vice-President.

Robin White is Professor of Law at the University of Leicester. He is a member of the University of Leicester Centre for European Law and Integration. He was until 2007 on the Editorial Board of the *European Law Review*.

PART I
INSTITUTIONAL QUESTIONS

1

The Functioning of the Court of Justice in an Enlarged Union and the Future of the Court

Konrad Schiemann[*]

I. Introduction

It functions and it has a future. I have still not lost the sense of astonishment which struck me when I first started looking at the European Communities and at the case law of the ECJ.[1] One is looking at an unprecedented legal order in which 27 nations have agreed on institutions which legislate for them all across a vast field of human activity; they have agreed on institutions which administer that legislation and they have agreed on a court which adjudicates on the constitutionality of the legislation, the legality of the decisions taken under it and the appropriate penalties for failure to abide by that legislation. The nations concerned have a wide variety of individual perceptions of the history of this continent and speak many different languages. Each of them has political tensions back home which result in forceful criticisms of whatever government is in power. Equally there are forceful criticisms of the European institutions. Yet the institutions of the Union are clearly functioning in a broadly effective way. More and more nations have joined and wish to join this novel polity.

Enlargement of the Community from its original six Member States to the current 27, the wide use made of the legislative and administrative competencies of the Union's institutions and the increase during the last 50 years in the competencies attributed to the Union and to the ECJ stimulate a consideration of the challenges facing the Union as regards the functioning of the Court. None of these challenges is new in itself.[2] There have been previous enlargements and

---

[*] The views expressed in this chapter are those of the author and may not be attributed to the institution of which he is a member.

[1] The nomenclature of the judicial institutions of the Union can be confusing. In this article I am primarily concerned with the Court of Justice set up pursuant to Art 221 EC and use the word 'Court' to refer to that Court. Many of the problems discussed are also encountered in the CFI and the Staff Tribunal.

[2] See, for instance, the report of the Court of Justice on certain aspects of the application of the Treaty on European Union, Luxembourg, May 1995, and the Due Report of January 2000.

increases in competencies and in the amount of legislation and decisions made pursuant to such legislation. To some extent these past challenges have been countered by the creation first of the Court of First Instance and more recently of the Staff Tribunal. This has resulted in some of the workload of the ECJ being transferred to these instances. There have been some alterations in the Rules of Procedure, a reduction in the amount of material which is translated and published, and a number of alterations in the internal practices of the Court which are designed to speed things up. Francis Jacobs presided over the Procedural Committee of the Court which has been the guiding motor of some of these changes. They have indeed resulted in some shortening of the time taken by the Court to provide judgments. Whether this is merely a temporary improvement which will be reversed once the new Member States start sending more work to the Court and once Member States start making references arising out of the increased competencies of the Court remains to be seen. It seems probable. Even the present improved position is far from satisfactory from a number of points of view. Seen from the perspective of many Member States and at any event some of the litigants, the time taken by the ECJ to produce its judgments still seems unconscionably long.

When I was appointed a High Court judge in England I was told by an Appeal Court judge that a desire to improve the legal quality of my judgments should not lead me to undue delay. In general, with luck, I would get the law right. It was for the Court of Appeal to improve the legal quality of the judgment if this proved necessary.[3] The ECJ, however, has no higher court which can improve its judgments. Although there is no formal doctrine of precedent, in practice the Court is extremely loath to depart from anything included in an earlier judgment. This is for the perfectly good reason that Member States and their citizens will have organized their affairs (including, it may well be, redrafting their legislation) on the basis that the interpretation given by the Court in the earlier judgment is definitive. It would cause widespread inconvenience and irritation if the Court were to make a practice of reversing its earlier judgments. Great care (which involves the work of many people) is taken in an effort to produce judgments with wording which will stand the test of time. Not merely do the parties have to live with those judgments but frequently they have an impact on all Member States and on innumerable persons throughout the Union. In those circumstances, in so far as there is a tension between attempts at quality and speed, the former tend to take precedence in the Court.

Moreover, it is important for the health of the Union that the judgments of the Court should not only aim to be technically the best that can be achieved, but they should also be acceptable in the Member States as a whole. From the beginning, Member States have insisted on being able to intervene in cases before the Court and thus make written submissions to the Court when they feel it

---

[3] Which occasionally indeed it did.

appropriate.[4] On many occasions that input from Member States has resulted in a better and more authoritative and acceptable judgment than might well have been the case without such an input. Even where the submissions of a Member State have not been accepted by the Court, the fact that the Court has received those submissions and has given reasons for not following them makes the judgment more acceptable in that state than it would have been if it were open to the criticism that the Court has simply not considered a point. However, the giving of an opportunity to make such observations undoubtedly results in substantial additions to the time taken to produce the judgment. Similarly, Member States have insisted on being given the right to have a case decided by the Grand Chamber,[5] yet it is probably true as a general rule that the greater the number of Judges involved in a decision, particularly in a judicial regime which permits only one judgment, the longer it will take to arrive at that decision.

II. The Language Challenge

Perhaps the biggest challenge of enlargement has been the result of the growth in number of the official languages of the Union. This has involved not only a vast expenditure of time and money[6] in communications between the Court and the outside world both in writing and at the oral hearing, but also increased difficulties in internal communications within the Court. One should take these points separately.

A. The External Dealings of the Court

One of the major, indeed indispensable, features of the Union is that each Member State regards the law of the Union as part of its own law which the state concerned and its citizens are bound to obey. One almost ineluctable consequence of this is that Union law should be available at least in the official language[7] of each Member State so that it can be understood by the judges, the administration and the citizens of that state. The institutions of the Union including the Court formally work on the basis that each language version of the legislation is equally authoritative.[8] In so far as the doctrine that all linguistic versions of legislation are of equal validity is based on a desire that the interpretation of a document should reflect the desires of the authors, the doctrine now has a certain air of unreality. Currently the majority of the legislators will not be able to read the legislation in the majority of the languages in which they have enacted it. However, it is equally

---

[4] Statute of the Court ('the Statute') Art 40.
[5] Rules of Procedure ('RP') Art 44(2).
[6] Nearly half of the budget of the Court is attributable to translation and interpretation.
[7] There can be additional problems where several languages are spoken in one state.
[8] Case 283/81 *CILFIT v Ministry of Health* [1982] ECR 3415, para 18.

true to say that those who are bound by legislation should be able to rely on it as it appears in their Member State's official language. There is something abhorrent in the thought that the citizen is bound by documents expressed in a language he cannot understand, even if one suspects that in each Member State it is a feature of life that its legislation and decisions which have nothing whatever to do with the Union are nevertheless frequently expressed in a terminology and style which, at best, only a few lawyers and administrators can understand.

One of the major achievements of the Union has been the close cooperation of the national administrations and courts and the ECJ. It is, after all, primarily the national administrations and courts which apply Union law. This state of affairs has been achieved by involving Member States in helping the ECJ to answer questions referred by national courts and by giving an extended right of audience to Member States. It is manifestly easier for a Member State to play an effective part in proceedings before the ECJ if it has access to all the relevant material in a language with which those concerned in that state are familiar and if these can express their thoughts in their own language.

The linguistic regime is broadly as follows. When a question for a preliminary ruling comes before the Court it is translated into the languages of Member States and transmitted to them.[9] When the replies come back they are translated. When the Court is dealing with direct actions, the claimant can in principle choose the language of the case but the exceptions to this rule have the result that in general the language of the case is that of the defendant.[10] All the pleadings have to be translated into the language of the case.

Translators and interpreters are therefore needed. The internal needs of the Court discussed below are such that there is a need for yet more translators and interpreters. The Court has a collection of them which certainly exceeds what is available in most Member States. Therefore there continues to be a strong case for concentrating the work of translation at the Court rather than putting the responsibility with each Member State. This in practice is what happens now.

The end result is that the quality and general acceptability of the judgments is increased in exchange for a substantial increase in time and cost for the Court. So far as I can see, this is a price which Member States are willing to pay in return for their administrations and their citizens being able to play a part in legal proceedings in their own languages. That seems to me a perfectly reasonable choice of principle, the more so since the extra time and expense for the Court is at least matched and probably exceeded by corresponding savings at Member State level. People are free to write in their own languages without themselves having to expend time and money in translations. Shifting the translation burden from the Court to Member States would not I suspect in the end result in speeding up the process or in any lowering of the total expenditure on litigation.

---

[9] Art 104(1) RP.
[10] Art 29 RP.

Let me now move on to consider communication at the Court itself. There are two aspects to this – what happens at the oral hearing and what happens in the Court's internal procedures.

B. The Oral Hearing

In principle, the hearing is conducted in the language of the case although Member States have the privilege of addressing the Court in their own languages.[11] The Commission and other institutions of the Union are, however, bound by the general rule. This can, not infrequently, have the disadvantage that the Court is addressed not by the person having conduct of the relevant field of activity but rather by someone who speaks the appropriate language.

The language problem in the oral hearing is significant. Understanding legal submissions can be difficult even in a monolingual setting. Even in their own language some advocates and judges are less good than others at making their meaning clear. Some people's mental processes are quicker than others. Not infrequently in the course of one hearing several languages will be spoken. Not all of those languages will be understood by each member of the Court and each participant in the hearing. In consequence submissions are simultaneously[12] translated into several languages. The quality of the interpretation is in general good and it is easy to blame an interpreter for what in fact is a fault in the original.[13] But the nature of the task is hugely difficult: *Traduttore, Traditore*. So the interpretation may be excellent in one language and less good in another.

My personal experience is that when I hear something in court which I do not immediately understand, if I wait a few sentences all will become clear. Sometimes this is not so but I do not always know whether my incomprehension is my fault, the fault of the interpreter or the fault of the advocate. It is a fact of life that everyone has their off-days. By the time I hear the translation of the passage following the phrase I did not understand, the speaker has moved on. By the time I have considered whether it is worth posing a question, and if so how and in what language to formulate it, he is a few more sentences on – sentences on which, meanwhile, it is difficult to concentrate. If I interrupt to pose a question this will sometimes puzzle some of my colleagues who do not share my difficulty – because my mind is slower that day, because their legal system is more similar to that of the speaker so that his thoughts are easier for them to understand or because their translation of the relevant sentences is clearer. One is aware that any question risks disturbing the advocate whose mind has moved on and who may come from a legal system where the questioning of advocates by the Court is all

---

[11] Art 29 RP.
[12] Not all that simultaneously when, as sometimes happens, the spoken word is translated into another language and then retranslated from that language into a third language.
[13] Consider Lady Brute's riposte in *The Relapse* to Belinda's comment 'you know we must return good for evil': 'That may be a mistake in the translation'.

but unknown. If every member of the Court were to pose a question every time one occurs to him the hearings would take much longer – certainly when we are dealing with cases with more than five Judges. In consequence the Court would not keep up with its case load and would take longer to produce judgments. The chances are that if one waits long enough the point will become clear, one of the other advocates will pick it up or a colleague can explain it during the break or after the hearing. So the tendency amongst most of us is to make a note to think about the point further and to look at the transcript of the hearing at leisure. Although I used to take a fairly active part in proceedings whilst a national Judge I have become much more silent for the sort of reasons described above. I doubt whether the oral hearings will ever become the centre of the Court's work in the way that they used, in any event, to be in England. Advocates who know their business will continue to put their arguments clearly in writing and not rely on the oral hearing.

The foregoing, however, lends force to those who say that the present prescription by the Statute[14] concerning references, namely that each party should only be allowed one set of pleadings, should be changed so as to provide for a second round of pleadings in these proceedings as well which would allow everyone a chance to reply in writing to the arguments of those who disagree with him. It may be that the Statute will be changed to allow this. If it is, however, then one ineluctable result will be to lengthen the time taken for the written proceedings yet further. While in some cases parties who had been allowed to put their case in writing would then be willing to forgo the oral hearing, I doubt whether this will be so in the majority. If that is right, such a change in the rules would probably result in a lengthening of the time before judgment. It is difficult to be certain because the availability of disciplined written arguments from the parties can facilitate and thus speed up the task of drafting the judgment.

C. The Internal Language Regime of the Court

The language regime adopted amongst the Judges and Advocates General in their dealings with one another in relation to a case is not prescribed in the rules. The members of the Court have worked out what suits them best. Although when the Court was founded it might have been practicable to use all the official languages of the Community, even then it was thought cheaper and wiser for the incoming documents to be translated into only one language and for the Judges to use just that language in their official communications with each other. At the present time it would be wholly impracticable for the documents to be translated into all the official languages of the Union and for each Judge to use his own language in his written or oral communications with the others – there are 23 official languages in the Union. No Judge speaks them all and if everything were to be

---

[14] Statute Art 23.

translated and interpreted into each language the cost in time, money and loss of spontaneity in judicial deliberations and confidentiality would be enormous.

This last point bears elaboration. Communications between the Judges in the context of the Court take two forms – written notes and oral discussion. It is obvious that a meaningful interplay between Judges from more than a score of different backgrounds and countries will present its difficulties at the best of times. Each Judge comes to the Court equipped with his own collection of self-evident truths and presuppositions acquired over a lifetime. In consequence, discussions between the Judges on cases can be long. It can at times be difficult to understand the problem which is vexing a colleague or to understand why he does not understand what is vexing you. The fact that most of the Judges are talking, writing and listening in a language which is not their own clearly adds to the problem. The Rules of Procedure provide that any Judge may require that any questions be formulated in the language of his choice and communicated in writing to the Court before being put to the vote.[15]

Everyone concerned is bound not to reveal the contents of the written notes and discussions[16] and only one judgment results.[17] In drafting their notes to each other the Judges have the help of their cabinets, and the Judges' skills, coupled with those resources, permit notes to be drafted relatively easily and quickly in the internal language of the Court without the intervention of translators. As for the oral discussion between the Judges, one has to accept that, particularly at the beginning of their mandate, some Judges find it difficult to communicate clearly in the internal language of the Court. Yet the Rules of Procedure provide that every Judge taking part in the deliberations shall state his opinion and the reasons for it.[18]

Theoretically this problem could be tackled by employing a sufficient number of interpreters but this would both be expensive in time and money and statistically increase the risk that some of the discussion would leak to the outside world. More important in my view is that the presence of non-judges would I think adversely affect the generally easy and relaxed communications between the Judges. This is partly a question of numbers – the more people that there are in a room the more difficult it is to be informal – and partly the result of the difficulties inherent in any interpretation process. In any event the Rules of Procedure currently forbid the presence at the deliberations of anyone other than the Judges.[19]

It would be possible to continue without interpreters and to use for judicial deliberations two languages (which is the practice in the European Court

---

[15] Art 27(4) RP. The precise import of this has not, so far as I know, ever been the subject of any ruling.
[16] Statute Arts 2 and 35.
[17] Art 63 RP.
[18] Art 27(3) RP.
[19] Art 27(2) RP.

of Human Rights) or even more. But even a modest extension of the linguistic regime is fraught with problems unless each Judge is familiar with all the languages used – in which case there seems little point in having more than one. Clearly the more languages one uses the more difficult it becomes for everyone to understand everything which is being said or written. Moreover, starting with a draft judgment written in one language would cause difficulty if each Judge were free to circulate alternative drafts of particular paragraphs in his preferred language. So my guess is that the Court will continue to have a one-language regime internally.

On the assumption that only one language is used, the question then arises as to which language this should be. At the moment it is French. One often hears surprise expressed – and not only by those coming from the United Kingdom – that it is not English. But such a change would not solve many of the problems which I have outlined above. While perhaps nowadays many can order a meal and chat about the weather in English, in most, if not all, Member States much more is required if one is to make a meaningful input into what is often a highly technical piece of litigation.

In my view the crucial question relates to the recruitment of Judges. When the Court was founded a knowledge of French was widely found amongst potential members of the Court. Even in the Union of 27 this may still be the case although I would doubt it. My guess is that as the older generation die out and (American) English continues its dominance of the spoken and written word, it will be easier for Member States to find potential members who have a good command of English than to find potential members who have a good command of any other of the official languages of the Union. If it is or becomes the case that a result of keeping French as the internal language of the Court is that the pool in which states fish for potential members is smaller than it would be if English were the internal language of the Court, then this would be an important matter.

However, even then there would be arguments for keeping French. First, at the moment it is difficult to recruit persons who are both jurists and linguists and are capable and willing to act as translators who have English as their mother tongue. There are not enough even now when English is not the internal language of the Court. If English were to become that language about twice as many as we currently have would be required. Second, the Court is situated in a country with two French-speaking neighbours and of which French is an official language. This implies that it is easier to recruit staff for many of the supporting services of the Court amongst French speakers than English speakers. The Judges must be able to communicate with the staff. Third, and this is a point worthy of a paper in itself, the case law of the Court has been crafted in French for the past 50 years and in consequence owes much to the way of thinking and expressing themselves which the French have evolved over the centuries. One finds a multitude of abstractions and a frequent use of the passive voice. There is a case for saying that the interpretative function imposed upon the Court by the preliminary reference procedure is easier to operate in French than in English. Any study of English legal history demonstrates how reluctant lawyers are to change their traditional language.

It is worth noting, however, that thought is being given by the Court, the Council, and the Commission both as to the amount of consultation of Member States there should be and as to the linguistic regime. This currently is in the context of proceedings involving children, loss of liberty and so on where speed may be even more important than in the run-of-the-mill cases. It may be that for urgent cases a different linguistic and consultation regime will be adopted which gives a greater emphasis to the requirement for speed.

III. The Members of the Court

A. One Judge per Member State

The Judges of the Court are chosen by common consent of all the Member States. The EC Treaty provides that there shall be one per Member State[20] and that the Judges are to be chosen 'from persons whose independence is beyond doubt and who possess the qualifications required for appointment to the highest judicial offices in their respective countries or who are jurisconsults of recognized competence'.[21] In practice, each Member State nominates a Judge from its citizens. In general, the other Member States concur in his or her appointment. Member States vary enormously in size and it is manifest that the smaller states will be fishing for Judges in a smaller pool of qualified persons than the larger states. There will never be an exact correlation between the amount of talent available and the total population, but statistically it must be probable that if Judges could be chosen without regard to the national limitation the choice would not fall on Judges each of which is of the nationality of a different Member State. So probably the present method of appointing Judges will have led to the appointment of some who would not have been chosen in an open competition across the Union if there had been no requirement of one Judge per state. However, here we come across another example of the typical political dilemma of seeking to achieve several different aims which are mutually contradictory.

The arguments in favour of the present system come both from the Member States and from the Court itself. Politicians currently regard it as essential from the point of view of achieving the acceptability in their countries of the judgments

---

[20] Art 221 EC. This was inserted by the Treaty of Nice. Previously there was no such rule. Art 1(20) of the Treaty of Lisbon repeats the requirement that there shall be one Judge from each Member State.
[21] Art 222 EC. That wording would seem to permit the appointment as the national Judge of someone who is a jurisconsult of recognized competence but comes from a different jurisdiction and is not eligible for appointment to the highest judicial office in the country concerned. However, this might be regarded as too literal an interpretation.

of the Court that there should be on the Court someone from their country. From the point of view of the Court it is important that we should have a feel of how the particular legislation or decision we are examining is operated in the country concerned, what is the national law and practice in the relevant field and what is the likely impact of a judgment going this way or that. So there are good grounds for the present system and I see no prospect of any change in that regard. That said, there is a case for changing the rules governing who sits on what case so as to follow the practice of the European Court of Human Rights and to provide that the composition of the chamber should include a Judge from the state from whom the reference comes or the legality of whose conduct is under examination. It is undoubtedly helpful to have amongst those ruling on the compatibility of a particular country's national law with the law of the Union a Judge from the jurisdiction in question. It is often very difficult for an outsider who does not speak the language in question and has no knowledge of the legal framework in which the law under examination is set to be completely sure that he has correctly understood the way the national law under examination works. When the language of the case is not spoken by any of the Judges it has happened that the Judges sign the definitive form of the judgment although, unknown to them, there has been a mistranslation into the language of the case. This can be rectified when spotted but the process is complicated.

B. The Independence of the Members of the Court

The independence of the Judges and Advocates General from the State which nominated them is manifestly desirable. The term of office of both Judges and Advocates General is six years renewable.[22] There have been some suggestions that the period of appointment should be longer, say 12 years, and that there should be no possibility of renewal. The aim behind such suggestions is to strengthen the independence of the Judges. Some feel that the Judge who wishes to be reappointed might be afraid that the direction of his vote in the deliberations might leak out into the wider world and that the Judge might for that reason be afraid to vote as he in truth thought best for fear that he might not be reappointed. I have no reason to suppose that this has ever been a consideration influencing any Judge in his vote, but one must accept that the possibility cannot be ruled out.

However, I think it highly unlikely that the result of the present term of the mandate is that the Court has delivered a judgment which it would not have delivered had the term been longer and unrenewable. First, one result of the requirements that there should be only one judgment and that the deliberations of the Judges be kept secret is that it is difficult for any state to be sure which way 'its' Judge voted in any particular case so the pressures are not all that great.

---

[22] Art 222 EC. In practice, as will appear below, the terms of the Advocates General from all but five of the Member States are not renewed.

Second, not only should the Judges be chosen from persons whose independence is beyond doubt, but also once they are there they find substantial internal social pressures in a small body like the Court which militate against partial behaviour. Judgments are the result of a team effort and the presence of a partial Judge is highly unlikely to have swung the case this way or that. Partiality in these circumstances would in general be obvious to the others sitting on the case.

A disadvantage of making the term longer than six years arises from a problem which besets all jurisdictions. It is in practice difficult to remove a Judge whose powers begin to fail during his mandate. It is much easier simply not to renew the mandate. The arguments are nicely balanced.

C. Choosing the Members of the Court

It has been left to each Member State to devise its own method of finding the Judge to nominate. In this context, as in others, a state may be subject to its internal political pressures of one sort or another. An increasing number of states, including the United Kingdom, have made the process more transparent than it was in the early days. The Treaty of Lisbon provides for the setting up of a panel comprising seven persons chosen from among former members of the Court of Justice and of the CFI, members of national Supreme Courts and lawyers of recognized competence one of whom shall be proposed by the European Parliament. That panel is to be set up in order to give an opinion on candidates' suitability to perform the duties of Judge and Advocate General.[23] The Treaty provides that the Judges shall be appointed by common accord of the governments of the Member States after consultation of the panel.[24] In the context of the appointment of members of the Staff Tribunal such a panel was set up[25] which made recommendations to the Council. Those recommendations were in fact followed by the Council although it was not obliged to do so. This was widely welcomed. There is a case for having the same sort of procedure in relation to the ECJ while still keeping the requirement that there should be one Judge nominated by each state. However, at present even that limited type of external quality control on the quality of applicants has not been introduced. But while this may seem regrettable to some, one must not forget that in practice it is not in the interest of any state that an unsuitable person be appointed: he would not carry weight in the deliberations of the Court. Moreover, the nominating state might well find opposition from other members of the Council if a candidate were manifestly unsuitable.

The position in relation to the Advocates General is similar in some ways, yet different. The arguments which are in play in the case of Judges about acceptability

---

[23] Art 2(204).
[24] Art 2(207).
[25] Pursuant to Art 3 of the Annex to the Statute.

and knowledge of the particular national law and system are of much less significance in the case of Advocates General. Moreover, the EC Treaty only provides for eight Advocates General.[26] There is currently an informal arrangement whereby five states[27] always have an Advocate General on the court whereas the rest take turns to provide the other three. The rule of one Advocate General per state having been abandoned, the case for seeking the best people that the Union can offer regardless of national origin increases. Moreover, people learn on the job. The Union is the poorer if it insists on replacing a first-class Advocate General[28] after his six-year mandate has expired just because he comes from a small country. It seems to me that a change in the system of appointment of Advocates General may well be desirable.

D. The Advocate General

Until recently an Advocate General was required to deliver an Opinion in every case. Now the Court has a choice as to whether to ask for such an Opinion if the case raises no new point of law.[29] That change has met with general approval. Some would go further and abolish the institution of the Advocate General altogether. Manifestly, the Court could function without any Advocates General. In effect, the reporting Judge's first draft of a judgment can fulfil many of the functions of the Opinion – ordering the material and providing a draft against which the Judges can, as it were, test their views before deciding the case.

I tend to the view, however, that the present situation is satisfactory, certainly if the rule as to there being only a single judgment is retained. There is a certain circularity in the arguments here. The style of the judgments of the Court is in part the result of the requirement that there be just one judgment. A reporting Judge inevitably will in general seek to produce a draft which is likely to meet with the acceptance of those sitting with him. This can lead him towards caution and lack of originality. The present style of the judgments is such that they tend not to record discussions of the advantages in going this way or that. An examination of the history of the Court will show that there have been significant changes of tack perhaps years after the delivery of an Opinion which first unsuccessfully advocated such a change. If there had been no such Opinion, the thoughts contained in it, whilst they might well have been put forward by one or more Judges in their deliberations, might well not have seen the light of day.

Not a large proportion of the time taken to produce a judgment is attributable to the Advocates General. If they delivered their Opinions before the oral hearing, a subject to which I return in Section 5 below, they would add even

---

[26] Art 222 EC.
[27] France, Germany, Italy, Spain and the UK.
[28] In practice, this may also well mean the loss to the Court of his legal secretaries who will also have learned on the job and may be replaced by neophytes.
[29] Statute Art 20(5).

less time to the total time required for decision and indeed might shorten it. The institution has proved valuable. It would be a pity to abolish it.

IV. The Rules of Procedure

The procedural rules which govern the functioning of the ECJ are laid down in part by the Statute, which cannot be altered save by unanimous agreement, and in part by the Rules of Procedure which require the approval of the Council acting by qualified majority.[30] These procedural rules govern a whole variety of matters – some manifestly of great importance to Member States, others, one would have thought, of a purely technical nature and of no intrinsic interest. Examples of the former are the rules indicating how the constitution of the chamber hearing a case is to be determined, how the Presidents of the Court and of the chambers are to be chosen, whether Member States must be notified of procedures to which they are not parties and the language regime to be followed in proceedings. An example of the latter is the rule which provides that documents must be served in writing on sheets of paper rather than by electronic means.

Somewhere in between are the rules which prescribe who may have access to the pleadings and supporting documents before the Court.[31] At present, there is no public right of access to these documents. This accords with the practice of some states but not with that of others. This rule helps safeguard confidentiality but has the disadvantage that it increases the difficulty facing anyone at the oral hearing who wishes to follow what is going on. The most important facts and arguments in any case should be in the pleadings. The Judges, in a desire to save time, tell the advocates not to repeat at the hearing what is already in their pleadings. In consequence, in so far as the advocates obey these instructions, the public and the press is left in the dark as to the arguments and facts advanced on each side.

Be that as it may, the present position is that, whether important or not, no rule change can be made without the approval of the Council. The obvious practical effect of this requirement is that changes thought to be desirable by most are not made because one or more Member State objects. A less obvious effect might be that the Court becomes reluctant even to propose changes because of a fear that any such proposal will involve a lot of work and wrangling and will in any event probably still come across some opposition.

The Court has thus in the past done its best to interpret the rules in a way which increases its efficacy. Thus although Article 20 of the Statute provides that 'The oral procedure shall consist of the reading of the report presented by a Judge acting as Rapporteur', in practice the President simply states that he considers

[30] Art 223 EC.
[31] Art 16 RP.

that the report may be taken as read. Similarly, although Article 37 provides 'Judgments... shall be read in open court', in practice only the order of the Court is read out. No-one has ever objected to the taking of these and similar short-cuts – indeed, some say that even now the time spent on this vestigial reading occupies thousands of man hours which could be more profitably employed.

It seems to me that there is a case for giving the Court greater discretion in prescribing its own Rules of Procedure and it may well be that this will come about.

V. The Timing of the Delivery of the Opinion

One result of the rules is that the Judges are usually compelled to consider a case in four separate stages usually separated by months rather than weeks – (i) at the time when, following the delivery of the Preliminary Report, the whole Court decides on the appropriate formation to hear the case and on the appropriateness of a Hearing and of an Opinion by the Advocate General, (ii) when preparing for the Hearing, (iii) on receiving the Opinion and (iv) following receipt of a draft judgment. For those not possessed of a prodigious memory, this involves refreshing one's memory three times. Time and energy could be saved if this were significantly reduced.

A possible way of doing this would be to change the time when the Advocates General deliver their Opinions. At present, this happens after the conclusion of the oral argument. One disadvantage of the present system is that, after the Hearing, there is often a delay of more than a month before the Reporting Judge starts preparing his draft judgment since he wishes to have the benefit of the Opinion before he does so. Since the preparation of the draft is interrupted by one or other of the stages of the other 50 or so cases which the Reporting Judge will have on his shelves, there is in general a much longer gap between the delivery of the Opinion and the deliberations on a draft judgment. The total gap between the Hearing and deliberations is, save on the rare occasions when the Opinion is delivered at the conclusion of the Hearing, of course longer still.

A further disadvantage of the present system is that the Judges are deprived of reasoned criticism of the Opinion by the parties. The inability of the parties to comment on the Opinion was challenged before the Court on the basis that it involved a breach of Article 6(1) of the European Convention on Human Rights and of the general principles of law the observance of which the Court secures. That challenge was rejected.[32] I assume for present purposes that the existing practice is compatible with the general principles but wish shortly to examine

---

[32] Case 17/98 *Emesa Sugar (Free Zone) NV v Aruba* [2000] ECR I-665. See also in this context the judgment of the ECtHR in *Kress v France*, App No 39594/98, Judgment of 7 June 2001, Reports of Judgments and decisions 2001-VI, and the Opinion of Advocate General Ruiz-Jarabo Colomer in Case C-466/00 *Kaba v SSHD* [2003] ECR I-2219.

the possibility of changing that practice in order to organize the business of the Court better.

There is significant pressure from various quarters arguing for delivery of the Advocate General's Opinion prior to the oral hearing. From the point of view of the public and the press attending the Hearing, the fact that they had already had an opportunity of reading the Opinion would undoubtedly produce a better comprehension of what was at issue and what were the arguments than the Report for the Hearing.

From the point of view of the parties, such a change in the practice would give them an opportunity of accepting parts of the Opinion and focusing on what was really contentious. It can happen that an Opinion canvasses something which was not argued either in the written material or at the Hearing. There is undoubtedly something to be said in such a case for giving the parties a chance to comment on this point. Under the present Rules, the Court has an option of reopening the Hearing after the delivery of the Opinion if it wishes.[33] This in theory gives the Judges the opportunity of considering whether, as a result of the points made in the Opinion or of points which have occurred to the Court in the course of drafting the judgment, there would be an advantage in hearing the parties again. While this has been done, there are strong practical considerations related to further expenditure of time and money which militate against this being done save in the rarest of cases. In any event, since, under current practice, there is then a further Opinion delivered after the parties' submissions, the problem could theoretically occur again.

From the point of view of the Judges, having the Opinion available before the Hearing would have the advantage that, when preparing for the Hearing, they would already have a reasoned impartial assessment of the arguments as presented in the written submissions, thus putting them in a position similar to that of Judges in Supreme Courts hearing appeals. It would have the further advantage that the Judges could move immediately after the Hearing to preparing and deliberating on the judgment. This would significantly reduce the element of repetition in the work carried out by Judges at different stages of the procedure to which I have referred above. From their point of view this would be a significant gain.

However, a move towards the delivery of Opinions before the Hearing undoubtedly has some possible disadvantages and views are divided as to its desirability. Notwithstanding the linguistic difficulties which attend the oral hearings, they can produce enlightenment as to facts or the way a party makes its submissions. Indeed, governments can and do make oral submissions without having made any written submissions at all. Particularly in reference cases, where there is only one round of pleadings and thus parties usually cannot comment in writing on some arguments which appear for the first time at that stage, the procedure of argument before the Court can lead to reformulations of position.

---

[33] Art 61 RP.

Thus if the Opinion were delivered before the Hearing it might turn out that it did not deal with an argument which appeared in a particular form for the first time at the Hearing or is seen as attacking the wrong target or proceeding from a false factual basis. A possible answer to this conundrum is for the Advocates General to deliver a provisional Opinion based only on the written material, and to be free to indicate at the Hearing whether that Opinion is to be regarded as final or whether they wish to deliver a new or revised Opinion in the light of what was said at the Hearing. This option, however, would involve more work for the Advocate General.

There are also in some quarters strongly held theoretical objections to giving a party the possibility of attacking the reasoning of a Member of the Court – which is indeed the formal position of the Advocate General albeit that he takes no part in the deliberations which lead to the formulation of the judgment and has no possibility of commenting on the draft judgment. It is rightly said that the position of the Advocate General would change so as to resemble more the position of a first instance judge vis-à-vis an appellate court. If the Opinion were to be delivered before the hearing the Advocate General would probably have to listen to criticisms of his work from one party and praise from another. Some may find this disagreeable[34] and some fear that the reaction of the Advocate General might be to enter into an argument with the advocate and thus disturb the smooth progress of the Hearing. Probably because it is nothing strange for an English judge to express a preliminary view early on in a case and then to have a civilized and instructive exchange with the advocates in open court about the correctness of his preliminary view, I do not find this horrifying. But there are those who do.

I would not be surprised if, at some time in the future, the rules were changed so as to permit or require the delivery of an Opinion before the Hearing. But it may never happen.

VI. Conclusion

In the life of the Court as in the rest of life there are choices to be made and each choice produces advantages and disadvantages. The system is such that the difficulties attendant upon making any changes mean that things change only slowly. The present system on the whole works reasonably well at trying to fulfil

---

[34] In *Kaba* (n 32 above) 110 the Advocate General went so far as to say 'the Advocate General, knowing that his Opinion would be the subject of a response from the parties, would inevitably take their reactions into account when drafting it, and would not therefore deliver it with "complete impartiality and independence" as required by Article 222 EC'. This would seem to imply a pessimistic view of the strength of character of Advocates General and also that first instance judges who know that they are subject to appeal do not act with impartiality and independence – a view which does not correspond with my personal experience both as a first instance judge and as a judge in the Court of Appeal.

conflicting demands. If Advocate General Sharpston has as long a tenure at the Court as Francis Jacobs, then I have no doubt that by the time of her retirement from the Court she will have seen some changes. My guess is that the procedures will in general still take over a year, and that the Court will still try to communicate with Member States and their citizens in their native tongue. While I consider that it is probable that the Court will still have only one internal language, this may well have changed to English. I suspect that the institution of the Advocates General will be retained but that their Opinions may become available to the parties before the Hearing. My hope is that the Court will be given a greater discretion as to its own Rules of Procedure.

2

The Changing Role of the Advocate General

*Eleanor Sharpston**

The Advocates General are an integral part of the Court of Justice – even if exactly what they do and why they do it sometimes needs explaining to puzzled outsiders. Over the years since Advocate General Lagrange delivered the first ever opinion, in *France v High Authority*,[1] 39 jurists from 15 Member States have served the Court in this capacity. Some – Gordon Slynn, Federico Mancini, José Luis Da Cruz Vilaça (who became the first President of the Court of First Instance), Claus Gulmann and Antonio Tizzano – having started as Advocates General, moved across to be judges. Others – Alberto Trabucchi, Francesco Capotorti, Antonio Saggio (who had been first judge and then President at the Court of First Instance) and Paolo Mengozzi (who had been judge at the Court of First Instance) – took the opposite route. One – Antonio La Pergola – even managed a 'double shuffle', starting as Judge, then spending nearly five years as an Advocate General and completing his time at the Court with a further spell as a Judge.

The role of the Advocate General is defined by the Treaties, simply yet eloquently, as being to 'assist' the Court,[2] just as the Court's own function is described, with equal simplicity, as being to 'ensure that in the interpretation and application of this Treaty the law is observed'.[3] Various distinguished academics and several former and serving Advocates General have sought, over the years, to 'unpack' that formula and explore, in greater detail, what it is that Advocates General do (and why).[4]

---

* The views expressed are personal to the author and do not bind the institution in which she serves. She would like to thank her colleague in chambers, Dr Geert de Baere, both for his helpful comments on the draft and for his sterling (and swift) assistance in tracking down elusive references and statistics and plugging gaps in footnotes.

[1] Case 1/54 *France v High Authority* [1954–6] ECR 1.
[2] Art 222(1) EC.
[3] Art 220(1) EC.
[4] See, for example, N Burrows and R Greaves, *The Advocate General and EC Law* (2007); J Kokott, *Anwältin des Rechts – Zur Rolle der Generalanwälte beim Europäischen Gerichtshof* (2006); C Ritter, 'A New Look at the Role and Impact of Advocates-General – Collectively and Individually' (2006) 12 Columbia Journal of European Law 751; K Mortelmans, 'The Court Under the Influence of its Advocates General: an Analysis of the Case Law on the Functioning of the Internal Market' (2005) 24 YEL 127; W Van Gerven, 'De Advocaat-Generaal in het EG-Hof van Justitie: een ware vriend?' in P Van Orshoven and M Storme (eds), *Amice curiae, quo vadis?*

As those commentators rightly conclude, the true contribution of the Advocates General is more elaborate than the bare formula suggests. To some extent, as the Court itself has evolved, the role played by the Advocates General has changed and developed with it. I shall suggest that further change is probably needed if the Court is to meet the challenges ahead with the effective assistance of its Advocates General.

I. The Early Days

How one starts to write on a blank sheet of paper is deeply important. It may or may not be true that the first preliminary reference to be lodged with the Court under what was then Article 177 EEC caused champagne to be broken out in celebration. It is certain that, in the early stages, every case represented a significant moment in the initial shaping of the structures and features of Community law. In comparison with today's Court, there was very little pressure of work in terms of the volume of the case load. Four cases (all direct actions) were brought in 1954 (by 2006, this figure had risen to 535).[5] Everyone – from the Member States to the High Authority to the Court itself – was feeling their way. The early Advocates General – initially, just Advocate General Lagrange, joined a few months later by Advocate General Roemer[6] – would necessarily have approached the drafting of their opinions conscious that they were helping to lay the foundations of the new system.

This is clear from the opening words of Advocate General Lagrange's first opinion. After quoting the pertinent passages from the Statute of the Court and the Treaty, he continued:[7]

I have the honour of presenting an opinion on the first action to come before the Court of the first European Community, and I shall strive to carry out that task to the best of my ability, in the spirit in which it has been defined by the Statute of the Court.

(2002) 195; T Tridimas, 'The Role of the Advocate General in the Development of Community Law: Some Reflections' (1997) 34 CML Rev 1349; N Fennelly, 'Reflections of an Irish Advocate General' (1996) Irish Journal of European Law 5; M Vranken, 'Role of the Advocate General in the Law-Making Process of the European Community' (1996) Anglo-American Law Review 39; CO Lenz, 'Das Amt des Generalanwalts am Europäischen Gerichtshof' in O Due, M Lutter and J Schwarze (eds), *Festschrift für Ullrich Everling* (1995) 719; K Borgsmidt, 'The Advocate General at the European Court of Justice: A Comparative Study' (1988) 13 EL Rev 106; AA Dashwood, 'The Advocate General in the Court of Justice of the European Communities' (1982) 2 Legal Studies 202; A Barav, 'Le commissaire du gouvernement près le Conseil d'Etat français et l'avocat-général près la Cour de Justice des Communautés européennes' (1974) RIDC 809.

[5] 201 direct actions, 251 references for a preliminary ruling, 80 appeals and three appeals concerning interim measures and interventions. Source: Statistics concerning the judicial activity of the Court of Justice in the 2006 Annual Report of the Court, available online at *http://curia.europa.eu/en/instit/presentationfr/rapport/stat/06_cour_stat.pdf*.

[6] Advocate General Lagrange took up office in December 1952; Advocate General Roemer in February 1953.

[7] Opinion of Advocate General Lagrange in Case 1/54 *France v High Authority* [1954–6] ECR 1, para 18.

Before coming to the Court of Justice, Advocate General Lagrange had, of course, been *commissaire du gouvernement* at the French *Conseil d'Etat*, the office that is often said to have served as the model for the Advocate General at the Court of Justice. I will let the words of the French delegation at the negotiations for the European Coal and Steel Community speak for themselves:[8]

C'est avec la conviction qu'une telle institution procurera à la nouvelle Cour ces mêmes effets bienfaisants que nos partenaires ont accepté de la faire profiter des fruits d'une expérience essentiellement française.

Advocate General Lagrange fulfilled the role with great style and showed an impressive grasp of the problems that Community law would face over the next decades.[9]

II. How Advocate General Francis Jacobs Saw the Role

As Advocate General, Francis set down his views on his job on a number of occasions.[10] He also gave many talks and presentations, some of which were subsequently formalized in writing.[11]

In a lecture given in the Grande Salle of the Court on 26 October 2005 – very shortly before he retired – Francis offered the following thoughts on the role of the Advocate General.

First, he stressed the 'internal' importance of the Advocate General to the work of the Court. The Advocate General follows a similar track to the *Juge Rapporteur* and he is there to assist the judges to decide. He is also there to develop the law – an important element, since the point at issue may not previously have been decided. Francis pointed out that references under Article 234 EC are accepted from all national courts at all levels. Some are, obviously, very inexperienced in referring and framing questions. Once the case is before the Court, the written and oral submissions of counsel are sometimes woefully inadequate.

Francis also highlighted the part played by the Advocate General's opinion within a system that delivers a single judgment to resolve any case, rather than allowing for dissenting judgments. He emphasized that Community law often synthesizes principles of differing national legal systems, through consensual

---

[8] Rapport de la délégation française sur le traité instituant la Communauté Européenne du Charbon et de l'Acier, Ministère des Affaires Etrangères, Paris, Octobre 1951, 32, quoted in Borgsmidt (n 4 above) 106.

[9] For a detailed analysis, see Burrows and Greaves (n 4 above) 59–88.

[10] See, for example, FG Jacobs, 'Advocates General and Judges in the European Court of Justice: Some Personal Reflections' in D O'Keeffe (ed.), *Judicial Review in European Union Law: Liber Amicorum in Honour of Lord Slynn of Hadley* (2000) 17.

[11] See, for example, FG Jacobs, 'Judicial Process in the European Court and the Role of the Advocate General' (The Dominik Lasok Lecture in European Community Law delivered in the University of Exeter on 2 February 1990).

judicial discussion, in order to develop the EU's own legal system. A true *communautaire* approach is therefore needed. The existence of separate concurring or dissenting judgments would weaken this. Indeed, there might well be a tendency for the dissenters to follow the thinking of their own national legal systems, thus undermining the whole process.

So far, so good; but, as Francis was quick to stress, a single judgment can be reached only through compromise. It follows all too easily that (particularly in a difficult or sensitive case) there may be lacunae in the reasoning. In such a context, the Advocate General's opinion may often provide more detailed reasoning than the judgment itself. For legal systems (such as the United Kingdom's) that place a premium on fuller reasoning, that is a way of satisfying 'users" demand. An Advocate General's opinion can also express doubts (whereas a judgment tends, by definition, to postulate certainties). If one supports a liberal concept of justice, identifying and recognising where the doubts lie is, however, important.

Finally, Francis stressed the increased transparency that flows from the existence of a published Advocate General's opinion. The judicial dialogue between Advocate General and Court is out in the open, and has led to many new and significant developments in EC law (for example, acceptance that transsexuals may be able, in certain circumstances, to obtain protection from EC sex equality law).[12] The importance of the Advocate General's role has been recognized both by national courts[13] and by the European Court of Human Rights.[14]

I would subscribe wholeheartedly to all these points.

III. The Court at the Start of the 21st Century

The rapid enlargement of the EU through the accession of 10 new Member States[15] in 2004, supplemented by the further accession of Bulgaria and Romania in 2007, has altered the balance within the Court and, as an inevitable corollary,

---

[12] See the opinion of Advocate General Tesauro in Case C-13/94 *P v S* [1996] ECR I-2143 and the opinion of Advocate General Ruiz-Jarabo Colomer in Case C-117/01 *KB v The National Health Service Pensions Agency and the Secretary of State for Health* [2004] ECR I-541, as well as the opinion of Advocate General Jacobs in Case C-423/04 *Sarah Margaret Richards v Secretary of State for Work and Pensions* [2006] ECR-3585. Note that, while Advocate General Elmer had held in his opinion in Case C-249/96 *Grant v South-West Trains* [1998] ECR I-621 that discrimination on the grounds of sexual orientation fell foul of Art 141 of the EC Treaty, the Court did not follow him.

[13] Francis pointed out that his opinion in Case C-338/95 *Wiener* [1997] ECR I-6495, in which he set out in detail the circumstances in which he felt that it was appropriate to make a reference under Art 234 EC, is frequently cited before national courts in the UK as a justification for *not* making a reference.

[14] See *Bosphorus Hava Yolları Turizm ve Ticaret Anonim Şirketi v Ireland*, App No 45036/98, judgment of 30 June 2005, described by Francis as 'a remarkable case', both for its recognition of the Court's human rights case law and in directing attention to the role played by the Advocate General.

[15] Cyprus, Czech Republic, Estonia, Hungary, Latvia, Lithuania, Malta, Poland, Slovakia and Slovenia.

the role of the Advocates General, in fundamental ways. In 2003, the Court was composed of the President, 14 other judges (who acted as *Juges Rapporteurs*) and eight Advocates General. In 2007, it consists of the President, 26 other judges (acting as *Juges Rapporteurs*) and eight Advocates General.

I draw attention here to three significant innovations.

First, the Treaty of Nice introduced the possibility of dispensing, in appropriate cases, with an Advocate General's opinion. Article 222 EC (ex Article 166), as amended, now provides:

> The Court of Justice shall be assisted by eight Advocates General. Should the Court of Justice so request, the Council, acting unanimously, may increase the number of Advocates General.
>
> It shall be the duty of the Advocate General, acting with complete impartiality and independence, to make, in open court, reasoned submissions on cases which, in accordance with the Statute of the Court of Justice, require his involvement.

Article 20(5) of the Statute of the Court gives the Court the discretionary power to proceed to judgment without an opinion of the Advocate General:

> Where it considers that the case raises no new point of law, the Court may decide, after hearing the Advocate General, that the case shall be determined without a submission from the Advocate General.

It may be that the intention was to reserve the (relatively) scarce advisory resource represented by the Advocates General for only the most significant cases, giving them back the time for reflection that their predecessors in the early days of the Court had enjoyed. I shall argue below that, if so, the intention has not wholly been fulfilled.

A second important innovation is the procedure whereby the First Advocate General serves as a filter for proposing the 'exceptional' review of Court of First Instance (CFI) judgments provided for by Article 225(2) EC, second paragraph.[16] Article 62 of the Statute of the Court provides that:

> in the cases provided for in Article 225(2) and (3) of the EC Treaty...where the First Advocate General considers that there is a serious risk of the unity or consistency of Community law being affected, he may propose that the Court of Justice review the decision of the Court of First Instance.
>
> The proposal must be made within one month of delivery of the decision by the Court of First Instance. Within one month of receiving the proposal of the First Advocate General, the Court of Justice shall decide whether the decision should be reviewed.

This means that the First Advocate General must now read each judgment of the CFI in an appeal from the Civil Service Tribunal (CST) and decide, within a relatively short time-frame, whether or not to recommend to the Court that it should

---

[16] A parallel provision is to be found in Art 225(3) EC, para 3, in respect of the (as yet hypothetical) case of review of CFI decisions on references for a preliminary ruling.

review that judgment.[17] This procedure will (by definition) also apply if, or when, further specialist panels are established. Ten appeals from the CST to the CFI were lodged in 2006.[18] There may well be a greater number in future years.

A third aspect is the new jurisdiction of the Court to hear references for a preliminary ruling in the area of freedom, security and justice. Article 68 EC puts an obligation on national courts of last resort to seek preliminary rulings on the interpretation of Title IV of Part Three of the EC Treaty, entitled 'Visas, asylum, immigration and other policies related to free movement of persons'. The Council, the Commission and the Member States are entitled to ask the Court for a ruling on how the provisions of the Title and acts adopted under it should be interpreted. Lower courts are, however, excluded from asking the Court for a preliminary ruling in cases under Title IV.[19] The drawbacks of this system have been pointed out by several authors.[20] Title IV of the EC Treaty is complemented by Title VI of the EU Treaty entitled 'Provisions on police and judicial cooperation in criminal matters'. Under Article 35 TEU, the Court of Justice has jurisdiction to give preliminary rulings in respect of a number of measures adopted under Title VI. However, only national courts of Member States who have declared that they accept the Court's jurisdiction in this respect are able to request such a ruling.

The overall effect is to confer upon the Court jurisdiction in respect of areas hitherto untouched by its case law. The need for a thoughtful contribution by the Advocates General to dissect the problems, map out the issues and suggest solutions would seem fairly evident.

A. The Parameters and the Issues

Simple arithmetic will show that, if it made sense to have a ratio of eight Advocates General to 15 judges in 2003 (just before the major enlargement in 2004), it

---

[17] Although, to lighten the workload, it is possible for the First Advocate General entirely informally to request another Advocate General to assist by taking a preliminary view as to whether a particular judgment should be reviewed, the actual decision whether or not to propose to the Court that it should exercise its power of review is one that can only be taken by the First Advocate General.

[18] Source: statistics concerning the judicial activity of the Court of First Instance in the 2006 Annual Report of the CFI, available online at *http://curia.europa.eu/en/instit/presentationfr/rapport/stat/06_trib_stat.pdf*.

[19] Note that Title IV of Part Three of the EC Treaty does not apply to the United Kingdom, Ireland or Denmark, except in certain circumstances specified in protocols Nos 4 and 5 annexed to the EU and the EC Treaties. There is a Commission proposal to extend the jurisdiction to make references to all courts: see Communication COM (2006) 346 final of 28 June 2006 from the Commission to the European Parliament, the Council, the European Economic and Social Committee, the Committee of the Regions and the Court of Justice of the European Communities on adaptation of the provisions of Title IV of the Treaty establishing the European Community relating to the jurisdiction of the Court of Justice with a view to ensuring more effective judicial protection, available online at *http://eur-lex.europa.eu/LexUriServ/site/en/com/2006/com2006_0346en01.pdf*.

[20] See, for example, A Arnull, *The European Union and its Court of Justice* (2nd ed, 2006) 132.

cannot be sensible to operate with a ratio of eight Advocates General to 27 judges *unless* there are significant changes in what the Advocates General do, or how they do it. The drafters of the Nice Treaty, in relaxing the requirement that there should be an Advocate General's opinion in every case, evidently recognized part of the problem. So far, it has been recognized but not, I would suggest, fully addressed.

Under Article 222 EC read in conjunction with Article 20(5) of the Statute of the Court, the *default* value is still that there *should* be an opinion.[21] The late Advocate General Geelhoed reckoned that an Advocate General could reasonably be expected to produce 30 opinions in a year. That yields, at a macro level, a total of 240 opinions per year from eight Advocates General. However, the decision whether to request the Advocate General to deliver an opinion in a particular case is taken at a micro level, on a case-by-case basis. The conundrum that needs to be solved is, therefore, how to get the two to coincide.

As a rule of thumb, one can say that a case that goes to a chamber of three judges will not have an opinion and a case that is allocated to the Grand Chamber will (of course) always have an opinion. What, however, of the significant percentage of cases that go to a chamber of five?

The Court has (naturally) sought informally to develop criteria so that decisions as to whether there is, or is not, to be an opinion are taken consistently. Its emerging practice, as can be seen (broadly) from recent cases,[22] is as follows.

First, the Court will wish to have an Advocate General's opinion in cases where there is a new question of law that is likely to have a systemic effect ('systemic' meaning an effect that impacts on the area of law in question as a whole, or more generally on the Community legal order).

Second, in the case of appeals from the CFI, the Court will wish to have an opinion where the subject matter has given rise to divergent decisions of the CFI, or where the CFI has decided cases in a way that is inconsistent with the case law of the Court of Justice.

Third, the Court is also prepared to hear the Advocate General on general questions of EC law where, even though the specific question of law is not new, there might be reason for the Court to reconsider its existing case law.[23]

Fourth, it is intended that there should be an opinion in any case in which the Court reviews a decision rendered by the CFI on appeal from a decision of one of the judicial panels set up under Article 220(2) EC (presently, therefore, the CST).

---

[21] Rather than that delivery of an opinion should be reserved for complex or difficult cases. That is because, unless the Court exercises the power given to it to take the positive step of deciding that there should *not* be an opinion, there will necessarily be an opinion.

[22] There may always be reasons why, in a particular case, the pattern that I outline here is not followed, and it is necessary for the Court to retain such flexibility. For example, a case that goes to the Grand Chamber solely because a Member State has insisted on that formation does not necessarily need an opinion.

[23] See, for example, the opinion of Advocate General Jacobs in Case C-50/00 P *UPA* [2002] ECR I-6677, the opinion of Advocate General Léger in Case C-147/02 *Alabaster* [2004] ECR I-3101 and the opinion of Advocate General Poiares Maduro in Case C-72/03 *Carbonati Apuani* [2004] ECR I-8027.

Since such review is intended to take place only 'exceptionally, where there is a serious risk of the unity or consistency of Community law being affected'[24] it is clear that the Court should have the benefit of the Advocate General's reflections when deciding such a case.[25]

B. Has the Role of the Advocate General Therefore been Redefined Adequately?

Although, as I have indicated, the Court has developed informal criteria for deciding whether or not an opinion is needed, there is no very obvious guarantee that, as a result, the total number of opinions in a particular year will approximate to the (informal) target (240) given by Advocate General Geelhoed. Moreover, if the criteria are not followed, it will tend to be in the sense of asking for opinions in additional cases that do not quite fit the criteria (rather than failing to ask for an opinion in a case that clearly fits the criteria). It is, of course, vital that the Court should retain sufficient flexibility to benefit from the Advocate General's formal assistance if it feels that would be helpful. At the same time, the effect of requesting an opinion in a marginal case, or a case that is for some reason exceptional, is inevitably to add to that Advocate General's workload.

The most visible part of the Advocate General's work has always been the delivery of full, formal opinions. In a Festschrift for Francis, one need only point to his opinions in, for example, *HAG II*,[26] *Säger v Dennemeyer*,[27] *Konstantinidis*,[28] *Commission v Greece*,[29] *Bosphorus*,[30] *Inter-Environnement Wallonie v Région Wallonne*,[31] *Silhouette*,[32] *Netherlands v Parliament and Council*[33] and *UPA*.[34]

However, as the commentators have rightly emphasized, Advocates General do not only contribute to cases by writing opinions. Each and every case that passes through the Court is assigned to an Advocate General, just as it is allocated to a *Juge Rapporteur*. From that point onwards, the case is shepherded through the Court by two members whose responsibility for its proper conduct goes beyond that of the *formation de jugement*. The Advocate General's view is thus sought, in parallel with that of the *Juge Rapporteur*, on every procedural question, great

---

[24] Cf Art 225(2) EC, para 2.

[25] Art 225(3) EC, para 2, provides the additional safeguard that, 'Where the Court of First Instance considers that the case requires a decision of principle likely to affect the unity and consistency of Community law, it may refer the case to the Court of Justice for a ruling'. It seems safe to assume that the Court would also wish to have the benefit of an Advocate General's opinion before delivering judgment in such a case.

[26] Case C-10/89 [1990] ECR I-3711.
[27] Case C-76/90 [1991] ECR I-4221.
[28] Case C-168/91 [1993] ECR I-1191.
[29] Case C-120/94 [1996] ECR I-1513.
[30] Case C-84/95 [1996] ECR I-3953.
[31] Case C-129/96 [1997] ECR I-7411.
[32] Case C-355/96 [1998] ECR I-4799.
[33] Case C-377/98 [2001] ECR I-7079.
[34] See n 23 above.

or small, that arises as the case proceeds – for example, when one of the parties requests that a language other than the language of the case be used for all or part of the proceedings,[35] or if in the course of the procedure one of the parties puts forward a new plea in law which is based on matters of law or of fact which come to light in the course of the procedure and the other party wishes to reply.[36]

The 'double scrutiny' that is provided by the Advocate General's involvement at every stage of the procedure is an important safeguard in a system where, for the majority of cases, the Court is the jurisdiction both of first and of last resort.[37] It also – necessarily – takes up time. There is a trade off to be assessed here, between the desirability of a true, detailed double scrutiny and use of a scarce resource.[38] Should the double scrutiny continue to apply to every element of case-handling or only to 'major' decisions (and, if so, how is 'major' to be defined)? Is double scrutiny really so necessary in a case that comes to the Court on appeal (where the file has already been subjected to careful and detailed judicial scrutiny by the CFI) as in infringement proceedings or a reference for a preliminary ruling?

Moreover, the decision as to whether or not an opinion is needed in any particular case is made by the *reunion générale* of the Court on the basis of the recommendations of *Juge Rapporteur* and Advocate General. By this point, the Advocate General and his cabinet will necessarily already have studied the file in some depth in order (in parallel with the *Juge Rapporteur*) to assess whether an opinion is in fact needed. Even in the case of uncontested, or barely contested, infringement proceedings, the Advocate General and his team will therefore have spent some time on the case before the (predictable) decision is taken by the *réunion générale* that an opinion is not required.

I have already drawn attention to the numerical balance (or imbalance) between *Juges Rapporteurs* and Advocates General. In purely practical terms, this means that each judge is dealing as *rapporteur* with less than a third of the cases that are attributed to each Advocate General (although, obviously, he is also sitting in other cases as a member of the *formation de jugement*). Cases can sensibly be handled by both *Juge Rapporteur* and Advocate General only after the last translation into the Court's working language (French) has become available. If individual *Juges Rapporteurs* each then start detailed work on their own case, the result may or may not be a balanced throughput of work for the Advocate General concerned.

The system presently operated can, and does, lead to curious anomalies. For example, if the Court decides at a *réunion générale* that a particular case is so clearly covered by the existing case law that it can be disposed of by reasoned order,[39]

---

[35] Art 29(2) RP.
[36] Art 42(2) RP.
[37] See Kokott (n 4 above) 9.
[38] Although the *référendaire* working on the case will come to the Advocate General with a suggestion as to how to deal with such a procedural question, the decision (and consequent formal view expressed in response to the *fiche verte* raising the procedural question) is that of the Advocate General.
[39] Under Art 104(3) RP.

the Advocate General remains involved, reviewing the draft order put forward by the *Juge Rapporteur* and, if appropriate, suggesting additions or modifications. In contrast, where the *réunion générale* decides to send a case to a chamber of three (implying that it is *not* sufficiently simple to be disposed of by reasoned order) the Advocate General will drop out of the case at that stage. The resulting paradox is that the Advocate General scrutinizes reasoned order cases to the bitter end, whereas a case before a chamber of three disappears off the Advocate General's books at a relatively early stage in the proceedings (even in a Grand Chamber case, the Advocate General's involvement – rightly – ends with the delivery of his opinion).

A more striking anomaly may be about to arise in the case of references for preliminary rulings treated under the new urgent preliminary ruling procedure (*procédure préjudicielle d'urgence* or PPU) currently under discussion to handle urgent cases in the area of freedom, security and justice.[40] These are, by definition, journeys into uncharted territory, where there is no pre-existing case law to which the Court can simply refer. Such preliminary references are likely to raise significant and sensitive new issues of EU law. They are, one would have thought, quintessentially cases in which the Court might be assisted by the reflections of the Advocate General; and in which the importance of a transparent, public judicial dialogue between the Advocate General and the Court can scarcely be over-emphasized.

There is, however, a genuine conundrum to resolve. By their very nature, a significant proportion of these cases are urgent. Because the issues raised are sensitive, Member States will naturally wish to preserve their right to intervene to make their views known. When the Member States intervene, they will of course wish to do so in their own official language. Trying to devise a procedure that satisfies those three core features is like trying to square a circle and then put a triangle inside.

In placing before the Council two discussion documents addressing the problem,[41] and in formulating, at the Council's request, draft proposals for the necessary modifications to the Statute of the Court[42] and the Rules of Procedure,[43] the Court has understandably been very concerned to try to shorten the time that will elapse before judgment is given in cases that are truly urgent. It is self-evident that the average 'normal' time for dealing with a reference for a preliminary ruling (at the last count in 2006, running at 19.8 months) would be quite unacceptable. The Court's recommendation to the Council is that judgment

---

[40] The Rules of Procedure were amended twice, in 2000, so as to permit, in some cases, recourse to an accelerated procedure (see Art 104a RP). However, the Court recognizes that recourse to the accelerated procedure would be unlikely to suffice to deal with urgent references under Title IV of Part Three EC and Title VI EU; and that, in any event, acceleration of one case is purchased at the cost of retarding other cases.

[41] Discussion paper of 25 September 2006, available online at *http://curia.europa.eu/en/instit/txtdocfr/documents/06208.pdf*, and supplementary discussion paper of 14 December 2006, available online at *http://curia.europa.eu/en/instit/txtdocfr/documents/08832EN.pdf*.

[42] Available online at *http://curia.europa.eu/en/instit/txtdocfr/documents/stat.pdf*.

[43] Available online at *http://curia.europa.eu/en/instit/txtdocfr/documents/rp.pdf*.

should be given 'after hearing the Advocate General' ('*l'avocat général entendu*'): the formula that is used in an accelerated procedure where no formal opinion is given.[44] There is thus, on the face of the text, no provision for the views of the Advocate General to be made public outside the *salle de délibéré*.

It may seem paradoxical that, having just stressed the Advocate Generals' existing workload, I should cavil at the idea that there might be no public Advocate General's opinion in such cases. I do so without apology, because there is no paradox. The Court needs its Advocates General to assist it with their reflections in this new, deeply important and deeply sensitive area of law as much as the early Court needed its Advocates General to assist in developing fundamental concepts of Community law that we now take for granted, such as primacy and direct effect.[45] By the same token, the 'users' of Community law – be they Member States' legal advisers, the Community institutions, the academic community, practitioners or (most importantly) the individuals who are affected by the Court's decisions – are surely entitled to greater clarity and transparency than a single succinct judgment produced under severe time constraints is likely to provide.

In advising in such cases, it is hardly likely that an Advocate General will walk into the *salle de délibéré* with a few notes jotted down on the back of an envelope. He and his *référendaires* will have invested considerable research and care in preparing the points that he will make.[46] In relative terms, transforming that oral advice (in appropriate cases) into a short opinion that is published is, I believe, a better use of an Advocate General's time than responding to a *fiche verte* about whether two counsel can be authorized to plead for a particular party. It would be possible to meet the (unquestionable) need for urgency simply by making provision for the Advocate General's opinion to be published *after* the judgment comes out, rather than holding up the procedure in order to get it out in published form before the Court proceeds to take the case *en délibéré*.[47] It is to be hoped that, as the Council considers the proposals before it, this will be amongst the issues that it examines.

---

[44] Compare Art 104a RP to the proposed Art 104b RP.

[45] On the role of the Advocates General in the development of the principle of direct effect, see Burrows and Greaves (n 4 above) 189–214.

[46] Since the Advocate General will necessarily be giving detailed oral advice in French (the Court's working language), whereas he would normally be using his mother tongue or another preferred pivot language (such as German or English) to write his opinion, it is extremely unlikely that he would not already have the beginnings of a prepared text (in French) of his advice. Interestingly, it seems likely that the Court may propose greater (apparent) flexibility as regards the Advocate General's input in the exceptional review cases under Art 225(2) EC (which are also meant to be urgent).

[47] After all, in pre-Internet times, subscribers to the roneo series received judgments and Advocate Generals' opinions in batches, and it was quite common to receive the Advocate General's opinion in a particular case after, rather than before, the judgment. In reviewing the proposed new procedure, the European Parliament's rapporteur, Mrs Diana Wallis, has openly expressed concern about the apparent absence of publication of the Advocate General's views. See *http://www.europarl.europa.eu/sides/getDoc.do?type=REPORT&mode=XML&reference=A6-2007-0451&language=EN*, explanatory statement, third para.

C. Can the System – and the Role – Go On Unchanged?

It seems to me (to put it bluntly) that the answer is probably 'no'. It is perfectly possible to preserve the essence of the system. As I shall argue, there are compelling reasons for doing so. However, it is not realistic to think that eight Advocates General can work in parallel with 26 *Juges Rapporteurs* in a Court that registers over 550 cases a year and still do exactly the same job as before in exactly the same way.

As I have emphasized, the Court has already recognized the problem and, in the informal criteria that it applies to deciding whether or not to ask the Advocate General to deliver an opinion in a particular case, is seeking to address it. Those criteria are assuredly part of the answer; but it is evident that there are other aspects that need to be addressed.

A different way of approaching the problem might be to increase the number of Advocates General. From the political perspective of ensuring that Member States which do not have one of the (unofficial) permanent 'slots' get a chance more often to nominate an Advocate General to the Court, there are obvious attractions. Such a course would also enable the Advocates General to play substantially the same role in the enlarged Union, within a Court with significantly enlarged jurisdiction and responsibilities, as they have played up till now.

The disadvantages are equally obvious. There is the increased cost and greater unwieldiness for the Court as a collegiate body that would follow from moving from the present 35 Members to, say, 38 (against a background in which at least some further accessions may take place, automatically adding a corresponding number of Judges to the Court[48]). A greater percentage of the 'corps' of Advocates General would be on single mandates. As a corollary, it is likely that there would be an increased degree of disruption to the Court's overall workflow. There is also the question of whether one feels that having more Advocates General would enable them to play the same role as they have played up till now in both case-handling and the delivery of opinions (with a greater diversity of vision) or whether, on the contrary, it might lead to a dilution in the clarity of the guidance that they are able to offer the Court.

---

[48] Art 221(1) EC now reads: 'The Court of Justice shall consist of one judge per Member State'. Pre-Nice versions of the Treaty specified the total number of Judges (which normally, coincidentally, resulted in one Judge per Member State). However, there have been instances where – in order to ensure the uneven number of Judges needed for the Court to take a valid decision (see Art 17 of the Statute) – there has been more than one Judge from a Member State. If the next accession involves only one new Member State, presumably some adjustment of this kind will likewise have to be made. In a Declaration on Art 222 EC annexed to the Lisbon Treaty, the Intergovernmental Conference indicated that if the Court so requests, the Member States will agree to increase the number of Advocates General by three, from eight to eleven (including a 'permanent' Polish Advocate General) – thus putting the issue back squarely before the Court.

D. So, Do We Still Need Advocates General?

In their recent book, Burrows and Greaves suggest that:

> there is no longer a need for Advocates General at the European Court of Justice. After all, the Community legal order has now reached a degree of maturity where the responsibility for enforcing Community law is continuously being placed on national courts and national authorities... many aspects of Community law are settled and clearly understood... Within such a mature system there may be no need for the post of Advocate General. Other mature systems of law operate without the benefit of an Opinion before the deliberation by the judges. In addition the background research that the Advocate General provides might no longer be needed given that the Court has at its disposal rich sources of legal advice ranging from academic writings to the written submissions of a number of law practitioners often from different legal systems. Furthermore, there is nothing to prevent the Court from appointing one of its members as Advocate General for a specific case where, for example, an issue of constitutional importance is raised or, for example, where the case-law on the issue was not consistent and there was a need for an independent analysis and summary. One of the benefits of dispensing with the role would be cost and time savings, an important consideration given the increased need to translate documents into so many different languages.[49]

Now, any reply to that argument from a serving Advocate General – particularly Francis' recently appointed successor who is loving the job – is likely to sound suspiciously like an *'apologia pro vita sua'*. Burrows and Greaves omit what, it seems to me, might be the truly provocative way of approaching the issue, namely, 'why not abolish Advocates General but allow dissenting judgments?' Perhaps *that* would be the hallmark of a mature legal system but, for the reasons Francis gave, I very much doubt that such a change is imminent.

The arguments on which Burrows and Greaves do rely are less convincing. Responsibility for enforcing Community law does indeed lie to a large extent with the national courts (described by David Edward as 'the powerhouse of Community law'[50]). However, it is wrong to conclude from that that many questions of Community law are therefore now so settled and well-rehearsed that they can be dealt with routinely. Though straightforward questions are sometimes referred to the Court under Article 234 EC, many are complex, some are both complex and sensitive, and many, even now, raise new points of law. Once the full effects of the last two enlargements are felt, it seems likely that the number of preliminary references will increase. The 'users' of the Court's jurisprudence seem, so far as one can judge, to continue to find that the Advocate General's opinion often provides an

---

[49] Burrows and Greaves (n 4 above) 298. The authors describe this suggestion as 'provocative'. One wonders, in the same spirit of academic flippancy, whether it was not also made a little tongue in cheek (after all, labelling Advocates General as dodos is a fun way to conclude a book that is devoted to studying them). The authors themselves say (ibid 297) that 'These ideas are presented simply to open up debate', suggesting that this is indeed the case.

[50] D Edward, 'National Courts – The Powerhouse of Community Law' (2002–3) 5 Cambridge Yearbook of European Legal Studies 1.

informative counterpoint to the Court's judgment. The CFI has experimented with ad hoc Advocates General, but has very rarely used them.[51] If there is an opinion, then (whoever wrote it) translation into other languages will be required.

As the Court's jurisdiction expands, there is more uncharted territory ahead, just as there was in the early days of the Court. Judicial thinking time is under pressure; and the need to compromise in order to agree a single (perhaps laconic) judgment is as present now as in 1952. A Court operating with a Grand Chamber and eight separate smaller chambers is more susceptible inadvertently to generate divergent strands of case law. In a world in which not all cases are properly pleaded and judges do not have the leisure to trawl through the extensive academic literature in the hopes of finding something interesting and pertinent, the Advocate General continues to provide open, public reflection on the present state of the case law, the possible directions in which that case law might now go and reasoned suggestions as to why it would be better for the case law to move in one direction rather than another. In short, I suggest that the public dialogue between the Court and its Advocates General is as relevant now as it has ever been. It would also be curious to abolish Advocates General at a time when the most recent Treaty amendments, in requiring the First Advocate General to act as a filter for reviews under Article 225 EC, have placed new and important responsibilities upon at least one of their number.

IV. Conclusion

Essentially, the Advocates' General contribution is, and remains, quasi-judicial. The Court does not deal with EU law in the abstract. It decides cases. The Advocates General are there to assist it to do that job as effectively as possible. In so doing, however, they also help to place the Court's decision-making in a wider context. They can make use of the individual freedom that they enjoy to explore, to advise and to warn. Provided the role of the Advocate General is enabled to evolve sensibly, Advocates General are as relevant now as when the Court was founded. It is, however, imperative to focus their time and efforts where these are really most effective and useful. The Court and the Member States will need to give further thought to how, precisely, that is to be achieved.

---

[51] A judge has been appointed to act as Advocate General at the CFI on four occasions. Judge Biancarelli delivered an opinion in Case T-120/89 *Stahlwerke Peine-Salzgitter* [1992] ECR II-279. Judge Edward delivered joined opinions in Case T-24/90 *Automec* [1992] ECR II-2223 and Case T-28/90 *Asia Motor France* [1992] ECR II-2285. Judge Kirschner delivered an opinion in Case T-51/89 *Tetra Pak* [1990] ECR II-309. Judge Vesterdorf delivered joined opinions in Case T-1/89 *Rhône-Poulenc* [1991] ECR II-867; Case T-2/89 *Petrofina* [1991] ECR II-1087; Case T-3/89 *Atochem* [1991] ECR II-1177; Case T-4/89 *BASF* [1991] ECR II-1523; Case T-6/89 *Enichem Anic* [1991] ECR II-1623; Case T-7/89 *SA Hercules Chemicals* [1991] ECR II-1711; Case T-8/89 *DSM* [1991] ECR II-1833; Case T-9/89 *Hüls* [1992] ECR II-499; Case T-10/89 *Hoechst* [1992] ECR II-629; Case T-11/89 *Shell International Chemical Company* [1992] ECR II-757; Case T-12/89 *Solvay & Cie* [1992] ECR II-907; Case T-13/89 *Imperial Chemical Industries* [1992] ECR II-1021; Case T-14/89 *Montedipe* [1992] ECR II-1155; and Case T-15/89 *Chemie Linz* [1992] ECR II-1275.

3

The Court of First Instance, its Development, and Future Role in the Legal Architecture of the European Union

Nicholas Forwood

I. Introduction

The 18 years during which Francis Jacobs was Advocate General at the Court of Justice saw an unparalleled development in the growth of the volume and complexity of Community law. Many have noted his key role in steering the Court in the delicate tasks of laying both the warp and weft of legal principle in new areas of judicial responsibility, such as EU citizenship; of pulling together loose threads of potentially divergent case law; and even, on several occasions, of explaining why it was necessary to unpick some earlier work altogether and start again – recommendations that, if not always followed by the Court, were nevertheless recognized by a wider audience as being intellectually convincing and even compelling. Thanks to his contribution, the tapestry of substantive Community law is notably richer in detail, and sounder in design than when he arrived.

On the procedural level, these same 18 years have also witnessed the start of a fundamental restructuring of the judicial architecture of the European Community, and latterly of the European Union. The institution that he joined in 1988 comprised a single court of 19 members (13 Judges and six Advocates General), supported by 593 officials, discharging all the judicial tasks entrusted to the Court of Justice by the Treaties. These ranged from disputes between Community institutions and Member States at one extreme, through the rich variety of preliminary rulings and direct actions, to staff cases at the other. By the time he left in 2006, the institution possessed a radically different structure, now comprising three courts (European Court of Justice (ECJ), Court of First Instance (CFI) and EU Staff Tribunal (EUST)) arranged in three distinct levels of jurisdiction, and with 65 judicial members supported by 1,648 officials and other staff, but still all working together to build and develop the 'community of law' on which the European Union is founded.

Symbolically, the rusty 'Palais' to which he came in 1988, and which had been the home of the Court since 1973, is no more. Mid-twentieth-century techniques of construction, though considered appropriate for their time, have with hindsight proved to be dangerous to health, even potentially fatal. The Palais has had to be completely dismantled, the dangerous and outdated components discarded, and the usable skeleton has been re-erected on a new base. The new buildings will hopefully provide a fitting home for the European Union's courts for at least the next 50 years.

At the functional level, too, the need for change in the Community's judicial architecture was arguably no less compelling. Even if, asbestos-like, the nature and extent of the risk was not at first easy to perceive, the dangers were as real as they were insidious. Those who are most directly affected by the results of the Court's work – be they national judges, politicians or administrators, or lawyers pleading before the courts or merely advising their clients – require three things from Community judges: clarity in their reasoning, coherence in their case law and a reasonable speed of decision-making. The challenges in meeting these demands, however, daily become greater. The number of Member States has more than doubled since 1988. More and more areas of our lives are directly affected on a daily basis by Community, and now Union, law, and legislation in these areas is becoming ever more complex.

Meanwhile, in fields such as asylum, immigration and family matters, it is simply not realistic or acceptable to expect national judges and the parties before them to wait for up to a year for a preliminary ruling, let alone for two years or more (still the current average for any but the most straightforward case). And as more and more individuals and businesses, and their advisers, realise how directly Community and Union law affects them, and increasingly turn to the courts, both national and Community, to resolve the legal issues that arise, the inevitable consequence will be even greater demands on the present structure.

One of the measures of success of any court is the degree of acceptance of its authority and integrity. In the case of Supreme Courts in particular, these are in turn particularly dependent on the intellectual rigour and coherence of their judgments. Confidence in the Court of Justice – as an effective arbiter of their rights and obligations under Community law – is central to the European citizen's view of the 'European Project'. One needs only to reflect on what might have been the result of the referenda on the European Constitutional Treaty if, in addition to their other criticisms, whether real or imaginary, its opponents had also been able credibly to claim that Community law – as interpreted and applied by the Community Courts – was unpredictable or irrational, or that the Community institutions were not subject to real and effective judicial control.

By these criteria, the Court of Justice as an institution in its first half century has generally been regarded a success. If it is to maintain that level of support, however, it needs to recognize the need for change in its institutional structure, and not respond only when pressures become irresistible even to the point of risking a loss of confidence. The present challenge for the Court of Justice – as an institution – is thus twofold. The first is the need to recognize, and wholeheartedly to accept, that, under the present allocation of judicial tasks between its different jurisdictions, the ECJ will not for much longer be able consistently to discharge all the tasks that it currently undertakes to the high standards that are, rightly, expected of it. If it is still, though only just, managing to do so, this is more due to the determination and efforts of its present President and members than to a sensible system of allocation of judicial tasks that would reserve to the highest Community court and give it more time to reflect on only those cases that truly merit the attention of a 'supreme' court.

The second challenge, which is conditional on the first, is the willingness of the Court as an institution to take the initiative even before the need for change has been definitely demonstrated. Changes to the Community judicial structure are notoriously slow to implement. Fortunately, the framework for further adjustments in the allocation of judicial tasks has already been put in place by the Member States in the Treaty of Nice, and restated in the Constitutional Treaty with the provision of a three-tier judicial structure with the ECJ still at the pinnacle, but with the central place in the new pyramid occupied by the CFI.

It is against this background that the present contribution examines the development of the CFI over the last 18 years, and offers some thoughts as to the possible evolution of its role.

II. Beginnings

On 24 October 1988, acting at the request of the Court of Justice, and pursuant to Article 168a of the EEC Treaty[1] – recently introduced by the Single European Act of 1986 – the Council adopted the decision creating a Court of First Instance of the European Communities (CFI).[2] While this decision formally marked the creation of the CFI, it was in fact also the final step in a long political process that had started some ten years earlier.

Even from the mid-1970s, and only shortly after the Communities' first enlargement, it had already become clear that the original judicial structure laid down by the EC Treaties, under which the ECJ exercised sole jurisdiction over

---

[1] See also the equivalent provisions of the ECSC and Euratom Treaties.

[2] For clarity, the expressions 'ECJ', 'CFI' and 'EUST' are generally used in this contribution to refer respectively to these courts exercising their judicial functions, while the term 'Court of Justice' is generally used to refer to the Community institution that comprises these three courts, and any further specialized courts that may be created in future. This approach parallels that of the Treaty establishing a Constitution for Europe (the 'Constitutional Treaty') which distinguishes between the institution, which it entitles 'The Court of Justice of the European Union', and its constituent courts, respectively the 'Court of Justice', the 'General Court' and the various 'specialized courts' (currently 'judicial panels') created pursuant to Article III-359 of the Constitutional Treaty (currently Article 225a EC).

the entire range of Community litigation from 'constitutional' disputes between Community institutions and Member States to, at the other extreme, staff cases involving EC officials, with preliminary rulings and much else in between, was not just less than ideal in certain respects, not least in the lack of an effective appeal structure, but was in any event unsustainable in the longer term because of the ever-increasing case load. The Commission had proposed reducing the case load by creating a special tribunal for staff cases, a step that could indeed have been taken by a relatively simple modification of the Staff Regulations. The Court of Justice, however, acting then with exemplary foresight, saw that this would not be enough, and that more fundamental changes would sooner or later be needed. In 1978 the then-President of the Court, Hans Kutscher, accordingly took the political initiative, and wrote to the President of the Commission proposing the creation of a new court of first instance, with a jurisdiction far broader than merely staff cases, and requested that the necessary process for revising the Treaties be started.[3] The request was repeated in 1985 by the then President of the Court in a letter to the Intergovernmental Conference, and it was this sustained political initiative that finally led to the adoption by the Member States, in the Single European Act, of the necessary Treaty changes to permit the creation of a new court, the CFI.

Two recitals of the founding Council decision are noteworthy, since they not only explain the direction of the development of the CFI over the subsequent 18 years, but also remain just as relevant for the decisions that need to be taken today with regard to the next stages in the evolution of the Community's judicial architecture. Immediately after referring to the new legal base for its action, the Council observed:

Whereas, in respect of actions requiring close examination of complex facts, the establishment of a second court will improve the judicial protection of individual interests;

Whereas, it is necessary, in order to maintain the quality and effectiveness of judicial review in the Community legal order, to enable the Court to concentrate its activities on its fundamental task of ensuring uniform interpretation of Community law.

While the benefits of a two-tier system of legal review, to both courts and parties alike, are now generally accepted, it was not universally so in 1986. Indeed, it is only since 1988 that Article 2 of Protocol 7 to the ECHR has expressly guaranteed the right of appeal in criminal matters. However, as the recitals to the Council's decision recognized, it was no longer realistic to believe that the judicial commitment that was needed for cases requiring a detailed examination of complex facts, particularly – but not exclusively – in competition cases, could be reconciled with the other demands on the ECJ. Indeed, removing these cases from the ECJ would enable the latter to concentrate on its fundamental task, which is indeed the defining characteristic of the Supreme Court of every judicial system, namely to ensure the consistency and uniform interpretation of the law.

---

[3] See Y Galmot, 'Le Tribunal de première instance des Communautés européennes' (1989) Revue française de droit administratif 568.

III. Progress Towards a More Rational Allocation of Judicial Tasks

The Single European Act provided only for the possible transfer to the CFI of direct actions brought by natural or legal persons, the precise categories of action to be specified in implementing Council decisions. Initially at least, there was thus no possibility of transferring to the CFI any part of the ECJ's jurisdiction over direct actions brought by Member States or by Community institutions,[4] still less of transferring its competence in relation to preliminary rulings.

If the 1988 decision – which provided for the transfer to the newly constituted CFI of competition and staff cases only – appears from today's standpoint to have been a rather tentative first step towards even this modest objective, at the time it was not seen as insignificant. A total of 151 cases of the ECJ's case load were being transferred to the CFI on 15 November 1989, the date on which the President of the Court formally declared that the CFI had been duly constituted. Roughly half were in the field of competition, cases which were (and still are) particularly demanding in terms of judicial effort, and there can be no doubt that, in terms of work load, the transfer represented an immediate benefit for the ECJ, even if it was to prove to be short-lived, at least when measured in numbers of pending cases. Thus, the number of pending cases in the ECJ throughout the mid-1980s had been broadly constant at about 600.[5] While this figure dropped to 501 at the end of 1989, immediately following the transfers to the CFI, by the end of 1990 it had risen again to 583 and, by December 1991, to 640. The purely short-term nature of the improvement in the ECJ's situation was also reflected in the average duration of preliminary ruling cases, which, though dropping slightly to a temporary low of 15.4 months in 1991 (the same level as in 1985), soon rose again so that by the end of the decade, it had reached 21.6 months, finally peaking in 2003 at 25.5 months.

The Council had, however, in Article 3(3) of its 1988 decision, prudently reserved to itself the power to review the position after two years of operation of the CFI with a view to making further transfers in other categories of direct actions, and – even more significantly – to do so without the need for a further formal request from the Court of Justice. This power was duly exercised, with the further transfer in 1993[6] of all remaining direct actions brought by natural or legal persons, except in the fields of dumping and subsidies (at the time an area of great political sensitivity), the decision to transfer this last category of direct actions only being finally taken the following year.[7]

---

[4] See Article 168a EEC and the equivalent provisions in the other Treaties.
[5] In total, 592 at the end of 1986, 618 at the end of 1987 and 605 at the end of 1988.
[6] Council decision 93/350 of 8 June 1993, OJ 1993 L144/21.
[7] Council decision 94/149 of 7 March 1994, OJ 1994 L66/29.

The next significant step forward had come with the Treaty of Maastricht which, again following a proposal from the Court of Justice, but this time supported by a separate submission from the Court of First Instance, further amended the founding Treaties to allow the transfer to the CFI of all direct actions, even those brought by Member States or Community institutions. However, while the Treaty basis for such a transfer was thus put in place, with effect from 1 November 1993, no formal request to that effect from the Court was forthcoming.

Instead, the issue of the future development of the Community's judicial architecture became the subject of an even more fundamental rethink. The British Institute of International and Comparative Law had produced a report in 1996 on the future of the Court of Justice, with some radical proposals for change. The CCBE and others, including again the House of Lords Select Committee, also made their contributions. By early 1999 the case for a more far-reaching reform of the Community's judicial system was clearly incontrovertible. Accordingly, encouraged by a far-reaching reflection paper prepared by the Court of Justice,[8] the Commission established a working group, chaired by former ECJ President Due and comprising former members of the ECJ and other eminent individuals, with a brief to review proposals for a structure that would enable the Community courts to meet the challenges of enlargement to a Community of 25 or more Members. The Due Working Group's report in turn gave rise to yet further proposals from the Commission and from the Court.

IV. The Nice Treaty and the 'New Judicial Architecture'

The results of all these efforts were then passed to an informal working group of representatives of the Member States, who came to be known as the *amis de la présidence*, and who in their turn produced for the Nice IGC a set of detailed proposals for Treaty changes that were duly adopted by the Member States in the Treaty of Nice. These changes have also been substantially readopted in the Constitutional Treaty. The changes represent a fundamental rethinking of the structure and roles of the Community's courts, and the relationships between them. While the detailed implementation of the changes was left to further decisions to be taken by the Council, the resulting package has nevertheless defined for the foreseeable future the intended framework for what can be called the judicial architecture of the European Community – or rather, if the Constitutional Treaty is eventually ratified in something resembling its present form – the judicial architecture of the European Union. Central to these changes is a fundamental redefinition of the role of the CFI, a redefinition that will also be reflected

---

[8] 'The future of the judicial system of the European Union (proposals and reflections)', sent to the Council on 10 May 1999.

in a change of name, if and when the Constitutional Treaty is ratified, to 'the General Court'[9] of the European Union.

From the architectural viewpoint, the main change introduced by the Nice Treaty was to provide for the creation of a new third tier of Community courts, hierarchically below the CFI. Article 225a EC, introduced by the Nice Treaty, gives the Council the power, acting either on a request from the Court of Justice or – in a possibly significant new development – on a proposal from the Commission, to create, in 'specific areas' of law, one or more specialized courts to hear and determine certain categories of direct action. From the decisions of these courts an appeal, normally limited to questions of law,[10] lies only to the Court of First Instance. These new specialized courts are, moreover, to be 'attached' to the CFI. Conversely, while the CFI had previously been 'attached' to the ECJ, this subordinate relationship was brought to an end by the new Article 220 EC, with the result that the CFI, like the ECJ, is now independently charged with the responsibility of carrying out the judicial tasks entrusted to it by the Treaties.

Within this new framework, the Nice Treaty also provided for four closely interrelated changes in the allocation of judicial functions as between these three levels of jurisdiction. The first was that all direct actions brought against any of the Community institutions – whether by natural or legal persons or even by a privileged applicant (Member State or Community institution) – are in principle to be assigned to the CFI. This exclusive competence is subject only, on the one hand, to the allocation of certain direct actions to the new specialized courts, as and when they are created, and, on the other hand, to a very limited category of cases – to be defined in the Statute of the Court – being reserved to the ECJ.[11]

The second change was that, while still remaining primarily a court of first instance, at least in functional terms, the CFI will now also become an appeal court – and normally the final appeal court – in respect of the decisions of the specialized courts, as and when the latter are progressively established. Thirdly, the Treaty provided expressly, for the first time, for the possible transfer to the CFI of competence in certain preliminary ruling cases, such a transfer again being limited to 'specific areas' of Community law. Lastly, and as a corollary to the new roles of the CFI, the ECJ was granted an entirely new judicial competence, namely the carrying out, under closely defined conditions, of an 'exceptional review' of those decisions of the CFI that, under the new structure, would otherwise be final, namely decisions on appeal from the new specialized courts, and preliminary rulings in those 'specific areas' transferred to the CFI.

---

[9] Articles I-29 and III-356 CT.

[10] The Council may, however, in the decision establishing any new specialized court, expressly provide for the possibility of an appeal on findings of fact – see Article 225a EC as amended by the Treaty of Nice.

[11] The definition of the direct actions reserved to the ECJ was effected by Council decision 2004/407 of 26 April 2004. See further n 12 below.

With the notable exception of the formal 'detachment' of the CFI from the ECJ, the Nice Treaty did not give immediate effect to these changes. While the new Treaty provisions unambiguously identified the key features of the judicial structure that the Member States wished to see in place, they have, at least for the present, left it to the Court of Justice both to take the initiative as to when the necessary works of construction should start, and to propose the finer details of the new edifice.

While this process is already under way, progress may not perhaps be as rapid as some Member states expected, and indeed wish. The first step was the revision of the Statute of the Court, by Council decision 2004/407[12] to provide for the transfer to the CFI of jurisdiction in certain classes of actions brought by Member States against acts of the Community institutions. These mainly concerned actions relating to clearance of accounts under the EAGGF and other Community regimes, and certain state aid cases, and 41 such pending cases were transferred to the CFI in late 2004, the decisive criterion for jurisdiction being now essentially the status of the defendant institution that adopted the act or omission challenged. As the Court of Justice pointed out when submitting its proposal, its choice of criterion involves reconciling 'simplicity, which favours the status of the defendant as the determining factor in jurisdiction, with the adjustments necessary to follow as closely as possible the guiding principle that the [ECJ] ought to retain jurisdiction at first and last instance only in connection with the basic legislative activity of the institutions'.

The first proposal for a new specialized court was for the creation of the EUST. Constituted by Council decision 2004/752/EC Euratom of 2 November 2004, it began work on 12 December 2005, when 117 staff cases pending before the CFI were transferred to it. In parallel, the Court of Justice had proposed changes to the Statute of the Court to provide for the 'exceptional review' procedure of CFI judgments on appeal from the EUST, and these were duly implemented by a Council decision of 3 October 2005.[13]

No other formal proposals for other specialized courts have yet been made, though the issue is currently the subject of active debate, outside as much as inside the Court. Also in abeyance is the issue of transfer of competences in relation to preliminary rulings. Before turning to discuss what further steps might be taken, it is instructive to look in more detail at how the work of the CFI has already developed over the last 18 years.

V. Eighteen Years of Experience – a Court Reaching Maturity

Throughout the whole of its 18 years' existence, the CFI's case load has grown in step both with the widening areas of its competence and with increasing activity,

[12] OJ 2004 L132/5.
[13] Council decision 2005/696/EC of 3 October 2005, OJ 2005 L 266/60–61.

and even a willingness to litigate, within those areas. In the result, the number of new cases arriving each year grew nearly five-fold in the decade to 2000, by which time the CFI was receiving 400 new cases a year, approximately the same number as the ECJ had received in its last years as the Community's sole court. Since 2000, the numbers have continued to grow, but more steadily, and by 2004, the last full year before the transfer of staff cases to the EUST, the number of new cases received was 536. The numbers of judgments delivered and of cases resolved by all means have also risen in parallel, though inevitably always a step behind, so that at times the CFI's task has been reminiscent of that of the sorcerer's apprentice in the film *Fantasia*. In both 2005 and 2006, however, for the first time in many years, the CFI (just) managed to dispose of more cases than arrived.[14] But the fact remains that the CFI, like the ECJ, is still faced with a work load significantly greater than that faced by the old Court of Justice in any year up to and including 1988, the year when that Court's case load was considered so great as to justify the creation of the Court of First Instance.

It should also be remembered that, while the total number of cases dealt with is broadly the same in both the CFI and ECJ, the factually intensive and complex nature of much of the CFI's work makes a simple one-for-one comparison inappropriate. Indeed, the tendency towards increasing complexity of the 'average' CFI case has been strengthened since 2004, first with the transfer to the CFI of cases involving detailed examination of the Commission's decisions in relation to subsidies payable to Member States under CAP or regional fund legislation, and second by the CFIs 'loss' to the EUST of the more numerous, but normally much less complex, staff cases.

A further indication – albeit a rough and ready one – of the trend towards a greater complexity of cases is the length of the judgments needed to dispose of the various arguments raised by the parties. In 1989, the last year of operation of the ECJ as the sole Community court, the ECR ran to about 4,500 pages. In 2000, the corresponding figure was over 16,500 pages.[15] In 2005, it was still 11,272 pages, though the figure would have been even higher but for intervening changes in publication policy which, in the case of the CFI at least, mean that now approximately one-third of its judgments or non-procedural orders are no longer published in full in the ECR.[16]

The creation of, and successive transfers of competence to, the CFI have been reflected in major changes in the pattern of the work of the ECJ. In 1989, requests for a preliminary ruling represented only just over a third of the ECJ's

[14] In 2005, after discounting the 117 pending staff cases transferred to the EUST in December 2005, the figures were 469 new cases and 493 cases completed. For 2006 the figures were 432 and 436.

[15] Due to changes in the style and content of case reports, including the fact that the ECR no longer publishes the Report for the Hearing, these figures in fact understate the extent of the growth.

[16] They are, however, still accessible on the Court's internet site in both French and the language of the case.

case load, whereas they now represent well over one half, most of the remainder (about 30 per cent) being infringement cases against Member States. In terms of demands on judicial resources, the proportion of judicial effort which the ECJ devotes to preliminary rulings is certainly even higher, since many infringement cases, typically those concerning non-implementation of directives, are uncontroversial and require minimal judicial input.[17] The remaining 10 to 15 per cent of the ECJ's case load concerns appeals from the CFI.

The CFI, meanwhile, has in effect evolved into what can be regarded as the general administrative law court of the European Communities, with general jurisdiction, subject only to the limited exceptions mentioned earlier, over the acts – and failures to act – of all the Community institutions. While the single largest category of cases, 143 trade mark cases, some 33 per cent of the total brought in 2006, involves appeals from decisions of the Boards of Appeal in Alicante in relation to Community trade marks, the remainder mainly involve direct action challenges to acts of the Community institutions or agencies. The subject matter of these cases is varied, even if it in no way parallels that of the ECJ, whose preliminary ruling competence covers many fields of Community law, such as social security, indirect taxation, environment and aspects of agricultural policy, that are normally litigated in the national courts. On the other hand, the corollary of the relative 'specialization' of the CFI, in those areas where it is most active, in particular competition and mergers, state aids and trade marks, is that it is in precisely these areas that the CFI, of the two Community Courts, now has the greater expertise.

From the viewpoint of reducing the work load of the ECJ, the creation of the Court of First Instance has thus been an undoubted success. Moreover, this would seem to have been achieved without adverse effects on the overall quality of justice on the results for the parties. This is most visible in the outcome of the proceedings. Since an appeal lies of right on any point of law from any final judgment or order of the CFI, the benefits of the transfers of competence would have been greatly reduced if they had simply led to a similar number of appeals to the ECJ. However, over recent years, the proportion of cases decided by the CFI in which appeals have been brought has remained fairly steady at between about one quarter and one third of the total. Looked at another way, the parties generally accept the CFI's judgment on law as well as fact (where, subject only to appeal on grounds of distortion of the evidence, the CFI's decision is final). In the remaining two thirds or so of all CFI cases, therefore, their transfer to the CFI has resulted in an unqualified benefit for the ECJ. And even in those instances where there is an appeal, moreover, the role of the ECJ and the demands on its judicial time are much more limited than if it had heard the case *de novo*. Last,

---

[17] Not only are such cases frequently straightforward, particularly when they relate to late or non-implementation of Community directives, but such cases are also normally dealt with in chambers of only three Judges, instead of the more usual five-judge chamber or even the Grand Chamber.

and perhaps most pertinently, in the vast majority of appeals the decision of the CFI is upheld.[18]

VI. The Possibilities and Challenges for the Future

The possibilities and challenges for the future of the CFI reflect, inevitably, those that face the Court of Justice as a whole. However, from the perspective of the CFI, the first priority has to be the handling of its current and anticipated future work load.

From that viewpoint, the three immediate possibilities are the creation of further judicial panels (specialized courts), the transfers of competence in relation to preliminary rulings in specific areas, to be laid down in the Statute, and the possible transfer of still further categories of direct action.

So far as further judicial panels are concerned, the two most-discussed candidates for relieving the CFI of part of its current work load are dedicated courts for trade marks (appeals from decisions of the Office for the Harmonization of the Internal Market in relation to Community trade marks) and for competition. Of these, the strongest candidate would appear to be a specialized trade mark court. The CFI currently handles even more trade mark cases than it did staff cases when the decision was taken to establish the EUST, and the number is predicted to increase.[19] The substantive law is relatively self-contained, and also relatively homogeneous, and should be easily amenable to a transfer. By contrast, the case for a dedicated competition court is – at least in the immediate future – less strong, though there has been some strong support for such a proposal, not least from some quarters of European industry. One particular problem is that the rules on competition cover a wide and, in some respects, almost continuous spectrum of cases, from pure Article 81 and 82 decisions, through merger cases, to state aids and decisions concerning public undertakings, all of which may require of the Court the judicial scrutiny of complex economic assessments, as well as detailed examination of common legal issues (such as effect on trade between Member States). It would clearly be inappropriate for all such cases to be transferred to a new specialized court, and it is not easy to see where a clear and workable line could be drawn. A further factor is that, as mentioned earlier, the CFI has already a high degree of expertise in competition cases, and so long as that remains the case there will be a natural unwillingness for its members to give up primary competence in a field that, for some Judges of the CFI at least, has been their primary raison d'être.

---

[18] Typically, in only about one appeal in six does the ECJ reverse or modify, even in part, the judgment of the CFI. The statistics are available in the Court's annual reports, and this figure has been relatively constant over the whole existence of the CFI.

[19] This prediction is based on the steadily-increasing trend in the number of filings for Community trade marks, the number of oppositions, and the number of appealable decisions by Boards of Appeal at Alicante hearing internal appeals against first level decisions of the Office.

A further candidate for a specialized court is a Community patent court. This proposal was first put forward formally by the Commission in December 2003, in conjunction with its proposal for a Regulation on the Community Patent. The creation of such a court would involve, for the first time, the exercise by a Community court of direct jurisdiction over disputes between private parties, a possibility that was introduced for the first time by the Treaty of Nice in Article 229a EC. The Commission's proposal made a certain amount of progress, but stalled for a period as a result of difficulties in relation to the language regimes to be applied. However, the Commission has recently announced that it intends to re-launch its proposal for a Community patent, but with modifications to allow for the creation of a 'unified and specialized patent judiciary with competence for litigation on European patents [granted under the European Patent Convention] and future Community patents'. This would comprise 'a limited number of first instance chambers as well as a fully centralized appeal court which would ensure uniformity of interpretation'. The chambers, which could make use of existing national structures, should form an integral part of the single jurisdictional system, which as a whole would have to 'respect the European Court of Justice as final arbiter in matters of EU law, including questions related to the *acquis communautaire* and to the validity of future Community patents'. While it is clear that this proposal remains to be developed, particularly as to its precise relationship to the EU's existing judicial architecture, and indeed the Commission's own earlier proposal, it will inevitably involve some role for one or more courts within the institution of the Court of Justice.

With regard to possible transfers of competence in relation to preliminary rulings, there are various factors to be considered. First, there is little short-term benefit to be expected – and probably the reverse – from transferring preliminary ruling competence in 'specific areas' where the CFI has, under present arrangements, no significant experience of the substantive EU law in the area. This would point against transfers in those areas of EU law that are generally implemented at the national level, such as VAT, social security, employee rights, consumer protection and even customs classification cases. Conversely, there would be a much stronger case for transferring preliminary ruling competence in specific areas where the CFI already has particularly strong expertise, such as competition or trade marks, or even state aid. That case would be further reinforced if and when, in relation to such specific areas, specialized courts were created so that the CFI had already become the final appellate court in direct actions in that field (subject only to the possibility of exceptional review under Article 225(2) EC).

Applying these criteria, there would already seem to be a compelling and urgent case for the creation of a specialized trade mark court to hear appeals from decisions of the Boards of Appeal in relation to Community trade marks. This step could be accompanied – though not necessarily simultaneously – with a transfer of preliminary ruling competence in relation to trade mark disputes involving Community trade marks under Regulation 40/94, and possibly also in relation to national trade marks issued under laws harmonized by the almost identically-worded Directive 89/104/EEC.

On the administrative level, there is also need for reflection. The Treaties and the Statute, while providing in detail for the judicial relationship between the three levels of courts within the institution of the Court of Justice, have remained totally silent on their administrative relationship. The position is made more confusing by a failure in the relevant texts to differentiate clearly between the institution of the Court of Justice, comprising all the courts, and the ECJ as a court. While the need to make such a distinction only first arose with the creation of the CFI in 1989, the practical problems were reduced by the implications of the CFI's 'attachment' to the ECJ.

It is also to be noted that the nature and implications of the 'attachment' of the new specialized courts to the CFI are not explicitly spelled out in the Nice Treaty.[20] Certainly, it is difficult to relate the concept of 'attachment' to the strictly judicial relationships between the respective courts, such as the conditions and scope of any appeal, since these are matters that in any event are laid down by other specific provisions of the Treaties and the Statute; this interpretation also seems to be confirmed by the fact that, despite the Nice Treaty unambiguously removing the CFI's status of attachment to the ECJ, the purely judicial relationship between the CFI and ECJ remained essentially unchanged. Instead, it seems more reasonable to infer that the Member States envisaged that the concept of 'attachment' would concern administrative and other related matters. While the new specialized courts, like the CFI and indeed the ECJ, are all now distinct jurisdictions within the single Community institution also known as the Court of Justice, and for reasons of administrative convenience share certain common services (such as translation and interpretation), it seems probable that the Member States envisaged that the CFI, together with its 'attached' specialized courts, should in future constitute a more distinct and independent entity, functionally separate from the ECJ but still within the umbrella institution of the Court of Justice, and that this entity be entrusted with a greater degree of responsibility for organizing its own administration and, in particular, for taking the political and other initiatives that will be necessary to improve the handling of all those cases that, both now and in the future, should come within the jurisdiction of the CFI and the specialized courts.

Certainly there is much to be said for such an approach, both in principle and at the practical level. In principle, the administration of groups of courts at a particular level is generally best executed with the active participation of the Judges of the courts in question, rather than of the Judges of some other level of courts. That is particularly true in respect of an institution such as the Court of Justice, where – unlike the situation in many national judicial systems – most of the Judges at the highest level have never acted as Judges at the lower levels of the

---

[20] Nor were they in Article 168a EEC.

judicial pyramid. At the practical level also, there would be benefits, not least in reducing the administrative burdens on the members of a court whose judicial workload continues steadily to increase.

More generally, however, the role of the CFI will in practice be determined by the willingness of the ECJ to take the decisions necessary to enable the Court of Justice, as an institution, to evolve in order better to deal with the challenges of today and tomorrow. In the past, as described at the outset of this chapter, the Court has shown itself willing and able to do so when the need became clear. But as the pace of change continues to accelerate, the ECJ, like the other Community courts, has to run ever faster just to stand still. Only bold initiatives and far-sightedness will give the ECJ, and indeed all the other courts within the new judicial architecture, a real chance to significantly reduce delays and improve their service for the users of the courts, both national judges and litigants alike, while maintaining the high standards that are rightly expected by Europe, its institutions and its citizens.

4

Litigating in Luxembourg and the Role of the Advocate at the Court of Justice

David Vaughan and Margaret Gray[1]

I. Introduction

The role of the advocate in litigation is always to persuade the bench resolving the dispute before it to find in favour of the party on whose behalf he pleads. This role is the same, whether the advocate appears before the Royal Courts of Justice or the Court of Justice. Precisely how the advocate goes about attaining his goal and any demystification of the so-called art of the advocate is beyond the scope of this essay,[2] which deals with how Community law and the Court of Justice affect the way the advocate carries out his task. However, it can be said that before the Luxembourg court,[3] as before national courts, the advocate who adheres to certain touchstones will go some way to success. As a long-standing former member of the Luxembourg bench has said, '[t]he basic rules of advocacy apply as much in pleading before the European Court of Justice as before any court or tribunal in the United Kingdom: *know your court; know your procedure; and know what you are trying to achieve*'.[4]

Yet anyone attending a hearing at the Court of Justice will realize that an advocate appearing before it must do a little more than adhere to those basic rules; he must adjust his matchplay. As Sir David Edward puts it, '[t]he technique of

---

[1] The provision of certain materials by Judge John D Cooke is gratefully acknowledged.
[2] It was Lord Justice Salmon in *Rondel v Worsley* [1967] 1 QB 443, 520 who said that 'advocacy is not an exact science. It is an art'. Little has been written about the subject, at least in English, as noted by David Pannick QC in *Advocates* (1992) 12. Neither does Pannick himself address that issue. On the subject of the task of the advocate, however, he says that it is to 'make mountains out of molehills, to find a point of law where none had previously been known to exist, to ensure that his client does not lose the case without everything possible (and, on occasion, some things impossible) being said on his behalf'.
[3] Litigation and the role of the advocate before the Court of First Instance is beyond the scope of this essay.
[4] Edward, 'Views from the European Courts – Advocacy before the Court of Justice: Hints for the uninitiated' in Barling and Brealey (eds), *Practitioners' Handbook of EC Law* (1998) at 3.1.1.

pleading before the Court of Justice needs to be different because the nature of the court is different, the procedure is different and the forms of action are different'.[5] The advocate before the Court of Justice therefore finds himself playing the same game but according to a different rule book. That rule book is affected by the nature of the Court's jurisdiction set down by the Treaties, its procedural rules governed by the Treaties, the Statute of the Court and its Rules of Procedure.[6] He also finds himself playing in unfamiliar conditions, those conditions being affected, in particular, by the melding of a number of legal families, systems and traditions, and the language regime which requires the Court to work on a daily basis in over 20 languages.[7] After all, the Court of Justice is 'unlike any other court in the world'.[8]

This essay considers some of the ways in which litigating before the Court of Justice is different from litigating before United Kingdom courts, and how those differences affect the manner in which the advocate appearing in Luxembourg performs his task. The first part of the essay will address the matter of who goes to court in Luxembourg and why. It looks at two specific questions: (a) what issues are litigated in Luxembourg; and (b) who may appear before the Court as parties and as legal representatives. This gives some context to an understanding of the role and task of counsel before the Court. The second part of the essay considers the way in which the Court's unique methods of working affect the written and oral stages of proceedings and the judgment, as well as the specific role played by advocates in those proceedings. The third part considers the impression that an advocate can make upon the Court, in particular, where its judgments have recorded a discernible win on the part of a claimant, or the reception into the case law of a legal principle enshrined in a national legal system. The final part addresses briefly the role of the advocate beyond Luxembourg.

Sir Francis Jacobs is no stranger to Kirchberg courtroom battles on both sides of the bar and this essay is the poorer for not having had the benefit of his sound opinion on the subject that it addresses. He would, however, in all likelihood, agree with those seasoned EU law practitioners who have commented that appearing before the Court of Justice affords those who have 'taken the trouble to learn the different legal techniques an unrivalled chance to appear in the challenging environment of a multi-national court with Judges coming from different backgrounds, different legal traditions and different political and social philosophies'.[9]

---

[5] D Edward, *Practitioners' Handbook of EC Law* (1998) 3.1.1.
[6] These and other factors affecting the conduct of litigation at the Court are identified by Edward in 'How the Court of Justice Works' (1995) 20 ELRev 539–540.
[7] There are currently 23 official languages.
[8] D Edward, *Practitioners' Handbook of EC Law* (1998) 3.1.2.1.
[9] Richards and Beloff, 'View from the Bar' in Barling and Brealey (eds), *Practitioners' Handbook of EC Law* (1998) at 2.48.

II. Who Goes to Court in Luxembourg?

A. The Jurisdiction of the Court: the Various Forms of Proceedings

An advocate either signing his name at the foot of pleadings to be lodged at the Registry of the Court or opening the doors of one of its courtrooms and stepping inside can find himself representing any one of a number of different parties to the various forms of proceedings litigated there. The principal forms of proceedings for which the Court has jurisdiction are: (i) direct actions; (ii) appeals; and (iii) references for preliminary rulings, typically pursuant to Article 234 EC.[10]

Direct actions are so called because they are brought directly before the Court by Community institutions or Member States. They arise most frequently where the Commission brings infringement proceedings against a Member State pursuant to Article 226 EC. In those cases, an advocate may be defending a Member State put in the dock by the Commission and brought before the Court to answer for its failure to meet obligations arising under the Treaties. Another type of proceeding arises whereby Member States and Community institutions may directly challenge certain Community measures seeking their annulment pursuant to Article 230 EC.[11] Thus, on rare occasions, counsel may be involved in proceedings where the institutions[12] go head-to-head before the Court. Even less likely to arise are those cases where one Member State has brought another before the Court pursuant to Article 227 EC. In each of these direct actions, the Court is a 'court of judicial review. It is not a "trial court". It is concerned with fact-finding only within very strict limits and the procedures available are not intended to cope with complex disputes of fact or opinion'.[13]

---

[10] Of the 537 new cases lodged in 2006, there were 201 direct actions, 80 appeals and 251 references.

[11] The Court of Justice has exclusive jurisdiction over actions brought by a Member State against the European Parliament and/or against the Council (apart from Council measures in respect of State aid, dumping and implementing powers). The Court of First Instance has jurisdiction, at first instance, in all other actions of this type and particularly in actions brought by individuals. Jurisdiction to hear actions for failure to act is shared between the Court of Justice and the Court of First Instance according to the same criteria as for actions for annulment. The Annual Report of the Court of Justice 2006 records four infringement actions brought by the Commission against the United Kingdom.

[12] Sir Francis Jacobs has commented that 'such inter-institutional proceedings are unfamiliar in national legal systems which have no Constitutional Court, but are less novel under, for example, the French and German constitutions, where the *Conseil Constitutionnel* and the *Bundesverfassungsgericht* respectively may be called upon to adjudicate at the instance of parliamentary organs': see F Jacobs, 'Is the Court of Justice of the European Communities a Constitutional Court?' in Curtin and O'Keeffe (eds), *Constitutional Adjudication in European Community and National Law* (1992) 25 at 27.

[13] D Edward, *Practitioners' Handbook of EC Law* (1998) 3.1.3.4. Facts play a more important part in those cases which come before the Court of First Instance, typically competition proceedings against Commission decisions and proceedings brought by individuals against the institutions concerning acts taken by them.

Appeals lie as regards questions of law and may only be brought against judgments and orders of the Court of First Instance. As appeal proceedings often concern trade mark or competition matters, it is common to find 'legal persons', such as companies, before the Court.[14] 'Natural persons', that is, individuals, may also appear as appellants, although their main route to the Court of Justice is by way of a reference for preliminary ruling.

References for preliminary ruling have for some years represented about half of the cases on the Court's docket. National courts may, and sometimes must, refer a question concerning clarification of a point of Community law to the Court, in order to determine whether national legislation complies with that law. A reference may also seek the review of the validity of a Community act. The aim of the procedure is to ensure the effective and uniform application of Community legislation and to prevent divergent interpretations. This is the type of proceeding in which a British advocate is most likely to become involved. He may represent either a private client or the United Kingdom as parties to the proceedings before the court which has sent the reference.[15] In those cases, the advocate will most likely have already played a formative role in shaping the conduct of the litigation before the case arrives at the Registry in Luxembourg, by assisting the national court with framing the questions and drafting the order for reference. In a significant number of other cases, a British advocate may act for the United Kingdom when it submits observations on a reference which has been sent by a court of another Member State.[16] It is by this procedure that a wide variety of questions of law falling within the scope of the Treaties which are matters of immediate pressing concern to individual litigants and also represent points of general public importance to European citizenry at large are answered by the Court on a daily basis.

B. Litigants and Advocates

The principal forms of proceedings outlined above dictate that there are certain 'repeat players' before the Court, namely the Community institutions, and the Member States. They must be represented by an agent appointed for each case, who may be assisted by an adviser or by a lawyer.

As regards the Community institutions, members of their respective internal legal services usually act as their agents before the Court.[17] An agent

---

[14] Of the 80 appeals lodged in 2006, 19 concerned the Community trade mark and 15 concerned competition.

[15] According to the Annual Report 2006, 10 references were sent by United Kingdom courts (on average, for the preceding five years, the annual number of references sent was around 20).

[16] In 2005, the United Kingdom made observations in writing in 90 references, and orally in 55 references. For 2006, the figures were 65 and 41 respectively. In some of those cases, both written and oral observations were submitted; in other cases, one was made without the other (figures supplied by the Treasury Solicitor's Department).

[17] On some occasions, the Commission will 'contract out' for the provision of legal services from external lawyers to assist it in the preparation of its cases, both at the written and oral stage.

of the Commission appears in almost every case. At oral hearings for reference proceedings, the Commission provides a reassuring point of constancy, occupying the advocates' table sited at the far left-hand side of the court room and exercising its conventionally acquired right to make its observations after the other parties have had their turn.

The United Kingdom is represented by an agent of the European Division of the Treasury Solicitor's Department, which conducts all of the government's litigation in Luxembourg. In most cases, the Treasury Solicitor's Department is assisted, both at the written and oral stage, by a barrister.[18] On rare occasions and where the constitutional importance of the case so requires, the Attorney General himself may appear. In recent years, the former Attorney General Lord Goldsmith QC has appeared in a few significant cases,[19] notably the Article 227 EC action brought by Spain against the United Kingdom by which Spain alleged that the United Kingdom had infringed Community law by virtue of the arrangements made by it for the inhabitants of Gibraltar to vote in European Parliament elections.[20] The Law Officers of the Crown made a number of appearances in the series of *Factortame* and related cases. Sir Nicholas Lyell QC represented the United Kingdom on the application for interim measures requesting an order suspending the application of the nationality requirements in sections 13 and 14 of the Merchant Shipping Act 1988[21] as Solicitor General, and at the hearing of *Brasserie du Pêcheur* and *ex parte Factortame*[22] on the issue of the conditions for state liability as Attorney General.

Other parties, namely those individuals and legal persons involved in reference and appeal proceedings, are generally represented by the lawyers who acted on their behalf before the national courts. Litigants in person may appear in reference proceedings.

---

[18] Barristers assisting the Treasury Solicitor are drawn from panels of Junior Counsel appointed by the Attorney General to undertake civil and European Community work or, in the case of Queen's Counsel, are nominated by the Attorney General.

[19] This is not necessarily limited to cases before the Grand Chamber. In recent years, the Attorney General has represented the United Kingdom in Case C-217/04 *United Kingdom v European Parliament and Council* [2006] ECR I-3771, concerning the regulation establishing the European Network and Information Security Agency, and in Case C-436/03 *European Parliament v Council* [2006] ECR I-3733, concerning the regulation on the Statute for a European Cooperative Society, which were heard by a Grand Chamber. However, the Attorney General also appeared in Joined Cases C-96/03 and C-97/03 *Templeman* [2005] ECR I-1895, heard by a five-judge chamber, which was a reference from a Dutch court concerning certain directives governing measures for the control of foot-and-mouth disease.

[20] Case C-145/04 *Spain v United Kingdom* [2006] ECR I-7917. The case revealed unprecedented political sensibilities even at the pre-litigation stage, with the Commission declaring that 'given the sensitivity of the underlying bilateral issue, the Commission at this stage refrains from adopting a reasoned opinion within the meaning of Article 227 [EC] and invites the parties to find an amicable solution' (para 32). The Grand Chamber dismissed Spain's action.

[21] Case C-246/89 R *Commission v United Kingdom* [1989] ECR 3125. See also Case C-213/89 *ex p Factortame* [1990] ECR I-2433 and Case C-246/89 *Commission v United Kingdom* [1991] ECR I-4585.

[22] Joined Cases C-46/93 and C-48/93 *Brasserie du Pêcheur* [1996] ECR I-1029.

Two features of the legal profession in the United Kingdom are particularly noteworthy at this point. The first feature is the existence and nature of an independent bar whose members are free to act for all parties across the board, the ability to do so and to give objective advice being considered a valuable part of the legal service provided.[23] This is the so-called 'cab rank rule'. It would be difficult to find someone who embodies the rule more than Sir Francis Jacobs himself who, according to the record, has appeared before the Court for the European Parliament,[24] Commission[25] and Council,[26] not only for the United Kingdom[27] but also for the Grand Duchy of Luxembourg,[28] as well as for individuals[29] and companies.[30] In practice, therefore, this means that Members of the Court of Justice may be, and often are, faced with the same advocate making submissions on behalf of the United Kingdom in one set of proceedings and against it in another.[31] This applies also to members of the Bar of Ireland.[32] While this ability of an advocate to switch horses is not a particularly noteworthy feature of litigation before the English courts, it may be considered more unusual in Luxembourg, where the institutions and other Member States tend to be represented by government agents who are unassisted by external lawyers.[33] It is well recognized that professional independence brings certain advantages for clients.[34]

The second feature is the ability to develop a specialized practice. While lawyers – either solicitors or barristers – with exclusively Community law practices are rare, there are some specializing in competition, public, employment,

---

[23] Claire Gibbs of the Treasury Solicitor's Department has spoken of the value attached to the legal services provided by counsel assisting with the United Kingdom's written and oral submissions, addressing the Irish Society of European Law, Dublin, on 8 February 2007 on the subject of United Kingdom interventions before the ECJ.

[24] Case 13/83 *European Parliament v Council* [1985] 1513 ('assisted by F. Jacobs, barrister in London and Professor at the University of London'). In the current style of the European Court Reports, the description of the professional status of lawyers is somewhat less prosaic.

[25] Case 119/77 *Nippon Seiko KK and others v Commission* [1979] ECR 1303 ('assisted by Francis Jacobs, Barrister of the Middle Temple').

[26] Joined Cases 260/85 and 106/86 *Tokyo Electric Company Ltd (TEC) and others v Council* [1988] ECR 5855 ('assisted by F. Jacobs QC').

[27] Case 84/85 *United Kingdom v Commission* [1987] ECR 3765 ('assisted by Francis Jacobs QC').

[28] Case 230/81 *Grand Duchy of Luxembourg v European Parliament* [1983] ECR 255 ('assisted by Francis Jacobs of the Middle Temple, Barrister'). Another case in which a barrister was instructed to act for other Member States is Case T-22/97 *Kesko Oy v Commission* [1999] ECR II-3775 (for Finland).

[29] Case 130/75 *Vivien Prais v Council* [1976] ECR 1589 ('represented by Francis Jacobs, Barrister, of the Middle Temple, London').

[30] Case114/81 *Tunnel Refineries Limited v Council* [1982] ECR 3189 ('represented by Francis Jacobs of the Middle Temple, Barrister').

[31] See Vaughan, '*Factortame* and After: A Fishy Story' [2005] EBLR 511.

[32] Although the tendency for this to happen is less marked, due to the fact that there are considerably fewer references made by the courts of Ireland than by the courts of the United Kingdom.

[33] Ireland being one exception.

[34] See, in particular, n 58 below.

intellectual property or tax whose practices are very heavily Community law based. Although Community law extends far beyond those subjects, familiarity with the principles upon which the Treaties are based and with Community law practice and procedure breeds expertise and inspires confidence. Often practitioners in these core fields are instructed when Community law issues arise in other fields. There is, therefore, considerable truth in the suggestion that the consideration of issues of Community law and, in particular, the making of Article 234 EC references is 'the province of a small, exclusive coterie of courts serviced by a specialist Bar'.[35]

But good advocacy crosses boundaries, and there is no reason to suppose that Community law ought necessarily to be the preserve of a specialist few. As Lord Denning pointed out as long ago as 1974, all lawyers qualified in the law of Member States are Community lawyers, who must all speak and think of Community law and of Community rights, a subject that will be revisited at section V below.

III. How Does the Court Work?

A. How the Court's Working Methods Affect the Role of the Advocate

The procedures and internal organization of the Court, which are governed by the Treaties, the Statute of the Court and its Rules of Procedure, as well as by some unwritten rules and conventions, determine its working methods. These working methods in turn affect the role played by an advocate in the Court's proceedings and the manner in which he carries out his task. Some of the particular, and in some instances peculiar, ways in which the Court works are examined below.

First, as regards the lodging of written pleadings, strict time limits are laid down, which may be extended only in certain proceedings and in exceptional circumstances. The Court has complete control over this aspect of procedure. Unlike in proceedings before the English courts, it is not possible for the parties to agree between themselves to extensions of time for the service of particular documents. A party who ignores or fails to meet court-imposed time-limits does so at his own peril.[36]

---

[35] Barnard and Sharpston, 'The Changing Face of Article 177 References' (1997) 34 CMLR 1113, 1168. See O'Leary, *Employment Law at the European Court of Justice* (2002) 49, who also cites de la Mare, 'Article 177 in Social and Political Context' in Craig and de Búrca (eds), *The Evolution of EU Law* (1999) 256, for the relative numbers of national lawyers appearing before the Court; and generally Mattli and Slaughter, *Constructing the European Community Legal System from the Ground Up: The Role of Individual Litigants and National Courts,* EUI WP RSC No 96/56, 18, who refer to the 'small size and relatively closely knit character of the legal community in each [Member State], forged by its ties of education, socialization and professional mobility between the professoriate, private practice and the judiciary'.

[36] For example, pursuant to Article 94(1) RP, if a defendant on whom an application has been duly served fails to lodge a defence to the application in the proper form within the time prescribed, the applicant may apply for judgment by default. A judgment by default shall be enforceable (Article 94(3) RP), although an application may be made to set it aside (Article 94(4) RP).

Second, extending the subject matter of pleadings beyond the original scope may be difficult and, in some instances, impossible. As regards references, Sir David Edward warns that since the Rules of Procedure require notice of the reference to be published in the Official Journal and the text to be sent to the Member States and institutions, 'the Court is reluctant to entertain new points which go beyond the scope of what has been notified and even more reluctant to hear oral argument on points that are not at least foreshadowed in the written pleadings'.[37]

Third, once registered, a case will be allocated by the President to a chamber of Judges and to a Judge Rapporteur. The Judge Rapporteur is responsible for the conduct of the case. This responsibility includes drafting a report summarizing the issues of fact and law arising and the arguments of the parties, which is called a Report for the Hearing, and a purely internal report for presentation to the Members at their weekly administrative meeting, which is called a Preliminary Report. The Judge Rapporteur also has carriage of draft judgments of cases assigned to him. Furthermore, for an advocate, convincing a few judicial voices may not be enough, as the Court of Justice delivers one collegiate judgment, and, in questions of law coming before it, is a court of last resort. The successful advocate must therefore rally the Judge Rapporteur, or another tenacious member of the formation, as well as a majority of the bench, to his side; otherwise, his client's cause is doomed.

There is no overt specialization of particular chambers; cases are allocated to chambers and Judges Rapporteurs on a fairly random basis, and a matter could be heard by any formation. It is therefore not unusual for the Judge from a particular Member State to be absent from a formation sitting either in a reference sent from a court in his Member State or in an infringement action against his Member State. In those circumstances there may be an additional responsibility on an advocate to provide details on points of substantive law or procedure pertaining to a national legal system which are necessary for a full understanding of the case. Sir David Edward has confirmed that, as regards references:

although the Court is in theory concerned only with questions of law, it frequently has to undertake what amounts to a process of preliminary 'fact-finding' on points of pure fact or aspects of national law or some of both. The member of the Court belonging to the country from which the reference comes from may be able to help, as may the Court's Research and Documentation Division. But the Court has to rely heavily on the parties, and particularly on the Commission, to fill in the factual and legal background.[38]

---

[37] D Edward, *Practitioners' Handbook of EC Law* (1998) 3.1.5.4. However, in some instances, the Court has, at the insistence of some parties, ruled upon Community law provisions pertinent to the dispute before the national court but not referred to in the questions referred. In such cases, the advocate has an important role to play in drawing the attention of such provisions to the Court. An example of such a case is Case 70/77 *Simmenthal SpA v Amministrazione delle finanze dello Stato* [1978] ECR 1453, where the Court interpreted a directive which had not been referred to by the national court, but had been mentioned in some of the written observations.
[38] D Edward, 'How the Court of Justice Works' (1995) 20 ELRev 545.

Fourth, the case will also be allocated an Advocate General who has responsibility for it as it moves through the procedural stages. Provided that the matter is not dealt with by reasoned order or otherwise without an opinion,[39] it is the duty of the Advocate General to assist the Court, by acting with complete impartiality and independence to provide reasoned submissions on cases. The Advocate General may make counsel's role either more easy or more difficult. An Advocate General's opinion may accept and improve upon certain of counsel's arguments, and adopt a conclusion finding in favour of the party he represents. It may reject counsel's arguments either in favour of those submitted by other parties or on an entirely new basis put forward by an Advocate General himself. Even the most cursory glance at the European Court Reports demonstrates that a fuller account of counsel's submissions is recorded in opinions than in judgments; that is the case now more than ever, since the Court has, in recent years, significantly reduced the proportion of its judgments that sets out the parties' arguments. Equally, opinions discuss in more detail comparative principles in national legal systems, particularly when they fall to be considered in cases of constitutional importance, and often provide more explicit reasoning for the derivation of a particular principle of Community law from national principles.[40] In the absence of dissenting opinions from the Court, an Advocate General's opinion which was not followed may provide a source of inspiration to advocates wanting to push the boundaries in a particular field of law.

Fifth, the Court has a unique language regime, which is shaped by two principal factors. In the first place, a case has its own language of procedure, generally the language chosen by the applicant. Member States plead in one of their official languages, and consequently many official languages of the Community are used daily.[41] In the second place, the Court's internal working language is French, which is used to draft the reports prepared by the Judge Rapporteur and is also used for the process of judicial deliberation among the Members. This language regime means that the written submissions of a British advocate will be translated, certainly into French, and possibly also into other languages.[42] Oral submissions at the hearing will be interpreted for the benefit of the other parties before the Court and the Members.

Finally, the workings of the Court are the product of an ongoing process of the mixing of a number of legal families, systems and traditions, given that 'the members and staff of the Court, as well as those who plead before it, have been bred in a variety of legal traditions spanning the historic divide between the

---

[39] As it may be pursuant to Article 20(5) EC where the case raises no new point of law.
[40] For example, see the opinion of Advocate General Tesauro in Case C-213/89 *ex p Factortame* [1990] ECR I-2433 which provides a masterly exposition of the legal basis for interim protection and a detailed comparative law survey.
[41] Exceptionally the Court may, on reasoned request, permit an advocate for a party to address the Court in a language other than the language of the case.
[42] Articles 29 and 30 RP. Any parts of a pleading still extant in the final judgment will be translated into the official Community languages.

so-called Civil Law and Common Law systems'.[43] Allowances may have to be made to accommodate such differences, and pleaded cases adjusted accordingly. As Judge Schiemann put it, 'What is a self-evident truth to a French lawyer is frequently not a self-evident truth to an English lawyer, and vice versa'.[44]

B. The Written and Oral Procedure

It seems obvious, but is worth repeating, that the procedure before the Court of Justice comprises two parts, written and oral,[45] which are then followed by a period of deliberation before judgment is handed down. The Court's working methods and its emphasis on comprehensive written pleadings means that, at the written stage, effective advocacy is equally, if not more, important than it is at the oral stage.

The written procedure consists of the communication to the parties and to the institutions of the Communities whose decisions are in dispute, of applications, statements of case, defences and observations, and of replies, if any, as well as of all papers and documents in support or of certified copies of them.[46] Pleadings are very different from the pithy formal style of those drafted by United Kingdom counsel and, by contrast, 'are expected to contain a full and authoritative statement of the relevant arguments of law and (where applicable) of fact'. In particular, in reference proceedings, their purpose is 'to suggest the answers which the Court should give to the questions referred to it, and to set out succinctly, but completely the reasoning on which those answers are based'.[47]

A number of characteristics of the Court's working methods identified in section III(A) above require counsel to take particular care when drafting pleadings.[48] First, the need to translate documents. A lovingly-crafted pleading over which the draftsman has laboured for hours in order to pin down that elusive phrase or the perfect bon mot may not survive the translation process: 'Counsel should always keep in mind, when drafting observations, that the pleadings will not necessarily be read by the judges in their original form or their original language... treasured nuances – especially of legal language – may be lost or

---

[43] D Edward, 'How the Court of Justice Works' (1995) 20 ELRev 540.
[44] Schiemann, 'The Application of General Principles' in Andenas and Jacobs (eds), *European Community Law in the English Courts* (1998) 139.
[45] Article 20 EC.
[46] Article 20 EC, para 2.
[47] Anderson and Demetriou, *References to the European Court* (2002) 10-013.
[48] In 'Notes for the Guidance of Counsel in written and oral proceedings before the Court of Justice of the European Communities', published most recently in January 2007 and available at *http://curia.europa.eu*, the Court uses the word 'counsel' in a non-technical sense so as to include all those appearing before the Court and acting as advocate, whatever their capacity or technical status. The CFI has recently amended its Instructions to the Registrar and Practice Directions for Parties (2007) OJL 232, to which reference should be made in relation to proceedings before that Court.

obscured'.⁴⁹ Pleadings which are not clearly structured or signposted may also fail to get the message across so effectively once translated. Documents indispensable to a proper understanding of the case must be annexed to the pleadings; however, given that annexes are not, as a rule, translated, essential passages of annexes ought to be included in the body of the pleading to ensure translation.⁵⁰ Second, the preparation of the Report for the Hearing and the significance of that report as a basis for the proceedings means that submissions ought to be capable of summary and easy presentation to the Members.⁵¹ Third, the need to address principles which may be peculiar to a national legal system and which are not necessary familiar, at least in a certain form or under a particular label, to all parties, requires a draftsman to take particular care when explaining legal provisions or principles which may be obvious to him but whose relevance and importance is not as clear to those who have undertaken their legal studies in another jurisdiction.⁵² The first reference from the United Kingdom courts in the *Factortame* cases,⁵³ which requested the Court to consider the principle in English law that there was no right to obtain injunctions against the Crown, is one such example. Another is that of *Courage and Crehan*,⁵⁴ where the Court of Appeal requested that the Court of Justice consider the compatibility with Community law of the English legal principle prohibiting a party to an illegal agreement to claim damages from the other party.

The Court itself makes a number of helpful suggestions which ought to be borne in mind when drafting:⁵⁵ the case is examined on the basis of the pleadings, and in order to facilitate that examination, documents must be structured and concise and must avoid repetition; pleadings will, as a general rule, be translated, and in order to facilitate translation and to make it as accurate as possible, sentences should be simple in structure and vocabulary should be simple and precise; and since the time needed for translation and for examination of the case file is proportionate to the

---

⁴⁹ D Edward, *Practitioners' Handbook of EC Law* (1998) 3.1.5.9. The same point has been made as regards the oral hearing: 'Unless the interpreter can interpret, one's choicest phrases are so much chaff – gone with the wind', Richards and Beloff, *Practitioners' Handbook of EC Law* (1998) 2.22.

⁵⁰ D Edward, *Practitioners' Handbook of EC Law* (1998) 3.1.5.13.

⁵¹ As Richards and Beloff put it at 2.16: 'If in the English Courts the degree to which the Judges are familiar with the case (notwithstanding the mandatory skeleton arguments) is moot, depending very much on the willingness and workload of the individual Judge, in the ECJ at least some members of the Court, as a result of the distinctive procedures, will truly be au fait'. For a discussion of the extent to which Judges may be familiar with the case file when attending the hearing but, in fact, may have had 'very little opportunity to examine the ramifications of the case or to identify the missing elements in the file', see O'Leary, *Employment Law at the European Court of Justice* (2002) 50–2.

⁵² The Court frequently draws on the resources of its Research and Documentation Division to carry out research concerning Community law or the law of one or more of the Member States and possibly the law of third states, examined from a comparative perspective.

⁵³ [1990] ECR I-1433 and the subsequent decision of the House of Lords at [1991] 1 AC 603.

⁵⁴ Case C-453/99 *Courage and Crehan* [2001] ECR I-6297.

⁵⁵ Court of Justice Practice Directions relating to direct actions and appeals (OJ 2004 L 361, 15) 43; Notes for the Guidance of Counsel 14(a).

length of the pleadings lodged, the shorter the pleadings, the swifter the disposal of the case.[56] In other words, 'brevity, simplicity and clarity'.[57]

It has been observed that a persuasive and concise written argument not only has the effect of getting a party's case off on the right track and getting into the mind of the Judge, but may also create a point of reference for the Court as regards submissions made by the same party in future proceedings. In the words of one former senior Judge:

> What has become more noticeable in recent years is the very high quality of British written pleadings, particularly those submitted by the United Kingdom government. More than one member of the Court has remarked that the quickest way to find out what a case is really about is to read the submissions of the UK government.[58]

Written pleadings form the bulk of a case file and their examination constitutes a large proportion of the time spent by a Judge or Advocate General's chambers when considering the merits of a case. Unlike in national proceedings, the Court's rules do not allow for written skeleton arguments to be added to a file.[59] Neither is it the case that written submissions are generally accepted by the Court following the hearing, either before or after the Advocate General has presented his opinion. Put simply, the importance of the written stage of proceedings cannot be overstated.[60]

---

[56] Sir David Edward says that, as 'a rule of thumb, observations should be no longer than 30 pages in complex cases and 10 pages in straightforward cases. Many excellent pleadings are even shorter than that'. See *Practitioners' Handbook of EC Law* (1998) 3.1.5.11. The Court itself advises that in its experience, 'save in exceptional circumstances, effective pleadings need not exceed 10 or 15 pages and replies, rejoinders and responses can be limited to 5 to 10 pages' (see Court of Justice Practice Directions relating to direct actions and appeals (OJ 2004 L 361, 15) 44). The Court of First Instance has also given directions as to the length of pleadings, and, in some cases, has adopted a practice of requesting that parties keep within the recommended length in order for the pleading to be accepted by the Registry. The Court of Justice does not appear to have adopted a similar practice.

[57] D Edward, *Practitioners' Handbook of EC Law* (1998) 3.1.5.10. Anderson and Demetriou quote an ex-President of the Court, Judge Due, in Gazette 90/14, 7 April 1993, 12 who contrasted 'the British tendency to overdo things in the written procedure' with the French practice of making submissions that were generally 'well made and well concentrated on the main issues' (Anderson and Demetriou, *References to the European Court* (2002) 10-033).

[58] D Edward, 'The development of law and legal process in the EU' in B Markesinis (ed), *The British Contribution to the Europe of the 21ˢᵗ Century* (2002) 31. This was attributed to two factors in particular, namely the use of independent advocates experienced in court work and consultation between United Kingdom government departments.

[59] See, in particular, 'Notes for the Guidance of Counsel' B.14(b). Exceptionally, the Court will accept documents which have been sent to the other parties where no objection has been raised to the introduction of new material.

[60] It was the view of Richards and Beloff in 1998 (*Practitioners' Handbook of EC Law* (1998) 2.16) that the 'importance attached to the written procedure can be illustrated by the fact that the author of the written submissions is identified in the case reports, giving a double chance of immortality'. While this was once true, sadly, it is no longer the case. The European Court Reports record the parties which submitted observations and the lawyers representing them without differentiating between the written and oral stages of procedure. However, despite this development, the written procedure is, on any view, of no less importance.

And yet, as with most litigation, it is the oral stage of proceedings which tends to capture the imagination. In all cases the purpose of the oral procedure and counsel's role in it is clear. He must recall, if necessary, by way of a highly condensed summary, the positions taken by the parties, with emphasis on the essential submissions in support of which written argument has been presented. He may submit any new arguments prompted by recent events occurring after the close of the written procedure which, for that reason, could not be set out in the pleadings. He may be required to explain and expound the more complex points and those which are more difficult to grasp, and to highlight the most important points. Finally, he may be called upon to answer any questions put by the Court. In references, the oral procedure enables lawyers to reply briefly to the main arguments set out in other written observations. The oral procedure must, however, be seen as supplementing the written procedure and should involve no repetition of what has already been stated in writing.[61]

The Court of Justice is a busy administrator of justice. This is reflected by the brief periods of time allotted to parties to make oral submissions and in the highly disciplined approach that the Court demands of those making them. As a general rule, the period initially allowed to each main party is limited to a maximum of 30 minutes, or 15 minutes before Chambers.[62] Interveners are allowed a maximum of 15 minutes.[63] A party's counsel may optimistically indicate – either by letter to the Registry or in the private meeting with the Members of the Court before the hearing – that he intends to be briefer than the maximum allowable period. Where he does so, he is estopped from changing his mind.[64]

There is an ongoing debate on the usefulness of the oral hearing. The inherent and inherited limitations are well rehearsed.[65] An oral hearing which adds nothing to the case as set out in the written pleadings is clearly not worth the delay which it adds to the time taken for judgment to be handed down. However, in most proceedings, the oral hearing will be the final occasion on which to address

---

[61] See 'Notes for the Guidance of Counsel', C.2.

[62] Composed of three Judges.

[63] It is of some consolation that these limits apply to a party's oral argument proper and do not include the time taken to reply to questions put by the Court. The time limits are strictly applied: 'The most spellbinding advocates can sometimes escape with an extra minute or two, but the Court enforces its time limits with great strictness and it would be rash to bank upon extra time being made available' (see Anderson and Demetriou, *References to the European Court* (2002) 11-036).

[64] Advice is to err on the side of caution. Beloff and Richards maintain that the 'trick is to ask for something imprecise and qualified – "I hope to be no more than twenty or so minutes" – which gives the impression of intended brevity, while – on close textual analysis – preserving one's right to the full half hour'. They also advise that, even though pleading may be in English, a rudimentary knowledge of French, at least 'French numbers between 10 and 30 is a great aid to confidence. But if in doubt about what has been said, seek confirmation in English rather than take the risk of stepping to the podium at the wrong time or presenting energetic submissions on a question that you have just been told it is unnecessary to address' (*Practitioners' Handbook of EC Law* (1998) 2.21).

[65] For a lively and informative discussion see O'Leary, *Employment Law at the European Court of Justice* (2002) 46–53.

Litigating in Luxembourg 61

those issues not dealt with in written submissions and to answer points made by other parties. This may be particularly important in references, where the exchange of observations is simultaneous and there is no further opportunity to lodge written pleadings in reply to the observations of other parties. A point which is often made as regards the Advocate General's opinion, but which may also apply to the hearing, is that it is only at the stage of oral submissions that the significance of certain issues will be clear to the Members of the Court.[66]

As with any proceedings before any court, it is clear that in certain cases effective oral advocacy can influence the outcome. In those circumstances, the advocate plays a vital role. It is also clear that it is the art of knowing what not to say as much as the art of knowing what to say that counts.[67] This is particularly so in Luxembourg, where timing is tight and where a number of parties may be making similar or identical submissions. The United Kingdom, which is the last of the Member States to appear at the oral hearing, has, and often takes, the opportunity to be more selective and focused in its submissions, avoiding the repetition of points which have been made clearly by other parties. The 'Notes for the Guidance of Counsel' give general encouragement to parties to adopt such an approach. In some cases, parties have coordinated submissions successfully.[68] This practice continues to find favour with the Court,[69] although it does have its limitations.

As regards the structure, content and delivery of submissions, there are a few golden rules. It has been remarked that if seeking guidance on the structure of oral submissions, 'the tradition of the Bars of the common law countries may serve as a model'.[70] One experienced member of the Luxembourg bench advises

[66] The different motives for attending the hearing have been listed as follows: 'The reasons for being present are manifold and vary from case to case: the need to comment on views presented by others; the need to avoid misunderstandings of one's own written observations; the need to develop, clarify or correct one's own views; a wish to be present in order to reply to questions from the Court; and a wish to be present in case "anything should happen"' (see Anderson and Demetriou, *References to the European Court* (2002) 11-008 citing L Mikaelsen, 'The Role of Government Representatives in Article 177 EEC Proceedings: the experience of Denmark', *Article 177: Experiences and Problems* (TMC Asser Instituut, 1987)).

[67] The more complex and complicated the oral argument, the less likely it is that the advocate will get his message across. Anderson and Demetriou, *References to the European Court* (2002) 9-045, refer to a litigant in person, the self-employed masseur and hydrotherapist Mr Christos Konstantinidis, who was 'praised by Advocate General Jacobs for presenting his oral argument "with a simple eloquence and brevity which many professional advocates would do well to emulate"' (Case C-168/91 *Konstantinidis* [1993] ECR I-1191).

[68] See Anderson and Demetriou, *References to the European Court* (2002) 11-032, who refer to the eight infringement actions relating to bilateral aviation agreements with the US: Cases C-466/98 *Commission v United Kingdom* [2002] ECR I-9427. The authors remark that 'informal allocation of topics between the eight Member States involved resulted in a productive use of time at the joint oral hearing'.

[69] Before the hearing in Case C-475/03 *Banca popolare di Cremona* [2006] ECR I-9373 the Court invited representatives of the Member State to coordinate their oral observations.

[70] 'Presenting the Case Orally – the Judge's View' in *Butterworths European Court Practice,* ii. Sir David Edward has remarked that although the oral submissions of advocates from the United Kingdom are generally 'much appreciated by the Court for their clarity and relevance', advocates

that it 'is best to begin the speech by indicating what points it is intended to cover and to make clear, as the speech proceeds, when counsel is moving from one point to another. This will help both the interpreters and the Judges. It is not necessary to rehearse facts which are set out in the Report for the Hearing. But it is useful to draw attention, very briefly, to the salient features of the case from the client's point of view so as to put the arguments in context'.[71]

If particular issues or questions have been raised by the Court either in writing or immediately before the hearing, this will give a steer as to what points counsel ought to dwell on in his speech and how he ought to tailor the content of his submissions. Oral submissions need to be carefully balanced to take account of the fact that not all members of the Court will be equally familiar with the issues in the case. At that stage, the Advocate General is likely to have formed a clear view of the case, and may even have a draft opinion with him at the oral hearing. The Judge Rapporteur and other members who have deliberated similar cases may also have a view as to the direction that a judgment may take. Others, by contrast, may have had less opportunity to review the pleadings and may be less familiar with the legal principles raised; in those circumstances, experienced advocates have suggested that these members 'may be more receptive to broader submissions on the merits'.[72]

The practice of delivering prepared speeches, which is common to many advocates appearing before the Court of Justice, is rather different from the style of delivery and frequent interruptions to counsel's arguments by the bench which is commonplace in the United Kingdom courts. On the one hand, it is quite understandable that clients – particularly Member States – are keen to keep a close eye on what counsel will say. On the other hand, reading from a text is not a particularly valuable way of communicating with the bench and does not leave much room for spontaneity. As ever, there is a happy medium, which is reckoned to produce a more successful outcome:

> [To read a speech] is much less likely to be effective than to speak from notes: the lawyer appearing before the European Court is still there as an advocate and a few strong submissions will catch the attention of the Court, attract the waverers, and maybe shake those who have already formed their preliminary view to the contrary on the basis of the pleadings.[73]

In any event, there may be limits to the impact of the submissions of even the most silver-tongued advocates. Unlike their brethren at the Court of First Instance, Judges at the Court of Justice do not, as a matter of course, deliberate over the outcome of the case immediately following the oral hearing, but rather wait for the circulation of a draft judgment by the Judge Rapporteur to discuss

---

from other Member States 'can display the same qualities in equal measure' (see 'The Development of law and legal process in the European' in Markesinis (ed), *The British Contribution to the Europe of the 21st Century* (2002)).

[71] D Edward, *Practitioners' Handbook of EC Law* (1998) 3.1.5.33.
[72] Anderson and Demetriou, *References to the European Court* (2002) 11-041.
[73] G Slynn, Litigating in Luxembourg (Counsel, 1988) 12.

the merits of the case either on paper or at a deliberation of the chamber or both. The presentation of the opinion of the Advocate General marking the close of the oral procedure, the preparation and proofing of a draft judgment, and the pressures of work at the Court requiring Judges to sit in or consider a substantial number of cases mean that it could be some time between the oral hearing and the deliberation before a Judge is required to reopen the file. In that intervening period, he will have listened to lawyers pleading in many other cases. And yet, as the reports show, fragments of oral pleadings have, in some very occasional cases, proven sufficiently memorable to form an essential part of the Court's reasoning and to warrant recording in the judgment.[74]

IV. The Impact of Advocacy and Advocates on the Court's Case Law

Curia novit iura.[75] Bearing this in mind, it would be unwise to give undue weight to any suggestion that the outcome of cases before the Court of Justice may be significantly affected by the work of an advocate. Certainly, it is not easy to discern to what extent an advocate may have got into the mind of the Court, and to draw any meaningful conclusions on whether he was responsible for a successful outcome for his client, or/and whether he may have left an impression on its jurisprudence.[76] However, the fact that an advocate, the principles of the legal system upon which he relies to found his arguments and the part played by advocacy itself in legal proceedings have, in some instances, influenced the course of litigation at the Court has been recognized by a number of commentators. Here a distinction can be made between the effect of advocacy generally on the Court's procedure, and its effect specifically on the substance of its case law.

Considering the Court's procedure, first, the common law style of advocacy is acknowledged to have left a mark. Writing generally on the influence of English

---

[74] It is worth considering that this may, in future, be less easy to spot, due to the tendency in recent judgments to reduce or omit those parts formerly either setting out the arguments of the parties or referring to them in the reasoning, a regrettable but seemingly necessary development due to the extraordinary demands placed on the translation service by the rules governing the Court's procedure.

[75] The court knows the law.

[76] Writing generally on the successes (and failures) of advocates, David Pannick QC expressed the view in *Advocates* (1992) 230 that '[i]mportant though the advocate is, his influence should not be exaggerated'. He cites Sir Patrick Hastings – Attorney General in 1924 and one of Britain's leading trial lawyers until well into the 1940s – who was 'satisfied that at least ninety per cent of all cases win or lose themselves, and that the ultimate result would have been the same whatever counsel the parties had chosen to represent them'. Hastings was sure that 'a case can be lost by bad advocacy'. On 'rare occasions... so rarely that perhaps they can be counted on the fingers of one hand', a case may be won by great advocacy (P Hastings, *Cases in Court* (1949) 109). Pannick concludes that '[i]nfrequently does great advocacy persuade judges to accept what they would otherwise reject'.

law on Community law, Sir Francis Jacobs made the following remark as regards the impression left by English counsel on the Court of Justice's proceedings:

> Even more pervasive has been the effect of the European Court's encounter with the English practitioner and with the English legal tradition: the English Bar has unquestionably had an impact on the character of the proceedings in the Court of Justice and given somewhat greater significance to the oral stage of the proceedings.[77]

Sir Francis is not the only former member of the Court to hold this view. The late Judge Mancini has also credited common law lawyers – in particular, the British and Irish Judges – with having altered the character of the oral hearing: he referred to the advent of the 'two insular Judges', and how their colleagues 'loved their refusal to listlessly accept the kind of assistance which the lawyers were prepared to give them and started to act in similar fashion. As a result, interruptions are now more frequent and a question period has become a permanent feature of the hearings, much to their advantage in terms of usefulness and liveliness'.[78] Clearly these were welcome changes, although, as mentioned above, the utility of a hearing at the Court of Justice still suffers by comparison with that of one before the High Court.

Second, there are other ways in which the English legal system has affected that of the European Community, such as influencing the Court's approach to the role of precedent and to the overruling of its own previous judgments. Professor Arnull has suggested that since the Court's encounter with the common law tradition it has been more explicit in its handling of its previous case law. Certainly, while the doctrine of precedent may not apply in the same way as in the English legal system, that may not necessarily be the same thing as saying that the Court is not – or does not consider itself to be – bound by its own decisions.[79] Others have feted the 'significant contribution' of the 'refined case law technique of the common law, which caused the Court to become more, as it were, precedent-conscious and therefore more skilful in distinguishing cases or in correcting itself when it felt that a case had been wrongly decided'.[80] Mancini

---

[77] 'Interpretation and Precedent in European Community Law' 125–9 in Andenas and Jacobs (eds), *European Community Law in the English Courts* (1998).

[78] Mancini and Keeling, 'Language, Culture and Politics in the Life of the European Court of Justice' (1995) Columbia Journal of European Law 397, 401.

[79] A Arnull, 'Interpretation and precedent in European Community law' 125–9 in M Andenas and F Jacobs (eds), *European Community Law in the English Courts* (1998). In *R v Henn and Darby* [1981] AC 850, 905C, Lord Diplock stated that:

the European Court does not apply the doctrine of precedent to its own decisions as rigidly as does an English court. Nevertheless, as any browsing in the Common Market Law Reports will show, the European Court too seeks to maintain consistency in its decisions in the interests of legal certainty. Consequently in the opinions of the Advocates General and the judgments of the court itself, citations of previous judgments of the court are as frequent as citations of previous authority in judgments of English courts.

[80] Mancini and Keeling, 'Language, Culture and Politics in the Life of the European Court of Justice' (1995) Columbia Journal of European Law 397, 401–2. They continue:

Civil law jurisdictions have never been quite as cavalier in their attitude towards precedent as is sometimes imagined in England and America, but it is true that the sophisticated case law apparatus developed by the common law – subtle distinctions between binding and persuasive authority,

and Keeling refer to the fact that in the decades following the 1970s, the practice of citing previous judgments became more commonplace and there is evidence of an attempt to build up a body of jurisprudence. They also note that while 'opinions may differ as to whether the common law influence was responsible for that change of approach, it is perhaps not without significance that when in 1990 the Court finally took the bold step of expressly overruling a previous judgment it did so at the instigation of a British Advocate General.'[81]

Considering the substance of the Court's case law, while the role of the advocate is designed to afford him the opportunity to exercise his talents of persuasion so that the bench may reach one conclusion over another, it would be unwise to overstate his case. There are, however, some instances where it can be said that an advocate has left indelible footprints in the sands of Community law. One such example is the case of *Barber*.[82] In those proceedings, the Court was required to rule on a number of questions regarding equal pay and equal treatment in the context of the right of a male employee to an early retirement pension on being made compulsorily redundant. The case is a frequently quoted example of the Court limiting the temporal effects of its judgment. Of particular note is the fact that the Court did so in response to the submissions of certain parties, namely the Commission and the United Kingdom. In the judgment, the Court made the following remarks:

In its written and oral observations, the Commission has referred to the possibility for the Court of restricting the effect of this judgment *ratione temporis* in the event of the concept of pay, for the purposes of the second paragraph of Article 119 of the Treaty ... For its part the United Kingdom emphasized at the hearing the serious financial consequences of such an interpretation of Article 119. The number of workers affiliated to contracted-out schemes is very large in the United Kingdom and the schemes in question frequently derogate from the principle of equality between men and women, in particular by providing for different pensionable ages.[83]

Another example is, as has been suggested above, where a 'striking or unusual phrase in written observations will sometimes find its way into the Report for the Hearing, the opinion of the Advocate General or even the judgment'.[84] David Anderson QC and Marie Demetriou refer to the phrase 'dumping fence', which was coined by the barrister assisting the Commission in *NMB v Commission*[85] and 'introduced into the standard terminology of anti-dumping law when it was taken up by the Court in its judgment'.[86]

or between *ratio decidendi* and *obiter dicta,* and fastidious (sometimes spurious) attempts to distinguish cases on their facts – has never held much appeal for lawyers on the European mainland.
[81] Mancini and Keeling (ibid) 402. The case was *Hag II* (Case C-10/89 *CNL v HAG GF* [1990] ECR I-3711, overruling Case 192/73 *Van Zuylen v HAG* [1974] ECR 731) and the Advocate General, as the reader might have guessed, was Francis Jacobs.
[82] Case C-262/88 *Barber v Guardian Royal Exchange* [1990] ECR I-1889.
[83] Para 40.
[84] Anderson and Demetriou, *References to the European Court* (2002) 10-035(5).
[85] Case C-188/88 *NMB v Commission* [1992] ECR I-1689, para 35. The barrister was Mark Cran QC.
[86] Anderson and Demetriou, *References to the European Court* (2002) 10-035(5).

In certain cases, the influence of a particular line of argument will be clear from the result reached by the Court. This is evident from the judgment in the seminal case, particularly for lawyers, of *AM & S Europe v Commission*.[87] In that case, the applicant, supported by the United Kingdom and the Consultative Committee of the Bars and Law Societies of the European Community (CCBE), argued successfully in favour of the protection of the confidentiality of written communications between lawyer and client in the context of requests by the Commission to produce documents during an investigation pursuant to Article 14(3) of Regulation No 17. While each of those parties pursued the same result, it can be detected from the Report for the Hearing (and is a matter of some legal folklore) that the CCBE played a formative role.

The impact made by the United Kingdom on court judgments was measured by Sir David Edward over a period of time in 1996. Sir David examined judgments rendered in 70 cases,[88] of which the United Kingdom had intervened in 23.[89] He recorded that:

in 11 of the cases in which the United Kingdom intervened, the arguments presented were wholly successful, in the sense that the Court's judgment coincided with the government's submissions both as to the result and as to the reasoning. In three cases, the judgment coincided with the government's submissions as to the proper result, but arrived at that result by different reasoning. In five cases, the United Kingdom was successful on some points but not on others.

He concluded that the 'success rate of the United Kingdom is, by any standards, very high'. This provides reason to suppose, therefore, that the practice of intervening may influence the outcome of cases and that a presence before the Court ought to continue to be encouraged.

V. The Role of European Advocates in National Courts

Appearing before the Court of Justice is, unquestionably, one of the high points of a European lawyer's career. However, it is more likely to be the case that a Euro lawyer will have to consider issues of the interpretation and application of EU law in national proceedings, and will find himself addressing a judge in London, rather than in Luxembourg. Just as before the Court of Justice, Community law issues in national proceedings arise in diverse fields, and can be raised in a wide range of courts and tribunals.

Many areas of public and administrative law are affected by Community law. Often, the legality of domestic acts and measures falls to be tested by judicial

---

[87] Case 155/79 *AM & S Europe v Commission* [1982] ECR 1575.

[88] Those judgments which had at that time been delivered in cases with docket numbers between 1/94 and 210/94.

[89] D Edward, 'The European Court of Justice – Friend or Foe?' Address to the European Atlantic Group, London, 18 July 1996, 13.

review by reference to whether the act or measure in question is compliant with Community law. As an experienced public law practitioner has put it, 'a breach of EC law is, therefore, an additional – and potentially very powerful – basis in an increasing number of cases for seeking relief in domestic judicial review proceedings'.[90] In employment cases before tribunals and appellate courts, advocates have to interpret national legislation in the light of Directives, and are frequently required to consider provisions previously not the subject of judicial determination either by the national courts or the Court of Justice. On a daily basis, the Competition Appeal Tribunal, whose procedure is modelled closely on that of the Court of First Instance, applies competition law as developed in Luxembourg. Before these and other national courts, in addition to relying upon the Treaties and secondary legislation, lawyers can draw on the general principles of Community law, such as proportionality, equal treatment, legitimate expectations and fundamental rights. Although there is a close connection between these principles and corresponding principles of English law, important distinctions remain and, in some cases, the notions have different substantive contents in Community as compared to domestic law. Lawyers may also rely on different interpretative techniques. In addition, United Kingdom courts are becoming the preferred route for challenging EU legislation, in cases in which the rules applying to actions before the Court of Justice would make a direct challenge inadmissible.[91]

The Chancery Division is also likely to be faced with advocates pleading Euro points, not least because, as a general rule, claims involving points of competition law must be commenced there. The Patents Court, in particular, has always been a fertile ground for lawyers sowing the seeds of novel pleas founded on the Treaties. It should come as no surprise that Sir Francis, before making the significant contribution to the development of the Court of Justice's jurisprudence on intellectual property for which he is widely acknowledged, was at the vanguard, appearing in such seminal cases as *EMI v CBS*.[92]

Lord Denning was right when he spoke of the giving effect to Community law requiring a 'great effort for the lawyers'.[93] This effort is not only for the lawyers, but also for the Judges. Evidently, such efforts have been, and continue to be, made. As David Anderson QC commented:

The number of references has never been very large, however, and increasingly the English courts have been showing the expertise and confidence to decide points of Community law for themselves. This is generally considered to be a positive tendency. It shortens

---

[90] Richard Gordon QC, *EC Law in Judicial Review* (2007) 1.04.
[91] For example, *ex parte Omega Air* [2000] EuLR 254.
[92] [1976] RPC 1. This was one of the first references from the United Kingdom. In his contribution in Andenas and Jacobs (eds), *European Community Law in the English Courts* (1998) 211, Mr Justice Jacob recalls that 'I was the junior for EMI before Graham J. I was led by one T.H. Bingham QC. He suggested that another junior from his chambers be added to the team because that junior knew rather a lot about EEC law. I supported the idea with vigour because this was all a new world. Thus in the ECJ you will see that one Francis Jacobs was the first junior'.
[93] *Bulmer v Bollinger* [1974] Ch 401.

litigation, and accords with calls from within the ECJ itself for 'self-restraint' from national courts as regards references. It has also resulted in a number of statements by English courts of their own opinions, informed by the case law of the ECJ, as to the future development on the general principles of Community law.[94]

This is how a developed system of Community law ought to work. The extensive case law of the Court provides sufficient detail to enable national courts and tribunals, at least at first instance, to decide many cases for themselves with a sufficient degree of confidence and without the need for a reference, a tendency making itself felt in the various jurisdictions in the United Kingdom and in Ireland. Since 1997, the most important judgments involving issues of Community law decided by the national courts or tribunals of England and Wales, Scotland, Northern Ireland and Ireland have been reported in the European Law Reports, enabling lawyers, judges and others to follow developments in these national jurisdictions; the breadth and depth of the decisions collected in the EuLRs is testament to the importance of judgments on Community law at the national level.[95]

Advocates do continue to have the opportunity to represent both private parties and the United Kingdom on references and direct actions before the Court of Justice. However, with the emphasis on national courts as fully empowered enforcers of Community law being stronger than ever,[96] all national lawyers ought, to a certain degree, also to consider themselves European lawyers. Looking around, they will find that there are more of them than they might have thought. The General Council of the Bar provides support to its members through the European Circuit of the Bar of England and Wales. Inaugurated in March 2001, it is the first Circuit to be founded in several hundred years, and, it has been said, marked a 'major evolution for the Bar'.[97] Associations such as the Bar European Group[98] and the United Kingdom Association of European Lawyers, in which Sir Francis has been heavily involved, as well as the Law Society European Group, provide opportunities for lawyers to debate current issues and exchange professional experiences with their colleagues in their own and in other Member States.

VI. Conclusion

Litigating in Luxembourg is a challenge. Carrying out his task before the Court can require the advocate to counter the positions of parties whose arguments

---

[94] David Anderson QC, 'The Application of the General Principles of Community Law by the Courts of England', Cour de Cassation, Paris Colloquium, 4–5 December 2000.
[95] See Editorial Introduction at [1997] EuLR 1.
[96] In particular, following the introduction of Regulation 1/2003 on the application of Articles 81 EC and 82 EC.
[97] The words of the present Circuit Leader, Lord Brennan QC. The Circuit brings together within one network barristers practising European law, barristers working in Europe and European lawyers with a link to the UK.
[98] In 2007, celebrating the 30th anniversary of its foundation.

are based on principles drawn from unfamiliar legal systems. It necessitates the translation and interpretation of his argument at various stages in proceedings. It requires adhering to strictly observed limits regarding both the points in time at which he can put his client's case before the court and the length of time he has to make oral submissions.

But, in many ways, the real challenge for the advocate is, to borrow a phrase of David Pannick QC, 'to find a point of law where none had previously been known to exist'. Despite the fact that now, almost 35 years after the Treaty of Rome was first referred to in an English court and English advocates pleaded a case in Luxembourg, previously unknown points of law are still to be found in the application of the Treaties, legislation and general principles of EU law. The EU legal system, with its ever expanding jurisdiction, continues to represent a new dimension for the legal profession. By assisting his client to enforce existing rights or to unearth new ones, the advocate, through his role in the litigation process, is presented with the opportunity to play a part in it.

5

Locus Standi of Individuals under Article 230(4): The Return of Euridice?

Takis Tridimas and Sara Poli[1]

I. Introduction

Sir Francis Jacobs has been one of the most influential Advocates General in the history of the Court of Justice. He became a member of the Court in October 1988 and served until October 2005, thus being the second longest-serving Advocate General and one of the longest-serving members of the Court.[2] The function of the Advocate General, which in the eyes of a common lawyer still remains a somewhat esoteric and quaint office, is 'to make, in open court, reasoned submissions' on cases 'acting with complete impartiality and independence'.[3] The opinion of the Advocate General fulfils essentially three functions.[4] It assists the Court to find a solution to the case and thus in preparing the judgment. It sheds light to the factual and legal background to the dispute. It thus complements and assists in explaining the judgment, which is collegiate and much more compact. It also offers an opportunity to analyse and, on occasion, re-evaluate the case law, taking a step back from the facts of the case and assessing the impact of possible solutions to the dispute on the wider matrix of the law. It is no secret that Sir Francis excelled in performing all these functions. In his years at the Court, he became renowned for his intellectual vigour, his persuasive arguments and his efficiency. He was a pioneer procuring by his opinion in *HAG II* the first ever express overruling of 'precedent' by the Court.[5] His opinions touched almost every aspect of European

---

[1] Takis Tridimas is the Sir John Lubbock Professor of Banking Law at Queen Mary College, University of London, and Professor at the Dickinson School of Law, Pennsylvania State University. He is a barrister at Matrix Chambers. Sara Poli is Lecturer in Law at the University of Rome. She has been primarily responsible for writing Sections 3–5 and 7 of this chapter and Takis Tridimas for the remaining sections.

[2] Karl Roemer AG served from 1953–1973. The longest serving Judges have been Andreas Donner (1958–79) and Pierre Pescatore (1967–85) who served for 21 and 18 years respectively.

[3] Art 222(2) EC.

[4] For more details, see T Tridimas, 'The influence of the Advocate General in the development of Community law: some reflections' (1997) 34 CMLRev 1349.

[5] Case C-10/89 *CNL-Sucal v HAG GF* [1990] ECR I-3711.

Community law. He was particularly present in some areas, such as free movement of goods and services, external relations, social security and taxation. In the field of human rights, especially, he often represented the Court's 'embodied conscience'[6] as his opinions in *Konstantinidis* and *Schmidberger* testify.[7]

This chapter focuses on his contribution on *locus standi* of individuals under Article 230(4), a particularly troubled area of Community law. Article 230(4) EC is one of the few provisions of the Treaty where, save with few exceptions, the case law has remained virtually unevolved. The ECJ has shown an uncharacteristic reluctance to broaden the *locus standi* of individuals, elevating the *Plaumann* formula[8] to an effective litigation filter. In determining *locus standi*, the ECJ is not preoccupied with injury-based considerations but follows an 'alternative forum' approach. This approach views national courts as the appropriate forum for challenges by individuals against the validity of Community acts of general application, irrespective of whether they are truly legislative or regulatory, and promotes a decentralized system of justice.

The 'closed category' test adopted in *Plaumann*[9] appears to be counter-intuitive and has been criticized as not corresponding to economic reality. A firm is denied *locus* where it is a member of a potentially open category which effectively limits standing to cases where some kind of a retroactive element is present.[10] It does not seem persuasive to deny *locus standi* to a person who is adversely affected by a measure on the ground that other persons may also be affected in the future.[11]

The contribution of Jacobs AG in this area of law can be traced primarily by reference to his opinions in *Extramet*,[12] *UPA*,[13] and, more recently, *ARE*.[14] This article focuses on his opinion in *UPA* and the resulting trialogue among Jacobs AG, the CFI and the ECJ as it unravelled in *UPA* and subsequent case law. There is no intention to be exhaustive and the examination of the case law is highly selective.

II. The Pre-*UPA* Case Law: Some Key Judgments

Before embarking on an examination of *UPA*, it may be interesting to recall briefly some key judgments delivered in earlier years. At an early stage, a consistent line

---

[6] This term was coined by C Hamson, *Executive Discretion and Judicial Control* (1954) 80.
[7] Case C-168/91 *Konstantinidis* [1993] ECR I-1191; Case C-112/00 *Schmidberger* [2003] ECR I-5659.
[8] Case 25/62 *Plaumann* [1963] ECR 95.
[9] In *Plaumann*, the ECJ held that persons other than those to whom a decision is addressed may only claim to be individually concerned if that decision affects them by reason of certain attributes peculiar to them or by reason of circumstances in which they are differentiated from all other persons and by virtue of these factors distinguishes them individually just as in the case of the person addressed.
[10] See Craig and De Burca, *EU Law, Text, Cases, and Materials* 462–3.
[11] ibid.
[12] Case C-358/89 *Extramet Industrie v Council* [1991] ECR I-2501.
[13] Case C-50/00 P *Unión de Pequeños Agricultores v Council* [2002] ECR I-6677.
[14] Case C-78/03 P *Commission v Germany* (*ARE case*), judgment of 13 December 2005.

of cases established that, as a general rule, an individual may only contest the validity of an act which is in substance a decision. Regulations are normative acts and as such were perceived to be, in principle, beyond the reach of individuals. The rationale of this approach was explained in *Koninklijke Scholten Honig*.[15] The Court stated that the objective of Article 173(2) (now Article 230(4)) is to prevent the Community institutions from being in a position, merely by choosing the form of a regulation, to exclude an application by individuals against a decision which concerns them directly and individually. It became, therefore, important to distinguish between normative acts and decisions although the distinction is by no means easy to draw and resulted in some complex case law.[16]

Although some allowances were made in the field of state aid, competition law and anti-dumping in view of the special features of these sectors, the interpretation of individual concern remained narrow and, save in the field of anti-dumping, the applicant had to establish in addition to direct and individual concern that the contested measure was in substance a decision.

The first case where the Court showed willingness to depart from its traditional strict approach was *Extramet*.[17] The Council had imposed anti-dumping duties on imports of calcium metal originating from China and the Soviet Union. The applicant was an independent Community importer whose prices were not taken into account for the determination of the export price and therefore, according to the case law as it stood, did not have *locus standi* to challenge the imposition of anti-dumping duty. The Court, however, led by Jacobs AG, held that, in the circumstances of the case, the applicant was able to establish individual concern. It was the largest Community importer. Its business activities depended on imports from China and the Soviet Union and were seriously affected by the contested regulation. There were effectively no alternative sources of supply as there was a limited number of manufacturers of the product concerned and the sole Community producer was a competitor of the applicant.[18] Although the result reached by the Court in *Extramet* was correct, its reasoning was limited to the facts. It focused on the prejudice which the regulation caused to the applicant in the circumstances and did not make any general pronouncements regarding *locus standi* in anti-dumping cases, despite being invited to do so by the Advocate General.

The Court went one step further in *Codorniu v Council*.[19] In 1989 the Council adopted a regulation by which it reserved the term '*crémant*' to certain quality sparkling wines produced in France and Luxembourg. The applicant was a

---

[15] Case 101/76 *Koninklijke Scholten Honig* [1979] ECR 797, para 6.
[16] See e.g. Joined Cases 789 and 790/79 *Calpak v Commission* [1980] ECR 1949; Case 138/79 *Roquette Frères v Council* [1980] ECR 3333; Joined Cases 41–44/70 *Fruit Company v Commission* [1971] ECR 411; Case 26/86 *Deutz and Gerldermann* [1987] ECR 941.
[17] Case C-358/89 *Extramet Industrie v Council* [1991] ECR I-2501.
[18] n 17 above, para 17.
[19] Case C-309/89 [1994] ECR I-1853.

Spanish company which had registered in Spain the graphic trademark AGran Cremant de Codorniu in 1924. It alleged that the regulation was discriminatory and deprived it of the right to use the terms it traditionally used for the description of its products. The Court accepted that the regulation was, by virtue of its abstract and general application, of a legislative nature. That, however, did not prevent it from being of individual concern to some traders. The applicant was able to establish individual concern because the contested regulation, by reserving the term *'crémant'* to French and Luxembourg producers, prevented it from using its graphic trademark.[20]

Codorniu is the first case outside the limited field of anti-dumping where the Court expressly acknowledged that an individual may challenge directly a true legislative measure. It may be taken as evidence that, where an applicant has a very strong case on the merits, the Court may be prepared to grant him *locus standi* to challenge a legislative measure despite the restrictive requirements of Article 230(4).[21] It may thus be viewed as a triumph of substance over form but, nonetheless, has remained very much the exception. It did not detract from the application of the *Plaumann* formula and the narrow interpretation of individual concern.

In *Campo Ebro*,[22] the Council adopted a regulation reducing sugar prices in Spain so as to align them with those in the rest of the Community. The applicants, who were producers of isoglucose, argued that the regulation discriminated against them because it did not grant them temporary aid to mitigate the reduction in prices whereas it granted such aid to sugar producers. The CFI held that, even if the applicants were the only producers of isoglucose in Spain, they were only affected in their objective capacity as isoglucose producers in the same way as any other trader in the sugar sector.[23] They were not, therefore, members of a closed class.

Similarly, in *Buralux*,[24] the appellants were undertakings carrying out the collection, shipment and dumping of household waste from Germany to France. They sought annulment of Article 4(3)(i)(a) in Council Regulation No 253/93, which authorized Member States to restrict the shipment of waste. The Court held that that provision concerned the appellants only in their capacity as economic operators in the business of waste transfer between Member States in the same manner as any other operator in that business. The fact that they were practically the only operators who transported waste from Germany to France was not sufficient to differentiate them nor was the fact that they had entered into long-term contracts with German public agencies for the shipment of waste

---

[20] n 19 above, paras 19–21.
[21] After declaring the application admissible, the Court proceeded to annul the regulation for breach of the principle of equal treatment. The regulation can be seen as a blatant disregard of acquired rights, indeed, as verging on expropriation; see T Tridimas, *The General Principles of EC Law* 58.
[22] Case T-472/93 *Campo Ebro v Council* [1995] ECR II-421.
[23] n 22 above, para 33.
[24] Case C-209/94 P *Buralux v Council* [1996] ECR I-615, paras 31–4.

before the regulation was issued. In response to the argument that such a restrictive approach to *locus standi* denies effective protection, the Court pointed out that the appellants could challenge before national courts the refusal of national authorities to ship waste based on the regulation and, in support of such challenge, claim that Article 4(3)(i)(a) was unlawful, thus obliging the national court to make a preliminary reference.

In *Campo Ebro* and *Buralux,* the Community courts applied the traditional approach according to which the possibility of determining more or less precisely the number or even the identity of the persons to whom a measure applies does not in any way imply that it must be regarded as being of individual concern to them, as long as it is established that such application takes effect by virtue of an objective legal or factual situation defined by the measure in question in relation to its purpose. For such persons to be capable of being regarded as individually concerned, their legal position must be affected because of a factual situation which differentiates them from all other persons and distinguishes them individually in the same way as a person to whom a measure is addressed.[25]

This test is detached from economic reality. It may lead to the refusal of *locus standi* even in cases where the applicant is the only person of a potentially open class at the time the contested measure is adopted and there is economically no realistic prospect that other undertakings will become part of the same group.[26]

III. The *UPA* Opinion

In his opinion in *Unión de Pequeños Agricultores v Council* (*UPA case*),[27] Jacobs AG criticized the restrictive interpretation of Article 230(4) and proposed an alternative definition of individual concern. The facts of the case, as such, are unremarkable. A Spanish trade association sought the annulment of a Council agricultural regulation. At first instance, the CFI rejected the action as inadmissible following the established case law.[28] On appeal, the applicant relied essentially on the right to judicial protection and Jacobs AG took the opportunity to revisit the case law. It is worth examining in some detail the arguments put forward in his opinion.

The Advocate General criticized the view, enshrined in traditional case law, that the preliminary reference procedure provided an effective alternative means of judicial review.[29] Preliminary references suffer from the disadvantages of

---

[25] See e.g. Case C-264/91 *Abertal and Others v Council* [1993] ECR I-3265, para 16; Case C-131/92 *Arnaud and Others v Council* [1993] ECR I-2573, para 13; Case 26/86 *Deutz und Geldermann v Council* [1987] ECR 941, para 9.

[26] That was argued to be the case in *Campo Ebro* (n 22 above), see paras 10, 25 and 33 of the judgment.

[27] Case C-50/00 P *Unión de Pequeños Agricultores v Council* [2002] ECR I-6677.

[28] Case T-173/98 *Unión de Pequeños Agricultores v Council* [1999] ECR II-3357.

[29] n 27 above, 6693 et seq.

extra costs and delay. They are contingent since they are for the national court to decide and access to the ECJ is not granted to an applicant as a matter of right. Furthermore, they make it impossible for individuals to challenge Community measures which do not require any implementing measures. Direct actions, by contrast, have procedural advantages since they entail a full exchange of pleadings and allow for the intervention of interested third parties. They also increase legal certainty since challenges must be brought within the short time limit of two months from the adoption of the contested measure.

The Advocate General then concentrated on how the annulment action could become more accessible to private applicants. One option might be to grant individuals standing to challenge a regulation where an examination of the particular case revealed that they would otherwise be denied effective judicial protection at national level. The applicant in *UPA* favoured this solution and some support for it could be drawn from previous case law, including the judgment in *Greenpeace*.[30] Jacobs AG, however, found this solution unsatisfactory for three reasons. First, Article 230 EC made no reference to the availability or absence in particular instances of alternative remedies in national courts. Second, Community courts were not competent and ill-equipped to rule on the interpretation of national law. Third, national rules on standing diverged: there were therefore risks that Community citizens, who were affected by a Community regulation in a similar way, might not enjoy the same possibilities to challenge it.

Another option, suggested by the Commission and the Council, was to shift the burden to Member States by requiring them not to apply rules of national law which rendered it difficult or impossible to challenge Community measures in the national courts. The Advocate General highlighted the weaknesses of this suggestion.[31] It would not resolve the problems linked to the preliminary procedure. It would make far-reaching intrusions into the national legal systems in the sensitive areas of remedies and procedure, which are viewed as falling within the national procedural autonomy. Finally, any required changes of national rules would be very difficult to monitor and enforce effectively.

According to the Advocate General, the time was ripe to give the notion of individual concern a wider reading. He proposed a new test according to which

---

[30] See Case C-321/95 P *Greenpeace, Council and Others v Commission* [1998] ECR I-1651, para 33. There, in rejecting the action brought by Greenpeace, the ECJ stated that the appellants did not remain without any effective judicial protection since in the circumstances their rights were 'fully protected by national courts'. This gave the impression that the Court might have rendered the action admissible if Greenpeace had no alternative possibility to pursue a claim in national courts. It is not, however, clear whether this was the Court's intention. The above dictum might have served to highlight that, in the specific circumstances of the case, the contested Commission decision which concerned the financing of a power station affected the applicant's interests only indirectly. See further Case C-300/00 *Federación de Cofradías de Pescadores de Guipúzcoa* P-R [2000] ECR I-8797, para 37, but see also the judgment in *Buralux v Council* (n 24 above), where reference to the preliminary reference procedure as an alternative remedy was made. For subsequent case law, see n 41 below.
[31] *UPA* (n 27 above) 6697–8.

a person was to be regarded as individually concerned 'where, by reason of his particular circumstances, the measure had, or was liable to have, a substantial adverse effect on his interests'.[32] This test does away with the closed category approach of the *Plaumann* case law. The Advocate General celebrated this extension pinpointing the fallacy of the traditional test.

Under *Plaumann*, the greater the number of persons affected by a measure, the less likely that an action under Article 230(4) would succeed. However, the fact that a measure adversely affected a large number of individuals, causing widespread rather than limited harm, provided 'a positive reason for accepting a direct challenge by one or more of those individuals'.[33]

The Advocate General then went on to explain the advantages of the proposed *locus standi* test and deal with possible objections to it. The new test would avoid a *déni de justice* and encourage the use of direct actions. This would have beneficial effects in terms of legal certainty and the uniform application of Community law. The new definition would bring clarity and simplicity to a compounded body of case law and remove a number of anomalies.[34] Finally, it would shift the emphasis of judicial review from questions of admissibility to questions of substance as is the case with actions in damages.

The Advocate General dismissed the argument that the new test was contrary to the wording of Article 230(4). Rather, it was one of the interpretations which the notion of individual concern was capable of carrying. He also found exaggerated the concern that the new test would open the floodgates. An increase in the number of annulment actions was to be expected but it would be manageable. In many cases, applicants would challenge the same act. Moreover, procedural and jurisdictional reforms of the Community judicial architecture would enable the system to cope with the growth of litigation. He further argued that the restrictive *locus standi* of individuals under Article 230(4) was increasingly out of line with the administrative laws of the Member States.

Finally, Jacobs AG drew attention to the evolving case law on the effective protection of Community rights in national courts. That principle was enunciated in 1986, in the case of *Johnston*,[35] and reaffirmed subsequent judgments such as *Factortame*[36] and *Verholen*[37] where it was held that the principle of effective judicial protection may require national courts to review all national legislative

---

[32] *UPA* (n 27 above) 6698, para 60 of the opinion.
[33] n 27 above, 6698, para 59 of the opinion.
[34] The opinion highlighted the following anomalies. First, the restrictive interpretation of the notion of individual concern contrasts with the generous and dynamic interpretation of other aspects of Article 230 adopted by the Court in cases such as Case 22/70 *Commission v Council (ERTA case)* [1971] ECR 263; Case 294/83 *Partie Ecologiste 'Les Verts' v European Parliament* [1986] ECR 1339; Case C-70/88 *Parliament v Council (Chernobyl case)* [1990] ECR I-2041. Second, there are no restrictions on the standing of individuals to bring actions for damages under Articles 235 and 288 EC.
[35] Case C-222/84 *Johnston v Chief Constable of the Royal Ulster Constabulary* [1986] ECR 1651.
[36] Case C-213/89 [1990] ECR I-2433.
[37] Joined Cases C-87/90, C-88/90 and C-89/90 [1991] ECR I-3757.

measures, to grant interim relief, and to grant individuals standing to bring proceedings, even where they would be unable to do so under national law. The Advocate General viewed the restrictive *Plaumann* formula as untenable in the light of the case law on judicial protection.

In its judgment, the ECJ did not heed to the recommendations of the Advocate General and reiterated the traditional case law. But the next act in this drama was to unravel not in the *UPA* litigation but in *Jégo-Quéré* which highlighted much more sharply the injustices of the *Plaumann* formula, and to which we now turn.

IV. The CFI's Test in *Jégo-Quéré v Commission*

In *Jégo-Quéré v Commission*,[38] a French fishing company sought to challenge a Commission Regulation which imposed minimum mesh sizes for fishing nets. The objective of the regulation was to protect the stock of hake. Jégo-Quéré claimed that, whilst it caught only a negligible quantity of hake, the enlargement of the mesh size prescribed by the regulation seriously reduced its catch of whiting which represented the bulk of its activity. It argued that the regulation penalized its business in violation of the principles of proportionality and equality.

The CFI had no difficulty in finding that the regulation was of direct concern to the applicant. It left no discretion to the Member States and no additional measures, either at Community or national level, were needed for its implementation. The crucial obstacle, however, was the condition of individual concern. The CFI found that Jégo-Quéré was not individually concerned within the meaning of the *Plaumann* test. The fact that it was the only operator fishing for whiting in the waters south of Ireland with vessels with a specific length was not sufficient to differentiate it from all operators specialized in fishing for whiting. The CFI then distinguished the case from '*Piraiki-Patraiki*'.[39] It held that the fact that a person was 'involved in some way or other in the procedure leading to the adoption of a Community measure was capable of distinguishing that person individually in relation to the measure in question only if the applicable Community legislation granted him certain procedural guarantees'.[40] Neither the EC Treaty, however, nor any Community measure required the Commission to hear Jégo-Quéré before adopting the regulation. In addition, the Court held that Jégo-Quéré was not in a special position comparable to that of the applicants in *Codorniu* and *Extramet*.

This would have been the end of the inquiry if it were not for another argument raised by Jégo-Quéré. It argued that, if the CFI held the action to be inadmissible, it would face a denial of justice since there were no alternative ways of

---

[38] Case T-177/01 *Jégo-Quéré v Commission* [2002] ECR II-2365.
[39] Case 11/82 *Piraiki-Patraiki v Commission* [1985] ECR 207.
[40] *Jégo-Quéré* (n 30 above), para 40.

challenging the regulation. This argument had been raised before[41] but the CFI had never upheld it on the ground that 'such circumstances, even if they [were] established, [could not] warrant modifying by way of judicial interpretation the system of legal remedies and procedures laid down in the Treaty'.[42] But in *Jégo-Quéré*, given the particular circumstances of the case, it underwent a change of heart, reasoning as follows.

The CFI acknowledged that access to the courts was one of the essential elements of a Community based on the rule of law and that the Treaty established a 'complete system of legal remedies'.[43] It then proceeded to examine whether the right to an effective remedy, based on Articles 6 and 13 of the ECHR and reaffirmed by Article 47 of the EU Charter of Fundamental Rights, could justify a relaxation of the *locus standi* conditions. The CFI first searched for alternative remedies and pointed out that neither the preliminary reference procedure nor an action in damages provided workable solutions. The applicant could not introduce an action under Article 234 since the contested regulation did not need any implementation measures in national law. The only chance for individuals to challenge it before a national court would be to violate its provisions and then contest its validity by way of defence in possible proceedings initiated against them. However, as Jacobs AG had already pointed out in *UPA*, requiring individuals to breach the law in order to gain access to justice fell short of the requirements of effective judicial protection. An action in damages did not offer a better alternative. The rationale of an action under Article 235 EC was to compensate for damages arising from the application of a Community measure and not to remove an illegal act from the Community legal order. Furthermore, the annulment action and the action for damages were based on different criteria of admissibility and substance. The review undertaken by the Court in an action for damages was not as comprehensive as in an annulment action since in the former the Court's scrutiny was limited in identifying a sufficiently serious breach and did not cover all

---

[41] This argument had been invoked, for example, in the following cases before the CFI: Joined Cases T-198/95, T-171/96, T-230/97, T-174/98 and T-225/99 *Comafrica SpA and Dole Fresh Fruit Europe Ltd & Co. v Commission* [2001] II-1975 para 111; Case T-172/98 *Salamander and others v Parliament/Council* case ECR [2000] II-2487, paras 72–3; Case C-321/95 P *Stichting Greenpeace* [1998] ECR I 1651, para 32; Case T-138/98 *Armement Coopératif Artisanal Vendéen* (ACAV) [2000] II-341, para 68; Case T-100/94 *Kapniki A. Michailidis AE* [1998] ECR II-3115, para 72; Cases T-14/97 and T-15/97 *Sofivo v Council* [1998] ECR II-4191, para 40; Case T-122/96 *Federazione Nazionale del Commercio Oleario (Federolio)* [1997] ECR II-1559, para 79. For examples of cases where parties had raised this argument in appeals before the ECJ, see Joined Cases C-300/99 P and C-388/99 P *Area Cova and others v Council* [2001] I-983, para 26; Case 87/95 P *Cassa Nazionale di Previdenza ed Assistenza a favore degli avvocati e dei Procuratori v Council* [1996] ECR I-2003, para 22.

[42] See *Armement Coopératif Artisanal Vendéen* (ACAV) (n 41 above), para 68. Similar wording was used in Case T-212/00 *Nuove Industrie Molisane v Commission* [2002] ECR I-347, para 48; Case T-339/00 *Bactria Industriehygiene-Service Verwaltungs GmbH*, judgment of 29 April 2002, para 54; Case T-172/98 *Salamander* (n 41 above), para 74; Case T-69/96 *Hamburger Hafen- und Lagerhaus Aktiengesellschaft* [2001] ECR II-1037, para 51.

[43] *Jégo-Quéré* (n 30 above), para 41.

the factors which might affect the legality of the measure in question. The CFI concluded that, in the light of Articles 6 and 13 of the ECHR and of Article 47 of the Charter of Fundamental Rights, Articles 234, 235 and 288(2) EC could not be regarded as guaranteeing individuals the right to an effective legal remedy.[44]

The CFI then proceeded to redefine the notion of individual concern to ensure private parties an effective judicial protection. Drawing inspiration from the wording of Article 47 of the Charter of Human Rights, it proposed the following new test of admissibility:

a natural or legal person will be regarded as individually concerned by a Community measure of general application that concerns him directly if the measure in question affects his legal position, in a manner which is both *definite* and *immediate*, by restricting his rights or by imposing obligations on him. The number and position of other persons who are likewise affected by the measure, or who may be so, are of no relevance in that regard.[45]

Applying the new test to the case in issue, the CFI concluded that Jégo-Quéré was individually concerned by the contested regulation since it imposed specific obligations on it concerning the mesh size of nets.

V. A Comparison of the Two Tests

There are obvious similarities between the test proposed by Jacobs AG in *UPA* and the test of the CFI in *Jégo-Quéré*. Both viewed the *Plaumann* formula as running counter to the fundamental right to judicial protection. They both considered the narrow interpretation of individual concern not as being dictated by the letter of the Treaty but as a judicial choice of construction. The broadening of *locus standi* endorses a hierarchy of remedies absent in the ECJ case law. Both the CFI and the Advocate General take the view that a direct annulment action should take precedence over a preliminary reference or an action for damages. This marks a stark contrast with past case law where individuals, wishing to contest the effects of a Community measure, were systematically redirected towards other remedies, mainly an indirect challenge in the national courts via the preliminary ruling[46] or, occasionally, the action in damages.[47] The Community judicature

---

[44] *Jégo-Quéré* (n 30 above), para 47.
[45] *Jégo-Quéré* (n 30 above), para 51, emphasis added.
[46] See e.g. Case T-244/00 *Coillte Teoranta* [2001] ECR II-1275, para 63; Case T-330/94 *Salt Union Ltd v Commission* [1996] ECR II-1475, para 39. There have been instances where the parties took up the suggestion of the Community courts and, after having unsuccessfully challenged a Community act through Article 230(4), they sought a preliminary ruling on the validity of the contested measure but their action was dismissed. See, for example, the reference in Case C-328/00 *Weber* [2002] ECR I-1461, where a party unsuccessfully attempted to challenge the validity of regulation via the preliminary ruling procedure after being denied individual concern by the CFI in Case T-482/93 *Weber v Commission* [1996] ECR II-609.
[47] See Case T-172/98 *Salamander* (n 41 above), para 77.

had pointed out to applicants (not vested with legal standing) the avenue of the preliminary ruling procedure without, however, considering whether that possibility was real or hypothetical.[48]

There are other similarities between the two tests. The number of parties which is affected by a given Community measure is irrelevant to pass the test of individual concern. Further, applicants are no longer required to show that the contested act is in substance a decision in order to challenge it. Although the importance of this requirement had declined since *Codorniu*,[49] the CFI had not been consistent in skipping the legal nature test. As a result, there was still some confusion as to whether or not the proof of the legal nature of an act was a preliminary requirement to claim individual concern.[50]

The two tests, however, are by no means identical. The *Jégo-Quéré* test is not as far-reaching as the test proposed by Jacobs AG in *UPA*. Semantically, the CFI test is drawn in narrower terms. It requires a 'definite and immediate effect' on the 'legal position' of the applicant, whilst Jacobs's test only demands a 'substantial' effect on his legal 'interests' and a potential effect seems to suffice. Further, the reasoning of the CFI suggests that the new test applies only where the contested Community measure requires no implementing measures 'capable of forming the basis of an action before national courts'.[51]

The CFI test is clearly less ambitious: understandably, the Court was preoccupied with the facts of the case and less concerned about articulating a general theory of *locus standi*. It identified an injustice and sought to avoid a *déni de justice* by doing away with the *Plaumann* formula in specific circumstances. The new test seems to be superimposed upon, and not change, the existing exceptions of *Codorniu* and *Extramet*. It preserves the possibility for private parties to attack a regulation where they have 'special rights' (as in *Codorniu*) or they establish the existence of a specific 'set of factors' (as in *Extramet*). Indeed, in considering whether Jégo-Quéré could rely on these cases to gain *locus standi*, the CFI stated that the applicant 'had not produced enough evidence' to that effect. By contrast, Jacobs's test, being broader, extinguishes the need to preserve *Codorniu*.

---

[48] This is effectively what the ECJ did in *Jégo-Quéré* on appeal. For a case where it was argued that it would be impossible to challenge a Community decision before national courts, see Case T-398/94 *Kahn Scheppvaart BV v Commission* [1996] ECR II-447, para 35.

[49] See A Ward, *Judicial Review and the Right of Private Parties in EC Law* (2000) 225.

[50] The expression 'legal nature test' is borrowed from A Albors-Llorens, *Private Parties in European Community Law* (1996). Note that in annulment actions against directives, the Community judicature continued to analyse whether the contested directive was in substance a decision. See, for example, Case C-321/95 *UEAPME v Council* [1998] ECR II-2335, para 63.

[51] *Jégo-Quéré* (n 30 above), para 45. The CFI stated that the *Jégo-Quéré* test applies to measures of general application. It did not consider whether the test is also applicable to individual acts such as decisions. It is submitted, however, that the test applies *a fortiori* in such measures since decisions, just as regulations, are directly applicable and may not require any implementing acts.

It would be interesting to speculate how certain cases that reached the ECJ might have been decided under each test. The test of Jacobs AG in *UPA* appears broad enough to provide *locus standi* to applicants in circumstances similar to those in *Plaumann*, *Buralux* and *Greenpeace*. Would the same be true for the *Jégo-Quéré* test? In our view, it is doubtful whether the applicant would have met the conditions for *locus standi* as defined in *Jégo-Quéré* in *Plaumann*. In that case, the direct annulment action did not appear to be, strictly speaking, the only available remedy to attack the validity of the Commission decision which appeared to require implementing measures by the German authorities. The applicant could therefore have challenged the national measure giving effect to the Commission decision before a national court. It is also uncertain whether the application of the *Jégo-Quéré* test would have been favourable to the applicants in *Buralux* and *Greenpeace* since the possibility of utilizing the preliminary reference procedure by challenging national measures appeared to exist. Also, it might be argued that the contested Community measures in those cases did not affect the legal position of the applicants in a manner which was both definite and immediate.

VI. The ECJ Judgment in *Jégo-Quéré*

On appeal by the Commission, the ECJ reversed the judgment of the CFI and reiterated the strict definition of individual concern. The following points may be made in relation to the judgment. The Court correctly confirmed that an action for annulment under Article 230(4) should not become available if it could be shown that national law does not allow the applicant to bring proceedings to contest the validity of the Community measure at issue. Such an interpretation would require the CFI or the ECJ to examine and interpret national procedural law in each individual case, and exceed their jurisdiction to review the legality of Community measures.[52] The Court felt unable to endorse the liberal interpretation of the CFI on the ground that, if it disregarded the requirement of individual concern, it would set aside a condition which is expressly laid down in the Treaty thus exceeding its jurisdiction. This is, however, a circular argument. As Jacobs AG observed in *UPA*,[53] and indeed the CFI in its judgment under appeal, there is nothing in the Treaty which dictates that the concept of individual concern should be interpreted so restrictively, that is, that the individual must be differentiated from all other persons: what the Court views as an inescapable constraint imposed by the letter of the Treaty is in fact no more than a constraint imposed by its own preferred interpretation of the provision.

[52] See *UPA* (n 27 above), paras 37 and 43.
[53] See para 59 of the opinion.

The Court then proceeded to shift the burden of providing an effective remedy to the national legal systems, following its judgment in *UPA*. It stated that the fact that the Commission's contested regulation applied directly, without intervention by the national authorities, did not mean that a party who was directly concerned by it could only contest its validity if he had first contravened it. It is possible for domestic law to permit an individual directly concerned by a general legislative measure of national law which cannot be directly contested before the courts to seek from the national authorities under that legislation a measure which may itself be contested before the national courts, so that the individual may challenge the legislation indirectly. It is likewise possible that under national law an operator directly concerned by the Commission regulation may seek from the national authorities a measure under that regulation which may be contested before the national court, enabling the operator to challenge the regulation indirectly.[54]

In effect, the Court identifies a gap in the system of judicial protection and requires the national legal systems to fill it, thus preserving the presumed integrity of the letter of the Treaty. It is, however, highly doubtful whether the alternative remedy proposed by the ECJ provides a workable solution. In many legal systems, a firm in the position of Jégo-Quéré would find it in practice very difficult to obtain a national act amenable to challenge given that a regulation of the type in issue would not normally require implementation. The success of any such action would be costly, time-consuming and highly uncertain. The judgment of the ECJ is based on an assumption, i.e. that indirect challenge in national courts provides an effective alternative, which is simply not valid.

The most striking aspect of the judgment is that it is so prescriptive as regards the remedies that should be available in national courts. The Court held that, in accordance with Article 10 EC, it is for the Member States to establish a system of legal remedies and procedures which ensure respect for the right to effective judicial protection and that therefore it is for the Member States to provide a remedy in a Jégo-Quéré situation. Ironically, this obligation finds much less of a basis in the letter of the Treaty than the more liberal interpretation of individual concern proposed by the CFI, or Jacobs AG in *UPA*.

Locus standi of individuals is an area where there has been consistent disagreement between the ECJ and the CFI and a higher than average success rate in appeals against decisions of the CFI.[55] The relationship between the two courts in this area seems to be an uneasy one, with the CFI pressing unsuccessfully for a liberalization of the case law.

---

[54] Para 35.
[55] This can be illustrated by reference to the litigation in Case T-32/98 *Nederlandse Antillen v Commission* [2000] ECR II-201 rvrsd C-142/00 [2003] ECR I-3483; *Jégo-Quéré* (n 30 above); Case T-54/99 *max.mobil Telekommunikation Service GmbH v Commission* [2002] ECR II-313; rvsd by Case C-141/02 P *Commission v T-Mobile Austria GmbH* [2005] ECR I-1283; *ARE* case, below.

It is notable that the EU Constitutional Treaty adopted the solution of the CFI in *Jégo-Quéré*.[56] Why then has the ECJ been so reluctant to accept the liberalization of *locus standi*? The following reasons may be given:[57]

(1) The ECJ and the CFI are already overburdened by a heavy work load. If *locus standi* was liberalized, that would open the floodgates and the judicial system would be unable to cope. This is particularly so in view of the impending enlargement of the Union.

(2) A class of litigants which would benefit particularly from liberalization of standing would be large corporations or associations of undertakings. These would be likely to challenge Community legislative measures which affected adversely their interests even if they had little chances of success on the merits, simply in order to delay the coming into effect of a measure.[58] This would still benefit them financially because it would postpone for a period the regulatory costs of compliance. This further stresses the danger of the proliferation of cases.

(3) Apart from those arguments which are costs-based, there is a majoritarian argument. Community legislative measures tend to have a long period of gestation and be the product of painstaking negotiations conducted by political actors who are directly or indirectly accountable to their electorates. The jurisdiction of the courts to annul such measures at the instigation of individuals should therefore be restricted.

(4) The limited standing of individuals to challenge legislative acts is in conformity with the constitutional traditions of most Member States.

(5) Every system of law has mechanisms which seek to restrict undesirable litigation. Common law systems tend to have more liberal rules of standing but this is counter-weighed by the fact that, traditionally, they exercise less rigorous review on the merits. In this light, a restrictive *locus standi* requirement can be seen as a quid pro quo for maintaining comparatively strict standards of substantive judicial review.

(6) In any event, the system as it currently stands has its own internal economy and works satisfactorily. The right to judicial protection is safeguarded since individuals may challenge the validity of Community acts indirectly before national courts.

These arguments are potent but none of them is without a counter-argument. Suffice it to say here that arguments of costs appear particularly important and

---

[56] See Article III-365(4) of the Constitutional Treaty and, for a discussion, T Tridimas, 'The European Court of Justice and the Draft Constitution: A Supreme Court for the Union?', in T Tridimas and P Nebbia (eds), *EU Law for the 21st Century: Rethinking the New Legal Order* (2004), 113–41.

[57] *EU Law for the 21st Century* (n 56 above), 123–4.

[58] For an example of a challenge before a national court, see Case C-491/01 *The Queen v Secretary of State for Health ex parte British American Tobacco Ltd*, judgment of 10 December 2002.

one assumes that they must have weighed specially in the policy of the ECJ not to liberalize standing for individuals.

VII. Post-*UPA* Developments

Although already in *UPA* the ECJ had rejected the invitation to revise its approach to Article 230(4), applicants continued to invoke the right to an effective remedy as an argument in favour of a more liberal interpretation. Such arguments were presented in direct actions against decisions,[59] regulations[60] and even directives.[61] In an attempt to circumvent the *Plaumann* straitjacket, the CFI was also asked to examine the substance before ruling on admissibility.[62] The CFI, however, reverted to the classic case law and rejected arguments based on the right to an effective remedy on the basis of the reasoning deployed by the ECJ in *UPA*. By way of exception, in two sets of cases, *Pfizer* and *Alpharma*[63] and *Sony*,[64] the application was held to be admissible but only in *Sony* did the party succeed on the merits.

In *Pfizer* and *Alpharma* the CFI ruled in favour of the applicants on the basis of *Codorniu*. It will be noted that the possibility to use *Codorniu* had cautiously been left open by the CFI in *Jégo-Quéré*.[65] Since both cases essentially shared the same legal and factual background, it suffices to refer to *Alpharma*. The applicant challenged a Council Regulation which withdrew authorization to market, among others, an antibiotic of which it was the only manufacturer and the largest supplier.[66] The CFI stated that the fact that, at the time when the contested regulation was adopted, the applicant was the only manufacturer and by far the largest supplier in the EU, was not in itself capable of distinguishing it from all other traders concerned. According to established case law, the fact that it is possible to determine the number or even the identity of the persons to whom a measure applies does not mean that they must be considered to be individually

---

[59] See e.g. Case T-45/02 *DOW AgroSciences BV* [2003] ECR II-1973; Case T-142/03 *Fost Plus* [2005] ECR I-589; Case T-141/03 *Sniace SA* [2005] ECR I-1197; Joint Cases C-346/03 and C-529/03 *Francesco Atzori, Giuseppe Atzeni, Giuseppe Ignazio Boi* [2003] ECR II-6037.

[60] See Case T-231/02 *Gonnelli* [2004] ECR II-1051; Case T-391/02 *Bundesverband der Nahrungsmittel* [2004] ECR II-1447.

[61] Case T-167/02 *Établissements Toulorge* [2003] ECR II-1111; Case T-154/02 *Villiger* [2003] ECR II-1921; Case T-321/02 *Paul Vannieuwenhuyze-Morin* [2003] ECR II-1997; Case T-213/02 *SNF SA v Commission* [2004] ECR II-3047; Case T-196/03 *European Federation for Cosmetic Ingredients* [2004] ECR II-4263.

[62] T-142/03, *Fost Plus VZW* (see n 59 above).

[63] Case T-13/99 *Pfizer Animal Health v Council* ECR [2002] II-3305, Case T-70/99 *Alpharma v Council* [2002] ECR II-3495.

[64] Case T-243/01 *Sony Computer Entertainment Ltd v Commission* [2003] ECR II-4189.

[65] See n 30 above.

[66] Regulation 2821/98 amending, as regards withdrawal of the authorization of certain antibiotics, Directive 70/524/EEC concerning additives in feedingstuffs (OJ [1998] L 351/4).

concerned as long as the measure applies by virtue of an objective legal or factual situation defined by it. It found, however, the applicant to be individually concerned because, as the firm first responsible for putting the product into circulation, under the Community rules applicable, it was the only person in a legal position enabling it to obtain authorization to market it. It enjoyed, therefore, legal safeguards which granted a specific right comparable to the applicant in *Codorniu*. Furthermore, the effect of the contested regulation was to suspend a procedure which had already been initiated by the applicant for the purpose of obtaining authorization for the antibiotic in question and in the course of which it enjoyed procedural rights. It thus affected the applicant by reason of a legal and factual situation which differentiated it from all other persons.[67]

Alpharma and *Pfizer* do not provide much of an extension to the *Codorniu* exception and reiterate, rather than question, the narrow reading of individual concern. Their distinct feature which enabled the applicants to be successful was that, under the applicable regime, the authorization of a product was linked to the person responsible for putting it into circulation. By contrast, the CFI rejected the action as inadmissible in *Bactria v Commission*[68] as it found no specific link between the product subject to regulation and the applicant. The legal background to that dispute was defined by Directive 98/8, the purpose of which was to establish Community rules for the authorization and placing on the market of biocidal products. The Directive provided that Member States may authorize a biocidal product only if its active substance is listed in the annexes to the Directive and introduced a procedure for inclusion of an active substance into them. The Directive also envisaged a ten-year programme for the systematic examination of all active substances already on the market on 14 May 2000. As a result, the Commission adopted a regulation which required producers to provide the Commission with information on existing active substances and introduced a notification procedure enabling producers and other interested parties to inform the Commission of their wish to request the inclusion of an existing active substance in the annexes to the Directive.

The applicant produced and marketed the active substance peracetic acid and biological products containing it. It sought the annulment of the regulation on the ground that it provided insufficient protection to commercially sensitive information. The CFI rejected the argument that the regulation applied only to a closed group of operators, namely companies who had placed a biocidal product containing existing active substances on the Community market before 14 May 2000. The regulation was addressed to all those who have an interest in the identification and notification of existing active substances and biological products and not only operators who placed such a product on the market before 14 May 2000. Given that the very argument of the applicant was that the regulation

---

[67] *Alpharma* (n 63 above), paras 87–90 and 96, and *Pfizer* (n 63 above), paras 93–8 and 104.
[68] Case T-339/00 [2002] ECR II-2287.

caused it harm precisely because it enabled companies not participating in the review process to profit without cost from the notifications made by diligent competitors, the narrow reading of individual concern appeared to lead to lack of judicial protection.

In *Sony Computer Entertainment Europe Ltd*,[69] the applicant sought to challenge a customs tariff classification regulation which applied to PlayStation2, a product of which Sony was the sole importer into the Community. Under the established case law, individuals may not normally challenge tariff classification regulations because, despite their apparent specificity, they concern all products of the type described regardless of their individual characteristics and origin, and take effect in relation to all customs authorities in the Community and all importers.[70] The CFI, however, found that there were special circumstances which made Sony individually concerned. As a result of the contested regulation, the UK custom authorities had revoked a Binding Tariff Information (BTI) which had been issued before its adoption and which was favourable to Sony. Also, the administrative procedure which led to the adoption of the contested regulation concerned specifically the tariff classification of the PlayStation2. No other similar product had been discussed before the Nomenclature Committee as part of that procedure. The applicant was, therefore, the only undertaking whose legal position was affected by the adoption of the regulation. Furthermore, a number of considerations showed that, although the contested regulation was worded in a general and abstract manner, it focused specifically on the classification of the PlayStation2: it described in detail all of the features of that product and there were no other products with identical features, at least not at the time the contested regulation entered into force. The description in fact corresponded exactly to the technical specifications of the PlayStation2 and it was so specific that it could not have applied to any other products.

Sony is the first case where an undertaking succeeds in annulling a customs classification regulation in a direct action. It is true that the position of the applicant was exceptional and 'hinged on quite particular circumstances'.[71] Still, the case evinces the willingness of the CFI to depart from established case law and might open up the possibility of Article 230(4) being applied more leniently in the area of custom law, as is the case in the areas of anti-dumping, competition law and state aids. An interesting aspect of the case is that the applicant could challenge the regulation through the plea of illegality: Sony could have attacked the revocation of the BTI by UK customs on the ground that it was based on an invalid Community act. It opted instead for a direct challenge on the ground that it was quicker to do so and because 'success in these proceedings would put it in a better financial position'.[72]

[69] Case T-243/01 *Sony Computer Entertainment Ltd v Commission* [2003] ECR II-4189.
[70] See e.g. Case 40/84 *Casteels v Commission* [1985] ECR 667, para 11.
[71] See Case T-243/01 DEP, *Sony Computer Entertainment Ltd v Commission*, judgment of 18 March 2005, para 25.
[72] Case T-243/01 *Sony Computer* (see n 71 above), para 55.

VIII. State Aid Proceedings

A final case that deserves consideration in this context is *Commission v Germany (ARE case)*.[73] The case is important because it provides a further illustration that the CFI is more liberal than the ECJ in granting standing to individuals and also because Jacobs AG proposed a reassessment of standing in state aid proceedings.

The origins of the case lie in the scheme for the privatization of agricultural land situated in the former East Germany introduced following reunification. Under the German Compensation Act, certain agricultural land held by the state could be acquired by eligible persons for less than half its market value. The Act gave priority to certain categories of persons, such as those who held a farming lease and the successors to the former cooperatives, provided that they fulfilled two conditions, namely that they were resident in the former German Democratic Republic on 3 October 1990 and had, on 1 October 1996, a long-term lease in respect of certain land owned by the state. By decision 1999/268, the Commission found the land acquisition scheme to be unlawful state aid in so far as it was tied to the condition of residence and also in so far as the purchase price exceeded the so-called maximum intensity rate, that is, it was available at a discount greater than 35 per cent below the actual value which was applicable under Community law.[74] Following the adoption of the Commission's decision, Germany produced an amended law which abolished the condition of residence and fixed the intensity rate at 35 per cent. The draft law was notified to the Commission which, without initiating the review procedure provided for in Article 88(2), authorized the amended aid. ARE, a representative association, sought to challenge the Commission's new decision. The CFI found that ARE was individually concerned in two respects.

First, it held that ARE was entitled to bring the action on behalf of those of its members whose competitive position was affected by the aid. Such members were parties concerned within the meaning of Article 88(2) EC and could have therefore challenged the Commission's decision individually. Second, the CFI held that ARE had *locus standi* because its negotiating position was affected by the Commission's decision.

The ECJ (and Jacobs AG) disagreed with the CFI. Recalling its case law, the ECJ drew a distinction between the procedure of Article 88(2) and that of Article 88(3). Where the Commission initiates the formal review procedure of Article 88(2), a competitor may challenge the Commission's decision finding aid compatible with the common market where its market position is substantially affected by the aid.[75]

---

[73] Case C-78/03 P *Commission v Germany (ARE case)*, judgment of 13 December 2005.
[74] See Council Regulation No 950/97 on improving the efficiency of agricultural structures, OJ 1997 L 142/1.
[75] See Case 169/84 *Cofaz and Others v Commission* [1986] ECR 391, Case C-406/96 P *Sveriges Betodlares [Centralförening] and Henrikson v Commission* [1997] ECR I-7531.

Where the Commission finds aid to be compatible with the common market at the end of a preliminary examination under Article 88(3), without initiating the formal procedure provided for in Article 88(2), a further distinction is drawn. A person who has the status of a 'party concerned' under Article 88(2) may challenge the Commission's decision in order to enforce the procedural rights available to him under Article 88(2). This includes persons, undertakings or associations whose interests might be affected by the grant of the aid, in particular competing undertakings and trade associations. There is, however, no need to show that the market position of the applicant has been affected in a substantial manner.[76]

Where, by contrast, the applicant does not merely seek to enforce the procedural rights of Article 88(2) but calls into question the merits of the decision appraising the aid, the mere fact that it may be regarded as concerned within the meaning of Article 88(2) cannot suffice to render the action admissible. It must then demonstrate that it has a particular status within the meaning of the *Plaumann* case law. That applies in particular where the applicant's market position is substantially affected by the aid to which the decision at issue relates.[77]

In the case in issue, the ECJ held that ARE was seeking to challenge the Commission's decision on substantive grounds but lacked individual concern since it had not been proved that the competitive position of its members was substantially affected by the aid scheme. The CFI had wrongly taken the view that the application of ARE should be construed as criticizing the Commission for failing to initiate the formal review procedure rather than the merits of the decision. The ECJ also rejected the view that ARE was individually concerned because it had participated actively in the formal review procedure leading to the adoption and implementation of the initial Commission decision. Its role was much less significant than that of the applicants in *Van der Kooy* and *CIRFS* where the ECJ had recognized standing to the applicant association.[78]

In his opinion, Jacobs AG criticized the case law on *locus standi* in state aid cases as being complex, unsatisfactory, and inconsistent.[79] In contrast to his opinion on *UPA*, Jacobs AG called here for narrowing rather than extending standing. His main points of criticism were as follows. The *Cook* and *Matra* line of case law[80] provided liberal standing to competitors in cases where the Commission decides not to initiate the Article 88(2) procedure to compensate for the fact that the applicant may not have sufficient information to establish individual concern. This, however, conferred standing to a very wide category of persons since many could claim that they would have been parties concerned if the Article 88(2) procedure had been

---

[76] Case C-198/91 *Cook v Commission* [1993] ECR I-2487; Case C-225/91 *Matra v Commission* [1993] ECR I-3203; Case C-367/95 P *Commission v Sytraval and Brink's France* [1998] ECR I-1719.

[77] See *ARE* (n 73 above), para 37 and also *Cofaz and Others v Commission* (n 75 above), paras 22–5; *Sveriges* (n 75 above), para 45.

[78] Joined Cases 67/85, 68/85 and 70/85 *Van der Kooy and Others v Commission* [1988] ECR 219; Case C-313/90 *CIRFS and Others v Commission* [1993] ECR I-1125.

[79] See paras 138–142 of the opinion.

[80] See n 76 above.

initiated. This led in turn to subsequent refinements that made the case law confusing and incoherent. Furthermore, Jacobs AG was not convinced that the more lenient interpretation of *locus standi* in the context of Article 88(3) was justified. He accepted that, because a decision under Article 88(3) is taken at an early stage, a person potentially affected by the proposed aid might have little information about its likely effect and therefore find it difficult to establish individual concern. He considered, however, that in the course of the proceedings before the CFI sufficient information would be produced by the Commission and possibly by the Member States concerned to enable the Court to decide on the existence of individual concern. In the view of the Advocate General, the best solution would be to apply in all cases where an applicant challenges a decision under Article 88(3) the test of direct and individual concern irrespective of the grounds on which the action is brought. The test of individual concern, however, should not be interpreted as narrowly as it was in *Plaumann* but in accordance with the broader approach taken in relation to competition and anti-dumping proceedings.[81]

IX. Conclusion

The opinion of Jacobs AG in *UPA* and the judgment of the CFI in *Jégo-Quéré* generated the hope that the ECJ would reconsider the much-criticized narrow construction of individual concern. But the ECJ reiterated *Plaumann*, signalling the 'return of Euridice'. Both the CFI and Advocate General Jacobs offered progressive interpretations of individual concern facilitating access to justice for private applicants. Post-*UPA* case law has developed within the constraints of *Codorniu* but this remains an area where the CFI and the ECJ frequently disagree, with the former favouring a less strict adherence to *Plaumann*. Although there are powerful arguments, mainly based on cost considerations, which would favour limiting the standing of individuals to challenge truly legislative acts, the current over-restrictive interpretation of Article 230(4) poses an obstacle to the right to judicial protection and is liable to cause injustice. The Constitutional Treaty extended somewhat *locus standi*, and it is a pity that in its judgment in *Jégo-Quéré* the ECJ declined the opportunity to anticipate it. The Court shows no appetite for a quantum leap so it seems that, at least in this area, and unlike the wider field of fundamental rights, the legacy of Advocate General Jacobs will remain that of a dissident.

---

[81] This line of reasoning, however, is not thoroughly persuasive. It is submitted that the protection of the rights of the applicant should not be left to the information that the Commission, being the opposite party in the litigation, might be required to produce in the proceedings. In any event, the ensuing argumentation as to whether the applicant is able to prove *locus standi* will be time-consuming and may lead to further nuances, and inconsistencies in the case law. Whilst acknowledging the need for simplicity, the present authors take the view that standing in state aid cases should be liberal rather than strict.

6

The EFTA Court, the ECJ, and the Latter's Advocates General – a Tale of Judicial Dialogue

Carl Baudenbacher

I. The EEA Agreement and the EFTA Court

The European Economic Area Agreement which was signed on 2 May 1992 and entered into force on 1 January 1994 aims at extending the internal market established within the EC to the EFTA States. The Agreement is based on a two-pillar approach with an EC and an EFTA pillar. The EFTA Surveillance Authority (ESA) monitors the fulfilment of the obligations of the EFTA States as well as the compliance of private actors with the competition rules. In that respect, the ESA functions as the counterpart of the Commission. The EFTA Court has been modelled on the template of the ECJ. When the EEA Agreement came into force, the Court consisted of five Judges from Austria, Finland, Iceland, Norway and Sweden. Since the accession of Austria, Finland and Sweden to the EC and of Liechtenstein to the EEA (that is, since mid-1995), it has been composed of three Judges nominated by Iceland, Liechtenstein and Norway. In addition, there are six ad hoc Judges. The EFTA Court's seat was originally Geneva, but on 1 September 1996 the seat was moved to Luxembourg. The case load of the EFTA Court is limited in terms of number of cases.[1] There are three main reasons for that: (1) The remaining three EEA/EFTA States are small states. Altogether they have five million inhabitants. (2) The national courts in EEA/EFTA States will hardly refer questions to the EFTA Court which have been answered by the ECJ in a Community or EEA law context. Moreover, courts of last resort are not obliged to refer, and it is possible that Nordic Judges tend to think that they have to preserve their sovereignty. (3) The EFTA Surveillance Authority has been reluctant to bring actions for alleged infringement of the EEA Agreement against EFTA States. If a legal question has been decided by the ECJ, the Authority will

---

[1] The most important judgments of the EFTA Court are summarized in C Baudenbacher, *EFTA Court – Legal Framework and Case Law* (2nd ed, 2006), which can be downloaded from the Court's website, *www.eftacourt.lu/default.asp?layout=article&id=348*.

in all probability first examine if it should try to persuade the EFTA States to comply with it.

II. The Homogeneity Goal in Particular

EEA law and EC law are two separate legal orders, but since EEA law originates from EC law,[2] they are largely identical in substance. With the establishment of the EFTA Court, a potential competition situation has been created that could, as a matter of principle, lead to forum shopping and a race to the bottom (or to the top). In order to avoid that and to secure a level playing field for individuals and economic operators, the fathers and mothers of the EEA Agreement have formulated special rules that should guarantee a homogeneous development of the case law in both EEA pillars. According to Article 6 EEA, the EFTA Court is supposed to interpret provisions of the EEA Agreement that are identical in substance to corresponding rules of the EC Treaty, in conformity with the relevant rulings of the ECJ given prior to the date of signature of the EEA Agreement (2 May 1992). Under Article 3(2) of the Agreement between the EFTA States on the establishment of a Surveillance Authority and a Court of Justice (SCA), the EFTA Court is required to take due account of relevant ECJ rulings rendered after that date. Five observations must be made in that respect: (1) The EFTA Court's case law is largely based on the ECJ's jurisprudence. The EFTA Court has, however, taken the liberty to go its own way in a number of cases without putting itself outside of the basic structures of ECJ case law.[3] (2) The homogeneity rules in question are, according to EFTA Court and ECJ case law, also relevant to rulings of the ECJ concerning the EEA Agreement.[4] (3) The EFTA Court has ruled that the term 'Court of Justice of the European Communities' in Article 6 EEA and in Articles 3(1) and 3(2) SCA includes the Court of First Instance of the European Communities.[5] (4) The distinction between old and new case law is politically significant, but has not been that important in reality. (5) The ECJ is under no written obligation to take account of the EFTA Court's jurisprudence. But the Community Courts and Advocates General of the ECJ have entered into a judicial dialogue with the EFTA Court whose features are the subject of the following sections.

---

[2] See Articles 97 ff. EEA.
[3] See C Timmermans, 'Creative Homogeneity', *Festschrift for Sven Norberg* (2006) 471 ff.
[4] See e.g. Cases C-452/01 *Ospelt and Schlössle Weissenberg* [2003] ECR I-9743; C-286/02, *Bellio F.lli Srl v Prefettura di Treviso* [2004] ECR, I-3465; E-1/04 *Fokus Bank ASA v Norwegian State* [2004] EFTA Court Report, 11.
[5] See Cases E-2/94 *Scottish Salmon Growers Association Limited v EFTA Surveillance Authority* [1994–5] EFTA Court Report, 59, para 13; E-2/02 *Technologien Bau- und Wirtschaftsberatung GmbH and Bellona Foundation v EFTA Surveillance Authority* [2003] EFTA Court Report, 52, para 40.

III. Dialogue with the Community Judiciary

A. Referring to EFTA Court Case Law as a Main or Leading Argument

(i) Courts

In a number of cases, the ECJ has referred to EFTA Court case law as a main or even a leading argument. In Joined Cases E-8/94 and E-9/94 *Mattel Scandinavia and Lego Norge*, the EFTA Court held in a judgment of 16 June 1995 that Articles 2(2) and 16 of the Television Directive 89/552/EEC must be interpreted as preventing an EEA State from applying a national general ban on television advertising specifically aimed at children if the advertisements are part of a television programme which is received from another EEA State. The EFTA Court added, however, that measures could still be taken by the receiving State under Directive 84/450/EEC concerning misleading advertising.[6] In its judgment of 9 July 1997 in Joined Cases C-34/95, 35/95, 36/95 *De Agostini and TV-shop i Sverige*, the ECJ fully endorsed the line previously taken by the EFTA Court. It reasoned that 'the Directive is to be interpreted as precluding the application to television broadcasts from other Member States of a provision of a domestic broadcasting law which provides that advertisements broadcast in commercial breaks on television must not be designed to attract the attention of children under 12 years of age'.[7] The ECJ noted, however, that Directive 84/450/EEC concerning misleading advertising 'could be robbed of its substance in the field of television advertising if the receiving Member State were deprived of all possibility of adopting measures against an advertiser and that this would be in contradiction with the express intention of the Community legislature' and referred to the EFTA Court's *Mattel Scandinavia/Lego Norge* judgment.[8]

In the mid-1990s, the EFTA Court and the ECJ were called upon by national courts to decide whether the succession of contracts – that is, the termination of a contract with an independent service provider followed by the conclusion of a new contract with a more competitive service provider – constituted a transfer of an undertaking within the meaning of the relevant Directive.[9] The EFTA Court held in a judgment of 19 December 1996 in Case E-2/96 *Ulstein and Røiseng*

---

[6] EFTA Court Report [1994–5] 113.
[7] Joined Cases C-34/95, *Konsumentombudsmannen v De Agostini (Svenska) Förlag AB* and C-35/95 and C-36/95 *Konsumentombudsmannen v TV-shop i Sverige AB* [1997] ECR I-3843, para 62 and operative part. These cases had originally been referred to the EFTA Court by the Swedish Market Court (Cases E-4/94 *Konsumentombudsmannen v De Agostini (Svenska) Förlag AB* EFTA Court Report [1994–95] 89, and E-5/94 *Konsumentombudsmannen v TV-shop i Sverige AB* EFTA Court Report [1994–95] 93). After Sweden's accession to the EU, that court withdrew the request for a preliminary ruling and, on 7 March 1995, referred it to the ECJ.
[8] ibid, para 37.
[9] See with regard to the state of the case law at the time C Baudenbacher, 'Auftragsnachfolge und Betriebsübergang im europäischen Recht' (1996) 49 Der Betrieb, 2177.

that a mere succession of two contracts for the provision of the same or similar services (*in casu* ambulance services for a hospital) will not, as a rule, be sufficient for there to be a transfer of an undertaking, business or part of a business within the meaning of the Transfer of Undertakings Directive.[10] Advocate General La Pergola had in his opinion of 15 October 1996 in Case C-13/95 *Süzen* proposed that the termination of a cleaning contract with an undertaking and the subsequent award of that contract to another undertaking should not, in the absence of other factors which may lead to a different classification, fall within the scope of the Directive.[11] The EFTA Court was aware of that opinion, but did not quote it. In its C-13/95 *Süzen* judgment of 11 March 1997,[12] the plenum of the ECJ did not qualify the replacement of a service provider as falling within the scope of the Transfer of Undertakings Directive. The EC Court noted that the decisive criterion for establishing the existence of a transfer within the meaning of the directive is whether the entity in question retains its identity, as indicated, *inter alia*, by the fact that its operation is actually continued or resumed and referred on that point to its longstanding case law and to paragraph 27 of the EFTA Court's *Ulstein* ruling.[13] In that paragraph, the EFTA Court had, in fact, made the said statement, but what is more important, it had concluded that a mere succession of contracts does not, as a rule, suffice for there to be a transfer of undertaking. One will have to assume that the citation in the ECJ's judgment was meant to relate to that finding, not least because it was the first time the ECJ had to deal with the issue. The EFTA Court confirmed its jurisprudence on 14 March 1997 in the judgment in Case E-3/96 *Ask v ABB and Aker*[14] and made three rather general references to the ECJ's *Süzen* ruling which had been rendered three days earlier.

In Cases E-2/95 *Eidesund*, E-2/96 *Ulstein and Røiseng* and E-3/96 *Ask v ABB and Aker*,[15] the EFTA Court held that the Transfer of Undertakings Directive was applicable where in the event of succession of contracts the new contract was awarded after a public tender had taken place. The ECJ (Sixth Chamber) followed this finding in its judgment of 25 January in Case C-172/00 *Oy Liikenne* and, referring to the EFTA Court's rulings in Cases E-2/95 *Eidesund* and E-3/96 *Ask and Others v ABB and Aker*,[16] held that the circumstance that a transaction comes under Directive 92/50 does not of itself rule out the application of Directive 77/187.

[10] Case E-2/96, EFTA Court Report [1995–96] 65, para 27.
[11] [1997] ECR I-1259.
[12] Case C-13/95 [1997] ECR I-1259.
[13] [1997] ECR I-1259, para 10.
[14] Case E-3/96, EFTA Court Report [1997] 1.
[15] Cases E-2/95 *Eilert Eidesund v Stavanger Catering A/S*, EFTA Court Report [1995–6] 1; E-2/96 *Jørn Ulstein and Peter Røiseng v Asbjørn Møller*, EFTA Court Report [1995–6] 65; E-3/96 *Tor Angeir Ask and Others v ABB Offshore Technology AS and Aker Offshore Partner AS*, EFTA Court Report [1997] 1.
[16] [2001] ECR, I-745, para 21: references to Cases E-2/95 *Eidesund*, para 50, and E-3/96 *Ask and Others v ABB and Aker*, para 33. Advocate General Léger had not mentioned the EFTA Court's judgments.

In Case E-3/00 *EFTA Surveillance Authority v Norway*, the so-called *Kellogg's* judgment,[17] the EFTA Court rejected the argument of the Norwegian government that in order to justify a marketing ban on cornflakes fortified with vitamins and iron which had been lawfully manufactured and marketed in other EEA States, it was sufficient to show the absence of a nutritional need for the fortification in the Norwegian population. At the same time, the EFTA Court found that in examining whether the marketing of fortified cornflakes with vitamins and minerals may be banned on grounds of the protection of human health, a national government may, in the absence of harmonization, invoke the precautionary principle. According to that principle, it is sufficient for a government to show that there is relevant scientific uncertainty with regard to the risk in question. The EFTA Court held that measures taken must be based on scientific evidence; they must be proportionate, non-discriminatory, transparent, and consistent with similar measures already taken. The potentially-negative health consequences had to be identified, and the risk to health had to be comprehensively evaluated on the basis of the most recent scientific information. The Norwegian fortification policy did not fulfil these requirements and was therefore held to be contrary to Article 11 EEA. No sufficient risk assessment had taken place, and the policy was incoherent because of the longstanding fortification of certain products initiated by the Government. That judgment had considerable influence on the case law of the ECJ and of the CFI. In Case C-192/01 *Commission v Denmark*,[18] the facts were similar to those of the *Kellogg's* case before the EFTA Court. In its judgment of 23 September 2003, the plenum of the ECJ rejected the position of the Danish government which had submitted that it was sufficient to show the absence of a nutritional need in order to justify a general prohibition on foodstuffs enriched with vitamins or minerals.[19] At the same time, the ECJ recognized the precautionary principle and formulated essentially the same conditions for its application as the EFTA Court had done in *Kellogg's*. The EC Court made reference to the latter's findings with regard to the fact that (1) a prohibition on the marketing of foodstuffs fortified with nutrients must be based on a detailed assessment of the risk alleged by the Member State; (2) the risk assessment cannot be based on purely hypothetical considerations; (3) it could be appropriate to take into consideration the cumulative effect of the presence on the market of several sources, natural or artificial, of a particular nutrient and of the possible existence in the future of additional sources which can reasonably be foreseen; (4) a proper application of the precautionary principle presupposes, first, the identification of the potentially negative consequences for health of the proposed fortification, and second, a comprehensive assessment of the risk based on the most reliable scientific data available and the most recent results of international

---

[17] EFTA Court Report [2001–2] 73.
[18] [2003] ECR I-9693.
[19] Paras 54 and 25.

research; (5) where the existence or extent of the alleged risk cannot be determined with certainty, but the likelihood of real harm to public health persists should the risk materialize, the precautionary principle justifies the adoption of restrictive measures; (6) such measures must not be allowed unless they are non-discriminatory and objective.[20] The Third Chamber of the ECJ also relied on the decision of the EFTA Court in *Kellogg's* in its 2004 judgment in Case C-41/02 *Commission v Netherlands* when it held that after having authorized the marketing of a foodstuff fortified with a given nutrient, the national authorities 'remain free to refuse a subsequent application for marketing authorization on the basis of the situation brought about by the first authorization'.[21] In September 2002, the CFI in the two cases T-13/99 *Pfizer Animal Health* and T-70/99 *Alpharma*, which involved the fortification of animal food with antibiotics, acknowledged the precautionary principle as being part of Community law.[22] The CFI considered that the existence of such a principle has in essence and at the very least implicitly been recognized by the ECJ, the CFI and the EFTA Court.[23] The CFI made further reference to the EFTA Court's *Kellogg's* judgment when emphasizing that preventive measures cannot properly be based on a purely hypothetical approach to the risk, founded on mere conjecture which has not been scientifically verified.[24]

The decision of the EFTA Court in *Kellogg's* also had an impact on the case law of the ECJ outside the field of the marketing of fortified foodstuffs and animal feedstuffs. In September 2003, the plenum of the EC Court in Case C-236/01 *Monsanto Agricoltura Italia* held in a case concerning the release of genetically modified maize[25] that the safeguard clause laid down in Article 12 of the so-called Novel Food Regulation No 258/97 must be understood as giving specific expression to the precautionary principle. Therefore, the conditions for the application of that clause were to be interpreted having due regard to this principle.[26] In that respect, the ECJ referred, *inter alia*, to the EFTA Court's *Kellogg's* judgment when stating that 'protective measures...may not properly be based on a purely hypothetical approach to risk, founded on mere suppositions which are not yet scientifically verified'.[27] In Case C-286/02 *Bellio Fratelli*, a consignment of fish flour imported from Norway had been confiscated after samples taken by the competent Italian authority showed that the fish meal contained fragments of unidentified animal bones.[28] The seizure was based on two decisions of the

---

[20] References to paras 29–32 of the EFTA Court's judgment in paras 47–53 of the ECJ's judgment.
[21] [2004] ECR I-11375, para 62.
[22] Cases T-13/99 *Pfizer Animal Health* [2002] ECR II-3305; T-70/99 *Alpharma* [2002] ECR II-3495.
[23] Cases T-13/99 *Pfizer Animal Health*, para 115; T-70/99 *Alpharma*, para 136.
[24] Cases T-13/99 *Pfizer Animal Health*, para 143; T-70/99 *Alpharma*, para 156.
[25] Reference to Case E-3/00, EFTA Court Report [2000–1] 73, paras 36–8, in Case C-236/01, *Monsanto* [2003] ECR I-8105, para 106.
[26] ibid para 110.
[27] ibid para 106.
[28] Case C-286/02, *Bellio Srl v Fratelli Prefettura di Treviso* [2004] ECR I-3465.

Council and the EC Commission on certain BSE protection measures which had been made part of EEA law. The Third Chamber of the ECJ found that the provisions on which the seizure had been based were compatible with EEA Article 13, the provision mirroring Article 30 EC. With regard to the precautionary principle and the conditions of its application, the ECJ referred to the decision of the EFTA Court in *Kellogg's* with respect to the following considerations: (1) That in the absence of harmonization and to the extent that uncertainties continue to exist in the current state of scientific research, it is for the Contracting Parties to decide on the level of protection of human health they wish to ensure, taking account of the fundamental requirements of EEA law and, in particular, the free movement of goods in the EEA;[29] (2) that a risk-management decision rests with each Contracting Party and that a Contracting Party may invoke the precautionary principle with regard to the risk in question if there is relevant scientific uncertainty with regard to the risk in question, but that the respective discretion must be open to judicial review; (3) that measures taken by a Contracting Party must be based on scientific evidence and must be proportionate, non-discriminatory, transparent, and consistent with similar measures already taken; (4) that even if the need to safeguard public health has been recognized as a primary concern, the principle of proportionality must be respected.[30]

In its judgment of 3 October 2006 in C-452/04 *Fidium Finanz*,[31] a case involving the granting of credit by a company incorporated under Swiss law with its registered office and central administration in Switzerland to residents of a Member State of the EC, the Grand Chamber of the ECJ held that, in principle, both the freedom to provide services within the meaning of Articles 49 ff. and the free movement of capital within the meaning of Articles 56 ff. EC were affected. In deciding which freedom prevailed over the other, the ECJ referred to the EFTA Court's judgment from 14 July 2000 in Case E-1/00 *State Management Debt Agency v Íslandsbanki-FBA*. In that case, the EFTA Court had applied a centre of gravity test and concluded that the '*predominant feature* of the case', which involved a national measure leading to a guarantee for loans from foreign lenders being more expensive than for loans from domestic lenders, constituted movement of capital.[32] The ECJ used the same test, but concluded that 'the *predominant consideration*' of the *Fidium Finanz* case was freedom to provide services.[33]

---

[29] References to Cases E-3/00 *EFTA Surveillance Authority v Norway*, EFTA Court Report [2000–1] 73, para 25; 174/82 *Sandoz* [1983] ECR 2445, para 16; C-192/01 *Commission v Denmark* [2003] ECR I-9693, para 42; C-24/00 *Commission v France* [2004] ECR I-1277, paras 49 and 57.

[30] References to Case E-3/00 *EFTA Surveillance Authority v Norway*, EFTA Court Report [2000–1] 73, paras 25, 26 and 27.

[31] Case C-452/04 *Fidium Finanz AG v Bundesanstalt für Finanzdienstleistungsaufsicht* judgment of 3 October 2006, nyr.

[32] EFTA Court Report [2000–1] 8, para 32, emphasis added.

[33] Para 49, emphasis added.

In Case C-434/04 *Jan-Erik Anders Ahokainen and Mati Leppik*, the ECJ (Third Chamber), when stating that national legislation under which undenatured ethyl alcohol of an alcoholic strength of more than 80 per cent may be imported only by a person who has obtained a licence to do so is in principle contrary to Article 28 EC, made not only reference to its own case law, but also to the EFTA Court's ruling in Case E-1/94 *Restamark*.[34]

In its judgment of 26 April 2007 in Case C-348/04 *Boehringer Ingelheim II*, the ECJ (Second Chamber) held that the condition that repackaging of pharmaceuticals must be necessary to gain market access is directed only at the fact of repackaging and not at the manner and style in which the product has been repackaged. The ECJ made extensive reference to the EFTA Court's considerations in Case E-3/02 *Paranova v Merck*.[35] In that judgment, the EFTA Court held that a parallel importer's strategy of product presentation, including the addition of new design elements on the boxes, could not mechanically be assessed on the basis of the necessity criterion developed by the ECJ with regard to the question whether the parallel importer obtained market access. Instead, a comprehensive balancing of the interests of the trade mark proprietor and the parallel importer must be undertaken.[36]

In Case T-308/00 *Salzgitter AG v Commission*,[37] the question at stake was whether provisions of the German law on the development of the border zone between the former German Democratic Republic and the former Czechoslovak Socialist Republic which provided for tax incentives for undertakings situated along the border area constituted state aid. The CFI held that it did not matter that the selective nature of the measure flowed from a criterion relating to geographic location in a defined part of a Member State's territory. What mattered was that the recipient undertakings belonged to a specific category determined by the application, in law or in fact, of the criterion established by the measure in question. In that respect, the CFI referred to the EFTA Court's judgment in Case E-6/98 *Norway v EFTA Surveillance Authority*[38] where the EFTA Court had dismissed an application brought by Norway for the annulment of a decision of ESA regarding state aid in the form of regionally differentiated social security taxation in that country.

(ii) Advocates General

The EFTA Court works without an Advocate General. That, however, does not mean that Advocates General do not play a role in the EFTA Court's

---

[34] References to Case 1/04, EFTA Court Report [1994–5] 15, paras 49 and 50 in Case C-434/04 *Criminal proceedings against Jan-Erik Anders Ahokainen and Mati Leppik*, judgment of 28 September 2006, nyr, para 20.
[35] Case C-348/04 *Boehringer Ingelheim II*, judgment of 26 April 2007, nyr, para 38 (reference to paras 41–5 in the EFTA Court's judgment).
[36] EFTA Court Report [2003] 101.
[37] Case T-308/00 [2004] ECR II-1933.
[38] Case E-6/98 *Norway v EFTA Surveillance Authority*, EFTA Court Report [1999] 74, para 37.

life. Advocates General will, as a matter of principle, take into account virtually every source of information which will help them to fulfil their task under Article 222(2) EC. EFTA Court case law constitutes such a source. Opinions of Advocates General are therefore an important gateway for EFTA Court case law into the ECJ's jurisprudence. Having said that, one may add that certain Advocates General are particularly open-minded when it comes to dealing with EFTA Court case law. In recent years, the EFTA Court, for its part, has started to reference Advocates' General opinions in certain cases.

In a number of cases, Advocates General have relied on EFTA Court case law as a main or even leading argument. In Joined Cases C-34/95, C-35/95 and C-36/95 *De Agostini/TV-shop i Sverige*, Advocate General Jacobs concluded that transfrontier advertising directed at children falls within the scope of the TV Directive and that by virtue of Article 2(2) of that Directive a receiving state may not restrict transmission on its territory. He noted that the EFTA Court had come to the same conclusion in Joined Cases E-8/94 and E-9/94 *Mattel Scandinavia/Lego Norge*.[39]

In Case C-126/01 *GEMO*, Advocate General Jacobs mentioned the EFTA Court's *Husbanken II* judgment as a reference for the so-called 'state aid approach' to the issue of whether financial compensation granted by a Member State to an undertaking providing a public service should be regarded as state aid.[40] The question was and partly still is one of the most controversial in EC state aid law and has been answered by the ECJ in *Ferring* and *Altmark* in favour of the so-called 'compensation approach'.[41] In Case E-7/97 *Husbanken II*,[42] the Norwegian Bankers' Association challenged a decision of the EFTA Surveillance Authority which had found that the state guarantee for Husbanken, the Norwegian State Housing Bank, amounted to state aid within the meaning of Article 61(1) EEA, but that it was essentially justified under Article 59(2) EEA as necessary for the operation of services of general economic interest. The EFTA Court held that an institution performing the tasks of Husbanken may be considered as an undertaking entrusted with the operation of a service of general economic interest within the meaning of that provision and that the aid in question was necessary for Husbanken to perform the tasks entrusted to it. However, the Court annulled the decision of the ESA on the grounds that the latter had not considered the following points to the extent necessary: the definition of the relevant market, the question of whether there were alternative means less distortive of competition, the issue of a cost-benefit analysis, and the application of a proportionality

---

[39] Opinion in Joined Cases C-34/95, C-35/95 and C-36/95 *De Agostini/TV-shop i Sverige* [1997] ECR, I-3843, pts 21, 46, 63.
[40] Opinion of 30 April 2002 in Case C-126/01 *GEMO* [2003] ECR I-13769, at fn 64, 77; references to Case E-4/97 *Husbanken II*, EFTA Court Report [1999] 1, fn 64, 77.
[41] Cases C-53/00 *Ferring* [2001] ECR, I-9067; C-280/00 *Altmark Trans* [2003] ECR I-7747; as a matter of interest see also Case E-3/03 *Transportbedriftenes Landsforening and Nor-Way Bussekspress AS v EFTA Surveillance Authority*, EFTA Court Report [2004] 1 (withdrawn).
[42] Case E-7/97 *Norwegian Bankers' Association v EFTA Surveillance Authority*, EFTA Court Report [1999] 1.

test. The ESA had thereby wrongly interpreted Article 59(2) EEA. The Court confirmed its stand in Cases E-1/00 *Íslandsbanki*[43] and E-9/04 *The Bankers' and Securities' Dealers Association of Iceland v EFTA Surveillance Authority (HFF)*.[44]

In *Commission v Denmark* and in *Greenham and Abel*, Advocate General Mischo advised the ECJ to follow the EFTA Court's 2001 *Kellogg's* ruling in so far as it recognized the right of Member States to invoke the precautionary principle when examining whether fortified food can be marketed or not.[45] The ECJ decided accordingly. In Case C-236/01 *Monsanto*, Advocate General Alber emphasized that action is appropriate even where cause for concern is based on preliminary scientific findings, but that in view of the free movement of goods, not every claim or scientifically unfounded presumption of potential risk to human health or the environment can justify the adoption of national protective measures. Rather, Advocate General Alber stated with reference to the decision of the EFTA Court in *Kellogg's* and that of the CFI in *Pfizer Animal Health*, 'the risk must be adequately substantiated by scientific evidence'.[46] The ECJ followed that advice. In *Commission v Netherlands*, Advocate General Poiares Maduro made reference to the *Kellogg's* judgment when stating that a preventive measure which bans the marketing of an enriched foodstuff based on health concerns cannot properly be based on hypothetical considerations.[47]

In Case C-452/01 *Ospelt*, Advocate General Geelhoed rejected the Austrian government's attempt to compare Article 40 EEA to Article 67 EEC in its pre-Maastricht version and referred to the decision of the EFTA Court in *Íslandsbanki*. Advocate General Geelhoed stated that according to the latter's case law the provisions on free movement of capital in the EEA Agreement have direct effect.[48]

Advocate General Poiares Maduro in Joined Cases C-232/04 and C-233/04 *Güney-Görres* referred to the EFTA Court's *Rasmussen* decision when concluding that the lack of transfer of ownership from one service provider to another does not prevent there being a transfer of assets, if it is established that the assets in question form part of the transferable entity.[49]

In Case C-537/03 *Candolin*, Advocate General Geelhoed proposed that Community law should preclude exclusions from cover by compulsory insurance against civil liability in respect of the use of motor vehicles other than the one explicitly referred to in the Second Motor Vehicle Insurance Directive (a

---

[43] EFTA Court Report [2000–1] 8, para 37.
[44] EFTA Court Report [2006] 42.
[45] References to Case E-3/00 *Kellogg's*, EFTA Court Report [2000–1] 73, in the opinions of AG Mischo in Case C-192/01 *Commission v Denmark* [2003] ECR I-9693, pts 81, 85, 87, 100, 125–8, and in Case C-95/01 *Greenham and Abel* [2004] ECR I-1333, pts 44, 53, 55.
[46] [2003] ECR I-8105, pts 137 and 138 of the opinion.
[47] ibid, pt 46.
[48] Reference to Case E-1/00 *Íslandsbanki*, EFTA Court Report [2000–1] 8, in opinion of AG Geelhoed in Case C-452/01 *Ospelt and Schlössle Weissenberg* [2003] ECR I-9743, fn 32.
[49] Reference to Case E-2/04 *Rasmussen*, EFTA Court Report [2004] 57, in opinion of AG Poiares Maduro in Joined Cases C-232/04 and C-233/04 *Güney-Görres* [2005] ECR I-11237, pt 15.

person voluntarily entered a stolen vehicle) from being relied on by the insurer as against the passengers. Advocate General Geelhoed referred to the EFTA Court's 1999 ruling in Case E-1/99 *Finanger* with regard to the following considerations: (1) That the exception provided for in case of theft of the vehicle had to be interpreted narrowly and as being exhaustive since it formed a departure from a general rule.[50] (2) That any other interpretation would have the effect of allowing Member States to limit payment of compensation to third-party victims of a road accident to certain types of damage, thus bringing about disparities in the treatment of victims depending on where the accident occurred, which is precisely what the directives are intended to avoid.[51] (3) That only in exceptional situations may the extent of the compensation paid to the victim be limited due to contributory fault on the basis of an individual assessment.[52]

In C-348/04 *Boehringer Ingelheim II*, Advocate General Sharpston stated that the precise manner and style of reboxing which affects only the outer packaging would not impair the guarantee of origin and that the notion of the condition of the goods being changed or impaired in Article 7(2) of the Trade Marks Directive should not be broadly interpreted.[53] The Advocate General cited the following passages from the EFTA Court's *Paranova v Merck* judgment which she characterized as 'certainly relevant':

[P]ermitting parallel imports and repackaging are means which aim at securing the free movement of goods... The parallel importer's right to repackage is, in other words, justified because it makes an important contribution to overcoming the partitioning of the EEA market along national boundaries. It is against this background that the Court of Justice [has] established the necessity test... It follows that the [test] is relevant to the issue of establishing the parallel importer's right to repackage as such, where the conduct of the trade mark proprietor and factual or legal trade barriers hinder effective access to the market of the state of importation. Where... the right to repackage is beyond doubt and the parallel importer has, in exercising it, achieved effective access to the market, the necessity requirement cannot be decisive when interpreting the term 'legitimate reasons' in Article 7(2) of the Directive... Imposing the necessity requirement on the market conduct of the parallel importer after having gained market access, in particular on its strategy of product presentation, such as advertising or packaging design, would constitute a disproportionate restriction on the free movement of goods.[54]

Eleanor Sharpston then laconically stated that she shared this view.[55] As already indicated, in its judgment of 26 April 2007, the ECJ (Second Chamber) decided

[50] Opinion of AG Geelhoed in Case C-537/03 *Candolin* [2005] ECR I-5745, pt 42 and fn 14.
[51] pt 42 and fn 15; in that regard, the Advocate General also referred to the ECJ's judgment in Case C-129/94 *Ruiz Bernáldez* [1996] ECR, I-1829.
[52] pt 51 and fn 17.
[53] References to Case E-3/02 *Merck v Paranova* EFTA Court Report [2003] 101, in opinion of AG Sharpston in Case C-348/04 *Boehringer Ingelheim II* of 26 April 2007, nyr, pts 49–55.
[54] pt 51 in Advocate General Sharpston's opinion in *Boehringer Ingelheim II*; paras 42–3 in the EFTA Court's *Merck v Paranova* judgment.
[55] pt 52.

accordingly and made reference to the EFTA Court's considerations in *Paranova v Merck*.[56]

In Case C-434/04 *Jan-Erik Anders Ahokainen and Mati Leppik*, Advocate General Poiares Maduro proposed that Article 28 EC should be held to preclude national legislation which requires a licence for the import of substances containing more than 80 per cent by volume of undenatured ethyl alcohol from another Member State. When rejecting the Portuguese government's contention that Article 28 EC did not preclude a system of prior import authorization for spirits because it constituted neither a quantitative restriction on imports, nor a measure having equivalent effect, Advocate General Poiares Maduro referred, *inter alia*, to the case law of the ECJ and to the EFTA Court's judgment in Case E-1/94 *Restamark*.[57]

B. Referring to EFTA Court Case Law as an Additional Argument

Occasionally, there may be a citation of EFTA Court jurisprudence in ECJ case law by way of supporting argument rather than main argument. That such additional reference may be important is demonstrated by Cases C-140/97 *Rechberger* and C-321/97 *Andersson*,[58] two cases originating from Austria and Sweden, whose facts occurred in 1994, when these two countries were EEA/EFTA States. In *Rechberger*, the plenum of the ECJ, consisting of nine Judges, denied jurisdiction to rule on whether the principle of state liability applied in Austria after that country's accession to the EEA on 1 January 1994, but added: 'Moreover, in view of the objective of uniform interpretation and application which informs the EEA Agreement, it should be pointed out that the principles governing the liability of an EFTA State for infringement of a directive referred to in the EEA Agreement were the subject of the EFTA Court's judgment of 10 December 1998 in *Sveinbjörnsdóttir*'.[59]

The EFTA Court in *Sveinbjörnsdóttir* had acknowledged state liability to be part of EEA law in spite of the resistance of the governments of Iceland, Norway and Sweden as well as of the Commission.[60] With its citation of the EFTA Court's decision in *Sveinbjörnsdóttir*, the ECJ avoided a gap in the EEA system of protection of individual rights. One will have to conclude from the reference that the Austrian Judge was at least indirectly encouraged to grant compensation, provided the conditions set out by the EFTA Court in *Sveinbjörnsdóttir* (which correspond to those developed by the ECJ in Community law) were fulfilled.

---

[56] Case C-348/04 *Boehringer Ingelheim II*, judgment of 26 April 2007, nyr, para 38 (reference to paras 41–5 in the EFTA Court's judgment).
[57] Case C-434/04 *Criminal Proceedings against Jan-Erik Anders Ahokainen and Mati Leppik*, opinion of 13 July 2006, nyr, paras 49 and 50.
[58] [1999] ECR, I-3499 and [1999] ECR I-3551.
[59] Case C-140/97 *Rechberger* [1999] ECR I-3499, para 39.
[60] Case E-9/97, EFTA Court Report [1998] 95.

That step was all the more important, as the governments of the EEA/EFTA states had excluded the competence of the EFTA Court to rule on requests for a preliminary ruling by courts in Austria, Finland and Sweden after 31 March 1995.[61] In its judgment in the *Andersson* case, which was delivered on the same day as *Rechberger* (15 June 1999), the plenum of the ECJ, consisting of 11 Judges, again stated that it lacked the competence to rule on the question of whether state liability applied in an EEA/EFTA state. The EC Court did not, however, make reference to the legal situation created in the EFTA states by the EFTA Court's *Sveinbjörnsdóttir* judgment. It appears that in *Rechberger* compensation was, in fact, paid in the framework of a settlement before the referring Austrian court. In *Andersson*, the referring *Stockholms tingsrätt* acknowledged that state liability was part of EEA law.[62] The Court of Appeal reversed that ruling, but the Swedish Supreme Court ultimately ruled that state liability was part of EEA law and granted the plaintiffs compensation. The Supreme Court made reference to both the EFTA Court's and the Icelandic Supreme Court's judgments in the *Sveinbjörnsdóttir* case.[63] The plaintiffs would probably have succeeded much earlier had the ECJ referenced the EFTA Court's jurisprudence.[64]

Advocates General too have referred to EFTA Court case law as additional information. A case in point is the opinion of Advocate General Lenz of 30 April 1996 in C-222/94 *Commission of the European Communities v United Kingdom of Great Britain and Northern Ireland*. When stating that the principal objective pursued by Council Directive 89/552/EEC is to remove barriers to the free provision of television broadcasting services, Advocate General Lenz referred to the judgments of the ECJ in Case C-412/93 *Leclerc-Siplec v TF1 Publicité and M6 Publicité* and of the EFTA Court in Joined Cases E-8/94 and E-9/94 *Forbrukerombudet v Mattel Scandinavia and Lego Norge*.[65] In Case C-189/95 *Criminal proceedings against Harry Franzén*,[66] the ECJ had to rule on the compatibility with Articles 28 and 31 of the EC Treaty of the Swedish legislation governing the retail sale of alcoholic beverages. Advocate General Elmer in his opinion of 4 March 1997 mentioned that, following the entry into force of the EEA Agreement on 1 January 1994, the EFTA Court had found, upon reference by a Finnish court in Case E-1/94 *Restamark*, that national measures which conferred on a statutory state monopoly

---

[61] Agreement on Transitional Arrangements for a Period After the Accession of Certain EFTA States to the European Union of 28 September 1994, EFTA Court Report [1994–5] 161 ff.

[62] Judgment in Case T-6-17/97.

[63] T-2595/01; see M Johansson, 'State liability within the EEA from a Swedish perspective – Sveinbjörnsdóttir confirmed', *European Law Reporter* (2005) 50 ff.

[64] The reasons for this omission are unknown. One will not, however, overlook that the composition of the ECJ differed in the two cases. The Swedish Judge Hans Ragnemalm participated in *Andersson*, but not in *Rechberger*. The Italian Judge Federico Mancini participated in *Rechberger*, but not in *Andersson*.

[65] [1996] ECR I-4025, pt 3: references to [1995] ECR I-179, para 28; EFTA Court Report [1994–5] 113, para 22.

[66] Reference to Case E-1/94 *Restamark*, EFTA Court Report [1994–5] 15 by AG Elmer in Case C-189/95 *Criminal proceedings against Harry Franzén* [1997] ECR I-05909, pt 3.

the exclusive right to import alcoholic beverages, or the application to intra-EEA trade of national provisions which require the authorization of the statutory state monopoly for the importation and putting into free circulation of such products, was incompatible with Article 11 EEA, even if such an authorization was granted automatically. Moreover, Advocate General Elmer stated that the EFTA Court had interpreted Article 16 EEA as meaning that, as from 1 January 1994, every state monopoly of a commercial character not covered by Protocol 8 EEA was to be adjusted so as to eliminate the exclusive right to import the goods subject to the monopoly into a Contracting Party from other Contracting Parties.[67] In Case 319/03 *Briheche*, Advocate General Poiares Maduro proposed that the Equal Rights Directive 76/207/EEC and Article 141(4) EC should be held to preclude national legislation that discriminates between widowers and widows who have not remarried as regards the age limit imposed on them for access to posts in the administration, without being aimed either at removing existing inequalities or at compensating them.[68] When emphasizing that measures that favour women in order to reduce their underrepresentation in professional life must be reconciled as far as possible with the equal treatment principle, the Advocate General referred, *inter alia*, to the EFTA Court's judgment in the *University of Oslo* case.[69] In that case, the EFTA Court held that 'earmarking' academic posts for women was contrary to the principle of equal treatment.[70]

C. Mutual References

The courts in both EEA pillars have made significant efforts to secure a homogeneous development of the case law. The EFTA Court in its very first case, E-1/94 *Restamark*, emphasized the importance of the objective of the Contracting Parties to create a dynamic and homogeneous EEA.[71] In Case E-9/97 *Sveinbjörnsdóttir*, the EFTA Court, when addressing the issue of EEA state liability, pointed to the fact that creating a homogeneous EEA was one of the main objectives of the Contracting Parties.[72] The CFI in its judgment of 22 January 1997 in Case T-115/94 *Opel Austria* stated that the two-pillar system underlying the EEA Agreement was reinforced, in addition to the similarity between the terms of the various provisions of the Agreement and the EC Treaty, by specific rules aimed at guaranteeing the homogeneous development of the case law and referred to the

---

[67] Case C-189/95 *Criminal proceedings against Harry Franzén* [1997] ECR, I-05909.
[68] Case 319/03 *Serge Briheche v Ministère de l'intérieur, de la sécurité intérieure et des libertés locales*, opinion of 29 June 2004 [2004] ECR I-8807, pts 34, 36 and 40; references to Case E-1/02 *EFTA v University of Oslo*, EFTA Court Report [2003] 1.
[69] ibid, pt 36, as well as fns 16 and 26.
[70] n 69 above.
[71] ibid, paras 24, 32–5, 44 ff.; see V Kronenberger, 'Does the EFTA Court interpret the EEA Agreement as if it were the EC Treaty? Some questions raised by the Restamark judgment', 45 Intl & Comp. LQ 198, 207.
[72] EFTA Court Report [1998] 95, paras 49 ff.

judgments of the EFTA Court in Cases E-1/94 *Restamark* and E-2/94 *Scottish Salmon Growers*.[73] A series of judgments rendered by the ECJ and the EFTA Court in the years 2003/2004 was particularly important for guaranteeing homogeneity. In Case C-452/01 *Margarethe Ospelt and Schlössle Weissenberg Familienstiftung* which involved national restrictions on the free movement of capital, the plenum of the ECJ saw it as its task to ensure that the rules of the EEA Agreement which are identical in substance to those of the Treaty are interpreted uniformly within the Member States.[74] In Case E-1/03 *ESA v Iceland*, the EFTA Court, when ruling on the compatibility of Icelandic legislation, which imposed a higher tax per air passenger travelling from Iceland to other EEA states than per passenger travelling on domestic flights, with the freedom to provide services, pointed to the homogeneity objective laid down in EEA law and referred to Case C-452/01 *Ospelt*.[75] The ECJ (Third Chamber) took up that ball in its judgment of 1 April 2004 in Case C-286/02 *Bellio Fratelli,* a case dealt with under EEA law, by emphasizing that:

> as Article 6 of the EEA Agreement states, the provisions of the agreement, in so far as they are identical in substance to corresponding rules of the EC Treaty and to acts adopted in application of that Treaty, must, in their implementation and application, be interpreted in conformity with the relevant rulings of the Court given prior to the date of signature of the EEA Agreement. Furthermore, *both the Court and the EFTA Court* have recognized the need to ensure that the rules of the EEA Agreement which are identical in substance to those of the Treaty are interpreted uniformly.[76]

On that point, the ECJ referred to its judgment in Case C-452/01 *Ospelt*,[77] and to the EFTA Court's ruling in Case E-1/03 *EFTA Surveillance Authority v Iceland*.[78] The EFTA Court, for its part, replied eight months later in Case E-1/04 *Fokus Bank*[79] by pointing to the importance of the homogeneity objective and referring to its judgment in Case E-1/03 *ESA v Iceland* and the ECJ's judgment in Case C-286/02 *Bellio Fratelli*. The ECJ's holding on the significance of homogeneity in *Bellio Fratelli* has since been used in two tax law cases involving the interpretation of the EC Treaty and of the EEA Agreement, C-471/04 *Keller Holding*[80] and Case C-345/05 *Commission v Portugal*.[81]

The EEA judicial dialogue was also crucial for ensuring identity in substance of the EC and EEA rules on free movement of capital. After the conclusion of the EEA Agreement, the Treaty on European Union introduced new provisions on 'capital and payments' in the EC Treaty, including Article 73b, which

---

[73] References to EFTA Court *Restamark*, paras 24, 33 and 34 and to *Scottish Salmon Growers*, para 29 in T-115/94 *Opel Austria GmbH v Council of the European Union* [1997] ECR, para 108.
[74] ibid, para 29.
[75] EFTA Court Report [2003] 143, para 27.
[76] Para 34, emphasis added.
[77] Para 34, emphasis added.
[78] 2003 EFTA Court Report 143, para 27.
[79] EFTA Court Report [2004] 11, para 22.
[80] Case C-471/04 *Keller Holding*, judgment of 23 February 2006, nyr.
[81] Case C-345/05 *Commission v Portugal*, judgment of 26 October 2006, nyr.

substantially reproduced the content of Article 1 of Directive 88/361/EEC. As a consequence of the Treaty of Amsterdam, Article 73b was renumbered as Article 56 EC. The provisions of the EEA Agreement on free movement of capital remained unchanged.[82] In Case E-1/00 *Íslandsbanki*,[83] the EFTA Court ruled on 14 July 2000 that Article 40 EEA precludes an EFTA state from maintaining rules that require borrowers benefiting from state guarantees to pay higher guarantee fees to the State Treasury on loans from foreign lenders than on loans from domestic lenders. Comparing Article 40 EEA to Article 56(1) EC, the EFTA Court found that it was *similar* to the latter.[84] In Case C-452/01 *Margarethe Ospelt and Schlössle Weissenberg Familienstiftung*, the ECJ held on 23 September 2003 that national rules making transactions relating to agricultural and forestry plots subject to administrative controls must, where a transaction is in issue between nationals of states party to the EEA Agreement, be assessed in the light of Article 40 of and Annex XII to the EEA Agreement, since these provisions possess 'the *same legal scope* as that of Article 73b of the Treaty, which is *identical in substance*'.[85] Advocate General Geelhoed for his part stated that the EFTA Court too had in Case E-1/00 *Íslandsbanki* compared Article 40 EEA with Article 56(1) EC and concluded that both provisions used comparable language.[86] In Case E-1/04 *Fokus Bank*, the EFTA Court, referring, *inter alia*, to the ECJ's judgment in *Ospelt* and the Advocate General's opinion in that case, held that the rules governing the free movement of capital in the EEA Agreement were essentially identical in substance to those in the EC Treaty.[87] Lastly, one may note that, in its judgment of 3 October 2006 in Case C-452/04 *Fidium Finanz AG*, the ECJ did not even discuss the question of substantive identity of EC and EEA law in the field of free movement of capital when referring to the centre of gravity test developed by the EFTA Court in Case E-1/00 *State Debt Management Agency/ Íslandsbanki-FBA* in order to demarcate the free movement of capital from the freedom to provide services.[88]

---

[82] Article 40 EEA provides: 'Within the framework of the provisions of this Agreement, there shall be no restrictions between the Contracting Parties on the movement of capital belonging to persons resident in EC Member States or EFTA states and no discrimination based on the nationality or on the place of residence of the parties or on the place where such capital is invested. Annex XII contains the provisions necessary to implement this Article'. Article 56 EC states: '1. Within the framework of the provisions set out in this chapter, all restrictions on the movement of capital between Member States and between Member States and third countries shall be prohibited. 2. Within the framework of the provisions set out in this chapter, all restrictions on payments between Member States and between Member States and third countries shall be prohibited'.
[83] Case E-1/00 *State Debt Management Agency v Íslandsbanki-FBA*, EFTA Court Report [2000–1] 8.
[84] ibid, para 16, emphasis added.
[85] [2003] ECR I-9743, operative part, answer 1, emphasis added.
[86] Opinion of Advocate General Geelhoed [2003] ECR I-9743, fn 32 with reference to Case E-1/00, *Íslandsbanki 2000*, EFTA Court Report [2000–1] 8, paras 16 ff.
[87] Case E-1/04 *Fokus Bank ASA v the Norwegian State, represented by Skattedirektoratet (the Directorate of Taxes)*, EFTA Court Report [2004] 11, para 22.
[88] EFTA Court Report [2000–1] 1, para 32.

After the series of references by the ECJ and the CFI to the EFTA Court's decision in *Kellogg's* in the years 2002–4 concerning the definition and scope of application of the precautionary principle,[89] the latter in its judgment of 25 February 2005 in Case E-4/04 *Pedicel* played the ball back and further elaborated on the scope of application of the precautionary principle.[90] The national court, *inter alia*, wanted to know whether there was room for the application of the precautionary principle when assessing the compatibility of the Norwegian ban on advertising alcoholic beverages with the provisions of the EEA Agreement on free movement of goods and of services. In its judgment of 25 February 2005, the EFTA Court made reference to its own *Kellogg's* judgment, to the ECJ's jurisprudence in *Commission v Denmark*, *Monsanto* and *Bellio* as well as the CFI's judgments in *Pfizer Animal Health* and in *Alpharma*, and concluded that in the case at issue there was no room for the application of the precautionary principle. The effects of excessive alcohol consumption on human health are not uncertain. Uncertainty with regard to the assessment of the effects of advertizing on the consumption of alcoholic beverages 'does not arise in a domain which would allow for the invocation of the precautionary principle as developed in the case law of the courts mentioned above' (the ECJ, the CFI and the EFTA Court).[91]

Mutual citations have also been made with regard to the question of whether state liability is part of EEA law. In Case E-4/01 *Karlsson*,[92] a reference from the Reykjavík District Court, the Norwegian government submitted observations under Article 20 of the EFTA Court's statute and under Article 97 of its Rules of Procedure and invited the EFTA Court to overrule its state liability jurisprudence as set out in Case E-9/97 *Sveinbjörnsdóttir*. As mentioned, the ECJ had endorsed *Sveinbjörnsdóttir* by referring to it in *Rechberger*.[93] In rejecting the Norwegian government's position, the EFTA Court in turn quoted the ECJ decision in *Rechberger*.[94] One commentator noted that with this, the EFTA Court had in a skilful way taken the ECJ on board as an ally.[95]

D. ECJ Reconsidering its Case Law in the Light of EFTA Court Jurisprudence

In a few cases, the ECJ has reconsidered its case law in view of a judgment of the EFTA Court. As already mentioned, the ECJ in Case C-13/95 *Süzen* followed the EFTA Court's finding in Case E-2/96 *Ulstein* that the succession

---

[89] Above.
[90] Case E-4/04 *Pedicel A/S v Sosial- og helsedirektoratet (Directorate for Health and Social Affairs)*, EFTA Court Report [2005] 1.
[91] ibid, para 61.
[92] See above.
[93] Above.
[94] EFTA Court Report [2002] 240, para 25.
[95] G Gorton, 'Bestätigung der Staatshaftungsrechtsprechung des EFTA-Gerichtshofs' (2002) *European Law Reporter* 260, 263.

of contracts – that is, the replacement of an independent service provider by a second one – does not normally constitute a transfer of an undertaking.[96] The EC Court had previously interpreted the notion of transfer of undertaking in a rather expansive way. This case law had culminated in the famous judgment in Case C-392/92 *Christel Schmidt*, in which the EC Court held that the succession of functions, that is, the outsourcing of a mere activity without any assets being transferred (*in casu* the cleaning of a small savings and loans bank), could amount to a transfer of undertaking.[97] In academic literature, *Süzen* has been called a quiet goodbye to *Christel Schmidt*.[98] Seen from that perspective, one is prompted to assume that the ECJ has reconsidered its case law in the light of the EFTA Court's jurisprudence.

As stated earlier, the EFTA Court found in Case C-3/00 *Kellogg's* that a Member State could not limit itself to invoking a lack of a nutritional need in order to justify a prohibition to market fortified foodstuffs. Rather, that state had to prove a possible harm to public health even if it could thereby rely on the precautionary principle. The ECJ had, for its part, in Case 174/82 *Sandoz* when interpreting Articles 28 and 30 EC, found that the Member States must give marketing permission for fortified foodstuffs, if the addition of vitamins will satisfy a real need, in particular, of technological or nutritional nature. At the same time, the ECJ held that a national regulation according to which the marketing approval for foodstuffs fortified with vitamins which have been lawfully put on the market in other Member States depends on whether the importer shows that there is a need on the market is incompatible with Community law.[99] In *Commission v Denmark*, the ECJ shared the opinion of the Commission, which by way of reference to the EFTA Court's decision in *Kellogg's* had argued that a general ban on the marketing of fortified foodstuffs could not be justified by the mere assertion that there was no respective nutritional need in the Member State concerned.[100] With this, the ECJ has at least clarified its *Sandoz* jurisprudence concerning the relevance of the nutritional need argument. Some commentators speak even of overruling.[101]

The ECJ's jurisprudence on the precautionary principle was subsequently developed further by way of dialogue with the EFTA Court in *Bellio Fratelli*. The plenum of the ECJ had in *Commission v Denmark* made reference to the

---

[96] Above.
[97] [1994] ECR I-1311.
[98] F Marhold, 'Der leise Abschied von Christel Schmidt' *St Gallen Europarechtsbriefe EU B* (1997) 162 ff.
[99] Case 174/82 [1983] ECR, 2445, para 24.
[100] [2003] ECR I-9693, paras 54 and 25.
[101] See Project on International Courts and Tribunals PICT, *www.pict-pcti.org/research/systemic_issues/news.html*: 'ECJ overrules its older case law with reference to EFTA Court's judgment'; M M Slotboom, 'Do Public Health Measures Receive Similar Treatment in European Community and World Trade Organization Law?' *Journal of World Trade* (2003) 37(3), 553, 585; M Bronckers, 'Exceptions to liberal trade in foodstuffs: the precautionary approach and collective preferences' in C Baudenbacher, P Tresselt and T Örlygsson (eds), *The EFTA Court Ten Years On* (2005).

EFTA Court's assertion that restrictive measures must be non-discriminatory and objective,[102] but not to the statement that they must be proportionate, non-discriminatory, transparent, and consistent with measures already taken, as did the Third Chamber in *Bellio*.[103] This fourfold requirement had already been formulated by the Commission in its 2000 Communication on the precautionary principle.[104]

In Case 1/99 *Storebrand Skadeforsikring AS v Veronika Finanger*[105], the EFTA Court on 17 November 1999 held upon a reference by the Supreme Court of Norway that a provision such as § 7 para 3 litra b of the Norwegian Automobile Liability Act, which basically excluded a passenger of an intoxicated motor vehicle driver from insurance coverage if he or she knew or must have known that the driver of the vehicle was under the influence of alcohol, was incompatible with the EEA Motor Vehicle Insurance Directives. The EFTA Court rejected the argument put forward by the insurance company Storebrand, the government of Iceland and the government of Norway that the Motor Vehicle Insurance Directives do not deal with rules relating to personal liability but only with insurance law. The EFTA Court made several references to the ECJ's judgment of 28 March 1996 in Case 129/94 *Ruiz Bernáldez*, where the EC Court had found that a provision of Spanish insurance legislation which excluded the victim of an intoxicated driver from insurance coverage was incompatible with the Directives.[106] So far homogeneity between the two EEA Court's case law seemed to be safeguarded. But on 14 September 2000, before the oral hearing took place in the Norwegian Supreme Court in the *Finanger* case, the ECJ (Fifth Chamber) rendered its judgment in Case C-348/98 *Ferreira*. There, the EC Court held, without mentioning the EFTA Court's *Finanger* ruling, that the Directives did not seek to harmonize the rules of the Member States governing civil liability. Based on this, the ECJ found unlawful a provision of the Portuguese Civil Code which stated that, in the case of transport provided free of charge, liability was incurred only if the passenger proved fault on the part of the driver and that this fault was the cause of the accident.[107] Whether the ECJ decision in *Ferreira* amounted to a departure from that of the EFTA Court in *Finanger*, may be left open. But what cannot be denied is that the *Ferreira* judgment lacked clarity. Proof of that is the reaction of the defendant and of the Norwegian government in the *Finanger* proceedings before the Norwegian Supreme Court. They pleaded that in *Ferreira* the ECJ had distanced itself from the EFTA Court's approach in *Finanger* and that the Norwegian Supreme Court

---

[102] Above.
[103] Case E-3/00 *EFTA Surveillance Authority v Norway*, EFTA Court Report [2000–1] 73, para 26.
[104] See Communication of the European Commission on the precautionary principle, COM 2000(1).
[105] EFTA Court Report [1999] 119.
[106] Case C-129/94 [1996] ECR I-1829.
[107] [2000] ECR I-6711.

ought to follow the ECJ's judgment.[108] The Supreme Court distinguished the two cases and followed the EFTA Court's *Finanger* ruling.[109] In its judgment in Case C-537/03 *Candolin* of 30 June 2005, a Finnish case in which the facts and the law were virtually identical to *Finanger*, the ECJ (First Chamber) eliminated any ambiguities and came to the same result as the EFTA Court in *Finanger*. It held that a provision of Finnish automobile liability law (that is, civil law), which excluded a passenger who took a ride in a car driven by an intoxicated driver, was incompatible with the Directives.[110] Although the ECJ did not refer to it, there are indications that the EFTA Court's *Finanger* judgment was in fact taken into account. Advocate General Geelhoed had concluded that the Directives 'do not preclude the partial exclusion of a passenger who has suffered loss or injury and who knew or should have known that the driver of the motor vehicle was driving under the influence of alcohol at the time of the accident from the right to compensation on the ground that he was partly to blame'.[111] He did not, however, mention the proportionality principle. The EFTA Court had stated in *Finanger* that a reduction of compensation due to contributory negligence must be possible in exceptional circumstances, but that a finding that a passenger who passively rode in a car driven by an intoxicated driver was to be denied compensation or that compensation was to be reduced in a way which is disproportionate to the contribution to the injury by the injured party would be incompatible with the Directives.[112] In its judgment, the ECJ, for its part, pointed out that the passenger's right to be compensated must not be limited in a disproportionate manner.[113]

E. National Courts of EC Countries Asking the ECJ to Clarify its Case Law in the Light of EFTA Court Jurisprudence

As far as I know, national courts of EC Member States have in three major cases referred questions to the ECJ under the Article 234 EC procedure on the ground that due to EFTA Court case law, there is doubt about the legal situation within the meaning of the CILFIT formula. As mentioned, the EFTA Court held in Case E-3/02 *Merck v Paranova*[114] that a parallel importer's and repackager's strategy of product presentation and the new design cannot mechanically be assessed on the basis of the necessity criterion as developed by the ECJ when assessing the lawfulness of the repackaging itself. Instead, the EFTA Court found, a comprehensive balancing of the interests of the trade mark proprietor and the

---

[108] See H Bull, 'European Law and Norwegian Courts' in P Müller-Graff and G Selvig (eds), *The Approach to European Law in Germany and Norway* (2004) 95 ff.
[109] See above.
[110] Case C-537/03 *Katja Candolin, Jari-Antero Viljaniemi and Veli-Matti Paananen v Vahinkovakuutusosakeyhtiö Pohjola and Jarno Ruokoranta* [2005] ECR I-5745.
[111] ibid, pt 52.
[112] ibid, para 34.
[113] ibid, paras 29, 34 and Operative Part.
[114] EFTA Court Report [2003] 101.

parallel importer must be undertaken. The EFTA Court emphasized the importance of free trade in markets partitioned along national boundaries, such as the pharmaceutical market, and held that once the right to repackage and to reaffix the original trade mark is established and market access is thereby ensured, the parallel importer is to be considered as an operator on a basically equal footing with the manufacturer and trade mark proprietor within the framework of the Trade Mark Directive. In the first *Boehringer* case, the EC Court had stated that repackaging of pharmaceutical products is objectively necessary if, without such repackaging, effective access to the market concerned, or to a substantial part of that market, must be considered to be hindered as the result of strong resistance from a significant proportion of consumers to relabelled pharmaceutical products.[115] In the second *Boehringer* case, the England and Wales Court of Appeal concluded that the law concerning the meaning of 'necessary' was not *acte clair*. It accordingly referred, *inter alia*, the question to the ECJ whether the use by a parallel importer and repackager of pharmaceuticals of its own design elements (referred to as 'co-branding') is in line with the Directive's provisions on the exhaustion principle and the ECJ's case law related thereto, in particular the 'necessity test'.[116] The Court of Appeal emphasized that with regard to this question, there appear to be two schools of thought in European justice: whereas the EFTA Court's jurisprudence shows a positive approach towards the parallel importer creating a package design of its own, the Supreme Courts of Austria, Denmark and Germany, as well as the Svea (Stockholm) Court of Appeal, apply a strict necessity test and tend to prohibit conduct such as Paranova's in the EFTA Court's judgment.[117] The Court of Appeal hinted that it tended to side with the EFTA Court and referred the question to the ECJ whether the condition that it must be shown that it is necessary to repackage the product in order that effective market access is not hindered, applies merely to the fact of reboxing '(as held by the EFTA Court in Case E-3/02 Paranova v Merck)' or also to the precise manner and style of the reboxing carried out by the parallel importer.

The second case of a national court reverting to the ECJ after a judgment of the EFTA Court concerns a reference for preliminary ruling by the Amsterdam Court of Appeal of 21 September 2005 regarding the compatibility of the Dutch dividend withholding tax exemption for intercompany dividend payments.[118] *Amurta* was a tax resident of Portugal and owned 14 per cent of the shares in a Dutch company. It objected to the imposition, at the rate of 25 per cent, of Dutch dividend withholding tax on the basis that the free movement of capital under Article 56 EC was violated since a company resident in the Netherlands would not have been subject to withholding tax. The Court considered that *Amurta*, being a non-resident, was in principle not in a situation comparable to that of a resident taxpayer, that there

---

[115] Case C-143/00 [2002] ECR I-3759 Operative Part, Answer 2.
[116] [2004] EWCA (Civ) 129.
[117] Case C-348/04.
[118] Case C-379/05, *Amurta*.

was no restriction of the free movement of capital, because the taxpayer was able to credit the Dutch withholding tax against the company's corporate tax liability in Portugal, and that even if the Dutch levy constituted a restriction of the free movement of capital, it was justified based on the coherence of the Dutch tax system. Nevertheless, in light of the EFTA Court's judgment in Case 1/04 *Fokus Bank*, the Court of Appeal considered that its preliminary conclusions were not free from all reasonable doubt. The EFTA Court in *Fokus Bank*[119] had declared the Norwegian imputation tax credit system according to which shareholders resident in Norway were granted an imputation tax credit, whereas this credit was not granted to shareholders non-resident in Norway to be in breach of Article 40 EEA. That Contracting Parties are, within the framework of double taxation agreements, at liberty to determine the connecting factors for the purposes of allocating powers of taxation as between themselves, but this was not held to mean that in the exercise of the power of taxation so allocated, a Contracting Party may disregard EEA law. The EFTA Court considered shareholders resident and non-resident in Norway, to be in an objectively comparable situation; it did not accept cohesion of the international tax system as a justification, since this would amount to giving bilateral tax agreements preference over EEA law. Also, the legislative history of the Corporate Tax Act gave rise to the assumption that the real purpose of the Act was not to preserve the cohesion of the international tax system but to protect the Norwegian tax base, a requirement of a purely economic nature. The Amsterdam Court of Appeal stayed the proceedings and referred the case to the ECJ.

The third case is a reference by the German Supreme Fiscal Court (*Bundesfinanzhof*) of 29 June 2006 in which that court submitted to the ECJ, *inter alia*, the question whether it is compatible with Articles 56 and 58 EC and with Article 43 EC for a national rule to provide for divergent set-off arrangements for the distribution of profits by a capital company using portions of its own capital, resulting in consequent tax liability even in cases in which the capital company demonstrates that it has distributed dividends to non-resident shareholders, even though, under national law, such non-resident shareholders, unlike resident shareholders, are not entitled to set off against their own tax the corporation tax thus determined. In its reasons, the *Bundesfinanzhof* made ample reference to the EFTA Court's *Fokus Bank* judgment.[120]

F. Advocates General Entering into a Substantive Discussion with the EFTA Court

Certain Advocates General are prepared to enter into a substantive or even dialectic debate with the EFTA Court. In his opinion of 17 September 1996 in Joined

---

[119] Case E-1/04 *Fokus Bank ASA*, EFTA Court Report [2004] 11.
[120] Case C-284/06 *Finanzamt Hamburg-Am Tierpark v Burda Verlagsbeteiligungen GmbH* (pending).

Cases C-34/95, C-35/95 and C-36/95 *De Agostini and TV-shop i Sverige*, Advocate General Jacobs advised the ECJ to follow the holding of the EFTA Court in *Mattel Scandinavia/Lego Norge* 1995 that the TV Directive prevents receiving states from controlling transfrontier TV broadcasts, but not the dictum that such control may be based on the Misleading Advertising Directive. Francis Jacobs stated:

> In an area where laws have already been harmonized, it is difficult to see any rationale for the view that those laws may be invoked against broadcasts in respect of which the Television Directive guarantees freedom of reception and retransmission. Moreover . . . the result of such a view would be both unsatisfactory and anomalous, requiring individual broadcasts to be conceptually dismantled in order to determine which fragments were within the scope of that directive and which were not.[121]

The ECJ followed the EFTA Court's approach.

In its judgment of 16 July 1998 in Case C-355/96 *Silhouette*, the ECJ held that rules of EC Member States providing for international exhaustion of trade mark rights were incompatible with Article 7(1) of the Trade Mark Directive.[122] According to that provision, the trade mark shall not entitle the proprietor to prohibit its use in relation to goods which have been put on the market in a Member State under that trade mark by the proprietor or with his consent. The ECJ's judgment was essentially based on the consideration that the result found was the only one in line with the goal of securing the functioning of the internal market. Seven months earlier, in Case E-2/97 *Maglite*,[123] the EFTA Court had concluded that Article 7(1) of the Trade Mark Directive was to be interpreted as leaving it up to the EFTA states parties to the EEA Agreement to decide whether they wish to introduce or maintain the principle of international exhaustion of rights conferred by a trade mark with regard to goods originating from outside the EEA. The EFTA Court emphasized that the principle of international exhaustion was in the interest of free trade and competition and thus in the interest of consumers, that it was in line with the main function of a trade mark, to allow consumers to identify with certainty the origin of the goods, and that this interpretation of Article 7(1) of the Trade Mark Directive was also consistent with the TRIPs Agreement. The ECJ in *Silhouette* did not mention the EFTA Court's *Maglite* ruling. But Advocate General Jacobs did. He distinguished the two cases on the facts (in *Maglite*, unlike in *Silhouette*, the parallel imports stemmed from the US – that is, from outside the EEA) and on the law (unlike the EC Treaty, the EEA Agreement has not established a customs union, but a free trade area in which sovereignty in foreign trade matters lies with the Contracting Parties). Advocate General Jacobs, moreover, found the argument put forward in *Silhouette* by the Swedish government that the function of trade marks is not to enable the trade mark owner to divide up the market and to exploit price differentials and that

---

[121] Opinion at pt 85.
[122] Case C-355/96 [1998] ECR I-4799.
[123] Case E-2/97, EFTA Court Report [1997] 127.

the adoption of international exhaustion would bring substantial advantages to consumers, and would promote price competition, 'extremely attractive'.[124] One will notice that the same approach underlies the EFTA Court's *Maglite* ruling. However, the Advocate General concluded that the ECJ's case law on the function of trade marks was developed in the context of the Community, not the world market, and to allow Member States to opt for international exhaustion would itself result in barriers between Member States.

In his opinions in Case C-95/01 *John Greenham and Leonard Abel* of 16 May 2002 and in C-192/01 *Commission v Denmark* of 12 December 2002, Advocate General Mischo advised the ECJ not to follow the EFTA Court's finding that a Member State may not rely on the nutritional need argument.[125] As already stated, the ECJ did not follow its Advocate General's proposal.

In Cases C-374/04 *Test Claimants in Class IV of the ACT Group Litigation* and C-170/05 *Denkavit International BV*, Advocate General Geelhoed asked the ECJ not to follow the EFTA Court's 2004 *Fokus Bank* ruling which found that a Member State which grants a tax credit to shareholders residing in that state on dividends paid by domestic companies, but denies such a favour to shareholders residing in other EEA countries (outbound dividends), violates the free movement of capital. The EFTA Court rejected the Norwegian attempt to justify this violation by invoking bilateral double taxation agreements (DTAs).[126] The ECJ for its part had ruled on 7 September 2004 in Case C-319/02 in *Manninen* that giving a tax credit to shareholders residing in the state of taxation on dividends paid by a domestic company and denying it to shareholders of companies from other Member States was incompatible with the rules on free movement of capital (inbound dividends). In *Test Claimants* and in *Denkavit*, Advocate General Geelhoed proposed that it should be held that the effects of DTAs should be taken into account in this assessment for two reasons. First, Member States are at liberty to apportion between themselves not only tax jurisdiction but also priority to taxation. It is therefore open to the source state to ensure, by DTA, that economic double taxation will be relieved by the home state. Second, not taking account of the effects of DTAs would ignore the economic reality of the taxable subject's activity and incentives in a cross-border context. It could distort the real effect on that taxpayer of the combination of home and source state obligations.[127] In *Test Claimants* the EC Court's Grand Chamber acknowledged, in

---

[124] Case 355/96 [1998] ECR I-4799, pts 48 f; see C Baudenbacher, 'Trademark Law and Parallel Imports in a Globalized World – Recent Developments in Europe with Special Regard to the Legal Situation in the United States' *22 Fordham Int'l LJ* 645 ff.

[125] Opinion of AG Mischo in Case C-95/01 *Criminal proceedings against John Greenham and Leonard Abel* [2004] ECR I-1333 pts 51–73 and 87.

[126] See above.

[127] Opinion of AG Geelhoed in Case C-374/04 *Test Claimants in Class IV of the ACT Group Litigation*, of 23 February 2006, nyr, pt 71, and in Case C-170/05 *Denkavit International BV, Denkavit France SARL v Ministre de l'Économie, des Finances et de l'Industrie*, of 27 April 2006, nyr, pt 39.

principle, that the effects of DTAs could be taken into account. It did not make reference to the EFTA Court's *Fokus Bank* judgment.[128] In *Denkavit*, the ECJ's First Chamber followed that line of argument.[129] Again, no reference was made to the EFTA Court's *Fokus Bank* judgment.

An interesting example of an Advocate General dealing with EFTA Court jurisprudence in substance is Paolo Mengozzi's opinion in Case C-170/04 *Klas Rosengren and Others v Riksåklagaren*.[130] The ECJ was asked whether a ban on private imports of alcoholic beverages such as that imposed by the Swedish Alcohol Law constituted a rule concerning the operation of a retail sales monopoly in the products in question which was to be examined under Article 31 EC. The EC Court had laid down in Case C-185/95 *Criminal Proceedings against Harry Franzén* a general test whereby 'the rules relating to the existence and operation of the monopoly' of a state retail alcohol monopoly are to be examined with reference to Article 31 EC, whereas 'the effect on intra-Community trade of the other provisions of the domestic legislation which [are] separable from the operation of the monopoly' are to be examined with reference to Article 28 EC.[131] Advocate General Tizzano, who had been assigned the *Rosengren* case first, found that since the Swedish retail sales monopoly Systembolaget had discretion to refuse orders from private parties that entail importing products from other Member States, the imposition of the ban on private parties importing those products themselves was contrary to Article 31 EC.[132] In view of its importance, the Third Chamber subsequently decided to submit the case to the plenum which assigned it to the Grand Chamber. Rosengren, the EFTA Surveillance Authority and the Commission argued that the ban fell to be considered under Article 28 EC. The governments of Sweden, Finland and Norway were of the opposite view. With regard to the question of whether such a ban was compatible with Article 31 EC, in his opinion of 30 November 2006, Advocate General Mengozzi concurred with (former) Advocate General Tizzano that Article 31 EC applied. In coming to that conclusion, he dealt extensively with the EFTA Court's judgment in Case E-4/05 *HOB-vín v The Icelandic State and Áfengis- og tóbaksverslun ríkisins* (the State Alcohol and Tobacco Company of Iceland) of 17 January 2006.[133] In that case, the EFTA Court held, *inter alia*, that the requirements that products of a certain quantity must be delivered on a pallet, and that the price of the pallet must be included in the price of the product, related to the operation of the monopoly. Since they exclusively applied to

---

[128] Case C-374/04 *Test Claimants*, judgment of 12 December 2006, nyr.
[129] C-170/05 *Denkavit*, judgment of 14 December 2006, nyr.
[130] Case C-170/04 *Klas Rosengren and Others v Riksåklagaren*, opinion of AG Mengozzi 30 November 2006, nyr.
[131] Case C-189/95 *Criminal Proceedings against Harry Franzén* [1997] ECR I-5909, paras 35 and 36.
[132] Case C-170/04 *Klas Rosengren and Others v Riksåklagaren*, opinion of AG Tizzano of 30 March 2006, nyr, paras 57 ff.
[133] EFTA Court Report [2006] 3.

the monopoly, they had to be considered inseparable from its operation.[134] The EFTA Surveillance Authority submitted in *Rosengren* that it followed from the EFTA Court's decision in *HOB-vín* that a provision of national law can only be deemed to be inseparable from the operation of the monopoly if it concerns the monopoly directly. Advocate General Mengozzi did not share that view and argued that it could not be deduced from the EFTA Court's judgment that national rules which concern other economic actors or private persons are necessarily separable from the operation of the monopoly.[135]

G. EFTA Court References to Advocates General

In recent times, the EFTA Court has referred to opinions of Advocates General on certain occasions. It is too early to tell how this policy will develop in the future, but the cases in point were characterized by the following features.

The EFTA Court made reference to opinions of Advocates General in two cases where there was no ECJ case law. In Joined Cases E-5/04, E-6/04 and E-7/04 *Fesil and Finnfjord and Others v EFTA Surveillance Authority* (2005),[136] the EFTA Court cited Advocate General Jacobs who had stated in his opinion in Case C-99/98 *Austria v Commission* that the new system established by Council Regulation No 659/1999 laying down detailed rules for the application of Article 93 EC 'strikes a somewhat novel and different balance between the interests of the Community, of Member States and of other interested parties... it would... be hazardous to isolate individual rules of that Regulation and to claim that those rules (which would be necessarily taken out of their context) codify the pre-existing state of the law'. The EFTA Court explicitly shared this view.[137] In Case E-3/05 *EFTA Surveillance Authority v Norway* ('*Finnmark*'), the EFTA Court held that a Norwegian regulation giving parents living together with their children in a certain region up to the age of 18 the right to obtain family allowances was compatible with Article 73 of Regulation 1408/71. It found the regional residence requirement to be indirectly discriminatory, but objectively justified on grounds of promoting sustainable settlement in an area which had experienced depopulation due to, *inter alia*, harsh climate and vast distances. With regard to the relationship between Council Regulation No 1408/71 on the application of social security schemes to employed persons, to self-employed persons and to members of their families moving within the Community and Council Regulation No 1612/68 on freedom of movement of workers within the

---

[134] ibid, para 25.
[135] Case C-170/04 *Klas Rosengren and Others v Riksåklagaren*, opinion of AG Mengozzi of 30 November 2006, nyr, pts 52–6.
[136] EFTA Court Report [2005] 117, rn 123.
[137] Reference to the opinion of AG Jacobs in Case C-99/98 *Austria v Commission* [2001] ECR I-1101 in Joined Cases E-5/04, E-6/04 and E-7/04 *Fesil and Finnfjord*, EFTA Court Report [2005] 117, para 123.

Community, the EFTA Court referred to the opinion of Advocate General Alber in Case C-35/97 *Commission v France*.[138]

On two occasions, the EFTA Court made reference to opinions of Advocates General despite there being relevant ECJ case law. In Case E-1/04 *Fokus Bank*, the EFTA Court held that provisions of the EEA Agreement on free movement of capital are essentially identical in substance to the ones of the EC Treaty as amended by the Maastricht Treaty. The EFTA Court referred to the ECJ's judgment in Case C-452/01 *Ospelt*, but also to the opinion of Advocate General Geelhoed in that case.[139] In Case E-1/02 *University of Oslo*, the EFTA Court decided that the earmarking of a certain number of academic posts for women was incompatible with the principle of equal treatment laid down in the relevant Directive. The EFTA Court first described the development of the ECJ's case law and cited two cornerstones in this development, the opinions of Advocate General Tesauro in Case C-450/93 *Kalanke* and of Advocate General Saggio in Case C-158/97 *Badeck*.[140]

In two important cases, the EFTA Court referred to the Advocate General's opinion although (or because) it pursued another line of argument than the ECJ's judgment. In light of the homogeneity rules laid down in EEA law, this is the most sensitive, but also the most interesting type of dialogue between the EFTA Court and an Advocate General. In Case E-8/00 *Norwegian Federation of Trade Unions*,[141] the Norwegian labour unions of municipal employees had sued the Norwegian Association of Local and Regional Authorities together with eleven municipalities before the Norwegian Labour Court. The unions alleged that the respective collective agreement had been violated. According to that agreement, all Norwegian municipalities had concluded their pension agreements with one supplier, *Kommunal Landspensjonskasse* (KLP), a private mutual life insurance company wholly owned by members of the Norwegian Association of Local and Regional Authorities. A change of the pension company was only possible after a discussion with union representatives. Moreover, relevant offers for a new occupational pension scheme had to be put before those members of the pension committee who represented the parties to the collective agreement, the occupational pension scheme had to be based on a financing system that was gender-neutral and did not have the effect of excluding older employees, approval from the Norwegian Public Service Pension Fund was needed, and the pension scheme

---

[138] Reference in Case E-3/05 *EFTA Surveillance Authority v Norway*, EFTA Court Report [2006] 101, para 63, to the opinion of AG Alber in Case C-35/97 *Commission v France* [1998] I-5325.

[139] Reference in Case E-1/04 *Fokus Bank*, EFTA Court Report [2004] 11, para 23, to the opinion of AG Geelhoed in Case C-452/01 *Ospelt* [2003] ECR I-9743.

[140] References in Case E-1/02 *University of Oslo*, EFTA Court Report [2003] 1, paras 37 and 40, to the opinions of AG Tesauro in Case C-450/93 *Kalanke* [1996] ECR I-3051 and AG Saggio in Case C-158/97 *Badeck* [2000] ECR I-1875.

[141] Case E-8/00 *Norwegian Federation of Trade Unions and Others v Norwegian Association of Local and Regional Authorities and Others*, EFTA Court Report [2002] 114.

had to be taken note of by the Banking, Insurance and Securities Commission. In its judgment of 22 March 2002, the EFTA Court held that articles of a collective agreement which pursue the aim of improving the conditions of work and employment do not fall within the scope of the EEA competition rules. This did not mean, however, that provisions of collective agreements were automatically sheltered from competition law. The EFTA Court allowed the parties to the agreement a certain margin of discretion. If, however, provisions of a collective agreement pursued the improvement of conditions of work and employment on the face, but their practical implementation was actually intended to further other interests, the protection of the agreement from EEA competition law could not be upheld. In that respect, the good faith of the parties in concluding and implementing a collective agreement was to be taken into account.[142] The ECJ for its part had a few years earlier in a series of judgments decided that collective agreements concluded in pursuit of social policy objectives such as the improvement of conditions of work and employment must, by virtue of their nature and purpose, be regarded as falling outside the scope of Article 85(1), now Article 81[1] of the Treaty.[143] In contrast to Advocate General Jacobs, the EC Court did not, however, examine the limits of such immunity. Francis Jacobs had carried out a comparative study which included the law of the United States and had come to the conclusion that, in all the systems examined, collective agreements are to some extent sheltered from the cartel prohibition, but that immunity is not unlimited.[144] The EFTA Court reproduced this statement almost verbatim and cited the respective point in the Advocate General's opinion.[145] The ECJ did not mention the opinion. The EFTA Court also held that the good faith of the parties in concluding and implementing a collective agreement had to be taken into account.[146] Advocate General Jacobs pointed to that requirement in his opinion,[147] but the ECJ did not. It may be added that on 23 May 2007, Advocate General Poiares Maduro in his opinion in Case C-438/05 *Viking Line* argued for a concept of 'limited antitrust immunity' of collective agreements and referred to Francis Jacobs' opinion in *Albany* and to the EFTA Court's *LO* judgment.[148]

In its judgment in Case E-2/02 *Bellona* of 19 June 2003,[149] the EFTA Court had to decide whether a Norwegian environmental foundation, and a German environmental consulting firm, had *locus standi* to challenge a decision of the

---

[142] ibid, para 55 ff.
[143] C-67/96 *Albany* [1999] ECR I-5751, paras 59–61; Joined Cases C-115/97, C-116/97 and C-117/97 *Brentjens* [1999] ECR I-6025; *Drijvende Bokken* [1999] ECR I-6121; C-222/98 *Van der Woude* [2000] ECR I-7111; Joined Cases C-180/98 to C-184/98 *Pavlov* [2000] ECR I-645.
[144] ibid, pt 109.
[145] Case E-8/00 *LO*, EFTA Court Report [2002] 114, para 35.
[146] ibid, para 56.
[147] ibid, pts 192, 194, 296.
[148] Case C-438/05 *The International Transport Workers' Federation and the Finnish Seamen's Union v Viking Line ABP and OÜ Viking Line Eesti*, nyr, pt 27, fn 24. In addition, there is a reference to the ECJ's ruling in Case C-222/98 *Van der Woude* [2000] ECR I-7111.
[149] EFTA Court Report [2003] 52, para 36 ff.

EFTA Surveillance Authority addressed to Norway under Article 36(2) EEA, the provision mirroring Article 230(4) EC. The ESA had found that the adoption of distinctly favourable depreciation rates for certain geographically-defined natural gas exploitation projects in Norway constituted state aid, but approved it as being compatible with EEA law. Bellona, and TBW, the second applicant, argued that under Article 3(1) SCA, the EFTA Court was not bound to follow the case law of the ECJ and the CFI on the question of admissibility of actions brought against Commission decisions. Referring in particular to Advocate General Jacobs' opinion in Case C-50/00 *Pequeños Agricultores*, they criticized the *Plaumann* test adopted by the ECJ in 1962[150] and used ever since, according to which persons other than those to whom a decision is addressed may claim *locus standi* in relation to a decision only if that decision affects them by 'reason of certain attributes which are peculiar to them, or by reason of circumstances in which they are differentiated from all other persons and by virtue of these factors distinguishes them individually just as in the case of the person addressed'.[151] Advocate General Jacobs had proposed in *Pequeños Agricultores* that the ECJ overrule its *Plaumann* jurisprudence and replace it by a more liberal approach. The EFTA Court observed introductorily that access to justice constitutes an essential element of the EEA legal framework. It also stated that it was aware of the ongoing debate with regard to the issue of the standing of natural and legal persons in actions against Community institutions and referred, *inter alia*, to the opinion of Advocate General Jacobs in *Pequeños Agricultores*,[152] but not to the judgment in that case.[153] The Court added that this discussion was important at a time when the significance of the judicial function which is inspired by the idea of human rights appeared to be on the increase, both on the national and international level. In the case at hand, the Court, however, concluded that the applicants lacked *locus standi*. Bellona was unable to demonstrate that its own commercial or financial interests were adversely affected; it is not an association and has no members. TBW was deemed not to be affected by any competition arising from the adoption of the contested decision.

IV. Assessment

A. The Dialogue Policy of the ECJ and its Advocates General

It may be concluded from the above that the ECJ is in general willing to enter a dialogue with the EFTA Court in cases concerning the interpretation of EC or EEA law, if the latter has answered a fresh legal question, provided the ECJ

---

[150] ibid, Report for the Hearing, pts 86 ff.
[151] Case 25/62, *Plaumann* [1963] ECR 95.
[152] Case C-50/00 *Pequeños Agricultores* [2002] ECR I-6677.
[153] ibid.

shares the EFTA Court's position with regard to the outcome and the reasons. In such cases, the ECJ is even willing to reconsider and to change its case law in the light of the EFTA Court's jurisprudence. Occasionally, the ECJ appears also to be prepared to make reference to the EFTA Court as a source of further information. The ECJ will, however, only refer to the EFTA Court's jurisprudence when dealing with the fresh legal issue for the first time. In subsequent cases, the EC Court will limit itself to citing its own case law (which in substance may be based on EFTA Court jurisprudence).[154] One could say that the EFTA Court's 'entitlement' to be quoted seems to be 'exhausted' after the first citation. There are, however, exceptions to that practice. The *Bellio Fratelli* judgment of the Third Chamber of the ECJ is a case in point.[155] The 'exhaustion principle' has in a way also been used in cases in which the ECJ applies EC and EEA law together. In Case C-471/04 *Keller Holding*, the ECJ referred to its own judgment in *Bellio Fratelli* and the EFTA Court's *ESA v Iceland* ruling when addressing the importance of a homogeneous development of the case law. In Case 345/05 *Commission v Portugal*, the ECJ cited only its own *Keller Holding* ruling (which, for its part, refers to an EFTA Court judgment).[156] In the latest case, the ECJ refrained from dealing with the homogeneity principle.[157]

In a small number of cases, the ECJ has given reasons that differ from the ones previously relied on by the EFTA Court. In such cases, the ECJ will not mention the EFTA Court's judgment.[158] One must therefore conclude that the judicial dialogue between the ECJ and the EFTA Court is essentially affirmative in nature.

---

[154] Cases in point concern the assessment of the succession or passing on of contracts under the Transfer of Undertakings Directive decided after C-13/95 *Süzen* (see e.g. Case C-340/01 *Abler* [2003] ECR I-14023, paras 29 ff; Joined Cases C-232/04 and C-233/04 *Güney-Görres* [2005] ECR I-11237, paras 31 ff), the recognition and the scope of application of the precautionary principle in food law and in related matters decided after C-192/01 *Commission v Denmark* (Cases C-24/00 *Commission v France* [2004] ECR I-1277, paras 55 ff; C-95/01 *Greenham and Abel* [2004] ECR I-1333, paras 42 ff; C-41/02 *Commission v Netherlands* [2004] ECR I-11375, paras 43 ff, but see the reference of the ECJ (Third Chamber) to EFTA Court *Kellogg's* with regard to fresh legal question in the same judgment, above.

[155] Above. The case was about the interpretation of EEA law.

[156] Above.

[157] Case C-104/06 *Commission v Sweden*, judgment of 18 January 2007, nyr.

[158] See the ECJ's 1997 judgment in Case C-189/95 *Criminal proceedings against Harry Franzén* [1997] ECR I-5909 and the EFTA Court's judgment in Case E-6/96 *Tore Wilhelmsen AS v Oslo kommune*, EFTA Court Report [1997] 53, concerning the relationship between Articles 28 and 31 EC in the assessment of a state alcohol retail monopoly; the ECJ's judgment in Case C-355/96 *Silhouette* [1998] ECR I-4799 and the EFTA Court's ruling in E-2/97 *Maglite*, EFTA Court Report [1997] 127, concerning the international exhaustion of trade mark rights; the ECJ's judgment in C-348/98 *Ferreira* [2000] ECR I-6711 and the EFTA Court's ruling in E-1/99 *Finanger*, EFTA Court Report [1999] 119, concerning the scope of application of the Motor Vehicle Insurance Directives; and the ECJ's judgments in Cases C-374/04 *Test Claimants in Class IV of the ACT Group Litigation*, judgment of 12 December 2006, nyr, and C-170/05 *Denkavit International BV, Denkavit France SARL v Ministre de l'Économie, des Finances and de l'Industrie*, judgment of 14 December 2006, nyr, on the one hand, and E-1/04 *Fokus Bank ASA*, EFTA Court Report [2004] 11 on the other, concerning the taxation of dividends.

As far as the dialogue with the CFI is concerned, it is difficult to draw any conclusions concerning that Court's policy in view of the low number of relevant cases. One must not overlook, however, that it was the CFI which opened the dialogue with the EFTA Court in Case T-115/94 *Opel Austria*.[159]

Advocates General pursue a different policy with regard to the dialogue with the EFTA Court than the ECJ. First of all, some of them tend to be more generous when referring to EFTA Court jurisprudence as an additional argument in cases in which they agree with it. Moreover, a number of Advocates General would in their opinions deal with the judgments of the EFTA Court in substance and enter a dialectic discussion with the latter.

B. Functions of Dialogue

Three functions of the dialogues between the ECJ and its Advocates General on the one hand and the EFTA Court on the other are of particular significance. First, judicial dialogue strengthens homogeneity. Second, the ECJ and the CFI by way of dialogue pay respect to the EFTA Court's contributions to the development of the case law in the EEA as a whole.[160] The same may be said of the dialogue between the EFTA Court and Advocates General. Third, judicial dialogue may amount to the ECJ lending support to the EFTA Court. In that respect, the judgment of the CFI in Case T-115/94 *Opel Austria* of 22 January 1997 is to be mentioned. In its first EEA opinion 1/91 of 14 December 1991, the ECJ had assumed that the EEA Agreement was essentially an agreement creating rights and obligations among governments and that, in view of the different goals and context, the principles of direct effect and primacy were not safeguarded by the identical wording of the EEA Agreement and the EC Treaty. In fact, the EC Court found that these principles were 'irreconcilable with the characteristics of the agreement'.[161] It should be recalled that when arguing against direct effect and state liability, the governments of the Nordic countries relied on opinion 1/91.[162] In *Opel Austria*, the CFI emphasized that '[c]ontrary to the Council's contention, the significance in regard to the interpretation and application of the Agreement

---

[159] Case T-115/94 *Opel Austria GmbH v Council of the European Union* [1997] ECR II-39; see the apt remarks of CFI President B Vesterdorf, 'EFTA Court 10th Anniversary' in C Baudenbacher, P Tresselt and T Örlygsson (eds), *The EFTA Court Ten Years On* (2005) 187 ff, 188. See with regard to CFI *Opel Austria GmbH v Council of the European Union* above.

[160] See C Timmermans, 'The European Union's Judicial System' (2004) 41 CMLRev 393, 400; V Skouris, 'The ECJ and the EFTA Court under the EEA Agreement: a paradigm for the international cooperation of judicial institutions' in C Baudenbacher, P Tresselt and T Örlygsson (eds), *The EFTA Court Ten Years On* (2005) 123 ff.

[161] Opinion 1/91 [1991] ECR I-6079 ff, para 28.

[162] See the pleadings of the government of Norway in Case E-1/94 *Restamark*, Report for the Hearing, EFTA Court Report [1994–5] 35, pt 91; further the pleadings of the governments of Iceland, Norway and Sweden in Case E-9/97 *Sveinbjörnsdóttir*, Report for the Hearing, EFTA Court Report [1998] 115, pts 54, 67, 79, of the government of Norway in Case E-4/01 *Karlsson*, Report for the Hearing, EFTA Court Report [2002] 155, pts 55 and 56.

of the Contracting Parties' objective of establishing a dynamic and homogeneous EEA has not been diminished by the Court of Justice in Opinion 1/91'.[163] As already indicated, the fact that EFTA Court case law had been endorsed by the ECJ also played a role when the EFTA Court in E-4/01 *Karlsson* rejected the Norwegian government's invitation to overrule its state liability case law.[164]

Opinions of Advocates General may also give moral support to the EFTA Court. In that respect, the references of Advocate General Geelhoed to the EFTA Court's E-1/00 *Finanger* ruling in Case C-537/03 *Candolin* were important. As mentioned above, the government of Norway had in Case E-1/99 *Finanger* unsuccessfully argued that a provision such as § 7 para 3 litra b of the Norwegian Automobile Liability Act which basically excluded a passenger of an intoxicated motor vehicle driver from insurance coverage if he or she knew or must have known that the driver of the vehicle was under the influence of alcohol was incompatible with the EEA Motor Vehicle Insurance Directives, was part of tort law, whereas the Motor Vehicle Insurance Directives were in its view only concerned with insurance law. When implementing the EFTA Court's ruling, the Norwegian Supreme Court unanimously held that Norway was in breach of the EEA Motor Vehicle Insurance Directives. By ten votes to five, the Chief Justice being in the minority, it declared, however, that it could not set aside a clear provision of Norwegian law.[165] The Norwegian legislature subsequently amended the Automobile Liability Act, and Veronika Finanger brought a second action, this time against the Norwegian state, under the EFTA Court's state liability jurisprudence. When Advocate General Geelhoed and the ECJ dealt with the *Candolin* case in the spring of 2005,[166] this second *Finanger* case was pending before the Supreme Court of Norway. In these proceedings, the Norwegian government did not uphold its opposition against state liability being part of EEA law,[167] but argued that the breach of EEA law by the Norwegian state was not sufficiently serious to trigger liability. At the same time, the Norwegian government submitted in *Candolin* before the ECJ that Community law, that is, the EC Motor Vehicle Insurance Directives, did not impose any limits on the appraisal under national law on civil liability of the extent to which a passenger contributed to the occurrence of his injuries.[168] In its judgment of 30 June 2005, the ECJ did not share that position, but held that the Directives precluded a national rule which allowed the compensation borne by the compulsory motor vehicle insurance to

---

[163] Case T-115/94 *Opel Austria GmbH v Council of the European Union* [1997] ECR II-39; see further C Baudenbacher, *The Legal Nature of EEA Law in the Course of Time – a Drama in Six Acts, and More May Follow* (2000) 39, 53 ff.
[164] See above.
[165] Supreme Court of Norway (Høyesterett), *Storebrand Skadeforsikring AS v Veronika Finanger*, 16.11.2000, Sivilsak Nr 55/1999, Inr 49B/2000, 1811.
[166] The opinion was rendered on 10 March 2005, the judgment on 30 June 2005.
[167] See above.
[168] Case C-537/03 *Katja Candolin, Jari-Antero Viljaniemi and Veli-Matti Paananen v Vahinkovakuutusosakeyhtiö Pohjola and Jarno Ruokoranta* [2005] ECR I-5745, para 25.

be refused or limited in a disproportionate manner on the basis of the passenger's contribution to the injury or loss he has suffered.[169] On 28 October 2005, the Norwegian Supreme Court ruled in favour of Veronika Finanger by nine votes to four, the Chief Justice being in the majority, and relied on the EFTA Court's and the Icelandic Supreme Court's judgments in the *Sveinbjörnsdóttir* case as well as on the ECJ's ruling in *Candolin*.[170] It does not take much to imagine what the Norwegian government would have stated in the *Finanger* proceedings before the Supreme Court, had the ECJ followed the Government's line of argument in the *Candolin* case.

V. Conclusions

The judicial dialogue between the ECJ, its Advocates General and the EFTA Court as described in this chapter has largely become a matter of course over the last 13 years. ECJ President Vassilios Skouris has stated that the results produced by the co-operation between the ECJ and the EFTA Court 'constitute a true paradigm for international cooperation between judicial institutions'.[171] At the same time, one will not overlook that the EEA type of dialogue is affirmative in nature, as far as the ECJ is concerned (but not as far as Advocates General are concerned); and it must be admitted that the framework conditions for judicial co-operation in the EEA are particularly favourable. There are special circumstances such as the identity in substance of the law, common values and personal contacts between the actors in Luxembourg which limit the risk of 'bricolage'. But even if the conditions are particularly good for cross-fertilization, whether dialogue takes place in a concrete case will to a large extent depend upon decisions by individual persons. Among Advocates General, Sir Francis G. Jacobs has been the EFTA Court's most important partner during the first 12 years of the latter's existence. This is due to his open mindedness and his curiosity in new developments on the one hand, and to the quality of his opinions on the other.

---

[169] See above.
[170] Supreme Court of Norway (Høyesterett), *Veronika Finanger v The State*, 28 October 2005, HR-2005-0169 – P, Case No 2005/412.
[171] 'The ECJ and the EFTA Court under the EEA Agreement' in C Baudenbacher, P Tresselt and T Örlygsson (eds), *The EFTA Court Ten Years On* (2005) 123, 129.

PART II
FUNDAMENTAL RIGHTS

7
The Role of the ECJ in the Protection of Fundamental Rights

Antonio Tizzano[1]

I. Introduction

I believe it is safe to say that the protection of fundamental rights is one of the fields of law where the intervention of the European Court of Justice has been most remarkable and far-reaching. Actually, using the words of my distinguished colleague to whom this study is dedicated, 'the whole foundations [of the protection of fundamental rights at the EU level] were the work of the Court'.[2]

As we shall see in greater detail below, the Court's approach in this area was developed progressively over several decades and different phases, through a number of judgments which were as bold as they were far-sighted. During his long tenure in Luxembourg, Advocate General Jacobs has certainly been one of the main contributors to the consolidation and further development of this jurisprudence, not only for the large number of cases, involving different aspects of fundamental rights protection, he directly dealt with[3] but also, and foremost, for the considerable influence his work exerted inside and outside the Court.

II. From Silence to Action

It is mainly on the basis of a systematic and teleological interpretation of the founding treaties that the Court has construed the inclusion of fundamental rights in the Community law system.

---

[1] The author wishes to thank Bruno Gencarelli and Luca Prete, référendaires in his chambers at the Court of Justice, for their precious assistance in the preparation of the present paper.

[2] F Jacobs, 'Human rights in the European Union: the role of the Court of Justice' (2001) 26 ELRev August 337.

[3] For a sample of Advocate General Jacobs' opinions in cases involving issues of fundamental rights, see e.g. opinions in Case 5/88 *Wachauf v Bundesamt für Ernährung und Forstwirtschaft* [1989] ECR 2609; Case C-177/95 *Ebony Maritime SA and Loten Navigation Co Ltd v Prefetto della Provincia di Brindisi and others* [1996] ECR I-1111; Case C-377/98 *Netherlands v European Parliament and Council* [2001] ECR I-7079, and Case C-167/04 P *JCB Services v Commission*, judgment of 21 September 2006.

As is well known, the three founding Treaties made no provision for the protection of human rights as such.[4] The reason lies probably in the fact that, at the time of their adoption, the economic integration undertaken by the six founding members of the Communities appeared a matter completely unrelated to that of fundamental rights. Such a reference might also have been considered unnecessary where all Member States had, a few years earlier, signed another pan-European instrument which specifically addressed the protection of fundamental rights: the European Convention for the Protection of Human Rights and Fundamental Freedoms.[5] Whatever the reason for the omission, in its early days the ECJ took the view that fundamental rights were not relevant for the application of the founding Treaties.[6] This was made particularly clear in the *Geitling v High Authority* judgment[7] in which the Court rejected the applicant's argument based on the protection of the right to property as provided for in the German Fundamental Law. In dismissing that argument, the Court expressly stated that it was only required to ensure the observance of Community law, not national law, and that Community law did not contain any general principle protecting the right in question. In other words, the Court lacked competence to enforce fundamental rights recognized in national systems.

These '*péchés de jeunesse*'[8] did not last long, though. The initial stance taken by the Court was subject to a progressive, but eventually radical, change as of the mid-sixties. This evolution is widely regarded as attributable to the affirmation in those years of the principles of direct effect and primacy of Community law and the reluctance of some national constitutional courts to acknowledge their full effectiveness. In particular, the German and Italian courts expressed concerns about whether EC law should also prevail in case of conflict with fundamental rights protected by their respective constitutions.

In this context, the lack of fundamental rights protection under Community law risked to undermine those very principles the ECJ was trying to establish, and first of all that of supremacy. How could the autonomy of the Community's

---

[4] This does not mean that fundamental rights were completely absent from the original Treaties. In particular, the EEC Treaty contained some specific provisions on the prohibition of discrimination on grounds of nationality and on the right of male and female workers to receive equal pay for equal work. Over the years, the Court gave an increasingly wide interpretation of both of these rights.

[5] The Convention was signed in Rome on 4 November 1950.

[6] See Case 2/56 *Geitling Ruhrkohlen-Verkaufsgesellschaft and Others v ECSC High Authority* [1957] ECR 9; Case 1/58 *Stork v High Authority* [1959] ECR 17; Joined Cases 36-41/59 *Simet and Others v ECSC High Authority* [1959] ECR 331, and Case 40/64 *Sgarlata v Commission* [1965] ECR 279.

[7] Joined Cases 36-38/59 and 40/59 *Geitling v High Authority* [1960] ECR 857, 889.

[8] J-P Puissochet, 'La Cour européenne des droits de l'homme, la Cour de justice des Communautés européennes et la protection des droits de l'homme' in P Mahoney, F Matscher, H Petzold and L Wildhaber (eds), *Protection des droits de l'homme: la perspective européenne. Mélanges à la mémoire de Rolv Ryssdal*, Koln, Heymanns (2000) 1139, 1140.

'own legal order'[9] and its uniformity of application be preserved if part of the protection of its citizens invoking rights they directly derived from the Treaty was left to national law? Conversely, how could national courts accept that EC law took precedence over all domestic law, including constitutional provisions, if the Community legal order did not provide for adequate human rights safeguards?

Hence, in 1969, 15 years after its first session, the Court stated – in a famous *obiter dictum* – that a certain provision in a Commission decision adopted in the framework of the Common Agricultural Policy did not prejudice 'the fundamental human rights enshrined in the general principles of Community law and protected by the Court'.[10] In practical terms, by including fundamental rights within the 'general principles of Community law' the observance of which it ensures, the Court meant that it was prepared to annul any EC law provision contrary to such rights. Thus, this ruling, soon followed by similar ones,[11] marked a first decisive step in the elaboration of a Community concept and judicial protection of human rights. Indeed, from then on, the Court considered, as it would stress some years later, that it had 'the duty... to ensure the observance of fundamental rights in the field of Community law'.[12]

III. A Judicial Bill of Rights

In *Stauder,* the Court referred to fundamental human rights as an integral part of the Community legal order without, however, dwelling upon what this body of rights actually included. Faced with the silence of the founding treaties, the ECJ filled this lacuna by taking inspiration and seeking guidance from a variety of sources and developing an autonomous and extensive catalogue of such rights.

The seminal *Internationale Handelsgesellschaft* judgment of 1970 identified a first source of inspiration in the 'constitutional traditions common to the Member States'.[13] Just a few years later, in the *Nold* ruling, the Court took a step further, stating that the ECJ was now 'bound to draw inspiration from'[14] common national constitutional traditions, adopting thus a non-written, yet solid and binding, legal source.

---

[9] Case 6/64 *Costa v Enel* [1964] ECR 585.
[10] Case 29/69 *Erich Stauder v City of Ulm – Sozialamt* [1969] ECR 419, para 7.
[11] See Case 11/70 *Internationale Handelsgesellschaft mbH v Einfuhr- und Vorratsstelle für Getreide und Futtermittel* [1970] ECR 1125 and Case 25/70 *Einfuhr- und Vorratsstelle für Getreide und Futtermittel v Köster* [1970] ECR 1161.
[12] Joined Cases 60 and 61/84 *Cinéthèque SA v Federation Nationale des Cinémas Français* [1985] ECR 2605, para 26.
[13] *Internationale Handelsgesellschaft*, para 4.
[14] Case 4/73 *Nold v Commission* [1974] ECR 491, para 13.

Interestingly, the Court's very early case law did not refer directly to the European Convention on Human Rights, which, however, would soon become its other main source of inspiration. This could be explained by a number of reasons, including the fact that France only ratified the Convention in 1974. This initial approach is reflected in the *Nold* judgment's general reference to 'international treaties for the protection of human rights on which the Member States have collaborated or of which they are signatories' which could possibly 'supply guidelines to be followed in the enforcement of Community law'.[15]

Despite this rather cautious language, it was not long before the Court started to rely more and more frequently and extensively on such international instruments, looking especially in the direction of Strasbourg.[16] There was a pragmatic and simple explanation for this change: the constitutional traditions of the Member States were not always so common. In other words, there appeared to be some inconsistencies between the substance and boundaries of the rights recognized as fundamental in the various national systems. As Advocate General Jacobs put it in his opinion on the *Schmidberger* case, 'despite a basic consensus...about a core of rights which must be regarded as fundamental, there are a number of divergences between the fundamental rights catalogues of the Member States, which often reflect the history and particular political culture of a given Member State'.[17]

In this context, the European Convention of Human Rights soon acquired a special and central role as a source for identifying fundamental rights. Not only was the Convention expressly relied on,[18] but in a number of cases it also constituted the deciding element in the Court's analysis.[19] This role was further strengthened by the Court's approach, consisting in referring, in addition to the Convention as such, also to the case law of the European Court of Human Rights. In essence, the Court came to de facto integrate the Convention, as well as the jurisprudence of its Strasbourg counterpart, in the Community legal order through its general principles. The following words written by a colleague of Advocate General Jacobs at the ECJ eloquently encapsulate this judicial incorporation process: 'tout se passe comme si la Cour de justice appliquait purement et simplement la convention'.[20] So profound is this integration that on some occasions the ECJ even decided to review its own case law having regard to Strasbourg's jurisprudence. This occurred, for instance, with respect to the protection of business premises (in the context of antitrust investigation) in the light of the right to

---

[15] ibid, para 13.
[16] Other treaties to which the Court has referred include the International Covenant on Civil and Political Rights of 1966 and the European Social Charter of 1961.
[17] Case C-112/00 *Eugen Schmidberger Internationale Transporte Planzügev Republik Österreich* [2003] ECR I-5659, para 97.
[18] See e.g. Case 36/75 *Roland Rutili contre Ministre de l'intérieur* [1975] ECR 1219, para 32.
[19] See e.g. Case 222/84 *Marguerite Johnston v Chief Constable of the Royal Ulster Constabulary* [1986] ECR 1651, paras 18 ff.
[20] Puissochet (n 8 above), 1143.

inviolability of the home enshrined in Article 8(1) of the Convention. In fact, in *Roquette Frères,* the Court appeared to almost rectify its previous *Hoechst* ruling by expressly observing that 'regard must be had to the case law of the European Court of Human Rights subsequent to the judgment in *Hoechst*'.[21]

But it would be wrong to describe the relationship between the two Courts as being a monologue. There are cases concerning, for example, transsexuals' rights, where the ECHR seems to have reconsidered its jurisprudence in the light of ECJ judgments. After more than 30 years of such dialogue, it seems fair to conclude that divergences in the case law of the two Courts seem quite rare and, when they do exist, the evolution of the jurisprudence of the two Courts appears capable of reducing them.

Using these two main guiding sources, over the years the ECJ 'discovered' a rich and diversified body of rights, expanding well beyond economic freedoms to include civil and political rights such as, *inter alia*, freedom of expression[22] and association,[23] right to manifest one's religion,[24] protection of privacy[25] and respect for family life[26] or the principle of non-retroactivity of penal provisions.[27]

Another important aspect of this phase of development of fundamental rights protection within the EC is the widening of the scope of such protection from a judicial review focusing solely on Community measures to a scrutiny extended to some national measures.

While the above-mentioned *Stauder, Internationale Handelsgesellschaft* and *Nold* rulings all concerned acts adopted by the Community institutions, the Court later established that national measures either implementing Community acts or derogating from the Treaty's provisions must also comply with Community standards of fundamental rights protection.

As to the first type of measures – that is, national measures implementing Community legislation – in the landmark *Wachauf* case Advocate General Jacobs stressed, in a key passage of his opinion which was followed by the Court, how it seemed 'self-evident that when acting in pursuance of powers granted under Community law, Member States must be subject to the same constraints, in any event in relation to the principle of respect for fundamental rights, as the Community legislator'.[28]

---

[21] Case C-94/00 *Roquette Frères v Directeur général de la concurrence, de la consommation et de la répression des fraudes* [2002] ECR 9011, para 29.
[22] See e.g. Case C-288/89 *Stichting Collectieve Antennevoorziening Gouda and Others v Commissariaat voor de Media* [1991] ECR I-4007.
[23] See e.g. Case 18/74 *General Union of Personnel of European Organizations v Commission* [1974] ECR 933.
[24] See e.g. Case 130/75 *Prais v Council* [1976] ECR 1589.
[25] See e.g. Case 165/82 *Commission v UK* [1983] ECR 3431.
[26] See e.g. Case 249/86 *Commission v Germany* [1989] ECR 1263.
[27] See e.g. Case 63/83 *Regina v Kent Kirk* [1984] ECR 2689.
[28] Case 5/88 *Wachauf v Bundesamt für Ernährung und Forstwirtschaft* [1989] ECR 2606, opinion of AG Jacobs, para 22.

With respect to the second category of national measures, the recent *Festersen* ruling contains an interesting illustration of the obligation imposed by the Court on Member States to comply with Community fundamental rights when invoking exceptions to, or derogations from, EC law. In this judgment, the Court took fundamental rights as one of the elements of the proportionality test when analysing whether a Danish measure, subjecting the acquisition of agricultural property to the obligation for the acquirer to fix his residence on that property, infringed the free movement of capital. In ascertaining whether this residence requirement constituted a measure proportionate to the legitimate aim of avoiding acquisitions of agricultural land for purely speculative reasons, the Court took account of the fact that this measure 'restrict[ed] not only the free movement of capital but also the right of the acquirer to choose his place of residence freely, a right which he is, however, guaranteed by Article 2(1) of Protocol No 4 to the [ECHR]'.[29] Accordingly, the Court considered that, '[g]iven that the residence requirement thus adversely affects a fundamental right guaranteed by the ECHR, [this measure] turns out to be particularly restrictive'.[30]

Mention should be made here of the fact that the case law developed vis-à-vis national measures restricting fundamental freedoms does not follow an entirely unilateral approach. The Court made it clear, notably in the well-known *Omega Spielhallen* judgment,[31] that a certain degree of flexibility and differentiation between domestic regimes is possible. This case concerned a German ban on laser games involving simulation of acts of homicide and the essential question was whether this restriction on the freedom to provide services had to be grounded on a conception of human dignity – this being the justification invoked by Germany on the basis of its constitutional provisions – common to all the Member States. After having recalled that human dignity constitutes a legitimate interest which is in principle capable of justifying a restriction of fundamental freedoms, the Court stated that to be deemed compatible with EC law it was not indispensable for the national measure in question to correspond to a conception shared by all Member States as regards the means of protecting human dignity. In other words, the Court accepted that different Member States can have different standards of protection of fundamental rights. This ruling seems somewhat to echo what Francis Jacobs had suggested a few years earlier regarding the standard of fundamental rights protection which a national court should apply: '[t]he Court of Justice is not in my view well placed to lay down that standard, nor I think has it ever sought to do so'.[32]

---

[29] Case C-370/05 *Festersen*, judgment of 25 January 2007, para 35.
[30] ibid, para 36.
[31] Case C-36/02 *Omega Spielhallen- und Automatenaufstellungs-GmbH v Oberbürgermeister der Bundesstadt Bonn* [ECR] I-9609. See also Case C-112/00 *Eugen Schmidberger, Internationale Transporte und Planzüge v Republik Österreich* [ECR] I-5659.
[32] Jacobs (n 2 above).

IV. The 'Masters of the Treaty' Step In

It is undisputed that the prominence given by the Court to the protection of fundamental rights prompted a series of major initiatives at both political and constitutional levels.

In 1977, the European Parliament, the Council and the Commission signed a Joint Declaration in which they expressed the 'prime importance' which they attached to the protection of fundamental rights arising from the two sources identified by the Court.[33] A further step was taken in 1986 with the preamble to the Single European Act containing, for the first time in a Community Treaty, a reference to fundamental rights.

But the most definitive recognition of the ECJ's pioneering role in the protection of such rights came in 1992 with the Maastricht Treaty on European Union (the 'TEU'). Giving tangible expression to the work carried out for more than 30 years by the Luxembourg Judges in this field, the authors of the TEU formally and unequivocally endorsed the Court's 'formula' by stipulating in Article F(2) (now Article 6(2) TEU) that '[t]he Union shall respect fundamental rights, as guaranteed by the European Convention for the Protection of Human Rights and Fundamental Freedoms signed in Rome on 4 November 1950 and as they result from the constitutional traditions common to the Member States, as general principles of Community law'. The inclusion of this provision in the TEU was not only of great symbolic significance, but also clearly imposed a legal obligation upon the EU institutions.

The seed was sowed in fertile ground. With the following revisions of the Treaties, this article directly rooted in the ECJ jurisprudence became the cornerstone of a whole corpus of rules on fundamental rights incorporated in primary Community law.

The Treaties of Amsterdam and Nice indeed strengthened the protection of fundamental rights in several ways.

First, a general clause was introduced in the first paragraph of Article 6 TEU stating that the Union is founded on a series of principles, including 'respect for human rights and fundamental freedoms', and Article 49 TEU formally makes compliance with such principles a precondition for joining the Union. As is well known, the level of fundamental rights protection attained by the countries of Central and Eastern Europe was the subject of intense scrutiny by the EU before their accession and is presently one of the most delicate issues discussed in the context of the enlargement negotiations with Turkey.

Second, the Amsterdam Treaty explicitly extended the jurisdiction of the ECJ to Article 6(2) TEU 'with regard to action of the institutions, insofar as the Court

---

[33] Joint Declaration of the European Parliament, the Council and the Commission [1977] OJ C103/1.

has jurisdiction under the [EC Treaty and the EU] Treaty' (Article 46(d) TEU), thereby further endorsing the Court's 'legacy'.

Finally, the insertion of Article 7 TEU attached new consequences to the breach of fundamental rights by a Member State, providing for the possibility of sanctions against the state in question, including the suspension of its voting rights, in case of serious and persistent violation of the principles laid down in Article 6(1). This mechanism was then strengthened by the Treaty of Nice which empowered the Council to address recommendations to the state concerned where there is clear risk of a serious breach of such principles.

Despite these important developments, many felt that the protection of fundamental rights in the EU legal system lacked, and was in urgent need of, a clear enunciation of the content of the rights the Union must respect and the Court must safeguard – especially in view of the continuous expansion of the EU's competences, including in areas capable of affecting the very heart of individual freedom such as cooperation in criminal matters.

A response to such mounting demand came with the Cologne European Council of June 1999, which decided to 'establish a Charter of Fundamental Rights in order to make their overriding importance and relevance more visible to the Union's citizens'.[34] A drafting committee (the so-called 'Convention') was established to elaborate such a text and on 7 December 2000 the European Parliament, the Council and the Commission 'solemnly proclaimed' the Charter, a declaratory text formally devoid – at least for the present – of legal effects.[35] Regardless even of the heavily-debated issue of the Charter's legal nature and binding force, there is no doubt that the work of the Court has greatly influenced what is today the most significant, detailed and visible EU instrument in the field of fundamental rights. The Charter, as envisioned by the representatives of the Member States and as drafted by the Convention, is indeed (mainly) an instrument of consolidation. That is to say, it does not amend substantive law in force but rather brings together in one single coherent text rights already guaranteed in the Community legal order, principally under the ECJ jurisprudence. In fact, in the words of the Cologne Council's mandate, the Charter had to bring together 'the fundamental rights and freedoms as well as basic procedural rights guaranteed by the European Convention for the Protection of Human Rights and Fundamental Freedoms and derived from the constitutional traditions common to the Member States, as general principles of Community law'.[36] And the Convention scrupulously respected its mandate, taking very often into consideration the Court's

---

[34] European Council Conclusions, Cologne, 3–4 June 1999.
[35] The Charter was proclaimed at the Nice European Council of December 2000 but was not included in the Treaty of Nice. After its promulgation, it was published in EC Official Journal in the C series, i.e. the section of the Official Journal covering non-binding documents (preparatory acts, notices, recommendations, etc.).
[36] Conclusions of the Presidency of the Cologne European Council, 3–4 June 1999, Annex IV.

case law,[37] so that the substance of the Charter has even been described as 'part of the *acquis communautaire*'.[38] Thus, in a certain sense, it could be said that the adoption of the Charter represented the zenith of the Court's contribution to, and influence on, the protection of fundamental rights in the EU.

V. Recent Trends and Future Prospects

Being a dynamic and ever-evolving subject, the protection of fundamental rights in the EU legal system continues to give rise to a number of novel and problematic issues. In their most recent jurisprudence, the Community courts have had the occasion to deal with some of these issues.

In recent years, the EU was deeply affected first by the adoption of the Treaty establishing a Constitution for Europe, then by the crisis which followed the French and Dutch referenda and finally by the relaunching of the EU, certainly one of the most debated issues. Once ratified, the Lisbon Treaty should eventually bring some clarity to this question by granting the Charter the same legal value as the Treaties (except with respect to the 'opting out' Member States).[39]

But even if currently lacking formal binding force, the significance and impact of this text should not be underestimated. The Charter cannot simply be described as a document of purely symbolic value but has progressively – yet surely – imposed itself as a main instrument of reference in the area of human rights, bringing an 'added value' both at the European and national level.

At EU level, for instance, shortly after the proclamation of the Charter at Nice, the Commission adopted an internal Communication directing its services to make the Charter 'an imperative in the daily action of the Commission'.[40] It notably provides that any proposal for a legislative or regulatory act which concerns one of the rights protected by the Charter should be the subject of prior control of its human rights compatibility. The Commission has been applying this human rights scrutiny to legislative proposals in particular in the sensitive areas of asylum, immigration and cooperation in criminal matters. The European Ombudsman is another EU actor who frequently invokes and 'enforces' the Charter. An example of this approach is to be found in The European Code of Good Administrative Behaviour, adopted by the Ombudsman and approved by the European Parliament, which specifically purports 'to explain in more detail

---

[37] See the many references to ECJ judgments in the 'Explanations relating to the Charter of Fundamental Rights' adopted by the Bureau of the Convention and which indicate the sources and the scope of each of the promulgated rights. Document Convent 49 of 11 October 2000.

[38] K Lenaerts and E De Smijter, 'A "Bill of Rights" for the European Union' (2001) 38 CMLRev 299.

[39] Please note that a new version of the Charter was proclaimed by the European Parliament, the Council and the Commission on 12 December 2007 and published in the [2007] OJ C303/1. This is the version that will be annexed to the Lisbon Treaty.

[40] Sec (2000) 380/3 of 13 March 2001.

what the Charter's right to good administration should mean in practice'.[41] Finally, there is no doubt that the Charter will be the main point of reference for the activities of the recently established EU Agency for Fundamental Rights, based in Vienna.[42]

Even more significantly for the purpose of this study, courts, including the Community judicature, have showed a growing interest for the Charter and have begun to use it and refer to it as a particularly authoritative evidence or confirmation of the existence of specific rights.

On the Kirchberg plateau, the Advocates General were the first to take possession and make use of the Charter in their opinions. Amongst these pioneers, Advocate General Jacobs has been particularly active. He expressly referred to the Charter when considering rights as diverse and different as, *inter alia*, the freedom of expression and assembly,[43] the prohibition of age discrimination,[44] the principle that every person has the right to have his or her affairs handled within a reasonable time by the institutions and bodies of the Union[45] and the importance of citizens' access to services of general economic interest.[46] In particular, in his opinion in *Netherlands v Parliament and Council*, he seems to have attributed an especially significant role and status to the Charter by directly and primarily basing on Article 3(2) thereof the rights to human dignity and to 'free and informed consent of the person concerned' in the fields of medicine and biology.[47] The Advocates General were soon emulated by the Court of First Instance which mentioned the Charter in a number of decisions, including the famous *Jégo-Quéré* ruling concerning access to Court to which I will return later.[48]

Despite these multiple references, the Charter has been for some time completely ignored in the Court's judgments, even in cases in which it followed the opinion of Advocates General who had drawn inspiration from such instrument. However, this approach has recently started to evolve, as the ECJ made its first references to articles of the Charter in the judgments rendered in *Parliament v*

---

[41] The European Code of Good Administrative Behaviour, 2005, 7. The full text of the Code is available at *http://www.ombudsman.europa.eu/code/pdf/en/code2005_en.pdf*.

[42] See Council Regulation (CE) No 168/2007 of 15 February 2007, establishing a European Union Agency for Fundamental Rights [2007] OJ L 53/1.

[43] Case C-112/00 *Eugen Schmidberger Internationale Transporte Planzügev Republik Österreich* [2003] ECR I-5659.

[44] Case C-227/04 P *Lindorfer v Council*, opinion of 27 October 2005.

[45] Case C-270/99 *Z v European Parliament* [2001] ECR I-9197.

[46] Case C-126/01 *Ministère de l'Économie, des Finances et de l'Industrie v GEMO SA* [2003] ECR I-13769. Interestingly, in this case AG Jacobs did not cite the Charter as an additional source among (many) others but quoted Article 36 of the Charter in parallel and on the same footing with Article 16 EC, thereby using it as a particularly relevant interpretative tool. See para 124 of the opinion.

[47] Case C-377/98 *Netherlands v Parliament and Council* [2001] ECR I-7079, paras 197 and 210.

[48] Case T-177/01 *Jégo-Quéré v Commission* [2002] ECR II-2365, para 42.

Council,[49] a case raising issues of validity of the directive on family reunification, and *Unibet*,[50] a reference from the Swedish Supreme Court concerning challenges to national provisions alleged to be contrary to Community law. In both judgments, the Court observed that the rights in question – respectively the right to respect for family life and the principle of effective judicial protection – were also recognized and reaffirmed by provisions of the Charter.

Further confirmations of the emergence of the Charter as a main human rights benchmark for all subjects involved, even outside the EU sphere of activity, come from references made to it by the European Court of Human Rights[51] and some national courts.[52]

However, leaving aside the issue of the substantial content of the rights protected, access to adequate judicial remedies has been pointed out by many commentators as a main shortcoming of the EU fundamental rights regime. According to these views, the 'procedural deficit' lies in the strict standing requirements imposed on private parties challenging a Community act under Article 230 EC as well as the even greater limitations applying to EU measures adopted on the basis of the Second and Third Pillars.

Sir Francis Jacobs certainly ought to be counted among these 'commentators', and as a particularly qualified one. Indeed, he should be credited for re-opening the debate on this issue by delivering in the famous *Unión de Pequeños Agricultores* ('UPA') case[53] an enlightening and detailed opinion inviting the Court to reconsider the notion of 'individual concern' as laid down in Article 230(4) EC. In his view, the interpretation made by the EC judicature of this requirement could in certain instances deprive individuals of an effective judicial protection and, in these cases, neither proceedings before national courts nor the possibility to resort to a preliminary ruling on the validity of a Community act constitute real and adequate alternatives. Consequently, he suggested broadening the standing rules, considering that:

the principle that an individual who considers himself wronged by a measure which deprives him of a right or advantage under Community law must have access to a remedy against that measure and be able to obtain complete judicial protection...is... grounded in the constitutional traditions common to the Member States and in Articles 6 and 13 of the European Convention on Human Rights [and recognized by] the Charter of fundamental rights of the European Union.

---

[49] Case C-540/03 *Parliament v Council*, judgment of 27 June 2006, paras 38 and 58.
[50] Case C-432/02 *Unibet v Justitiekanslern*, judgment of 13 March 2007, para 37.
[51] See e.g. *Goodwin v United Kingdom* App No 28957/95 (2002) 35 EHRR 18, and *Vo v France*, App 53924/00 (2005) 40 EHRR 12.
[52] See e.g. Tribunal Constitucional de España (Spain), judgment No 292/2000 of 30 November 2000, Corte Costituzionale (Italy), judgment No 135 of 11-24 April 2002, and Eesti Vabariigi Riigikohus (Estonia), judgment No 3 of the Constitutional Review Chamber of the Supreme Court of 21 January 2004.
[53] Case C-50/00 P *Unión de Pequeños Agricultores v Council* [2002] ECR I-6677.

A person should be regarded as individually concerned by a Community measure where, 'by reason of his particular circumstances, the measure has, or is liable to have, a substantial adverse effect on his interests'.[54]

The CFI was evidently influenced by this opinion when in its *Jégo-Quéré* ruling, issued a few weeks later, it held that the *locus standi* requirements applicable to private applicants could 'no longer be regarded, in the light of Articles 6 and 13 of the ECHR and of Article 47 of the Charter of Fundamental Rights, as guaranteeing persons the right to an effective remedy enabling them to contest the legality of Community measures of general application which directly affect their legal situation'[55] and needed therefore to be reconsidered.

As it will be recalled, however, the Court declined to follow either Advocate General Jacobs or the CFI. In its UPA judgment, it stated that, although the 'individual concern' requisite must be interpreted in light of the principle of effective judicial protection, such an interpretation 'cannot have the effect of setting aside the condition in question, expressly laid down in the Treaty, without going beyond the jurisdiction conferred by the Treaty on the Community Courts'.[56]

In his opinion in the *Jégo-Quéré* appeal, Advocate General Jacobs had thus to acknowledge the Court's position on this issue, but he also took the opportunity to stress that, in his view, an action by the Member States to amend Article 230(4) EC was necessary as 'there are powerful arguments in favour of introducing a more liberal standing requirement in respect of individuals seeking to challenge generally applicable Community measures in order to ensure that full judicial protection is in all circumstances guaranteed'.[57]

The message was definitely heard by the members of the Convention on the Future of Europe and then by the drafters of the Lisbon Treaty. The latter would indeed, if ratified, bring some significant changes in this area by extending the Court's jurisdiction to matters presently subject to important restrictions (essentially, police and judicial cooperation in criminal matters), as well as modifying the requirements that natural or legal persons have to satisfy in order to bring an action for annulment. As regards the latter aspect, under Article 263(4) of the Treaty on the functioning of the European Union (that is, Article 230(4) EC, as amended by Article 2.214.C of the Lisbon Treaty, '[a]ny natural or legal person may, under the conditions laid down in the first and second paragraphs, institute proceedings against an act addressed to that person or which is of direct and individual concern to them, and against a regulatory act which is of direct concern to them and does not entail implementing measures'. With this provision, it is clear that the authors of the Treaty have intended, albeit cautiously, to widen the *locus*

---

[54] Opinion of 21 March 2002, paras 38–9 and 60.
[55] Case T-177/01 *Jégo-Quéré v Commission* [2002] ECR II-2365, para 47.
[56] *Unión de Pequeños Agricultores v Council*, para 44.
[57] Case C-263/02 P *Commission v Jégo-Quéré* [2004] ECR I-3425, opinion of 10 July 2003, para 46.

standi of private parties, thereby trying to do away with some of the limitations of the current Treaty rules.

While waiting for the ratification of the Lisbon Treaty and when assessing the 'quality' of the protection of fundamental rights currently afforded by the EU, from both a substantial and procedural point of view, it is necessary to take into account the approach adopted by other judicial systems.

In that respect, there has been recently a remarkable development in the case law of the European Court of Human Rights. In the *Bosphorus* case[58] concerning an Irish measure implementing an EC Regulation which had been previously challenged and upheld before the ECJ, the Strasbourg Court appears to signal its readiness to review, although indirectly, the compatibility with the Convention of Community acts. Most importantly, after closely considering the guarantees offered by the EU system of fundamental rights protection and specifically the treatment of this case by the Court of Justice, the ECHR came to the conclusion that there was no need to re-examine the applicant's claims concerning an alleged violation of his rights to property. In short, it found that the EU system of protection can be considered to be 'equivalent' to that of the ECHR and that therefore it was not necessary to scrutinize in detail the case before it.

A similar trend can be observed at national level. More than 30 years of affirmation of the protection of fundamental rights in the EU have dissipated, at least in part, some of the old fears. This is the case, for example, of the German *Bundesverfassungsgericht* – originally one of the national constitutional courts which expressed most scepticism about the Community capacity to safeguard human rights – which in the so-called *Solange II* judgment of 1986 declared to be satisfied with the general level of fundamental rights protection afforded by the ECJ, considering it comparable to the one provided under its Fundamental Law, and therefore held that in the future it would refrain from reviewing acts of the Community institutions, so long as that equivalence was maintained.[59] A very recent example of such spirit of *détente* is to be found in the *Arcelor* ruling rendered last February by the French Conseil d'Etat.[60] In that case, the plaintiffs alleged that a decree, implementing an EC Directive establishing an emission trading scheme under the Kyoto Protocol, infringed the right to property and to trade freely as well as the principle of equality, all guaranteed by the French Constitution. In stark contrast with its previous practice, the French supreme administrative court did not rule on the legality of the decree under its national law, but instead gave full effect to the supremacy of Community law by referring the case to the ECJ after having found that the fundamental rights in question are afforded similar protection under Community law and under the French Constitution.

---

[58] *Bosphorus Hava Yollari Turizm Ve Ticaret Sirketi v Ireland* App No 45036/98 (2006) 42 EHRR 1.
[59] *Wünsche Handelsgesellschaft* [1987] 3 CMLR 2225.
[60] Case No 287110, *Société Arcelor Atlantique etorraine et autres*, judgment of 8 February 2007.

These are all tangible signs of an emerging climate of mutual trust and reciprocal enrichment between the various, and ever increasing, actors involved in the protection of fundamental rights in Europe. The overview provided in this paper has attempted to briefly explain the significance of the unique contribution given by the Court of Justice to the development of this community of principles and values.

VI. Concluding Remarks

I believe that in the future the Court will continue to effectively ensure protection of fundamental rights under EU law, in spite of the well-known obstacles and difficulties which the Community process still encounters along the way and the extension of its jurisdiction to new and more sensitive areas, such as – to mention but the most significant – criminal law.

The Court will do this notwithstanding the criticisms which have been made and are made from time to time with respect to its supposed 'activism'. In fact, it is well known that the role played by the Court in the field of fundamental rights has been sometimes criticized as excessively interventionist or creative.

In this respect, I would like to point out that these criticisms need to be clarified; that is to say, the critics need to explain what else the Court should have done, while remaining faithful to its mission, other than contribute to the construction of the edifice whose fundamental elements (the Treaties) had been placed in its care – and do so consistently with the defining characteristics of a Community that is first of all a community of principles and values at the heart of which are fundamental rights, constitutionalism, democracy and the rule of law.

Therefore, I would rather say that the Court has undertaken a dynamic interpretation of Community law, developing to their full extent principles inherent in the legal order originally created by the Treaties. After all, it is not by chance that its jurisprudence has been, in all evidence, fully endorsed by Member States and the other institutions which have progressively enshrined in the Treaty the Court's legacy.

I do think, therefore, that the Court has carried out its mission and fulfilled its role in a consistent manner and I would add that it is fortunate that such an evolution has taken place. Otherwise we probably could not speak today of a truly Community legal order and perhaps not even of a genuine European Union.

8

The Strasbourg Perspective and its Effect on the Court of Justice: Is Mutual Respect Enough?

Robin CA White

I. Background and Context

The European Convention on Human Rights applies to states, and is concerned with violations of human rights by states in relation to those within their jurisdiction.[1] The European Court of Human Rights[2] can only concern itself with any issue of a violation of Convention rights which results from the actions of an institution in so far as that institution acts through the states which are its Contracting Parties. Over the years, attempts have been made to make applications against states in respect of actions which seem at first sight to be those of international organizations or institutions. The Strasbourg organs have avoided deciding that the personality of an international organization is separate from that of its members. But the Commission has decided that it cannot review actions of the institutions of the European Communities per se since the Communities are not a party to the Convention.[3] Nevertheless, in 1975 the Commission decided that Contracting Parties are responsible for acts of their national institutions which constitute violations of the Convention regardless of whether the impugned act results from the operation of national law or from compliance with international obligations.[4]

Although the Strasbourg Court has taken a broad view of a state's responsibility under the Convention through its development of the concept of jurisdiction in Article 1 of the European Convention, it has not used this notion to encompass examination of the actions of international organizations. So, for example,

---

[1] C Ovey and R White, *The European Convention on Human Rights* (4th ed, 2006) ch 2.
[2] Referred to in this essay as 'the Strasbourg Court'.
[3] *CFDT v European Communities*, App No 8030/77, decision of 10 July 1978 (1978) 13 DR 231, and *D v European Communities*, App No 13539/88, decision of 19 January 1989.
[4] *Ilse Hess v United Kingdom*, App No 6231/73, decision of 28 May 1975 (1975) 2 DR 72.

the Court has consistently found that Turkey is responsible for conduct in the northern part of Cyprus which has been carried out by the so-called 'Turkish Republic of Northern Cyprus'.[5] Yet in the *Banković* case[6] the Court refused to accept the jurisdictional link between the respondent states and air strikes carried out by NATO countries, though it was significant for the Strasbourg Court that the Federal Republic of Yugoslavia was not a party to the Convention. The Convention was said to operate within the 'legal space' (*espace juridique*) of the Contracting States.[7]

In 1990 the Commission invented the equivalent protection doctrine under which it would defer to fundamental rights protection inherent in the operation of an international organization of which a Contracting Party was a member. In the *M & Co* case[8] a company had been fined under the Community competition rules after the Commission had concluded that there was a concerted practice for the prevention of parallel imports of hi-fi equipment from Germany into France. The company had sought the annulment of the Commission decision imposing the fine before the Court of Justice.[9] Among the grounds on which annulment was sought was a complaint that guarantees contained in Article 6 of the European Convention were not present in proceedings of the Commission. The Luxembourg Court had concluded that the Commission was not a court for the purposes of Article 6, but that certain procedural guarantees were an inherent feature of Community law. The Commission's decision was annulled in relation to certain dates, and a different fine substituted for that imposed by the Commission.[10] There followed attempts by the German company to prevent the execution of the writ of execution in Germany in respect of the fines which had been imposed. These were ultimately unsuccessful and the applicant brought a complaint before the Strasbourg organs alleging violations of Article 6 of the Convention. The essence of the applicant's complaint is neatly summarized in the decision of the Commission:

the competent Minister, before issuing a writ of execution, should examine whether or not the judgment of the European Court of Justice had been given in proceedings respecting the guarantees set out in Article 6 of the Convention. As this was not the case the granting of the writ of execution, so the applicant company argues, gave effect to the violations complained of and therefore violated the provisions involved.[11]

---

[5] See *Loizidou v Cyprus (Preliminary Objections)*, App No 15319/89, judgment of 23 March 1995 (1995) 20 EHRR 99, and *Cyprus v Turkey*, App No 25781/94, judgment of 10 May 2001 (2001) 35 EHRR 731.

[6] *Banković and Others v Belgium and 16 other Contracting States*, App No 52207/99, admissibility decision of 12 December 2001.

[7] ibid, para 80 of the decision.

[8] *M & Co v Federal Republic of Germany*, App No 13258/87, decision of 9 February 1990 (1990) 64 DR 138.

[9] Referred to in this essay as 'the Luxembourg Court'.

[10] Joined Cases 100–103/80 *SA Musique Diffusion Française and Others v Commission* [1983] ECR 1825.

[11] *M & Co v Federal Republic of Germany*, App No 13258/87, decision of 9 February 1990 (1990) 64 DR 138, 143.

The Commission, recapitulating earlier decisions, reaffirmed that a transfer of a state's powers under an international agreement does not necessarily exclude a state's responsibility for violations of the Convention arising from the exercise of the transferred powers. There then follows the key determination: 'the transfer of powers to an international organization is not incompatible with the Convention provided that within that organization fundamental rights will receive an equivalent protection'.[12] The Commission goes on to determine that the Community legal order does provide protection for fundamental rights notwithstanding the absence of a catalogue of rights in the EEC Treaty. The Commission concluded:

the Court of Justice underlined in the present case that the right to a fair hearing is a fundamental principle of Community law. It stated that Community law contained all criteria which are prerequisites not only to examine but, if necessary, to remedy the applicant company's complaint that its right to a fair hearing was violated . . . However, it came to the conclusion that the complaint was unfounded.

The Commission has also taken into consideration that it would be contrary to the very idea of transferring powers to an international organization to hold the Member States responsible for examining, in each individual case before issuing a writ of execution for a judgment of the European Court of Justice, whether Article 6 of the Convention was respected in the underlying proceedings.[13]

The application was found to be incompatible with the provisions of the Convention *ratione materiae* and was accordingly ruled to be inadmissible.

In 1994 the Commission held, in relation to the European Patents Convention, that the transfer of powers by the Contracting States to an international organization is compatible with the Convention, provided that fundamental rights receive, within the organization, an equivalent protection. It ruled that it was.[14]

In 1998 the Strasbourg Court ruled that time taken to provide a preliminary ruling did not count towards the computation of time in order to decide whether a national court had given judgment within a reasonable time:

95. As regards the proceedings before the Court of Justice of the European Communities, the Court notes that the Athens District Court decided on 3 August 1993 to refer a question to the Court of Justice, which gave judgment on 12 March 1996. During the intervening period the proceedings in the actions concerned were stayed, which prolonged them by two years, seven months and nine days. The Court cannot, however, take this period into consideration in its assessment of the length of each particular set of proceedings: even though it may at first sight appear relatively long, to take it into account would

---

[12] ibid 145.
[13] ibid 145–6.
[14] *Heinze v Contracting Parties who are also Parties to the European Patent Convention*, App No 12090/92, decision of 10 January 1994 (1994) 76A DR 125; (1994) 18 EHRR CD168.

adversely affect the system instituted by Article 177 of the EEC Treaty and work against the aim pursued in substance in that Article.[15]

The pattern was set for a policy of mutual respect. So far as the principle applies to the European Communities, the Luxembourg Court has reciprocated by increasingly referring to the European Convention in its judgments.[16] It has also acknowledged that it has not always got Convention law right. So, in the *Roquette Frères* case,[17] the Luxembourg Court tacitly acknowledged that it had erred in its interpretation of Article 8 of the Convention in its earlier decision in the *Hoechst* case.[18]

II. The *Matthews* Case

The Strasbourg Court considered the status of the European Parliament and the application of Article 3 of Protocol 1 in the *Matthews* case.[19] The applicant was a British citizen living in Gibraltar, which is a dependent territory of the United Kingdom with its own legislature. The EC Treaty applies to Gibraltar, although the operation of parts of the Treaty is excluded in relation to Gibraltar under the terms of the Treaty of Accession. Elections to the European Parliament are governed by the Act Concerning the Election of the Representatives of the European Parliament by Universal Suffrage of 20 September 1976; that Act was signed by the ministers of foreign affairs of the Member States and attached to Council Decision 76/787.[20] The Act provided for elections to take place only in the territory of the United Kingdom but not in Gibraltar.

The Strasbourg Court rejected the argument of the United Kingdom government that the European Parliament should be excluded from the ambit of elections within the scope of Article 3 of Protocol 1 on the ground that it is a supranational rather than a national representative organ. The Government then argued that it lacked the attributes of a legislature, which it defined as the power to initiate and adopt legislation. After analysing the powers of the European Parliament and their impact upon Gibraltar, the Strasbourg Court concluded that the European Parliament constitutes 'part of the legislature of Gibraltar for the purposes of Article 3 of Protocol 1'.[21] The Commission had taken a different

---

[15] *Pafitis v Greece,* App No 20323/92 (1999) 27 EHRR 566, para 95 of the judgment.
[16] For example, in Case 36/75 *Rutili* [1975] ECR 1219; Case 222/84 *Johnston* [1986] ECR 1651; Case C-13/94 *P & S* [1996] ECR I-2143; Case C-109/01 *Akrich* [2003] ECR I-9607; and Case C-112/00 *Schmidberger* [2003] ECR I-5659.
[17] Case C-94/00 *Roquette Frères SA* [2002] ECR I-9011, para 29 of the judgment.
[18] Joined Cases 46/87 and 227/88 *Hoechst AG v Commission* [1989] ECR 2859.
[19] *Matthews v United Kingdom,* App No 24833/94, judgment of 18 February 1999 (1999) 28 EHRR 361.
[20] [1976[IJ L278/5.
[21] *Matthews v United Kingdom,* App No 24833/94, judgment of 18 February 1999 (1999) 28 EHRR 361, para 54 of the judgment. For the 2004 elections to the European Parliament, Gibraltar

view by 11 votes to six, but in his dissenting opinion, Schermers concluded: 'I consider it essential to underline that the Contracting States remain responsible for infringements of human rights if they do not provide for adequate protection of these rights by the institutions to which powers are transferred'.[22] For the Court, it was significant that the Community Act could not be challenged before the Luxembourg Court because it amounted to a treaty within the Community legal order.[23]

Two subsequent cases might have addressed more directly Strasbourg supervision of fundamental rights by the Community. Both concerned the application of Article 6 of the Convention within Community law proceedings, but neither reached the merits stage. The *Emesa Sugar* saga concerned a challenge to the absence of any ability by parties to litigation in Luxembourg to make further representations between the delivery of the Advocate General's opinion and the Court's judgment.[24] The *Senator Lines* saga concerned a challenge to the refusal to suspend the operation of a competition fine pending an application for annulment before the Court of First Instance.[25]

III. The *Bosphorus Airways* Case

The judgment of the Grand Chamber in the *Bosphorus Airways* case[26] represents the modern restatement of the position of the Strasbourg Court to supervision of fundamental rights within the Community legal order. It is also of considerable importance because it touches on possible supervision of the decisions of international organizations.[27] The *Bosphorus Airways* case concerned the implementation in Ireland of an EC Regulation imposing sanctions against Serbia and Montenegro. These sanctions were in turn required by a resolution of the UN Security Council. Two aircraft owned by Yugoslav airlines (JAT) had been leased to Bosphorus Airways, which is a Turkish company. This company had only two

---

was added to the constituency which included Cornwall. On the case, see I Canor, '*Primus inter pares*. Who is the ultimate guardian of fundamental rights in Europe?' (2000) 25 ELRev 3.

[22] ibid, dissenting opinion of H G Schermers.

[23] And so there was no equivalent protection within the Community legal order. See para 33 of the judgment.

[24] See C-17/98 *Emesa Sugar* [2000] ECR I-675 for the Luxembourg case, and *Emesa Sugar BV v Netherlands* App No 62023/00, decision of 13 January 2005, for the Strasbourg admissibility decision.

[25] See Joined Cases T-191/98, T-212/98, T-213/98 and T-214/98 *Senator Lines* [1999] ECR II-2531 for the Luxembourg case, and *Senator Lines v the Fifteen Member States of the European Union*, App No 56672/00 (2004) 39 EHRR SE3.

[26] *Bosphorus Hava Yollari Turizm ve Itcaret Anonim Şirketi v Ireland*, App No 45036/98, judgment of 30 June 2005 (2006) 42 EHRR 1.

[27] For the definitive consideration of the implications of this case, see C Costello, 'The *Bosphorus* ruling of the European Court of Human Rights: fundamental rights and blurred boundaries in Europe' (2006) 6 HRLRev 87.

aircraft, both on lease. The lease had been entered into prior to the passing of the UN Security Council resolution. One of the aircraft was seized in Ireland on 28 May 1993 just before take-off. This resulted in the Turkish authorities grounding the second Bosphorus Airways aircraft and cancelling the licence for it to operate as a commercial airline, since Turkish law required commercial operators to have a minimum of two aircraft in service.

There then followed two decisions of the High Court in Ireland. Both quashed the seizure order. The first decision was taken on appeal to the Supreme Court, which made a reference to the Luxembourg Court. The ruling of the Luxembourg Court on that reference was that the interference with Bosphorus Airways' property rights was justified by the EC Regulation.[28] Acting on this ruling, the Supreme Court in Ireland found the seizure of the aircraft to be lawful, and indeed to be required by the terms of the EC Regulation. Bosphorus Airways then pursued its remedies under the European Convention on Human Rights, complaining of interference with its property rights. The European Commission was an intervener in the case.

Costello has neatly summarized the judgment of the Strasbourg Court on the responsibility of Ireland for the seizure:

The ECtHR accepted that 'the impugned interference was not the result of an exercise of discretion by the Irish authorities, either under EC or Irish law, but rather amounted to compliance by the Irish State with its legal obligations flowing from EC law'. The reasons for this conclusion were three-fold. First, the Regulation required Ireland to act in the manner that it did. Second, Ireland was obliged under the duty of loyal cooperation embodied in Article 10 EC to appeal the High Court's ruling to the Supreme Court. Third, the Supreme Court was obliged to refer the matter to the ECJ under Article 234 EC and obliged to apply the resultant ruling, which left no discretion to the national court and 'the only conclusion open to the [latter] was that EC Regulation 990/93 applied to the applicant's aircraft'. Crucially, the ECtHR emphasized that 'a state would be fully responsible under the Convention for all acts falling outside its strict international legal obligations' and explained its previous rulings on state responsibility for Member State implementation as examples of this principle in action.[29]

The key paragraphs from the Grand Chamber's judgment on compatibility with Convention rights reads:

154. In...establishing the extent to which state action can be justified by its compliance with obligations flowing from its membership of an international organization to which it has transferred part of its sovereignty, the Court has recognized that absolving Contracting States completely from their Convention responsibility in the areas covered by such a transfer would be incompatible with the purpose and object

---

[28] Case C-84/95 *Bosphorus Hava Yollari Turizm ve Ticaret AS v Minister for Transport, Energy and Communications and Others* [1996] ECR I-3953.

[29] C Costello (n 27 above), 100 (footnotes omitted).

of the Convention: the guarantees of the Convention could be limited or excluded at will thereby depriving it of its peremptory character and undermining the practical and effective nature of its safeguards...The state is considered to retain Convention liability in respect of treaty commitments subsequent to the entry into force of the Convention...

155. In the Court's view, state action taken in compliance with such legal obligations is justified as long as the relevant organization is considered to protect fundamental rights, as regards both the substantive guarantees offered and the mechanisms controlling their observance, in a manner which can be considered at least equivalent to that for which the Convention provides... By 'equivalent' the Court means 'comparable': any requirement that the organization's protection be 'identical' could run counter to the interest of international cooperation pursued... However, any such finding of equivalence could not be final and would be susceptible to review in the light of any relevant change in fundamental rights' protection.

156. If such equivalent protection is considered to be provided by the organization, the presumption will be that a state has not departed from the requirements of the Convention when it does no more than implement legal obligations flowing from its membership of the organization.

However, any such presumption can be rebutted if, in the circumstances of a particular case, it is considered that the protection of Convention rights was manifestly deficient. In such cases, the interest of international cooperation would be outweighed by the Convention's role as a 'constitutional instrument of European public order' in the field of human rights (*Loizidou v Turkey (preliminary objections)*, judgment of 23 March 1995, Series A no 310, § 75).

There could be no more ringing endorsement of the principle of equivalent protection than this from the Strasbourg Court. The Grand Chamber went on to find that the systems for the protection of human rights at the material time were equivalent under Community law to those offered under the European Convention. Hence the presumption of compliance applied, and it had not been rebutted in the case before the Court. Costello is critical of the requirement that the equivalent protection must be 'manifestly deficient',[30] arguing that it is difficult to see why the presumption should be 'rebuttable only on this high standard'.[31] On the substantive point, the Strasbourg Court found that the interference with the applicants' property rights in the aircraft was justified within the limitations permitted by Article 1 of Protocol 1.[32]

The existence of the reference and preliminary ruling from the Luxembourg Court were clearly significant factors in persuading the Strasbourg Court that there was a presumption of compliance in this case. It follows that a Member State taking action required, or perceived to be required, by Community law, which

---

[30] See para 156 of the judgment, quoted above.
[31] C Costello (n 27 above), 102.
[32] For a discussion of these, see C Ovey and R White, *The European Convention on Human Rights* (4th ed, 2006) ch 15.

may be challengeable on human rights grounds, should consider arguing in any litigation for its courts to make a reference to the Luxembourg Court in order to provide some protection against a finding that it has breached Convention rights.

It also follows that in cases where there is no possibility of making a reference to the Luxembourg Court, or where that possibility is heavily circumscribed, then Community law may fail to provide equivalent protection. Such situations arise in relation to Title IV of the EC Treaty on visas, asylum, immigration and other policies related to the free movement of persons. In the broader context of European Union law, the absence of the ability to have decisions in the spheres of the common foreign and security policy, and of police and judicial cooperation in criminal matters, also exposes the Union to a human rights deficit. Finally, as the *Matthews* case demonstrated, where the failure to secure Convention rights flows from primary law of the Community, there is no possibility of any form of judicial review by the Luxembourg Court.

IV. Should the European Union Accede to the European Convention?

As long ago as 1977, the political institutions of the Communities issued a Joint Declaration[33] indicating the importance of fundamental rights as part of the general principles of law recognized by the Communities, and noting the key role played by the European Convention.

The current conventional wisdom is that all problems would be resolved if the European Union became a party to the European Convention on Human Rights. The decisions of the Luxembourg Court, and the absence of a detailed catalogue of fundamental rights, led to proposals for the Community to accede to the European Convention and so subject itself to the jurisdiction of that Court as a supranational organization. In 1979, the Commission first proposed that the Communities should accede to the European Convention.[34] The proposal was made again in 1989.[35] The Council of the European Union responded to the Commission's proposal by seeking an opinion of the Luxembourg Court under what is now Article 300 EC. The outcome was a ruling that 'as Community law now stands, the Community has no competence to accede to the European

---

[33] Joint Declaration of the European Parliament, the Council and the Commission of 5 April 1977 [1977] OJ C103/1.
[34] 'Accession of the Communities to the European Convention on Human Rights' (1979) EC Bull Supp 2/79.
[35] Press Release IP(90) 892 of 31 October 1990.

Convention'.[36] Some Member States had argued that the Community was competent to accede to the European Convention because of the penetration of the protection of fundamental rights through the general principles of law. This is referred to in the Court's reasoning, but accession would, in the Court's view, require the integration of two separate systems for the protection of human rights. Such changes 'would be of constitutional significance and would therefore be such as to go beyond the scope of Article 235' and could only be brought about by way of amendments to the EC Treaty. The opinion is very clever; it is argued that the response is legally correct in the context of the timing and the question asked.[37] It serves to preserve in full the power of protection of fundamental rights by way of the application of the general principles of law. Few reading the opinion can be left in any doubt about the complexities of integrating the European Community system and the Strasbourg system.[38]

However, the issue has not gone away. The waters have been further clouded by the solemn proclamation of the Charter of Fundamental Rights of the European Union on 7 December 2000 at the Nice Council.[39] This document has no legally-binding force for the Member States,[40] and there remain intriguing questions about its impact on the protection of fundamental rights within the European Union. It is divided into six sections[41] and includes rights for citizens of the European Union as well as certain rights which are to be applicable to all within the jurisdiction of the Member States. The rights are said to be based on the rights guaranteed by the European Convention, but in many cases there are intriguing differences of wording.[42] Its scope is considerably wider than the rights protected in the European Convention. A limited welcome can be offered

---

[36] Opinion 2/94 on accession by the Community to the European Convention on Human Rights [1996] ECR I-1759.

[37] On opinion 2/94, see J Duvigneau, 'From advisory opinion 2/94 to the Amsterdam Treaty: human rights protection in the European Union' (1998) 25 LIEI 61; S O'Leary, 'Accession by the European Community to the European Convention on Human Rights – The Opinion of the ECJ' [1996] EHRLR 362; G Gaja, 'Opinion 2/94' (1996) 33 CMLRev 973; and N Burrows, 'Question of Community Accession to the European Convention Determined' (1997) 22 ELRev 58.

[38] See also Study of the Technical and Legal Issues of a Possible EC/EU Accession to the European Convention on Human Rights. Report adopted by the Steering Committee for Human Rights (CDDH) at its 53rd meeting 25–8 June 2002, DG-II(2002)006 (CDDH(2002)010 Addendum 2) (referred to in this essay as 'the Lathouwers Study').

[39] Referred to in this essay as 'the EU Charter'. See, generally, S Peers and A Ward, *The EU Charter of Fundamental Rights. Politics, Law and Policy* (2004). See also speech by P-H Imbert, Director General of Human Rights of the Council of Europe at the Judge's [sic] Symposium on the relationship between the European Convention on Human Rights and the Charter of Fundamental Rights of the European Union, 16 September 2002, available at *www.coe.int*.

[40] Though it can be argued that it binds the political institutions since they signed it.

[41] Dignity, freedoms, equality, solidarity, citizens' rights and justice.

[42] For example, Art 9 of the EU Charter provides, 'The right to marry and the right to found a family shall be guaranteed in accordance with the national laws governing the exercise of these rights'. This could be interpreted as decoupling the right to marry and the right to found a family which are coupled in Art 12 of the Convention. Elsewhere there is a more sweeping approach to limitations which may be applied to certain rights.

to the EU Charter. As a declaratory document standing behind the legal recognition of fundamental rights, it is probably as good as it could be given that its purpose was not formally decided in advance of the Nice Council and given the manner in which it was constructed.[43] Following a number of references to the Charter by Advocates General and the Court of First Instance, the Luxembourg Court itself referred to the EU Charter for the first time in June 2006 in an inter-institutional case[44] in which the European Parliament challenged the compatibility of provisions of Directive 2003/86 on the right to family reunification[45] with requirements in Articles 8 and 14 of the Convention. The Court concluded that there was no incompatibility. On the EU Charter, the Court said:

> The Charter was solemnly proclaimed by the Parliament, the Council and the Commission in Nice on 7 December 2000. While the Charter is not a legally binding instrument, the Community legislature did, however, acknowledge its importance by stating, in the second recital in the preamble to the Directive, that the Directive observes the principles recognized not only by Article 8 of the ECHR but also in the Charter. Furthermore, the principal aim of the Charter, as is apparent from its preamble, is to reaffirm 'rights as they result, in particular, from the constitutional traditions and international obligations common to the Member States, the Treaty on European Union, the Community Treaties, the [ECHR], the Social Charters adopted by the Community and by the Council of Europe and the case law of the Court... and of the European Court of Human Rights'.[46]

So the EU Charter joins the European Convention and the constitutional traditions of the Member States as a source of inspiration in determining the fundamental rights protected by the Union.

The EU Charter has been included as Part II of the Treaty establishing a Constitution for Europe, which was signed in Rome on 29 October 2004.[47] Article I-9(2) provides that the Union *shall* accede to the Convention. On the Council of Europe side, Article 17 of Protocol 14[48] makes provision for Union accession by adding a new paragraph to Article 59 of the Convention in the following terms: '2. The European Union may accede to this Convention'.

The future of the Treaty establishing a Constitution for Europe has, however, been thrown into considerable doubt following its rejection in referendums in France and The Netherlands. It now seems certain that it will not be adopted in its current form.

What then are the arguments for accession, and the arguments against?

---

[43] See G de Búrca, 'The drafting of the European Union Charter of Fundamental Rights' (2001) 26 ELRev 126.
[44] Case C-540/03 *European Parliament v Council* [2006] ECR I-5769.
[45] Directive 2003/86 on the right to family reunification [2003] OJ L251/12.
[46] Case C-540/03 *European Parliament v Council* [2006] ECR I-5769, para 38 of the judgment.
[47] [2004] OJ C310/1. See now amendments made by the Treaty of Lisbon to the same effect in relation to the Charter and accession to the ECHR.
[48] ETS No 194. Not yet in force, all Contracting Parties except Russia have now ratified Protocol 14.

A. The Arguments for Accession

These operate principally at the political and philosophical level. As the Union increasingly holds itself out as a human rights institution, it is anomalous that it is not formally a party to the human rights treaty which has been described as 'part of the cultural self-definition of European civilization'.[49] Alston and Weiler have noted:

> As the Council of Europe grows, as the European Convention on Human Rights adapts and absorbs new Member States and new legal traditions and understandings, it is regrettable that there will be no explicit Community voice within the European Convention on Human Rights. Such a voice would have enabled the sensibilities and experiences of the Community to form an integral part of the evolving jurisprudence and extra-juridical activity of the European Convention system. This, almost as much as any other reason, requires that accession to the European Convention remain a live objective.[50]

In addition to this contribution to the development of European human rights law, the Union's willingness to submit itself to scrutiny by the Strasbourg Court would indicate a genuine commitment to human rights in relation to matters at the core of fundamental rights protection within Europe. It would reinforce the status of the European Convention as 'a constitutional instrument of European public order'.[51] It would reflect the core values of the Union as expressed in the Draft Treaty establishing a Constitution for Europe:

> The Union is founded on the values of respect for human dignity, freedom, democracy, equality, the rule of law and respect for human rights, including the rights of persons belonging to minorities. These values are common to the Member States in a society in which pluralism, non-discrimination, tolerance, justice, solidarity and equality between men and women prevail.[52]

On the practical side, the necessary accommodations to enable the Strasbourg Court to deal with applications against the Union can, it is argued, be readily overcome.[53]

---

[49] P Alston and J Weiler, 'An "ever closer union" in need of a human rights policy: the European Union and human rights' in P Alston (ed), *The EU and Human Rights* (1999) 3, 30. See also S Besson, 'The European Union and Human Rights: Towards a Post-National Human Rights Institution' (2006) 6 HRLRev 323.

[50] P Alston and J Weiler (n 49 above), 30–1.

[51] *Loizidou v Cyprus (Preliminary Objections)*, App No 15319/89, judgment of 23 March 1995 (1995) 20 EHRR 99, para 75 of the judgment.

[52] Art I-2. See now new Art 1a TEU added by the Treaty of Lisbon to the same effect.

[53] The Lathouwers Study (n 38 above). This sets out the practicalities and indicates that amendments to the Convention do not, of themselves, present an insuperable problem. It remains an open question whether the Union should also become a party to the Statute of the Council of Europe, ETS No 1; the Statute is currently only open to membership by 'European States' (Art 4).

B. The Arguments Against Accession

Much of the argument against accession relates to the status of the Luxembourg Court and the Strasbourg Court as courts of equal standing in the international legal order. Each should retain its own supreme position in its sphere of influence. Furthermore, the political institutions of the Union have now committed themselves, through their signature to the Charter of Fundamental Rights, to a modern catalogue of rights applicable to the Union, and pay due regard to the content of the European Convention in developing its own standing as a human rights institution. The Luxembourg Court has developed its own approach to the protection of human rights in the Union legal order, which respects the significant position of the European Convention in the constitutional orders of each of the Member States setting the base line of human rights protection.

Perhaps more significantly it is argued that virtually all of Community law is implemented through the actions of the Member States, which are, following the exhaustion of domestic remedies, subject to international supervision by the Strasbourg Court when someone within their jurisdiction raises before that court a complaint of a violation of Convention rights. If the Union becomes a party to the European Convention, there are likely to be demarcation issues. The Union would only be responsible for a violation of Convention rights which arose from action of the Union. In other words, the Convention would only apply when the Union was exercising its own competences and not acting through the Member States. But the prudent applicant may, following accession, choose to make the application against the Member State and the Union. That would then add to the work of the Strasbourg Court, because there would be argument about whether one or other, or both, of the respondents bore responsibility for the alleged violation of the Convention. Indeed, the Lathouwers Study[54] went so far as to suggest that there might be a need to oblige the Union to intervene in cases concerning an alleged violation of the Convention by a Member State by reason of action it had taken in implementing Community law. The alternative which was canvassed was of joining the Union as a co-defendant in such cases.

On substance, the European Convention (and its Protocols) contains a somewhat restricted list of human rights. The rights in the Protocols are not binding on all the Member States, since not all their provisions have been ratified by all Contracting States. Although the Convention establishes minimum standards for states, its application to the work of an international organization is more questionable. It may be better for the Union to develop its own internal standards which build on the foundations of the European Convention.

---

[54] The Lathouwers Study (n 38 above).

C. Key Issues Arising from Accession

The Lathouwers Study[55] suggested that the accommodations required for the Union to accede to the Convention could be achieved through a Protocol or through an accession treaty. The preference in the study would seem to be for an accession treaty. If a Protocol procedure were adopted, that would require ratification by all the Contracting Parties to the Convention before accession by the Union could follow. An accession treaty could combine amendments to the text of the Convention and its Protocols, supplementary provisions clarifying the scope of terms in the Convention,[56] and technical and administrative issues, such as the contribution to the running costs of the Strasbourg Court to be paid by the Union. However, the presence of Article 17 of Protocol 14 amending the Convention to permit the accession of the Union rather suggests that the protocol route will be taken if the proposal for accession is implemented.

Other issues related to the ability of the Union to use the inter-state procedure in Article 33 of the Convention, or to be a respondent in such cases. The Lathouwers Study[57] regarded the option of having no judge on the Strasbourg Court representing the Union as one which should be discarded. The possibility of using an ad hoc judge was canvassed but was seen potentially to be impracticable if a significant number of cases involved the Union as respondent. The preferred option seems to be for a full-time judge representing the Union who would participate on an equal footing with other judges on the Strasbourg Court. The Lathouwers Study[58] expresses some distaste for the idea of special panels composed only of judges from the Member States of the European Union and of the judge appointed in respect of the Union, since this would 'run counter to the philosophy of the Convention system'.[59]

The final idea which is canvassed is the introduction of a new procedure[60] permitting either of the Luxembourg Courts to request an interpretation of the European Convention from the Strasbourg Court. The principal purpose of such a procedure would be to avoid divergences in the case law. There is, of course, a case which can readily be made for the introduction of such a procedure for the current Contracting Parties.

The current treaty amendments on both sides refer to the Union acceding to the European Convention. The Union, however, has a much broader range of competences than the Communities, and some competences and actions of

---

[55] The Lathouwers Study (n 38 above).
[56] Which currently uses the language of states throughout, with corresponding references to nationals of the states which are Contracting Parties.
[57] The Lathouwers Study (n 38 above).
[58] ibid.
[59] ibid para 74.
[60] Distinguishable from the advisory opinion procedure in Art 47 of the Convention, on which see C Ovey and R White, *The European Convention on Human Rights* (4th ed, 2006) 12–14.

the Union are not subject to the same level of judicial review as actions of the Communities. This presents a further area in which demarcation issues are likely to arise. However, accession on this basis would extend the fundamental rights protection of the European Convention to areas which are now within the zone of the human rights deficit of the Union. It would enable direct challenges to be made to aspects of Community and Union action which are currently outside the judicial review competence of the Luxembourg Court. The actions of the Luxembourg Court itself could be subject to scrutiny under the wide case law under Article 6 of the European Convention. As the United Kingdom found when it incorporated the European Convention under the Human Rights Act 1998, applications tend to increase rather than decrease because of the higher profile the Convention enjoys in the national legal order.[61]

It has to be acknowledged that it is taking significant periods of time for Protocols which require ratification by all Contracting Parties to come into force. Protocol 11 was first proposed in 1993, was signed on 11 May 1994 and entered into force on 1 November 1998. Protocol 14 was first proposed in 2001, was signed on 13 May 2004, and has yet to come into force.

D. Can We Live with the Status Quo?

It will be some years at the earliest before the Convention regime could apply to the Union, even if steps were taken immediately to enable the Union's accession; so the status quo is with us for some time come what may.

From rather humble beginnings, the Luxembourg Court has developed a significant case law on fundamental rights.[62] Bruno de Witte has described accession to the European Convention and the creation of a Community catalogue of rights as spectacular reforms attractive to some but repulsive to others, which have failed to prove attractive to the Member States.[63] There is now a catalogue of rights of sorts in the EU Charter, and the way for accession is being paved. But sceptics will be able to argue convincingly that the status quo may well be better than accession, and that the arrival of the EU Charter obviates the need for accession to the European Convention. There would remain a human rights deficit, since failings at Union level would continue to be subject to Strasbourg scrutiny only where an applicant could show that action by a Member State in implementation of requirements under Community or Union law was the source of the violation. Such a situation leaves some actions of the Union exempt from

---

[61] As at 1 April 2007, there are 2,400 pending cases against the United Kingdom before the Strasbourg Court.
[62] See generally D Spielmann, 'Human Rights Case Law in the Strasbourg and Luxembourg Courts: Conflicts, Inconsistencies and Complementarities' and B de Witte, 'The Past and Future Role of the European Court of Justice in the Protection of Human Rights' in P Alston (ed), *The EU and Human Rights* (1999) 757 and 859.
[63] B de Witte (n 62 above) 859, 889–90.

scrutiny. In some cases, such as access to a court for the action for annulment, the imagination of the Court is hidebound by the text of the EC Treaty.[64]

V. Could the Strasbourg Court Cope?

The cultural shift which the Strasbourg Court would face if the Contracting Parties included a supranational organization as significant as the European Union would be enormous. There is universal agreement that the current work load of the Strasbourg Court is way beyond its current capacity. As at 1 April 2007, the Strasbourg Court had 94,300 pending cases.[65] That includes the following applications against some of the Member States of the European Union:

Member State	No of Pending Cases
Romania	11,500
Poland	7,700
France	4,400
Germany	3,800
Italy	3,500
Czech Republic	3,400
Slovenia	2,400
United Kingdom	2,400
Bulgaria	2,200[66]

The backlog is growing at a rate in excess of 1,000 cases per month. It is already acknowledged that the changes to be brought about by Protocol 14 are not enough to address the problem of the Court's growing case load, and the Council of Europe has undertaken work on longer-term measures to address the problem. Protocol 14, like Protocol 11, is only a partial remedy to the problems presented by the exponential increase in applications to the Strasbourg Court.[67] For this reason the Declaration at the end of the Third Summit of the Council of Europe held in Warsaw in May 2005 included a commitment to the establishment of a group of 'wise persons to draw up a comprehensive strategy to secure the

[64] Notwithstanding efforts by Advocate General Jacobs to persuade the Luxembourg Court to take a different approach to the interpretation of Article 230 EC. See R White, 'Citizenship of the Union, Governance, and Equality' (2006) 29 Fordham ILJ 790, 802–6.
[65] Statistical information available on the Court's website *www.echr.coe.int*.
[66] Cases against the other Member States of the European Union form part of a figure of 17,900 cases for all other Contracting Parties.
[67] See address by Luzius Wildhaber at the high level seminar on the reform of the European human rights system, held at Oslo on 18 October 2004, available at *www.echr.coe.int*. See also Final Declaration of the Heads of State and Government of the Member States of the Council of Europe, and its accompanying Action Plan (CM(2005)80 final), 17 May 2005.

effectiveness of the system in the longer term' but these proposals are to preserve the basic philosophy underlying the Convention. In his speech at the Summit, the then President of the Court said:

> We therefore need to look beyond Protocol No 14 and address the issue of the long-term future of the system, and we should start doing so now. What kind of international protection mechanism do we need in the Europe of the 21st century? Are the present procedures still adjusted to the pan-European character which the system has acquired since its creation? What will be the impact of the projected accession of the European Union to the Convention? How can the system best provide the guidance expected from it by authorities and citizens alike in an ever faster changing world? These are some of the crucial questions which we urgently need to start addressing, if we want to have a chance to enable the system to face up in time to the new challenges awaiting it.
>
> Now is not the time for a quick fix, but for vision. A vision on how to ensure that the European Court of Human Rights remains what it has been since its creation, for the benefit of nearly two generations of citizens: the tangible symbol of the effective preeminence on our continent of human rights and the rule of law.[68]

One is forced to conclude that, although the political will at the institutional levels is there on both sides,[69] the practical capacity of the Strasbourg Court is not there. The case for extending the jurisdiction of the Strasbourg Court accordingly needs to be especially compelling if accession is to go ahead. Neither the Council of Europe, nor the Union has yet put in place the legal basis for accession, though the Council of Europe is ahead of the European Union since Protocol 14 will come into force once it has been ratified by Russia.

VI. Concluding Remarks

The question posed in this essay is whether mutual respect between the two Courts is enough to secure guarantees for the protection of human rights in the European Union. The answer must be a tentative view that it is sufficient in the current state of development of the protection of human rights by international organizations, but nevertheless leaves a human rights deficit. That refers to areas where there is no judicial supervision of compliance with human rights obligations. The European way is to view the existence of judicial protection and individual application complaining of violations as keys to implementation of human rights standards. The Strasbourg system has been spectacularly successful in

---

[68] Address by the President of the European Court of Human Rights, Luzius Wildhaber, to the Third Summit of the Council of Europe, 16–17 May 2005. See also speech by the President of the European Court of Human Rights at the Colloquy on 'Future Developments of the European Court of Human Rights in the light of the Wise Persons' Report' in San Marino on 22 March 2007; both available at *www.coe.int*.

[69] As distinct from the political will of the Member States of the Union and the Contracting Parties to the European Convention.

securing recognition of such measures of implementation among 46 states of a wider Europe representing 800 million people. The foundation of the European system is the European Convention and its Protocols. It was in a sense logical to see the European Union joining that system as a supranational organization. However, detailed examination of the implications of accession by the European Union indicates that this may not be the best way forward.

It is trite to say that the European Convention system is based upon a partnership between national courts and the Strasbourg Court. It is also trite to say that the European Union is not a state. If the European Union accedes to the Convention, then the role of the Luxembourg Court in the operation of the Convention system should be no greater than the role of a supreme court in one of the Contracting Parties. Yet there is discussion of a special partnership between the two Courts. Central to that dialogue is the suggestion that it might be possible for the Luxembourg Court to make a reference to the Strasbourg Court for interpretation of the Convention. If such a procedure is offered to the Luxembourg Court, why should it not be extended to supreme courts in the national legal orders?

Furthermore, accession by the European Union[70] would open all the activities of the Union to scrutiny against the standards set out in the European Convention.[71] That would immediately raise difficulties in that many areas of activity outside the so-called First Pillar of the European Communities are not susceptible to judicial review by the Luxembourg Court.

A catalogue of rights like that contained in the EU Charter presents fewer difficulties than is sometimes suggested in terms of the potential for conflict with the standards of the European Convention. The European Convention system requires Contracting Parties to offer the guarantees contained in the Convention as minimum standards. It establishes only the ground floor; Contracting Parties can build on those foundations but must not descend into the basement. Of course, despite that, virtually all states still fail from time to time to meet the base line requirements; and it has to be remembered that the Convention is a living instrument whose standards have developed over time.

Finally, from the perspective of the European Union, if the Union accedes to the European Convention, why should it not accede to other international human rights instruments both within the European arena and in the broader international community?[72]

---

[70] It should be borne in mind that both proposed treaty changes refer to accession by the Union rather than the Community.

[71] Including such Protocols as would be included in the instruments of accession.

[72] Alston and Weiler have proposed, by way of example, that the Community should accede to the European Social Charter, the Convention for the Protection of Individuals with regard to Automatic Processing of Personal Data, and to the Vienna Convention on Human Rights and Application of Biology and Medicine. See P Alston and J Weiler, 'An "Ever Closer Union" in Need of a Human Rights Policy: The European Union and Human Rights' in P Alston (ed), *The EU and Human Rights* (1999), 3, 31.

From the perspective of the Strasbourg Court, contemplating a significant development in its jurisdiction to include the capacity to deal with complaints against a supranational organization as complex as the European Union when it cannot cope with its current case load seems foolish. There are few signs of the political will among the Contracting Parties to a massive increase in funding which would enable the Court to deal with its increased case load and to move into new areas. Indeed, taking an objective view of the achievements of the European Convention, efforts might be better directed at modernizing the catalogue of rights covered by the European system for the protection of human rights.

The advantage of continuing the pragmatic approach which has seen the Strasbourg Court subject actions of the Union's Member States to a gentle scrutiny when they are implementing Community requirements is that it permits organic development of a system of supervision of actions of the European Union at a time when it is itself struggling to develop a clearer set of constitutional principles in a new treaty.

9

The EU Charter of Fundamental Rights, Not Binding but Influential: the Example of Good Administration

Jacqueline Dutheil de la Rochère

I. The Charter's Lack of Binding Force

The Cologne mandate (3–4 June 1999) indicated that once a Charter of fundamental rights was adopted by the Convention, the European Council should decide if and how it should be included in the treaties. The question of the binding force of the Charter could therefore have polluted the entire discussion on the substance – the United Kingdom being fundamentally hostile while Germany was in favour of binding force – had not the German President of the Convention, Roman Herzog, had the wisdom to impose his views at the time. He managed to convince the participants to the Convention that the Charter should be drafted 'as if' it were to become compulsory at a certain stage, so that the language adopted would be sufficiently rigorous but that no time would be spent on a matter which belonged to the discretion of the European Council. Subsequently, the draft Charter was approved without any modification by the European Council at the pre-summit of Biarritz (13–14 October 2000) and then solemnly and conjunctly proclaimed by the Council, the Commission and the European Parliament at Nice on 7–9 December 2000. The intergovernmental conference of revision of the treaties which was held in Nice at the same time did not discuss the question of a possible inclusion of the Charter; it did not even take notice of the proposal of the European Parliament to amend Article 6.2 TEU to add a reference to the Charter as a major expression of the fundamental rights the European Union undertakes to comply with.[1]

Following a commitment made in declaration No 23 annexed to the Final Act of the Nice Conference, one of the key points for the future of the European Union defined in the Laeken Declaration (15–16 December 2001) was nevertheless the

---

[1] On 15 November 2000 the European Parliament approved the Charter: 410 in favour, 93 against and 27 abstentions. The Parliament requested that the question of the inclusion of the Charter into the treaties be scheduled and, subsidiarily, that Article 6.2 be amended.

future legal status of the Charter and the complementary question of a possible adhesion of the Union to the European Convention on Human Rights. At the convention presided over by V Giscard d'Estaing, the working group II, chaired by former commissioner A Vitorino, worked on the question of the Charter with the result that the convention agreed to include the Charter as part II of the Constitutional Treaty, without any modification of the substance considered as an *acquis* due to the large consensus obtained at the first convention. The final clauses (Articles II-111 to II-114 of the Constitutional Treaty, replacing Articles 51 to 54 of the Charter) devoted to interpretation and implementation of the Charter were modified, in some cases cosmetically,[2] in other cases more significantly with a clear intention of preventing extensive interpretation. For instance, a new Article II-112, para 5, introduces a distinction between rights and principles and requires any judge not to use principles inscribed in the Charter for any purpose other than interpreting provisions which implement EU law. One will observe that the distinction between rights and principles is difficult to make when reading the Charter; a number of provisions refer to both – take, for instance, equality between men and women. However, even if the legal reasons behind these amendments were questionable, they contributed to the easy acceptance by the intergovernmental conference of the inclusion of the Charter in the Constitutional Treaty. Subsequently, in certain Member States like France, such provisions helped the constitutional judge to give to the Charter a certificate of conformity with the French Constitution when the Constitutional Treaty was under scrutiny.[3]

Following the negative result of the referenda on the Constitutional Treaty organized in France and The Netherlands, respectively on 29 May and 2 June 2005, the question of the legal destiny of the Charter is to be raised again. Is it condemned to the same lot as the Treaty itself or should it be allowed a different fate? Whatever the future of the Charter and its binding effect, it is noticeable that it has become a document of reference for the Union, either in decision-making or through case law. We will try to analyse this phenomenon and give some practical examples in the area of good administration.

II. The Influential Effect of the Charter of Fundamental Rights

If the Charter were to be included in the EU Treaties, either the Constitutional Treaty as it is or in any other combination of texts to be agreed on, it would acquire

---

[2] For instance, two paragraphs (Article II.112 paras 4 and 6) have been unnecessarily added to underline the respect due to national law of the Member States.

[3] In its decision of 19 November 2004 (No 2004–505DC), the French *Conseil constitutionnel* refers, among others, to the distinction between rights and principles and, taking account of the new final provisions of the Charter, concludes that part II of the Constitutional Treaty, neither by its content nor through its effects, would undermine 'the essential conditions of exercise of national sovereignty'.

according to Article II-111 (replacing Article 51.1) binding force on institutions, bodies and agencies of the Union and on Member States when they are implementing Union law.[4] It means that the Charter would create for Member States and EU institutions, to the extent the provisions of the Charter are enforceable, legal obligations. On the other hand it appears that, considering its format, its substance and the way it is drafted, borrowing a lot from existing sources such as widely agreed international or regional conventions, common constitutional traditions of the Member States or case law of the European Court of Justice, the Charter through its underlying concepts and principles is capable of influential effect.

A. The Charter as Interinstitutional Agreement

Formally the Charter was published in the Official Journal of the Communities[5] as an interinstitutional agreement between the European Parliament, the Council and the Commission. At the time this type of act did not appear in the official catalogue of EC/EU acts; it was mentioned for the first time in a Declaration of the Final Act of the Nice conference. An interinstitutional agreement is a commitment to behave according to a given way; it creates political and moral obligations for the institutions which have subscribed to it even if it does not confer rights on third parties. It is an expression of the duty of loyal cooperation referred to in Article 10 EC.[6] As regards the Charter, the Commission and the Parliament have clearly expressed the extent of their commitment; as actors in the legislative procedure, they have to take account of the provisions of the Charter in any policy or legislative measure which has connections with fundamental rights.[7]

Following a public commitment made by R Prodi and A Vitorino, the Commission decided to submit any proposal of legislative or regulatory measure to a preliminary test of compatibility with the Charter.[8] It was also decided that any proposal of a legislative measure which had a specific connection with fundamental rights should contain a visa expressing formally that compatibility with the Charter had been checked; a special sentence could be added mentioning

---

[4] We set aside for the time being the discussion of the meaning of the exact formula used in the Charter: 'the Member States only when they are implementing Union law'.

[5] [2000] OJ C364/8.

[6] Declaration No 3 to the Nice Treaty related to Art 10 EC. The ECJ has occasionally referred to certain interinstitutional agreements (Case 302/87 *Parliament v Council* [1988] ECR 5615; Case C- 25/94 *Commission v Council* [1996] ECR I-1469). The Constitutional treaty, in line with existing practice, recognizes the right of the European Parliament, the Council and the Commission to conclude interinstitutional agreements which may have a binding force (Art III-397).

[7] Presentation by Mrs N Fontaine, President of the European Parliament, for the proclamation of the Charter at Nice, 7 December 2000; Communications of the Commission 13 September 2000, the Charter of Fundamental Rights of the European Union, Doc.COM (2000) 559 final, and 11 October 2000, The nature of the Charter of Fundamental Rights of the European Union, Doc.COM (2000) 644 final.

[8] Communication of 13 March 2001, Implementation of the Charter of Fundamental Rights of the European Union, SEC (2001) 380/3.

the relevant provisions of the Charter. In a communication of 27 April 2005 the Commission specified that the visa 'Charter' made sense either when the legislative proposal aimed at implementing or promoting fundamental rights or when, by contrast, it implied a limitation of such rights.[9]

(i) Legislative Practice

The legislative practice offers a number of examples of acts which refer to the Charter in their preamble. For instance, a formal declaration of conformity appears in the third paragraph of the preamble of the Directive 2002/73/CE of 23 September 2002 of the European Parliament and Council, modifying the Directive 76/207/CEE of the Council, on the implementation of the principle of equal treatment between men and women;[10] in the second paragraph of the preamble of the Directive 2003/86 CE of the Council of 22 September 2003 on the right to family reunification of third countries' nationals;[11] and in the third paragraph of the preamble of the Directive 2003/109 CE of the Council of 25 November 2003 on the statute of long-term residents originating from third countries.[12] There are other, less formal ways of referring to the Charter. The second paragraph of the preamble of the Regulation (CE) No 1049/2001 of the European Parliament and the Council of 30 May 2001 on public access to European Parliament, Council and Commission documents states that, 'Openness contributes to strengthening the principles of democracy and respect for fundamental rights as laid down in Article 6 of the EU Treaty and in the Charter of Fundamental Rights of the European Union'.[13] Paragraph 1 of the Directive 2004/38/CE of the European Parliament and the Council of 29 April 2004 on the rights of citizens of the Union and members of their family to move and reside freely within the territory of the Member States invites said Member States to implement the directive without the discriminations prohibited by Article 21 of the Charter.[14] Finally, the fourth paragraph of the preamble of

---

[9] Communication of 27 April 2005, the respect for the Charter of Fundamental Rights in the legislative proposals of the Commission – methodology for a rigorous and systematic control, Doc. COM (205) 172 final.

[10] Directive 2002/73/EC of the European Parliament and of the Council of 23 September 2002 amending Council Directive 76/207/EEC on the implementation of the principle of equal treatment for men and women as regards access to employment, vocational training and promotion, and working conditions; [2002] OJ L 269/15.

[11] Council Directive 2003/86/EC of 22 September 2003 on the right to family reunification; [2003] OJ L 251/12.

[12] Council Directive 2003/109/EC of 25 November 2003 concerning the status of third-country nationals who are long-term residents; [2004] OJ L 16/44.

[13] Regulation (EC) No 1049/2001 of the European Parliament and of the Council of 30 May 2001 regarding public access to European Parliament, Council and Commission documents; [2001] OJ L 145/43.

[14] Directive 2004/38/EC of the European Parliament and of the Council of 29 April 2004 on the right of citizens of the Union and their family members to move and reside freely within the territory of the Member States amending Regulation (EEC) No 1612/68 and repealing Directives

Directive 2004/113/CE of the Council of 13 December 2004 implementing the principle of equal treatment between men and women in the access to and supply of goods and services characterizes this principle as fundamental and refers back to Articles 21, 23 and 24 of the Charter.[15] All these provisions underline the influential role of the Charter as expression of values and principles.

On the other hand one may regret the absence of similar references to the Charter in a number of directives in social matters, related to the rights of workers, such as Directive 2002/14 CE of the European Parliament and the Council of 11 March 2002 establishing a framework for informing and consulting employees in the European Community;[16] Directive 2003/88 of the European Parliament and the Council of 4 November 2004 on certain aspects of organization of working time;[17] and Directive 2004/40 CE of the European Parliament and the Council of 29 April 2004 on minimum health and safety requirements regarding the exposure of workers to the risks arising from electromagnetic fields.[18] Article 27 of the Charter deals with workers' rights of information and consultation within the undertaking; Article 31 with fair and just working conditions, namely health, safety and working time. One explanation for the absence of reference to these provisions of the Charter in recent directives may very well be the traditional reluctance of some Member States as to any extensive interpretation of European social rights; the drafting of Title IV of the Charter ('Solidarity') was at the time the result of a difficult transaction. The same sort of comment could be made when observing that the administrative arrangement of February 2006 between Spain and the Council of the European Union[19] does not mention Article 22 of the Charter on linguistic diversity. This agreement which authorizes, in the relations with European institutions, the use of regional languages recognized by the national constitution (Catalan, Basque and Galician), states in the third paragraph of its preamble that 'within the framework of the efforts developed in order to bring together the Union and its citizens the richness of linguistic diversity must be taken into account more systematically'. This is exactly what Article 22

64/221/EEC, 68/360/EEC, 72/194/EEC, 73/148/EEC, 75/34/EEC, 75/35/EEC, 90/364/EEC, 90/365/EEC and 93/96/EEC; [2004] OJ L 158/77.

[15] Council Directive 2004/113/EC of 13 December 2004 implementing the principle of equal treatment between men and women in the access to and supply of goods and services; [2004] OJ L 373/37.

[16] Directive 2002/14/EC of the European Parliament and of the Council of 11 March 2002 establishing a general framework for informing and consulting employees in the European Community; [2002] OJ L 80/29.

[17] Directive 2003/88/EC of the European Parliament and of the Council of 4 November 2003 concerning certain aspects of the organization of working time; [2003] OJ L 299/9.

[18] Directive 2004/40/EC of the European Parliament and of the Council of 29 April 2004 on the minimum health and safety requirements regarding the exposure of workers to the risks arising from physical agents (electromagnetic fields) (18th individual Directive within the meaning of Article 16(1) of Directive 89/391/EEC); [2004] OJ L 159/1.

[19] Administrative arrangement between the Kingdom of Spain and the Council of the European Union; No 2006/C/40/02; [2006] OJ C 40/2.

implies; but we know how difficult and acute the linguistic question has become in the Union!

(ii) Institutional Practice

Even if a specific reference to the Charter does not appear in EU/EC legislation every time it would make sense, the institutions of the Union take seriously their commitment to comply with the Charter as an inter-institutional agreement. Following the proclamation of the Charter, various initiatives have been taken in order that the fundamental rights dimension be more effectively taken into account in the elaboration of EU policies and their implementation. To that effect, following a recommendation of the European Parliament, the Commission created in September 2002 a network of independent experts whose mission is to collect information concerning the situation of human rights in each Member State; a first report was made public on 31 March 2003. Subsequently, the Commission presided over by M Barroso instituted in December 2004 a group of commissioners to watch over the respect of fundamental rights in Community action;[20] following the methodological prescriptions of the Communication (already mentioned) of 27 April 2005, further than a simple statement of reasons, a proper impact analysis in terms of conformity with the Charter must be made for any text or initiative which has implications in the area of fundamental rights. The Commission could thus avoid the criticism of pure formalism of a textual reference to the Charter.

Worth mentioning are other initiatives such as the creation on the basis of Article 308 EC of an Agency of Fundamental Rights of the European Union to be effective as from 1 March 2007.[21] Its name is inspired by that of the Charter. Its role is to provide the institutions and bodies of the Union, as well as the Member States when they implement Community law, with assistance and expertise in the area of fundamental rights. The Council will have the opportunity to require the agency to contribute to an expert evaluation in the framework of Article 7 TEU procedures; the agency will use the provisions of the Charter as a document of reference (see recital 2 of the preamble). The contemplated European Institute for equality between men and women is also inspired by provisions of the Charter (Articles 21 and 23)[22] while it has its legal basis in the EC Treaty (Articles 13 and 141 EC). As Advocate General Ruiz-Jarabo Colomer observes in a recent opinion: 'More relevant is the Charter of Fundamental Rights of the European Union, proclaimed on 7 December 2000 at the Nice European Council, since, apart from the controversy regarding its legal nature, it has had a significant influence on legislation planned and approved since it was proclaimed'.[23] These various texts

---

[20] SEC [2004] 1617.
[21] Council Regulation (EC) No 162/207 of 15 February2007 establishing a European Agency for Fundamental Rights; [2007] OJ L 53/1.
[22] Proposition of regulation of the European Parliament and the Council presented on 8 March 2005, doc.COM (2005) 81 final.
[23] Case C-207/04 *Vergani* [2005] ECR I-7453; Concl Point 27.

and initiatives contribute to promoting at the European Union level, at the time of new important enlargements, a common European culture of fundamental rights for which the Charter is the agreed reference. One may wonder if, for the promotion of such a 'cultural' policy, the use of the open method of coordination would not be appropriate: more than under compulsion, much improvement might be obtained in the area of fundamental rights through exchange of experiences and good practices between Member States, increased involvement of regional and local actors of civil society, benchmarking, peer review and so on.

Apart from the European Parliament, the Commission and the Council, the other institutions and bodies of the Union have not made any commitment as to the respect of the Charter. However, the European Ombudsman, in his annual report, refers to it recurrently, namely to Article 41 on the right to good administration. Other EU institutions, bodies and agencies could also take account of this provision.

B. The Influence of the Charter on European Case Law

At their respective levels, the various actors of the European Union judiciary – the Court of First Instance, the Advocates General and the European Court of Justice – have used the Charter as a source of inspiration, as a relevant formulation of those fundamental rights which qualify as general principles of Community law. Its influence goes even beyond the EU circle.

(i) Influence of the Charter on the Court of First Instance Case Law

Prompted by the parties to the cases, the CFI has been inclined quite early to give life to the Charter as a document 'reaffirming' the fundamental rights which count among general principles of Community law. These series of decisions are well known, related either to the right to good administration,[24] the right to an effective remedy,[25] the presumption of innocence[26] or the right to respect for private and family life.[27] According to the CFI, 'although it is deprived of legal binding force, the Charter demonstrates the importance in Community legal order of the rights it states'.[28]

Worth mentioning is the use made by the CFI of Article 47 of the Charter (right to an effective remedy) in order to refute the traditional strict interpretation of Article 230, fourth paragraph, EC on *locus standi* of natural and legal persons

---

[24] Case T-54/99 *Max. mobil Telekommunikation* [2002] ECR II-313; case T-242/02 *The Surinder Corp v OHMI* [2005] ECR II-2793.
[25] Case T-377/00, T-379/00, T-380/00, T-260/01 and T-272/01 *Philip Morris International v Commission* [2003] ECR II-1; Case T-116/01 and T-118/01 *P&O European Ferries* [2003] ECR II-2957.
[26] Case T-67/00, T-68/00, T-71/00 and T-78/00 *JFE Engineering Corp v Commission* [2004] ECR II-1575.
[27] Case T-165/03 *Vonier v Commission* [2004] ECR II-1575.
[28] *Philip Morris International*, point 122.

to institute proceedings contesting the legality of EC acts. Inspired by the audacious position of Advocate General Jacobs in *Unión de Pequeños Agricultores* (opinion of 31 March 2002), the Court of First Instance proposed a new reading of the concept of 'direct and individual concern' in order to open more widely the access to Community courts for individuals.[29] The Court of Justice did not follow that approach and maintained its restrictive interpretation as long as the terms of the Treaty are not modified.[30]

The CFI proved to be much more reserved as regards the use of the Charter as a direct source of positive law. In two cases related to the age limit for recruitment by the Commission, the claimant based arguments on Article 21 of the Charter which prohibits any discrimination based on age. The Court dismissed the plea, stating that 'although it is established that [the Charter] has been referred to on various occasions by the Community judge as a source of inspiration for the recognition and protection of the rights of citizens and as a test of measure of the rights granted in the legal Community order, it remains that, presently, the Charter is deprived of legal binding force.'[31] It appears that the Court of First Instance makes a difference between the provisions of the Charter expressing rights which are already part of the corpus of general principles of Community law and those which imply new developments. As regards the prohibition of discrimination based on age, this right is not mentioned in Article 14 'Prohibition of discrimination' of the ECHR, but in Article 13 EC, both provisions being referred to in the 'explanations' under Article 21 of the Charter; however, the drafting of Article 13 EC is such that the newly recognized rights it contains, such as non-discrimination based on age, are deprived of direct effect, appropriate measures having to be adopted by secondary legislation.

(ii) *The Charter in Advocates' General Opinions*

The opinions of the Advocates General do not have the same legal force as Court decisions, but they are illuminating. The most vigorous statements in favour of the Charter were expressed as early as 2001; they are well known.[32] In most cases where it is relevant, Advocates General make reference to the Charter either in the text of their opinions or more unobtrusively in footnotes, quoting a provision which confirms the existence of a fundamental right protected by Community law. A wide range of various rights, classical or more new, has up to now been

---

[29] Case T-177/01 *Jégo-Quéré* [2002] ECR II-2365.
[30] Case C-50/00 P *Unión Pequeños Agricultores* [2002] ECR I-6677; Case C-263/02 P *Jégo-Quéré* [2004] ECR I-3425.
[31] Case T-219/02 and T-337/02 *Lutz Herrera v Commission* [2004] ECR II-1407, point 88 (our translation from Spanish); Case T-256/01 *Pyres v Commission* [2005] ECR II-25, point 66 (our translation from French).
[32] Opinion of Advocate General Tizzano of 8 February 2001, point 28, in Case C-178/99 *BECTU* [2001] ECR I-4881; opinion of Advocate General Léger of 10 July in Case C-359/99 *Hautala* [2001] ECR I-9565.

alluded to: right to property,[33] freedom of movement and residence,[34] freedom of association,[35] right of access to services of general economic interest,[36] right of every worker to working conditions which respect his or her health and safety,[37] a worker's right to information and consultation within the undertaking,[38] right to social security and social assistance,[39] respect of linguistic diversity,[40] environmental protection,[41] and protection of personal data.[42] The provisions of the Charter are used in support of a reasoning of the kind proposed by Advocate General Ruiz-Jarabo Colomer, according to which 'the Charter of Fundamental Rights of the European Union, proclaimed in Nice on 7 December 2000, which, whilst not having genuine legislative scope in the strict sense, as it is not in itself binding, is an invaluable reflection of the common denominator of the legal values paramount in Member States, from which emanate, in their turn, the general principles of Community law'.[43] Very similarly, Advocate General Poiares Maduro indicates that 'although it does not as yet have binding legal effects, the abovementioned Charter nonetheless serves as a guide to and point of reference for the rights guaranteed by the Community legal order'.[44] It appears that the Advocates General very unanimously invite the Court to use the Charter not as an autonomous source of Community law, but as a useful expression, utterly accomplished, of general principles of Community law.

(iii) Influence of the Charter on the European Court of Justice Case Law

For months, the ECJ reacted to these invitations with a prudent silence. It seemed to imply that for the Court it belonged to the 'constitutional authorities' to decide what should be the destiny of the Charter and its level of binding force in the Community legal order. Considering the now-established failure of

---

[33] Opinion of Advocate General Mischo of 10 July 2003 in Case E620/00 and C-64/00 *Booker Aquaculture and Hydro Seafood* [2003] ECR I-7411.
[34] Opinion of Advocate General Geelhoed in Case C-209/03 *Bidar* [2005] ECR I-2119.
[35] Opinion of Advocate General Ruiz-Jarabo Colomer in Case C-499/04 *Werhof* [2006] ECR I-2397.
[36] Opinion of Advocate General Albert in Case C-340/99 *TNT Traco SpA* [2001] ECR I-4109.
[37] Opinion of Advocate General Stix-Hackl in Case C-49/00 *Commission v Italy* [2001] ECR I-8575.
[38] Opinion of Advocate General Kokott in Case C-220/02 *Österreichischer Gewerkschaftsbund* [2004] ECR I-5907.
[39] Opinion of Advocate General Poiares Maduro in Case C-181/03 P *Nardone v Commission* [2005] ECR I-199.
[40] Opinion of Advocate General Poiares Maduro in Case C-160/03 *Spain v Eurojust* [2005] ECR I-2077.
[41] Opinion of Advocate General Ruiz-Jarabo Colomer in Case C-176/03 *Commission v Council* [2005] ECR I-7879.
[42] Opinion of Advocate General Léger of 25 November 2005 in Case C-317/04 *European Parliament v Council* [2006] ECR I-4721.
[43] Opinion of Advocate General Ruiz-Jarabo Colomer, point 59, in Case C-208/00 *Überseering* [2002] ECR I-9919.
[44] Opinion on *Nardone*, point 51 (n 38 above).

prompt ratification of the Constitutional Treaty incorporating the Charter, it is not impossible that new evolutions take place. It is only fair to underline that the presence of the Charter in the Constitutional Treaty has never been objected to by the opponents to the Treaty in France or The Netherlands. The presence of Part III was more heavily criticized; the situation would very likely have been different in the UK.

On some occasions it has been observed that, although the ECJ does not explicitly refer to the provisions of the Charter, it makes use of it as a source of inspiration. This is noticeable as regards the principle of human dignity. In the case *Netherlands v European Parliament and Council*,[45] The Netherlands had contested the legality of the Directive 98/44/CE of the European Parliament and the Council of 6 July 1998 on the legal protection of biotechnological inventions. It argued, among others, that the possibility of obtaining a patent for parts of the human body was a blow to human dignity. In his opinion of 14 June 2001, Advocate General Jacobs underlined that 'The right to human dignity is perhaps the most fundamental right of all, and is now expressed in Article 1 of the Charter of Fundamental Rights of the European Union' (paragraph 197). The ECJ confirmed the legality of the Directive. The main interest of its decision is that for the first time it characterized the right to human dignity as a fundamental right in line with the provisions of the Charter: 'It is for the Court of Justice, in its review of the compatibility of acts of the institutions with the general principles of Community law, to ensure that the fundamental right to human dignity and integrity is observed' (point 70). One may observe that the principle of human dignity appears in the preamble of the Universal Declaration of Human Rights of 1948, but not in the ECHR.

Commenting on this approach of the ECJ in her opinion of 18 March 2004 on the *Omega* case,[46] which related to trade distribution of games centred on homicide, Advocate General Stix-Hackl observes: 'The Court of Justice therefore appears to base the concept of human dignity on a comparatively wide understanding, as expressed in Article 1 of the Charter of Fundamental Rights of the European Union. This article reads as follows: Human dignity is inviolable. It must be respected and protected' (point 91). In its subsequent decision the Court accepted that the distribution of such games could be prohibited by national measures on the basis of considerations of human dignity. The Court stated that, 'Community legal order undeniably strives to ensure respect for human dignity as a general principle of law' (point 34). By quoting its Advocate General and, therefore, indirectly the Charter, the Court confirms, even if it is indirectly, that it adheres to its ethos.

In other examples the influence of the Charter on ECJ case law is even more indirect. This is apparent in a case related to a transsexual who wanted to marry

---

[45] Case C-377/98 [2001] ECR I-7079.
[46] Case 36/02 *Omega* [2004] ECR I-9609.

after having gone through an operation in order to have his sex modified.[47] Such marriage is not allowed under English law; therefore the woman partner, Mrs KB, was not allowed the benefit of a pension, for which the fact that the couple is married is a condition. The ECJ recalled that, according to the case law of the European Court of Human Rights, these provisions of the English statute infringe Article 12 ECHR interpreted in the light of Article 9 of the Charter on the right to marry. In fact, it has been observed that on the question of marriage, the Charter is more 'modern' than the ECHR in the sense that, not mentioning explicitly men and women, it implies that persons of the same sex should not necessarily be excluded of the right to marry. Various decisions of the European Court of Human Rights referring to the Charter and on which the ECJ builds its reasoning in the *KB* case[48] illustrate the complex way through which the provisions of the Charter seep into Community law. More generally, the judges of the ECtHR do not hesitate to quote the Charter. For instance, Article 21 on non-discrimination is mentioned in the partly-dissenting opinion of Judges Bratza, Fuhrmann and Tulkens in the *Fretté* case,[49] where they underline that this provision gives evidence that 'a European consensus is now emerging' on prohibition of any discrimination based on sexual orientation. A significant role was attributed to the Charter in the *Bosphorus* case of 30 June 2005[50] in relation to the implementation in Ireland of an EC regulation. The ECtHR observes that, unless a specific failure is demonstrated in a particular situation, the protection of fundamental rights guaranteed by EC law is equivalent to that guaranteed by the ECHR; and among the elements referred to by the Strasbourg Court appear the provisions of the Charter 'although not fully binding' (point 159).

---

[47] Case -117/01 *KB* [2004] ECR I-541.
[48] *Goodwin v United Kingdom,* App No 28957/75, judgment of 11 July 2002; *I v United Kingdom,* App No25680/98, judgment of 11 July 2002.
[49] *Fretté v France* App No 36515/97, judgment of 26 February 2002.
[50] *Bosphorus Hava Yollari Turizm ve Ticaret anonim sirketi v Ireland,* App No 45036/98, judgment of 30 June 2005, 159. The Court has described (at paras 73–81) the fundamental rights guarantees of the EC which govern Member States, Community institutions together with natural and legal persons ('individuals'). While the constituent EC Treaty did not initially contain express provisions for the protection of fundamental rights, the ECJ subsequently recognized that such rights were enshrined in the general principles of Community law protected by it and that the Convention had a 'special significance' as a source of such rights. Respect for fundamental rights has become 'a condition of the legality of Community acts' (paras 73–5, together with the opinion of the AG in the present case at paras 45–50) and in carrying out this assessment the ECJ refers extensively to Convention provisions and to this Court's jurisprudence. At the relevant time, these jurisprudential developments had been reflected in certain Treaty amendments (notably those aspects of the Single European Act 1986 and of the TEU referred to at paras 77–8). This evolution has continued thereafter. The Treaty of Amsterdam 1997 is referred to at para 79. Although not fully binding, the provisions of the Charter of Fundamental Rights of the European Union were substantially inspired by those of the Convention and the Charter recognizes the Convention as establishing the minimum human rights standards. Article I-9 of the later Treaty establishing a Constitution for Europe (not in force) provides for the Charter to become primary law of the European Union and for the Union to accede to the Convention (see paras 80–1).

It would, therefore, be possible to conclude that slowly but surely, even if the Charter does not formally become part of EU constitutional law, as long as the Constitutional Treaty is not ratified it plays an influential and significant role in the building of a European corpus of law protecting fundamental rights. The Charter is referred to in the preambles of texts of secondary legislation and used as a document of reference by the various EC/EU institutions. On the other hand the Charter, although not binding, influences the case law of European courts. Recent signs indicate that the two trends could meet. In a case where the European Parliament contested the validity of certain provisions of the Directive 2003/86/CE on family reunification for the reason that they did not comply with the principle of non-discrimination,[51] the ECJ confirmed the validity of the Directive indicating, among others, that 'while the Charter is not a legal binding instrument, the Community legislator has intended to recognize its importance by stating in the second paragraph of the preamble of the Directive that said Directive respects the principles which are recognized not only by Article 8 ECHR but equally by the Charter'. This is the first time the Court refers to the fact that the Charter is quoted in the preamble of a text of secondary legislation to recognize the importance of the Charter as a legal document. This is a first step which might be followed by many others in various domains.

III. The Example of the Right to Good Administration

The right to good administration as expressed in Article 41 of the Charter has no precedent in any international or European documents on human rights. The national laws of the founding Member States do not refer to a right to good administration as a fundamental right, even if their statutes and case law have developed rules of good administrative behaviour. However, the more recent constitutions of Member States such as Spain or Portugal include specific provisions aiming at protecting individuals from unfair procedures. At a time when the debate on good administration, sometimes referred to as 'good governance', developed in Europe, together with a more general need to reform the EU administration criticized for its lack of efficiency, of transparency and its remoteness from individuals, it is not surprising that the Finnish proposal to include in the Charter a right to good administration was welcome. What is really innovative in the drafting of the Charter is that principles of administrative law are not put in terms of objective legality in the public interest, but in the language of subjective public rights. The Charter tends to recognize the status of fundamental rights to procedural rights: access to justice, access to documents, the right to complain to the Ombudsman and the right to good administration. Further, the constitutionalization of these new rights enjoyed by the individuals vis-à-vis the

---

[51] Case C-540/03 *European Parliament v Council* [2006] ECR I-5769 (point 38).

administration can be seen as giving a new dimension to European citizenship (they appear in title V of the Charter: 'Citizen's rights').

However, as regards the right to good administration, the drafting of the Charter, although innovative, remains prudent. The scope of Article 41 is strictly limited *ratione materiae* and *ratione personae* in order to not interfere with the procedural autonomy of the Member States, which have their long-established rules and practices of judicial review in the area of administrative law. As to the substance of good administration in Article 41 of the Charter, the rights concerned are based on the Treaty although they do not exactly reproduce the corresponding Treaty articles. The first basic 'right of every person to have his or her affairs handled impartially, fairly and within a reasonable time by the institutions and bodies of the Union' is drafted very similarly to Article 47(2) of the Charter (right to an effective remedy) and Article 6(1) ECHR. This right in turn includes three sub-rights enumerated in a non-exhaustive manner: the right of every person to be heard before any individual measure which would affect him or her adversely is taken, the right of access to individual file and the obligation for the administration to give reasons for its decisions. These various rules have been developed in numerous cases decided by the ECJ and the CFI, the most important of which are mentioned in the 'explanations' under Article 41. As regards the right to a reasoned decision, the Charter departs significantly from the wording of the Treaty. Article 253 EC imposes a duty to provide reasons for regulations, directives and decisions whereas the Charter limits the scope of this obligation to administrative decisions. Such a narrow formulation fits into the notion of good administration; the obligation to give reasons is not motivated here by the care for democracy and political accountability: 'According to the case law of the Courts, the duty to state reasons has two objectives: it is necessary in order to ensure that the individual has an opportunity to consider whether it is feasible to challenge a given measure and it serves to ensure that the Court can exercise its power to review the legality of the measure'.[52]

Two other rights follow: the right to compensation for damage done by the Community institutions or officials and the right to correspond in one of the Community languages. These rights are based on Article 288 EC and Article 21(3) EC respectively. The list of rights contained in Article 41 is intentionally non-exhaustive. Many more rights could have been enumerated under the umbrella of the right to good administration. There are two good reasons for such self-restraint on the part of the drafters: one is the respect for the terms of the Treaty and the rights already agreed on by Member States, the other is that the principle of good administration will continue to develop according to effective needs through case law and the practice of the institutions. This care

---

[52] See K Kanska, 'Towards Administrative Human Rights in the EU. Impact of the Charter of Fundamental Rights' European Law Journal 10, 3 (May 2004) 296–326, 320; this article offers a textual analysis and commentary of Article 41.

for limitations agreed on by Member States is obvious as one considers the scope *ratione personae* of Article 41 of the Charter. The obligations stemming from Article 41 extend to institutions, bodies and agencies of the Union; unlike most other Charter rights, Article 41 does not apply to Member States when implementing EU law. The intention behind such drafting is to reassure Member States that they will not have to take into account the principle of good administration in purely national administrative procedures, including those involving application of Community law. However, such limitation may in fact prove to be unpractical given that much of Community administration is indirect and that the case law of the Court of Justice showed a tendency towards imposing common standards on the Member States when implementing EU law.[53]

These various elements put together show how the drafters of Article 41, while promoting a new concept of subjective public right of the individual to a good administration, have simultaneously carefully adhered to a prudent wording which does not transgress existing obligations inscribed in the Treaty and sometimes even stays behind. It is in this ambivalent context that the influential effects of these provisions of the Charter have developed through institutional practice and case law. We will give some examples. After the resignation of the Santer Commission and the publication of the Committee of Independent Experts' First Report in March 1999, the Commission launched a White Paper on Administrative Reform[54] which, apart from matters connected with better management and prevention of fraud, insists on an improvement of procedural rules governing the exercise of Community administrative activities. A few months later the Commission, in a Communication on the Charter, confirmed its view that the Charter 'enshrines certain "new" rights which already exist but have not yet been explicitly protected as fundamental rights, notwithstanding the values they are intended to protect, such as . . . the right to good administration'.[55] Soon after, in a Decision of 2001,[56] the Commission gave effect to the right to be heard enshrined in Article 41. The Decision concerned duties of a hearing official in competition proceedings, the necessity of his independence and integrity; in recital 2 of the preamble we read: 'The Commission must ensure that the right of the parties concerned and of third parties to be heard before a final decision affecting their interests is taken is guaranteed in its competition proceedings, having regard in particular to the Charter of Fundamental Rights of the European Union'. On one side the Commission makes express reference to the Charter and to the fundamental right to be heard which it promotes; on the other the Decision of the Commission retains a wider scope of this right, not limited to the parties concerned as provided for in Article 41, but extended to third parties.

---

[53] Case 222/86 *Unectef v Heylens* [1987] ECR- 4097.
[54] 'Reforming the Commission. A White paper' COM(2000) 200 final 2, 5 April 2000.
[55] Communication of the Commission on the Charter of Fundamental Rights (n 7 above).
[56] Commission Decision 2001/462/EC-ECSC.

In so doing, the Commission indicates that it accepts the influential effect of the Charter but does not feel bound by the limits imposed by its exact wording.

As mentioned above, the Ombudsman also makes frequent references to Article 41 of the Charter in his annual report on maladministration, although 'maladministration' as a non-legal concept is certainly not the antithesis of the right to good administration deeply rooted in the rule of law.[57] Finally, references to Article 41 appear directly or indirectly in the case law of the European Courts. As an example, we cannot do better than quoting the laconic remark of Advocate General Jacobs on the right to have one's affairs handled in a reasonable time: 'slow administration is a bad administration'.[58] In his opinion he made an express reference to Article 41(1) of the Charter and stated that it 'proclaims a generally recognized principle'. In its subsequent decision, the Court characterizes the right to a good administration as a 'general principle of Community law' without making any reference to common constitutional traditions or the ECHR or any other international documents in order to identify the source of such general principle. Therefore, by simply following the opinion of its Advocate General who quoted the relevant passage of the Charter, the Court has indirectly confirmed the authoritative value of this provision of the Charter. These are some examples, among many, of the complex process through which the terms of the Charter have been drafted, agreed on and now, although not binding, exert influence on EU law in the making.

[57] The 'Explanations' under Article 41 of the Charter confirm this approach by stating: 'Artcle 41 is based on the existence of a Community subject to the rule of law whose characteristics were developed in the case law which enshrined inter alia the principle of good administration'.

[58] Opinion of Advocate General Jacobs in Case C-270/99 P, *Z v Parliament* [2001] ECR I-9197, para 40.

10

Administrative Justice and Standards of Substantive Judicial Review

Jeffrey Jowell

I. Introduction

Francis Jacobs was the first to ask many important questions. The one I want to consider is whether there is or should be a single test for judicial review of the substance of a public authority's decision.[1] When he posed that question the test for substantive review in the United Kingdom's domestic law was *Wednesbury* unreasonableness, under which the courts would only interfere with decisions which were 'so unreasonable that no reasonable authority could so decide'.[2] As Lord Bingham has said, under this test the claimant making a challenge has 'a mountain to climb'.[3] In 1999 Jacobs noted the alternative test of proportionality as it was applied in European Community law by the European Court of Justice and by the European Court of Human Rights in interpreting the European Convention on Human Rights. He wondered how much longer we could or should continue with dual or multiple standards of review.

Does one test of substantive review fit all decisions? Is there a single way to approach these issues in a modern European democracy? To answer that question we must first consider three preliminary questions:

(a) whether administrative justice is integral to the required elements of a modern European democracy;

(b) if so, whether substantive review is an essential element of administrative justice; and

(c) if so, whether there is just one standard which the courts must apply when reviewing the substantive decisions of administrative authorities.

---

[1] F Jacobs, 'The Influence of European Community Law on Public Law in the United Kingdom' (1999) 2 CYELS 1.
[2] *Associated Provincial Picture Houses v Wednesbury Corporation* [1948] KB 223.
[3] *R v Lord Chancellor, ex p Maxwell* [1997] 1 LR 104, 109.

II. The Democratic Necessity of Administrative Justice

Good comparatists over the years have intoned the mantra of context, insisting that the law of any one country can only be understood in the light of the history, traditions and culture of that country. It is of course difficult to argue with that assertion. But this kind of cultural relativism can come into sharp conflict with the kind of democratic absolutism that is increasingly being demanded. In the old days we were indulgent to a degree in accepting the appellation 'democracy' for countries governed by parties alone; or for a government which, although freely elected, decided, with popular support, to suppress its opposition. Nowadays we are more certain that a country that denies at least a basic catalogue of human rights does not merit a democratic designation.

To what extent is administrative justice a universal democratic requirement, and to what extent are the standards of administrative justice universal? In the UK the history is well known of the way in which the judges pulled the rabbit of administrative justice out of the hat of a non-written constitution. Yet the notion of administrative justice as a human right is gaining ground. The first constitutions to incorporate administrative justice were those of Namibia and South Africa. Article 18 of the Namibian Constitution states that:

> Administrative bodies and administrative officials shall act fairly and reasonably and comply with the requirements imposed upon such bodies by common law and any relevant legislation, and persons aggrieved by the exercise of such acts and decisions shall have the right to seek redress before a competent Court or Tribunal.

Section 33 of the current South African Constitution is more extensive, providing that:

(1) everyone has the right to administrative action that is lawful, reasonable and procedurally fair;

(2) everyone whose rights have been adversely affected by administrative action has the right to be given written reasons;

(3) national legislation must be enacted to give effect to these rights, and must:
    (a) provide for the review of administrative action by a court or, where appropriate, an independent and impartial tribunal;
    (b) impose a duty on the state to give effect to the rights in subsection (1) and (2); and
    (c) promote an efficient administration.[4]

---

[4] Under s24 of the 1994 Interim South African Constitution administrative justice was defined as the right to administrative action which is 'lawful', 'procedurally fair', and 'justifiable in relation to the reasons given for it'. Reasons for decisions were also required.

In the early 1990s, when the South African constitution was so painstakingly negotiated, administrative justice was not an obvious candidate for inclusion.[5] Opposition was initially voiced against a bill of rights at all, and to administrative justice as a right in particular – opposition from those who finally saw the chance of coming to power, yet harboured legitimate concerns about the possibility of being constrained by the countervailing power of unelected (and then unrepresentative) judges. Other opponents of the constitutionalization of administrative justice, while not necessarily quarrelling with the intent of administrative law, preferred its development on a case-by-case elaboration of the common law (as in England, where the principles of administrative law have never formally been codified). In the end, however, in recognition of the fact that the apartheid regime was characterized not only by racial discrimination but also by bureaucratic oppression, it was accepted that administrative justice should be entrenched as a foundational value in the new South Africa. Traces of the tensions during the drafting process of section 33 remain only in the cautionary note in subsection 3(c) which draws attention to the necessity of 'efficiency' as a quality of administrative justice.

Inspired by South Africa's example, the concept of administrative justice as a constitutional right is being actively considered by the new democracies, such as countries of the former Soviet Union. Not all of them have accepted South Africa's decision to codify its administrative law principles (now under the terms of the Promotion of Administrative Justice Act 2002). Even the Charter of Fundamental Rights of the European Union has adopted a modified version of South Africa's section 33. Under Chapter V of that Charter, which provides for 'citizen's rights', Article 41 confers a 'right to good administration', which is phrased as follows:

(1) Every person has the right to have his or her affairs handled impartially, fairly and within a reasonable time by the institutions and bodies of the Union.
(2) The right includes:
    - The right of every person to be heard, before any individual measure which would affect him or her adversely is taken;
    - The right of every person to have access to his or her file, while respecting the legitimate interests of confidentiality and of professional and business secrecy;
    - The obligations of the administration to give reasons for its decisions.

A. Does the Right to Administrative Justice Include Substantive or Merely Procedural Protections?

The incorporation of a right to good administration in the European Charter (whatever the present uncertain status of the Charter) is a signal example of the

---

[5] See the account in L de Plessis and H Corder, *Understanding South Africa's Transitional Bill of Rights* (1994).

progressive and incremental articulation of administrative justice as a democratic necessity. However, the rights that it protects are largely procedural (the right to a hearing, access to information and reasons for a decision). They do not go as far as the South African constitution in incorporating the right to a 'reasonable' decision. However, the Charter is set in the context of the European Court of Justice's recognition of 'fundamental principles' by which to assess substantive interference with Treaty obligations by the standards of equality, legal certainty and proportionality. In addition, the ECJ applies Convention rights, some of which protect substantive rights, such as Article 5 (the right to the liberty and security of the person) and Article 14 (equality).

In addition, in the UK, as elsewhere, the rule of law as a constitutional principle provides the justification for much of administrative justice.[6] Some see the rule of law as embodying formal qualities in law (such as clarity, prospectivity, stability, openness and access to an impartial judiciary).[7] Others criticize that view as a 'rule-book conception' of the rule of law and prefer the 'rights conception', under which legal rules contain inherent moral content.[8] In so far as the rule of law is a principle guiding the way power is deployed by government in a democracy (rather than a general theory of law, or of 'good' law), it highlights a number of values inherent in administrative justice.[9] These include: *legality* (which requires all decisions and acts of public officials to be legally authorized); *certainty* (which allows affected persons to know what they are required to do – or not do – in advance of any sanction for breach of a rule);[10] *consistency* (which requires even-handed application of standards, and like cases can then be treated alike); *access to justice* (which forbids measures which prevent or preclude judicial review) and *due process* (requiring a fair hearing by an unbiased tribunal). Many of these values are substantive, including even that of due process[11] which, in the course of providing full and fair consideration of the issues and evidence, as

[6] See P Craig, 'Formal and substantive conceptions of the rule of law: an analytical framework' [1997] PL 467; N Barber, 'Must legalistic conceptions of the rule of law have a social dimension?' (2004) Ratio Juris 474.

[7] J Raz, 'The rule of law and its virtue' (1977) 93 LQR 195; *The Authority of Law* (1979). Compare Lon Fuller's requirements of 'legality': generality, clarity, public promulgation, stability, consistency, fidelity to purpose and prohibition of the impossible (L Fuller, *The Morality of Law* (1964) 153. See also R Summers, 'The principles of the rule of law' (1999) Notre Dame LR 1691; J Waldron, 'Is the rule of law an essentially contested concept?' (2002) Law and Philosophy 137.

[8] R Dworkin, *A Matter of Principle* (1985) 1, 11 ff.

[9] See J Jowell, 'The Rule of Law and its Underlying Values' in J Jowell and D Oliver (eds), *The Changing Constitution* (6th ed, 2007); Lord Bingham, 'The Rule of Law', Sir David Williams Lecture, Cambridge, December 2006; compare Sir John Laws, 'The Rule of Law: Form or Substance', London School of Economics, November 2006.

[10] Certainty in that sense has an instrumental value in that it allows decisions to be planned in advance and people to know clearly where they stand. However, the value of legal certainty is also based in substantive *fairness*. It is unfair to penalize someone for an action which was lawful when it was carried out and it is unfair to punish someone for the breach of a law which they were not able to discover.

[11] For a full account of the variety of justifications for procedural protections, see DJ Galligan, *Due Process and Fair Procedures* (1996).

Lord Steyn has said, plays 'an instrumental role in promoting [substantively] just decisions'.[12]

Whatever the content of its constituent parts, administrative justice is integral to constitutional democracy because it requires individuals to be treated lawfully and with due regard to the proper merits of their cause. Failure to provide that treatment diminishes a person's sense of individual worth. In a democracy properly so-called everyone has the right to equal respect, and it is this respect and dignity that administrative injustice denies. The claim of administrative justice for our attention is based therefore on the assumption that in a properly democratic society no public official should close his ears to legitimate claims or abuse the authority with which he has been entrusted.

III. Standards of Substantive Review

If, as I contend, administrative justice is an inherent feature of constitutional democracy and substantive judicial review is a necessary feature of administrative justice, to what extent can divergence be permitted in the standards and intensity of review? Should the *Wednesbury* standard of unreasonableness (later called 'rationality' – the terms will be used interchangeably) be abandoned in favour of proportionality?

This question assumes that the distinction between proportionality and rationality is clear, but that is not the case (or is no longer the case). I shall in the next section show how the contours of unreasonableness have themselves been altered recently and mingled with those of proportionality.

In addition, it should be noted that proportionality is used in two different senses. In its first sense it requires a *fair balance* to be struck between two or more decisional referents, or between the ends and means of a decision. In its second sense proportionality is, as Lord Steyn said in *Daly*,[13] 'more sophisticated than the traditional [that is, rationality] ground of judicial review'.[14] Proportionality in this more complex sense is what I shall call a *structured test of justification*. It is 'structured' in that it asks a series of integrated questions, the purpose of which is to consider whether the breach of a fundamental norm is 'justified'. It is applied in that sense by the European Court of Justice to assess infringements of EU law, and by the European Court of Human Rights to assess infringements of the qualified rights set out in the Convention.

---

[12] *Raji v General Medical Council* [2003] UKPC 24.
[13] *R (Daly) v Home Secretary* [2001] 2 AC 532 at [27].
[14] Although in *Brown v Stott* [2003] 1 AC 681, 728, it was alluded to as a 'fair balance' test by Lord Hope.

A. The Mingling of Proportionality and Rationality

The distinction between unreasonableness and proportionality (in both its senses) is, however, particularly unclear for the following reasons:

(a) there are aspects of proportionality deep within rationality;

(b) there are aspects of irrationality deep within proportionality;

(c) the intensity of review in both rationality and proportionality is variable.

(i) Proportionality within Rationality

The initial reason given by English courts for rejecting proportionality was that it required an assessment of the facts or merits of the case – an assessment not permitted under judicial review.[15] This was a misunderstanding and belied the fact that proportionality was already inherent in the notion of unreasonableness. A dissection of cases under the wide *Wednesbury* umbrella reveals two situations where the impugned decision could, with more precision, be described as disproportionate rather than unreasonable: (i) excessively onerous or oppressive penalties or infringements of rights or interests, and (ii) manifest imbalance of relevant considerations. In both these cases, it should be noted that proportionality is used as a general test of unfair balance, rather than the structured test of justifiability identified above.

a) Penalties and infringements of rights or duties

Courts expressly employ the notion of proportionality when reviewing harsh penalties. Article 20 of Magna Carta provides that, 'For a trivial offence, a free man will be fined only in proportion to the degree of his offence, and for a serious offence correspondingly, but not so heavily as to deprive him of his livelihood'. A very early case concerning land involved the Commissioner of Sewers imposing on one landowner alone charges for repairs to a river bank from which other riparian owners had also benefited. This decision was held to be contrary to the law and reason.[16] More recently the actions of a local authority were held unlawful when, in order to avoid raising rents generally, they charged the whole of required rent increases upon a single property.[17] Lord Denning would have struck down a decision suspending a stallholder's licence on the ground that 'the punishment is altogether excessive and out of proportion to the occasion'.[18]

---

[15] See in particular the speeches of Lords Lowry and Ackner in *R v Secretary of State for the Home Department ex p Brind* [1991] 2 AC 696.

[16] *Rooke's* case (1598) 5 Co Rep 99b.

[17] *Backhouse v Lambeth LBC*, The Times, 14 October 1972.

[18] *R v Barnsley MBC, ex p Hook* [1976] 1 WLR 1052, 1057. The offence was urinating in the street and using offensive language. The Court of Appeal struck down the suspension on the ground of the lack of a fair hearing. See also *R v Secretary of State for the Home Department, ex p Benwell* [1984] ICR 723, 736 where Hodson J said that 'in an extreme case an administrative or

A resolution of a local authority banning a member of the public from local authority property was held to be 'out of proportion to what the applicant had done',[19] and proportionality was expressly used to test the Government's suspension of the permits of Romanian pilots.[20] Town and country planning provides countless examples where planning conditions have been held unreasonable because of their unnecessarily onerous impact. Although the legislation permits the local authority, or the Secretary of State on appeal, to attach conditions to planning permissions as they 'think fit',[21] conditions have been held unreasonable which, in effect, require the developer to dedicate part of his land for public use,[22] or otherwise require the developer to provide the off-site physical infrastructure necessary to unlock the development.[23] Similarly, a planning condition was held unreasonable which, in effect, required the developer to construct housing to local authority standards and rents, and to take tenants from the council's waiting list.[24]

The focus of attention in these cases will be principally the *impact* of the decision upon the affected person. The outcome or end-product of the decision-making process will thus be assessed, rather than the way the decision was reached (although the factors taken into account in reaching the decision may also be – or may be assumed to be – incorrectly weighed) and the courts in effect are pronouncing the decision to have a disproportionate effect on the rights or interests of the claimant. As Laws LJ recently said: 'Clearly a public body may choose to deploy powers it enjoys under statute in so draconian a fashion that the hardship suffered by affected individuals in consequence will justify the court in condemning the exercise as irrational and perverse'.[25]

b) Manifest imbalance of relevant considerations

The weight attached to a consideration that is lawfully relevant is normally regarded, under judicial review, as a matter within the discretion of the primary decision-maker. However, the courts do intervene where excessive or manifestly

---

quasi-administrative penalty can be attacked on the ground that it was so disproportionate to the offence as to be perverse'.

[19] *R v Brent LBC, ex p Assegai* (1987) 151 LGR 891. The reason for the ban was the applicant's unruly behaviour at previous meetings.

[20] *R v Secretary of State for Transport, ex p Pegasus Holidays (London) Ltd and Airbro (UK) Ltd* [1988] 1 WLR 990.

[21] Town and Country Planning Act 1990, s70(1).

[22] *Hall & Co Ltd v Shoreham-by-Sea UDC* [1964] 1 WLR 240. The purpose of the condition was to ensure safe access to the site, a purpose well within the 'four corners' of the legislation.

[23] *City of Bradford MC v Secretary of State for the Environment* [1986] JPL 598. But such a condition may survive if framed in negative terms. See *Grampian RC v Aberdeen CC* (1984) 47 P and CR 633, HL.

[24] *R v Hillingdon LBC, ex p Royco Homes Ltd* [1974] 1 QB 720.

[25] *R (Khatun) v Newham LBC* [2004] EWCA Civ 55; [2005] QB 37, 41 (neither oppressive, perverse or disproportionate for the council to require a claimant who had not viewed an offered property to accept it on pain of his existing accommodation being cancelled if he did not).

inadequate weight is accorded to a relevant consideration.[26] Although not normally referred to as proportionality the courts are in effect asking whether a fair balance has been struck between competing considerations.

Thus where the police, in the face of disruptive demonstrations by animal welfare groups, withdrew protection from the exporters of animals for certain days of the week, it was held by the House of Lords that the considerations taken into account (such as pressures on police protection elsewhere in the county) had been fairly balanced against the danger to the rule of law that the withdrawal of protection would entail.[27]

In licensing cases it has also been held that too much weight had been placed by an authority upon recent precedent refusing refreshment licences, and too little on the 50-year previous enjoyment of the licence by the claimant.[28] Similarly, an adjudicator on an asylum appeal, who had reversed the Secretary of State's decision to deport an asylum seeker who had served a prison sentence in the UK, had placed excessive weight upon the risk of the appellant re-offending, and insufficient weight upon the character of the offence.[29]

Although the courts will normally leave the balancing of 'material' planning considerations to the judgment of the planning authority, they are not 'shy in an appropriate case of concluding that it would have been irrational of a decision-maker to have had regard to an alternative proposal as a material consideration or that, even if possibly he should have done so, to have given it any or any sufficient weight'.[30]

(ii) Rationality within Proportionality

When the courts test whether an official decision is unreasonable in domestic law, one of the features assessed is whether the decision bears a 'rational connection' to the ends which the decision seeks to achieve. Such a test was applied, for example, in a recent case where a non-statutory scheme was introduced to provide compensation for British civilians interned during World War II by the Japanese. The scheme excluded individuals whose parents or grandparents were not born in the UK. The Court of Appeal examined carefully whether the exclusion bore a rational connection to the 'foundation' and 'essential character' of the scheme,

---

[26] See J Silber in *Secretary of State for Trade and Industry, ex p BT3G Ltd* [2001] EWCA Civ 1448; [2001] EuLR 325, 187.
[27] *R v Chief Constable of Sussex, ex p International Trader's Ferry* [1997] 3 WLR 132. See Lord Hoffmann, 'A sense of proportion' (1997) The Irish Jurist 49.
[28] *R v Flintshire County Licensing Committee, ex p Barrett* [1957] 1 QB 350.
[29] *N (Kenya) v Secretary of State for the Home Department* [2004] EWCA Civ 1094 (May and Judge LJJ, Sedley LJ dissenting). See also *R (Harris) v Secretary of State for the Home Department* [2001] INLR 584 where it was held unreasonable to refuse leave to re-enter the UK to a person who had made a brief visit to a dying relative abroad, on the ground of a previous conviction which itself would not have been a ground for deportation.
[30] *R (Mount Cook Land Ltd) v Westminster City Council* [2003] EWCA Civ 1346, per Auld LJ, 33.

but held in the circumstances that the scheme did not fail the *Wednesbury* test.[31] The House of Lords had adopted a similar approach in a case where, under an ex-gratia compensation scheme, British soldiers injured in Bosnia were accorded treatment different from those injured in Northern Ireland.[32]

When courts apply proportionality in the sense of structured justification (in relation to EU law or when interpreting the European Convention on Human Rights) the issue of a rational relationship between ends and means also applies. In *Daly*,[33] the House of Lords adopted the set of interrelated criteria set out in the Privy Council in *de Freitas v Permanent Secretary of Ministry of Agriculture, Fisheries, Land and Housing*[34] asking whether, in determining whether a limitation (by an act, rule or decision) of a Convention right is arbitrary or excessive the court should ask itself:

whether: (i) the legislative objective is sufficiently important to justify limiting a fundamental right; (ii) the measures designed to meet the legislative objective are rationally connected to it; and (iii) the means used to impair the right or freedom are no more than is necessary to accomplish the objective.

Both in EU law and in Convention law we see proportionality as a more sophisticated and structured test of justifiability than the mere 'fair balance' test that we have identified under the umbrella of domestic rationality, but nevertheless containing at its core the notion of 'rational connection'.

The Canadian Supreme Court has also adopted the test of structured proportionality to assess whether a breach of the rights set out in their Charter meet the test of 'reasonable limits...demonstrably justified in a free and democratic society'.[35] *R v Chaulk*[36] defined the notion of 'rational connection' as implying that 'the measures must be carefully designed to meet the objective in question. They must not be arbitrary, unfair or based on irrational considerations'.

B. The Intensity of Review and Burden of Justification

As they initially emerged, unreasonableness and proportionality were employed in very different situations. Unreasonableness was employed as a test to judge the exercise of discretion which was normally conferred upon the decision-maker in

---

[31] *R (Association of British Civilian Internees: Far East Region) v Secretary of State for Defence* [2003] QB 397, 40.

[32] *R v Ministry of Defence, ex p Walker* [2000] 1 WLR 806. Lord Slynn, at 812, said that, 'It is not for the courts to consider whether the scheme...is a good scheme or a bad scheme, unless it can be said that the exclusion is so irrational or unreasonable that no reasonable minister could have adopted it'. Lord Hoffmann considered the distinction to be 'fine' but not irrational: 'That is too high a hurdle to surmount'.

[33] [2001] 2 AC 532.

[34] [1999] 1 AC 69, 80, per Lord Clyde.

[35] Under s1 of the Canadian Charter of Rights and Freedoms. The test was first established in *R v Oakes* [1986] 1 SCR 103, 137–8.

[36] [1990] 3 SCR 1303, per Dickson CJ.

broad and apparently subjective terms. In order to assert anything other than a literal interpretation of those terms, the courts required the decision-maker to act in a way that was 'perverse'[37] or 'absurd' – implying that the decision-maker had 'taken leave of his senses'.[38]

Whether the criterion for judicial intervention is termed irrationality or unreasonableness, where discretionary power is conferred on a decision-maker in domestic law, the burden is on the *claimant* to show that it was wrongly exercised. The essential difference between that approach and that of proportionality (as structured justification), as we have discussed, is that in the latter case the question is whether the defendant (the public authority) has properly departed from a fundamental norm (EU duties or Convention rights). The burden in these cases is therefore upon the *defendant* to justify that departure.

In recent years, however, the *Wednesbury* test has been reformulated. In the *GCHQ* case,[39] in the famous passage where he enunciated the 'grounds' of judicial review, Lord Diplock eschewed the term 'unreasonable' in favour of 'irrational', defining an irrational decision as one 'which is so outrageous in its defiance of logic or accepted moral standards that no sensible person who had applied his mind to the question to be decided could have arrived at it'. This test seems to widen the criteria for judicial interference by permitting an evaluation of the decision-maker's 'moral standards'. However, the decision still has to be 'outrageous' before the courts may properly intervene.

More recently, Lord Cooke opined that *Wednesbury* was 'an unfortunately retrogressive decision in English administrative law, insofar as it suggested that there are degrees of unreasonableness and that only a very extreme degree can bring an administrative decision within the legitimate scope of judicial invalidation'.[40] This view seems now to be generally accepted and the definition of an unreasonable or irrational decision seems to have settled into: 'a decision which is not within the range of reasonable responses'.[41]

(i) Variable Levels of Intensity

Despite the reformulation of the *Wednesbury* test, until the House of Lords determines otherwise, it may still be too early to pronounce the demise of unreasonableness and its substitution by proportionality.[42] In some recent cases

---

[37] Lord Brightman in *Pulhofer v Hillingdon LBC* [1986] AC 484, 518.
[38] Lord Scarman in *R v Secretary of State for the Environment, ex p Notts CC* [1986] AC 240, 247–8.
[39] *Council of Civil Service Unions v Minister for the Civil Service* [1985] AC 374.
[40] *R v Secretary of State for the Home Department, ex p Daly* [2001] 2 AC 532; [2001] UKHL 26, 32.
[41] *R (Daly) v Secretary of State for the Home Department* [2001] 2 AC 532.
[42] In *R (Association of British Civilian Internees: Far East Region) v Secretary of State for Defence* [2003] QB 1397, 35, Dyson LJ clearly felt that *Wednesbury* should now be conflated with proportionality, but it was not for the Court of Appeal to 'perform its burial rights'.

it has been retained in its rawest state.[43] However, the new formulation opens the door to variable degrees of intensity for reasonableness review. They are as follows.

a) Anxious scrutiny

Since 1987, it has been held that decisions which interfere with what the courts recognize as a fundamental right, such as the right to life, should receive the 'most anxious scrutiny of the courts'.[44] The notion of 'anxious scrutiny' is difficult to define with any precision, but it does indicate that the full rigour of *Wednesbury* is softened, and that the burden shifts towards the public body to justify its actions. In *Brind*, (a case in which the House of Lords resolutely refused to employ proportionality rather than unreasonableness to test an incursion into freedom of expression), the 'anxious scrutiny' test required the Home Secrtetary to justify his decision by 'an important competing public interest'.[45] In *R v Ministry of Defence ex p Smith*[46] (where there was a challenge to the exclusion of homosexuals by the Ministry of Defence in the armed forces) Bingham MR accepted that 'the more substantial the interference with human rights, the more the court will require by justification before it is satisfied that the decision is reasonable' – a formulation which again goes some way towards asking the decision-maker, rather than the claimant, to justify that the decision was 'reasonable'. However, when the European Court of Human Rights considered *Smith,* it was made clear that the Court of Appeal's review in that case was not as intense as that applied in the structured proportionality test applied by the Strasbourg court.[47]

b) Constitutional rights and legality

To add to the diversity of approach, in some cases English courts have identified a common law 'constitutional right'. In *Leech,*[48] the Court of Appeal held that a prisoner's right to communicate with his solicitor was a 'constitutional right' – that of access to justice. As such, it could only be interfered with when there was a 'pressing need' and the intrusion even then should be the minimum necessary to ensure that the correspondence was bona fide. The Home Secretary, it was held, had not discharged the burden of satisfying that test.

---

[43] e.g. in *R (on the application of Pro-Life Alliance) v BBC* [2003] 2 WLR 1403, where the House of Lords held that the prohibition of the showing of aborted foetuses in a party election broadcast could not be interfered with unless the decision was 'arbitrary'. Lord Scott, dissenting, held that since free expression was engaged a structured proportionality test ought to be employed. See E Barendt, 'Free speech and abortion' (2003) PL 580; J Jowell, 'Judicial deference: servility, civility or institutional capacity?' (2003) PL 592.

[44] Lord Bridge in *Bugdaycay v Home Secretary* [1987] AC 514, 531, speaking of the right to life in a deportation case. Such decisions, he said, would be subject to a 'more rigorous examination'. See also Lord Templeman 537–8. See A Le Sueur [2005] JR 52; J Rivers (2006) CLT 174.

[45] *R v Secretary of State for the Home Department, ex p Brind* [1991] 1 AC 696, 749–75, Lords Bridge and Roskill.

[46] [1996] QB 517.

[47] *Smith and Grady v UK* (1999) 29 ECHR 493.

[48] *R v Secretary of State for the Home Department, ex p Leech* (No 2) [1994] 2 QB 198.

This kind of review is similar to structured proportionality and was applied in other cases where a constitutional right, including or based upon the rule of law, was infringed.[49] It has been buttressed by the principle of 'legality', which provides that:

> a power conferred by Parliament in general terms is not to be taken to authorize the doing of acts...which adversely affects the legal rights of the citizen or the basic principles on which the law of the United Kingdom is based unless the statute conferring the power makes it clear that such was the intention of Parliament.[50]

c) No latitude

In some cases the reasonableness of a decision is assessed by the courts without permitting the decision-maker *any* degree of latitude. The term 'abuse of power' is increasingly being employed to describe the ground under which the courts assess these decisions. They include:

(a) decisions taken in bad faith.[51] In view of the fact that such decisions are by definition irrational, this is a strict test and does not vary in any way with the subject matter or context. The question whether bad faith motivated the decision is one entirely for the court on the basis of the available evidence.

(b) Cases where no evidence for the decision exists, or where a decision is taken in ignorance of an established or relevant fact.[52] Here too, there is no place for any leeway or latitude to the decision-maker, as such a situation renders the decision unreasonable *ipso facto*.

(c) Decisions where the decision-maker disappoints a substantive legitimate expectation. In many such cases the courts will defer to the decision-maker who wishes to alter his policy in the public interest. However, in *Coughlan*,[53] where the authority reneged on a promise of a 'home for life' for chronically sick patients, and where the class of promisee is limited and the promise was in the 'nature of a contract', the Court of Appeal held that it could determine the unfairness of the breach of promise without the need to defer to the authority's judgment on the basis of the *Wednesbury* formula.

---

[49] *R v Secretary of State for the Home Department, ex p Witham* [1997] 1 WLR 104 (access to the courts); *R v Secretary of State for the Home Department, ex p Simms* (blanket ban on prisoners' access to press infringed freedom of expression).

[50] Lord Browne-Wilkinson in *R v Secretary of State for the Home Department, ex p Pierson* [1998] AC 539, 575. See also Lord Hoffmann's formulation in *Simms*, above, at 412–13. Compare *R v Secretary of State for the Home Department, ex p Brind* [1991] AC 696, where the House of Lords held that the discretion conferred on the Home Secretary impliedly overrode the presumption that the European Convention on Human Rights would apply as a treaty obligation in international law if the provision in question was ambiguously worded.

[51] Such decisions could be described offending the ground of irrationality but could also fit into the ground of illegality where the offence is taking improper motives into account.

[52] *E v Secretary of State for the Home Department* [2004] EWCA Civ 49; [2004] QB 1044.

[53] *R v North and East Devon Health Authority, ex p Coughlan* [2000] QB 213.

d) Deference on the ground of lack of institutional capacity

At the other end of the spectrum are decisions where the courts recognize the superior capacity of the decision-maker and therefore defer to their assessment of the facts or judgment. Deference of this kind occurs whether or not the court is engaged in an unreasonableness review or proportionality review under the structured test. In EU law, even in the context of structured proportionality, the ECJ requires 'manifest' disproportionality before interfering with certain decisions.[54] Varying levels of the intensity of review will be appropriate in different categories of case. For example, in respect of measures involving the European Commission in 'complex economic assessment', such as in the implementation of anti-dumping measures, the ECJ will display 'extreme self restraint'[55] and only substitute its own discretion for that of the Commission if it can be shown that the conclusions of the Commission were 'manifestly' or 'patently' wrong.[56]

Similarly, in relation to Convention rights, the courts tend to defer to the legislature or administration in decisions involving 'broad social policy'[57] or the allocation of finite financial resources.[58] Decisions taken by experts,[59] those best able to calculate risk,[60] also indicate some measure of respect.

---

[54] See e.g. *R v Ministry of Agriculture, Fisheries and Food, ex p Astonquest* [2000] EuLR 371, for Robert Walker LJ using the test of 'manifest inappropriateness'. For an excellent account of the use of proportionality in EU law, see P Craig, *EU Administrative Law* (2006) chs 17 and 18.

[55] A Egger, 'The principle of proportionality in community anti-dumping law' (1993) 18 ELRev 367.

[56] See Case 57/72 *Westzucker v EVS Zucker* [1973] ECR 321; Case 136/77 *Racke v HZA Mainz* [1978] ECR 1245.

[57] This point has been made most forcefully by Lord Hoffmann. See his 'Separation of Powers' [2002] JR 137 and his statement in *R (Alconbury) v Secretary of State for the Environment and the Regions* [2001] 2 WLR 1389, where he distinguished a 'policy decisions' from a 'determination of right'. Policy decisions should be made not by the courts, he said, but in a democracy by 'democratically elected bodies or persons accountable to them'. 'The more the legislation concerns matters of broad social policy the less ready will be a court to intervene': *Wilson v First County Trust Ltd* [2003] UKHL 40, 70, Lord Nicholls. 'A very considerable margin of discretion must be accorded to the Secretary of State. Difficult questions of economic and social policy were involved, the resolution of which fell within the province of the executive and the legislature rather than the courts', Laws LJ in *R(Hooper) v Secretary of State for Work and Pensions* [2003] 1 WLR 2623, 63–4. See also Laws LJ in *R v Secretary of State for Education and Employment, ex p Begbie* [2000] 1 WLR 1115, 1131, who states that less intrusive judicial review should apply to decisions in the 'macro-political field'.

[58] Brooke LJ, '[T]his is pre-eminently a field in which the courts should defer to the decisions taken by a democratically elected Parliament, which has determined the manner in which public resources should be allocated for local authority housing' in *Michalak v Wandsworth LBC* [2003] 1 WLR 617, 41.

[59] See e.g. *R v Home Secretary, ex p Swati* [1986] 1 WLR 477; *R v Chief Constable of the Merseyside Police, ex p Calveley* [1986] 1 QB 424; *Pulhofer v Hillingdon LBC* [1986] AC 484. See also *R v Secretary of State for Social Services, ex p Stitt* [1990] COD 288. Sedley LJ, 'A youth court has expertise which a higher court lacks' in *R (W) v Thetford Youth Justices* [2002] EWHC 1252, 40.

[60] *R (Farrakhan) v Secretary of State for the Home Department* [2002] QB 1319; cf *R v Secretary of State for the Home Department, ex p Turgut* [2001] 1 All ER 719, 729, Simon Brown LJ: 'The court is hardly less well placed than the Secretary of State himself to evaluate the risk once the relevant material is placed before it'.

A sensitive appreciation of relative institutional capacity must, however, be qualified in two respects. First, institutional deference does not mean constitutional deference. The courts ought not automatically to kowtow to Parliament (when legislation is being reviewed under the Human Rights Act or EU law) or to the executive or other officials, on the ground that they are accountable to the electorate and the courts are not.[61] In the recent case of *Huang*,[62] the House of Lords found unpersuasive the submission of the Secretary of State that the decision-maker and the court should assume that the immigration rules adopted by the responsible minister and laid before Parliament 'had the imprimatur of democratic approval and should be taken to strike the right balance between the interests of the individual and those of the community'.[63]

Secondly, the acceptance of institutional imperfection on the part of the courts, or of a superior institutional capacity on the part of the primary decision-maker (for example, on the ground that he had access to 'special sources of knowledge and advice'[64]) should not inevitably signal a low level of scrutiny of the decision. As was said in *Huang*, although the authority may be better placed to investigate the facts and test the evidence, the court cannot abdicate its responsibility of ensuring that the facts are properly 'explored and summarized in the decision, with care'.[65] We do not have any carefully calibrated theory of institutional capacity, but even where the courts recognize their lack of relative capacity or expertise to make the primary decision, they should nevertheless not easily relinquish their secondary function of probing the quality of the reasoning and ensuring that assertions are properly justified.

IV. Towards a Culture of Justification

I have in this chapter argued that substantive administrative justice is a democratic necessity. That proposition of course begs many questions about the separation of powers in a constitutional democracy – in particular, to what extent the

---

[61] See J Jowell, 'Judicial deference and human rights: a question of competence' in P Craig and R Rawlings (eds), *Law and Administration in Europe: Essays in Honour of Carol Harlow* (2003) 67; J Jowell, 'Judicial deference: servility, civility or institutional capacity?' [2003] PL 592; R Clayton, 'Judicial deference and "democratic dialogue": the legitimacy of judicial intervention under the Human Rights Act 1998' [2004] PL 33. This view was accepted by Lord Bingham in *A v Secretary of State for the Home Department* [2004] UKHL 56 (the Belmarsh case). See also Lord Steyn, 'Deference: a tangled story' [2005] PL 346; Lord Steyn, '2000–2005: laying the foundations of human rights law in the United Kingdom' [2005] EHRLR 349, 359 ff.
[62] *Huang (FC) v Secretary of State for the Home Department* [2007] UKHL 11.
[63] At 17. Compare *Kay v Lambeth LBC* [2006] UKHL 10, where such an assumption was made in relation to housing policy. In *Huang*, however, the Lords made clear the distinction between a housing policy, where the result represented 'a considered democratic compromise' and where all parties were represented in the debate, and where the issue involved the allocation of finite resources, and the situation in immigration where those elements were not present.
[64] ibid, 16.
[65] ibid, 15.

courts should intervene with the substance of decisions taken by other branches of government.

For many years courts in the United Kingdom were diffident in pronouncing upon the reasonableness of the decisions of the executive and administration. While that approach has not wholly been replaced by the more intrusive standard of proportionality, we have seen that the two approaches have become inextricably intertwined. In particular, the use of structured proportionality has changed our expectations of how decision-makers ought to behave. It has introduced what has been called a 'culture of justification',[66] which requires decision-makers not only to act in accordance with bare rationality, but also to consider carefully the relationship between the means of a decision and its ends, to insist upon the consideration of less oppressive alternatives in appropriate cases and to ask for more cogent justification than bare *Wednesbury* permits when decisions interfere with established rights and significant interests.

If these expectations are confirmed in the case law of the future, the abandonment of the test of unreasonableness will not have breached the line between judicial review and appeal. We shall still not have adopted merits review. The courts will simply require more fulsome justification of a decision whose merits still lie within the scope of the primary decision-maker's discretion. However, instead of getting away with simply stating that he has carried out a proper balancing exercise and that he has not crossed the barrier of the 'absurd' or 'outrageous', the decision-maker will be required positively to 'identify the factors he has weighed and explain why he has given weight to some factors and not to others',[67] and to support his conclusions by 'evidence and argument'.[68] After all, probing and assessing the quality of justification is the function that courts have always been best equipped to perform.

---

[66] E Mureinik, 'A bridge to where? Introducing the interim bill of rights' (1994) 10 SAJHR 31. Referring to the shift in post-apartheid South Africa from a 'culture of authority' to a 'culture of justification'. See also D Dyzenhous, 'Law as justification: Etienne Mureinik's conception of legal culture' (1998) 14 SAJHR 11. See also two excellent chapters on this subject in N Banforth and P Leyland (eds), *Public Law in a Multi-Layered Constitution* (2003): M Taggart, 'Reinventing administrative law' and M Hunt, 'Sovereignty's blight: why contemporary public law needs a concept of due deference'. Hunt assumes that I propose institutional deference (in the articles cited in n 64 above – although he seems only to have seen a bare summary of them elsewhere) as a way of excusing justification of decisions, but I was in that article aiming at a particular target (inappropriate constitutional deference) and wholly agree with Hunt's position about justifiability.

[67] *R (X) v Chief Constable of Midlands Police* [2004] 1 WLR 1518, 101.

[68] *R (Hindawi) v Secretary of State for the Home Department* [2004] EWHC 78, 29. Both these cases involved Convention rights, but the standards they require seem appropriate for all public decisions.

PART III

INTERNAL MARKET AND ECONOMIC AND MONETARY UNION

11

The Definition of Measures Having Equivalent Effect

Laurence W Gormley

I. Introduction

The definition of measures having equivalent effect to quantitative restrictions has given rise to some of the most vigorous debates in Community law;[1] in part because it goes to the heart of the degree of permissible state interference in economic activities, and in part because the Court of Justice, while seeking to maintain the appearance of consistency, has over the years done more twisting and turning than the renowned Vicar of Bray. Among the great Advocates General there has never been a reluctance to confront the Court with its inconsistencies, infelicities and infidelities or to provide intellectual guidance of tremendous import,[2] and Francis Jacobs has maintained and built on this 'soul of the Court' function of the Advocate General's work.

---

[1] See further, *inter alia*, LW Gormley, *Prohibiting Restrictions on Trade within the EEC* (1985); C Gulman, *Handelshindringer I EF-Retten* (1980); MA Jarvis, *The Application of EC Law by National Courts, The Free Movement of Goods* (1998); A Mattera, *Le marché unique européen – ses règles, son fonctionnement* (2nd ed, 1990); M Poiares Maduro, *We, the Court, The European Court of Justice and the European Economic Constitution* (1998); P Oliver, *Free Movement of Goods in the European Community* (4th ed, 2003); C-M von Quitzow, *Fria varurörelser i den Europeiska Gemenskapen* (1995); W-H Roth, *Freier Warenverkehr und staatliche Regelungsgewalt in einem Gemeinsamen Markt* (1977); J Snell, *Goods and Services in EC Law, A Study of the Relationship Between the Freedoms* (2002); H Weyer, *Freier Warenverkehr und nationale Regelungsgewalt in der Europäischen Union* (1997), all of which contain further extensive bibliographies with references to the now vast periodical literature. See also e.g. D Chalmers (1993) 42 ICLQ 269 and (1994) 19 ELRev 385; L Defalque (1987) 23 CDE 471; LW Gormley (1989) 9 YEL 197, (1990) 27 CMLRev 825, (1996) 19 Fordh. Int'l L J 866; R Joliet (1995) 1 Columbia J. Eur. Law 146; P Koutrakos (2001) 26 ELRev 391; G Marenco (1984) 20 CDE 291; A Mattera (1994) RMUE 117; K Mortelmans (1991) 28 CMLRev 115; P Oliver (1999) 36 CMLRev 783; P Oliver and W-H Roth (2004) 41 CMLRev 407; T Schilling (1994) EuR 50; N Nic Shuibne (2002) 27 ELRev 408; J Steiner (1992) 29 CMLRev 749; W van Gerven (1996) 2 Columb. J Eur. L 217; H Weyer (1998) EuR 435; S Weatherill (1996) 33 CMLRev 885 and (1999) 36 CMLRev 51; W Wils (1993) 18 ELRev 475, and EL White (1989) 26 CMLRev 235.

[2] See e.g. Case 13/61 *Kledingverkoopbedrijf de Geus en Uitdenbogerd v Robert Bosch GmbH et al* [1962] ECR 45 at 56 et seq, Case 8/55 *Fédération Charbonnière de Belgique v High Authority*

This contribution looks at the definition of measures having equivalent effect: it therefore does not deal substantively with the justifications known to Community law for such measures, although there is inevitably some tangential discussion of them.[3] It is, however, appropriate to set to rest two very old canards about justifications. First, the finding that a measure is justified does *not* mean that such a measure ceases to be a measure having equivalent effect; it merely means that in the instant case it is acceptable in all the circumstances (having regard to the purpose, the necessity and the proportionality of the measure).[4] This distinguishes the justifications from obstacles to trade which are deemed not to fall within the definition of measures having equivalent effect under the *Keck* approach.[5] Second, there is still a clear distinction between the Treaty-based justifications and those finding their basis solely in case law under the 'mandatory requirements'; to assimilate them,[6] is, it is respectfully submitted, a fundamentally flawed approach. While both sets of justification are subject to the same requirements of necessity, proportionality and not amounting to a means of arbitrary discrimination or a disguised restriction on trade between Member States, the case law-based exceptions will only benefit measures which apply to domestic and imported products alike[7] – the well-known

---

[1954–6] ECR 245, Case 3/54 *Associazione Industrie Siderurgique Italiane (ASSIDER) v High Authority* [1954–6] ECR 63, Cases 7/56 & 3–7/57 *Algera et al v Common Assembly* [1957–8] ECR 39 (Lagrange); Cases 7 & 9/54 *Groupement des Industries Sidérugiques Luxembourgeoises v High Authority* [1954–6] ECR 175, Case 5/71 *Aktien-Zukerfabrik Schöppenstedt v Council* [1971] ECR 975 at 988 et seq (Roemer); Case 113/79 *NTN Toyo Bearing Co Ltd et al v* Council [1979] ECR 1185 (Warner); Case 155/79 *AM & S Europe Ltd v Commission* [1982] ECR 1575 (Warner and Slynn); Case 60/81 *International Business Machines Corporation v Commission* [1981] ECR 2639 at 2660 et seq (Slynn); Case C-292/92 *Hünermund et al v Landesapothekerkammer Baden-Württemberg* [1993] ECR I-6787 (Tesauro); Case C-412/93 *Société d'importation Édouard Leclerc v TFI Publicité SA et al* [1995] ECR I-179 (Jacobs); sometimes they succeed in persuading the Court to revisit earlier positions, e.g. in celebrated fashion Van Gerven in Case C-70/88 *European Parliament v Council* [1990] ECR I-2041 and Jacobs in Case C-10/89 *SA CNL-SUCAL NV v HAG GF AG* [1990] ECR I-3711. See, further, Tridimas (1997) 34 CMLRev 1349 and literature cited there.

[3] These are in practice either those stemming from Art 30 EC or from the case law-based justifications sometimes referred to as the rule of reason exceptions or, in the language of the Court, 'mandatory requirements' (or in other fields such as the freedom to provide services they are often called public interest requirements). As to the origin and function of the rule of reason in the free movement of goods see LW Gormley, in A Schrauwen (ed), *The Rule of Reason* (2006) 14. As, for the purposes of this analysis, the renumbering of the EC Treaty at Amsterdam (the old Art 30 became Art 28 EC; the old Art 34, Art 29 EC, and the old Art 36, Art 30 EC) is of no consequence, the new Article numbers are used throughout this contribution, although in square brackets where a quotation referred to the original numbering.

[4] Although this is a fairly obvious point, it always surprised the present writer how many of his former colleagues in the Commission in the 1980s thought otherwise!

[5] Cases C-267 and 268/91 *Keck & Mithouard* [1993] ECR I-6097 at 6131, as to which, see below.

[6] As in Oliver (see note 1, (2003), 216 et seq and (1999) 36 CMLRev 783 at 804 (he acknowledges that his view is not shared by the majority of writers). See further LW Gormley, in A Schrauwen (ed), note 3, 25 et seq.

[7] e.g. Case 788/79 *Gilli & Andres* [1980] ECR 2071 at 2078; Case 251/82 *Walter Rau Lebensmittelwerke v De Smedt PvbA* [1982] ECR 3961 at 3972; Case 59/82 *Schutzverband gegen Unwesen in der Wirtschaft v Weinvertriebs GmbH* [1983] ECR 1217 at 1227; Cases C-158 & 159/04 *Alfa Vita Vassilopoulos AE et al v Elliniko Dimosio* [2006] ECRI-nyr (14 September 2006), although

breach of this rule in relation to environmental protection[8] has not constituted a general retreat from this rule; and the case law-based exceptions come into play only if the alleged justification is not one listed in Article 30. Moreover, the Court maintains that the heads of justification in the first sentence of Article 30 are not capable of expansion,[9] and it is clear that the case law-based exceptions are not merely aspects of public policy (and thus of Article 30 itself).[10] While justifications under Article 30 and those under the case law are interim justifications pending the adoption of Community measures occupying the field concerned, they are unlikely to become entirely dead-letter provisions.[11]

II. The Early Approaches

It has been clear from the very beginning of the attempts to define the notion of measures having equivalent effect that it should be viewed as an effects doctrine rather than dependent upon the nature or contents – or even purpose – of the measure; the Commission rightly emphasized this,[12] subsequently noting that Article [28] EC, applied not merely to legal and administrative measures, but also administrative practices;[13] significantly, though, it took the view that measures, which were equally applicable to imports and national products would not in most cases fall within the ambit of Article [28] EC.[14] This initial approach of the Commission excited a torrent of academic writing. Put briefly, commentators divided into three groups: those who took the view that only discriminatory measures were caught by the notion of measures having equivalent effect;[15] those

---

equal applicability on the face of the measure is not enough, the Court will look behind the face of the measure: Case 207/83 *Commission v United Kingdom* [1985] ECR 1205 at 1212 (the *origin marking* case).

[8] Case 2/90 *Commission v Belgium* [1992] ECR I-4431 (the *Walloon waste* case).

[9] e.g. Case 13/80 *Commission v Ireland* [1981] ECR 1625 at 1638; Case 229/83 *Association des Centres Distributeurs Édouard Leclerc v Au Blé Vert Sàrl* [1985] ECR 1 at 35.

[10] Case 177/83 *Theodor Kohl KG v Ringelhan and Rennett SA* [1984] ECR 3651 at 3663.

[11] Simply because if nothing else, public morality, public policy and interests such as press freedom are most unlikely ever to be the subject of Community harmonization measures. It is now accepted that the case law-based justifications, like those under Art 30, cannot be invoked to satisfy economic purposes: Case C-203/96 *Chemische Afvalstoffen Dusseldorp BV et al v Minister van Volkshuisvesting, Ruimtelijke Ordening en Milieubeheer* [1988] ECR I-4075 at 4127, confirming the view advanced by LW Gormley (note 1, 1985) 66–7 (discussing earlier literature).

[12] Reply to Written Question 118 (Deringer) [1967] J O 901/67 See also D Ehle (1967) AWD 453 at 455.

[13] Reply to Written Question 64 (Deringer) [1967] J O 169/12.

[14] ibid.

[15] M Seidel (1967) NJW 2081 at 2084, 2086; G Meier (1967) AWD 219 at 220 and in D Ehle and G Meier, *EWG-Warenverkehr* (1971); M Graf, *Der Begriff, Massnahmen gleicher Wirkung wire mengenmässige Einfuhrbeschränkungen'in dem EWG-Vertrag* (1972), and, broadening the narrow approach somewhat, finding 'material discrimination' (i.e. in fact if not in law) enough, E Steindorff in M Lagrange et al, *Dienstleistungsfreiheit und Versicherungsaufsicht im Gemeinsamen Markt* (1971) 79, 83.

who took a wider view looking at obstacles to trade between Member States;[16] and those who took a view broadly supportive of the Commission.[17] The wide divergences of views in the literature well demonstrated the difficulty of achieving a balance between the understandable desire of the Member States to continue to enforce the legislation on the one hand and integrationist demands of the Community on the other.[18] The narrow interpretation of Article 28 would have allowed the Member States to frustrate the achievement of the free movement of goods envisaged in the Treaty. And yet the wider view gave rise to fears that in important sectors effective right of the Member States to legislate would be eroded. Although the use of the principle of proportionality by the Commission[19] and the observation by VerLoren van Themaat that many equally applicable obstacles would be likely to benefit from Article [30][20] represented an attempt to find a balance between the demands of the Community and the claims of the Member States, it was not until the judgment of the Court of Justice in *Dassonville*[21] that the primacy of Community interests was firmly established in relation to Article 28. This was, however, accompanied by a recognition that, pending action at the Community level to afford guarantees of certain interests or values, national measures taken in order to secure those guarantees or values would be acceptable subject to certain conditions; thus the Court admitted a rule of reason – later designated mandatory requirements – which tempered, albeit only on a provisional basis, the rigours of the principle of the free movement of goods.[22]

III. Applying the Basic Principle in *Dassonville*

A. The Path to *Keck*

The judgment in *Dassonville* is celebrated not merely for the statement of the basic principle, the definition of measures having equivalent effect, but also for the first mention of the case law based justifications which were to be worked

---

[16] P VerLoren van Themaat (1967) SEW 632 and (1970) SEW 258 (in the latter article criticizing the Commission's standpoint in Directive 70/50 ([1970] OJ English Special Edition (I) 17); M Waelbroeck in J Mégret et al, *Le droit de la Communauté Economique Européenne* Vol 1 (1970) 102–103. See also, subsequently, AWH Meij and JA Winter (1976) 13 CMLRev 79.

[17] D Ehle (1967) AWD 453, 455; R-C Béraud (1968) RTDE 265; W Dona-Viscardini (1973) RMC 224; P Ulmer (1973) GRURInt 502 (also critical of the Commission's viewpoint), and C-D Ehlermann (1973) EuR 1.

[18] LW Gormley (1985), note 1, 18.

[19] In Directive 70/50, note 16.

[20] (1967) SEW 632, 634.

[21] Case 8/74 *Procureur du Roi v Dassonville et al.* [1974] ECR 837, 852.

[22] ibid. The provisional basis of the case law-based justifications is evident from the formulation in *Dassonville*: 'In the absence of a Community system guaranteeing for consumers the authenticity of a product's designation of origin' [1974] ECR 837, 852.

out further.[23] That basic principle was expressed in resounding terms: 'All trading rules enacted by Member States which are capable of hindering, directly or indirectly, actually or potentially, intra-Community trade are to be considered as measures having an effect equivalent to quantitative restrictions'.[24]

In subsequent cases the specific reference to trading rules has sometimes been omitted,[25] although on other occasions it is still mentioned,[26] but apart from that, the *Dassonville* basic principle has survived as a constant feature throughout the roller-coaster case law in this field. The basic principle remains wide indeed in its potential scope, but on occasions the Court has been willing to sacrifice coherent reasoning on the altar of expediency in no small measure: sometimes this results from the political sensitivity of the measure,[27] but more usually it has had to do with the scant integrationist merit of some of the cases presented to the Court. Thus cases such as *Blesgen*,[28] had in reality little or nothing to do

---

[23] Many authors believe that justifications such as consumer protection and the prevention of unfair commercial practices originated in Case 120/78 *Rewe-Zentral AG v Bundesmonopolverwaltung für Branntwein* [1979] ECR 649 (more commonly known as *Cassis de Dijon*). They did not: they originate from *Dassonville* in the very next paragraph after the statement of the basic principle (para 6 on p 852). Two further mistakes frequently made in relation to *Cassis de Dijon* were made by the Court itself: first, speaking of products 'lawfully produced and marketed in a Member State' rather than lawfully produced *or* marketed (the Court's formulation must be incorrect, as the free movement of goods benefits goods in free circulation within the Community, irrespective of their origin); second, the Court listed the protection of public health as a separate head of justification. This added nothing to the terms of Article 30 EC itself, and in Cases C-1 and 76/90 *Aragonesa de Publicidad Exterior SA et al v Departamento de Sanidad y Seguridad Social de la Generalitat de Cataluña* [1991] ECR I-4151 at 4183–4 the Court stated that the protection of public health fell exclusively within the realm of Article 30, as opposed to the mandatory requirements.

[24] Case 8/74 *Procureur du Roi v Dassonville et al* [1974] ECR 837, 852.

[25] e.g. Case 190/73 *Officier van Justitie v van Haaster* [1974] ECR 1123 (in relation to a scheme of common organization which repeated the wording of Article 28 EC verbatim); Case 104/75 *Officier van Justitie v de Peijper* [1976] ECR 613; Case C-63/94 *Groupement National des Négociants en Pommes de Terre (Belgapom) v ITM Belgium SA et al* [1995] ECR I-2467; Cases C-158 and 159/04 *Alfa Vita Vassilopoulos AE et al v Elliniko Dimosio, Nommarkhiaki Aftodiikisi Ioanninon* [2006] ECR I-nyr (14 September 2006); Case C-54/05 *Commission v Finland* [2007] ECR I-nyr (15 March 2007).

[26] e.g. Case C-420/01 *Commission v Italy* [2003] ECR I-6445, 6466; Case C-434/04 *Ahokainen & Leppik v Virallinen syyttäjä* [2006] ECR I-nyr (28 September 2006), and (rather unusually as 'all commercial rules') Case C-192/01 *Commission v Denmark* [2003] ECR I-9693, 9736.

[27] e.g. Case C-2/90 *Commission v Belgium* [1992] ECR I-4431 (*Walloon waste*) in which the Court having decided that waste fell to be treated like any other goods, went on to find that because of its special nature it was not a discriminatory measure and would be upheld on environmental protection grounds when it was manifestly discriminatory: cf Case C-21/88 *Du Pont de Nemours Italiana SpA v Unità Sanitaria Locale no. 2 di Carrara* [1990] ECR I-889 which in legal terms is the parallel of *Walloon waste* in another context. A controversial example of the Court being prepared to stand earlier analysis on its head under considerable political pressure, this time in relation to what is now Art 29 EC, is Case C-388/95 *Belgium v Spain* [2000] ECR I-3123 reversing the finding in Case C-47/90 *Éts Delhaize Frères et Compagnie Le Lion SA v Promalvin SA et al* [1992] ECR I-3669 (*Rioja*). Outside the free movement of goods, the political controversies surrounding Case C-379/89 *Groener v Minister for Education et al* [1989] ECR 3967 and Case C-159/90 *The Society for the Protection of Unborn Children Ltd v Grogan et al* [1991] ECR I-4685 are well-known examples.

[28] Case 75/81 *Blesgen* [1982] ECR 1211.

with intra-Community trade; while justification on the ground of public policy or the protection of health and life of humans could perfectly well have been used to uphold the national measure; the Court was under a high degree of pressure not to hand down a finding that the Belgian rule in principle infringed Article 28 EC.[29] More difficult cases on Sunday trading,[30] sex shop licensing,[31] and worker protection[32] in particular followed, and the warnings against misuse of Article 28 EC went unheeded.[33] The Court was at first reluctant to give clear guidance,[34] but when it did[35] was dismayed to find that lawyers were not listening, carried away with the exuberance of litigation for a cause.[36]

These more 'police powers' cases formed but one front of attack on perceived restrictions of commercial freedom. A second front can also be identified: a number of cases started to appear in which various national prohibitions on the use of particular types of selling techniques that were authorized in some Member States were challenged.[37] In these latter cases, the use of the *Dassonville* basic principle, combined with an evaluation of the alleged justifications under the

---

[29] The Court was under pressure not to find that the measure was indeed a measure having equivalent effect but justified, because the legislation involved was ostensibly designed to protect the young from the evils of strong drink; it is understood that inspiration was drawn from the American police powers concepts, but this shows the danger of looking just at the conclusion, rather than at the reasoning in the case law as a whole: non-discriminatory liquor licensing measures were found to be capable of hindering interstate commerce, but acceptable because of their purpose. The better policy for the Court would be to have gone down that route (either on health grounds or on public policy (in the sense of public order) grounds). In any event, a few years later the Belgians replaced the legislation involved with a licensing system (as much as anything as a revenue-raiser). See further LW Gormley, in L Krämer et al (eds), *Law and Diffuse Interests in the European Legal Order* (Liber Amicorum Norbert Reich, 1997) 11, 19–20.

[30] Case C-145/88 *Torfaen Borough Council v B & Q PLC* [1989] ECR 3851; Case C-312/89 *Union départementale des syndicates CGT de l'Aisne v SIDEF Conforama et al* [1991] ECR I-997; Case C-332/89 *Marchandise et al* [1991] ECR I-1027; Case C-169/91 *Council of the City of Stoke-on-Trent et al v B & Q plc* [1992] ECR I-6635; Case C-306/88 *Rochdale Borough Council v Anders* [1992] ECR I-6457; Case C-304/90 *Reading Borough Council v Payless DIY Ltd et al* [1992] ECR I-6493.

[31] Case C-23/89 *Quietlynn & Richards v Southend Borough Council* [1990] ECR I-3059; Case C-350/89 *Sheptonhurst Ltd v Newham Borough Council* [1991] ECR I-2387.

[32] Case 155/80 *Oebel* [1981] ECR 1993 (this pre-dated *Blesgen*); also in *Conforama* and *Marchandise* clear worker protection arguments were advanced.

[33] LW Gormley (1990) 27 CMLRev 141, 150.

[34] In *Torfaen* it bounced the ball back to the national court to decide on the proportionality issue.

[35] In *Conforama* and *Marchandise*.

[36] Hence *Stoke-on-Trent*, *Rochdale*, and *Reading*. This actually even carried on after *Keck*: see Cases C-401 & 402/92 *Tankstation't Heuske vof & Boermans* [1994] ECR I-2199; Cases C-69 & 258/93 *Punto Casa SpA et al v Sindaco del Commune di Capena et al* [1994] ECR I-2355; Cases C-418–421/93 etc *Semeraro Casa Uno Srl et al v Sindaco del Commune di Erbusco et al* [1996] ECR I-2975.

[37] Case C-286/81 *Oosthoek's Uitgeversmaatschappij BV* [1982] ECR 4575; Case 382/87 *Buet & Educational Business Services (EBS) SARL v Ministère public* [1989] ECR 1235; Case C-362/88 *GB-INNO-BM v Confédération du commerce luxembourgeois* [1990] ECR I-667; Case 60/89 *Monteil &* Samanni [1991] ECR I-1547; Case C-369/88 *Delattre* [1991] ECR I-1487; Case C-239/90 *SCP Bosscher, Studer & Fromentin v SA British Motors Wright et al* [1991] ECR I-2023; Cases C-1 & 176/90 *Aragonesa de Publicidad Exterior et al v Departamento de Sanidad y Seguridad Social de la Generalitat de Cataluña* [1991] ECR I-4151; Case C-126/91 *Schutzverband gegen unwesen in der Wirtschaft e V v Yves Rocher GmbH* [1993] ECR I-2361.

headings in particular of consumer protection and the prevention of unfair commercial practices, caused a stream of attacks on national measures which traders felt restricted their ability to sell abroad in the same manner as they did at home; in one spectacular instance, the high-water mark of the pro-active, informed consumer, the power of the consumer's right to information carried the day.[38]

At the same time as an increased use was being made of Article 28 EC sometimes in circumstances of scant integrationist merit, concerted attacks on a wide application of the basic principle started to appear. To some extent, these were echoes of the old discrimination school;[39] to some extent they were conceived as a vehicle for seeking to rein in the increasing importance of the free movement of goods in the Commission's complaints, infringement procedures and preliminary rulings workload.[40] White's submissions on behalf of the Commission in *Torfaen* were reflected in his influential contribution to the academic debate, which stimulated numerous other views.[41] However, the judgment in *Torfaen* did not follow the Commission's submissions; the Court clearly felt that the Sunday trading legislation was capable of hindering trade between Member States but left the assessment of the justification (in particular as to proportionality) firmly to the national court,[42] and the Commission subsequently retreated from White's approach.[43] By the time of the judgments in *Keck* and *Hünermund*, however, the judicial tide seemed to turn, and sentiments of White's reasoning undoubtedly lay behind the tortuous reasoning in the immaculate misconception which is *Keck*.[44]

B. *Keck*

The debate around *Keck* has rightly been described by Oliver as a cottage industry in its own right,[45] and the positions on *Keck* are well known.[46] Before examining the effect of *Keck* in the light of the title of this *Festschrift*, however, it may be useful to make a few points about the drafting of that judgment.

---

[38] Case C-362/88 *GB-INNO-BM v Confédération du commerce luxembourgeois* [1990] ECR I-667.
[39] See in particular G Marenco (1984) CDE 291; more nuanced, L Defalque (1987) CDE 471.
[40] EL White (1989) 26 CMLRev 235.
[41] K Mortelmans (1991) 28 CMLRev 115; J Steiner (1992) 29 CMLRev 749.
[42] [1989] ECR I-3851 at 3889, see LW Gormley (1990) 27 CMLRev 141.
[43] In the oral proceedings in *Quietlynn* it abandonded the position it took in *Torfaen*; the Court simply adopted a *Blesgen* approach and applied a remoteness test: [1990] ECR I-3059 at 3081; the same approach occurred in *Sheptonhurst*: [1991] ECR I-2387 (summary publication).
[44] Cases C-267 & 268/91 *Keck & Mithouard* [1993] ECR I-6097.
[45] P Oliver, see note 1 (2003) 124.
[46] The list of annotations of Keck is enormous: see, further in particular, PJG Kapteyn and P VerLoren van Themaat, LW Gormley (ed), *Introduction to the Law of the European Communities* (3rd ed, 1998) 631–7 and A Arnull, *The European Union and its Court of Justice* (2nd ed, 2006) 427–38 and the bibliographic references mentioned there; see also F Picod (1998) RTDE 169, JHH Weiler in P Craig and G de Búrca (eds), *The Evolution of EU Law* (1999) ch 10 and S Weatherill (1996) 33 CMLRev 885 and the literature cited below.

First, there was a change in the wording of paragraph 15 of the judgment (in English at least) between publication of the judgment in the text originally pronounced and the publication in the European Court Reports. Originally, paragraph 15 read:

In '*Cassis de Dijon*' (Case 120/78 *Rewe-Zentral v Bundesmonopolverwaltung für Branntwein* [1978] ECR 649) it was held that, in the absence of harmonization of legislation, measures of equivalent effect prohibited by Article 30 include obstacles to the free movement of goods where they are the consequences of applying rules that lay down requirements to be met by goods (such as requirements as to designation, form, size, weight, composition, presentation, labelling, packaging) to goods from other Member States where they are lawfully manufactured and marketed, even if those rules apply without distinction to all products unless the application can be justified by a public interest objective taking precedence over the free movement of goods.

By the time of publication in the European Court Reports, that had become:

It is established by the case law, beginning with '*Cassis de Dijon*' (Case 120/78 *Rewe-Zentral v Bundesmonopolverwaltung für Branntwein* [1978] ECR 649) that, in the absence of harmonization of legislation, obstacles to free movement of goods which are the consequence of applying, to goods coming from other Member States where they are lawfully manufactured and marketed, rules that lay down requirements to be met by such goods (such as those relating to designation, form, size, weight, composition, presentation, labelling, packaging) constitute measures of equivalent effect prohibited by Article 30. This is so even if those rules apply without distinction to all products unless the application can be justified by a public-interest objective taking precedence over the free movement of goods.[47]

Explicably, if infelicitously, the first version has remained in some contributions to the literature.[48]

Second, it is distinctly unfortunate that the Court seems to have been unable to reach agreement on precisely which judgments were being overruled: the mere phrase 'contrary to what has previously been decided' scarcely amounts to a clarification of the case law, even if it indicates a re-examination of it. This has all the hallmarks of the judgment being the product of a distinctly divided Court.[49] Some members of the Court were apparently prepared to give their views on overruling on the student lecture circuit; Joliet in particular launched an infamous attack on (in particular) Mattera's criticism of *Keck*, but he was unable to say what judgments were overruled, for the simple reason that a number of cases were still pending before the Court and he understandably felt

---

[47] [1993] ECR I-6097, 6131.

[48] Those writing shortly after the judgment will have relied on the roneo text (e.g. Gormley (1994) EBLR 63) and simply repeated that subsequently (Gormley (1996) 19 Fordh. Int'l LJ 866, 869), as, clearly, did Oliver (n 1 above) 100 and 4th ed (2003) 123; Craig and De Búrca, *EU Law* (2nd ed (1999) 618 and 3rd ed (2003)) 647 also still cite the roneo version.

[49] Obviously only those who took part in the judgment know how the voting went, but history is littered with momentous consequences decided by a majority of one!

unable to indicate his position extra-judicially.[50] No such constraints bound academic commentators or even Advocates General![51] The confusion becomes even greater because within a very short while the Court was referring to judgments which appeared to be overruled – at least on whether the measure was a prohibited one under the *Dassonville* basic principle as nuanced in its interpretation by *Keck* – in order to discuss the justification of the measure on the grounds of consumer protection and/or the prevention of unfair commercial practices.[52] Some judgments were overruled for some purposes, then, but not for others.

Third, it is clear that the basic principle in *Dassonville* survives *Keck*; certain selling arrangements are now deemed to fall outside the definition in the basic principle, even though they may have (potential) trade-restricting effects; this is a strange analysis indeed, and might be thought to indicate the introduction of a *de minimis* approach. Fortunately, however, that was to prove not to be the case. Fourth, perhaps evidently – but students often forget this – it is not enough to characterize a measure as a 'selling arrangement' to take it outside the definition of a measure having equivalent effect; it must also fulfil two conditions; these conditions are considered further below.

Finally, the only reason given for re-examining and clarifying the case law given in *Keck* was 'the increasing tendency of traders to invoke Article [28] of the Treaty as a means of challenging any rules whose effect is to limit their commercial freedom even when such rules are not aimed at products from other Member States'. This is more of a managerial reason than a legal reason, and clearly expressed a certain degree of exasperation at the increasing number of cases which arose through failure to understand correctly earlier judgments: the Sunday trading line of authority was already clearly saying that the Court was not prepared to condemn non-discriminatory local regulation of socio-economic life in this sort of situation;[53] but the judgments in the more clearly sales methods (as opposed to when and where) cases were in fact sending out the signal that

---

[50] The attack was originally delivered in a speech to a group of visiting judges: it was published in German (1994) in GRUR Int 979; in French (1994) in JdT (Dr. Eur.) 145, and in English (1995) in 1 Columbia J. Eur. Law 146.

[51] e.g. AG Lenz in Case C-391/92 *Commission v Greece* [1995] ECR I-1621; AG Jacobs in *Société d'importation Édouard Leclerc v TFI Publicité SA et al* [1995] ECR I-179.

[52] e.g. Case C-315/92 *Verband Sozialer Wettbewerb e V v Clinique Laboratoires SNC et al* [1994] ECR I-317, 336 (citing *Buet* as to the principle of proportionality); Cases C-277, 318 and 319/91 *Ligur Carni Srl et al v Unità Sanitaria Locale no XV di Genova et al* [1993] ECR I-6621, 6661 (citing *Aragonesa* as to the discriminatory scope of the measure); Case C-370/93 *Verein gegen Unwesen in Handel und Gewerbe Köln e V v Mars GmbH* [1995] ECR I-1923, 1941–2 (citing *Yves Rocher* as to the principle of proportionality).

[53] Case C-332/89 *Marchandise et al* [1991] ECR I-1027; Case C-169/91 *Council of the City of Stoke-on-Trent et al v B & Q plc* [1992] ECR I-6635; Case C-306/88 *Rochdale Borough Council v Anders* [1992] ECR I-6457; Case C-304/90 *Reading Borough Council v Payless DIY Ltd et al* [1992] ECR I-6493. See also the sex shop licensing judgments in Case C-23/89 *Quietlynn & Richards v Southend Borough Council* [1990] ECR I-3059; Case C-350/89 *Sheptonhurst Ltd v Newham Borough Council* [1991] ECR I-2387.

the Court of Justice was encouraging such cases;[54] the blame for more litigation can partly be laid at the door of the litigants, but in part it must lie at the door of the Court itself. For selling arrangements, at least, discrimination seemed to become the touchstone to take them outside the scope of Article 28 EC. The trouble with this is that a discrimination test applied to an effects doctrine simply is a nonsense; discrimination is a sufficient but not a necessary element to find a hindrance to trade between Member States.[55]

C. Post-*Keck*

While *Keck* itself was scarcely a model of clarity, it is indeed now much clearer what should be made of that judgment. In part this stems from the Court's undoubted reaction to the deafening chorus of criticism heaped upon the drafting of *Keck* – a point which united opponents and proponents of the *Keck* approach – and in part from the opportunities presented by various cases for the Court to give some refining indicators. Thus the concept of a selling arrangement clearly now covers legislation restricting who may sell goods and/or where they may be sold and/or when they may be sold,[56] advertising restrictions[57] (other than those which are related to the presentation or packaging of the product itself[58] or which act as a total barrier to market entry[59]) and price control legislation,[60] but legislation controlling

---

[54] Case C-286/81 *Oosthoek's Uitgeversmaatschappij BV* [1982] ECR 4575; Case 382/87 *Buet & Educational Business Services (EBS) SARL v Ministère public* [1989] ECR 1235; Case C-362/88 *GB-INNO-BM v Confédération du commerce luxembourgeois* [1990] ECR I-667; Case 60/89 *Monteil & Samanni* [1991] ECR I-1547; Case C-369/88 *Delattre* [1991] ECR I-1487; Case C-239/90 *SCP Bosscher, Studer & Fromentin v SA British Motors Wright et al* [1991] ECR I-2023; Cases C-1 & 176/90 *Aragonesa de Publicidad Exterior et al v Departamento de Sanidad y Seguridad Social de la Generalitat de Cataluña* [1991] ECR I-4151; Case C-126/91 *Schutzverband gegen unwesen in der Wirtschaft e V v Yves Rocher GmbH* [1993] ECR I-2361.

[55] If it were otherwise, equally applicable measures could never fall within the ambit of Art 28 EC, and abundant case law makes it clear that they do (now with the exception of selling arrangements which meet the *Keck* conditions); see e.g. Case C-434/04 *Ahokainen & Leppik v Virallinen syyttäjä* [2006] ECR I-nyr (28 September 2006), para 18.

[56] Case C-391/92 *Commission v Greece* [1995] ECR I-1621; Cases C-401 & 402/92 *Tankstation't Heuske vof & Boermans* [1994] ECR I-2199; Cases C-69 & 258/93 *Punto Casa SpA et al v Sindaco del Commune di Capena et al* [1994] ECR I-2355; Case C-387/93 *Banchero* [1995] ECR I-4663; Cases C-418–421/93 etc. *Semeraro Casa Uno Srl et al v Sindaco del Commune di Erbusco et al* [1996] ECR I-2975. But see the discussion of Case C-254/98 *Schutzverband gegen Unlauteren Wettbewerb v TK Heimdienst Sass GmbH* [2000] ECR I-151, below.

[57] Case C-292/92 *Hünermund et al v Landesapothekerkammer Baden-Württemberg* [1993] ECR I-6787; Case C-412/93 *Société d'importation Édouard Leclerc v TFI Publicité SA et al* [1995] ECR I-179.

[58] Case C-370/93 *Verein gegen Unwesen in Handel und Gewerbe Köln e V v Mars GmbH* [1995] ECR I-1923; Case C-368/95 *Vereinigte Familiapress Zeitungsverlags-und vertriebs GmbH v Heinrich Bauer Verlag* [1997] ECR I-3689.

[59] Cases C-34–36/95 *Konsumentenombudsmannen (KO) v De Agiostini (Svenska) Förlag AB et al* [1997] ECR I-3843, 3891–2; Case C-405/98 *Konsumentenombudsmannen (KO) v Gourmet International Products AB (GIP)* [2002] ECR I-1795, 1823–4.

[60] At least in so far as it concerns resale conditions: see *Keck* itself and Case C-63/94 *Groupement National des Négociants en Pommes de Terre (Belgapom) v ITM Belgium SA et al* [1995] ECR I-2467.

the conditions under which goods are sold may not be so clear cut.[61] The Court has rightly rejected all invitations to expand the scope of 'selling arrangements' to apply the *Keck* reasoning outside the field of the free movement of goods;[62] and requirements which necessitate a change in the product or affect its packaging will clearly not constitute selling arrangements.[63]

Once a measure has been classified as a selling arrangement the next step is to consider whether it satisfies the two conditions from *Keck*. The first of these, that the measure applies to all affected traders operating within the national territory, has been the subject of relatively little discussion;[64] an argument that such a measure in fact operates to penalize small traders more heavily than larger firms got short shrift,[65] and it seems that the purpose of this test is simply to ensure that there is no distinction (on the basis of nationality or residence in particular) as to the scope of those affected by the measure. The second criterion, that the measures affect in the same manner, in law and in fact, the marketing of domestic products and of those from other Member States, has given rise to more interesting analysis. Despite an unpromising start,[66] there has been some considerable movement in the Court's approach. In *TK-Heimdienst*[67] the Court looked at Austrian legislation preventing bakers, butchers and grocers from making sales on rounds in a given administrative district unless they also carry on their trade at a permanent establishment situated in that district or in an adjacent municipality, where they also offer for sale the same goods as they do on their rounds. While it had no difficulty concluding that this was a selling arrangement, and, implicitly that it applied to all market participants, it quickly found that it did not affect in the same manner the marketing of domestic products and that of products from other Member States. Local operators could meet this requirement of permanent establishment, but operators from other Member States would be forced to bear additional costs to comply with that requirement. Even though the measure was equally applicable to domestic and foreign butchers, bakers and

---

[61] Contrast the analysis in Case C-416/00 *Morellato v Comune di Padova* [2003] ECR 9343 with that in Cases C-158 and 159/04 *Alfa Vita Vassilopoulos AE et al v Elliniko Dimosio* [2006] ECR I-nyr (14 September 2006) and Case C-82/05 *Commission v Greece* [2006] ECRI-nyr (14 September 2006) relating to the marketing of 'bake-off' products.

[62] e.g. Case C-384/93 *Alpine Investments BV v Minister van Financiën* [1995] ECR I-1141, 1177–8; Case C-415/93 *Union Royale Belge des Sociétés de Football Association ASBL et al v Bosman et al* [1995] ECR I-4921, 5070–1. See also Tesauro (1995) 15 YEL 1, 7.

[63] The Court has held that the need, resulting from the measures at issue, to alter the packaging or the labelling of imported products prevents those measures from concerning selling arrangements for the products within the meaning of the judgment in *Keck and Mithouard* (see Case C-33/97 *Colim* [1999] ECR I-3175, paragraph 37, Case C-12/00 *Commission v Spain* [2003] ECR I-459, para 76, and Case C-416/00 *Morellato* [2003] ECR I-9343, para 29).

[64] It is relatively easy to ascertain whether this condition is met.

[65] Cases C-418–421/93 etc *Semeraro Casa Uno Srl et al v Sindaco del Commune di Erbusco et al* [1996] ECR I-2975.

[66] Case C-391/92 *Commission v Greece* [1995] ECR I-1621.

[67] Case C-254/98 *Schutzverband gegen Unlauteren Wettbewerb v TK Heimdienst Sass GmbH* [2000] ECR I-151.

grocers, the Court noted that it was unnecessary for a measure to have the effect of favouring national products as a whole or of placing only imported products at a disadvantage and not national products for the measure to be found to have discriminatory or protective effects in relation to the free movement of goods.

Taking this approach further, in *Doc Morris*[68] the Court observed that 'even if the measure is not intended to regulate trade in goods between the Member States, the determining factor is its effect, actual or potential, on intra-Community trade'.[69] The Court gave the following summary of the second *Keck* criterion:

In order to ascertain whether a particular measure affects in the same manner the marketing of both domestic products and those from other Member States, the scope of the restrictive measure concerned must be ascertained. Thus, the Court has found that a prohibition on pharmacists from advertising quasi-pharmaceutical products outside the pharmacy, which they were authorized to offer for sale, did not affect the ability of traders other than pharmacists to advertise those products (see *Hünermund*, paragraph 19). Similarly, the prohibition on broadcasting the advertising at issue in *Leclerc-Siplec* was not extensive, since it covered only one particular form of promotion (television advertising) of one particular method of marketing products (distribution) (see *Leclerc-Siplec*, paragraph 22).

By contrast, the Court has accepted the relevance of the argument that a prohibition on television advertising deprived a trader of the only effective form of promotion which would have enabled it to penetrate a national market (see *De Agostini and TV-shop*, paragraph 43). Furthermore, the Court has found that in the case of products such as alcoholic beverages, the consumption of which is linked to traditional social practices and to local habits and customs, prohibiting all advertising directed at consumers in the form of advertisements in the press, on the radio and on television, the direct mailing of unsolicited material or the placing of posters on the public highway is liable to impede access to the market for products from other Member States more than it impedes access for domestic products, with which consumers are instantly more familiar (see Case C-405/98 *Gourmet International Products* [2001] ECR I-1795, paragraphs 21 and 24).[70]

The Court went on to note that it was undisputed that there was a requirement that certain medicines be sold only in pharmacies and a prohibition on mail-order sales of medicines; while the latter prohibition could be regarded as merely the consequence of the first requirement, the emergence of the Internet as a method of cross-border sales meant that the scope and effect of the prohibition had to be viewed broadly. It found that the prohibition was more of an obstacle to pharmacies outside Germany than to those in Germany; while there was little doubt that as a result of the prohibition, pharmacies in Germany could not use the extra or alternative method of gaining access to the German market consisting of end consumers of medicinal products, they were still able to sell the

---

[68] Case C-222/01 *Deutscher Apotherkerverbund eV v 0800 Doc Morris NV et al* [2003] ECR I-14887.
[69] ibid, 14984.
[70] ibid, 14986.

products in their dispensaries. But for pharmacies not established in Germany, the Internet offered a more significant way to gain direct access to the German market. Given that a prohibition which had a greater impact on pharmacies established outside German territory could impede access to the German market for products from other Member States more than it impedes access for domestic products, the Court concluded that the prohibition did not affect the sale of domestic medicines in the same way as it affected the sale of those coming from other Member States. In effect, the foreign pharmacies were being completely kept out of the market, while the domestic pharmacies had their marketing possibilities curtailed but not wholly closed.

In more recent case law, the Court has seemed a little unwilling in Article 234 EC references to come to a concluded view on whether the second condition in *Keck* is satisfied, preferring to leave it to national courts to conduct the factual analysis, although this had more to do with the paucity of information available to it than anything else. Thus in Case C-20/03 *Burmanjer et al*[71] dealing with itinerant sales, the Court found that it did not have sufficient information to reach a conclusion; in Case C-444/04 *A-Punkt Schmuckhandels GmbH v Schmidt*,[72] it was unable to decide whether the prohibition on marketing in private houses would affect the sale of imported products more than that of domestic products.

The willingness of the Court to ensure that local-grab measures will not be accepted on the selling arrangements bandwagon without more ado mirrors to some extent the changed emphasis in the free movement of workers, the freedom of establishment and the freedom to provide services away from merely discrimination-based concepts to become more potentially and even (indirectly) effect-oriented.[73] Indeed, the move to a broader interpretation of those freedoms makes it all the more necessary for the Court to be willing to look behind the nature of selling arrangements to maintain the integrationist effects of intra-Community market penetration. In practice the Court's refusal to allow *Keck* to become a general escape clause subject to practically no review has greatly mitigated the damage which was feared and even done when the judgment in *Keck* was handed down; to coin a Dutch phrase, soup is always served hotter than it is consumed!

The possibility of *Keck* perhaps signalling a *de minimis* approach was noted above, but it is now clear that this was not the Court's intention.[74] Indeed, in

---

[71] [2005] ECR I-nyr (26 May 2005).
[72] [2006] ECR I-nyr (23 February 2006).
[73] e.g. Case C-415/93 *Union Royale Belge des Sociétés de Football Association ASBL et al v Bosman et al* [1995] ECR I-4921, 5068–71.
[74] This is implicit in the rejection of the plea for a *de minimis* approach by AG Jacobs, discussed in the text. See also Case C-309/02 *Radlberger Getränkegesellschaft mbH & Co KG, S Spitz KG v Land Baden-Württemberg* [2004] ECR I-nyr (14 December 2004), para 68. The Court has also recently confirmed in relation to a transport ban that the fact that there are alternative routes or other means of transport capable of allowing the goods in question to be transported does not negate the existence of an obstacle arising through a ban on the use of a particular route: Case C-320/03 *Commission v Austria* [2005] ECR I-nyr (15 November 2005), para 67.

the course of his significant criticism of *Keck* in his opinion in *Leclerc-Siplec*,[75] Advocate General Jacobs made an eloquent plea for a *de minimis* approach instead. However, that plea fell on stony ground and deaf ears. With respect, the Court was right not to follow that path. Several reasons militate against accepting a *de minimis* rule in the free movement of goods. Most practically, where should the line be drawn? A percentage of GDP; a percentage of the value of the market (and what would be the relevant market); the value of a daily penalty on the Commission's guideline scales for penalizing Member States under Article 228 EC;[76] the value of a day's imports? Advocate General Tesauro felt that this would be a 'very difficult, if not downright impossible' exercise.[77] The position of the free movement of goods as a fundamental freedom and foundation of the Community would indeed be jeopardized by the introduction of a *de minimis* rule, and the Court has (on this point at least) been consistent in rejecting it.[78] Moreover, the Member States are under a particular duty by virtue of Article 10 EC to secure the free movement of goods,[79] and that militates against accepting chinks in the armour. This last argument is also an argument against the whole approach of treating selling arrangements as a special case outside the scope of Article 28.[80]

IV. Applying *Dassonville* More Generally

While it is not appropriate here to shower examples of typical measures having equivalent effect,[81] one or two individual observations on developments seem appropriate. Infamously, the Court declined to apply the *Dassonville* basic principle without more ado in the context of Article 29 EC in relation to measures applicable irrespective of the destination of the product.[82] This demonstrates the truth of the old adage that hard cases make bad law, and the Court was clearly

---

[75] Case C-412/93 *Société d'importation Édouard Leclerc v TFI Publicité SA et al* [1995] ECR I-179, 194–7.

[76] See [1997] OJ C63/2.

[77] Case C-292/92 *Hünermund v Landesapothekerkammer Baden-Württemberg* [1993] ECR I-6787, 6810–11.

[78] As to earlier authorities rejecting a *de minimis* argument, see Case 16/83 *Prantl* [1984] ECR 1299, at 1326; Cases 177/82 and 178/82 *Van de Haar* [1984] ECR 1797 at 1812–13; Case 269/83 *Commission v France* [1985] ECR 837, 846, and Case 103/84 *Commission v Italy* [1986] ECR 1759, 1773.

[79] See Case C-265/95 *Commission v France* [1997] ECR I-6959, 6999; Case C-112/00 *Eugen Schmidberger, Internationale Transporte und Planzüge v Österreich* [2003] ECR I-5659, 5714–15.

[80] The dangers of a slippery slope of exceptions can be seen now that AG Kokott has sought to exclude arrangements for use from the scope of Art 28 EC, see Case C-142/05 *Åklagaren v Mickelsson & Roos* (pending, opinion of 14 December 2006).

[81] See LW Gormley, *EU Law of Free Movement of Goods and Customs Union* (forthcoming, 2008); P Oliver (2003, see n 1 above), ch VII.

[82] e.g. Case 15/79 *P B Groenveld BV v Produktschap voor Vee en Vlees* [1979] ECR 3409; Case 155/80 *Oebel* [1981] ECR 1993.

swayed in *Groenveld*[83] by the point that if the Dutch prohibition were to be condemned it was likely that exports of Dutch processed meat products (particularly to Anglo-Saxon countries) would suffer. One consolation is that the formula adopted in *Groenveld*, although contrary to Advocate General Capotorti's suggestion that the basic principle in *Dassonville* be applied, nevertheless was sufficiently wide to catch 'local grab' measures.[84] However, apart from that distinct aberration, for which the wording of the EC Treaty itself provides no justification, the *Keck*-style circumstances, and those rare cases where the Court found any effect on trade between Member States 'too uncertain and indirect',[85] the line of the basic principle in *Dassonville* has held firm.

The range of measures caught by Article 28 EC is truly remarkable, but one of the most interesting developments is how the concept of the mutual acceptance of goods, which gave rise to strong emotions in some quarters,[86] and which certainly is not the panacea it once seemed,[87] has developed new energy with the idea of an obligation on the Member States to take account of the need for mutual recognition clauses in national legislation.[88] Another interesting development is the Court's idea that it does not follow that Article 28 EC is inapplicable merely because all the facts are confined to one Member State.[89] This will not

---

[83] 15/79 *PB Groenveld BV v Produktschap voor Vee en Vlees* [1979] ECR 3409.

[84] e.g. Case 173/83 *Commission v France* [1985] ECR 491. As Case C-388/95 *Belgium v Spain* [2000] ECR I-3123, reversing the finding in Case C-47/90 *Éts Delhaize Frères et Compagnie Le Lion SA v Promalvin SA et al* [1992] ECR I-3669 (*Rioja*) demonstrates, even local-grab measures may be justified (although it has to be said that the justification for reversing *Delhaize* was thin indeed and more politically than legally motivated).

[85] Case 379/92 *Peralta* [1994] ECR I-3453, 3497; Case C-140/94 *DIP SpA et al v Commune di Bassano di Grappa et al* [1995] ECR I-3257, 3297; Case C-96/94 *Centro Servizi Spediporto Srl v Spedizione Marittima del Golfo Srl* [1995] ECR I-2883, 2914; Case C-134/94 *Esso Española SA v Comunidad Autonoma de Canarias* [1995] ECR I-4223, 4249; Case C-266/96 *Corsica Ferries France SA v Gruppo Antichi Ormeggiatori del Porto di Genova Coop. Arl et al* [1998] ECR I-3949, 3992–3; Case C-44/98 *BASF AG v Präsident des Deutschen Patentamts* [1999] ECR I-6269. These cases are all post-*Keck*. There were a few cases decided pre-*Keck* in which a similar approach was taken (*Blesgen*, *Quietlynn* and *Sheptonhurst* mentioned in the discussion above, Case C-69/88 *H Krantz GmbH & Co v Ontvanger der Directe Belastingen et al* [1990] ECR I-583, 597 and Case C-93/92 *CMC Motorradcenter GmbH v Baskiciogullari* [1993] ECR I-5009, 5021) but those cases would all now fall within the *Keck* approach. The idea of uncertain and indirect is, it is respectfully submitted, rather different from a *de minimis* test, and has more to do with perceived abuse of Community law than with the backdoor introduction of a *de minimis* provision or even of a genuine remoteness test. Oliver (see note 1 (2003)) 103, 206–7 rightly argues, referring to this case law, that there is no general rule of remoteness in Art 28 EC.

[86] See LW Gormley (1981) 6 ELRev 454, discussing reactions to the Commission's famous Communication on the consequences of the *Cassis de Dijon* judgment [1980] OJ C 256/2.

[87] See Case 188/84 *Commission v France* [1986] ECR 419 (type approval for woodworking machines) and Case C-293/93 *Houtwipper* [1994] ECR I-4249 (hallmarking of jewellery).

[88] Case C-184/96 *Commission v France* [1998] ECR I-6197 (*foie gras*). See further A Mattera (1998/4) RMUE 113. There may be health considerations which may justify limits, see e.g. Case C-24/00 *Commission v France* [2004] ECR I-1277 and Case C-95/01 *Greenham & Abel* [2004] ECR I-1333.

[89] Cases C-321–324/94 *Pistre et al* [1997] ECR I-2343, 2374–5; Case C-448/98 *Guimont* [2000] ECR I-10663, 10688.

sound so strange to those familiar with Community competition law, where the concept of barriers to entry to the territory of a Member State arising through action by a cartel in that Member State is familiar, or even to those familiar with the developments in relation to the other freedoms as to disincentives to exercising the freedoms granted by the Treaty; a reminder, if any were needed of the strength of the terms indirect or potential in the basic principle of *Dassonville* itself. Whatever the reactions to perceived abuse of the freedoms granted by Community law – and the *Keck* judgment shows how monumental a change in the wind can be (at least initially) – the Court is still not afraid to develop Article 28 EC in the interest of the proper functioning of the internal market and indeed the common market.

V. Conclusions

The above case law has demonstrated just how dynamic Community law is; on the one hand there are clear signs of continuity and consistency, on the other hand those of change, reassessment and new developments. The free movement of goods remains, now with developments in the other freedoms and in Union citizenship, a dynamic and far-reaching area of Community law. Just as some people start to think it is coming to maturity, so the case law moves on and reveals new facets. Undoubtedly the Court of Justice could improve its consistency, particularly in its reasoning, but the overall state of the free movement of goods case law is happier now than it seemed in the immediate aftermath of *Keck*. The free movement of goods – and in particular the definition of measures having equivalent effect – is a fitting subject indeed for study in the light of the theme Continuity and Change.

Valedictory

As the present writer has stated elsewhere,[90] Francis Jacobs has been one of the great Advocates General, but he has been so much more than that as well; his contributions to academic life and to legal practice in the field of European Law (conceived broadly and including human rights) have been legion and his indefatigable energy continues to grace the Law School at King's: he giveth them good doctrine and his law will not be forsaken.[91]

---

[90] LW Gormley (2006) 29 Fordham Int'l LJ 665, 689.
[91] See Proverbs 4, ii (King James version).

12

The Concept of Abuse in the Freedom of Establishment of Companies: a Case of Double Standards?

Vanessa Edwards and Paul Farmer

Following a visit to the European Court of Justice shortly after the United Kingdom's accession to the European Communities, Lord Denning put his newly-acquired knowledge to good use when, in his inimitable style, he summed up the ECJ's judicial method in *Buchanan v Babco*:

> They adopt a method which they call in English by strange words – at any rate they were strange to me – the 'schematic and teleological' method of interpretation... They... interpret the legislation so as to produce the desired effect. This means that they fill the gaps, quite unashamedly, without hesitation. They ask simply: what is the sensible way of dealing with this situation so as to give effect to the presumed intention of the legislature?... To our eyes – short-sighted by tradition – it is legislation pure and simple. But to their eyes it is fulfilling the true role of the courts. They are giving effect to what the legislature intended, or may be presumed to have intended.[1]

Lord Denning went on to declare that the method was in fact no more than he himself had advocated in a ruling in 1949, several years before the ECJ was established. We do not know what Lord Denning would have made of the concept of abuse of rights. Though just as strange to the English judicial ear, the doctrine is closely related to the teleological or purposive method of interpretation which he so brilliantly described. Indeed recent case law on the doctrine of abuse increasingly supports the view that it is simply one instrument in the teleological tool chest, to be used in the presence of a particular pattern of circumstances.[2] More pragmatically, and in language which would surely have been music to Lord Denning's ears, the doctrine has been described as simply enabling the Court 'to prevent Community law from being applied in

---

[1] *James Buchanan & Co Ltd v Babco Forwarding & Shipping (UK) Ltd* [1977] QB 208, CA.
[2] Para 68 of the opinion of AG Poiares Maduro in Case C-255/02 *Halifax* [2006] ECR I-1609.

a way which went against common sense and ignored obvious and undeniable realities'.[3]

Abuse of rights is a doctrine known to many legal systems. Its status varies. In Community law, as the case law stands at present, it appears to serve as a principle of construction.[4] Provisions of Community primary or secondary law are to be interpreted as permitting or requiring the denial of a right where, although the formal conditions laid down are met, the exercise of the right would be abusive. The Community rights in question may derive from the Treaty or from a regulation or directive. They may be denied by national authorities under domestic trading, professional or other regulations, domestic abuse of law provisions or Community regulations.[5] This article considers aspects of the doctrine in the context of companies' right of establishment under Articles 43 and 48 EC.

I. Development of Abuse of Rights in Community Law

The origins of the doctrine in EU law can be traced back to the 1974 ruling in *Van Binsbergen*[6], where the ECJ stated:

A Member State cannot be denied the right to take measures to prevent the exercise by a person providing services whose activity is entirely or principally directed towards its territory of the freedom guaranteed by Article [49 EC] for the purpose of avoiding the professional rules of conduct which would be applicable to him if he were established within that state.

Van Binsbergen concerned the freedom to provide services. The doctrine was further developed in that context 20 years later in *Veronica*[7] and *TV10*.[8] In the meantime the Court had applied it to other Treaty freedoms.[9] In the context of freedom of

---

[3] Para 34 of the opinion of AG Mischo in Case C-45/90 *Paletta* [1992] ECR I-3423, referring to the approach taken by the Court in Case 130/88 *Van de Bijl* [1989] ECR 3039. AG Poiares Maduro similarly described the principle prohibiting abuse of Community law as 'an indispensable safety-valve for protecting the aims of all provisions of Community law against a formalistic application of them based solely on their plain meaning' (para 74 of the opinion in *Halifax*).

[4] See further the discussions in the opinions of AG Tesauro in Case C-367/96 *Kefalas* [1998] ECR I-2843, paras 18–27, and AG Poiares Maduro in *Halifax*, paras 62–71. For different views, see L Neville Brown, 'Is there a general principle of abuse of rights in European Community law?' in D Curtin and T Heukels (eds), *Institutional Dynamics of European Integration, Vol II* (1994) 511 and K Sørensen, 'Abuse of rights in Community law: a principle of substance or merely rhetoric?' (2006) 43 CMLRev 423.

[5] In areas of Community policy administered by the Community authorities, the rights could presumably be administered by those authorities.

[6] Case 33/74 [1974] ECR 1299.

[7] Case C-148/91 [1993] ECR I-487. See also Case C-19/92 *Kraus* [1993] ECR I-1663 and, most recently, Case C-147/03 *Commission v Austria* [2005] ECR I-5969.

[8] Case C-23/93 [1994] ECR I-4795.

[9] See Case 115/78 *Knoors* [1979] ECR 399, Case 39/86 *Lair* [1988] ECR 3161, Case C-61/89 *Bouchoucha* [1990] ECR 1-3551 and Case C-370/90 *Singh* [1992] ECR I-4265 concerning freedom of movement for persons and freedom of establishment, and Case 229/83 *Leclerc* [1985] ECR 1 concerning the free movement of goods. See also more recently Case C-109/01 *Akrich* [2003] ECR I-9607 concerning freedom of movement for persons.

establishment, the Court stated in *Knoors* in 1979 that it was 'not possible to disregard the legitimate interests which a Member State may have in preventing certain of its nationals, by means of facilities created under the Treaty, from attempting wrongly to evade the application of their national legislation as regards training for a trade'.[10]

The Court has also applied the doctrine of abuse in other areas of Community law,[11] and indeed it was the field of agriculture which provided the Court with the opportunity to develop it more fully. In *Emsland-Stärke* the Court had to consider whether an exporter lost its right to an export refund under a Community regulation where goods were exported and released for home use in a non-EU country (Switzerland) but were immediately re-imported into the Community (Italy). Although the formal conditions for the grant of the refund under Regulation No 2730/79[12] were met, the German authorities sought repayment of the export refunds on the ground that the goods were never intended for export but for the Italian market.

The Court held that the Regulation was to be interpreted as meaning that the right to the refund could be forfeited in cases of abuse despite the formal conditions which it laid down being fulfilled. It then set about defining the notion of abuse. An abuse presupposed, first, a combination of objective circumstances from which it was apparent that, despite formal observance of the conditions laid down by the Community rules, the purpose of the rules had not been achieved and, second, an intention to benefit from an advantage conferred by the Community rules by artificially creating the conditions for obtaining it. It was for the national court to determine whether those two conditions were met, subject to the effectiveness of Community law not being undermined.

The *Emsland-Stärke* decision prompted a series of references in the VAT area from the UK courts.[13] The context of the cases in which the question of abuse has

---

[10] Para 25. Described as an obiter dictum by AG Darmon in *Van de Bijl* (see para 11 of the opinion). In *Knoors*, the Court found that on the facts there was no risk of such abuse. In *Bouchoucha*, in contrast, the Court ruled that France, which required osteopathy to be performed by a doctor, was not required to recognize the UK qualification of osteopath.

[11] In the field of agriculture, see Case 125/76 *Cremer* [1977] ECR 1593, Case C-8/92 *General Milk Products* [1993] ECR I-779, and more recently Case C-110/99 *Emsland-Stärke* [2000] I-11569, Case C-137/00 *Milk Marque and National Farmers' Union* [2003] ECR I-7975, Case C-515/03 *Eichsfelder Schlachtbetrieb* [2005] ECR I-7355 and Case C-279/05 *Vonk* [2007] ECR I-239. In the field of shareholder rights, see *Kefalas* and Case C-373/97 *Diamantis* [2000] ECR I-1705. In the field of maritime cabotage, see Case C-456/04 *Agip Petroli* [2006] ECR I-3395. In the field of social security, see Case C-206/94 *Paletta II* [1996] ECR I-2357. In the context of the common system of taxation for mergers, see Case C-321/05 *Kofoed*, judgment of 5 July 2007. In the context of capital duty, see Case C-178/05 *Commission v Greece*, judgment of 7 June 2007.

[12] Commission Reg (EEC) No 2730/79 of 29 November 1979 laying down common detailed rules for the application of the system of export refunds on agricultural products [1979] OJ L317/1 as amended by Commission Reg (EEC) No 568/85 of 4 March 1985 [1985] OJ L65/5.

[13] *Halifax*, Case C-419/02 *BUPA Hospitals* [2006] ECR I-1685 and Case C-223/03 *University of Huddersfield Higher Education Corporation* [2006] ECR I-1751. See M Ridsdale, 'Abuse of rights, fiscal neutrality and VAT' (2005) 14 EC Tax Review 82 and O Rousselle and H M Liebman, 'The doctrine of the abuse of Community law: the sword of Damocles hanging over the head of EC Corporate Tax law' (2006) 46 European Taxation 559.

arisen thus varies.[14] In the area of Treaty freedoms, however, there is inevitably a consistent pattern: a legal or natural person seeks to carry out a cross-border activity which is prohibited or impeded by legislation of one of the Member States involved; that person challenges the legislation on the basis that it is contrary to a fundamental freedom.

In the framework of the freedom of establishment, two parallel phenomena have contributed to the more recent development of the doctrine of abuse. First, the Court has been confronted on several occasions – and will doubtless continue to be so – by cases in which nationals of one Member State have used a company incorporated in another Member State as a vehicle to do business in the first Member State with the explicit intention of avoiding certain features of their national company law. Second, ever more sophisticated national legislation designed to target tax avoidance[15] has prompted corporate taxpayers to invoke the freedom of establishment in order to legitimate the arrangements they have put in place wholly or partly with tax considerations in mind.

With regard to the first group of cases, the fact that the allegedly abusive activity involves the use of a company has meant that the Court's earlier analysis of abuse in the context of the freedom of establishment of individuals has had to be refined in a number of ways. With regard to the second group, the Court has had to juggle the different but analogous concepts of abuse of the freedom of establishment, unlawful circumvention of national legislation, and tax avoidance or evasion. What is striking is that, although the case law has developed in parallel in certain respects, the Court appears to have adopted significantly different approaches to the relevance of genuine establishment in the Member State of incorporation of the company involved. This article examines the similarities and differences in the recent case law and suggests an analysis which might have enabled the Court's case law in the field of company law to have evolved in the same way as its case law in the field of tax.

II. Pre-emption or Justification?

The question of abuse had arisen in the earlier cases more often than not in the context of whether the Treaty freedom invoked was applicable at all.[16] Thus

---

[14] For a comprehensive review of the case law spanning the different areas, see A Kjellgren, 'On the border of abuse – the jurisprudence of the European Court of Justice on circumvention, fraud and other misuse of Community law' (2000) 11 EBLR 179.

[15] Confusingly, 'tax avoidance', which in conventional English usage suggests technically lawful transactions undertaken with a view to paying less tax, is translated in French as 'évasion fiscale', while 'tax evasion', which is used to describe unlawful transactions, is translated as 'fraude fiscale'. This has unfortunately led to frequent errors of the English translations of judgments of the ECJ.

[16] This corresponds to the analysis in *Emsland-Stärke* (and indeed the other cases involving secondary legislation rather than Treaty freedoms), where the Court held that the individual forfeited his rights under the relevant provision of secondary legislation in certain circumstances.

the issue in *Knoors* was whether Mr Knoors, a Netherlands national resident in Belgium, where he worked as a self-employed plumber, who wished to establish himself in the Netherlands in the same line of business, was a beneficiary of the freedom of establishment.[17] In *Bouchoucha* the principal argument of the applicant, who held an English diploma in osteopathy but was not medically qualified and who wished to practise in France, which required osteopathy to be performed by a doctor, was that Community law (in particular the freedom of establishment) was applicable to him and the case was not purely internal to France. In *Lair*, in which the question arose whether a Member State could require a national of another Member State to have worked for a minimum period within its territory before applying for a student grant, the Court considered the argument that such a requirement was motivated by a desire to prevent certain abuses, for example the entry of a worker into a Member State for the sole purpose of enjoying a student grant after a very short period of work, and ruled that 'such abuses are not covered by the Community provisions in question'.[18]

In the areas of other freedoms, the question referred in *Van Binsbergen* was 'what is the meaning of Articles [49 and 50 EC]'; although the Court's judgment is framed in general terms, it appears to have been directing itself to the question whether the situation at issue (a requirement of Netherlands law that legal representatives be established in the Netherlands) fell within the scope of those articles. In *Leclerc*, the Court stated that its previous finding that legislation fixing the price of imported books constituted a measure equivalent in effect to a quantitative restriction on imports 'is not applicable where it is established that the books in question were exported for the sole purpose of re-importation in order to circumvent legislation of the type at issue'.[19]

Once a company incorporated in another Member State is being used as a vehicle for trade in the host Member State, however, and it is precisely the use of the company which is allegedly abusive, a clearer focus is required. The argument that the Treaty does not apply because the situation is internal and that the company's founders are simply committing a 'U-turn' can be maintained only if the founders and the company are regarded as a single entity.

This situation first came before the Court in 1986 in *Segers*.[20] That case concerned the compatibility with the freedom of establishment of Netherlands legislation which, as interpreted by the national courts, excluded Mr Segers, sole director of and (with his wife) sole shareholder in a company incorporated in the United Kingdom which conducted all its business in the Netherlands,

---

[17] At that time, and in that field, governed by Council Directive 64/427 of 7 July 1964 laying down detailed provisions concerning transitional measures in respect of activities of self-employed persons in [certain manufacturing and processing industries] (OJ English Special Edition, 1963–4, 148).
[18] Para 43.
[19] Para 27.
[20] Case 79/85 [1986] ECR 2375.

from a sickness insurance benefit scheme solely on the ground that the company was incorporated in another Member State. It was argued on behalf of the relevant national authority that the fact that the case concerned a Netherlands national residing in the Netherlands where he in practice conducted all his business meant that it was a purely internal matter, even though all that business was conducted by a company incorporated in the United Kingdom. That proposition was considered and (clearly correctly) rejected by Advocate General Darmon on the grounds that the different treatment in question was based exclusively on the location of the company's seat. That was sufficient to bring the case within the scope of Article 43 EC. Unfortunately the Court did not deal directly with this argument. Nor, in consequence, did it consider whether the fact that the company conducted no business in the Member State of its incorporation might affect the question whether Mr Segers could be said to have genuinely exercised his right of establishment in incorporating the company and using it as he did.

The question arose again in *Centros*.[21] That case concerned two Danish nationals who had formed a company in the United Kingdom with the sole purpose of carrying on business in Denmark through a branch and thus of avoiding the Danish legislation on the formation of private limited companies, and in particular the requirement for a minimum share capital, which would have been applicable had they incorporated a Danish private limited company. The company which they incorporated in the United Kingdom conducted no business there. The Danish authorities refused to register a branch of the company on that ground. The question referred to the Court was whether that refusal was compatible with Articles 43 and 48 EC.

Denmark argued before the Court that Article 43 EC was not applicable since the situation was purely internal: in such circumstances the formation by nationals of one Member State of a company in another Member State did not amount to a relevant external element in the light of Community law and, in particular, freedom of establishment.

Clearly that argument, narrowly put as it was, could succeed only if the company and its shareholders were regarded as a single entity – it required the Court to lift the corporate veil. Unsurprisingly the Court was not prepared to do this. There was manifestly an issue of cross-border establishment by the *company*, notwithstanding that it conducted no business in the Member State where it was incorporated, and the Court focused on that rather than considering whether the circumstances might suggest that the founders of the company had not genuinely

---

[21] Case C-212/97 [1999] ECR I-2357. Among the wealth of literature, see R Crauford Smith, 'The establishment of companies in European Community law: choice of law or abuse of rights?' European Current Law (November 1999) xi; A Looijestijn-Clearie, 'Centros Ltd – a complete U-turn in the right of establishment for companies?' (2000) 49 ICLQ 621 and P Cabral and P Cunha, '"Presumed innocent": companies and the exercise of the right of establishment under Community law' (2000) 25 ELRev 157.

exercised *their* right of establishment, and whether, if so, that might be relevant to the question before the Court.[22]

Having reached the view that the formation by Centros of a branch in Denmark was covered by Articles 43 and 48, the Court made it clear that abuse could nonetheless be relevant at a different stage in the analysis: 'The question of the application of Articles [43 and 48 EC] is different from the question whether or not a Member State may adopt measures in order to prevent attempts by certain of its national to evade domestic legislation by having recourse to the possibilities offered by the Treaty'.[23] The Court went on to consider whether, given that the freedom of establishment in principle applied to such a situation, the doctrine of abuse none the less entitled Denmark to refuse to register a branch in such circumstances in order to prevent abuse of the freedom of establishment. It ruled that, since that freedom conferred the very right which was alleged to constitute abuse, namely the formation by a company incorporated in one Member State of a branch in another Member State, there could be no abuse.[24] Despite that ruling, the Court entertained arguments analogous to those based on abuse at a third stage in the judgment, when considering whether the practice of refusing to register a branch in such circumstances could be justified by the need to combat fraud. Although the classic language of abuse was not used at that point, the concepts appear to be similar. The Court ruled in effect that national measures found to impede the freedom of establishment may in principle be justified by the need to combat abuse, although that justification was not made out in *Centros* itself.

The Court's approach was developed further in *Inspire Art*.[25] That case concerned Netherlands legislation attaching additional conditions[26] to the establishment in the Netherlands of a company incorporated in another Member State[27] with the sole aim of securing certain advantages compared with companies incorporated in the Netherlands, which are subject to stricter rules concerning, in particular, minimum share capital.[28] The Court was asked essentially whether

---

[22] The question referred in *Centros* in fact specifically mentioned this point, noting that the incorporation of the UK company 'must be regarded as having been employed in order to avoid paying up [Danish minimum] company capital' (see para 13).

[23] Para 18.

[24] The Court's analysis of this argument is considered in more detail in the following section.

[25] Case C-167/01 [2003] ECR I-10155. See A Looijestijn-Clearie, 'Have the dikes collapsed? *Inspire Art*, a further breakthrough in the freedom of establishment of companies' (2004) 5 EBOR 389 and M Rehberg, '*Inspire Art* – Freedom of establishment for companies in Europe between "abuse" and national regulatory concerns' (1-2004) European Legal Forum 1.

[26] Again, the condition principally at issue was the requirement of a minimum share capital, backed by the imposition in default of personal liability on the company's directors.

[27] In *Inspire Art*, as is usually the case in such contexts, the company was incorporated in the UK.

[28] A Looijestijn-Clearie explains the background to the Netherlands legislation as follows:

Since the 1980s an increase in the number of formally foreign or pseudo-foreign companies had been detected in the Netherlands. Persons wishing to do business in the Netherlands through the medium of a small or single member company have increasingly made use of a company incorporated and registered in the most exotic of jurisdictions for the sole purpose of circumventing Dutch company law rules... Companies formed in the Dutch Antilles as well as in the UK and the state

such national legislation was compatible with Articles 43 and 48 EC. Here the argument that the national legislation sought to combat improper recourse to freedom of establishment was explicitly analysed (and rejected) by the Court as a justification.[29] Similarly in *Commission v Portugal*[30] it was argued that a requirement that foreign undertakings wishing to operate in a particular sector had to have a minimum share capital sought to prevent any attempt to circumvent national rules on share capital. The Court dealt squarely with that argument in the context of justification (and again rejected it).[31] The point at which the principle of abuse may be raised by a Member State thus appears to have shifted.[32]

In the field of tax there has been a parallel convergence of the notions of abuse of rights in the classic sense and abuse in a more general sense as a justification. For tax lawyers abuse and avoidance are familiar concepts. Indeed, it is the daily business of tax professionals to explore ways of minimizing the tax liability of individuals and companies, and large swathes of forest have been sacrificed in a largely vain attempt to define the borderline between legitimate tax planning and unacceptable avoidance or abuse. It is not surprising, therefore, that the tax area, and more specifically value added tax, has provided Community law with some of the leading cases on the notion of abuse.

In *Halifax, BUPA* and *University of Huddersfield*,[33] the Court was asked to apply to VAT the principles on abuse laid down in *Emsland-Stärke*. In parallel to the development of the 'classic' abuse of rights doctrine in the VAT cases,[34] the

---

of Delaware (USA) have become popular. The classic example is the window-cleaning firm operating in a small Dutch village (Appingedam) which was incorporated under the law of the state of Delaware. Advertisements for the use of such companies were regularly found in several newspapers and legal journals. The only link which such pseudo-foreign companies have with the state of incorporation is the fact that they have their registered office in this country (n 25 above) 396–7.

It appears that *Inspire Art* was a test case initiated by one of the organizations advertising foreign companies, which offered a wide variety of offshore companies on its website: see H-J de Kluiver, 'Inspiring a new European Company law?' (1/2004) ECFR 121, 123.

[29] See paras 136–9.

[30] Case C-171/02 [2004] ECR I-5645.

[31] Para 56. Similarly, in *Commission v Austria* (n 7 above), the Court unambiguously dealt with a classic abuse argument (in the context of the freedom to provide services) as a justification: see paras 67–8. AG Geelhoed expresses the same view in *Akrich*, stating that 'the Court, where it accepts that abuses may be combated, applies the following reasoning in that regard. National legislation which is justified on overriding public interest grounds may be applied to the Member State's own nationals who are using community law purely and simply in order to evade that legislation' (para 105).

[32] In *TV10* the Court had already treated abuse as a justification, although in *Veronica* (where AG Tesauro had considered it in the context of justification) it is not clear whether the Court did so too. In *Segers*, similarly, the Netherlands authority had additionally pleaded the need to combat possible abuse as a justification for its refusal to grant Mr Segers sickness insurance cover. The Court summarily rejected that argument on the basis that it did not fall within Art 46 EC (see para 17).

[33] See n 13 above.

[34] It may be noted that in Case C-425/06 *Part Service* (pending), also in the field of VAT, the Court has been asked whether the concept of abuse of rights, defined in *Halifax* as 'transactions, the essential aim of which is to obtain a tax advantage', corresponds to the definition 'transactions

Court has had occasion to consider the legitimacy of direct tax restrictions on the freedoms, particularly establishment. In *ICI*,[35] the Court accepted that a fiscal restriction could in principle be justified by the imperative interest in preventing tax avoidance.[36] Such a restriction must have the specific purpose of preventing wholly artificial arrangements set up to circumvent domestic tax rules.[37] The language used is therefore similar to the language of abuse; and indeed in some recent cases the Court has referred in the same breath to 'tax avoidance' and 'abusive practices',[38] although always at the level of justification. In similar vein, Advocate General Léger has expressed the view that the language of the formula developed by the Court in assessing justification of national legislation on the ground of counteraction of tax avoidance (namely that the legislation must be specifically designed to exclude from a tax advantage wholly artificial arrangements aimed at circumventing national law) 'reproduces that of the doctrine of "abuse of rights"'.[39]

A good illustration of the tendency to elide the two concepts is *X and Y*,[40] where the Member State concerned had pleaded both abuse in the conventional context and justification by reference to the imperative requirement based on the risk of tax avoidance. The Court dealt with both arguments at the level of justification, stating in particular that refusal by a Member State of a tax advantage in a cross-border context 'cannot be justified on the ground of abuse of freedom of establishment'[41] (and going on to rule that, although the prevention of tax avoidance was an overriding requirement of general interest, the measure in question was not proportionate).

Two more recent cases illustrate the evolving scope of the concept of abuse in the context of freedom of establishment and national legislation aimed at tax avoidance.

---

carried out for no commercial reasons other than a tax advantage', or whether it is broader or more restrictive than that definition.

[35] Case C-264/96 *Imperial Chemical Industries* [1998] ECR I-4695.
[36] The Court has confirmed this proposition in numerous subsequent cases.
[37] *ICI*, para 26, Case C-324/00 *Lankhorst-Hohorst* [2002] ECR I-11779, para 37. This proposition has been confirmed on several occasions (Case C-9/02 *de Lasteyrie du Saillant* [2004] ECR I-2409, para 50; Case C-446/03 *Marks & Spencer* [2005] ECR I-10837, para 57; Case C-196/04 *Cadbury Schweppes* [2006] ECR I-7995, para 51; Case C-524/04 *Test Claimants in the Thin Cap Group Litigation* ('*Thin Cap*') [2007] ECR I-2107, para 72). See more recently, however, Case C-231/05 *AA*, judgment of 18 July 2007, where the Court found that national legislation which allowed a resident subsidiary to deduct an intra-group financial transfer except where the transferee was a foreign company was justified on the ground, *inter alia*, of the prevention of tax avoidance, even if it was not specifically designed to exclude from the tax advantage it conferred purely artificial arrangements (para 63).
[38] See e.g. *Cadbury Schweppes*, paras 48 and 55; *Thin Cap*, paras 73, 74, 77 and 80.
[39] Para 88 of the opinion in *Cadbury Schweppes*.
[40] C-436/00 [2002] ECR I-10829.
[41] Para 45. See also para 47 of the opinion of AG Mischo, who refers to 'the possibility of justifying the discrimination at issue in this case on the grounds that it is intended to prevent tax evasion or abuse of the freedoms conferred by Community law'.

It is clear first that a Member State may rely on the justification where the establishment at issue is an artifice designed solely to circumvent tax laws. In such a situation the notion of tax avoidance and the classic notion of abuse (in the sense of the Treaty provision not being applicable at all) coincide.

In *Cadbury Schweppes* the Court had occasion to consider whether UK anti-avoidance rules imposing a charge on a UK parent company in respect of the undistributed profits of its Irish subsidiary on account of the low rate of tax in that latter state were compatible with Article 43 EC. The Court dealt initially with abuse in the 'classic' sense[42] and ruled that the fact that the subsidiary was established in Ireland for the purpose of benefiting from more favourable legislation did not in itself suffice to constitute abuse of the freedom of establishment.[43] Having found there to be a restriction, it moved on to consider whether the legislation was justified because it was necessary to prevent wholly artificial arrangements. In doing so the Court not only drew on the previous case law on tax avoidance[44] but also referred to the principles on abuse articulated in *Emsland-Stärke* and *Halifax*.[45] It concluded that a Member State was entitled to impose restrictions only where the taxpayer did not genuinely establish an economic activity but incorporated a purely artificial subsidiary solely with the intent of circumventing UK tax rules. The finding of economic activity had to be based on objective factors which were ascertainable by third parties with regard in particular to the extent to which the subsidiary physically existed in terms of premises, staff and equipment. The legislation at issue in *Cadbury Schweppes* was capable of covering abuse in the classic sense, but also potentially went beyond such cases. This explains the Court's ruling that it was not abuse simply to seek to benefit from a foreign regime and its assessment of the permitted limits of the legislation in the context of justification.

In *Thin Cap*, the Court took the convergence of abuse and tax avoidance a step further. It did not deal with abuse in the 'classic' sense at all, although the questions referred made separate mention of both abuse of rights and artificial arrangements designed to circumvent national tax law: instead, it dealt with the compound argument of the 'prevention of abusive practices' at the level of justification.[46] The Court held that that justification can also be relied upon in cases where there has unquestionably been a genuine exercise of the freedom of establishment for purposes other than circumventing national tax rules but where the tax arrangements accompanying the establishment are artificial and lead to a circumvention of domestic tax law. In *Thin Cap*, the UK subsidiaries set up by the

---

[42] Paras 34–8.
[43] Paras 48–68.
[44] *ICI, Lankhorst-Hohorst*.
[45] For a comparison of the Court's approach in *Halifax* and *Cadbury Schweppes*, see F Vanistendael, '*Halifax* and *Cadbury Schweppes*: one single European theory of abuse in tax law?' (2006) 15 EC Tax Review 192.
[46] Paras 71–80.

claimants, established in other Member States, were undeniably conducting genuine businesses in the United Kingdom. The issue which arose was whether the United Kingdom was entitled to limit the amount of interest on intra-group loan finance which could be deducted in computing the UK subsidiaries' corporation tax liability when it imposed no equivalent limitation where the parent was resident in the United Kingdom. The Court held that, although such a limitation constituted a restriction on the parent companies' freedom of establishment, the restriction was justified in so far as it was necessary to prevent wholly artificial arrangements. Here the Court was referring not to the artificiality or otherwise of the establishment but to whether the level of debt and interest paid was commercial. For that purpose a Member State was entitled to apply an objective arm's length test providing that it was possible for the taxpayer to demonstrate that there were commercial reasons for the arrangements (even if not strictly arm's length).

The recent tendency in the cases on corporate establishment in both the tax and company law fields to analyze abuse at the level of justification has the consequence that abuse is no longer an 'all or nothing' argument, simply displacing the Treaty freedom if successful. If it is assessed in the context of justification, a national measure aimed at preventing abuse will be legitimate only if it satisfies the requirements the Court has developed in its case law: in particular, it must be justified by imperative requirements in the general interest, it must be suitable for securing the attainment of the objective which it pursues and it must not go beyond what is necessary in order to attain it.[47] Justification seems an appropriate instrument for reviewing the legitimacy of complex fiscal measures – and indeed of national provisions seeking to regulate companies – since it enables the Court to evaluate legislation which, like the curate's egg, is only bad in part.

III. Abuse of Which Right?

Although the analysis in *Van Binsbergen* starts with a reference to the objective of Article 49 EC,[48] it is interesting to note that in most of the early cases the Court, while focusing on the motives of the person concerned in carrying on the activity in question[49] and/or the aim of the national legislation being challenged,[50] does not explicitly consider the purpose of the Treaty rule invoked.

Ultimately, however, whether abuse is considered to pre-empt the application of the Treaty or to be a justification for a restriction, a proper analysis of the purpose of the provisions on freedom of establishment is crucial, as is a proper analysis of which right is at stake. This is demonstrated by a comparison of the company law and tax case law.

---

[47] See, for example, *Centros*, para 34.
[48] See para 11.
[49] See *Van Binsbergen, Knoors, Lair, Veronica* and *TV10*.
[50] See *Van Binsbergen, Lair, Veronica* and *TV10*.

In *Centros* and *Inspire Art*, it was explicitly argued that it was an abuse of Articles 43 and 48 EC for nationals of one Member State to use a company incorporated in another Member State for conducting business in the first Member State with the sole aim of avoiding national company law requirements. As Advocate General Darmon had stated in *Segers*, however, that 'operation is made possible by the combination of the right which is accorded to natural persons of setting up a company in another Member State and that, for legal persons, including companies created in that way, of conducting their business through the intermediary of a [branch or] subsidiary in the country of origin of the natural person'.[51] Does the argument that such operations constitute abuse of the right of establishment therefore beg the question?[52]

That argument was raised only briefly in *Segers*[53] and dealt with as such by Advocate General Darmon, who, anticipating the analysis in *Centros*, focused on the purpose of the Treaty right of establishment and concluded that exercising that right by forming a company in another Member State to do business exclusively in the host Member State could not be assumed to be an abuse. On the contrary, that situation, albeit 'paradoxical', was 'the logical consequence of the rights guaranteed under the Treaty [and] consistent with the objective behind the inclusion of the freedom of establishment in the EEC Treaty, namely the need to promote the free movement of persons'.[54] Unfortunately, the Court in *Segers* did not analyse this question in any depth, and in particular did not separate the two elements of the composite operation underlying the reference, namely (i) the exercise by Mr Segers of his freedom to establish a company in another Member State and (ii) the exercise by that company of its freedom to set up a secondary establishment in another Member State.

It was not until *Centros* that the issue came before the Court again. In his opinion in *Centros*, Advocate General La Pergola echoed much of the analysis of Advocate General Darmon in *Segers*, repeating, for example, that the situation before the Court in *Centros* was 'the logical consequence of the rights guaranteed under the Treaty [and] consistent with the objective behind the inclusion of the freedom of establishment in the Treaty'.[55] The Court took a similar approach,

---

[51] Para 6 of the opinion in *Segers*. Arts 43 and 48 EC confer on Community nationals 'the right...to set up and manage...companies...under the conditions laid down for its own nationals by the law of the country where such establishment is effected' and prohibit restrictions on the setting up of branches or subsidiaries by companies formed in accordance with the law of a Member State and having their registered office, central administration or principal place of business within the Community.

[52] AG La Pergola in *Centros*, para 20 of his opinion.

[53] The issue was less clear cut in *Segers* than in *Centros* and *Inspire Art*, in which the references to the ECJ were essentially prompted by the host Member State's anti-abuse measures. In *Segers*, in contrast, the dispute arose out of the host Member State's refusal to extend to the company's director social security benefits to which he would have been entitled had the company been incorporated in that Member State. See also n 78 below.

[54] Para 6.

[55] Para 20.

ruling that, although a Member State was entitled to take measures designed to prevent abuse in the classic sense,[56] so that national courts could, case by case, take account of abuse or fraudulent conduct in order, where appropriate, to deny the persons concerned the benefit of the provisions of Community law on which they sought to rely, they must nevertheless assess such conduct in the light of the objectives pursued by those provisions.[57]

The Court went on to note that in the case before it the provisions of national law application of which the parties concerned had sought to avoid were rules governing the formation of companies and not rules concerning the carrying on of certain trades, professions or businesses[58] and that the Treaty provisions on freedom of establishment were intended specifically to enable companies formed in accordance with the law of a Member State and having their registered office, central administration or principal place of business within the Community to pursue activities in other Member States through an agency, branch or subsidiary. That being so, the fact that a national of a Member State who wished to set up a company chose to form it in the Member State whose rules of company law seemed to him least restrictive[59] and to set up branches in other Member States could not, in itself, constitute an abuse of the right of establishment. The right to form a company in accordance with the law of a Member State and to set up branches in other Member States was inherent in the exercise, in a single market, of the freedom of establishment guaranteed by the Treaty.[60] The Court has since reaffirmed the above distillation in its judgment in *Inspire Art*.[61]

In *Cadbury Schweppes* the Court similarly held in effect that the fact that a company is established in another Member State in order to escape the tax regime of its founder's state of residence and benefit from the more favourable tax regime in the other state does not in itself constitute abuse.[62] Again this flows directly from the purpose of Article 43 EC: the fundamental freedom enshrined by that provision (in conjunction with Article 48 EC) is intended to enable a company established in one Member State to set up a subsidiary in any other Member

---

[56] The Court cited, inter alia, *Van Binsbergen*, *Veronica*, *TV10*, *Knoors*, *Bouchoucha*, *Leclerc*, *Lair* and *General Milk Products*.

[57] Paras 24–5.

[58] Harking back to the original formulation in *Van Binsbergen* framed in terms of activities with 'the purpose of avoiding the professional rules of conduct ['*règles professionnelles*'] which would [otherwise] be applicable' (para 13). Similarly *Knoors* was framed in terms of 'training for a trade' ['*formation professionnelle*'] (para 25), *Van de Bijl* in terms of 'rules relating to occupations' ['*règles professionnelles*'] (para 26) and *Bouchoucha* in terms of 'vocational training' ['*formation professionnelle*'] (para 14).

[59] Again echoing AG Darmon in *Segers*, who said that the fact that a national of a Member State may take advantage of the flexibility of United Kingdom company law must be viewed in the context of the objective of the freedom of establishment (para 6 of the opinion).

[60] Paras 26–7.

[61] Paras 137–8. See also para 56 of the judgment in *Commission v Portugal* and para 44 of the judgment in *X and Y*.

[62] *Cadbury Schweppes*, paras 36–8.

State.⁶³ Ultimately tax is a business cost, and the ability for companies to take advantage of lower costs in other Member States is inherent, in a single market, in the exercise of the right of establishment.

However, the Court added an important caveat in *Cadbury Schweppes*: it made it equally clear that Article 43 EC does not confer on companies the right to incorporate subsidiaries in other Member States in order to move taxable profits from one state to another unless the subsidiary is genuinely established in the Member State where it is incorporated. In the absence of genuine establishment, a Member State is justified in imposing restrictions to prevent the circumvention of its tax laws.

By imposing a requirement for genuine establishment of the subsidiary, the Court seems to be diverging significantly from its approach in *Centros* and *Inspire Art*, where it was clear that the company whose right of establishment was allegedly thwarted had no genuine economic activity in the Member State where it was incorporated.

It might be argued that there is no inconsistency because *Cadbury Schweppes* concerned the question whether, where a company exercises its right of secondary establishment by setting up a subsidiary, that subsidiary must engage in genuine economic activity in the Member State where it was incorporated. In *Segers*, *Centros* and *Inspire Art*, in contrast, this was not in issue: the question there was whether, where a company exercises its right of secondary establishment by setting up a branch, that company must engage in genuine economic activity in the Member State where it was incorporated. However, this masks a fundamental confusion in the Court's analysis of the framework in the company law cases.

The real issue underlying the questions referred in *Centros* and *Inspire Art* at least⁶⁴ related not to the right of establishment of the company which was relying on that right to challenge national legislation but to the right of establishment of its founders: did Community law give them the right to incorporate a brass-plate company in another Member State purely for the purpose of avoiding the company law requirements in their state of residence? Or, more accurately, is it right for Community law to be used to strike down national legislation aimed at combating such arrangements?

In other words, the issue in those cases was the same as that in *Cadbury Schweppes*: can it be said that incorporating in another Member State a company which carries on no business at all in that Member State fulfils the objective of the freedom of establishment? Even before the recent tax cases, there was authority (in fact relied on by the Court in *Cadbury Schweppes*⁶⁵) to the effect that the concept of establishment requires some degree of genuine economic integration

---

⁶³ Para 41 of the opinion of AG Léger. See also para 46.
⁶⁴ The situation was arguably different in *Segers*; see n 53 above and n 78 below.
⁶⁵ See para 54.

in the host state.⁶⁶ Interestingly, the analysis at that point in the judgment in *Cadbury Schweppes* starts with the proposition, for which *Centros* is cited as the original authority, that it is necessary, in assessing the conduct of the taxable person, to take particular account of the objective pursued by the freedom of establishment.⁶⁷ In the following paragraph in *Cadbury Schweppes* the Court states that that objective is to allow a national of a Member State to set up a secondary establishment in another Member State to carry on its activities there and thus assist economic and social interpenetration within the Community; to that end, freedom of establishment is intended to allow a Community national to participate, on a stable and continuing basis, in the economic life of a Member State other than his state of origin and to profit therefrom. The Court concludes from those two paragraphs that, having regard to the objective of integration in the host Member State, the concept of establishment involves the actual pursuit of an economic activity through a fixed establishment in that state for an indefinite period, and consequently pre-supposes actual establishment of the company concerned in the host Member State and the pursuit of genuine economic activity there. The requirement of a genuine establishment which the Court imposed in *Cadbury Schweppes* has a direct line of ascent to *Centros*, where the Court reached the opposite conclusion.

The recent case law thus supports the proposition that, if the cross-border incorporation of a company leads to no economic integration at all of that company in the Member State of incorporation, the operation can hardly be said to be an exercise of the right of establishment. This is, moreover, surely true whether the founders of the company are natural persons (exercising their right of primary establishment) or another company (exercising its right of secondary establishment).⁶⁸ In response to the question put by Advocate General La Pergola, it is submitted therefore that it is not begging the question to consider the genuineness of the establishment of the company by its founders before considering

---

⁶⁶ See Case C-221/89 *Factortame* [1991] ECR I-3905 (*Factortame II*), paras 20 and 34, and Case C-246/89 *Commission v United Kingdom* [1991] ECR I-4585. There is a more developed analysis in the opinion of AG Mischo (given for both cases, published with *Factortame*), paras 43–6, drawing on the opinion of AG Darmon in Case 81/87 *Daily Mail* [1988] ECR 5500, where the concept of establishment as genuine integration made its first judicial appearance (see paras 3–8).

⁶⁷ Para 52.

⁶⁸ Art 48 EC provides that companies formed in accordance with the law of a Member State and having their registered office, central administration or principal place of business within the Community are, for the purposes of Chapter 2 EC on the right of establishment, to be treated in the same way as natural persons who are nationals of Member States. The reverse must also be true (as is indeed suggested by the Court's statement that Arts 43 and 48 EC 'guarantee nationals of Member States of the Community who have exercised their freedom of establishment and companies or firms which are assimilated to them the same treatment in the host Member State as that accorded to nationals of that Member State': see para 34 of the judgment in Case C-307/97 *Saint Gobain* [1999] ECR I-6161). And the contrary view would mean, at least since *Cadbury Schweppes*, that, although Mr and Mrs Bryde could, with impunity from national anti-avoidance legislation, incorporate a company in one Member State which carried out its entire business in another Member State, Bryde plc could not.

whether the company has abused its right of establishment by operating wholly in another Member State.[69]

Advocate General La Pergola in *Centros* was also of the view that the practical difficulties of determining whether the company carried on business in the Member State of incorporation militated against regarding this issue as relevant. Stating that he was unconvinced by the argument advanced by the Danish authorities that, as the company established in the United Kingdom did not conduct any business there, it had no real and continuous link with the economic life of that country and that in consequence there was patently a case of abusive and devious exercise of the right of establishment enshrined in the Treaty, the Advocate General expressed the view that the requirement that the parent company effectively carry on business was not only debatable as to substance but also difficult to apply owing to its indeterminate nature: what kind of business must the parent company conduct, for how long and on what scale, for it to be at liberty to exercise the right to set up a secondary establishment?[70]

However, that argument now seems untenable in the light of the approach taken by the Court in *Cadbury Schweppes*. In that case, the Court apparently had no difficulty in requiring that, in order for the taxpayer to be able successfully to challenge the national legislation at issue on the basis that it was contrary to Community law, the incorporation of a given subsidiary 'reflect economic reality' and 'correspond with an actual establishment intended to carry on genuine economic activities', as distinct from 'the case of a "letterbox" or "front" subsidiary'.[71] The Court even gave specific guidance, saying that the finding of an actual establishment intended to carry on genuine economic activities must be based on objective factors which are ascertainable by third parties with regard in particular to the extent to which the company physically exists in terms of premises, staff and equipment.[72]

---

[69] Again, the analysis of AG Darmon in *Daily Mail* is helpful: see in particular para 9, where he expresses the view, essentially, that where the effect of a corporate structure is 'to cause the company to cease to be subject to legislation which would otherwise apply to it' that may be a factor suggesting that what is involved is not genuine establishment, in which case the national court may assess whether there is a suggestion of abuse of a right or circumvention of the law and whether it should decide not to apply Community law.

[70] Para 17.

[71] Paras 65, 66 and 68.

[72] Para 67. It may also be noted that the Community legislature has apparently not regarded evidential problems as insurmountable. Most recently, recital 10 in the preamble to Dir 2006/48/EC of the European Parliament and of the Council of 14 June 2006 relating to the taking up and pursuit of the business of credit institutions (recast) [2006] OJ L177/1 states:

The principles of mutual recognition and home Member State supervision require that Member States' competent authorities should not grant or should withdraw an authorization where factors such as the content of the activities programmes, the geographical distribution of activities or the activities actually carried on indicate clearly that a credit institution has opted for the legal system of one Member State for the purpose of evading the stricter standards in force in another Member State within whose territory it carries on or intends to carry on the greater part of its activities.

Essentially the same statement appears in the preamble to the following directives: Second Council Dir 89/646/EEC of 15 December 1989 on the coordination of laws, regulations and administrative

IV. The Relevance of Motive

If, as is submitted above, on a correct analysis the decisive issue in assessing the lawfulness of a national measure seeking to counter abuse is whether the allegedly abusive conduct fulfils the objective of the Treaty provision invoked to invalidate the national measure, the logical consequence would seem to be that the motive for that conduct is no longer relevant.

That approach seems to be consistent with recent case law on freedom of establishment in the fiscal arena. In *Cadbury Schweppes*, for example, Advocate General Léger echoed the approach of Advocate General La Pergola in *Centros*, summarizing the case law as deciding that 'when the objective pursued by freedom of establishment is fulfilled, the reasons for which the Community national or company concerned wished to exercise that freedom cannot call into question the protection they derive from the Treaty'.[73] Advocate General Léger went on to say that 'it can be inferred [from *Centros* and *Inspire Art*] that as long as there is genuine and actual pursuit of an activity by the controlled subsidiary in the Member State in which it was established, the reasons for which the parent company decided to establish the subsidiary in that host state cannot call into question the rights which that company derives from the Treaty'.[74] The Court in *Cadbury Schweppes* took essentially the same view, stating that the fact that the parent decided to establish subsidiaries 'for the avowed purpose of benefiting from the more favourable tax regime which that establishment enjoys does not in itself constitute abuse'.[75]

If, therefore, there is genuine establishment, the fact that it is tax-driven is irrelevant: a taxpayer is entitled to choose his place of establishment for tax

---

provisions relating to the taking up and pursuit of the business of credit institutions and amending Dir 77/780/EEC [1989] OJ L386/1; Council Dir 93/22/EEC of 10 May 1993 on investment services in the securities field [1993] OJ L141/27; European Parliament and Council Dir 95/26/EC of 29 June 1995 amending Dirs 77/780/EEC and 89/646/EEC in the field of credit institutions, Dirs 73/239/EEC and 92/49/EEC in the field of non-life insurance, Dirs 79/267/EEC and 92/96/EEC in the field of life assurance, Dir 93/22/EEC in the field of investment firms and Dir 85/611/EEC in the field of undertakings for collective investment in transferable securities (UCITS), with a view to reinforcing prudential supervision [1995] OJ L168/7; Dir 2000/12/EC of the European Parliament and of the Council of 20 March 2000 relating to the taking up and pursuit of the business of credit institutions [2000] OJ L126/1; Dir 2001/107/EC of the European Parliament and of the Council of 21 January 2002 amending Council Dir 85/611/EEC on the coordination of laws, regulations and administrative provisions relating to undertakings for collective investment in transferable securities (UCITS) with a view to regulating management companies and simplified prospectuses [2002] OJ L41/20; and Dir 2004/39/EC of the European Parliament and of the Council of 21 April 2004 on markets in financial instruments amending Council Dirs 85/611/EEC and 93/6/EEC and Dir 2000/12/EC of the European Parliament and of the Council and repealing Council Dir 93/22/EEC [2004] OJ L145/1.

[73] Para 43.
[74] Para 49.
[75] Para 38, citing *Centros*, para 18, and *Inspire Art*, para 98.

reasons. If, on the other hand, there is no genuine establishment, then a Member State is free to apply restrictions designed to prevent tax avoidance and abuse, and there is no need for evidence as to whether this was the taxpayer's sole or main motive.

The *Thin Cap* judgment shows, however, that motive is not always altogether irrelevant. It is clear from that judgment that in order to determine whether a Member State is justified in applying thin capitalization restrictions on grounds of preventing tax avoidance or abuse it is necessary to establish whether there are commercial reasons for the arrangements. That is, however, not a subjective exercise. It does not involve an inquiry into the inner motivation of the company's directors. It involves an assessment of whether, considered objectively, there is evidence of genuine commerical reasons for the transaction. Put another way, if there are no valid commercial reasons then a tax avoidance motive can be presumed.[76]

Although the Court in *Cadbury Schweppes* drew on *Centros* as authority for its dicta concerning the relevance of motive, its analysis in the latter case is somewhat less lucid. Where, as in *Centros*, a company is incorporated in one Member State and subsequently carries on its entire business in another Member State with more onerous company law requirements, the question of potentially abusive motive will arise at an earlier stage in the operation: is it relevant that the founders of the company intended to avoid those requirements by operating within that structure?

That question did not arise as such in *Segers*: an English company had been chosen because it was quicker to form than the Netherlands equivalent and because Mr Segers thought that the designation 'Ltd' was more attractive than 'BV'[77] and no argument was raised as to intent to avoid any more onerous provisions of Netherlands company law.[78] It arose in stark form in *Centros*, however: the founders of the company had openly declared before the national court that 'It's easier to find £100 than DKK 200,000'.[79]

---

[76] This echoes the language which the Court has used in its judgments on abuse of rights in the field of secondary legislation. See e.g. *Halifax*, where it summarized its earlier case law in the area of agriculture thus: 'The application of Community legislation cannot be extended to cover abusive practices by economic operators, that is to say transactions carried out not in the context of normal commercial operations' (para 69).

[77] See para 1 of the opinion of AG Darmon.

[78] AG Darmon states that the Netherlands authority had acknowledged at the hearing that its refusal was not based on any attempt at fraud on the part of Mr Segers. It was also reportedly 'admitted by [the relevant Netherlands authority] in the course of the national proceedings that no…abuse [of foreign company law for purely "Dutch" activities] or fraud had been established or could be alleged in the specific case', IGF Cath, 'Freedom of establishment of companies: a new step towards completion of the internal market' (1993) 13 YEL 247, 248, written by Mr Segers' lawyer. AG La Pergola in *Centros* nonetheless drew support for his analysis from *Segers*.

[79] E Werlauff, 'Using a foreign company for domestic activities' (1999) European Business Law Review 306, 309. The authorized capital of Centros Ltd (none of which was paid up) was £100; the minimum paid-up capital required of a Danish private limited company was DKK 200,000 (see

Advocate General La Pergola gave a robust response: so long as the right of establishment, exercised by setting up the company in accordance with the law of the Member State of incorporation, was exercised in accordance with the formal requirements of the Treaty, 'the motives, calculations and particular personal interests underlying the choice do not come into consideration and are consequently not open to judgment'.[80] The Court, while noting that the fact that the founders had formed the company in the United Kingdom 'for the purpose of avoiding Danish legislation requiring that a minimum amount of share capital be paid up has not been denied', simply stated that that did not mean that the formation by that company of a branch in Denmark was not covered by freedom of establishment.[81] Essentially the same statement was made in *Inspire Art*.[82]

The motives of the founders of the company are therefore irrelevant to the right of the company to establish a branch in another Member State. The Court did not consider the logically prior question whether those motives might be relevant to the right of the founders to incorporate a company solely for the purpose of circumventing the company law rules of the Member State in which the company was intended to do business. It is submitted that, on the basis of the more recent tax cases, that question also calls for a negative answer. That does not, however, legitimate the operation. Where the company carries on no genuine economic activity in its Member State of incorporation, the objective of the Treaty right of establishment cannot be said to have been attained and there is scope in principle for the application of national anti-abuse measures. The fact that the company carries on no genuine economic activity in its Member State of incorporation may be ascertained without inquiry into motives.

It will be recalled that in the areas of agriculture and VAT the Court made it clear in *Emsland-Stärke* and *Halifax* that abuse presupposes, in addition to an objective element, an intention on the part of the individual to benefit from an advantage by artificially creating the conditions for obtaining it. In *Halifax*, Advocate General Poiares Maduro expressed the view, similar to that proposed above, that the necessary finding of artificiality should be based on an assessment not of the subjective intentions of those claiming the Community right but of

---

paras 3 and 7 of the judgment of the ECJ). Interestingly, Latty, a US commentator writing in the 1950s, reported that:

England apparently was the Delaware of the second half of the nineteenth century for French enterprises seeking to incorporate but to avoid the rigorous French law. In one litigated case, it appears that an attempt was even made to anglicize the Moulin Rouge ... Promoters ... liked the Anglo-Saxon idea of 'authorized' capital, whereby with little outlay they could represent that their authorized capital was millions of francs – which, translated into French, apparently gave the empty shell the aura of a great enterprise.

Although a minimum capital requirement (of £50) for limited liability companies had been enacted in 1855, it was repealed in 1856, and has never been re-introduced for private companies. (E R Latty, 'Pseudo-foreign corporations' (1955) 65 Yale Law Journal 137, n 130.)

[80] Para 20.
[81] Para 18.
[82] Para 98.

a set of objective circumstances verified in each case. Although those objective circumstances will reveal that the person engaged in the activity probably had the intention of abusing Community law, it is not that intention that is decisive for the assessment of abuse: rather, it is the activity itself, objectively considered. The intentions of the parties improperly to obtain an advantage from Community law are merely inferable from the artificial character of the situation to be assessed in the light of a set of objective circumstances.[83]

V. Proportionality and Presumptions

In *Centros*, the Court conceded that the fact that a Member State could not refuse to register a branch of a company incorporated in another Member State did not preclude that first state from adopting measures for preventing or penalizing fraud. Since, however, any such measure would be liable to restrict the freedom of establishment, it must be justified by imperative requirements in the general interest and be proportionate.[84] The Court found that the national legislation at issue did not meet those requirements, limiting itself to the assertion that, in any event, combating fraud could not justify a practice of refusing to register a branch of a company which had its registered office in another Member State.

Although the Court was laconic on this point, it may perhaps be assumed that what it found particularly objectionable was the practice of *automatically* refusing to register a branch in circumstances such as those at issue, rather than the practice of refusing to register a branch *in a given case* where there was evidence of fraud or abuse: the Court had already stated earlier in its judgment that national courts could, *case by case*, take account of abuse or fraudulent conduct.[85] It may be noted that Advocate General Tesauro had made precisely that point in the context of the freedom to provide services in *Commission v Belgium*,[86] stating that *Van Binsbergen* authorized a Member State 'to adopt specific measures in an individual case of abuse and certainly not to exclude an entire category of operators from its market'. The Court echoed the point, noting that for a Member State to prohibit altogether the provision of certain services by operators established in other Member States would be tantamount to abolishing the freedom to provide services.[87] In the context of the free movement of workers the Court has taken a similar approach.[88] Once the analysis has shifted to the level of justification, it is in any event obvious that a presumption that a given situation is abusive solely by virtue of a cross-border element is liable to fall foul of the principle of proportionality.

[83] Paras 70–1; see also para 117 of the opinion of AG Léger in *Cadbury Schweppes*.
[84] Paras 38 and 34.
[85] Para 25. See to similar effect the opinion of AG Darmon in *Segers*, para 6.
[86] Case C-211/91 [1992] ECR I-6757, para 4 of the opinion.
[87] Para 12.
[88] For recent examples, see Case C-464/02 *Commission v Denmark* [2005] ECR I-7929 and Case C-151/04 *Nadin and Nadin-Lux* [2005] ECR I-11203.

In the tax field the Court, while also reluctant to allow Member States to justify restrictions on the freedom of establishment by reference to presumed abuse, has developed a more nuanced analysis. In *ICI* the Court, consistent with the approach described above, noted that the national legislation at issue (by which a form of group tax relief was not available where a majority of a company's subsidiaries were established in another Member State) did not have the specific purpose of preventing wholly artificial arrangements, set up to circumvent national tax legislation, from attracting tax benefits, but applied generally to all situations in which the majority of a group's subsidiaries were established, for whatever reason, in another Member State. The Court pointed out that the establishment of a company in another Member State did not, of itself, necessarily entail tax avoidance, since that company would in any event be subject to the tax legislation of the state of establishment.[89] Thus the existence of a general presumption meant by definition that the net cast by the legislation was too wide: the catch would not necessarily be limited to wholly artificial arrangements set up to circumvent tax legislation.

The Court has subsequently refined that analysis in *Cadbury Schweppes* and *Thin Cap*. In those cases, it essentially accepted that a presumption of abuse or tax avoidance could be justified provided that the presumption itself incorporated the notion of artificiality.[90] Thus a presumption that a company was avoiding tax merely by setting up a subsidiary in a lower-tax jurisdiction would not be proportionate since it might catch structures where there were genuine commercial reasons for the establishment. A presumption that a company was avoiding tax by incorporating a subsidiary in a lower-tax jurisdiction *where it pursued no genuine economic activity* would, in contrast, be proportionate.[91]

It is difficult to see why an analogous analysis could not be applied to cases such as *Centros* and *Inspire Art*. In those cases, the national practice or legislation which was impugned consisted in refusing to register a branch of a company incorporated in another Member State where it carried on no business (*Centros*) or in requiring compliance with certain domestic company law provisions by a company incorporated in another Member State which carried on its activities entirely or almost entirely in the host Member State and which did not have any real connection with the Member State of incorporation (*Inspire Art*). Thus in

---

[89] Para 26.
[90] This approach was anticipated by the legislature: Art 11(1)(a) of Council Dir 90/434/EEC of 23 July 1990 on the common system of taxation applicable to mergers, divisions, transfers of assets and exchanges of shares concerning companies of different Member States [1990] OJ L225/1, which permits Member States to refuse to apply or withdraw the benefit of the tax regime instituted by the directive where it appears that a given operation has as its principal objective or as one of its principal objectives tax evasion or tax avoidance, provides that the fact that the operation 'is not carried out for valid commercial reasons such as the restructuring or rationalization of the activities of the companies participating in the operation may constitute a presumption that the operation has tax evasion or tax avoidance as its principal objective or as one of its principal objectives'.
[91] The taxpayer must in addition be given an opportunity to rebut the presumption where appropriate: see *Cadbury Schweppes*, para 70 of the judgment and paras 143–4 of the opinion of AG Léger.

each case the measure did not presume that any company incorporated in another Member State and seeking to do business in the host Member State was thereby abusing the freedom of establishment: it targeted only companies incorporated in another Member State *where they pursued no genuine economic activity*, to adopt the language of *Cadbury Schweppes*. It is not obvious why such a response to the phenomenon of 'formally foreign companies'[92] used to avoid the application of national company law should not be regarded as proportionate in the same way as the analogous response of Member States to the phenomenon of 'controlled foreign companies'[93] used to avoid the application of national tax law.

VI. Conclusion

The recurrent question in the cases considered above is whether a Member State is entitled to restrict corporate establishment in order to prevent avoidance of company law or tax rules. Ultimately, in terms of result, it probably matters little whether a party is denied the opportunity to challenge a national measure because the Court considers that, by abusing his freedom of establishment, he has put himself beyond the pale of Community law rights or because a Member State is allowed to plead that a national measure restricting the exercise of the Treaty freedom is justified on the basis of abuse (in one guise or other). Either approach requires an examination of the objective of the Treaty freedom concerned and a rigorous analysis of the rights at stake.

The recent tax cases have given the Court the opportunity to clarify the purpose and scope of Article 43 EC in that respect. In short, it is within the aim of the Treaty to allow a company established in one Member State to effect a genuine establishment in another Member State and as a consequence to benefit from a more favourable tax regime. In contrast it is not within the aim of the Treaty to allow a taxpayer to obtain tax advantages by incorporating a company in another Member State without genuine establishment and integration into the economy of that State. Arguably a more rigorous analysis of the rights at stake in the company law cases would have led to a similar distinction being made in those cases. The Court could thus have built on the foundations originally laid by Advocate General Darmon in *Daily Mail*, and subsequently developed by Advocate General Mischo and by the Court in *Factortame* and *Commission v United Kingdom*, and developed the principle that the right of a company to set up a secondary establishment in another Member State presupposed (as is suggested by the very concept of 'secondary') a genuine establishment, in the sense

---

[92] The term used by the Netherlands legislature at issue in *Inspire Art* (the Wet op de Formeel Buitenlandse Vennootschappen of 17 December 1997).
[93] The term used by the national legislation at issue in *Cadbury Schweppes* to describe foreign subsidiaries of a UK parent incorporated in a lower-tax jurisdiction.

of some degree of economic integration, by that company in the Member State of incorporation. Such an approach would serve to distinguish cases where an already established company wishes to exercise its Treaty right to set up a cross-border secondary establishment from those where nationals of a Member State use a brass-plate company incorporated in another Member State to carry on business in their Member State, thus conferring on them the benefits of limited liability but allowing them to elude the obligations which that Member State regards as an apposite counterpart for the enjoyment of those benefits. It is difficult to understand how the second situation can be regarded as promoting the single market. It is submitted that in the latter cases the Court has fallen on the wrong side of 'the dividing line between misuse of EC law and use of EC law for a purpose which in actual fact was not contemplated by the Community legislature though rendered possible by it'.[94]

On the question of analysis it is perhaps more satisfactory that situations involving abuse of the Treaty freedoms should be examined using standard principles of intepretation. In cases like *Emsland-Stärke* and *Halifax* the Court, if it wished to defeat artificial planning, had no choice but to depart from standard methods of intepretation. In *Emsland-Stärke* in particular the company's situation seemed to fall within the scope of the provisions of Community secondary law on any normal interpretation, and yet it had somehow contrived to defeat the purpose of the provisions in a manner that was so blatant and damaging for the Community regime that the Court felt constrained to prevent it from benefiting from its ingenuity. Departing from standard interpretation in this way is, however, inherently unsatisfactory and should be seen to be highly exceptional. The shift towards dealing with abuse at the level of justification is therefore welcome and in addition has the advantage of allowing – and indeed requiring – a simultaneous evaluation of proportionality. The reference in *Emsland-Stärke* to a subjective component of abuse is also dangerous, and Advocate General Poiares Maduro was rightly at pains to qualify it in *Halifax*. In the present context it is not necessary for a national court to make any finding as to the intention of the individual or company to circumvent domestic company law or tax rules. The national court's inquiry should limit itself to determining whether there was genuine establishment and integration into the local economy and/or whether there were valid commercial reasons for the arrangements.

---

[94] Advocate General Geelhoed in *Akrich*, para 178 of the opinion.

13

Recurring Cycles in the Internal Market: Some Reflections on the Free Movement of Services

Andrea Biondi

I. Introduction

It is always tempting to use history, or at least historical metaphors, to explain developments in any kind of human affairs. So it is with the law. Most fittingly for the European Union legal system, for which its youth makes it easy and its chaotic developments make it necessary, characterization in terms of ages, periods and stages is often deployed. One of the most *célèbres* is the 'generations' allegory used by Professor Weiler to describe the developments in the law of the free movement of products as 'the heart of the Community'. In his *The Constitution of the Common Market Place*,[1] Weiler focuses on one of the principal actors in the process of European integration, the European Court of Justice, and proposes to divide the Court of Justice's case law into five generations: the foundational period, the free market heroic days of the *Dassonville* prohibition on any unjustified obstacles whether protectionist or not;[2] a consolidation period, which solved the questions opened by such a broad approach by insisting on possible derogations (*Cassis de Dijon* et al[3]); a third, entirely legislative, generation – the White Paper Commission and the 1992 programme days;[4] followed by a fourth, self-restraint period – the 'end-game' epitomized by the *Keck* judgment;[5] and finally, a fifth generation, encapsulating a personal reconstruction for the future.

Without wishing to be the depositary of a Weilerian legacy, it is intriguing to use his five generations as a guide for a short journey through the freedom

---

[1] J Weiler, 'The constitution of the common market place' in P Craig and G De Burca (eds), *The Evolution of EU Law* (1999), 349.
[2] C-8/74 *Dassonville* [1974] ECR 837.
[3] C-120/78 *Rewe-Zentrale AG v Bundesmonopolverwaltung fur Branntwein* [1979] ECR 649.
[4] European Commission White Paper on Completing the Internal Market, COM (85) 310 final.
[5] Joined Cases C-267 and C-268/91 *Keck and Mithouard* [1993] ECR I-6097.

to provide and receive an economic service, another and slightly newer heart of Community law.

The importance of this area is self-evident. The reader will be spared the usual Lisbon rhetoric about the expansion of the services sector and its growing expansion in terms of market operators, consumers, providers and recipients' activities. Suffice to say that according to a study of the European Commission, services constitute the engine of economic growth and account for 70 per cent of GDP and employment in most Member States.[6] Not knowing how such data could have been calculated, another easy-to-check and useful statistic concerns instead the numbers of cases decided by the European Court of Justice. According to Hatzopoulos, another author inclined to historical reconstructions,[7] the ECJ has gone from deciding 40 cases on Article 49 EC in the five-year period between 1995 and 1999 to deciding over 140 cases based on the same article between 2000 and 2005.[8] Such a steep increase in litigation is evidence of how much still has to be achieved in terms of integration of national markets. It is also a sign of the continuous expansion of the scope of application of the Treaty provisions. Such an expansionary process, however, is not without its problems as those fast developments may lead to clashes between the requirements of free trade and the preservation of national powers, with the readily-enclosed criticisms of excessive deregulatory effects and competence creep. This contribution will focus mainly on the possible boundaries of Article 49 EC, and attempt to delineate what is 'outside' more than on what is 'inside'.[9] Particular attention will thus be devoted to the 'self-restraint' and 'legislative' generations, where the parallels with the law on free movement of goods seem to provide for some contradictory results. On the surface at least, history seems not to repeat itself. As Giambattista Vico would probably have said, however, although historical

---

[6] Communication from the Commission to the Council and the European Parliament entitled 'An internal market strategy for services': COM (2000) 888; Bull. 12–2000.

[7] Hatzopoulos provided for his generations charts on the developments of Article 49 EC case law. After a first generation essentially tackling discriminatory measures and a second generation which clearly set out the principle that the freedom to provide services requires the abolition of all restrictive or hindering measures, we are currently faced with a third generation of cases whereby the ECJ specifies, on an ad hoc basis, the extent and the limitations of the application of Article 49 EC. This is certainly a correct and convincing reconstruction, but for our purposes it is preferable to use the Weiler generations. V. Hatzopoulos, 'Recent developments of the case law of the ECJ in the field of services 1994–1999 (2000) 37 CMLRev, 43.

[8] V Hatzopoulos and T H Do, 'The case law of the ECJ concerning the free provision of services: 2000–2005' (2006) 43 CMLRev, 923.

[9] Certain important issues are overlooked here. Other possible outer limits such as the 'purely internal rule' should have been included. As a formal defence, editorial strictness can be mentioned. In terms of a substantial defence, these areas do not present particular difficulties. It cannot be denied that one way or another, either by relying on the so-called *Guimont/Anomar* case law – C-448/98 *Guimont* [2000] ECR I-10663 and C-6/01 *Anomar and Others* [2003] ECR I-8621 – or by simply ignoring the problem altogether, the purely internal situation is something of mere archaeological interest. See for recent examples Case C-60/00 *Carpenter* [2002] ECR I-6279 and Joined Cases C-94/04 and C-202/04 *Cipolla and Others* [2006] ECR I-11421. See further C-293/02 *Jersey Potato* [2005] ECR I-9543 noted by A Tryfonidou (2006) 43 CMLRev 1727.

recurring cycles endlessly replicate themselves, their evolutions need not be a perfect match.[10]

II. Foundation and Consolidation

The foundation and consolidation eras in the free movement of goods and the free movement of services share common features and evolutions, although not the same time frame, as it took much longer for the case law on services to develop fully. The beginning of the journey is, however, the same – 1974 – a date which will always be remembered as the year of the *Dassonville* judgment. The other 'big' case of that year was the *Van Binsbergen* case in which the Court held a Dutch law requiring all lawyers to be resident in the Netherlands to be incompatible with EC law free movement principles. Mr Van Binsbergen, a Dutch national who was resident in Belgium, was prevented from providing his professional services in the country of his birth. The Court held that Article 59 EEC (now Article 49 EC) not only prohibits any restrictions imposed on the basis of nationality or the habitual residence of the service provider, but also *'all requirements which may prevent or otherwise obstruct his/her activities'*.[11] The essential issue in the case was clearly one of discrimination – a protectionist measure aimed at sheltering the Dutch legal profession from 'outside' disturbances. The Court, in stating that a residence requirement is very likely to favour national operators against out-of-staters, did not, however, miss the opportunity to add that there might have been other requirements that could affect the free flow of services, and would therefore also be prohibited. This reconstruction might be a bit too empathic; nonetheless, the reading of Article 49 given by the Court is certainly an extensive one, as this provision provided, and still provides, that 'the person providing a service may, in order to do so, temporarily pursue his activity in the state where the service is provided, *under the same conditions as are imposed by that state on its own nationals'*.[12] Although less evidently than in *Dassonville*, the seeds for an approach based on the effects on trade in services, rather than one based merely on protectionist intent, had been planted. The full blossoming of the principle of unfettered access to the services market can be found, however, in the opinion of Advocate General Jacobs in the *Säger* case of 21st February 1991.[13] The issue was whether Article 49 EC prevented German law from requiring lawyers and patent agents, who wanted to provide certain services for monitoring patents and advising the

---

[10] T G Bergin and M H Fisch, *The New Science of Giambattista Vico*, revised translations of the third edition of 1744, Itacha, (1948), 448.
[11] Case 33/74 *Van Binsbergen* [1974] ECR 1299, para 10.
[12] After all, just a few months before, in a nearly identical case, the Court limited itself to holding that criteria, such as the place of origin or residence, are equivalent to discrimination on the grounds of nationality. Case C-152/73 *Sotgiu v Deutsche Bundespost* [1974] ECR 153, para 11.
[13] Case C-76/90 *Säger* [1991] ECR I-4221. See also Case 279/80 *Webb* [1981] ECR 3305.

proprietors of the patents when renewal fees were due, to have an established office in Germany. Such a requirement was applicable to national agents as well as to agents from other Member States. The parties had variably tried to demonstrate the presence of an element of discrimination, either overt or covert, or, as the German government argued, that it was impossible to extend Articles 49 and 50 EC to indistinctly applicable measures. In what have since become famous passages, AG Jacobs concentrated first on the nature of the provision of services, by definition a flexible one, which covers 'a *vast spectrum of different types of activity*', thus making it difficult to accept the assumption that there should be a general rule that a measure lies wholly outside the scope of Article 49 simply because it does not in any way discriminate between domestic undertakings and those established in other Member States. As for the claim that indistinctly applicable measures did not fall within the scope of Article 49, AG Jacobs opined that:

> If such a view were accepted, it would mean that restrictions on the freedom to provide services would have to be tolerated, even if they lacked any objective justification, on condition that they did not lead to discrimination against foreign undertakings... The principle should, I think, be that if an undertaking complies with the legislation of the Member State in which it is established it may provide services to clients in another Member State, even though the provision of such services would not normally be lawful under the laws of the second Member State. Restrictions imposed by those laws can only be applied against the foreign undertaking if they are justified by some requirement that is compatible with the aims of the Community.[14]

The Court fully endorsed this view and rapidly developed a consistent body of case law, which centred on the relevance of a restrictive effect in the market as a criterion for determining the scope of application of the Treaty provisions. In well known cases such as *Alpine Investments* or *De Agostini*, for instance, the Court found that national provisions restricting advertising had to be considered as depriving their commercial operators of their most effective weapon for accessing other Member States' markets, independently of the identification of specific recipients of the service in question.[15] The core of the Court's approach is thus that Article 49 EC prohibits '*any restriction, even if it applies to national providers of services and to those of other Member States alike, which is liable to prohibit, impede or render less advantageous the activities of a provider of services established in another Member State where he lawfully provides similar services*'.[16]

Although the debate on the precise nature of the test applied by the Court still continues, regardless of the name given to it – direct; formal; substantive[17] – the fact of the matter is that the access to market principle has been effectively deployed

---

[14] *Säger*, para 27.
[15] Case C-384/93 *Alpine Investments* [1995] ECR I-1141 and C-34, 35 and 36/95 *KO v De Agostini* [1997] ECR I-3843.
[16] Case C-58/98 *Corsten* [2000] ECR I-7919, para 3323.
[17] See for example E Spaventa, *The Free Movement of Persons in the EU: Barriers to Movement and their Constitutional Context* (2007), ch 4.

as a very powerful pro-integrationist tool. This integration is not, however, without its limits.

To go back in time once again, besides being foundational, in *Van Binsbergen*, the Court provided for some consolidation – read 'moderation'. The central passage of the judgment, anticipating what *Cassis de Dijon* would further develop, immediately acknowledges that a wide and thorough prohibition on restrictions should correspond to an equally wide and extensive recognition of its limits. The Court emphasized that the obstacles on the exercise of the profession of lawyers could be justified by an argument based on the *general good* and a need to guarantee the organization, qualifications, and professional ethics of that profession. Therefore – as well as for the consolidation era in free movement of goods – the excessive application of the free movement of services has been tempered by reliance on possible justifications and derogations. As such, Article 49 EC is counterbalanced by Article 46 EC and by a case law-made list of imperative requirements to be used by Member States to justify restrictive measures. The Court has generally responded positively to the pleas of national governments. Thus, the ECJ has been very flexible on the supposedly strict interpretation of the Treaty derogations – for instance, inserting into the notion of public health the need to preserve some money in the state coffers to fund social security services,[18] or by reading public policy as possible grounds to protect human dignity.[19] The list of imperative requirements has been kept open as well. The reputation of financial markets, child protection and the preservation of the urban environment have all been accepted by the Court as 'lawful' state policies.[20] The balancing approach adopted by the Court worked quite well; still, no matter how wide the list of justifications might be, Member States are required to fully discharge the burden of proof and show that their actions are proportionate. Although variable in its intensity, the national measure is therefore always subject to some form of scrutiny, either in Luxembourg or before the national court. A different question is, instead, whether it should be accepted that the *acquis communitaire* on Article 49 EC should be taken to mean that any regulation that imposes or implies any kind of restriction should fall within the scope of the Treaty, or whether instead, there are any areas of national regulation that could be excluded *in limine* from the application of Article 49 EC, thereby making the same provision inapplicable. The now-famous question, formulated by AG Tesauro as far as the free circulation of goods was concerned, whether Article 28 EC was to be considered as a provision intended to liberalize intra-Community trade or whether it was intended more generally to encourage the unhindered pursuit of commerce in individual Member States,[21] is equally applicable as regards Article 49 EC. The Court, so

---

[18] Case C-158/96 *Kohll* [1998] ECR I-1931 and Case C-120/95 *Decker* [1998] ECR I-1831.
[19] Case C-36/02 *Omega* [2004] ECR I-9609.
[20] Respectively *Alpine Investments* (n 15 above), *De Agostini* (n 15 above) and Case C-17/00 *De Coster* [2001] ECR I-9445.
[21] Case-292/92 *Hunermund* [1994] ECR I-6787.

far, has been rather reluctant to draw any boundaries, instead always preferring a two-step approach, whereby everything starts off as a breach, but can then be justified. New eras may, however, be on the horizon.

III. Retreat: the Strange Case of the Services Directive

When looking at the free movement of goods generations, after the epic foundation and the skilful consolidation periods came the political responsibility generation. The judgments of the ECJ had never existed in a constitutional vacuum for they served the supreme Treaty objective of approximation and harmonization of national trade standards. *Dassonville* and *Cassis de Dijon* and many other Court judgments, as noted by Weiler, are evidence of market failure, and/or of the State's inability to take into account the effect of its regulation on free movement.[22] The final settlement has to be achieved through a full economic and political process carried out by the Community legislator. The Delors Commission's vivacious list of initiatives within the 1992 programme represented political acceptance of the responsibility of ensuring the full effectiveness of such a process. In parallel with Article 28 EC developments, the ECJ case law in the areas of services is equally seen as a call for a harmonized settlement and an assumption of political responsibility. Already in *Van Binsbergen* such an incitement was indeed very vocal, as the Court, by holding Article 49 EC to be directly applicable, implicitly reminded the Council and the Commission of their obligation to implement the necessary legislation in the area.[23] The same can be said with reference to more recent case law. For instance, in a now rather well established line of case law, the Court held that national systems of prior authorization imposed on patients wishing to receive medical treatment in another Member State were incompatible with the free movement of services.[24] These judgments have been widely discussed and debated, especially with regard to the relationship between trade integration and welfare protection.[25] Whatever one thinks of the Court's approach, it must be admitted that there are at least two clear messages being sent from Luxembourg: first, that the existing legislation in the area, notably Regulation 1408/71,[26] had to be considered as out of date and inappropriate; and second, through a very in-depth assessment of the

---

[22] Weiler (n 1 above), 362.
[23] See for further examples of the Court policy-making relationship in the area of services S O'Leary, 'The free movement of persons and services' in Craig and De Burca (eds) (n 1 above) 376, 380–2.
[24] *Kohll*; *Decker* (n 20 above); Case C-368/98 *Vanbraekel* [2001] ECR I-5363; Case C-157/99 *Smits & Peerbooms* [2001] ECR I-5473; Case C-385/99 *Müller-Fauré* [2003] ECR I-4509; Case C-372/04 *Watts* [2006] ECR I-4325.
[25] See *inter alia* G Davies, 'Welfare as a service' (2002) LIEI, 27.
[26] Council Regulation (EEC) No 1408/71 of 14 June 1971 on the application of social security schemes to employed persons, to self-employed persons and to members of their families

proportionality of the authorization systems, the Court managed to sketch at least a draft directive imposing minimum guarantees for parties wishing to receive treatment abroad.[27] Another good example of a positive use of the free movement of services provisions can be drawn from the very recent and robust case law on government concessions. In a series of decisions starting from the *Coname* case, the Court found that a municipal concession awarded without an invitation to tender amounted to a violation of Article 49 EC in that it prevented an undertaking located in the territory of a Member State other than that of the municipality in question to have access to appropriate information regarding that concession, so that, if that undertaking had so wished, it would have been in a position to express its interest in obtaining that concession.[28] In substance the Court extended the requirement of transparency and information as provided for by the Public Works directives[29] into a non-harmonized area creating therefore the conditions for an extension of those Directives in the area of municipal concessions as well.

The calls of the Court of Justice did not, this time around, produce a 1992 programme but, instead, the Services Directive.[30] The controversies, deceits, political calculations, folkloristic anecdotes and urban myths surrounding the adoption of the final text of the Directive make its objective assessment difficult and an article-by-article assessment is beyond the scope of this contribution.[31] A few observations on the policy model adopted by the Community legislator should, however, be made. The measure – the notorious Bolkenstein draft directive – was born with two main aims: to provide for administrative simplification and the

---

moving within the Community (see the version amended and updated by Council Regulation (EC) No 118/97 of 2 December 1996, OJ 1997 L 28, p 1).

[27] For instance, in the *Peerbooms* case, the Court accepted that such an authorization could be based on the criteria of normality and of necessity of the treatment requested. As for the proportionality of both conditions, the Court spelt out a series of very specific requirements: for instance, as far as treatment of the 'normal' condition was concerned, not only national but also international medical opinion had to be taken into account, while, with regard to 'necessity', the Court stated that authorization should be refused only if the patient could receive the same or equally effective treatment without undue delay from an establishment with which his sickness insurance fund had contractual arrangements. Authorities had to take account of all the circumstances, including the patient's past and present medical records. Only by satisfying these requirements could Member State measures be compatible with EC law. *Peerbooms* (n 24 above).

[28] Case C-231/03 *Coname* [2005] ECR I-7287; Case C-458/03 *Parking Brixen* [2005] ECR I-8612 and Case C-410/04 *ANAV* [2005] ECR I-3303.

[29] Council Directive 92/50/EEC of 18 June 1992 relating to the coordination of procedures for the award of public service contracts or Council Directive 93/38/EEC of 14 June 1993 coordinating the procurement procedures of entities operating in the water, energy, transport and telecommunications sectors OJ 1992 L 209, p 1 as replaced by Directive 2004/18/EC of 31 March 2004 on the coordination of procedures for the award of public works contracts, public supply contracts and public service contracts, OJ 2004 L 134, p 114.

[30] Directive 2006/123/EC of 12 December 2006, OJ L376/36.

[31] See for a masterful and rather entertaining reconstruction G Berardis, 'La direttiva generale in materia di servizi' in L Radicati di Brozolo and L Bestagno (eds), *La Libera Circolazione dei Servizi in Europa* (2007). See also Editorial Comment, 'The services directive proposal: striking a balance between the promotion of the internal market and preserving the European social model?' (2006) 43 CML Rev, 307.

codification of existing ECJ case law, putting the state of origin principle as its general regulatory principle.[32] The final text, based on Articles 47 and 52 EC, declares that the Directive has as its credo the facilitation of the exercise of the freedom of establishment for service providers and the free movement of services, while maintaining a high quality of services. Curiously, such a positive intention is, however, defined in the negative, as there are more than 20 exceptions that can hardly be considered as facilitators. Article 1 requires, in fact, that the Directive would not affect a wide range of activities that extends from very broad economic areas such as state aid, the liberalization of services of general economic interest or monopolies to encompass equally broad non-trade related areas, such as Member States' rules of criminal law, *'labour law, that is any legal or contractual provision concerning employment conditions, working conditions, including health and safety at work and the relationship between employers and workers'*, social security legislation of the Member States, and *'the exercise of fundamental rights as recognized in the Member States and by Community law'* including *'the right to negotiate, conclude and enforce collective agreements and to take industrial action'*. Article 2 reinforces this idea, by providing another list of excluded activities including financial services or transport, and, puzzlingly, gambling, private security services and services provided by notaries. Most notably, healthcare and pharmaceutical services are also excluded while the regulation of reimbursement of medical expenses incurred by a patient in another Member State is postponed to a future Community legal instrument in order to achieve greater legal certainty and clarity of this issue.[33] Finally, the Directive does not apply to the field of taxation. The principle of the country of origin is nowhere to be found in the final text, replaced by some broad formulae such as non-discrimination or proportionality (Article 16).

The very extensive list of excluded activities is problematic, first with regard to identifying which activities have been inserted into the list, and second, as regards the constitutional significance of adopting such a model. As for the specific activities, for most of them, such as state aid, there was absolutely no need to mention them, as they are clearly covered by other Treaty provisions and/or EC secondary legislation. Moreover, the Court has consistently ruled that Article 49 of the Treaty also applies in regulated fields such as transport.[34] The main concern, however, is the clear political decision to draw a line between what belongs to the state (criminal law, labour law, healthcare and so on) from what belongs to the Community (not much if the Directive is to be taken literally). Sophisticated interpretations on the meaning of expressions such as 'does not affect' will certainly be proposed to moderate the Directive's impact. It is nonetheless maintained that, while the Directive is a clear attempt to formulate a response to the expansion of the law

---

[32] Proposal for a Directive on Services in the Internal market, COM (2004) 2/3 final.
[33] Directive 2006/123 (n 30 above), preamble, 23.
[34] See for instance Case C-381/93, *Commission v France* [1994] ECR I-5145.

on free movement of services and to tackle the questions of its limits, the model adopted is a retrograde one, based on a mere repatriation of powers to the national legislator – a settlement influenced by a traditional and fearful view of sovereignty. More particularly, from the perspective of the achievement of an internal market, there is an undoubted tension between the competence model adopted by the Directive and the case law of the Court. To go back to the foundational generation, one of the postulates of the *Dassonville* and *Van Binsbergen/Säger* approach is that the ascertainment of a 'restriction' to the free flow of trade is entirely independent from the area of state regulatory competence upon which the measure in question has been adopted. Thus, it is now a well-established principle that the existence of a certain competence is one thing, and how such a competence is exercised, no matter if a certain case deals with national criminal law, labour law or taxation, is quite another. To take criminal law, for instance, in cases such as *Cowan* or *Calfa* the Court held that although in principle criminal legislation is a matter for which the Member States are responsible, '*Community law sets certain limits to their power, and such legislation may not restrict the fundamental freedoms guaranteed by Community law*'.[35] Certainly those two cases are examples of the progressive identification of free movement and individual rights but the same principle has also been applied in a purely economic context, such as, for instance, the imposition of criminal sanctions on internet betting.[36] The Court *acquis* has to be explained in terms of supremacy and of the need to ensure the full effectiveness of the obligations imposed by the Treaty on the Member States. Arguably, a 'hard list' of included and excluded activities such as the one adopted by the Services Directive does not do justice of the complexities of the European constitutional order and might endanger the achievement of the core objectives of the Treaty. One could, of course, respond therefore that, in reality, there will not be any real problems as for clear-cut constitutional reasons, Article 49 EC, and the interpretation given to it by the Court, will always prevail over the provisions of a Directive. Still, this policy decision does not bode well for the future, as it seems a rather clumsy attempt to reintroduce a misguided idea of protectionism. Perhaps it is better to stick with history once again.[37]

IV. Repositioning: Judicial Retuning of Article 49 EC

It has now become a sort of cliché to recite that one of the main distinctions between the different economic freedoms is that the Court has only accepted to

---

[35] Case 186/87 *Cowan v Trésor Public* [1989] ECR 195, para 15 and Case C-348/96 *Calfa* [1999] ECR I-11, para 17.
[36] Case C-243/01 *Gambelli and Others* [2003] ECR I-13031 and Joined Cases C-338/04, C-359/04 and C-360/04 *Placanica* [2007] ECR I-1891.
[37] The prophecy of this author is that despite its intention, and perhaps inadvertently the directive will end up producing many more effects than envisaged.

acknowledge an outer limit to its case law with regard to the free movement of goods. In the *Keck* judgment, the ECJ held that national provisions restricting or prohibiting certain selling arrangements are not liable to hinder intra-Community trade, so long as they apply to all relevant traders operating within the national territory and so long as they affect in the same manner, in law and in fact, the marketing of domestic products and of those from other Member States.[38] Not only is this supposed to be a difference between the different freedoms but it is generally accepted that the *Keck and Mithouard* principle should not actually be transposed to the other freedoms including that of providing and receiving services.[39] AG Stix Hackl in the *Omega* case argued that a *Keck* transplant:

is unpersuasive because, where there are sufficient international implications, a rule on arrangements for the provision of any service – irrespective of location – must constitute a restriction of relevance to Community law simply because of the incorporeal nature of services, without any distinction at all being permissible in this respect between rules relating to arrangements for the provision of services and rules that relate directly to the services themselves.[40]

These kinds of arguments are misplaced. For many years the debate on *Keck* has been excessively focused on the notion of selling arrangements and mostly on that of discrimination, while the thrust of the judgment is instead a judicial attempt to decide what kind of regulatory national competence should fall outside the scope of European law. The Court seeks to accomplish this by looking at the specific context in which those rules operated. The question of what an obstacle to trade is would in fact depend on the economic and legal context in which the national measure was concluded, its object, its effects, and whether it affects intra-Community trade, taking into account the economic context in which the national rule operates, the products or services covered by the measure, the structure of the market concerned and the actual conditions in which it functions.[41] The case law on advertising is probably the best example to explain such an approach,[42] with the opinion of AG Jacobs in the *Leclerc-Siplec* case being a useful term of reference.[43] This is probably the most quoted opinion in the 50 years that Advocates General have existed, but invariably all the comments concentrate on the criticisms of *Keck*, or on whether the opinion is insisting on the concept that only rules which substantially hinder access to another Member State's

---

[38] *Keck* (n 5 above).
[39] See *inter alia* JL Da Cruz Vilaça, 'On the application of *Keck* in the field of free provision of services', 25 and M Poiares Maduro, 'Harmony and dissonance in free movement', 41 in M Andenas and P Roth, *Services and Free Movement in EU Law* (2002).
[40] *Omega* (n 21 above) para 36.
[41] Paraphrased from competition law cases such as Case 22/71 *Béguelin Import* [1971] ECR 949, para 13 and Case C-399/93 *Oude Littikhuis and Others* [1995] ECR I-4515, para 10.
[42] Although the Court distinguishes between restrictions on free movement of goods and restrictions on services the outcome is practically identical.
[43] Case C-412/93 *Leclerc-Siplec v TFI Publicité and M6 Publicité* [1995] ECR I-179.

market should be caught by the free movement provisions, and thereby envisages the introduction of a *de minimis* test, to which the usual response is that it is impossible to introduce any numerical threshold into internal market law. While these might all be very valid comments, if the opinion is read in its entirety, it is clear that its approach is purely 'qualitative'.[44] It is a thorough and sophisticated analysis of the function of advertising in an integrated market as a tool to promote trade. The opinion goes as far as to sketch the content of a freedom to advertise by suggesting, for instance, that a total ban on advertising would never be considered as neutral from the perspective of free movement, whilst a partial ban would need to be carefully analysed in the context of the specific economic sector (for example, distribution – as in the instant case) and of the medium chosen (TV or other more traditional advertising methods). The Court's case law clearly embodies the Advocate General's opinion. In *Alpine Investments*[45] – a judgment usually relied upon to dismiss a possible application of *Keck* to services – particular emphasis is placed by the Court on the fact that the commercial operators had been deprived of a particular, efficient technique to penetrate Member State markets. Cases such as *De Agostini*, and more emphatically *Gourmet* and *Doc Morris*, are also illustrations of a refined contextual analysis whose starting point is the ascertainment of the nature of the market in question. In *Gourmet* in particular, the Court confirmed that a total ban can never be considered neutral. The Court did accept the argument presented by a Swedish company against the Swedish legislation in that a national measure, which prohibited alcohol advertising, deprived it of the possibility of offering advertising spaces to potential clients abroad.[46] Thus, in this case, the Court sanctioned not only the potential restrictions to another state market; but also the fact that a total ban had the effect of preventing the development of a domestic market. The *Doc Morris* judgment concerned a partial ban – a restriction imposed by Germany on the sale and advertising of medicine on the Internet – and contains another highly-developed analysis of the role of advertising within the specific medium of the Internet as a method of cross-border sales. The terms of reference of the judgment – that is, the effect of the prohibition – are thus dependent on the scale of importance that the Internet has assumed.[47] In short, in all the advertising cases, once it was 'proved' that advertising belongs fully to the remit of an integrated market, the Court was bound to refuse any analogy with *Keck*. Conversely some areas of national regulatory competence might not have the same implications and effects for an integrated market on services and might well fall outside the scope of Article 49 EC. In our opinion, the Court has already embraced the idea of drawing some outer limit to the Treaty provision. Two examples are very significant in this context.

[44] S Weatherill, 'After *Keck*: some thoughts on how to clarify the clarification' (1996) 33 CMLR 885, 906.
[45] *Alpine Investments* (n 15 above).
[46] C-405/98 *KO v Gourmet International Products* [2001] ECR I-1795.
[47] Case C-322/01 *Deutscher Apothekerverband v Doc Morris* [2003] ECR I-14887.

The first is the *Deliège* case, where the question was whether selection rules for sporting events could be regarded as an obstacle to the freedom to provide a service. The Court held that although selection rules inevitably have the effect of limiting the number of participants in a tournament, *'such a limitation is inherent in the conduct of an international high-level sports event, which necessarily involves certain selection rules or criteria being adopted'* and therefore could not constitute a restriction on the freedom to provide services prohibited by Article 49 EC.[48] Such an approach has been recently confirmed in a case dealing with anti-doping rules. The Court established that although they might have the effect of limiting athletes' freedom of action, *'such a limitation is inherent in the organization and proper conduct of competitive sport and its very purpose is to ensure healthy rivalry between athletes'*.[49] The 'inherent restriction' test, lifted from the case law on competition and transplanted in the context of free movement of services, confirms that a national regulation can only be construed as a restriction after having fully examined the legal and economic context within which the measure operates and the aims – most notably in this context, fairness in sport – that it seeks to achieve.[50] The second example comes from cases dealing with indirect taxation on services. In two relatively recent judgments, both dealing with the imposition of municipal taxes on the provision of services, the Court found that Article 49 EC was not applicable. In *Viacom II*, a French company refused to reimburse the payment, made by an advertising agency, of an Italian municipal tax on advertising, which was imposed on all public bills. The French company claimed that such a tax had to be considered as in breach of Article 49 EC. The municipal advertising tax was incurred for advertising by means of bill-posting that was carried out for domestic and foreign customers and by domestic and foreign suppliers. The Court found that the taxes were applied without any distinction between in-state and out-state operators and the amount was rather modest.

Thus *'the levying of such a tax is not on any view liable to prohibit, impede or otherwise make less attractive the provision of advertising services to be carried out in the territory of the municipalities concerned, including the case in which the provision of services is of a cross-border nature on account of the place of establishment of either the provider or the recipient of the services'*.[51]

---

[48] Case C-51/96 and C-191/97 *Christelle Deliège* [2000] ECR I-2549.
[49] Case C-519/04 P *David Meca-Medina* [2006] ECR I-0000. In *Wouters* the ECJ, applying the same test to competition and free movement of services, found that rules on multi-disciplinary practices 'despite the effects restrictive of competition that are inherent in it' were deemed necessary for the proper practice of the legal profession, as organized in the Member State concerned. Case C-309/99 *Wouters* [2002] ECR I-1577.
[50] Case 26/76 *Metro I* [1977] ECR 1875 and Case 250/92 *Gottrup-Klim* [1994] ECR I-5641. See further K Mortelmans, 'Towards convergence in the application of the rules on free movement and on competition' (2001) 38 CMLRev, 613; G Monti, 'Article 81 and Public Policy' (2002), 39 CMLRev, 1057 and P Stuyck, 'Libre circulation et concurrence: les deux piliers du marché commun' in *Mélanges en hommage à Michel Waelbroeck* vol II (1999) 1499.
[51] Case C-134/03 *Viacom Outdoor* [2005] ECR I-1167, para 38.

In *Mobistar* the question was whether Article 49 EC must be interpreted as precluding the introduction, by legislation of a national or local authority, of a tax on mobile and personal communications infrastructures, which were used to carry on activities provided for in licences and authorizations. The Court held: '*By contrast, measures, the only effect of which is to create additional costs in respect of the service in question and which affect in the same way the provision of services between Member States and that within one Member State, do not fall within the scope of Article 49 of the Treaty.*' [52]

Apart from the linguistic similarities (in law and fact), *Viacom II* and *Mobistar* seem to embrace the *Keck* rationale and go some way to improving upon it by avoiding any attempt to categorize those rules, thus avoiding the 'selling arrangement' trap.[53] More importantly, the Court's judgments are based on a full analysis of the legal and economic context and on the relevance of the context – taxation – of the national measures in question. Without having been mentioned, there are echoes of the traditional case law of the Court in the area of indirect taxation imposed on goods where the objective of the Treaty is to ensure neutrality of taxes in relation to imported goods.[54] In that area, the Court has always resisted the temptation not to consider the specific function of indirect taxation as a lawful fiscal policy so long as it does not discriminate against imported products, for instance by refusing to apply Art 28 EC in relation to an obstacle of a fiscal nature.[55] Thus in *Viacom II* and *Mobistar*, the two elements taken into account by the Court are the neutrality of the tax and the absence of any real burden on the free provision of services.

In conclusion, although the case law mentioned is still not notable in numerical terms, the recent repositioning of the Court in the area of services reflects a savvier knowledge of the market place and a more refined attitude to the questions of its limits; there is therefore no obstacle on the free movement either – to use another, often misinterpreted, opinion – when the restrictive effect of a certain national regulation does not, in principle, 'exceed the effects intrinsic to rules of that kind'[56] such as in the *Deliège* case or when in the Court's assessment, state legislation distributes benefits and burdens equally between national and non-national operators such as in the *Mobistar* and *Viacom II* cases. In those situations, there is no need for judicial intervention as there are no market failures to

---

[52] Joined Cases C-544/03 and C-545/03 *Mobistar and Belgacom Mobile* [2005] ECR I-7723, para 31.

[53] See further Hatzopoulos (n 8 above), 960. He interestingly argued that another benefit of a Mobistar test would be to accommodate the very evanescent case law on the 'tenuous and remote effect' never really well-explained by the Court. See cases such as Case C-379/92 *Peralta* [1994] ECR I-3453; Case C-96/94 *Centro Servizi Spediporto* [1995] ECR I-288; Case C-266/96 *Corsica Ferries III* [1998] ECR I-3949.

[54] Case C-47/88 *Commission v Denmark* [1990] ECR I-4509; Case C-375/95 *Commission v Greece* [1997] ECR I-5981; Case C-101/00 *Tulliasiamies and Siilin* [2002] ECR I-7487.

[55] C-383/01 *De Danske Bilimportører* [2003] ECR I-6065, para 32 and Case C-313/05 *Maciej Brzeziński* [2007] ECR I-0000.

[56] See the opinion of Van Gerven AG in Case 145/88 *Toerfen* [1989] ECR 3851, para 17.

correct, and the national political process can be said to have functioned properly, in that out-of-state interests have been fully represented.

The introduction of a jurisprudential outer limit for Article 49 EC is thus desirable both in constitutional terms, so as to avoid an excessive expansion of EC law, and in terms of efficiency of the market. It may be argued that the different tests used by the Court – 'inherent restrictions', 'in law and fact' – lack sufficient precision and clarity and ultimately fail to provide national courts with specific guidelines for their judgments. A certain degree of flexibility, however, might indeed be attractive. A linking factor in all of these cases is the clear attempt of commercial operators to use EC law to get rid of rules they did not like and that variably affected their business. A general but adaptable principle that would exclude artificial cases could thus be useful to prevent those cases from even reaching Luxembourg.[57]

V. Recurring Cycles

To go back to our historical metaphors, the conclusions should be the following: after an expansionary period, a self-restrained one was bound to follow, both politically and judicially. As is hopefully apparent from the above arguments, the political and judicial self-restraint generations do not merit an equally positive assessment. The differences between the two could appear more superficial than substantial: after all, both the Services Directive model and the judicial repositioning struggle to achieve the same result – that is, a clearer delimitation of the scope of application of the free movement of services, and both dealt with the same constitutional question of the boundaries of European Union competences. The two paths are, however, markedly different. The model, upon which the Directive is based, is an ex-ante assessment, totally removed from a contemporary social and economic reality and inspired by a very divisive idea of Europe. The failed attempt to introduce a hard competence list during the debate on the future Constitutional Treaty seems to have eventually succeeded. To paraphrase a critique moved against such an attempt, the Services Directive hard list of excluded activities '*set up antagonisms and rigidities that would cause damage worse than the cure, in particular because the imposition of an inflexible division between Union and state competences is likely to harm the EU's capacity to fulfil its mission by denying it an adaptable and efficiently functioning system of governance that*

---

[57] See, for instance, *The Countryside Alliance and Others and the Secretary of State for Environment* [2006] EWHC 817 (Court of Appeal). In this case the English Court of Appeal found that the act which bans fox hunting in England could not be considered as an obstacle to the free movement of goods (horses, rifles) or to services (the right, for instance, to rent a dog pack). The Court extended the ratio of *Keck* and found that the only effect was to render less attractive the market and to remove some factual opportunity to engage in a certain trade.

properly implicates several levels.[58] The battle for the preservation of social values and a balanced welfare system can be much more effectively fought and won by instruments other than a directive on trade. Without advocating a *gouvernement des juges*,[59] the more nuanced approach adopted by the Court is instead much more in line with what is usually termed the Community method. This method is founded on the constitutional principle of attributed powers and operates with the full acknowledgement of the simultaneous necessity of national and supranational regulation and on the need for a fair balancing of conflicting interests, with a call for all the different political and economic actors to be fully involved.[60] As such, the development of the law on the free movement of services is based on a historical method where the recurring cycles effortlessly give way to one another.

[58] S Weatherill, 'Better competence monitoring' (2005) 20 ELRev 23, 32.

[59] See on this point the observations of Professor Edward. He rightly draws attention to the paradox of criticizing the Court for being too active and then later complaining when the legislator does not act in a way that one would wish. D Edward 'Will there be honey still for tea' (2006) 43 CML Rev, 623. Interestingly, the ECJ is soon going to be called upon to decide a very controversial case dealing with the question of whether a collective agreement can be considered as restriction of the free movement of services and establishment. Reference for a preliminary ruling from the Court of Appeal, Case C-438/05 *Viking Line Abp v The International Transport Workers' Federation and the Finnish Seamen's Union*, pending. Although several comments have already appeared it might be wise to wait for the judgment. See, however, B Bercusson, 'The trade union movement and the EU: judgment day' (2007) 13 ELJ 279.

[60] C-376/98 *Germany v Parliament and Council* [2000] ECR I-8419.

14

Continuity and Change in the Law Relating to Services

David Edward[1] and Niamh Nic Shuibhne[2]

I. Introduction

What are 'services' and how should they be regulated? In so far as the Treaty answers these questions at all, the answer is sketchy and not entirely coherent. Until the much-disputed 'Bolkestein Directive',[3] legislative activity was patchy, and the task of bringing coherence to this aspect of the Treaty was left to the Court of Justice. Although the Court's case law on services, stimulated by Francis Jacobs, has been innovative and quite far-reaching, there has been little by way of academic discussion and analysis in comparison with the very extensive work undertaken on goods or persons. Services have been the academic Cinderella of the four freedoms. In that respect at least there has been continuity.

Where there has been change (and the change has been dramatic), it has been in the scope, volume and character of the economic activities with which the Services provisions of the Treaty have to deal. Fast, low-cost travel has transformed the ease of personal movement. More efficient telephones, fax and email, Internet buying and selling, and other technological developments have recast the boundaries of 'movement' more fundamentally still. A 'service' transaction can now come within the scope of the Treaty with minimal (if any) degree of commitment on the part of the service provider outside the home state. Since recipients as well as providers are covered, few of us now escape the personal scope of services and neither we nor the providers necessarily have to move so that we can receive them. In consequence, services sit – sometimes uncomfortably – on the borderline between, on the one hand, the law regulating the freedom to market (particularly the freedom to market 'invisibles') and, on the other, the law

---

[1] Judge of the Court of Justice 1992–2004; honorary Professor of the University of Edinburgh.
[2] Reader in EC Law, Europa Institute, University of Edinburgh.
[3] The original Commission proposal was published as COM (2004) 2 final/3; a second, heavily revised proposal was published in summer 2006 (COM (2006) 160 final), now enacted as Directive 2006/123/EC on services in the internal market, [2006] OJ L376/36.

governing the personal right of free movement of the service provider,[4] or in the case of corporations, of the provider's employees.

During the period spanning Francis Jacobs' time at the Court, immediately following the Cockfield White Paper[5] and the Single European Act, the basic ideas underlying the law of the internal market and the four freedoms came under repeated and intense scrutiny. *Keck and Mithouard*[6] generated impassioned debate about the scope of Treaty rights and the relative importance of discrimination on the one hand and market access on the other. There was significantly less effort to analyse the comparable issues raised by *Grogan*[7] and *Alpine Investments*.[8] Later on, judgments like *Chen*[9] and *Bidar*[10] transplanted the seedling of EU citizenship in *Martínez Sala*[11] in a way that some did not anticipate into the field of freedom of movement, including the freedom to provide services. Francis Jacobs' contribution to all these discussions will remain for the enlightenment of posterity in his lucid and often challenging opinions.

As our contribution to this tribute to a fine jurist and a good friend, we do not attempt to give a comprehensive survey of the law of services as it developed over the period from 1988 to 2006. Rather, we offer a sketch map of the territory of 'services', and its place in the wider map of the internal market. We suggest that this neglected area of free movement law, particularly as regards its future development, deserves greater attention on the part of explorers. Perhaps one of them will be Cinderella's fairy prince.

II. Mapping the Scope of Services

A. The Treaty

The Treaty defines the Four Freedoms as 'freedom of movement for goods, persons, services and capital' (Article 3(1)(c) EC). According to this definition, it is the 'service' as such that should be free to move. However, the structure and wording of the chapter on services (part two, title III, chapter 3) suggest a different, though not entirely consistent, approach.

---

[4] But not necessarily the personal right of the service recipient, as confirmed recently in Case C-290/04 *FKP Scorpio Konzertproduktionen GmbH v Finanzamt Hamburg-Eimsbüttel* [2006] ECR I-9461, discussed further below.
[5] European Commission, *Completing the Internal Market*, COM (85) 310.
[6] Case C-267–268/91 *Criminal Proceedings against Keck and Mithouard* [1993] ECR I-6097.
[7] Case C-159/90 *SPUC v Grogan* [1991] ECR I-4685.
[8] Case C-384/93 *Alpine Investments v Minister van Financiën* [1995] ECR I-1141.
[9] Case C-200/02 *Zhu and Chen v Secretary of State for the Home Department* [2004] ECR I-9925.
[10] Case C-209/03 *Bidar v London Borough of Ealing; Secretary of State for Education and Skills* [2005] ECR I-2119.
[11] Case C-85/96 *Martínez Sala v Freistaat Bayern* [1998] ECR I-2691.

Chapter 3 opens with a prohibition of 'restrictions on the freedom to *provide* services' (Article 49), suggesting that we are concerned with restrictions on the freedom of the provider – a 'person' – rather than on the freedom to move of the 'service' as some sort of abstract entity. This is echoed in Article 50 (first paragraph, second sentence) which illustrates the meaning of 'services' by reference to human 'activities' (industrial, commercial, craft and professional). Similarly, Article 50 (second paragraph) provides that 'the person providing the service may... temporarily pursue his activity in the state where the service is provided'.

Article 55 incorporates Articles 45 to 48 of chapter 2 into chapter 3, so linking the chapter on services to the chapter on establishment. The chapter on establishment is clearly about 'persons', and the reference in Article 50, second paragraph, to 'pursuit of activities' echoes the wording of Article 47. In this perspective, services and establishment are different aspects of the law of free movement of persons, the former involving temporary movement, the latter permanent.

But Article 50 is not wholly consistent with this approach since the first sentence defines 'services' in a negative way as being services that are '*not* governed by the provisions relating to freedom of movement for goods, capital and persons'. This suggests that what the Treaty has to say about 'persons' has been exhausted by chapters 1 ('workers') and 2 ('establishment'). 'Services' are about something else.

One reason for this lack of textual clarity may lie in the historical context in which this part of the Treaty was conceived and drafted – a world characterized by limited and generally slow means of cross-frontier transport; limited and generally slow cross-frontier postal services; very limited and very slow cross-frontier telephone services; no telex; no fax; no mobiles; no emails. Consequently, for most practical purposes, from the perspective of the Treaty-makers, movement of a service almost inevitably involved movement of the person of the service provider (or, as Directive 73/148[12] and *Luisi and Carbone*[13] later pointed out, of the recipient).

It is perhaps also true that, when the Treaty was written, services, with certain exceptions, were not regarded as being economically all that important. The exceptions were transport, banking and insurance, each of which is expressly mentioned in Article 51. Transport was the most obvious example of 'temporary' cross-frontier services (temporary from the point of view of the user) but was excluded from the scope of title III and made the subject of a separate title. Banking and insurance were the most obvious (and perhaps at that time the only) examples of 'invisible' cross-frontier services capable of performance without personal displacement. Although not excluded, they were linked to freedom of movement of capital.

---

[12] OJ 1973 L172/14, now repealed and replaced by Directive 2004/38/EC on the right of citizens of the Union and their family members to move and reside freely within the territory of the Member States, OJ 2004 L229/35.
[13] Joined Cases 286/82 and 26/83 *Luisi and Carbone v Ministero del Tesoro* [1984] ECR 377.

Since 1957, the services sector has grown and diversified to such an extent that the reference to the activities of craftsmen in Article 50 seems almost quaint. The importance of the sector for the economic future of Europe has been recognized and emphasized. The Union also faces the challenge of compliance with GATS, which arguably imposes a limit on the Union's power to maintain (far less to extend) a protectionist internal regime. Yet the text of the chapter on services remains the same, and the Convention on the Constitution, which was supposed to provide us with a template for the next half-century, did not appear even to have asked itself whether the substantive Treaty provisions needed fresh appraisal. This legislative myopia persisted in the Bolkestein debate.

B. The 'Residual' Scope of Services

According to the Treaty definition, the scope of services is 'residual' vis-à-vis persons, capital and goods. An activity is considered to fall within the services provisions only when it is not, or indeed cannot be, covered by one of the other freedoms – an approach recently reaffirmed and applied in *Burmanjer*.[14] Perhaps it is this residual character that has contributed to services' Cinderella status (of being in the background, second best, the poor relation, and so on).

But it should be remembered that the Cinderella story has a happy ending, and a more positively spun assessment of the Treaty provisions would be that the residual scope of services allows this chapter to perform an all-encompassing sweeper function, bringing activities and transactions within the scope of Community law that could not otherwise have been captured. It is fair to say that the drafters of the services provisions probably did not intend this; they could not possibly have envisaged the way in which we trade today. But, although the force and potential of services' residual scope may be accidental, it is nonetheless potentially very important as a way of adapting the Treaty provisions as a whole to the effects of technological progress.

C. The 'Personal' Scope of Services

Personal service providers or recipients must have the nationality of a Member State, like workers or 'natural persons' who seek to exercise the right of establishment. This is formally true also of corporations and other 'legal persons', in the sense that it is their 'nationality' that matters.[15] Article 48 is very clear in attributing rights under chapters 2 and 3 to the legal person as such (a point persistently

---

[14] Case C-20/03 *Criminal proceedings against Burmanjer* [2005] ECR I-4133, paras 33–5, citing Case C-275/92 *Her Majesty's Customs and Excise v Schindler* [1994] ECR I-1039, para 22; Case C-390/99 *Canal Satélite Digital v Administración General del Estado, and Distribuidora de Televisión Digital SA (DTS)* [2002] ECR I-607, para 31; and Case C-71/02 *Karner Industrie-Auktionen GmbH v Troostwijk GmbH* [2004] ECR I-3025, para 46.

[15] This point is clearly evidenced by the judgment in Case C-290/04 *Scorpio* (n 4 above). Even though the 'service' passed from one Member State to another, and the service recipient was a legal person with Member State 'nationality', the third country nationality of the provider was found to

overlooked by the numerous critics of the Court's judgment in *Centros*[16]). It is the corporation or other 'fictional' entity (as opposed to its directors or operative personnel, irrespective of their nationality or domicile) that is viewed as providing the service and is accorded the right to do so.

Where corporations are concerned, many 'service' activities nowadays are archetypically economic or financial activities which, from a regulatory point of view, have more in common with trade in goods or movement of capital than free movement of persons. It is not essential that either the provider or the recipient of the service (any more than the importer or exporter of goods or the dealer on the capital market) should physically move in order to trigger Community protection. A service can move 'virtually' or 'abstractly', such as financial advice received over the telephone or the purchase of an insurance policy, where the only thing that moves will be the policy document.

Nevertheless, services provided by legal persons are provided only through the agency of human beings. Especially in the construction industries, it is artificial wholly to divorce the freedom of the employer to provide construction services from the rights of skilled employees (craftsmen) to deploy their skills where the market offers the opportunity to do so – a consideration underlying Court's reasoning in judgments such as *Corsten, Arblade* and *Schnitzer*.[17]

Perhaps most importantly, there are many reasons nowadays, including tax considerations, why individuals engaged in quite modest self-employed activities pursue those activities through the medium of a company. There are many species in the corporate zoo, and the small family company is one of them.

So, although Article 48 of the Treaty might appear indifferent to the rights of the human beings who are hidden behind the corporate veil of service providers, to ignore them would hardly be consistent with the intention of the Treaty which, notably in its reference to craftsmen and professionals in Article 50, clearly envisages that chapter 3 has something to do with the economic opportunities of real people. This may, at least psychologically, affect the view one takes of the nature of the activity, the rights that should attach to it and the way in which it should be regulated.[18]

D. The 'Private' Scope of Services

The scope of responsibility for compliance with the Treaty freedoms was extended in *Walrave* beyond the Member State (and its emanations) to 'rules of any other nature aimed at regulating in a collective manner gainful employment and the

---

take the situation outwith the scope of Community law on the basis of the inference to be drawn from Article 49, para 2 (although not in the view of Advocate General Léger).

[16] Case C-212/97 *Centros* [1999] ECR I-1459.

[17] Case C-58/98 *Corsten* [2000] ECR I-7919; Case 369/96 *Criminal proceedings against Arblade and Others* [1999] ECR I-8453; Case C-215/01 *Schnitzer* [2003] ECR I-14847.

[18] Again, see the reasoning of Advocate General Léger in this vein, in his opinion on Case C-290/04 *Scorpio* (n 4 above), especially from para 106 onwards.

provision of services'.[19] Here we are looking, not at the provider of services, but at the private individual or organization that might seek to impede the freedom of the provider. Does chapter 3 impinge on private relationships or on the actions of non-state actors that may obstruct the freedom to provide services?

In the case of workers, the decision in *Angonese* extended the scope of Article 39 into the sphere of (individual) private employment.[20] But the reference in *Walrave* to 'provision of services' has not led to any comparable development (for the time being at least) in the field of services and there are several pointers in a different direction. For example, Directive 2006/123 seems to be inspired by the Court's solution (instituted in the *Strawberries* case and widened considerably in *Schmidberger*[21]) to the problem of non-state obstacles to free movement of goods. This draws, at various points,[22] from Article 10 EC and establishes a legally defensible halfway house by imposing responsibility on the state to control the protectionist effects of private action. In the field of legislation, recent initiatives on air passenger compensation and mobile phone roaming charges, for example,[23] have proceeded down the effective but politically difficult route of harmonizing regulations, perhaps demonstrating a preference *against* enhanced horizontal obligations being placed directly on service providers.

E. Import and Export of Services

Whatever other similarities or comparisons there may be between services and goods, the chapter on services does not distinguish between export and import as does the chapter on goods (Articles 28 and 29 EC, exemplified by *Groenveld*[24]). *Alpine Investments* is the benchmark for services.

F. The Factual Scope of 'Services' and their Relationship with the Other Freedoms

As we have noted, the Treaty treats the scope of services as residual vis-à-vis the other freedoms. But as we have also noted, the service sector has expanded out

---

[19] Case 36/74 *Walrave and Koch v Union Cycliste Internationale* [1974] ECR 1405, para 17 (with para 18 onwards setting out the reasoning of the Court).
[20] Case C-281/98 *Angonese v Cassa di Risparmio di Bolzano* [2000] ECR I-4139.
[21] Case C-265/95 *Commission v France* [1997] ECR I-6959 and Case C-112/00 *Schmidberger v Austria* [2003] ECR I-5659.
[22] See, especially, Article 20 of the Directive ('non-discrimination'), which compels '*Member States* [to] ensure that the recipient is not made subject to discriminatory requirements based on his nationality or place of residence' (emphasis added).
[23] See Regulation 261/2004 establishing common rules on compensation and assistance to passengers in the event of denied boarding and of cancellation or long delay of flights [2004] OJ L46/1, and Regulation 717/2007 on roaming on public mobile telephone networks within the Community [2007] OJ L171/32.
[24] Case 15/79 *Groenveld v Produktschap voor Vee en Vlees* [1979] ECR 3409; more recently, see Case C-108/01 *Consorzio del Prosciutto di Parma and and Salumificio S Rita v Asda Stores Ltd and Hygrade Foods Ltd* [2003] ECR I-5121.

of all recognition since the Treaty was written. The apparently simple, 'residual' approach of the Treaty is easy to state but less easy to apply in the modern context. In particular, it is not easy to define the point at which pursuit of an activity in another Member State ceases to be 'temporary' (Article 60, second paragraph) and constitutes establishment. On this point, there seemed at one stage to be a fundamental difference of approach between the Community legislator and the Court of Justice.[25]

From the point of view of the Treaty-makers back in 1957 when travel and communications were slow, the distinction between permanent establishment and temporary provision of services may have appeared rather obvious. Except in frontier areas, there were practical obstacles to carrying on economic activities in more than one Member State at the same time, so the temporary/permanent distinction was probably felt to be adequate. This is no longer so, and in *Gebhard*[26] and more recently in *Schnitzer*,[27] the Court sought to offer guidelines as to how the national courts should approach the distinction between establishment and services.

In the run-up to enactment of the Bolkestein Directive, the political institutions appeared either to have been ignorant of the Court's case law, or to have been willing deliberately to ignore it in their attempt to create a form of 'deemed establishment' whenever the work involved in provision of a service extended beyond a specified period of time. So it is important to stress that, as the judgment in *Schnitzer* explains, 'temporary' does not necessarily mean 'brief' or 'of short duration'.[28]

The logic can best be illustrated by reference to construction contracts.[29] A contractor, particularly an SME, that seeks to enter the market in another Member State will normally wish to test the market before committing capital and manpower to a permanent establishment in that Member State. Construction contracts may last several months, if not years. The contractor who bids successfully for a first (and perhaps only) contract in another Member State should not be deemed to have become established there by reason only of the duration of that contract. The extent to which the contractor should be subjected to local labour and other laws is a separate question and, as the Court has said,[30] is essentially a matter of proportionality. That analysis should not be confused by creating a false doctrine of deemed establishment.

A further 'factual' difficulty relates to the fuzziness with which one is faced when trying to attach appropriate weight to the different elements within a

---

[25] See the original Commission proposal for the Bolkestein Directive (n 3 above).
[26] Case C-55/94 *Gebhard v Consiglio dell' Ordine degli Avvocati e Procuratori di Milano* [1995] ECR I-4165.
[27] n 17 above.
[28] See, in particular, paras 31–2 of the judgment in *Schnitzer* (n 17 above).
[29] See also the opinion of Advocate General Jacobs in Case C-76/90 *Säger v Dennemayer* [1991] ECR I-4221, para 25.
[30] See again the judgments in n 17 above.

mixed activity that has multiple elements – for example, where an information, registration or maintenance service is linked to the purchase of goods, or where the recipient of medical services has to purchase medicines as an integral part of the treatment received. The Court recently summarized the applicable rules in *Burmanjer*,[31] outlining a test based on the primary/secondary purposes of the activities in question viewed from the perspective of each of the four freedoms. Services come into play only if none of the others applies. Application of this test, although enjoined by the Treaty, ought not, however, to lead to a situation in which obstacles to the provision of services are viewed as of secondary importance as compared with obstacles to the other three freedoms.

In determining the components of an activity, advertising presented an especially thorny issue in *Grogan*.[32] It had been established in the case law on the free movement of goods that a restriction on advertising is capable of violating Article 28 EC.[33] Plainly, in *Grogan*, there was no question of obstructing the marketing of goods, and the subject matter of the case could fall within the scope of the Treaty only under the chapter on services.

In order to resolve the issue, the Court distinguished between information 'distributed on behalf of an economic operator established in another Member State' and student-led provision of information on abortion and abortion clinics. The latter was described as information that constituted 'a manifestation of freedom of expression and of the freedom to impart and receive information which is independent of the economic activity carried on by clinics established in another Member State'.[34] To this distinction the Court added the absence of 'remuneration' (see below), thus enabling the finding that 'the link between the activity of the students' associations... and medical terminations of pregnancies carried out in clinics in another Member State is too tenuous for the prohibition on the distribution of information to be capable of being regarded as a restriction within the meaning of Article [49 EC]'.[35]

The *Grogan* judgment generated heated commentary on the Court's dipping into the 'moral plane' of abortion issues,[36] and the Court's legal construction of

---

[31] See again paras 33–5 of the judgment in *Burmanjer* (n 14 above).

[32] n 7 above; we return to the more thematic point underlying case law on advertising, that of market access, further below.

[33] See especially, Case C-362/88 *GB-INNO-BM* [1990] ECR I-667.

[34] *Grogan*, para 26.

[35] *Grogan*, para 24; cf the opinion of Advocate General Van Gerven, especially para 18 onwards.

[36] *Grogan*, para 20; key literature here includes J Coppel and A O'Neill, 'The European Court of Justice: taking rights seriously?' (1992) 29 *Common Market Law Review* 669; JHH Weiler and NJS Lockhart, '"Taking rights seriously" seriously: the European Court of Justice and its fundamental rights jurisprudence' (1995) 32 *Common Market Law Review* vol 32:1, 51, vol 32:2, 579; DR Phelan, 'Right to life of the unborn v promotion of trade in services: the ECJ and the normative shaping of the European Union' (1992) 55 *Modern Law Review* 670, and G de Búrca, 'Fundamental rights and the reach of European Community law' (1993) 13 *Oxford Journal of Legal Studies* 283.

services/advertising was strongly criticized.[37] But the judgment conceals a much wider and deeper debate about whether the Treaty compels only the removal of discriminatory obstacles for the benefit of service providers or realization of the broader goal of creating a free market in services for the benefit of European citizens in general, a debate to which we return in section III below.

G. The Criterion of Remuneration

Article 50 provides that 'Services shall be considered to be "services" within the meaning of this Treaty where they are normally provided for remuneration'. This criterion has long formed a critical element of the definition of services that fall within the scope of the Treaty and, as noted above, was invoked, gratefully if inelegantly, as part of the Court's solution to the problem in *Grogan*. As a criterion, it suffers from two uncertainties. First, by whom must the service provider be remunerated? Second, what is the significance of the word 'normally'? Where a service is provided without remuneration, does it nevertheless fall within the scope of the Treaty if it is 'normally' provided for remuneration? If so, in what context and by whom must it 'normally' be so provided?

As regards the first question, the Court gave a clear answer in *Bond van Adverteerders*.[38] It is not necessary that the remuneration should pass directly from the beneficiary of the service to the provider. In the same year, however, the Court in *Humbel*[39] adopted a different approach as regards payment for vocational training within the public educational system. More recently, the Court has been more flexible in its case law on cross-border health care provision,[40] and citizenship enabled the Court to give a fresh answer to the problem of access to publicly funded education (and/or related benefits) in *Grzelczyk*, *D'Hoop* and *Bidar*[41].

A source of further tension on this point between the legislator and the Court could yet be simmering under the surface. Directive 2006/123 (particularly Recital 34 of the preamble) purports to exclude publicly funded education from the purview of services. But it is not at all clear that the exclusion is valid in light

---

[37] See especially S O'Leary, 'Freedom of establishment and freedom to provide services: the Court of Justice as a reluctant constitutional adjudicator: an examination of the abortion information case' (1992) 17 *European Law Review* 138; O'Leary captures the *Grogan* judgment astutely when she comments (139) that '[the Court] appears eager to assert its role as a legitimate participant in the legal issue but shies away from any concrete resolution of the matter'.

[38] Case 352/85 *Bond van Adverteerders v Netherlands* [1988] ECR 2085, especially para 16.

[39] Case 263/86 *Belgium v Humbel* [1988] ECR 5365.

[40] For a useful review of the evolution and principles of the medical services case law, see the opinion of Advocate General Geelhoed in Case C-372/04 *Watts v Bedford Primary Care Trust and Secretary of State for Health* [2006] ECR I-4325, from para 46 onwards.

[41] Case C-184/99 *Grzelczyk v Centre public d'aide sociale d'Ottignies-Louvain-la-Neuve* [2001] ECR I-6193, and Case C-224/98 *D'Hoop v Office national de l'emploi* [2002] ECR I-619 and Case C-209/03 *Bidar v London Borough of Ealing; Secretary of State for Education and Skills* [2005] ECR I-2119.

of the evolving case law on the citizen's right of access to education as a publicly funded service.[42]

It may therefore become important to determine the answer to the second question – what does 'normally' mean? Clearly, a service does not fall outside the scope of the Treaty simply because, in the instant case, it is not provided for remuneration. The question is whether it is 'normally' provided for remuneration. The original intention of the Treaty-makers may have been to deal with a situation where a service provider is denied access to another Member State simply because, in the instant case, he/she does not intend to charge for the service, although this would not normally be so, and perhaps also to avoid bureaucratic arguments about whether the sum paid is sufficient to constitute 'remuneration'. But the scope of the question is wider and it may be necessary to determine whether, in assessing 'normality', we are to look at the normal practice of the individual service provider involved in the transaction at issue, at that of service-providers in that particular sector more generally, or at the normal situation in other Member States as well as the State immediately concerned. This problem does not appear to have arisen as yet.

H. The Link between the Service and the Right Claimed

The legislative and judicial extension of Treaty coverage to receipt as well as provision of services raises a further issue as to the extent to which there must be a direct link between the service in question and the right claimed.

In *Luisi and Carbone*,[43] the services in question were health care services in another Member State. The right claimed by the recipients of those services was the right to export sufficient currency from the home state to pay for them, thereby exceeding the national currency control limit. The link between the service and the right was therefore indirect, although obvious enough. In *Carpenter*,[44] the threatened deportation of Mrs Carpenter from the UK was found to be detrimental to the conditions under which Mr Carpenter provided services in other Member States. But the link between the fundamental right of respect for the Carpenters' family life in the UK and the actual exercise of Mr Carpenter's service activities in other Member States was tenuous, to say the least, and the Court, perhaps wisely, did not seek to analyse it.

---

[42] In Case C-147/03 *Commission v Austria* [2005] ECR I-5969, para 31 onwards, Advocate General Jacobs argued for the preservation of strictness with regard to publicly funded education in contrast to developments in respect of healthcare – although he did attach a rider should the law change in respect of entitlement to student maintenance grants, a proposition that has since been realized in *Bidar*. See now also Joined Cases C-11/06 *Morgan v Bezirksregierung Köln* and C-12/06 *Bucher v Landrat des Kreises Düren*, opinion of 20 March 2007 (especially paras 97–103) and judgment of 23 October 2007.

[43] n 13 above.

[44] Case C-60/00 *Carpenter v Secretary of State for the Home Department* [2002] ECR I-6279.

In other cases, the Court has simply *presumed* that there was a link between the service and the right. In *Cowan*,[45] the Court presumed that Mr Cowan, as a tourist, was necessarily a recipient of services in France – 'tourists, among others, *must* be regarded as recipients of services'.[46] But there was no other link between any of the services Mr Cowan was presumed to have enjoyed in France (except conceivably transport services on the Metro) and the right he claimed – the right to receive compensation for criminal injuries. The presumption was more extreme still in *Bickel and Franz*,[47] as we have no idea whether Mr Bickel, in particular, ever got out of his lorry to receive services in Italy. The judgment is suitably vague in applying Article 12 EC on this point, so it is unclear whether the law protected Mr Bickel under Article 49 or Article 18 EC.

Problems thrown up by this type of reasoning[48] clearly demonstrate the strains inherent in claiming rights on such an ephemeral basis as services, and it is no surprise that many of these situations are now overtaken by citizenship, a change in approach that began to unfold in *Bickel* itself.

Lastly, on this point, it should be noted that an actual, 'real life' recipient does not need to be identified when the freedom to provide services is being considered.[49]

III. The Place of Services in the Wider Map of the Internal Market

How does the law on services fit into the more general law of the internal market? Recent scholarship has involved tracing patterns and symmetries (or the absence of them) across the four freedoms. Do the rules and principles of the internal market fit into a coherent framework, irrespective of whether goods or people or companies are involved, and *should* there be a coherent framework that achieves this in any event? If a rule or principle has had a ripple effect across the freedoms, it might be thought that it must have started from one of them and, more particularly, as Oliver and Roth suggest, that 'free movement of goods was once the

---

[45] Case 186/87 *Cowan v Trésor Public* [1989] ECR 195; the splitting of personal and substantive or material scope in this way is widely considered to have laid the foundations for the Court's landmark decision on EU citizenship just over a decade later, Case C-85/96 *Martínez Sala v Freistaat Bayern* [1998] ECR I-2691.
[46] *Cowan*, ibid, para 15 (emphasis added).
[47] Case C-274/96 *Criminal proceedings against Bickel and Franz* [1998] ECR I-7637.
[48] Described as the 'functional method of the Court' to the non-discrimination principle in C Tomuschat, case comment on Case C-85/96 *Martínez Sala v Freistaat Bayern* (2000) 37 *Common Market Law Review* 449–57, 451, i.e. where '[t]he Court simply asks whether the legal proposition or practice under review exerts any impact on one of the freedoms under the Treaty'.
[49] See, for example, *Alpine Investments* (n 8 above), para 35, and Case C-405/98 *Konsumentombudsmannen (KO) v Gourmet International Products AB (GIP)* [2001] ECR I-1795, para 39, extending the *Alpine* reasoning more overtly to potential advertisers (para 38); see also Case C-70/95 *Sodemare and Others v Regione Lombardia* [1997] ECR I-3395.

trailblazer, [but] the other freedoms have now caught up and in some cases have even overtaken it'.[50] We suggest that this approach is misleading, and that the case law on services was just as important as the case law on goods. Goods were the trailblazer only in the sense that there were more cases about them and that, for a period, the trail led down a *fausse piste*.

The legal infrastructure of the internal market, underpinning the Single European Act and the 1992 programme, is usually traced back to *Dassonville*[51] and *Cassis de Dijon*.[52] It is often overlooked that *Van Binsbergen*[53] was virtually contemporaneous with *Dassonville* and predated *Cassis* by several years.

In *Dassonville*, the definition of measures having equivalent effect to a quantitative restriction was genuinely expansive. As it turned out, the *Dassonville* formula[54] – borrowed from competition law – was probably too expansive and led to difficulties later which *Keck and Mithouard* failed to resolve. The formulae adopted in *Van Binsbergen* were more careful and more precise:

[T]he restrictions to be abolished pursuant to [Article 49 EC] include *all requirements* imposed on the person providing the service by reason *in particular* of his nationality or of the fact that he does not habitually reside in the state where the service is provided, which do not apply to persons established within the national territory *or which may prevent or otherwise obstruct* the activities of the person providing the service...

[T]he *precise object of [Article 49 EC] is to abolish restrictions* on freedom to provide services imposed on persons who are not established in the state where the service is to be provided.[55]

The judgment in *Van Binsbergen* also introduced the idea of 'rules justified by the general good' – in that case '[professional] rules relating to organization, qualifications, professional ethics, supervision and liability'. This formula was repeated in the context of establishment in *Thieffry*[56] with the rider that application of the admissible rules must be 'effected without discrimination'. Again, it can be argued, this was a clearer and more precise version of the 'mandatory requirements' criterion enunciated in *Cassis*.[57]

The crucial point, so it seems to us, is not which came first, or which was the trailblazer, but that, already in the early 1970s, the Court was formulating a gen-

---

[50] P Oliver and W-H Roth, 'The internal market and the four freedoms' (2004) 41 *Common Market Law Review* 407, 439, continuing that 'it is widely considered that the provisions on workers and services have taken over the role of pioneer since the early 1990s and especially since *Keck*'.
[51] Case 8/74 *Procureur du Roi v Dassonville* [1974] ECR 837.
[52] Case 120/78 *Rewe-Zentrale AG v Bundesmonopolverwaltung für Branntwein (Cassis de Dijon)* [1979] ECR 649.
[53] Case 33/74 *Van Binsbergen v Bestuur van de Bedrijfsvereniging voor de Metaalnijverheid* [1974] ECR 1299.
[54] *Dassonville* (n 51 above), para 5.
[55] See *Van Binsbergen* (n 53 above), paras 10 and 11 (emphasis added).
[56] Case 71/76 *Thieffry v Conseil de l'Ordre des avocats à la cour de Paris* [1977] ECR 765.
[57] *Van Binsbergen* (n 53 above), para 12; *Thieffry* (n 56 above), para 12; *Cassis* (n 52 above), para 8.

eral internal market approach, whose common concern was to cut through legislatively authorized, and therefore stubbornly resistant, obstacles to intra-state trade that were not overtly discriminatory though their application might have that effect. The wider ambition of realizing a genuine internal market, rather than freedom of movement for goods or services as such, is a better descriptor of the 'trailblazer' of that time.

It was this simple internal market approach that got lost in the case law on goods leading up to *Keck* – a trend that the judgment in *Keck* sought to correct but only succeeded in confusing. The trend was due to an extravagant interpretation of the *Dassonville* formula which, as noted, had been borrowed from competition law without, however, allowing for any *de minimis* or rule of reason exception. Any imagined limitation of the freedom to market imported goods was thought to fall within the scope of the formula and did not need to be tested against the reality of access to the actual marketplace where domestic and imported goods were to compete for the attention of the consumer. *Keck* sought to focus attention on the domestic marketplace of the Member State of import by referring to *modalités de vente* (inadequately and inelegantly translated 'selling arrangements'[58]). But this only made the confusion worse since it did not define at what point or points in the supply chain the 'selling arrangement' might apply.

An early opportunity to make clear the intention of *Keck* came in *Alpine Investments*, where it was argued that cold-calling was a form of 'selling arrangement' and therefore fell outside the scope of the Treaty. In one paragraph,[59] the Court resumed and explained what had been said in *Keck*:

[T]he application to products from other Member States of national provisions restricting or prohibiting, within the Member State of importation, certain selling arrangements is not such as to hinder trade between Member States so long as, first, those provisions apply to all relevant traders operating within the national territory and, secondly, they affect in the same manner, in law and in fact, the marketing of domestic products and of those from other Member States. The reason is that the application of such provisions is not such as to prevent access by the latter to the market of the Member State of importation or to impede such access more than it impedes access by domestic products.

Keck was not as restrictive nor *Alpine Investments* as radically innovative an interpretation of the principle of market access as they might have seemed at the time.[60] Together they established or reasserted the twofold test of discrimination and access to the domestic market. This has become clearer in subsequent judgments, discrimination being treated as one (but only one) category of obstacles to

---

[58] The inadequacy of the translation and the confusion to which it has led illustrate the problem of agreeing a text in one language without making sure that it can be adequately translated into others. One of the present authors pleads guilty in this respect.
[59] Para 37.
[60] See N Nic Shuibhne, 'The free movement of goods and Article 28 EC: an evolving framework' (2002) 27 *European Law Review* 408; S Enchelmaier, 'Four freedoms, how many principles?' (2004) 24 *Oxford Journal of Legal Studies* 155.

market access, rather than the other, more restrictive way around.[61] So, in *Säger*, the Court stressed that:

Article [49 EC] requires *not only the elimination of all discrimination* against a person providing services on the ground of his nationality but also *the abolition of any restriction, even if it applies without distinction* to national providers of services and to those of other Member States, when it is liable to prohibit *or otherwise impede* the activities of a provider of services established in another Member State where he lawfully provides similar services.[62]

If market access is ultimately the best criterion, applicable across the range of internal market law, there must nevertheless be some way of delimiting the scope of the freedoms in relation to non-discriminatory obstacles. Otherwise, there is a danger of setting off again down the *fausse piste* that ended with *Keck*.

Here, the immature concept of remoteness might have a part to play. As we have noted, *Dassonville* imported the breadth of the competition test ('actually or potentially') without the limitations of a *de minimis* test. In competition law, however, the *de minimis* principle is a *quantitative* one, relating directly to volume, and this aspect of the principle was rejected in the ambit of free movement law.[63] The *qualitative* aspect of the principle – remoteness – has sometimes been applied in free movement cases, though sporadically and therefore somewhat unsatisfactorily.

Thus a test of remoteness ('too tenuous') was adopted for services in *Grogan*,[64] and a similar test ('too uncertain and indirect') was adopted for goods in *Krantz*[65] and for workers in *Graf*.[66] It is arguable that the Court in *Alpine Investments* was careful to establish, at the start of its analysis,[67] that the barrier to movement was *not* too remote.

---

[61] See especially, Case C-254/98 *Schutzverband gegen unlauteren Wettbewerb v TK-Heimdienst Sass GmbH* [2000] ECR I-151 and Case C-405/98 *Konsumentombudsmannen v Gourmet International Products AB (GIP)* [2001] ECR I-1795; in *Gourmet*, see also the opinion of Advocate General Jacobs, paras 29–31 in particular.

[62] Case C-76/90 *Säger v Dennemeyer* [1991] ECR I-4221, para 12. The April 2006 editorial in the *Common Market Law Review* describes *Säger* as the 'grandfather' of the country of origin principle – arguably making the watered-down Directive 2006/123 more 'revolutionary' (albeit in a negative or 'reverse' sense) than the originally conceived Bolkestein version (see (editorial), 'The services directive proposal: striking a balance between the promotion of the internal market and preserving the European social model?' (2006) 43 *Common Market Law Review* 307, 309).

[63] In respect of goods, see the classic authority in the Danish Beekeeping Case (Case C-67/97 *Criminal Proceedings against Bluhme* [1998] ECR I-8033).

[64] Para 24.

[65] In earlier case law, see the decisions in Case C-69/88 *Krantz* [1990] ECR I-583 and Case C-93/92 *CMC Motorradcenter* [1993] ECR I-5009; more recently, see *Burmanjer*, para 31 ('if those rules did have such an effect, it would be *too insignificant and uncertain* to be regarded as being such as to hinder or otherwise interfere with trade between Member States', emphasis added) and para 32.

[66] Case C-190/98 *Graf v Filmoser Maschinenbau GmbH* [2000] ECR I-493.

[67] *Alpine Investments*, para 24; this is fleshed out by A Arnull, *The European Union and its Court of Justice* (2nd ed, 2006), 491; he pursues the thread through to *Deliège* and Joined Cases C-544/03 and C-545/03 *Mobistar v Commune de Fléron* [2005] ECR I-7723.

The Court has not adopted a remoteness test as part of the three-stage obstacle/objective justification/proportionality approach required by *Gebhard* and, more recently, *Bacardi France*.[68] But apart from that, remoteness as a concept (or any variant of it) raises problems that are familiar to lawyers practising in the field of personal injuries where cases can be bedevilled by problems of causation of philosophical complexity. If application of the test – 'Is the causal connection too remote?' – is not to depend on the length of the judge's foot, it calls for some explanation of how it is to be applied. But the search for that explanation leads too often to much spilling of ink inventing what turn out to be no more than different ways of saying the same thing.

Perhaps, therefore, the simplest solution is *not* to create a separate test or criterion of remoteness, but to treat remoteness as being an aspect of the question 'is there an "obstacle" to freedom of movement?' The issue is more economic and practical than legal: 'what is the obstacle and how does it work?' The answer will, of course, depend on judicial assessment of the facts but that assessment need not be arbitrary and should be evidence-based. If, as a practical matter, there is no obstacle, then the situation in question is too 'remote' to fall within the scope of Community law.

Up to now, we have focused on the parallels between goods and services. The relationship between services and persons is a good deal fuzzier, though not as regards the establishment of individual professionals and services provided by them. The main issue in *Gebhard*[69] was, after all, to determine the line of demarcation between establishment and services, and the three-stage obstacle/justification/proportionality test was enunciated for both. In addition, the Treaty provisions on citizenship and the Court's interpretation of them have strengthened the commitment to freedom of movement, freedom of establishment and freedom to provide services as *personal* rights.

It seems to us that this commitment is subject to strain at two points – in both cases because, nowadays, service providers are so often legal rather than natural persons and therefore entitled to the benefits of Article 48. (The recent decision in *Scorpio*[70] excludes third country corporations from the benefit of the Treaty provisions on services, but that can normally be got round by incorporation of subsidiaries within the EU.)

As we have noted, the services sector covers many activities of an economic or financial nature which involve 'invisible' or 'virtual' transactions across frontiers without any physical movement at all. These activities are almost always conducted by corporate entities – frequently multinationals or their subsidiaries – and increasingly call for regulation for a variety of public interest reasons, including compliance with competition law and consumer protection. The frontiers across

---

[68] Case C-429/02 *Bacardi France v Télévision française 1 SA (TF1), Groupe Jean-Claude Darmon SA and Girosport SARL* [2004] ECR I-6613, para 34.
[69] n 26 above.
[70] n 4 above.

which these activities are conducted are not confined to the internal frontiers of the European Union, which is, moreover, bound by the rules of GATS.

One question which seems to us to call for deeper analysis is whether the extent, manner and intensity of regulation of corporate activities in the field of services has any logical connection with regulating 'personal' free movement rights. Does it make sense for financial services sold over the Internet to be discussed in the same terms as the personal services of the individual craftsman? Is it appropriate to analyse the rights of a multinational law firm or accountancy firm with limited liability on the same basis as those of the local practitioner whose involvement in cross-frontier transactions is liable to be sporadic and infrequent?

Questions such as these were probably at the root of the objections to the 'country of origin' principle underlying the original Bolkestein proposal, on the view that it is unrealistic to assume that the authorities of Member States are in a position to police the Union-wide, and in some cases worldwide, policies and practices of their corporate 'nationals'. Given the range and complexity of the transactions that have to be regulated, one must ask whether the sketchy Treaty provisions, even if fleshed out by the case law of the Court, are an adequate legal basis for effective regulation. It is not enough to say that the Union legislator can make good the lacunae or deficiencies of the Treaty since these lacunae and deficiencies can be made good only within the limits of the Treaty.

A comparable, but quite different, point of strain exists in relation to the rights of the individual worker who exercises his/her skills as an employee of a corporate entity (whether a large-scale operator, such as a construction company, or a small family company). The Treaty gives 'workers' extensive rights and these have been jealously protected by the Court and the legislator. Article 15(1) of the Charter of Fundamental Rights proclaims the 'right to engage in work and to pursue a freely chosen or accepted occupation'. But where the individual worker is the employee of a corporate service provider whose efficiency (not necessarily low-wage efficiency[71]) threatens to disturb the comforts of a protected 'social market', then the right of the individual (the dreaded 'Polish plumber') to pursue his/her chosen occupation must, it appears, give way to the avoidance of 'social dumping'.

One does not need to be a neocon (or in some vocabularies, a neoliberal) to ask whether this approach is consistent with the intentions of the Treaty-makers. Their intention was decidedly not to promote 'the unhindered pursuit of commerce'.[72] On the other hand, it is surely to their credit that they recognized and proclaimed, as part of the internal market idea, the right of human beings to realize their potential, if necessary in competition with each other. There are both legal and moral reasons for questioning the sort of regime to which some at least of the Masters of the Treaties appear to be committed – a regime under which

---

[71] In *Corsten* (n 17 above), the Dutch company offered to lay composition floors for 'considerably less' (almost 50 per cent less) than German companies protected by the *Handwerksordnung*.
[72] See, especially, the opening line of the opinion of Advocate General Tesauro in Case C-292/92 *Hünermund v Landesapothekerkammer Baden-Württemberg* [1993] ECR I-6787.

a high-sounding preoccupation with the human right to realize one's potential ignores the reality of the way in which that right is exercized in modern conditions. 'Competition' is not a dirty word to be eliminated from the aims of the Treaty: it is a counterpart of the economics of free movement of real people.

IV. Concluding Remarks

Our brief journey into the territory of services has, we hope, exemplified the core themes of this volume: *continuity*, especially the jurisprudential thread reaching back to *Van Binsbergen* to which Advocate General Jacobs contributed his own characteristic powers of analysis; and *change* – the transformed services environment, and perhaps also the new political environment, in which the Treaty principles must now be applied.

The function of the Court in an Article 234 reference is to provide guidance to the referring court in dealing with the case before it. Where the Treaty remains vague, it is inevitable (and, looking to Article 220 EC, expected) that the Court will also offer some general propositions to substitute for that vagueness. Experience of the case law on goods from *Dassonville* to *Keck and Mithouard* is a warning against excessively broad judicial pronouncements. Judges best maintain the 'logic or symmetry of the law'[73] on a case-by-case basis.

So perhaps it is somewhat unreasonable for us to complain when the political institutions seek to provide us with new textual bricks. We are, however, entitled to ask whether the new bricks are good bricks, fit for purpose. It remains to be seen whether Directive 2006/123 in its final form passes this test. We must also ask whether the formulae of a Treaty 50 years old are adequate as a basis for regulating the market in services in the economic and technological conditions of the 21st century. So we may wonder why the substantive provisions of the Treaty seemed so irrelevant in the recent intense discussions of Treaty reform. We may, nevertheless, be forced to answer that the levity with which today's Treaty-makers are prepared to tinker with the text of the Treaty over the dinner table suggests that it is better to leave the texts as they are and trust to the pragmatic instincts of the Court.

Since this article was submitted, the Court has issued its judgments in Cases C-76/05 *Schwarz and Gootjes-Schwarz v Finanzamt Bergish Gladbach* and C-318/05 *Commission v Germany*, judgment of 11 September 2007, and Joined Cases C-11/06 *Morgan v Bezirksregierung Köln* and C-12/06 *Bucher v Landrat des Kreises Düren*, judgment of 23 October 2007. These illustrate the complex interaction between the laws on services, education, personal taxation and citizenship.

---

[73] AV Dicey, *Law and Opinion in England* (2nd ed, 1914), Lecture XI, 364.

15

The Financial Services Single Market and the Interface between Community Law and Domestic Law

Eva Lomnicka

I. Introduction

The fact that each of the Member States of the EU has its own legal system has been a major inhibitor of the achievement of the single market. Multiple legal systems lead to the potential application of the private and public laws of more than one legal system to cross-border activities. There is also the possibility that the institutions, whether judicial or regulatory, of more than one Member State will claim jurisdiction over those activities and seek to exercise such powers as they have over them. This is a recipe for the fragmentation of markets, not their integration. Hence the single market is achievable only if the consequent potential for confusion and duplication is tackled.

Community law – whether Treaty law or the many secondary law initiatives – has sought to address the problems posed by multiple legal systems. But these problems already have solutions – of sorts – in the traditional rules of domestic private international law (applicable in the private law sphere) and the principle of territoriality (applicable to regulatory law). These long-standing domestic law solutions clearly need to be modified significantly if the single market is to be achieved, but the precise extent of their modification also needs to be very clear, otherwise the consequent uncertainty merely compounds the problems. For example, a common feature of secondary Community legislation[1] is that it seeks to 'harmonize' Member States' laws. But it is important to note that Community harmonization measures operate in two distinct ways, each having a different impact on those traditional domestic law principles.

---

[1] And of the 1980 Rome Convention, [1980] OJ L226/1, which is not strictly a 'Community' measure (see n 7 below).

The first type of harmonization technique does not challenge, but works within, the established framework of traditional principles of private international law or territoriality, as the case may be. Here the rules applicable in each Member State are harmonized. Hence multiple legal systems continue to be potentially applicable but the consequences are less problematic. This is because a firm operating in a way that satisfies the laws of its home Member State is likely to satisfy the laws of every other Member State in which it wishes to do business. The only form of harmonization that can work in this way is 'maximum' harmonization, with Member States not being permitted to impose additional requirements above those that have been harmonized. But maximum harmonization as a mechanism for facilitating a single market has serious shortcomings. First, there are politically sensitive areas where Member States are reluctant to compromise on harmonized rules, if they are to forgo their power to impose additional rules in their domestic arena. Second, there are the inevitable discrepancies that result from each Member State transposing[2] and then interpreting the 'harmonized' rules. And there are practical limits to the extent to which Community institutions can eliminate those discrepancies of implementation and interpretation.[3]

Harmonization can also be used in a more radical way as the basis on which to challenge, rather than accept, the applicability of multiple legal systems. Once common rules are agreed upon, there is less justification for each Member State continuing to apply its own version to incoming business. The obvious next step is to concede that one or other – but not both – Member State's laws apply. The 'home country control' concept[4] illustrates this more radical use of harmonization. Here, once a firm complies with its 'home' Member State's rules, the 'host' Member State should not be able to insist that the firm also complies with its own equivalent rules. When harmonization becomes the mechanism justifying the choice of one Member State's legal system over another's, there is less need to insist on maximum harmonization.[5] As only one Member State's law applies, all that is needed is so-called 'minimum' harmonization at a level that persuades Member States to surrender their competence to impose their own rules. Minimum harmonization of 'key' or core principles can thus be the basis of mutual recognition of legal systems.

This second, more radical harmonization technique is an example of Community law adopting an approach that departs from traditional domestic law principles. But it is not always obvious exactly how Community law interacts with and affects the domestic rules that prima facie apply to determine issues of jurisdiction and applicable law in relation to cross-border activity. And this

---

[2] Assuming the Community measure (e.g. a Directive) needs transposing.
[3] See, most recently, the introduction of the third and fourth 'levels' of the Lamfalussy process which seek to address this issue.
[4] Considered further below.
[5] Although there appears to be a move towards maximum harmonization even in this context, see, most recently, MiFID (Section III(B)(ii)(b) below).

uncertainty is itself a significant threat to the single market. The nature of the problem will now be considered in the financial services sector, starting with the traditional rules themselves and going on to examine some examples of Community law and how they apparently adjust those rules to the needs of a single market.

II. Traditional Domestic Law Approaches

A. General

In the private law sphere, resolving jurisdictional and choice of law problems in the context of cross-border activity is nothing new. Each law district has developed its own rules for determining when its courts have jurisdiction to try contested issues and what the applicable law to those issues is. These rules are often far from ideal in supplying clear answers, but they do at least provide a tried and tested analytical approach to identifying and answering the question of which courts can act and which country's law they should apply.

But in the financial services sector, firms need to have regard not only to private but also to public law. Therefore, as well as ensuring that their dealings are effective under private law principles, they also need to comply with requirements imposed by regulators and hence to know which regulatory requirements apply to them. And they also need to know which of those regulators have enforcement powers over them. In the public law sphere, principles of territoriality have traditionally determined the reach of regulatory power and have compartmentalized – on territorial lines – the competence of national regulators to impose and enforce their own rules. Thus it is accepted that each State's regulator is competent to impose and enforce its own regulatory rule book on activities within its borders (to the extent that practical considerations allow) and against firms based in its territory.

It follows that, in the financial services context, the question of which Member State's legal system applies needs to be broken down into a number of components. The first main question addresses the 'choice of law' issue: which Member States' rules apply to the cross-border activity? And this, in turn, depends on whether those rules are of a private or public law nature. The second question addresses the 'jurisdiction' or competence issue: which Member States' institutions have competence to apply and enforce those rules? This question also needs to be subdivided, depending on whether the institution exercising the power is a judicial body or a regulator.

B. Whose Law(s)?

In examining the first 'choice of law' question of which Member States' rules apply to cross-border activity, a distinction needs to be drawn between private and public law. As already mentioned, private international law principles provide the answer in relation to private law issues whilst the principle of territoriality applies when it comes to regulatory rules. In practice these traditional principles are notoriously uncertain in their application. This uncertainty is, in itself, enough to impede cross-border activity. However, in addition, they often lead to the applicability of more than one legal system and the extra burdens this duplication imposes also makes cross-border activity unattractive.

Starting with those private law issues, private international law is well known for producing unpredictable results.[6] Moreover, as different Member States each have their own legal systems, they each have their own private international law rules. So, depending on the forum in which a dispute arises, the solution provided by private international law in choosing the applicable law may differ from Member State to Member State. This adds a further layer of unpredictability of result that depends on which Member State provides the forum for the litigation. The latter problem was initially tackled within the EU by the 1980 Rome Convention,[7] which has harmonized the private international rules applying to choice of law in contract. Thus providers of cross-border services in the EU can be confident that every Member State will, in theory, agree which legal system applies to the contracts they make. Of course, discrepancies may still arise as Member States — despite the oversight of the ECJ[8] — in practice take different views of how the harmonized rules apply in particular cases, but in general a uniform approach operates. Moreover, it is an approach that generally leads to the application of a single law.[9] So, in sum, these harmonization measures have, in theory, significantly reduced the doubt as to which law applies to contractual issues arising in cross-border activity and have resulted in one law predominantly applying. The doubts that remain are those inherent in a single market that maintains different legal systems that are capable of interpreting the measures differently.

Turning to regulatory matters, the picture is less encouraging for cross-border service provision. The principle of territoriality enables each Member State to insist that activities within its borders are undertaken in compliance with its regulatory laws. This leads to the application of multiple laws with no mechanism of choosing one rather than the other. Recognizing the clear inhibitory

---

[6] Not only are the rules themselves difficult to apply, but if they result in the choice of a foreign (non-forum) law, evidence of that law may be unreliable.

[7] On the Law Applicable to Contractual Obligations [1980] OJ L226/1. This is a traditional international Convention initially entered into by the (then) EC Member States and not 'Community Law' derived from the (then) Treaty of Rome. See now the proposal for the 'Rome 1' Regulation to amend and replace the Rome Convention: COM (2005) 650 final. In relation to insurance concerning risks in an EEA State, there are specific 'choice of law' provisions in Directive 2002/83/EC, [2002] OJ L345, Arts 32–6 (life assurance) and Directive 88/357/EEC, [1988] OJ L172, Art 7, as amended by 92/49/EEC, [1992] OJ L228 (non-life insurance).

[8] The two 1988 Protocols provide for the ECJ to have jurisdiction over the interpretation of the Rome Convention.

[9] But see Section III.A below.

effect of having to comply with a new set of regulatory rules every time activity extends to another Member State, the Community law-makers have been active in this sphere also[10] and eventually developed the ingenious 'single passport/ home country control' concept as a means of allocating regulatory rule-making responsibility,[11] so firms only needed to look to one Member State for the applicable rules.

C. Whose Institution(s)?

But deciding which Member States' rules apply to cross-border activity is not the end of the inquiry. There is the further question of which Member States' institutions have competence to apply and enforce those rules.

In the private law sphere, the issue of jurisdiction (which courts have competence to try the issue) is clearly recognized as distinct from the issue of choice of law (which law applies). Hence it is not unusual for the courts that have jurisdiction over an issue to determine, through the application of their choice of law rules, that a law other than the *lex fori* is the applicable law. And as noted above, if the dispute relates to contractual obligations, the Member States will generally[12] apply the rules set out in the Rome Convention and (in theory) come to the same conclusion as to the applicable law no matter where the litigation occurs. When it comes to jurisdiction, each State again has its own rules as to when its courts have power to determine an *inter partes* dispute. Within the single market, these rules in the context of civil and commercial disputes have also been harmonized and are now generally contained in the Judgments Regulation,[13] so again there is broad agreement as to which courts have jurisdiction in relation to private law disputes. And the rules of the Judgments Regulation seek to ensure that, although a number of Member States may initially have jurisdiction, litigation only proceeds in one of them.[14]

But in the regulatory sphere this distinction between jurisdiction (or competence) to exercise regulatory power on the one hand, and choice of law on the other, has hitherto not been drawn. Because of the territorial principle, each regulator has always applied its own rule book – and no other – to activities within its territory. And, as there has been no question of regulatory rules being enforceable extra-territorially, the issue of whether a regulator should apply the regulatory rules of some other State never arose. However, once the territoriality principle

---

[10] Reliance on the Treaty freedoms also being of limited efficacy, see Section III B(i).
[11] See Section III.B (ii)1 below.
[12] See n 7 above as to the position in insurance.
[13] Council Regulation (EC) No 44/2001 of 22 December 2000, [2001] OJ L12/1. The Brussels Convention 1968 still applies in Denmark. In Iceland and Norway the Brussels 1968 and Lugano Conventions still apply. For a full discussion, see AV Dicey and JHC Morris, *The Conflict of Laws* (14th edn), chaps 11–12.
[14] Arts 26–9.

Financial Services 265

begins to be modified, for example by the 'home country control' approach, the distinction between jurisdiction (or competence) and choice of law becomes relevant. It becomes important to determine whether the modification operates at the 'jurisdiction' or the 'choice of law' level or at both. As will be considered further below,[15] Community legislative measures do not always give a clear answer to this question.

III. Accommodating the Single Market

A. The Rome Convention

Although it is not always obvious how Community law interacts with the traditional domestic law principles noted above, the nature of the impact of the Rome Convention[16] and Judgments Regulation[17] is explicit and clear. The former harmonizes Member States' choice of law rules in contract and the latter harmonizes, *inter alia*, their rules as to jurisdiction in civil and commercial matters. Given this clarity of approach, there is no doubt what they seek to achieve.

Taking the example of determining which law applies to cross-border contracts effected by financial services providers (other than insurers[18]), the Rome Convention sets out reasonably clear rules for each Member State to adopt. These rules confirm the principle of autonomy in choice of law, subject to the application of certain mandatory laws[19] and supply a presumption that the law of the provider of the service generally applies in default.[20] In practice, providers usually include a choice of law clause in their contracts and so, to that extent, can decide which legal system applies to their contracts. If the service is provided to consumers, then the incentive to choose the applicable law is strong as otherwise the law of the consumer's habitual residence is likely to apply.[21] A choice of law

---

[15] See Section III.B(ii)(b).
[16] Which is not strictly 'Community law' (see n 7 above). For a full discussion, see AV Dicey and JHC Morris, *The Conflict of Laws* (14th edn), chap 32.
[17] See n 13 above.
[18] See n 7 above.
[19] Art 3. As to mandatory rules, see Art 3(3) (contracts otherwise connected with other country), Art 5(2) (consumer contracts), Art 6(1) (employment contracts), Art 7(1) (if applicable, mandatory rules of other country), Art 7(2) (mandatory rules of forum). See also Art 16 (public policy).
[20] Art 4(2). More precisely, absent a choice of law, the applicable law is generally the law of the place where the provider has its central administration or, if performance is effected through it, the law of that secondary place of business or branch
[21] Art 5(3), in the circumstances set out in Art 5(2) (i.e. if the consumer was canvassed and they acted in their country or if the consumer's order was received there). But note the exclusion in Art 5(4)(b) (supply of services exclusively in country other than consumer's habitual residence). The application of these provisions to online and other forms of 'distance' contracting is problematic. See AV Dicey and JHC Morris (n 16 above), paras 33.017–33.023. As litigation is likely to occur in the place of consumer's domicile (see Judgments Regulation, Art 16(2)), then Art 7(2) enables the forum to apply its own (and therefore the consumer's habitual residence's) mandatory rules.

clause will generally be effective even in relation to consumers, except that it cannot deprive the consumer of the 'mandatory' rules of the law of the consumer's habitual residence.[22] Thus, the general picture is clear: a provider can be confident that the law it chooses will govern its contracts, wherever in the EU it operates, subject to having to take account of the 'mandatory' laws of each Member State in relation to consumers.

The overriding nature under the Rome Convention of the 'mandatory' laws – in particular, Member State's consumer protection laws – remains a major obstacle to cross-border activity. An obvious way to reduce this obstacle is to harmonize those 'mandatory' measures throughout the single market. If 'maximum' harmonization is adopted, with Member States not being permitted to impose additional protections, then major disparities between Member States are reduced, although never eliminated.[23] An alternative, more radical approach is to adopt a mutual recognition approach based on a sufficient degree of harmonization so that the Member State of the consumer's habitual residence has to recognize the degree of protection afforded by the applicable law and concede that its law is no longer applicable. But given the 'general good' exceptions – one of which is the interests of consumers – it would seem that Community secondary legislation is needed to achieve this result.

In sum, the Rome Convention has gone some way towards facilitating the single market by injecting considerable certainty as to which law(s) apply to contractual issues. But being a choice of law measure, operating within the framework of each Member State's legal system, it is still subject to discrepancies inherent in having multiple fori applying their rules. Moreover, although in general resulting in one applicable law, certain mandatory laws (especially of the consumer's habitual residence and the forum) still apply. And even if those mandatory laws are 'harmonized', there are again the inevitable discrepancies which arise due to the fact that each Member State may take a different view of the effect of a 'harmonized' measure.

B. Community Law

(i) *The EC Treaty*

There is no doubt that the EC Treaty has an impact on the traditional approaches outlined above – including the application of the Rome Convention[24] – in so far as they inhibit cross-border activity. However, its impact is *ex post facto* and limited. It does not seek to modify the approaches themselves but only their results.

---

[22] Art 5(3). Again, how this operates in relation to online and other forms of 'distance' contracting is problematic, see previous note, including the reference to Art 7(2).

[23] Because, as noted above, there are the inevitable discrepancies resulting from differences in transposition and/or interpretation in each Member State.

[24] Art 20 of the Rome Convention gives precedence to Community law provisions (and 'national laws harmonized in implementation of such acts') which 'lay down choice of law rules'. The problem is, as explored below, that it is rarely clear when Community law provisions do 'lay down choice of law rules'.

Thus Member States are free to apply their private international law rules and/or territoriality principles unless these result in cross-border activity being hindered in a way that contravenes the Treaty freedoms. And even then the impact of the Treaty is limited to ensuring that those freedoms are safeguarded.

There have been a number of ECJ cases where Member States' ability to impose regulatory requirements on financial services firms operating within their territory has been challenged on the basis that they contravened the Treaty freedoms.[25] They demonstrate that the EC Treaty itself does not challenge the traditional approaches but merely modifies the results they give rise to, to the extent necessary to give effect to the Treaty freedoms. The deficiencies of this limited, ad hoc judicial approach in furthering the single market are obvious and explain why more drastic intervention in the form of secondary Community legislation was regarded as necessary.

(ii) The Directives
a) General
The Directive has now become a major Community law instrument in seeking to reduce the barriers to cross-border financial services activity. Rather than overtly operating within traditional principles, Directives often adopt less orthodox methods to tackle the problems posed by multiple legal systems. However, in being more innovative, these methods suffer from two conceptual shortcomings.

First, there is often no clear indication of how they interface with the traditional principles outlined above in that they rarely address the core legal issue of how the two sources of legal rules – the traditional rules and the community rules – are supposed to interact. This is problematic as Directives – or rather the measures implementing them in each Member State – do not operate in a legal vacuum. Ultimately they need to be applied by lawyers acting for clients or regulators in each of the Member States. And the starting point will be familiar domestic principles of private international law or territoriality (depending on the issue) and the question will be asked, and will need to be answered, as to how the Directives change the way these are to be applied. Unlike Community law derived from the EC Treaty itself, which clearly leaves these traditional principles alone until they reach a result which undermines the Treaty freedoms,[26] Community law derived from the Directives appears to have a more drastic impact. Yet, as will be demonstrated below, the precise impact is often unclear.

---

[25] See the early 'insurance' cases invoking Article 49 (ex 59) EC: Case C-205/84 *Commission v Germany* [1986] ECR 3755; Case 252/83 *Commission v France* [1986] ECR 3663. See more recently Case C-101/94 *Commission v Italy* [1996] ECR I-2691 and Case C-222/95 *Société Civil Immobolière Parodi v Banque H Albert de Bary et Cie* [1997] ECR I-3899. For a challenge to the home Member State's ability to extend its regulatory regime extra-territorially, see Case C-384/93 *Alpine Investment BV v Minister van Financien* 1995] ECR I-1141. And see, on Art 43 EC, Case C-442/02 *Caixa-Bank France v Ministère de l'économie* [2004] ECR I-8961.
[26] See Section III.B(i) above.

Second, the Directives have not been consistent in the approaches they have adopted. Their common core is a degree of harmonization: they all oblige Member States to adapt their domestic law, often by requiring them to impose regulatory requirements[27] but sometimes by requiring them to change their private law.[28] Thereafter a variety of means are used to try resolve the problems of multiple legal systems. Sometimes the 'home' and 'host' State[29] or 'country or origin' and 'country of destination'[30] are given spheres of responsibility, but it is by no means clear if this responsibility is meant to operate in a way that is consistent with traditional principles or whether entirely new methods of allocating enforcement responsibility and choosing applicable laws are envisaged.

b) The single market directives

The original single market directives in banking,[31] insurance[32] and investment services[33] were concerned with the barriers to the single market presented by the different regulatory systems in the Member States in relation to those sectors. Regulatory systems are aspects of public law and so the territorial principles outlined above[34] operated in this context and meant that each Member State had a regulator that imposed and enforced its own regulatory rules on activities within its territory.[35] Inspired by the *Cassis de Dijon* case,[36] a radical new approach that challenged the supremacy of the territorial principle was articulated in the famous White Paper of 1985[37] which launched the 1992 Internal Market Programme. Once Member States agreed to harmonize certain 'key' aspects of their national

---

[27] See, for example, the single market Directives, considered under (b) below.

[28] See, for example, the Distance Marketing of Consumer Financial Services Directive (DMD) and the Electronic Commerce Directive (ECD), considered at (c) and (d) below.

[29] See again, for example, the single market and related Directives, considered under (b) below.

[30] See again, for example, the Electronic Commerce Directive (ECD), considered under (c) below – although, as there noted, the ECD does not actually use those terms.

[31] The 1st Directive (No 77/780, [1977] OJ L322/30) and the Second Banking Co-ordination Directive 89/646 [1986] OJ L386/1 were amended and consolidated, with other banking Directives, in the Banking Co-ordination Directive 2000/12/EC [2000] OJ L126/1. See now Directive 2006/48/EC (hereafter 'BCD').

[32] For non-life insurance, see the 1st (No 73/239/EEC), 2nd (88/357/EEC) and 3rd (No 92/49/EEC) Directives. For life insurance, see now the consolidation Directive No 2002/83/EC (hereafter 'ICD').

[33] The Investment Services Directive 93/22 [1993] OJ L141/27, replaced by the Markets in Financial Instruments Directive, 2004/39/EC [2004] OJ L145/1 (hereafter 'MiFID').

[34] See Section II.

[35] Although there was always the possibility of a challenge on the basis of the Treaty freedoms, see Section III.B(i) above.

[36] Case 120/78 *Rewe-Zentral AG v Bundesmonopolverwaltung fur Branntwein* [1979] ECR 649 – a free movement of goods case. For the application of the 'Cassis' concept to services, see Case 262/81 *Coditel and others v Cine-Vog Films and Others* [1982] ECR 3381 and Case 76/90 *Sager Dennemeyer* [1991] ECR I-4221.

[37] *Completing the Internal Market: White Paper from the Commission to the European Council*, COM (85) 310 final. There was already some precedent for this approach in the 'UCITS passport' conferred on UCITSs (Undertakings for collective investment in transferable securities) by the UCITS Directive, 85/611, [1985] OJ L375/3 (as subsequently amended).

Financial Services   269

regulatory systems, the justification for the cumulative application of these rules by 'home' and 'host' State regulators fell away. Hence, only one regulatory system – that of the 'home' Member State – was to apply in relation to authorization and prudential supervision.[38] The 'home' state is defined as, essentially, the Member State where the undertaking has its registered and/or head office.[39] Thus authorization by the 'home' Member State gives rise to the so-called 'single passport', enabling home-state authorized undertakings to establish branches and provide cross-border services[40] without needing to comply with additional authorization or prudential requirements in other 'host' Member States. The 'host' Member State is generally[41] defined as the Member State 'in which'[42] an undertaking establishes a branch or provides services.[43] However, the Directives are less than clear on the respective roles of the 'host' and 'home' Member States' regulatory systems.

In denying the 'host' Member State the power to impose its authorization and prudential requirements on financial service providers who are already authorized in their 'home' Member State, the single market Directives clearly modify the territoriality principle. But the extent of that modification is uncertain. As regards initial authorization and ongoing prudential supervision, it seems clear that it is generally only the 'home' state rules that apply.[44] Which rules apply to other aspects of regulation, in particular conduct of business regulation, is less clear. To take the example of MiFID,[45] Article 32(7) provides that the 'host' Member State of a branch (but not that of a firm merely providing cross-border services[46]) must ensure compliance with certain (especially conduct of business) provisions listed in that Directive.[47] However, those listed provisions merely talk of 'Member States' having to impose them, without being clear (in contrast to the position in relation to authorization requirements[48]) whether it is the 'home'

---

[38] The relevant provisions are now: BCD, Art 40; ICD, Art 4; 1st non-life Directive (No 73/239/EEC), Art 6 (as substituted by 3rd non-life Directive (No 92/49/EEC), Art 4); MiFID, Art 16.

[39] The relevant provisions are now: BCD, Art 4.1(7) and Recital (10); ICD, Art 1.1(e); 3rd non-life Directive (No 92/49/EEC), Art 1(c); MiFID, Art 4.1(20).

[40] The relevant provisions are now: BCD, Art 23; ICD, Art 5.1; 1st non-life Directive (No 73/239/EEC), Art 7 (as substituted by 3rd non-life Directive (No 92/49/EEC), Art 5); MiFID, Arts 31 and 32.

[41] The position in insurance is different, but the effect is analogous.

[42] There is much controversy as to when services are provided 'in' a Member State – yet the same definition is adopted in the BCD and MIFID. See the Commission's Interpretative Communication, *Freedom to Provide Services and the Interest of the General Good in the Second Banking Directive* SEC (97) 1193 final (20 June 1997).

[43] BCD, Art 4.1(8); MIFID Art 4.1(21).

[44] BCD, Art 22; ICD, *passim*; MiFID, Art 5(1), 13(1).

[45] See n 33 above.

[46] There is no equivalent provision to Art 32(7) in Art 31 in relation to the provision of services so it is clear that the 'home' Member State has sole responsibility if its firms merely provide cross-border services and do not set up branches.

[47] Those in Arts 19, 21, 22, 25, 27 and 28.

[48] i.e. 'organisation requirements': Art 13 explicitly obliges the 'home' Member State to 'require' the firm to comply with detailed 'organisational requirements', Art 13(9) making provision for the 'host' State ('without prejudice' to the powers of the 'home' State) to enforce the requirement as to records.

or 'host' State's rules which actually apply. Although these requirements will be harmonized,[49] it will still be necessary to be clear which Member State's 'harmonized' rules actually apply. It requires a very close reading of other MiFID provisions[50] to justify the prevailing view[51] that the 'host' state's responsibility extends to imposing its own rules rather than just enforcing the relevant 'home' State rules. Thus for situations outside Article 32(7) (including situations where only services are provided in the 'host' Member State) it must follow, at least implicitly, that it is the 'home' State's rules that apply in relation to all matters covered by the Directive.[52]

The single market Directives illustrate how, if traditional principles (in their case, the territorial principle applicable to regulatory law) are to be modified in pursuit of the single market, the extent of that modification needs to be very clear. If it is not, then it is hardly surprising that Member States continue to apply familiar principles which at best continue to present obstacles to cross-border provision but at worst, in combination with the confusion engendered by differing views of the impact of the modification, make those obstacles worse.

c) The Electronic Commerce Directive (the ECD)

This Directive,[53] although superficially similar in concept to the single market Directives is, on closer examination,[54] a very different measure. It identifies a wide 'co-ordinated field',[55] comprising both public and private law rules which apply to 'information society services' (ISSs) and providers of such services. It then introduces a (small) degree of harmonization of some of those rules[56] – but is explicitly 'without prejudice to future Community harmonization relating to [ISSs] and to future legislation adopted at national level in accordance with Community law'.[57] Finally, Article 3, the so-called 'internal market' clause,[58]

---

[49] See MiFID Implementing Regulation (EC) 1287/2006 and Directive 2006/73/EC, supplementing Arts 22(7), 27 and 28.

[50] Primarily Art 61.2, which talks of 'standards set by the host Member State that apply... for the cases provided for in Article 32(7)'. Moreover, a comparison of the last paragraph of Art 31(1) (in relation to services) and of Art 32(1) (in relation to branches) suggests that 'host' Member States may 'impose additional requirements... allowed under' Art 32(7).

[51] Confirmed by the Commission's Document: *Supervision of branches under MiFID*; MARKT/ G/3/MV D(2007) 2386 (18 June 2007).

[52] Again, confirmed by ibid.

[53] Directive 2000/31/EC [2000] OJ L178/1, as amended. See J Hornle, 'Country of origin regulation in cross-border media: one step beyond the freedom to provide services' (2005) 54 ICLQ 89.

[54] The *travaux preparatoires* and subsequent Commission Communication on *E-Commerce and Financial Services* COM (2001) 66 final (9 Feb 2001) 'explain' that it extends the 'home country control' principle in relation to the 'country of origin', but the actual text of the Directive (as will be considered below) is more equivocal. As many Member States (although not the UK) have used the 'copy out' method of implementing the Directive, the actual text is likely to be determinative of how it is interpreted in those Member States.

[55] Defined in Art 2(h).

[56] Arts 4–15.

[57] Recital (21).

[58] That being the article's title.

makes special provision in relation to the 'co-ordinated field' rules in the Member States involved in cross-border electronic commerce.

The first surprising feature is that the ECD makes no explicit mention either of a 'home' or 'host' state. The corresponding concepts adopted by commentators – although these terms are also not expressly used in the ECD – are 'country of origin' and 'country of destination'.[59] Although broadly corresponding to the 'home' and 'host' State in the single market Directives, in the sense that the ECD imposes different obligations on each of those Member States, it must not be assumed that they correspond in meaning. The 'country of origin' is the Member State where the ISS provider is 'established', the term 'established service provider' being defined to mean one 'who effectively pursues an economic activity using a fixed establishment for an indefinite period'.[60] Thus if an ISS provider has a registered and head office in Member State A, provides the ISS from a branch in Member State B, with customers in Member State C accessing its internet site, then State A is the 'home' state for the purposes of the single market Directives,[61] State B is the 'host' state for the purpose of those Directives[62] but the 'country of origin' for the purposes of the ECD,[63] with State C being the 'country of destination' for the purposes of the ECD.[64]

The 'internal market' clause addresses the responsibilities of the 'country of origin' and the 'country of destination'. As regards the 'country of origin', Article 3(1) provides that this Member State: 'shall ensure that the [ISSs] provided by a service provider established on its territory comply with the national provisions applicable in the Member State in question which fall within the co-ordinated field.' As regards the country of destination, Article 3(2) provides that this Member State: 'may not, for reasons falling within the co-ordinated field, restrict the freedom to provide [ISSs] from another Member State'.[65]

Reading these provisions in isolation, it is by no means clear how – if at all – they are meant to affect traditional domestic law principles of private international law

---

[59] Recital (5) talks of 'services *originating* from another Member State' and Recital (22) talks of the Member State 'where services *originate*' (emphasis added). The *travaux preparatoires* and subsequent Official Community documents have adopted the terms 'country or origin' and 'country of destination'. See Thunken (2002) 51 ICLQ 909; Hornle (2005) 54 ICLQ 89.

[60] Art 2(c). It adds: 'The presence and use of the technical means and technologies required to provide the service do not, in themselves, constitute an establishment of the provider'.

[61] See Section III.B(ii)(b) above.

[62] See n 43 above.

[63] See n 60 above.

[64] Some argue that it may also be a 'host' Member State for the purposes of the single passport Directives, but this depends on whether giving access to its internet site is the provision of services 'in' Member State C. See n 42 above.

[65] There are significant derogations, especially in the Annex (see Art 3(3)) and Art 3(4)–(6)). There is already a Commission Interpretative Communication on the latter: *Application to Financial Services of Art 3(4) to (6) of the Electronic Commerce Directive* COM (2003) 259 final (14 May 2003).

and territoriality, considered above.[66] This is because Article 3 merely addresses the position, first in one Member State (the 'country of origin') and then the other (the 'country of destination'), without indicating how the laws and institutions of the two legal systems are meant to work together.

Starting with Article 3(2), this in terms appears to do no more than reinforce the Treaty freedom to provide services. If that is its only effect, then (like the EC Treaty)[67] it has no impact on the traditional principles but merely comes into play if those principles reach a result that restricts the freedom to provide services in the country of destination. Whether it goes any further depends on the effect of the words 'for reasons falling within the co-ordinated field' – an apparent reference back to Article 3(1). But the effect of Article 3(1) is equally obscure. In obliging the 'country of origin' to 'ensure' that its ISS providers abide by its (public and private) 'co-ordinated field' rules, it clearly requires Member States to revise their domestic 'co-ordinated field' rules so that these rules apply to their ISS providers irrespective of where, in the single market, they provide ISSs. Whether it goes further and interferes with the traditional domestic law principles outlined above depends on what 'ensuring compliance' with the co-ordinated field rules actually means and how this relates to the 'country of destination's' responsibilities under Article 3(2).

One possibility is that the internal market clause operates as a choice of law rule which chooses the 'country of origin's' rules – those private and public rules comprising the co-ordinated field – as the rules applicable wherever, within the single market, the ISS providers operate.[68] If this is its effect, it has a major impact on the traditional rules. In so far as the co-ordinated field comprises regulatory rules, the territoriality principle is modified: the rules of the 'country of origin' operate extraterritorially.[69] In so far as the co-ordinated field comprises private law rules, then again private international law rules are modified in so far as they would reach a contrary conclusion as to the applicable law.[70] In the contractual context, as demonstrated above,[71] the Rome Convention often leads to the application of the service provider's law – which may well be the law of 'country of

---

[66] Section II. See Fawcett, Harris and Bridge, *International Sale of Goods in the Conflict of Laws* (2005), 1226–33; Dicey and Morris, *The Conflict of Laws* (14th ed), para 35–158 et seq.

[67] See Section III.B.(i).

[68] See Thunken (2002) 51 ICLQ 909, 940–1, especially footnote 171 (for the debate on this issue in Germany).

[69] Although regulators have increasingly sought to regulate how firms established in their territory operate, even as regards activities *outside* their territory. And see the *Alpine Investments* case (n 25 above) where such a rule (outlawing cold-calling of investments in commodities) survived EC Treaty challenge. And, of course, the single market Directives have this effect as regards authorization and prudential supervision, see section III.B(ii)(b) above.

[70] As noted in n 24 above, Art 20 of the Rome Convention makes it clear that Community provisions 'which...lay down choice of law rules' take precedence over the rules in the Convention.

[71] Section III.A.

origin' – but this is by no means always the case.[72] However, as for the overriding effect of mandatory consumer protection rules, the ECD excludes these from the co-ordinated field[73] and hence, to that extent, the ECD has no effect on the operation of the normal private international rules.

As well as addressing the choice of law issue, the internal market clause could also – or possibly alternatively – be addressing the 'jurisdiction' issue. Thus it may be addressing the competence of the institutions of the two relevant Member States to enforce the 'co-ordinated field' rules. In the private law context, there is nothing to suggest that the jurisdiction of the Member States' courts to try *inter partes* disputes is being disturbed – although wherever litigation ensues (according to the rules of the Judgment Regulation[74]), those courts will have to face the choice of law issue explored above: should they apply their own private international law rules, merely making sure that the result does not entail a restriction of the freedom to provide services, or does the internal market clause require them to choose the law of the 'country of origin' as the applicable law from the outset? In the regulatory context it is more arguable that the internal market clause has an impact on the competence of the regulators to act against ISS providers. Normal territorial principles would allow each regulator in each Member State to decide when it can act against ISS providers operating within its territory, so regulators in both the 'country of origin' and 'country of destination' would have competence. In this case, the regulator in the 'country of destination'[75] would face the 'choice of law' question: should it be enforcing its own 'co-ordinated field' rule book, except to the extent that it restricts the freedom of ISS provision, or should it be enforcing the 'co-ordinated field' rules of the 'country of origin'? Whatever the answer to the 'choice of law' issue is, by requiring the 'country of origin' to 'ensure' that ISS providers 'comply' with its rules and by precluding the country of destination from 'restrict[ing] the freedom to provide services', it may be that the internal market clause is seeking to disturb the normal territorial distribution of regulatory competence. Like the single market Directives, it may be conferring on the 'country of origin' regulator, sole competence to 'ensure compliance' with and hence enforce its own regulatory rules. The issue may often not be that

---

[72] Thus ISS providers may (say) choose the law of the place of their head office, irrespective of which branch provides the ISS, in which case (according to the Rome Convention rules) the applicable law will not be the law of the 'country of origin' but the chosen (place of head office) law.

[73] Art 3(3) and hence the Annex exclude 'contractual obligations concerning consumer contracts' and see Recital (55) which makes it clear that the Rome Convention still applies ('this Directive cannot have the result of depriving the consumer of the protection afforded to him by the mandatory rules relating to contractual obligations of the law of the Member State in which he has his habitual residence').

[74] See Section II.C above. If a consumer is being sued, this is likely to be the place of his domicile (see Judgment Regulation, Art 16(2)) i.e. usually the country of destination.

[75] As the 'country of origin' would have changed its law (in accordance with Art 3(1)) so that its domestic 'co-ordinated field' rules apply to its ISS providers, wherever in the single market they act, it would be clear that the regulator on the 'country of origin' should enforce those 'country of origin rules'.

important in practice, as the lack of physical presence of the ISS provider in the 'country of destination' will usually mean that its regulator will be unable to enforce whatever powers it may claim to have. However, there may be occasions – for example, if the 'country of destination' is a place where the ISS provider has assets or keeps 'the technical means and technologies required' to support its website'[76] – when the exercise of 'country of destination' regulatory power against the ISS provider will, as a matter of practicalities, be possible.

So far, the internal market clause has been considered in isolation without reference to its wider ECD context. Unfortunately, the rest of the ECD sends mixed messages as to the precise effect of the internal market clause. Article 1(4) states that it 'does not establish additional rules on private international law nor does it deal with the jurisdiction of the courts'.[77] The corresponding Recital[78] adds, 'provisions of the applicable law designated by rules of private international law must not restrict the freedom to provide' ISS. This appears to rule out the possibility explored above that the internal market clause operates as a 'choice of law' provision in the private law context as this would give rise to an 'additional' rule of private international law. And the proviso in the Recital appears to assume that the normal private international law principles will continue to apply to 'designate' the 'applicable law', with Article 3(2) operating *ex post facto* if the applicable law's provisions restrict the freedom to provide services. However, if private international law principles would lead to the application of a law other than the 'country of origin',[79] then Article 3(1) is deprived of much of its effect in the private law context – unless it is envisaged as converting all 'country of origin' rules in the co-ordinated field into mandatory rules which over-ride the applicable law.[80] On the other hand, Recital (5) talks of ISS provision being hampered by 'legal obstacles to the proper functioning of the internal market...aris[ing] from the legal uncertainty as to which national rules apply' – which suggests that the Directive is addressing choice of law 'uncertainties' and hence providing a clear ('country of origin') choice of law rule. Moreover, Recital (22) states that ISSs 'should in principle be subject to the law of the Member State in which the service provider is established', again supporting the view that a choice of law rule is intended. One possible interpretation of Article 3(1), which gives it a 'choice of law' force whilst not contradicting Article 1(4), is to make a distinction between private and regulatory law. Thus Article 3(1) might be regarded as choosing the

---

[76] Which, in itself, is not sufficient to constitute that place the 'country of origin': Art 2(c).

[77] And note the derogation in the Annex for 'the freedom of the parties to choose the law applicable to their contract'.

[78] Recital (23). Recital (55), cited at n 73 above, seems ambiguous. It may merely be confirmatory of the application of the Rome Convention (in relation to consumers), or it may be implying that, in other cases, normal 'Rome' rules do *not* apply.

[79] See n 72 above.

[80] But then only those 'country of destination' Member States which have adopted Art 7(1) of the Rome Convention (of which the UK is not one) would be obliged to apply the 'country of origin' co-ordinate field rules.

'country of origin's' regulatory rules as applicable to ISS providers, whilst leaving private international law intact to determine the choice of law in contractual and other private law disputes.[81] This might result in a mismatch between the applicable laws in relation to the private and regulatory aspects of ISS cross-border distance provision, with the result that only complying with the 'country of origin' regulatory rules might not protect the supplier from private law liability.[82] However, Article 3(2) would then become relevant so that the 'additional' private law liability might well be regarded as a restriction of 'the freedom to provide ISSs from another Member State' and hence could be held not to arise.

The conclusion that the ECD has no impact on the rules as to the courts' jurisdiction appears correct in the light of Article 1(4)'s denial that it deals 'with the jurisdiction of the courts', as there is nothing in the Recitals which undermines this conclusion. But when it comes to regulatory competence the position is less clear. As suggested above, the terms of the internal market clause, in particular the obligation of the 'country of origin' to 'ensure compliance' with its 'co-ordinated field' rules, are ambiguous in this regard. However, the Recitals suggest that some interference with regulatory competence may be envisaged. Thus Recital (5), referred to above, also notes that 'legal uncertainty exists with regard to the extent to which Member States may control services originating from another Member State'. Assuming 'control' is a reference to the exercise of regulatory power, this suggests that the Directive addresses this 'uncertainty'. Moreover, Recital (22), also referred to above, states that ISSs 'should be supervised at the source of the activity' and talks of the necessity 'to state clearly this responsibility on the part of the Member States where the services originate'. But there is nothing in the ECD which comes near to the elaborate and relatively precise provisions in the single market Directives which explicitly re-allocate regulatory responsibility.[83]

Therefore it is tempting to conclude that all the internal market clause does is positively to oblige the legislators of the 'country of origin' to make rules and enforce them over their ISS providers even when they act extraterritorially, but no more. In particular, there is nothing explicit to deprive the regulators of the 'country of destination' of their traditional powers to use such powers as they have against ISS providers who operate within their territory – assuming that the ISS provider is practically amenable to such regulatory power. And, unless the internal market clause is a choice of law clause, those 'country of destination' regulators may impose their own 'co-ordinated field' rules on such ISS providers – save where

---

[81] This appears to be the view taken by the UK regulatory authorities. See FSA CP192, para 4.18–4.29. And see the ECO Module of the FSA Handbook, made in implementation of the ECD.

[82] As far as contractual liability is concerned, the provider would be well advised to choose the law of the 'country of origin' so that, mandatory rules apart, contractual and regulatory duties would be co-extensive. But if the applicable law is not the law of the country of origin (for example, in relation to delictual claims arising from advertising – which is within the 'co-ordinated field') then liability may arise under it even if the 'country of origin' regulatory rules have been complied with.

[83] See Section III.B(ii)(b).

this constitutes a restriction on the freedom to provide ISSs[84] or more generally interferes with the Treaty freedoms.[85] Similarly, any judicial tribunal may determine the applicable law by applying traditional principles of private international law (including the Rome Convention in relation to non-insurance contractual issues) and if these rules lead to some law other than that of the 'country of origin' applying then so be it – unless again this results in a restriction on the freedom to provide ISSs[86] or more generally interferes with the Treaty freedoms.[87]

In conclusion, the ECD, whilst attempting to tackle the 'legal obstacles' which the multiple legal systems of the Member States present and to remove the consequent 'uncertainty',[88] has created uncertainties of its own. This is because it has not spelt out with any clarity how it has modified – if at all – those traditional rules which give rise to those 'legal obstacles'. The major question is whether it contains a choice of law rule, rendering the 'co-ordinated field' private and/or public law rules of the 'country of origin' applicable to ISS provision, wherever in the internal market this provision occurs.[89] But there is also uncertainty as to the extent the ECD interferes with the competence of the regulators of the 'country of destination' to exercise their traditional territorially based powers to act against ISS providers operating within their territory.[90]

(d) The Distance Marketing Directive (the DMD)

On the face of it, the DMD[91] is an example of a maximum harmonization measure,[92] illustrative of the first type of harmonization technique considered above.[93] It appears, in terms, to have no direct impact on traditional principles

---

[84] Within Art 3(2).

[85] As it may well do because these rules are likely to be duplicative of the 'country of origin's' rules and hence the 'Cassis' approach (as extended to services) will apply, see n 36 above.

[86] Within Art 3(2).

[87] For example, by imposing liabilities which do not exist under the law of the 'country of origin', see text following n 82 above.

[88] Recital (5).

[89] In the UK, the DTI, Treasury and FSA have taken the view that, in the regulatory context, they should disapply the UK regulatory regime in relation to ISS provided from an establishment in another EEA Member State; see (i) DTI *Consultation Document on implementation of the E-Commerce Directive* (August 2001); (ii) HMT's Consultation Documents on the *Implementation of the E-Commerce Directive in Financial Services*, December 2001 and March 2002; (iii) the FSA's Consultation Paper No 129, *Implementing the Electronic Commerce Directive* (March 2002) and Policy Statement, *Feedback on CP129* (August 2002). For the detail, see the Electronic Commerce (E.C. Directive) Regulations 2002, SI 2002/2013 and the FSA's E-Commerce Directive Sourcebook (the ECO), which forms part of its handbook.

[90] Although the UK has decided to forgo its powers over 'incoming' ISS providers from other Member States, whether other Member States will be similarly abstemious remains to be seen. The FSA notes in CP129, para 4.13 that 'The way in which these provisions are implemented across the EEA will determine how much benefit consumers and providers of financial services derive from the opportunities offered by the ECD'.

[91] Directive 2002/65/EC, [2002] OJ L 271/16.

[92] See Recital (13). But Art 4(2) permits Member States to impose 'more stringent information requirements when the provisions are in conformity with Community law'.

[93] See Section I.

of private international law or territoriality[94] but merely seeks to harmonize Member States' domestic law so that the inhibitory effects of applying those traditional principles on cross-border activity are reduced.[95] That it operates within the framework of traditional private international law principles seems to be confirmed by Recital (8), which states that the Directive 'does not affect the applicability to the distance marketing of consumer financial services' of the Judgment Regulation or the Rome Convention.[96] Of course, some distance marketing will be done electronically – in which case, the ECD will become relevant[97] – but, as noted above, that hardly clarifies the position and will bring problems of its own.

The DMD lays down a number of consumer protection measures in relation to 'distance contracts'.[98] In essence, the consumer must receive certain information from the supplier prior to the conclusion of a 'distance contract'[99] and must generally have a right to cancel the contract.[100] Thus it operates both at the private law level (the relevant contracts are cancellable, the information may give rise to private law liabilities on the part of the supplier) and at the regulatory level (suppliers need to comply with regulatory rules obliging them to confer these rights on consumers), Member States being obliged to implement the Directive by adapting their domestic laws to give effect to it. And, on the face of it, traditional domestic law principles will still operate to determine which law applies to the contract and to the supplier's liabilities and which institutions are able to enforce those consumer protection rules. Thus, although the individual Member States' laws will have been harmonized, a particular Member State's law will still be applicable and a particular Member State's institutions will still have competence to enforce that law, in any given case, according to those traditional principles.

In the private law sphere, the Rome Convention rules – as implemented in the relevant Member State in which the contractual issue is being decided – will generally operate to identify the applicable law(s).[101] Indeed, one of the items of information which the consumer must be given is 'any contractual clause on law

---

[94] There are only two oblique references to the different Member States involved in distance marketing. The first is Recital (7): 'This Directive [is]...without prejudice to...where applicable, host Member State control and/or authorisation or supervision systems in the Member States.' The second is Art 16, which appears to refer to the supplier's 'country of origin', considered further, below. Recitals (4) and (28) also talk of Member States where the supplier is 'established' and see Art 3.1(1)(a) (address where supplier is 'established' to be given to consumer).

[95] And, perhaps, so that the *Cassis* doctrine might be invoked (see n 36 above) – although the impact of this doctrine on consumer protection measures is uncertain, given the inclusion of consumer protection in the 'general good' exceptions list.

[96] And see Art 3.1(e) and (f) (on the applicable law before and after contracting) and Art 12.2 (reference to loss of protection through choice of law of non-member country).

[97] Recital (6) confirms that the DMD 'should be applied in conformity with the Treaty and with secondary law, including [the ECD]'. But note the ECD exclusion for 'consumer contracts' (n 73 above).

[98] Defined in Art 2(a).

[99] Arts 3–5.

[100] Called a 'right of withdrawal' in the Directive: Arts 6–7.

[101] See Section III.A above.

applicable to the distance contract'.[102] Assuming the supplier has chosen his own law,[103] this will apply together with any relevant mandatory laws, in particular of the consumer's habitual residence.[104] It is when these individual Member States' laws fall to be applied that the inevitable discrepancies which harmonization cannot eliminate come to the fore. Ideally, if both the applicable law and the law of the consumers habitual residence have implemented the DMD and the supplier has complied with the former, it will also have complied with the law of the latter. But this may not always be the case. For example, there may be disagreement as to when the DMD protections apply[105] so that according to the applicable law the DMD requirements do not apply whilst according to the law of the consumer's habitual residence they do and have not been fulfilled. Assuming that the DMD requirements would be regarded as 'mandatory' laws, the law of the consumer's habitual residence would generally[106] apply to, *inter alia*, confer a right of cancellation in situations where one did not exist under the applicable law.

Turning to the regulatory context, financial services regulators in each Member State are obliged to ensure that consumers obtain the DMD protections and hence that suppliers comply with the DMD requirements.[107] Applying ordinary territorial principles, it would be up to each regulator to exercise such powers as it had under its domestic legal system over its territory. There is no clear indication in the DMD[108] as to which regulators – those where the supplier has its registered office (the 'home' State regulators, using the single market Directive terminology)[109] or those where the supplier has its branch from which the distance services are provided (the 'country of origin' state, using the ECD terminology)[110] or those where the consumer is (the 'country of destination'

---

[102] Art 3.1(3)(f). See also Art 12.2, which assumes that a distance contract can *prima facie* choose the law of a non-Member State and provides against this if the result would be a loss of the DMD protection (although Art 5(2) of the Rome Convention – if applicable – would lead to that result anyway) and see Case C-381/98 *Ingmar GB Ltd v Eaton Leonard Technologies Inc* [2000] ECR I-9305.

[103] Either the law of the place of its head office or, if it has branches, the law of the place where the relevant branch is. In the former case, this will not be the law of the 'country of origin' in the ECD sense (see n 72 above).

[104] As noted above (n 21), under the Judgments Regulation, this will usually also be the law of the forum. But as also there noted, the application of Art 5(2) and (3) to distance-contracting, especially online contracting, is problematic.

[105] Member States may, in transposing the Directive or interpreting the resulting domestic law, disagree as to whether the contract is a 'distance contract'. Or Member States may have used the derogation in Art 6.3 (enabling them to provide that certain contracts are not cancellable) differently.

[106] Unless the view were take that Art 5(2) or (3) (as the case may be, dependant on whether there was a choice of law clause or not) did not apply in relation to that particular 'distance contract'.

[107] Art 11: 'Member States shall provide for appropriate sanctions in the event of the supplier's failure to comply with national provisions adopted pursuant to this Directive'. And see Art 13 (judicial and administrative redress).

[108] But see Art 16, considered below.

[109] See Section III.B (ii)(b).

[110] See Section III.B(ii)(c) – which is the 'host' Member State under the single passport Directives (see n 43 above).

Financial Services

State, using the ECD terminology) – have competence to enforce the DMD requirements. Therefore, the preliminary conclusion must be that normal territorial principles apply and so any given regulator has competence to enforce the DMD requirements in such circumstances as local regulatory rules (and practical considerations) permit. In the distance marketing context, the regulator in the consumer's Member State is unlikely to have any practical means of enforcement against the (distance) supplier, although there will be situations where this might be a possibility,[111] in which case there seems no reason why it could not rely on normal territorial principles to do so. But whichever regulator acts, the 'choice of law' question will again arise: which Member State's DMD protections is the consumer entitled to? As noted above, even assuming each Member State has implemented the DMD, there may be discrepancies between the various local laws, in which case it will become important to know whether it is the regulator's Member State's DMD rules which operate or the consumer's Member State's or a combination of the two.

There is one mysterious provision in the DMD which suggests that the intention is that traditional domestic law principles do not operate. Article 16 is headed 'Transitional Measures' and it provides: 'Member States may impose national rules which are in conformity with this Directive on suppliers established in a Member State which has not yet transposed this Directive and whose law has no obligations corresponding to those provided for in this Directive.' The implication appears to be that Member States may only impose their DMD rules on suppliers 'established'[112] elsewhere if that Member State has not yet transposed the DMD and has no other corresponding provisions; that if the 'country of origin' has transposed the DMD or already has corresponding provisions, then these provisions apply instead. Yet, as explained above,[113] traditional principles of both private international law (in relation to private law) and territoriality (in relation to regulatory law) enable a Member State to 'impose' its national private and regulatory rules on suppliers from other Member States in the circumstances outlined above. The law of the 'country of origin' may well be the applicable law in contract – but this is not necessarily or exclusively the case.[114] And although the law of the 'country of origin' will be the law applied by the 'country of origin' regulators, regulators from other Member States will expect to apply their own DMD provisions to protect their own consumers. Hence it must be concluded that Article 16 implies that traditional principles do not apply when it comes to

---

[111] See text accompanying n 76 above.
[112] The term 'established' is not defined, but given the reference to the ECD in Recital (6), it seems likely (and that is certainly the view in the UK, see the Consultation Documents referred to at n 119 below) that the term refers to the 'country of origin' within the meaning of the ECD (although Recital (7) talks of 'host' State control – which echoes the single market Directives). The term 'supplier established' is also used in Recitals (4) and (28) – and see Art 3.1(1)(a), all referred to at n 94 above.
[113] See Section II.
[114] See n 72 above.

DMD requirements. Which leads again to the question: to what extent are they modified?

Given the clear provision in the preamble[115] that the Directive 'does not affect the applicability' either of the Judgments Regulation or the Rome Convention, it would seem that Article 16 cannot be referring to the private law context. In particular, if the Rome Convention rules lead to the conclusion that some law other than the law of the 'country of origin' applies, then that law must be 'imposed' on the parties. Therefore, it would seem that Article 16 is referring to the regulatory context and implies that country of destination regulators cannot 'impose' their DMD 'national rules' on suppliers 'established in' other Member States, the further implication being that the regulatory rules of the 'country of origin' will apply instead. Whether Article 16 has any (implicit) effect on the competence of regulators to enforce whichever DMD rules apply is less clear. Moreover, if this reading of Article 16 is correct, there is again[116] a mismatch between the private law and public law which applies to cross-border distance provision. If there are discrepancies in the transposition of the DMD between the 'country of origin' and the 'country of destination' – for example, the former does not regard certain contracts as 'distance contracts' entailing the DMD protections whilst the latter does – then in contractual and other private law[117] matters, suppliers must have regard to the DMD rules in the 'country of destination',[118] whereas in regulatory matters they need only satisfy their 'country of origin's' rulebook.

In the UK, the view has been taken by the regulators that 'the DMD is intended to operate on a country of origin basis'[119] – although it is conceded that this is not 'expressly stated within its text'.[120] Thus, the UK has changed its law[121] so that the UK's DMD provisions (a) apply to firms operating from a UK establishment whether they target the UK or other Member State market(s)

---

[115] Recital (8).

[116] As there is under the ECD, if such a distinction between 'private' and 'regulatory' rules is made. See text accompanying n 82 above.

[117] For example, delictual liability.

[118] Assuming that Art 5(2) or (3) (as the case may be) applies to the distance contract (about which there may be doubt; see further n 21 above) and that DMD rules would be regarded as 'mandatory'. It may be that this is what Recital (7) is referring to when it states that the Directive is 'without prejudice to...where applicable, host Member State control' – yet it is unclear which is the 'host' State (for the purposes of the single passport Directive, see n 43 above and accompanying text).

[119] FSA Consultation Paper No 196, *Implementation of the Distance Marketing Directive: proposed rules and guidance*, September 2003, para 3.21. See also HM Treasury Consultation Document, *Implementation of the Distance Marketing of Consumer Financial Services Directive*, paras 21–5.

[120] See the FSA's paper, para 3.21. The HMT Consultation Document also admits (at para 21) that 'nowhere in the DMD is there an explicit provision as to whether it is the competent authorities of the supplier's or the consumer's state that should be responsible for enforcing its provisions'.

[121] See, especially, the Financial Services (Distance Marketing) Regulations 2004, SI 2004/2095. And see the changes made by the FSA to its handbook.

and (b) do not apply to firms operating from an establishment elsewhere in the EEA.[122] In the regulatory sphere, the UK is clearly entitled to determine the territorial reach of its own rules and enforcement powers, in so far as their exercise in the UK is concerned. However, whether other Member States will also take that view and agree that their 'country of destination' rules and enforcement powers do not apply to UK established distance providers targeting their consumers is another matter. Moreover, in the private law sphere, again the UK is entitled to determine that its DMD protections do not apply to its consumers when dealing with suppliers established elsewhere in the EEA. But it remains to be seen if other Member States will take a similar view of their DMD protections in relation to suppliers from the UK. If, because of differences in transposition, the 'country of origin's' DMD protections are not as extensive as those of the consumer's country, the pressures to use traditional principles of private international law[123] or territoriality[124] to override the law of the 'country of origin' on the basis that the DMD does not, in clear terms, change them may be overwhelming.

IV. Conclusion

Facilitating the single market clearly requires a rethinking of traditional methods of determining both which Member State's laws (whether private or public) apply to cross-border activity and which Member State's institutions (whether judicial or regulatory) have competence to enforce those laws. It is not enough to continue to permit Member States to invoke those traditional principles of private international law (in relation to private law) and territoriality (in relation to regulatory law) and to fall back on the Treaty freedoms or to attempt harmonization, without more, to overcome the impediments to cross-border activity that those traditional methods give rise to. Those traditional methods were developed in the context of independent states, jealously asserting and guarding their autonomy to devise and enforce their own laws. Membership of the EU – and the commitment to a single market – challenges this attitude, as does harmonization which challenges the wisdom of insisting on the cumulative application of Member States' laws that are (in theory) the same.

The 'home country control' principle, based on an appropriate degree of harmonization, constitutes such a re-thinking of traditional principles: the choosing of one Member State – the home Member State – as having the sole competence to impose its own rules and the primary competence to enforce them. In the

---

[122] See HM Treasury Consultation Document, *Implementation of the Distance Marketing of Consumer Financial Services Directive*, para 22, stating: 'since it is the rules of that state – the country of origin – that will apply'.

[123] Which are likely to result in the application of the consumer protection provisions of the consumer's habitual residence, assuming Art 5(2) or (3) (as the case may be) applies.

[124] Which permits a regulator to apply its own rule book within its territory.

narrow regulatory context of authorization and prudential supervision of financial services firms, the principle was introduced successfully by the single market Directives which made it relatively clear – at least in relation to those core responsibilities – that the traditional territorial principle which gave host Member States competence to impose and enforce their own legal requirements had been modified. But subsequent Directives, in particular the ECD and the DMD, although apparently seeking to apply a similar principle – based this time on the 'country of origin' – to electronic commerce and distance marketing, have singularly failed to make clear precisely how (if at all) the traditional principles are to be modified. Instead of increasing certainty, they have left more confusion in their wake and potentially put back rather than furthered the achievement of the single market in financial services.

16
Equal Before the Law? Not if You Want to Register a Trade Mark

*David T Keeling**

I. The Principle of Equal Treatment

Trade mark applicants who are told that their trade mark cannot be registered because, for example, it is devoid of distinctive character or descriptive, frequently argue that other trade marks no more distinctive than theirs have been placed on the register. How, they complain, can it be fair to deny them the advantages of registration when these same advantages have been granted to other firms, perhaps even their most feared competitors, in respect of comparable trade marks?

Trade mark applicants who make this complaint are, whether they know it or not, invoking the principle of equal treatment, also known as the principle of non-discrimination. One might expect this argument to be taken rather seriously by the European Court of Justice and the Court of First Instance, which would surely take the trouble to examine the previous examples of favourable treatment cited by the party in question and consider whether the case they are required to adjudicate on merits the same treatment.

The principle of equal treatment is, after all, one of the fundamental principles of the Community legal order; it 'requires that similar situations shall not be treated differently unless differentiation is objectively justified'.[1] Indeed, it could be argued that a general principle of non-discrimination is the foundation of law itself. The very concept of law presupposes the existence of clear, predetermined rules which will be applied objectively and consistently to specific situations. Total consistency is, of course, impossible, especially in an area like trade mark law where the objective application of rules is difficult because so much depends on subjective appraisals. The same could, however, be said about

---

* Member of the Board of Appeal of the Office for Harmonization in the Internal Market (Trade Marks and Designs).

[1] Joined Cases 117/76 and 16/77 *Ruckdeschel v Hauptzollamt Hamburg–St Annen* [1977] ECR 1753, para 7.

virtually any branch of law, but that is not an excuse for abandoning any attempt to apply the law consistently. Arbitrary conduct on the part of administrative bodies is unacceptable. That, in a nutshell, is what the principle of equal treatment is about.

II. The Doctrine of Circumscribed Powers

Why, then, have the ECJ and CFI handed down a number of judgments that have made it practically impossible for trade mark applicants to invoke the principle of equal treatment? Why have the Courts produced case law that legitimizes arbitrary conduct on the part of the authorities, both administrative and judicial, responsible for applying trade mark law in the European Union? For let there be no mistake! That is what the Courts have done. If a trade mark applicant goes to Luxembourg and argues that the Office for Harmonization in the Internal Market (Trade Marks and Designs) (OHIM) and its Boards of Appeal should not have rejected his trade mark on grounds of descriptiveness because they had accepted three dozen equally descriptive trade marks, even in relation to similar goods or services, it is unlikely that he will persuade the CFI or ECJ even to look at any of the three dozen earlier cases and consider whether his application is on all fours with them and entitled to equal treatment. The discrimination argument will not get off the ground.

Our putative trade mark applicant will be fobbed off with a piece of ingenious sophistry that calls itself the doctrine of circumscribed powers. This curious doctrine of law, the provenance of which is unknown,[2] made its first appearance in *Streamserve Inc v OHIM*, a case decided in February 2002.[3] In that case Streamserve Inc, a company from North Carolina, applied to register Streamserve as a Community trade mark for various goods, including 'apparatus for recording, transmitting and reproducing sounds and images; data processing equipment, including computers, computer memories, viewing screens, keyboards, processors, printers and scanners; computer programs stored on tapes, disks, diskettes and other machine-readable media' in Class 9 of the Nice Classification. An OHIM examiner refused the application and the decision was confirmed by the Board of Appeal. The basis for the refusal was that the

---

[2] The concept of *compétence liée* exists in French administrative law but it does not, so far as I can establish, have the effect attributed to it by the CFI. *Compétence liée* is the opposite of *pouvoir discrétionnaire*. It means that the administration, having established the existence of certain facts, is compelled to take a particular decision and has no choice in the matter. A decision dictated by a *compétence liée* will not be annulled even though it was vitiated by a formal defect. That appears to be the significance given to the concept of *compétence liée* in French administrative law. It does not have the effect of rendering the principle of equal treatment irrelevant. For further information and cases, see René Chapus, *Droit Administratif Général* (2001), para 1251.

[3] Case T-106/00 *Streamserve Inc v OHIM* ('Streamserve') [2002] ECR II-723.

trade mark was devoid of distinctive character under Article 7(1)(b) of Council Regulation (EC) No 40/94 on the Community trade mark[4] and 'descriptive' of the goods under Article 7(1)(c) of the same regulation (hereafter referred to as 'the CTMR').

Streamserve Inc challenged the refusal in the CFI. One of its arguments was that OHIM had infringed the principle of discrimination inasmuch as an OHIM Board of Appeal had previously accepted the trade mark Imagestream for partially identical goods. At first blush the difference in treatment is hard to justify. In computer jargon the expression to 'stream' refers to techniques for transmitting a large amount of data over a computer network in a short time. 'Serve' and 'server' are well-known computer terms. 'Image', of course, requires no definition. No amount of ingenuity could explain why Imagestream is inherently distinctive for computer goods but Streamserve is not. So the applicant had a valid point. Two highly similar trade marks had been treated differently. Another undertaking – probably a direct competitor of the applicant since the two firms apparently traded in the same goods – had received more favourable treatment.

Instances of unequal treatment are hardly a rarity in the trade mark world. Absolute consistency is impossible to attain in a field in which thousands of decisions are taken each month by scores of officials who have to apply difficult legislation and carry out appraisals that are inevitably subjective in part. There are several legitimate ways in which a judicial body can react when the principle of non-discrimination is invoked in such a case. Some of them will be examined in the rest of this article. In *Streamserve Inc* the CFI adopted an approach which, it is submitted, cannot be legitimate because it renders the principle of equal treatment inapplicable in the field of trade mark. The Court stated:

66. [D]ecisions concerning registration of a sign as a Community [trade] mark which the Boards of Appeal are called on to take under Regulation No 40/94 are adopted in the exercise of circumscribed powers and are not a matter of discretion. Accordingly, the legality of the decisions of Boards of Appeal must be assessed solely on the basis of that regulation, as interpreted by the Community judicature, and not on the basis of a previous decision-making practice of those boards.

67. Two hypotheses therefore exist. If, by accepting, in a previous case, the registrability of a sign as a Community [trade] mark, the Board of Appeal correctly applied the relevant provisions of Regulation No 40/94 and, in a later case comparable to the previous one, the Board of Appeal adopted a contrary decision, the Community judicature will be required to annul the latter decision because of infringement of the relevant provisions of Regulation No 40/94. In this first hypothesis, the plea alleging breach of the principle of non-discrimination [does not, therefore, come into play].[5] On the other hand, if, by

---

[4] OJ EC 1994 L 11, 1.

[5] The official English version contains an inaccurate translation. It says that if the Board of Appeal's decision in the previous comparable case was correct, the plea based on the principle of non-discrimination 'must therefore fail'. The French text says 'le moyen tiré de la violation du

accepting in an earlier case the registrability of a sign as a Community [trade] mark, the Board of Appeal erred in law and, in a later case, comparable to the previous one, the Board of Appeal adopted a contrary decision, the first decision cannot be successfully relied on to support an application for the annulment of the latter decision. It is clear from the case law of the Court of Justice that observance of the principle of equal treatment must be reconciled with observance of the principle of legality according to which no person may rely, in support of his claim, on unlawful acts committed in favour of another (see, to that effect, Case 134/84 *Williams v Court of Auditors* [1985] ECR 2225, para 14, and Case 188/83 *Witte v Parliament* [1984] ECR 3465, para 15). On the basis of this second hypothesis, the plea alleging breach of the principle of non-discrimination must therefore also fail.

68. It follows that the plea alleging breach of the principle of non-discrimination must fail.

What the Court is saying is that the principle of equal treatment has no role whatsoever in this field because the only cases in which it could ever be successfully invoked are the ones in which it could never be needed. A doctrine that renders a fundamental principle of law redundant must, one suspects, be seriously flawed. In fact, the doctrine of circumscribed powers is a flimsy piece of sophistry. On a first reading it may look like a clever solution to an awkward problem. On closer inspection it turns out to be based on specious reasoning.

III. Legal Formalism

The doctrine of circumscribed powers is founded on the idea that there is always a single correct solution to any legal problem. According to this school of jurisprudence, any lawyer sufficiently skilled in the art will, by carefully applying legal rules and methodology, arrive at the right answer; those who come up with a different answer have misdirected themselves and 'got the law wrong'. The technical name for this theory of law is 'legal formalism'.[6]

There is no place for legal formalism in trade mark law. It is breathtakingly naive to believe that there is invariably a single right answer to the question whether a particular trade mark is inherently distinctive. In some cases, of course, there is an obvious, incontestably right answer. When the trade mark Kodak was coined it had no meaning in relation to photography and was clearly adapted to

---

principe de non-discrimination est, dès lors, inopérant'. The position taken by the Court is simply that the plea is irrelevant and does not come into play because the decision taken by the Board of Appeal in the later case must, in this hypothesis, have been unlawful and will therefore be annulled regardless of any discrimination. The point that I am making in this article is that the theory breaks down because in many cases there is no clearcut distinction between lawful and unlawful decisions in an area where much depends on subjective appraisals.

[6] For criticism of legal formalism, see my article (and works cited there), 'In praise of judicial activism. But what does it mean? And has the European Court of Justice ever practised it?' *Scritti in Onore di Giuseppe Federico Mancini* vol II, 504, 507 et seq.

the task of distinguishing Mr Eastman's photographic products from anybody else's.[7] Pampers is, by the same token, a very good trade mark for nappies. But what about Sharp-Pix for photographic equipment and Baby-Dry for nappies? These are surely more difficult cases. Sharp-Pix tells people that the equipment takes sharp pictures (that is, photographs that are not fuzzy but clear and well-focused), and Baby-Dry conveys a clear message about the urine-absorbing capacity of the product. But do such 'signs' (for want of a better term) merely suggest information about the nature of the product in question or do they describe the product's function so clearly that they ought to be considered prima facie not eligible for registration? There is no obviously correct answer to these questions, just as there is no obviously correct answer to the question whether Streamserve and Imagestream are distinctive.

The beauty of trade mark law is that it is full of problems of this nature. Many of the issues that trade mark examiners are required to rule on in their daily work contain a subjective element that simply cannot be removed. Is Baby-Dry distinctive for nappies?[8] Is Screw You offensive and therefore unfit for protection as a trade mark for clothing or condoms on grounds of public morality?[9] Is Cotonnelle deceptive for toilet paper not made of cotton?[10] Are Bass and Pash likely to be confused if they are used for clothing in Germany?[11] Will the distinctive character of Duplo, a reputed trade mark for chocolate bars, suffer detriment if it is used as a trade mark for office requisites?[12] If someone files an application to register Teleye as a trade mark for surveillance systems and later informs OHIM that he really meant to register Teleeye, does that amount to a 'substantial change' of the trade mark as originally filed?[13] These are just some examples of the awkward questions that confront trade mark examiners on just about every day of their working lives. Often there is no obviously correct answer to these questions. In many cases equally knowledgeable experts in trade mark law will defend conflicting outcomes. And the wisest of them will agree to disagree, recognizing that it is ultimately a matter of opinion.

Trade mark law is not so different from many other branches of law in this respect. The law governing tax, social security, employment, agricultural subsidies and many other areas of human activity is complex. In all these areas complicated

---

[7] George Eastman obtained several photographic patents and registered the trade mark Kodak in 1888. He also coined the not-very-distinctive slogan 'you press the button, we do the rest', but does not appear to have made any attempt to register this.

[8] Case C-383/99 P *Procter & Gamble v OHIM* [2001] ECR I-6251; Case T-163/98 *Procter & Gamble v OHIM* [1999] ECR II-2383. See also the two decisions of the OHIM Boards of Appeal in Case R 35/1998–1 (31 July 1998) and Case 35/1998–3 (17 July 2002). All the decisions of the Boards of Appeal are published in the language of the case on the OHIM website, *www.oami.europa.eu*.

[9] Case R 495/2005–4 G *Jebarah Kenneth trading as Screw You* ('Screw You'), 6 July 2006.

[10] Case C-313/94 *Graffione* [1996] I-2727.

[11] Case T-292/01 *Phillips-Van Heusen Corp v OHIM* ('Bass/Pash') [2003] ECR II-4335.

[12] Case R 802/1999–1 *Ferrero oHG mbH v Duplo Corporation* ('Duplo/Duplo'), 5 June 2000.

[13] Case T-128/99 *Signal Communications v OHIM* ('Teleye') [2001] ECR II-3273.

facts have to be evaluated and decisions have to be taken that involve a power of appraisal.[14] Most lawyers would probably agree that legal formalism is a sterile doctrine and that there are few, if any, areas in which it produces satisfactory results. In trade mark law it is particularly inappropriate because of the subjective nature of many of the appraisals that have to be made. Tragically, trade mark law seems to be the one field in which the CFI and ECJ have embraced legal formalism with unabated enthusiasm. Their entire case law on trade marks reeks of formalism. For example, the Judges are very fond of telling us that the Board of Appeal has committed an error in finding that a trade mark is not distinctive or that there is or is not a likelihood of confusion between two trade marks; what they really mean in most cases is that their own appraisal differs from that of the Board of Appeal. To speak of errors in such cases is itself the true error.[15] We are dealing with issues on which equally competent and well-qualified experts can reach opposing results without either of them being wrong or misapplying the law.

I am not suggesting that trade law is totally different from any other branch of law in this respect. On the contrary, the point that I am making is that trade mark law is similar to many other areas in which decision-making involves the application of criteria that are to some extent subjective. That is the very point that the judges appear to miss. In no other area does the CFI have recourse to the doctrine of circumscribed powers as a device for rendering the principle of equal treatment devoid of any scope of application. There is not a single case in the European Court Reports, apart from cases concerning the registration of Community trade marks, in which the CFI or ECJ has rejected out of hand an attempt to invoke the principle of equal treatment by resorting to the doctrine of circumscribed powers.

IV. An Alternative Approach

It is surely clear from the above that the CFI's approach to the discrimination argument is wrong. What, then, is the correct approach? It is submitted that the answer can be found in a number of decisions issued by the OHIM Boards of

---

[14] In the *Ruckdeschel* case (n 1 above), for example, the Court had to consider whether quellmehl and pre-gelatinized starch were in comparable situations, in the sense that pre-gelatinized starch could be substituted for quellmehl in the specific uses to which the latter product was traditionally put.

[15] The latest example of this attitude is to be found in Case T-137/05 *Gruppo La Perla SpA v OHIM* ('Nimei La Perla Modern Classic/La Perla [fig.]), judgment of 16 May 2007. The CFI tells us, at para 52, that the Board of Appeal committed an error by considering that the marks in question were not sufficiently similar to justify the view that the use of Nimei La Perla Modern Classic in relation to 'jewellery, gold articles, watches; precious metals; pearls; precious stones' might take advantage of, or be detrimental to, the reputation or distinctive character of a figurative mark dominated by the term La Perla (Italian for 'the pearl') and protected in respect of clothing *inter alia*.

Appeal in the course of the last nine years. I propose to look at some of these decisions.

An argument based on the principle of equal treatment was first put forward in Case R 20/1997–1 *Xtra*. The decision, issued on 27 July 1998, was the very first by an OHIM Board of Appeal on absolute grounds. The appellant, USA Detergents, Inc, applied to register Xtra as a Community trade mark for a variety of detergent products in Class 3 of the Nice Classification. The OHIM examiner rejected the application on the ground that the mark, being an obvious phonetic equivalent of 'Extra', was devoid of distinctive character within the meaning of Article 7(1)(b) CTMR. The Board of Appeal shared that view (and also observed that Article 7(1)(c) CTMR was relevant). One of the appellant's arguments was that Xtra was comparable to Shoe4You, a trade mark that had been accepted by the Office for footwear in Class 25. The appellant's point was that in both cases a non-distinctive sign (Extra and Shoe for You) had been transformed into a distinctive sign by recourse to a deliberately incorrect phonetic spelling. Why then was one application accepted and the other refused? Could it truly be said as a matter of law or fact that Xtra was not distinctive for detergents but that Shoe4You was distinctive for footwear?

The Board did not say anything about the circumscribed powers of the examiner and most certainly did not suggest that trade mark law was one area in which the principle of equal treatment had no application. The Board began by pointing out that the decision to accept Shoe4You was not in issue in the proceedings before the Board. It observed that the Board must in each case consider the merits of the decision under appeal and could not, for practical reasons, compare that decision with all the other decisions – which might number many thousands taken in relation to other applications. The Board went on to make some comments that provide a fascinating contrast to the approach taken by the CFI and ECJ in later cases:

The assessment of the distinctiveness of a trade mark is a complex exercise which involves a combination of objective and subjective elements. The examiner must have regard to the general impression created by the mark as a whole, taking into account the nature of the goods or services, the level of awareness of the likely consumers of those goods or services, and any other relevant factors. While the examination procedure must be as objective as possible and the examiners must strive, individually and collectively, to achieve the greatest possible consistency, it must be borne in mind that in each case the examiner enjoys a certain margin of discretion and that the decision on distinctiveness depends to some extent on the examiner's subjective appraisal. It is inevitable therefore that certain decisions will be perceived by some observers as reflecting a more restrictive approach than others. The validity of a decision which, in itself, is reasonable and in conformity with the law cannot be called in question on the ground that in other decisions relating to different trade mark applications a less restrictive approach appears to have been followed, unless the difference in approach is sufficiently apparent to constitute a breach of the principle of non-discrimination. That principle is infringed when:

identical situations receive dissimilar treatment for which there is no objective justification (see, for example, Joined Cases 103 and 145/77 *Royal Scholten-Honig v Intervention Board for Agricultural Produce* [1978] ECR 2037, at para 27)'.[16]

That, it is submitted, is the correct way to go about the business of reviewing the legality of decisions taken by trade mark examiners. If the CFI had adopted such an approach in these matters, it would have saved itself much grief and would have a far lighter docket. Moreover, practitioners and trade mark applicants would find it much easier to predict whether a trade mark had a reasonable chance of being registered. OHIM would have been able to perform the task implied by its name, since it would have been encouraged to develop a truly consistent approach, in collaboration with the national trade mark Offices, and the law would have been harmonized in practice as well as in theory.

V. 'No Discretion' Does Not Mean 'No Power of Appraisal'

Of course some will object that the Board of Appeal committed a crass error by saying that trade mark examiners enjoy a margin of discretion. It is true that under the law now in force in the European Union trade mark examiners, both at OHIM and in the national Offices, do not enjoy the broad discretion that was formerly conferred on the UK Registrar by section 17(2) of the Trade Marks Act 1938.

It is true that if a mark is found not to be subject to any of the absolute grounds of objection laid down in Article 7, OHIM must publish the application. Thus if the examiner considers that the mark is not devoid of distinctive character, descriptive, generic, deceptive, contrary to public morality and so forth, the Office cannot refuse to publish it on account of some vague feeling that the registration of the mark would be inappropriate. In that sense there is no discretion and the Office's powers are circumscribed. Nonetheless, in deciding whether any of those grounds of objection apply, the examiner has to exercise judgment. There are many borderline cases in which the decision could easily go either way.[17] Even the most committed formalist must concede that there is no single, legally correct answer to questions such as whether Sat.2 is distinctive for broadcasting services[18] or whether Screw You would be offensive to public morality if used as a trade mark for clothes or condoms. Discretion may not be quite the right word

---

[16] Case R 20/1997–1 *USA Detergents Inc* ('Xtra'), 27 July 1998, para 18.
[17] For more discussion of the nature of the examiner's task, see Case R 118/2003–2 ('Whitening Multi-Action'), 22 June 2004. See also the commentary on that decision by Ilanah Simon, 'Trade Marks in Trouble' [2005] EIPR 71.
[18] Case C-329/02 P *SAT.1 Satellitenfernsehen GmbH v OHIM* ('SAT.2') [2004] ECR I-8317, Case T-323/00 *SAT.1 v OHIM* [2002] ECR II-2839 and Case R 312/1999–2, 2 August 2000.

but examiners surely have a margin of appraisal within which more than one decision can be reached without infringing the law. Continental lawyers would talk about a *pouvoir d'appréciation* or *Beurteilungsraum* as opposed to a *pouvoir discrétionnaire* or *Ermessensspielraum*.

In the *Xtra* case the Board of Appeal went on to consider in more detail the trade mark examiner's duty when an applicant invokes the principle of equal treatment:

When an applicant for a Community trade mark draws the examiner's attention to an apparently similar case which has been the subject of a favourable decision by the Office, the examiner is under a duty, both at the time of the original decision and at the stage of interlocutory revision, to consider whether the two cases are so similar as to require identical treatment. That duty is particularly onerous when the goods or services in respect of which registration is sought are in a competitive relationship. The Board of Appeal does not consider that the examiner infringed the principle of non-discrimination by deciding that the trade mark XTRA is not eligible for registration in respect of detergents in Class 3, whereas an examiner had previously allowed the publication of the trade mark SHOE4YOU in respect of a range of goods, including footwear, in Classes 18, 25 and 28. Both are decisions that a skilled examiner could reasonably take in the exercise of the discretion conferred on him by the terms of Article 7 CTMR.

VI. Two Wrongs Do Not Make a Right, but Nevertheless...

It is, of course, well established that there is no right to claim equality of treatment with someone who has benefited from an unlawful act. That principle is self-evident: if Company X has received an illegal subsidy, that does not entitle Company Y to claim an illegal subsidy on the ground that it is in the same situation as Company X and should be treated in the same way. The solution in such a case is to recover the money illegally paid to Company X. Two wrongs do not make a right, so the wrong that has been done must be undone in so far as possible, not repeated again and again. All this was recognized by the Board of Appeal in two decisions given in November 1998.[19] An OHIM examiner had refused to register Easi-Card and Easi-Cash for, *inter alia*, 'banking and financial services' on the ground that the marks were devoid of distinctive character. The Board of Appeal agreed with that assessment. The appellant complained that OHIM had accepted a number of trade marks composed of 'Easi' or 'Easy' plus a purely descriptive word. On the face of it, the Office had been inconsistent. The difference in treatment was hard to justify. This placed the Board of Appeal in an awkward position since it clearly thought that Easi-Cash and Easi-Card, even on the most generous view of the law, were not eligible for registration. That finding could not change simply because marks like Easyprint for 'photographic chemicals and apparatus

---

[19] Cases R 96/1998–1 and R 99/1998–1 *Oversea-Chinese Banking Corporation Limited* ('Easi-Cash' and 'Easi-Card'), 20 November 1998.

used in the printing of photographs' had somehow slipped through the net. Faced with this dilemma, the Board of Appeal again referred to the principle of equal treatment and cited *Royal Scholten-Honig* but went on to point out that that principle must be reconciled with the principle of legality, according to which no person may rely, in support of his claim, on an unlawful act committed in favour of another. On that point the Board cited a case in which an official of the Court of Auditors had claimed the same treatment, in terms of grading and seniority in step, as that accorded to other officials by the Court of Auditors in comparable situations. The claim had failed because the generous treatment given to the other officials had clearly been contrary to the Staff Regulations of Officials of the European Communities.[20]

It is implicit in the Easi-Cash and Easi-Card decisions that the Board of Appeal was not inclined to follow the precedent set by the Easyprint decision for the simple reason that it thought the decision wrong. In other decisions the Boards of Appeal have gone further and pointed out that there are procedures for cancelling trade marks that have been registered as a result of an erroneous decision by an examiner.[21] The wording of Article 51(1)(a) CTMR expressly empowers OHIM to invalidate a Community trade mark which OHIM has registered 'in breach of the provisions of Article 7'. That provision recognizes that, no matter how exhaustive the *ex parte* examination on absolute grounds may be, mistakes are bound to be made and some trade marks will find their way on to the register as a result of these mistakes. The difficulty for the Board of Appeal is that it cannot openly say that a trade mark should never have been registered in proceedings in which the proprietor of the trade mark is not involved and has no chance to defend the registration. The most the Board can do is to hint at the possible invalidity of the registration.

It is all very well to point out that each case must be dealt with on its merits and that one bad decision must not lead to another. This must never be turned into an excuse for disregarding the principle of equal treatment and licensing arbitrary conduct on the part of Trade Mark Offices. The inadequacy of such an approach was highlighted by the Board of Appeal in relation to Elsevier Inc's application to register its slogan 'Building Insights. Breaking Boundaries' as a Community trade mark for books, magazines, newspapers and such like.[22] The appellant had drawn attention to a large number of analogously constructed slogans that had been accepted and registered. Typically the argument was given short shrift by the examiner. The Board of Appeal had the following to say:

In the contested decision the examiner dismissed the argument founded on the principle of equal treatment with the comment that each case must be dealt with on its merits, having

[20] Case 134/84 *Williams v Court of Auditors* [1985] ECR 2225, para 14.
[21] See, for example, Case R 862/2004-2 *Procter & Gamble* ('Device of Backgrounds with Coloured Granules [fig. mark]'), 17 December 2004, para 20.
[22] Case R 407/2004-2 *Elsevier Inc* ('Building Insights. Breaking Boundaries'), 26 November 2004.

regard to the characteristics of the mark applied for and to the goods and services for which protection is sought. That is true so far as it goes. It is also true that bad precedents should not be followed and that an isolated instance of extreme leniency should not become a model for the future conduct of the Office. It is important to emphasize nonetheless that the Office must strive for consistency and must attempt to apply uniform criteria. Nothing less would satisfy the requirements of the principle of equal treatment. When an applicant cites a large number of registered CTMs that appear prima facie to be no more distinctive than the mark applied for, the Office should make a genuine attempt to determine whether the mark applied for should, on grounds of consistency, be given the same treatment. To hold otherwise would be to deprive the principle of equal treatment of any meaning.[23]

The Board went on to apply the principle of equal treatment by comparing the slogan at issue in that case with some of the other slogans that had sailed through the supposedly rigorous examination procedures that OHIM is, according to the Court of Justice, supposed to apply. The Board had this to say:

In the present case it is difficult to see how the Office could justify rejecting the mark applied for in the light of some of the registrations cited [by the appellant]. GLOBAL VIEW LOCAL INSIGHT for 'travel information services' hardly seems more distinctive than BUILDING INSIGHTS. BREAKING BOUNDARIES for 'magazines and educational services'. The same could be said of INSIGHT INTO THE ENERGY FUTURE for 'consultancy services relating to the economical tendencies and situations on the world markets of oil, gas, electricity and other energy sources', BREAKING THE PERFORMANCE BARRIER for 'razors, razor blades and shaving instruments', BUILDING RELATIONSHIPS SOLUTION BY SOLUTION for 'advertising, business management; business administration', TOGETHER WE CREATE INSIGHT for 'computer software for systems inventory, trading and reporting' or MEDIA INSIGHT for 'advertising, promotional, sales and marketing services, business and business management services, publicity services, market research and market analysis, media research and consultancy'. The refusal of the mark applied for in the present case seems more than a little arbitrary in the light of such a long series of comparable cases that led to a different outcome. This is clearly a case in which the principle of equal treatment can be successfully invoked.[24]

Obviously the principle of equal treatment would not have been of much avail to Elsevier Inc if its slogan 'Building Insights. Breaking Boundaries' had been manifestly devoid of distinctive character. Before concluding that this was a case in which the principle of equal treatment could be successfully invoked, the Board had examined the mark applied for on its merits and had decided that it would be 'somewhat harsh to dismiss it as devoid of any distinctive character'. The slogan's laudatory message was 'subtle and indirect'. It was 'thought-provoking'. It offered 'a vague promise of some sort of cultural enrichment and an expansion of one's intellectual horizons'.[25]

[23] Para 17.
[24] Para 18.
[25] Para 14.

VII. Patrolling the Grey Zone

At no point did the Board pretend that 'Building Insights. Breaking Boundaries' must, as a matter of legal science, necessarily be regarded as distinctive. The Board did not say that the examiner committed an error of law by holding the slogan to be devoid of distinctive character. The crucial point is that 'Building Insights. Breaking Boundaries' was, like so many of the marks that are the subject of appeal proceedings, 'on the cusp'. It was a borderline case. On a strict view it could be refused; on a more lenient view it could be accepted. There are arguments in favour of either approach, and many will agree that Trade Mark Offices should in general attempt to steer a middle course.

What matters above all is consistency. The law must be predictable. Trade mark registration must not be arbitrary. In a properly run Trade Mark Office steps will be taken to identify similar cases, common standards will be applied, a uniform approach will be adopted. An overall pattern of consistency will emerge. The courts should do everything to encourage Trade Mark Offices to harmonize the work of their examiners. They should always be ready to castigate blatant inconsistency.

The need for a consistent approach to borderline cases was stressed by the Board of Appeal in relation to Volcano Corporation's application to register Virtual Histology for 'intravascular ultrasound imaging systems'.[26] These were exactly the kind of goods that might be used by a histologist (someone who studies plant or animal tissues) to view an image of tissue on a computer screen, so the 'trade mark' was plainly descriptive. OHIM had accepted marks such as Virtual Album and Virtual Video for various computer and electronic goods. The applicant asked the examiner for equally lenient treatment and was, as tends to happen in such cases, fobbed off with a reference to *Streamserve* and the doctrine of circumscribed powers. The Board of Appeal had this to say:

> It is true that the powers of the Office are circumscribed, in the sense that it must accept marks that are clearly eligible for registration and must refuse marks that are clearly not eligible for registration. However, it is not always easy to determine whether the conditions for registration are satisfied. The assessment of distinctiveness is notoriously subjective. It is not an exact science. Many marks hover on the borderline. Between the white area occupied by marks that are unquestionably distinctive and the black area occupied by marks that are clearly not distinctive, there is a grey zone. When operating within that grey zone, trade mark examiners may not possess discretionary powers but they do have a margin of appraisal. In this limited area the principle of equal treatment has a role to play. The Office must not act arbitrarily. It must apply uniform standards and develop a common approach. Genuinely comparable marks that fall within the grey zone should receive the same treatment, at least if the goods or services covered by the respective

---

[26] Case R 1029/2004-2 *Volcano Corporation* ('Virtual Histology'), 7 December 2005.

applications are in competition. To hold otherwise would be to permit discrimination for which there would be no objective justification.[27]

The Board went on to hold that there was no scope for applying the principle of equal treatment in favour of Volcano Corporation because Virtual Histology was situated a good distance to the wrong side of the borderline. It was not in the grey zone at all.

VIII. The Way Forward

It is submitted that the approach taken by the Board of Appeal in Virtual Histology is correct. If such an approach is to be implemented in the European Union, a number of things will have to happen. The starting point is to persuade the CFI and ECJ to abandon legal formalism. No progress can be made until this is done. Oliver Wendell Holmes was writing of law in general when he said: 'The life of the law has not been logic; it has been experience'.[28] Nevertheless, his words are especially true in the field of trade marks. Trade mark law cannot be dealt with 'as if it contained only the axioms and corollaries of a book of mathematics'.[29] The Courts must stop believing in fairytales. They must stop peddling the myth that assessing distinctiveness, descriptiveness, likelihood of confusion and so forth is an objective science with a book of rules that can be applied mechanically so as to deliver the one and only legally correct solution each time. The Courts must recognize that trade mark examination involves a subjective element. They must admit that there is a grey zone, that there are borderline cases where contrasting outcomes are legally defensible.

The corollary of abandoning legal formalism is the recognition that trade mark examiners have a margin of appraisal and that their powers are circumscribed only in the sense that they must not stray outside the limits of that margin of appraisal. That is not to say that examiners can do anything they like in the exercise of their powers of appraisal. Quite the opposite! They must not act arbitrarily. They must not treat applicants or other parties to proceedings in a discriminatory fashion. They must, as the Board of Appeal said long ago in the twice-annulled BABY-DRY decision, 'strive, individually and collectively, to achieve the greatest possible consistency'.[30]

Trade mark registration today is in danger of becoming a lottery.[31] The danger can only be averted if the CFI and ECJ start stressing the Office's duty to act

---

[27] Para 16.
[28] Oliver Wendell Holmes, *The Common Law I* (1881). The book is available in electronic form at *www.gutenberg.org/dirs/etext00/cmnlw10.txt*. The passage quoted is on the first page of the book.
[29] ibid.
[30] Case R 35/1998–1 *Procter & Gamble* ('Baby-Dry'), 31 July 1998, para 18.
[31] See Case R 1206/2006–2 *The Coca Cola Company*, 22 December 2006, para 17. The Board of Appeal said that 'getting a three-dimensional trade mark registered should not be equivalent to

consistently, to apply common standards, to identify analogous cases and to give them similar treatment. When applicants point out that numerous applications comparable to their own have been treated favourably, examiners should not be allowed to get away with trotting out a tired old line about each case being dealt with on its merits. Before issuing a negative decision they should be compelled to ask themselves whether the case they are examining lies in the grey zone and, if it does, whether in the name of consistency and equal treatment the applicant should receive a positive decision. People who pay good money for the services of a Trade Mark Office are entitled to expect a bit of consistency. They should not have to put up with meaningless cant about circumscribed powers.

Finally, the CFI and ECJ need to understand that genuine consistency in decision-making practice can only be achieved at the purely administrative level. It cannot be done by judges. Judges are independent and do not work within a hierarchical framework.[32] If the judges take an interventionist stance and insist on substituting their own appraisal for that of the examiners and other first-instance bodies, they will – unintentionally of course – have a divergent influence on the law. The law will only become predictable if the judges, in the first place, recognize that examiners have a power of appraisal and, second, emphasize that examiners and their managers have a duty to act consistently, coordinate their work and apply common standards. A uniform approach to the subjective issues that bedevil trade mark examination can only be achieved by an organization that is structured in a hierarchy. A Trade Mark Office can be organized in departments and sub-departments. Instructions can be given, top-down, as to how to deal with applications to register bottle shapes, single-letter word marks, colour marks and so on. Difficult cases can be referred to supervisors. Heads of unit can get together and coordinate their approach. No trade mark office wants to acquire a reputation for unpredictability. If the managers and workers 'at the coal face' are left to get on with the job, consistency will be achieved. OHIM is uniquely placed to pursue such a goal and can help to harmonize practice throughout the European Union through regular meetings with representatives from the national Offices. OHIM could even live up to its grandiose name and become a genuine Office for Harmonization in the Internal Market.

---

winning *el Gordo* in the Spanish national lottery'. By a remarkable coincidence the decision was signed on the date on which the draw for *el Gordo* takes place.

[32] The OHIM Boards of Appeal are, of course, in exactly the same position as the judges in this respect by virtue of the independence bestowed on their members by Article 131 CTMR. No one seriously doubts the judicial or quasi-judicial nature of the Boards of Appeal: see Case R 22/2003–2 *Yamaha Kabushiki Kaisha* ('Junior Kit'), 4 July 2005, paras 18 and 23, and the extensive literature and case law cited there. The realization that the Boards of Appeal would, as a result of their independence, be a divergent influence on the case law unless they adopted a 'hands-off' approach explains why the Board of Appeal, in the very first Baby-Dry decision, stressed the examiner's margin of 'discretion' and duty to strive for the greatest possible consistency. One can only regret that this approach was not endorsed by the CFI and ECJ.

17

The Evolution of Economic and Monetary Union – Some Legal Issues

JA Usher

I. Introduction

Fifteen of the 27 Member States of the European Union participate in Economic and Monetary Union, making it one of the major areas of differentiated integration in the EU. That apart, it is an area which involves questions of exclusive Community competence, a special system of enforcement, and a special institutional structure; its genesis, in its present form, may be regarded as a development from the completion of the internal market, and the original timetable for its implementation was inextricably linked with the evolution of the rules on capital movements.

The form of Economic and Monetary Union introduced into the EC Treaty by the Treaty of Maastricht largely follows the Report of a Committee chaired by Jacques Delors, then President of the Commission, which was set up following a meeting of the European Council in Hanover in June 1988 and which reported back in April 1989.[1] The Delors Committee took as a starting point the view that the development of the single market necessitated a more effective coordination of economic policy between national authorities, pointing out that with full freedom of capital movements and integrated financial markets, incompatible national policies would quickly translate into exchange rate tensions and put an increasing and undue burden on monetary policy[2] – a prediction which was subsequently proved correct in 1992 and 1993. They did, however, point out that Economic and Monetary Union would be a quantum leap implying far more than the single market programme.[3]

The Report briefly suggested that Economic and Monetary Union implied complete freedom of movement for persons, goods, services and capital, as well

---

[1] Agence Europe Documents No 1550/1551, 20 April 1989.
[2] Paras 10–12.
[3] Para 14.

as irrevocably fixed exchange rates and, finally, a single currency.[4] It was also expressly pointed out that it would require a transfer of decision-making power from Member States to the Community as a whole, particularly in the fields of monetary policy and macro-economic policy. With regard to the question of monetary union, the Delors Report[5] expressly referred to the 1970 Report of the Werner Committee, which had been set up to look at the question of Economic and Monetary Union at the end of the original transitional period. While it was drafted in a world of fixed exchange rates under the Bretton Woods system, and the assumptions underlying it were therefore destroyed when the US dollar was decoupled from gold and world currencies began to float in 1971, the Werner Committee's Report[6] reached the fundamental conclusion that in an Economic and Monetary Union, 'the Community currencies will be assured of total and irreversible mutual convertibility free from fluctuations in rates and with immutable parity rates, or preferably they will be replaced by a sole Community currency'. The Delors Committee similarly concluded that if there was an irrevocable locking of exchange rate parities, a single currency would be a natural and desirable further development, showing the move was irreversible and avoiding the transaction costs of converting currency.[7]

The Werner Committee had also pointed out that monetary and credit policy would have to be centralized, and that external monetary policy would fall within Community competence, the first and third of which have indeed happened under the Maastricht Treaty,[8] and they also recognized that regional and structural policies would no longer fall under exclusive national competence. Other aspects of their report were not, however, followed by the Delors Committee; in particular, the Werner Committee had suggested that essential features of public budgets would be decided at the Community level, and that it would be necessary to develop a centre of decision for economic policy. In the Delors Report, on the other hand, the concept of economic union was described as comprising four basic elements: the single market, competition policy, common policies aimed at structural change and regional development, and macro-economic policy coordination.[9] With regard to the last of these, it was acknowledged that since the Community budget would remain very small, the task of setting a Community-wide fiscal policy stance would have to be performed through the coordination of national budgetary policies.[10]

Finally, at the institutional level, it was recognized, as the Werner Committee had also recognized, that a new monetary institution would be required to

---

[4] Para 16.
[5] 1989 Report, para 22.
[6] EC Bulletin 1970 Supplement 11.
[7] Para 23.
[8] EC Treaty Arts 105 and 111.
[9] Para 25.
[10] Para 30.

operate a single Community monetary policy, and the report recommended the creation of a European System of Central Banks with the status of an autonomous Community institution.[11] In effect, therefore, the model of Economic and Monetary Union adopted in the EC comprises a single monetary policy set by the European Central Bank[12] and coordinated national economic policies policed by the Commission and Council.[13] These issues will be considered further later in this paper.

It may also be noted that the Werner Committee observed that in the long run Economic and Monetary Union could not do without the development of political union. As we survey the failure to ratify the Treaty establishing a Constitution for Europe, this has clearly not occurred, but may help explain why the Maastricht package which introduced the provisions on Economic and Monetary Union into the EC Treaty also introduced the Second Pillar on Common Foreign and Security Policy and the Third Pillar on (originally) Home Affairs and Justice.

With regard to the mechanisms for achieving Economic and Monetary Union, the Delors Committee recommended a three-stage process. The first stage did not require any Treaty amendments, and in fact the European Council meeting in Madrid in June 1989 decided that it should start on 1 July 1990,[14] which also happened to be the date by which Member States were due to implement Council Directive 88/361[15] on the free movement of capital – the only Treaty freedom to be achieved (more than 20 years late) solely by legislation rather than through the case law concept of direct effect. In the economic field, this stage would see the completion of the internal market and the doubling of the structural funds under existing legislation, and it was recommended that the 1974 decision[16] on economic convergence should be replaced by a system of multilateral surveillance of economic developments and policies. This recommendation was followed by the Council of Ministers in decision 90/141 on the attainment of progressive convergence of economic policies and performance during stage one of Economic and Monetary Union.[17]

In the monetary field, it was suggested that the first stage could see the implementation of the objective of a single financial area in which all monetary and financial instruments circulate freely, and banking, securities and insurance services were offered uniformly throughout the Community; it may be suggested that this takes a somewhat generous view of the scope of the relevant Community legislation. It was further asserted that it would be important to include all

---

[11] Para 32.
[12] EC Treaty Art 105(2).
[13] Under the excessive deficits procedure set out in EC Treaty Art 104.
[14] See e.g. the recitals to Council decision 90/141 on the progressive convergence of economic policies and performance during stage one of Economic and Monetary Union (OJ 1990 L78/23).
[15] OJ 1988 L178/5.
[16] Council decision 74/120 (OJ 1974 L63/16).
[17] OJ 1990 L78/23.

Community currencies in the EMS exchange rate mechanism subject to the same rules; even the UK joined the exchange rate mechanism in 1990, but unfortunately in 1992 both the UK and Italy had to leave the system, although Italy rejoined in November 1996 during the second stage of Economic and Monetary Union. After suggesting that all impediments to the private use of the ECU, the basket unit of account used for EC accounting purposes, should be removed, it was also recommended that the structure and functions of the Committee of Governors of Central Banks of the EC[18] should be amended in various specific ways, recommendations which were largely followed in Council decision 90/142.[19]

In stage two, which the Maastricht Treaty defined as beginning on 1 January 1994,[20] the fundamental recommendation was that the institutional structure should be established.[21] This was not wholly followed in the Maastricht Treaty, which provided for the creation of a transitional European Monetary Institute[22] able to exercise some, but not all, of the powers to be enjoyed by the European Central Bank in the third stage. However, perhaps its most important feature was the establishment of the criteria determining whether progress may be made towards the third stage, in Article 121. This was based on a system of reports by the Commission and the European Monetary Institute to the Council on the progress made in the fulfilment by the Member States of their obligations regarding the achievement of Economic and Monetary Union. These reports included an examination of the compatibility between each Member State's national legislation, including the statutes of its national central bank, and Articles 108 and 109 on the independence of the European Central Bank and of national central banks, and the Statute of the European System of Central Banks.

Finally, it was foreseen that in the third stage, which began, as required under the final deadline set by the Maastricht provisions, on 1 January 1999, the irrevocably locked exchange rates would begin to be replaced by a single currency, and the relevant monetary and economic competences would be transferred to Community institutions, and it was pointed out that they would have to have authority to impose constraints on national budgets to the extent to which this was necessary to prevent imbalances that might threaten monetary stability.[23] Presumably this is the source of Article 104, requiring Member States[24] to avoid excessive government deficits and laying down procedures to enforce that obligation.

---

[18] The functions of this body were taken over by the European Monetary Institute in 1994 under Art 117(1) of the EC Treaty, and then subsumed in the activities of the European Central bank following its establishment in 1998 by virtue of Art 123(2).
[19] OJ 1990 L78/25.
[20] EC Treaty Art 116(1).
[21] Para 57.
[22] Art 117.
[23] Para 59.
[24] With an exception for the UK under its Protocol. However, by virtue of a reference to Art 116(4), the UK must 'endeavour' to avoid excessive government deficits.

II. EMU and Capital Movements

As mentioned above, the first stage of EMU began on 1 July 1990,[25] which happened also to be the date by which Member States were due to implement Council Directive 88/361[26] on the free movement of capital, and the commencement of the second stage was also the date of entry into force of the current capital movement rules of the EC Treaty.[27] The fundamental rules are set out in paragraph 1 of Article 56 EC, which states that within the framework of the provisions set out in that chapter, all restrictions on the movement of capital between Member States and between Member States and third countries shall be prohibited; paragraph 2 states that, within the same framework, all restrictions on payments between Member States and between Member States and third countries shall be prohibited.

At first sight, a fundamental distinction between these provisions and the original provisions – and indeed from the situation reached under the 1988 Directive – is that it appears that movements to and from third countries are to be treated the same way as movements between Member States. The substantive link to EMU is that, with hindsight, this can be seen as anticipating the need to reassure the international money markets with regard to the external movement and availability of the euro. However, in reality, there are differences which remain. Under Article 57, the provisions of Article 56 are stated to be without prejudice to the application to third countries of any restrictions which existed on 31 December 1993 under national or Community law adopted in respect of the movement of capital to or from third countries involving direct investment (including investment in real estate), establishment, the provision of financial services or the admission of securities to capital markets; in other words, they do not require existing lawful restrictions to be abolished in these (admittedly limited) areas.

Be that as it may, to the extent that a payment or capital movement is not excluded, Article 56 has been held to be directly effective even with regard to capital movements to third countries such as Switzerland and Turkey.[28] This in itself is an interesting development, given the Court's reluctance in earlier case law automatically to extend concepts developed in the context of the internal market to situations governed by similar language in relations with third countries.[29] Nevertheless, despite the fact that free movement of capital rules now apply to movements into and out of the Community, the 1988 definitions drafted to cover movements within the Community continue to be used. This was made clear when the Court confirmed that a mortgage fell within the scope of a capital movement as defined in the

---

[25] See e.g. the recitals to Council decision 90/141 on the progressive convergence of economic policies and performance during stage one of Economic and Monetary Union (OJ 1990 L78/23).
[26] OJ 1988 L178/5.
[27] Arts 56–60 of the EC Treaty.
[28] See Cases C-163, 165 and 250/94 *Sanz de Lera* [1995] ECR I-4821.
[29] Case 270/80 *Polydor v Harlequin* [1982] ECR 379.

Directive in *Trummer and Meyer*,[30] and further held that this interpretation should continue to apply to the free movement of capital under Article 56.

Many of these definitions clearly overlap with freedom of establishment and freedom to provide services, but there has been a lack of consistency in determining whether an activity falling within the lists in the Annex to the Directive should be categorized as a capital movement or as falling within the scope of another 'freedom'. The question then arises as to whether the current capital movement provisions effectively extend the other freedoms to third-country nationals or residents. It is against this background that in Case C-452/04 *Fidium Finanz*[31] the Grand Chamber held that the residual nature of 'services' under Article 50 is a matter of definition, and does not establish an order of priority between services and, for example, capital. However, it seems to accept that the same national measure may relate to services and capital at the same time, but it will in principle consider a measure in relation to only one of those freedoms if it appears that one of them is entirely secondary in relation to the other. The case involved a Swiss firm offering credit on the internet into Germany. The Court expressly noted the difference between the capital movement rules and the services rules with regard to third-country providers, but accepted that the activity of granting credit on a commercial basis concerns both the freedom to provide services and the free movement of capital. However, it took the view that the German rules at issue, which related to authorization of financial service undertakings and required a permanent establishment (therefore by definition breaching the services rules) should be categorized as restrictions of the freedom to provide services – which could not be invoked by a Swiss company (at the time the facts occurred). It further held that any restriction on free movement of capital was 'merely an unavoidable consequence of the restriction on the freedom to provide services'. Similarly, in recent cases involving alleged tax discrimination categorized as involving freedom to provide services[32] or freedom of establishment,[33] the Court expressly observed that the rules on freedom to provide services and the rules on freedom of establishment could not be invoked by those established in third countries – the implication appears to be that if those cases had been categorized as involving free movement of capital, the Treaty rules could be invoked by those established in third countries.

III. EMU and Differentiated Integration

The price for the inclusion of legally-binding provisions on EMU in the Maastricht Treaty was special treatment for the UK and Denmark, in the form

---

[30] [1999] ECR I-1661.
[31] 3 October 2006.
[32] Case C-290/04 *FKP Scorpio Konzertproduktionen* (3 October 2006).
[33] Case C-292/04 *Meilicke* (6 March 2007).

of Protocols under which most stage 3 rules do not apply to them, and they are not to be considered for membership of EMU unless and until they give notice of their desire to participate. However, in the case of EMU, the situation arises not just from the special treatment accorded to the UK and Denmark by special Protocols, but also from the fact that it was appreciated that not all Member States would meet the criteria for economic convergence laid down as the precondition for participation in the monetary union; such states are referred to as 'Member States with a derogation'.[34] It may in any event be suggested that participation in EMU is in fact voluntary; voluntary participation in Community activities may arguably be said to have started in this area given that membership of the European Monetary System is and always was voluntary.[35] The voluntary nature of the European Monetary System has had important legal consequences in the context of the application of the convergence criteria set out in Article 122 of the EC Treaty. Two of these criteria expressly relate to membership of the European Monetary System:

- the observance of the normal fluctuation margins provided for by the Exchange Rate Mechanism of the European Monetary System, for at least two years, without devaluing against the currency of any other Member State;
- the durability of convergence achieved by the Member State and of its participation in the Exchange Rate Mechanism of the European Monetary System being reflected in the long-term interest rate levels.

Sweden, which joined the Community in 1995, had not participated at all in the ERM, and was known politically not to wish to participate in stage three of EMU, but did not have the benefit of a special protocol like the UK or Denmark. There is no mention of this last point in the Commission's Report, which instead observes that the Swedish crown had never participated in the ERM, and that during the relevant two years it had fluctuated against the ERM currencies, 'reflecting, among other things, the absence of an exchange rate target', and the formal Council decision[36] uses very similar wording. Both then conclude that Sweden did not fulfil the third convergence criterion. The conclusion may therefore be drawn that while this criterion has not been interpreted literally, a Member State which does not participate at all in the ERM will not be regarded as meeting the criterion, at least if it has suffered currency fluctuation (which is highly likely to be the case). The practical consequence, therefore, may be said to be that to the extent that membership of the ERM was and is voluntary, participation in the third stage of Economic and Monetary Union was and is also voluntary, even if no new Member States were offered the special treatment given to the UK and Denmark.

---

[34] Art 122 of the EC Treaty.
[35] European Council Resolution of 5 December 1978 Art 3, European Council Resolution of 16 June 1997, para 1.6.
[36] Council decision 98/317 (OJ 1998 L139/30).

In this context, it must be emphasized that the convergence criteria are not simply a set of tests which were applied once in 1998; they remain relevant so long as there are non-participant Member States, and in the context of the successive enlargements of the Community. Thus, they were applied in 2000 to admit Greece to the eurozone, in 2006 to admit Slovenia (when Lithuania's application was rejected) and in 2007 to admit Cyprus and Malta. The status of a Member State with a derogation is envisaged as being transitional rather than permanent. Under Article 122(2), at least once every two years, or at the request of a Member State with a derogation, the Commission and the European Central Bank must report to the Council in accordance with the procedure laid down in Article 121(1). After consulting the European Parliament and after discussion in the Council, meeting in the composition of the Heads of State or of Government, the Council, acting by a qualified majority on a proposal from the Commission, is then to decide which Member States with a derogation fulfil the necessary conditions on the basis of the convergence criteria set out in Article 121(1), and abrogate the derogations of the Member States concerned. This process led in 2000[37] to the admission of Greece to the eurozone with effect from 1 January 2001, but in 2000, 2002, 2004 and 2006 Sweden was found not to meet the criteria because of its non-participation in the Exchange Rate Mechanism. On the other hand, in 2006 Slovenia, which joined the EU in 2004, was found to meet the convergence criteria,[38] and joined the eurozone, as did Cyprus and Malta in January 2008.

A further problem arises from the very fact that these two criteria for convergence relate to the exchange rate mechanism of the European Monetary System, the original version of which required the maintenance of bilateral exchange rates derived from central rates against the ECU defined as a 'basket' of sums expressed in national currencies of Member States.[39] Such a system clearly could not be maintained when the ECU and most of the national currencies had been replaced by the euro, and this led to the adoption of a Resolution introducing the European Monetary System Mark II,[40] given the failure of the Treaty itself to deal with the question of an exchange rate mechanism in relations between Member States which participate in Economic and Monetary Union and those which do not. The main features of the European Monetary System Mark II include the fact that, like the first version, participation in the exchange rate mechanism is voluntary for the Member States outside the euro area, so that the Swedish precedent appears to remain valid. This raises the question whether, with hindsight, the UK and Danish Protocols were really necessary – to which the answer is probably yes, since, for example, Denmark does in fact participate

---

[37] Council decision 2000/427 on the adoption by Greece of the single currency (OJ 2000 L167/19).
[38] Council decision 2006/495 on the adoption by Slovenia of the single currency (OJ 2006 L195/25).
[39] See JA Usher, *The Law of Money and Financial Services in the EC* (2nd ed, 2000) 173–8.
[40] European Council Resolution of 16 June 1997 ('Rapid', Information Service 18 June 1997).

in the exchange rate mechanism but its electorate voted in a referendum not to join the eurozone, a situation which would not be possible without its Protocol. Nevertheless, it is stated that Member States with a derogation can be expected to join the mechanism.[41]

In September 1998, agreement was reached between the finance ministers of the then Euro-11, the ECB and the ministers and Central Bank governors of Denmark and Greece that Denmark would participate in ERM II within a narrow band of fluctuation of 2.25 per cent, and that Greece would participate within the standard band of plus or minus 15 per cent.[42] However, Greece went on to join the eurozone in January 2001, having been found to meet the convergence criteria,[43] leaving Denmark as the only participant in ERM II until the accession of 10 new Member States in 2004, and that of Romania and Bulgaria in 2007. Thereafter, Slovenia (which went on to join the eurozone in 2007), Lithuania, Estonia, Latvia, Slovakia, Cyprus and Malta (which entered the eurozone in 2008) have joined the exchange rate mechanism of EMS II,[44] but the UK and Sweden remain outside the system.

The question therefore has arisen as to whether and how Community legislation binding only on the eurozone Member States may be extended to others where there is no possibility of opt-in to the legislation as such. A practical example may be seen in the provisions governing the operation of Target (Trans-European Automated Real-time Gross settlement European Transfer system), the payments system for the euro. While the fear that the 'outs' would be excluded has proved to be unfounded, the price of permitting them to use it is a complex legal framework. This framework is based on a combination of an ECB guideline[45] adopted by the Governing Council of the ECB addressed to and binding upon the national central banks of the eurozone, and the Target Agreement between the ECB and the national central banks of the Member States which have not adopted the euro but which wish to connect to Target. Effectively the Agreement incorporates the provisions of the guideline, which can only apply as such within the eurozone, to apply its terms outside the eurozone.[46]

However, there may be a simpler solution within the framework of Community law. It may respectfully be suggested that there is a long history of using general powers to legislate on matters which fall outside the scope of the specific Treaty provisions, and that the real question is that of knowing where to draw the line between circumvention and filling a gap. Article 308 provides that if action by the Community should prove necessary to attain, in the course of the operation

---

[41] European Council Resolution of 16 June 1997, para 1.6.
[42] Bulletin Quotidien Europe No 7310, 28 and 29 September 1998.
[43] Council decision 2000/427 on the adoption by Greece of the single currency (OJ 2000 L167/19).
[44] See MEMO/05/147 of 2 May 2005 and MEX/05/1128 of 28 November 2005.
[45] Similar in legal nature to an EC Directive; see JV Louis, 'A legal and institutional approach for building a Monetary Union' (1998) CMLRev 33, 54–8.
[46] ECB Third Progress Report on the Target project, November 1998, 18.

of the Common Market, one of the objectives of the Community and the Treaty has not provided the necessary powers, the Council shall, acting unanimously on a proposal from the Commission and after consulting the Parliament, take the appropriate measures. By way of example, Article 123(4) of the EC Treaty can, on its express terms, only be used by the Member States without a derogation; that is, the participants in Economic and Monetary Union, and Council Regulation 1338/2001[47] laying down measures necessary for the protection of the euro against counterfeiting was enacted under this provision. It was obviously desirable, however, that such measures should apply throughout the Community, and so Council Regulation 1339/2001 was contemporaneously enacted under Article 308 to apply the substantive provisions of Regulation 1338/2001 to the Member States which are not in the eurozone. It may be suggested that there could hardly be a more obvious example of using a general provision to circumvent the limits of the specific provision, so as to ensure that the same rules can be applied both to the 'ins' and to the 'outs'. This pattern has subsequently been followed in Council decisions 2003/861 and 2003/862 on analysis and cooperation with regard to counterfeit euro coins[48] and Council decisions 2006/849 and 2006/850 on an exchange, assistance and training programme for the protection of the euro against counterfeiting.[49]

Differentiation also creates problems at the level of the institutions themselves, particularly with regard to the compositions and functioning of the Council of Ministers. Evidence on this last point may be gleaned from the European Council meeting in Luxembourg in December 1997. A resolution was there agreed on economic policy coordination under Article 99 of the EC Treaty in stage 3 of EMU,[50] Article 99 being a provision with regard to which there is no derogation or opt-out. Article 6 of the resolution recognizes that the ECOFIN Council (including everyone) is the only body empowered to formulate and adopt 'the broad economic policy guidelines which constitute the main instrument of economic coordination' but at the same time accepts that 'the Ministers of the States participating in the euro area may meet informally among themselves to discuss issues connected with their shared specific responsibilities for the single currency'. If they wish to do that in this context, it can hardly be imagined that they would wish non-participants to be present in discussion of what to them is their domestic monetary policy. This is reflected in the Protocol on the Euro Group annexed to the 2004 Constitutional Treaty.[51] Its recitals declare an aim 'to develop ever-closer coordination of economic policies within the euro area' and recognize 'the need to lay down special provisions for enhanced dialogue between the States in the euro area, pending the accession of all EU Member States to the euro area'.

[47] OJ 2001 L181/6.
[48] OJ 2003 L325/44 and 45.
[49] OJ 2006 L330/28 and 30.
[50] Annex I to the Conclusions of the Luxembourg European Council, 12 and 13 December 1997.
[51] Protocol No 12.

Article 1 of the Protocol states that the ministers of the states in the euro area are to meet 'informally', and that such meetings are to take place, when necessary, to discuss questions related to the specific responsibilities they share with regard to the single currency. It is further provided that the Commission and the ECB are to be invited to take part in such meetings, which are to be prepared by the representatives of the ministers with responsibility for finance participating in the euro area – in other words, a special version of COREPER. Article 2 then envisages that 'the ministers of the Member States whose currency is the euro shall elect a president for two and a half years, by a majority of those Member States'. It may be suggested that this hardly seems to be an informal arrangement.

The timetable for the creation of the ECB and ESCB was laid down in Article 123, which required that immediately after the decision on the date for the beginning of the third stage had been taken in accordance with Article 121(3), or, as the case may be, immediately after 1 July 1998, the Council should adopt certain provisions required by the Statute,[52] and the governments of the Member States without a derogation but only those governments, should appoint the President, the Vice-President and the other members of the Executive Board of the ECB. The decision appointing the members of the Executive Board was in fact taken on 26 May 1998[53] at a meeting which, though it occurred during a British Presidency of the Council, was chaired by the Austrian Chancellor (Austria being the next Member State to hold the Presidency) in the absence of the United Kingdom.

The exclusion of a Member State with a derogation and its national central bank from rights and obligations within the ESCB is laid down in Chapter IX of the Statute of the ESCB. The consequence very briefly is that for most purposes in those Statutes, 'Member States' means those without a derogation, and 'national central banks' means the central banks of Member States without a derogation. In other words, Member States with a derogation are largely excluded from its operation.

However, not every case where the 'ins' might wish to exclude the 'outs' is expressly envisaged in the Treaty. A specific example arose in relation to the adoption of Council Regulation 2532/98 on the powers of the ECB to impose sanctions.[54] By virtue of Article 122(3) and the UK and Danish Protocols, Article 110(3) on the imposition of fines or penalty payments by the ECB does not apply to the 'outs'. However, the Regulation was made under the specific powers set out in Article 107(6) of the EC Treaty, from which there is no derogation, and it would appear that the UK (followed by the other 'outs') therefore asserted that it was entitled to take part in the vote on the adoption of the Regulation even though it would not apply in the UK. Eventually, in November 1998, the UK agreed that the Regulation could be adopted by the votes of the 'ins', but a year later the UK made

---

[52] See Art 106(6).
[53] Decision 98/345 (OJ 1998 L154/33).
[54] OJ 1998 L318/4. An account of the legal debates is given in Vigneron and Mollica, 'La différenciation dans l'Union économique et monétaire' (2000) Euredia (Revue européenne de droit bancaire et financier) 197, 219–27.

a declaration recorded in the Council minutes that in its view all Member States could participate in the adoption of legislation under Article 107(6), whereupon nine of the 'ins' (Belgium, Germany, Spain, France, Ireland, Italy, Luxembourg, Austria and Portugal) recorded their view that only the Member States which had adopted the euro had the right to vote on such regulations. It would therefore appear to be a matter on which there continues to be a difference of opinion.[55]

IV. Monetary Policy – Exclusivity and Independence

The core of monetary policy is in Article 4(2) of the EC Treaty, which under the Protocol[56] is not binding on the UK following the UK's notice given in November 1997 that it would not participate in stage three of Economic and Monetary Union. Article 4(2) states that as provided in the Treaty and in accordance with the timetable and the procedures set out therein, the activities of the Member States and of the Community shall include the irrevocable fixing of exchange rates leading to the introduction of a single currency, the ECU, and the definition and conduct of a single monetary policy and exchange rate policy the primary objective of both of which shall be to maintain price stability and, without prejudice to this objective, to support the general economic policies in the Community, in accordance with the principle of an open market economy with free competition.

Article 118 introduced by the Maastricht Treaty stated categorically that the currency composition of the ECU basket could not be changed, no doubt with the intention of building confidence in the international money markets. It further provided that from the start of the third stage, the value of the ECU should be irrevocably fixed in accordance with Article 123(4), which in turn laid down that from that date, the Council should, acting with the unanimity of the Member States which were able and willing to participate, adopt the conversion rates at which their currencies should be irrevocably fixed and at which irrevocably fixed rate the ECU should be substituted for these currencies, and the ECU would become a currency in its own right – which it did as the 'euro'.

A. Replacement of the ECU by the Euro

The replacement of the ECU by the euro is a matter which was not foreseen by the Maastricht Treaty, since it was only decided at the meeting of the European Council in December 1995 that the name to be given to the European currency should be the 'euro' rather than the term ECU used in the Treaty. As recorded

---

[55] This is reflected also in the academic literature: the UK view is in effect supported by JV Louis, 'A legal and institutional approach for building a Monetary Union' (1998) CMLRev 33, 65, but Vigneron and Mollica (see n 54 above) argue on a teleological basis in favour of the majority view.
[56] Para 5.

in the recitals to Council Regulations 1103/97,[57] and 974/98,[58] at the meeting of the European Council in Madrid on 15 and 16 December 1995, the decision was taken that the term 'ECU' used by the Treaty to refer to the European currency unit was a generic term, and the governments of the then 15 Member States reached the common agreement that this decision was 'the agreed and definitive interpretation of the relevant Treaty provisions' and that the name given to the European currency should be the 'euro'. Thus, without changing the Treaty, the Treaty term was changed. The use of the term 'euro' was, in fact, judicially challenged by a member of the European Parliament,[59] but the action was held inadmissible since he attempted to challenge the proposal which eventually became Regulation 1103/97 rather than a binding legal act. In a second action, Case T-207/97 *Berthu v Council*,[60] he sought the annulment of Council Regulation 1103/97 itself, but this action was held inadmissible on the ground that the Regulation was not of individual concern to the applicant.

Regulation 1103/97[61] was adopted in June 1997 under Article 308 of the EC Treaty to deal with the problems of conversion; it was adopted therefore contemporaneously with the Amsterdam Treaty, even if that Treaty did not make any formal amendment to introduce the term 'euro'. It would appear that political agreement had been reached that the Amsterdam IGC would not alter any of the EMU provisions of the EC Treaty, so as to avoid upsetting the money markets. Under Article 2 of this Regulation, every reference in a legal instrument to the ECU as defined under Community law was to be replaced by a reference to the euro at a rate of one euro to one ECU, and in an effort to cover the private sector use of the ECU, references in a legal instrument to the ECU were deemed to be references to the ECU as defined in Community law, subject to the intentions of the parties. A contrary intention was found in Case C-49/92P *Commission v Anic Partecipazioni*;[62] this involved a fine imposed in 1986 under the competition rules where the Commission had expressly converted ECU to national currency in its decision, and the Court held that the sum in ECU could not simply be treated as the same number of euro.

It might finally be observed in this context that under Article 4(4), monetary amounts to be converted from one participant national currency unit into another were first to be converted into a monetary amount expressed in the euro unit, and were then to be converted into the other national currency unit. This reflects the fact that even during the transitional period before euro notes and coins were introduced, the currency unit was the euro,[63] so that there were no

---

[57] OJ 1997 L162/1.
[58] OJ 1998 L139/1.
[59] Case T-175/96 *Berthu v Commission* [1997] ECR II-811.
[60] [1998] ECR II-509.
[61] OJ 1997 L162/1.
[62] [1999] ECR I-4125.
[63] Council Regulation 974/98 Art 2.

bilateral exchange rates between the former national currencies except as a consequence of the conversion rate against the euro. It was further provided in Article 4(1), presumably for the same reason, that the conversion rates should be adopted as one euro expressed in terms of each of the national currencies of the participating Member States.

B. Replacement of National Currencies by the Euro

In order to give the markets maximum notice as to legal rules applicable on the replacement of national currencies by the euro, even though no formal legislation could be issued until the decision had been taken on which countries should participate in the third stage of Economic and Monetary Union,[64] the Council published a resolution in July 1997[65] setting out what it expected to be the text of the legislation. Following the decision to move to the third stage of Economic and Monetary Union, a formal Regulation was adopted on 3 May 1998[66] which, apart from filling in the blanks, is virtually identical to the text published in the resolution. This Regulation declared unequivocally in Article 2 that as from 1 January 1999 the currency of the participating Member States should be the euro, that the currency unit should be one euro, and that one euro should be divided into 100 cents (which again is a matter with which the Treaty does not expressly deal). The euro was substituted for the currency of each participating Member State at the conversion rate[67] set at the start of the third stage under Article 123(4) of the Treaty, and it became the unit of account of the European Central Bank (ECB) and of the central banks of the participating Member States.[68]

While the euro may have become the currency of the participating Member States in 1999, euro banknotes and coins were not introduced until January 2002.[69] During the intervening period, and for up to six months thereafter, national notes and coins remained in use, but their legal nature changed: under Article 6 of the Regulation they became divisions of the euro rather than continuing as currencies in their own right. They were only legal tender, however, within their territorial limits as of the day before the commencement of Economic and Monetary Union.[70] The Regulation provided that where in a legal instrument reference was made to a national currency unit, 'this reference should be as valid as if reference were made to the euro unit according to the conversion rates'.[71]

---

[64] EC Treaty Art 123.
[65] European Council Resolution of 7 July 1997 on the legal framework for the introduction of the euro (OJ 1997 C236/7).
[66] Council Regulation 974/98 of 3 May 1998 on the introduction of the euro (OJ 1998 L139/1).
[67] Art 3. The rates were set by Council Regulation 2866/98 (OJ 1998 L359/1).
[68] Art 4.
[69] Art 10.
[70] Art 9.
[71] Art 6(2).

Furthermore, the substitution of the euro for the currency of each participating Member State did not in itself have the effect of altering the denomination of legal instruments in existence on the date of substitution.[72]

Banknotes denominated in euro, and coins denominated in euro or in cents were to be (and were) put in circulation in the participating Member States as from 1 January 2002[73] and, subject to a changeover period of up to six months,[74] became the only banknotes and coins which have the status of legal tender in all these Member States. Nevertheless, issuers of national banknotes and coins were required to continue to accept the banknotes and coins previously issued by them against euros at the conversion rate.[75]

With a view to further accessions to the eurozone, Council Regulation 974/98 was amended by Council Regulation 2169/2005.[76] Whilst keeping a maximum three-year changeover period,[77] this period can be reduced to zero.[78] Thus, when Slovenia joined the eurozone, the euro adoption date and the cash changeover date both occurred on the same day – 1 January 2007 – and the same policy was pursued in Cyprus and Malta in January 2008.

C. The Role of the ECB

Authority to issue notes and coins stems from Article 106 of the EC Treaty. Article 106(1) sets out a fundamental monetary function of the ECB, going to the heart of what has been traditionally regarded as a function of the state:[79] for the participating Member States, the ECB has the exclusive right to authorize the issue of bank notes within the Community. The ECB and the national central banks may issue such notes, and the bank notes issued by the ECB and the national central banks are the only such notes to have the status of legal tender within the Community. With regard to coins, Article 106(2) permits participating Member States to issue coins subject to approval by the ECB of the volume of the issue. The Council may, acting in accordance with the cooperation procedure[80] and after consulting the ECB, adopt measures to harmonize the denominations and technical specifications of all coins intended for circulation to the extent necessary to permit their smooth circulation within the Community, resulting in the enactment of Council Regulation 975/98 of

---

[72] Art 7.
[73] Art 10.
[74] Art 15.
[75] Art 16.
[76] OJ 2005 L346/1.
[77] Under a new Art 1(h).
[78] Recital 6 and Art 1(2), introducing a new Art 1a of the 1998 Regulation.
[79] See the judgment of the European Court in Case 7/78 *R v Thompson* [1978] ECR 2247.
[80] Art 252. The failure of the Amsterdam Treaty to amend any of the provisions relating to EMU means that this is the only sector where the cooperation procedure is encountered after the entry into force of that Treaty.

3 May 1998 on the denomination and technical specifications of euro coins intended for circulation.[81]

The move to a single currency was envisaged in parallel with the creation of the ECB. It was provided in Article 123(4) that at the starting date of the third stage, the Council should, acting with the unanimity of the Member States without a derogation, on a proposal from the Commission and after consulting the ECB, adopt the conversion rates at which their currencies shall be irrevocably fixed and at which irrevocably fixed rate the euro should be substituted for these currencies. This was effected by Council Regulation 2866/98 on conversion rates for the euro.[82]

A requirement of independence similar to if not stronger than that imposed on members of the Commission by Article 213(2) of the EC Treaty is laid down by Article 108 (which, however, does not apply to the United Kingdom).[83] When exercising the powers and carrying out the tasks and duties conferred upon them by the Treaty and the Statute of the ESCB, neither the ECB, nor a national central bank, nor any member of their decision-making bodies may seek or take instructions from Community institutions or bodies, from any government of a Member State or from any other body. Conversely, the Community institutions and bodies and the governments of the Member States undertake to respect this principle and not to seek to influence the members of the decision-making bodies of the ECB or of the national central banks in the performance of their tasks. Linked to this, Article 109, which similarly does not apply to the United Kingdom, imposes the obligation on each Member State to ensure, at the latest at the date of the establishment of the ESCB, that its national legislation including the statutes of its national central bank is compatible with the Treaty and the Statute of the ESCB. This strong statement of independence has led to critical comment as to the lack of democratic control over the ECB,[84] though others have argued in favour of a separate status.[85]

However, it has now become clear that there are limits to this independence. In Case C-11/00 *Commission v ECB*,[86] the Commission sought the annulment of the ECB's decision on fraud prevention, which had been adopted on the basis of the view held by the ECB that its independence under the EC Treaty meant that it was not subject to EP and Council Regulation 1073/1999 concerning investigations conducted by the European Anti-Fraud Office (OLAF). The Court in fact held that while the ECB had independence in relation to the exercise of its

---

[81] OJ 1998 L139/6.
[82] OJ 1998 L359/1.
[83] UK Protocol Art 5.
[84] Gormley and De Haan, 'The democratic deficit of the European Central Bank' (1996) ELRev 95. For a detailed comparative analysis see Amtenbrink, *The Democratic Accountability of Central Banks* (1999).
[85] Zillig and Selmayr, 'The ECB: an independent specialized organisation of Community law' (2000) CML Rev 591.
[86] 10 July 2003.

specific powers, that did not have the consequence of separating it entirely from the EC and exempting it from every rule of Community law; in the result it was found that the adoption by the ECB of its own decision infringed the general Regulation on OLAF investigations. This was then reflected in the ECB's decision 2004/11 on OLAF investigations of the ECB.[87]

More specifically, Article 14.2 of the Statute, which does not apply to the UK,[88] requires that the statutes of the national central banks should, in particular, provide that the term of office of a governor of a national central bank shall be no less than five years. Furthermore, a governor may be relieved from office only if he no longer fulfils the conditions required for the performance of his duties or if he has been guilty of serious misconduct. A decision to this effect may be referred to the Court of Justice by the governor concerned or the Governing Council of the ECB on grounds of infringement of the Treaty or of any rule of law relating to its application – a unique example of a national official becoming subject to Community jurisdiction.

A further possible limit on the independence of the ECB results from Article 111 of the EC Treaty. This provision envisages the possible need (or hope) for an exchange rate policy following the introduction of the euro, and it does not apply to Member States with a derogation[89] or to the United Kingdom.[90] Article 111(1) operates by way of derogation from Article 300, which sets out the general procedure for the negotiation of international agreements between the Community and non-Member States or international organizations; it empowers the Council to conclude formal agreements on an exchange rate system for the euro in relation to non-Community currencies – which seems to contemplate a return to something like the former IMF system – and lays down a special procedure for this to be achieved.

However, in the absence of an exchange rate system negotiated under Articles 111(1) and (3) in relation to one or more non-Community currencies, Article 111(2) provides for the Council to formulate general orientations for Community exchange rate policy in relation to these currencies, though these general orientations must be without prejudice to the primary objective of the ESCB to maintain price stability. While the Council may act by a qualified majority either on a recommendation from the Commission and after consulting the ECB or simply on a recommendation from the ECB, which again shows the power of initiative of the ECB in this area, there would seem little point in formulating orientations if the ECB is not obliged to take any notice of them.[91] Nevertheless, what is novel about Article 111, but a recurring characteristic of the third stage of

---

[87] OJ 2004 L230/56.
[88] UK Protocol Art 8.
[89] Art 122(3) and (4).
[90] UK Protocol Art 5.
[91] Indeed, Art 105(1) requires the ECB to conduct foreign exchange operations 'consistent with the provisions of Article 111'.

Economic and Monetary Union as it results from the Maastricht Treaty, is that international agreements may be entered into in the name of the Community which will be binding on some but not all of the Member States.

V. Economic Union – Coordination and Enforcement

One of the convergence criteria set out in Article 121 of the EC Treaty is not simply a hurdle to be passed in order to gain entry to the eurozone but reflects a continuing obligation and requirement. This is the second criterion, which relates to the sustainability of the government financial position. This is stated to be apparent from having achieved a government budgetary position without a deficit that is excessive as determined in accordance with Article 104(6). Under Article 104(2), the relevant criteria relate to the ratio of the planned or actual government deficit to gross domestic product and to the ratio of government debt to gross domestic product. These criteria are further refined in the Protocol on the Excessive Deficit Procedure, according to which government deficit must not exceed 3 per cent of GDP, and government debt must not exceed 60 per cent of GDP, but they are not absolute. Thus it is stated that a Member State which breaches the deficit ratio will not be regarded as having an excessive government deficit if the ratio has declined 'substantially and continuously' and reached a level that comes close to the reference value, or, alternatively, the excess over the reference value is only 'exceptional and temporary' and the ratio remains close to the reference value.[92] Furthermore, a higher ratio of government debt will not be regarded as excessive if the ratio is 'sufficiently diminishing' and approaching the reference value 'at a satisfactory pace'.[93] Thus both Belgium and Italy had a ratio of government debt to GDP above 120 per cent when the assessment of compliance with the convergence criteria was made[94] yet were not regarded as having an excessive deficit. However, the obligation to avoid an excessive government deficit remains in perpetuity,[95] and its enforcement is the subject of the Stability and Growth Pact.[96]

During the second stage, Member States were merely under the obligation to 'endeavour' to avoid excessive government deficits,[97] and this remains the situation for the United Kingdom under its Protocol. Nevertheless, for Member

---

[92] Art 104(2)(a).
[93] Art 104(2)(b).
[94] Commission Report of 25 March 1998 on Progress towards Convergence, 1.3.1 and 1.3.7.
[95] See Hahn, 'The stability pact for European Monetary Union: compliance with deficit limit as a constant legal duty' (1998) CMLRev 77.
[96] European Council Resolution (OJ 1997 C236/1) on the Stability and Growth Pact; Council Regulation 1466/97 on the strengthening of the surveillance of budgetary positions and of the surveillance and coordination of economic policies (OJ 1997 L209/1); Council Regulation 1467/97 on speeding up and clarifying the implementation of the excessive deficit procedure (OJ 1997 L209/6).
[97] Art 116(4).

States wishing to participate in the third stage of Economic and Monetary Union, compliance with this obligation is an absolute necessity in the third stage. The structure of the excessive deficits procedure is that it:

- sets out the obligation to avoid excessive government deficits;
- establishes machinery for determining whether there is an excessive deficit, which applies to all Member States;
- sets out its own enforcement machinery which, however, does not apply to Member States with a derogation,[98] to Denmark (which is treated as if it did have a derogation[99]) or to the United Kingdom.[100]

If the Commission considers that an excessive deficit in a Member State exists or may occur, the Commission addresses an opinion (by definition a non-binding act) to the Council, and the Council, acting by a qualified majority on a recommendation from the Commission, and having considered any observations which the Member State concerned may wish to make, has to decide after an overall assessment whether an excessive deficit exists.[101]

Where it decides that there is an excessive deficit the Council makes recommendations to the Member State concerned with a view to bringing that situation to an end within a given period. However, these recommendations are not to be made public, unless it is established that there has been no effective action in response to its recommendations within the period laid down, in which case the Council may make its recommendations public.[102] It may, nevertheless, be observed that under the Resolution of the European Council on the Stability and Growth Pact,[103] Member States are 'invited' to make such recommendations public on their own initiative. In any event, however, the Treaty itself does not lay down any time limits for the conduct of this assessment procedure.

So far as enforcement is concerned, it is expressly provided in Article 104(10) that the rights for the Commission or other Member States to bring actions against the State concerned before the European Court provided for in Articles 226 and 227 may not be exercised within the framework of paragraphs 1 to 9 of that article. However, the article sets out its own enforcement mechanism, providing that if a Member State persists in failing to put into practice the recommendations of the Council, the Council may decide to give notice to the Member State to take, within a specified time limit, measures for the deficit reduction which is judged necessary by the Council in order to remedy the situation.[104] In such case, the Council may request the Member State concerned to submit reports

---

[98] Art 122(3).
[99] Danish Protocol, para 2.
[100] UK Protocol, para 5.
[101] Art 104(6).
[102] Arts 104(7) and (8).
[103] OJ 1997 C236/1.
[104] Art 104(9).

in accordance with a specific timetable in order to examine the adjustment efforts of that Member State. Finally, it is provided that as long as a Member State fails to comply with a decision taken in accordance with paragraph 9, the Council may decide to apply or, as the case may be, intensify one or more of the following measures:

- to require the Member State concerned to publish additional information, to be specified by the Council, before issuing bonds and securities;
- to invite the European Investment Bank to reconsider its lending policy towards the Member State concerned;
- to require the Member State concerned to make a non-interest-bearing deposit of an appropriate size with the Community until the excessive deficit has, in the view of the Council, been corrected; and
- to impose fines of an appropriate size.

In taking decisions as to the existence of an excessive deficit and in imposing remedial measures or sanctions, the Council is required to act on a recommendation from the Commission by a special majority of two-thirds of the weighted votes of its members, excluding the votes of the representative of the Member State concerned. This is a slightly lower majority than the normal qualified majority, though it is the same proportion of the available votes as the qualified majority among the participants in Economic and Monetary Union when the votes of Member States with derogations are excluded.[105] In that case, under Article 122(5), a qualified majority is defined as two thirds of the votes of the representatives of the Member States without derogation weighted in accordance with Article 205(2) – a proportion which seems particularly low in the light of the 2004 and 2007 enlargements[106] – and unanimity of those Member States alone is required for an act requiring unanimity. The anomaly with regard to qualified majorities would have been removed by the Constitutional Treaty: this envisaged that, with effect from 1 November 2009,[107] a normal qualified majority would require the votes of 55 per cent of the members of the Council comprising at least 15 members representing 65 per cent of the EU's population, but coupled with a requirement that a blocking minority must include at least four Council members. A similar pattern would be followed in areas in which not all Member States participate: in the context of enhanced cooperation[108] and Economic and Monetary Union,[109] a qualified majority would be the votes of 55 per cent of the

---

[105] Art 122(5).
[106] Following the 2004 accessions a qualified majority represented 72.27 per cent of the weighted votes, and following the 2007 accessions it represents 73.91 per cent of the weighted votes, subject to an overall requirement in Art 205(4) that it should be formed by Member States representing at least 62 per cent of the population of the EU.
[107] Art I-25(1).
[108] Art I-44.
[109] Art II-194 etc.

participant Member States, comprising at least 65 per cent of their combined population, and a blocking minority would be the minimum number representing more than 35 per cent of the population of the participating States, plus one member. The same reforms are in fact envisaged in the Treaty of Lisbon 2007, but with effect from 1 November 2014.

A common thread running through this enforcement machinery as set out in Articles 104(8) to (11) is that it is discretionary – it states what the Council 'may' do, but does not require it to take any action. This may be contrasted with the situation where the Council withdraws its measures. Under Article 104(12), the Council 'shall' abrogate some or all of its decisions as to the existence of an excessive deficit or imposing remedial measures or sanctions to the extent that the excessive deficit in the Member State concerned has, in the view of the Council, been corrected. In particular, if the Council has previously made public recommendations, it must, as soon as the decision to make the recommendation public has been abrogated, make a public statement that an excessive deficit in the Member State concerned no longer exists. In sum, therefore, although Article 104 maintains the excessive deficit criteria as continuing obligations for participants in the eurozone, it does so by provisions which lay down no time limit for the process of assessment and which do not oblige the Council to impose sanctions. This gave rise to the feeling,[110] particularly in Germany,[111] that this was not a sound basis on which to proceed to Economic and Monetary Union. The resultant political pressure led to the adoption in Amsterdam in June 1997 of a group of measures compendiously known as the Stability and Growth Pact, which has introduced an element of automaticity into the process.

The Stability and Growth Pact consists of a European Council Resolution[112] on the Stability and Growth Pact, together with Council Regulation 1466/97,[113] subsequently amended by Council Regulation 1055/2005,[114] on the strengthening of the surveillance of budgetary positions and the surveillance and coordination of economic policies, and Council Regulation 1467/97[115] on speeding up and clarifying the implementation of the excessive deficit procedure, subsequently amended by Council Regulation 1056/2005.[116] To the extent that reliance is placed on a Resolution of the European Council, its status is the same as both versions of the European Monetary System, and the same arguments arise as in relation to the European Monetary System Mark II with regard to the

---

[110] See Gros, 'Towards a credible excessive deficits procedure' in Andenas, Gormley, Hadjiemmanuil and Harden (eds), *European Economic and Monetary Union: The Institutional Framework* (1997) 241–56.
[111] See the sources cited in Hahn, 'The stability pact for European Monetary Union: compliance with deficit limit as a constant legal duty' (1998) CMLRev 77, 79 and 80.
[112] OJ 1997 C236/1.
[113] OJ 1997 L209/1.
[114] OJ 2005 L174/1.
[115] OJ 1997 L209/6.
[116] OJ 2005 L174/5.

legitimacy of an institution of the European Union acting in an area subject to the express competence of the European Community.

The Resolution describes itself as providing 'firm political guidance to the parties who will implement the Stability and Growth Pact' and sets out what it calls 'guidelines' for the Member States, the Commission and the Council. This clear political commitment to use the sanctions machinery is reflected and supplemented in the legally binding obligations set out in Council Regulation 1467/97 on speeding up and clarifying the implementation of the excessive deficit procedure.[117]

With regard to the imposition of sanctions, Regulation 1467/97 provides that whenever the Council decides to apply sanctions to a participating Member State in accordance with Article 104(11), a non-interest-bearing deposit shall, 'as a rule', be required, though the Council may decide to supplement this deposit by the measures provided for in the first and second indents of Article 104(11),[118] that is, by requiring the Member State concerned to publish additional information, to be specified by the Council, before issuing bonds and securities, or by inviting the European Investment Bank to reconsider its lending policy towards the Member State concerned.

However, the fundamental substantive problem with Regulation 1467/97 was that under its original Article 2(2) an excessive deficit could only be regarded as 'exceptional'[119] in terms of Article 104(2) if there was an annual fall in real GDP of at least 2 per cent. In effect, therefore, short of economic disaster, no deficit could be regarded as 'exceptional', and it may be suggested that this is part of the background to Case C-27/04 *Commission v Council*,[120] which also illustrates that while the Council must act within the parameters of the Stability and Growth Pact in this context, it can only do so if it obtains the necessary majority. In that case, following decisions finding that Germany and France had excessive deficits, the Commission took the view that those countries were failing to take the appropriate steps to remedy the situation, and therefore recommended to the Council that it should make its recommendations public and that it should require France and Germany to take specific measures for deficit reduction. The Council failed to achieve the necessary majority to follow these recommendations, but instead adopted 'conclusions' which held the excessive deficits procedures against France and Germany in abeyance. The Commission then challenged both the failure to adopt the measures set out in its recommendations (which it categorized as a decision not to follow its recommendations) and the conclusions holding the procedure in abeyance. While the Court accepted that the procedure might de facto be held in abeyance if there was not a majority in the Council to take the matter forward, it held that there was no power under the Treaty provisions on

[117] OJ 1997 L209/6.
[118] Art 11.
[119] Therefore not breaching the excessive deficits requirements.
[120] 13 July 2004.

the excessive deficits procedure or under the secondary legislation on the Stability and Growth Pact formally to decide to hold the matter in abeyance. The Court therefore annulled the Council's conclusions even if the lack of a majority meant it could take no further action.

Following this judgment, the Stability and Growth Pact was revised in 2005, and Council Regulation 1467/97 was substantially amended by Council Regulation 1056/2005.[121] This has replaced the text of Article 2(2) so that an excess resulting from a severe economic downturn may be regarded as 'exceptional' if it results from a negative annual GDP volume growth rate (rather than minus 2 per cent) or 'from an accumulated loss of output during a protracted period of very low annual GDP volume growth relative to its potential'. It may be suggested that this is a totally different concept from the original version. Furthermore, under new Articles 2(5) and 2(7), in all budgetary assessments in the framework of the excessive deficits procedure, the Commission and the Council are required to 'give due consideration to the implementation of pension reforms introducing a multi-pillar system that includes a mandatory fully-funded pillar', and they must also consider the cost of the reform to the publicly managed pillar. Again, it would appear that pension policy was a factor in the French and German deficits. Dare it be suggested that the changes effected by Regulation 1056/2005 reflect the principle of proportionality in operation, even if that word was not actually used?

VI. Conclusion

While EMU may be regarded as a matter not of direct concern in the United Kingdom, it is one of the major examples of differentiated integration in the EU. As such, it illustrates that there can be exclusive Community competence in relation to a group of Member States rather than the Community as a whole, and it also shows that rules relating to the group have been extended to the Community as a whole through the use of Article 308. It has created a new institutional structure, with an apparently enormous degree of independence, which has been tempered by a judgment of the ECJ. In the context of economic policy, it has created new enforcement machinery, based on what some would regard as a rather arbitrary choice of figures for government debt and deficits. This also has been tempered, this time by a combination of political will and a judgment of the ECJ. Finally, it may be suggested that it is EMU which is responsible for the fact that the current rules on capital movements and payments involve a third-country effect, an effect which also appears to have been limited, by the ECJ categorizing situations as falling under other Treaty freedoms.

[121] OJ 2005 L174/5.

PART IV

EXTERNAL RELATIONS

18

A Panorama of Two Decades of EU External Relations Law

Piet Eeckhout

I. Introduction

In the two decades during which Sir Francis Jacobs was Advocate General at the Court of Justice, EC and EU external relations law grew exponentially, reflecting the expansion and diversification of Europe's external policies. In the late 1980s the Community was primarily engaged in trade policy and development aid. The former was confined to trade in goods, even if the Community was negotiating in the Uruguay Round which would lead to the establishment of the WTO, with its much broader conception of trade. There were some attempts at foreign policy coordination through the vehicle of European Political Cooperation (EPC), but the Pillar structure of the European Union was still to be created, and those attempts were but the nucleus of today's Common Foreign and Security Policy (CFSP). The contrast with current EU external policies is stark. Throughout both the political and economic spheres the EU has become an important international actor. It is true that particularly in the political field the EU does not always manage to speak with one voice and to be effective, but there is a presence and there is activity, even in defence matters. EU external relations law reflects this expansion and diversification. The current EU concludes international agreements which touch upon virtually all economic matters: trade, investment, intellectual property, technical regulations and standards, competition policy, even taxation. Increasingly there is activity in non-economic areas such as conflict of laws, criminal law, even human rights law. In foreign policy the EU is becoming an active player in international crises, and has been driving economic sanctions and anti-terrorism policies. The EU is a member of some international organizations, such as the WTO, and an important actor also in others, such as the UN, notwithstanding its mere observer status. All of this means that EU external relations law has had to adapt and develop. The new legal order is increasingly a legal order confronted also with the outside world. The development of external relations law is partly an internal affair, in the sense that it is based on the core legal principles of Community law. But the expanding external policies also expose the EU ever more to international law and its rapid development. The Community legal order constituted itself in *Van Gend en Loos*[1] as distinct and different from public international law, but the last decade witnesses ever greater interaction between these two legal systems, and arguably greater convergence too.[2]

All of this would suggest that EU external relations law has been fundamentally transformed. However, in line with the theme of this volume, there is both continuity and change. The foundations of EU external relations law are still pretty much the same as 20 years ago, and change and development can only be understood in the light of those foundations. This short contribution aims to sketch a panorama of two decades of external relations law, focusing on continuity and change. It is but a sketch, not an elaborate painting, and it is incomplete, as many parts of the landscape will be left blank. The parts I will try to sketch are twofold. They are at the heart of external relations law. First, the evolving external powers of the EU, where the focus will be on the interaction between trade and foreign policy. Second, the effects which international agreements, and international law more broadly, produce in EU law.

In sketching those parts I will, of course, highlight the contributions by Advocate General Jacobs. This also permits me to indicate that I had the enormous privilege and good fortune to be able to work with him for a number of years, including on some of the cases to which I will refer. This was simply the most rewarding experience in my professional life.

II. External Powers – Trade and Foreign Policy

As mentioned, trade was the Community's predominant external policy two decades ago. EPC had just been formalized through the Single European Act, but constituted little else than limited coordination of Member States' foreign policies, expressed in political declarations. The collapse of the Soviet bloc and the destruction of the Iron Curtain made the further development of a common foreign policy both possible and indispensable. The response was set out in the Maastricht Treaty on European Union (TEU), which created the pillar structure in which foreign policy was institutionally separated from other external policies. Since then, the CFSP has developed into a policy of its own. Public debate often concentrates on the CFSP's flaws and defects, the emblem of which is the failure to construct a common approach towards the Iraq crisis. Such a focus risks concealing the importance of the CFSP. Whilst obviously not as 'thick' as trade policy, the CFSP grew enormously since its conception. This can be seen at both institutional and legal level. Within the Council of Ministers an elaborate framework of

---

[1] Case 26/62 *Van Gend en Loos v Nederlandse Administratie der Belastingen* [1963] ECR 1.
[2] CWA Timmermans, 'The EU and public international law', 4 EFA Review (1999) 181–94.

committees and agencies has been set up, headed by the High Representative for the CFSP. The ill-fated Constitutional Treaty's attempt to transform that function into a genuine EU Foreign Affairs Minister did not suffer from delusions of grandeur, but correctly reflected the growing importance of the EU's foreign policy.[3] At a legal level it is remarkable how broad the terrain of the CFSP actually is. Under the terminological veil of the innocent and uncommon denominations of 'common positions' and 'joint actions', CFSP legal instruments include acts which are wide-ranging and meaningful.[4]

The institutional separation of the CFSP from other external policies is an accident of the EU's constitutional history rather than an optimal organization of policy-making. 'Foreign policy' is an ill-defined and broad term, and in nation states it encompasses a wide range of policies, many of which, in the EU's structure, are located, not in the Second but in the First Pillar.[5] The Constitutional Treaty therefore rightly made an attempt to remove part of the pillar structure, and to integrate external policies. The interaction between foreign policy, *sensu stricto*, and 'other' external policies is most evident with respect to trade policy. In the 1980s the Community became active in the sphere of economic sanctions, which often involved trade embargos.[6] Community involvement was unavoidable because of the exclusive character of the Community's external competence in trade matters. It was further pushed to increase the effectiveness and immediacy of sanctions: EC Regulations – the instruments used – are directly applicable in all Member States and endowed with the primacy of Community law. But economic sanctions are, of course, primarily foreign policy instruments, and the TEU therefore set up a special mechanism to adopt them. Articles 301 and 60(1) EC permit the Community to interrupt or reduce economic relations with one or more third countries, including the movement of capital and payments, but on the basis of a prior CFSP joint action or common position. There are other areas where trade and foreign policy interact, such as export controls on so-called dual-use goods.[7]

This interaction, and the parallel development of trade policy and foreign policy, are fascinating corners of the EU external relations law landscape. The common commercial policy is an exclusive Community competence,[8] exercised through qualified majority voting by the Council and with a central role for the Commission. Member States can only take commercial policy measures where

---

[3] See further M Cremona, 'The Draft Constitutional Treaty: external relations and external action' 40 CMLRev (2003) 1355.
[4] See P Eeckhout, *External Relations of the European Union – Legal and Constitutional Foundations* (2004) 398–409; R Gosalbo Bono, 'Some reflections on the CFSP legal order', 43 CMLRev (2006) 337–94.
[5] Compare with E Denza, *The Intergovernmental Pillars of the European Union* (2002) 85–6.
[6] P Koutrakos, *Trade, Foreign Policy and Defence in EU Constitutional Law* (2001).
[7] Council Regulation 1334/00 setting up a Community regime for the control of exports of dual-use items and technology [2000] OJ L 159/1.
[8] Opinion 1/75 re Understanding on a Local Cost Standard [1975] ECR 1355.

specifically authorized by the Community.[9] Foreign policy, by contrast, used to be the sole preserve of Member States. The TEU aimed to construct a common policy, but one not subject to the strictures of Community law, and definitely not an exclusive EU competence. The Constitutional Treaty, notwithstanding its ambition to remove some of the pillar separations, did not even go so far as to classify the CFSP in the system of EU competences.[10] Conceiving of the CFSP as a shared or parallel competence was a bridge too far. The foreign policy is common only if, when, and where Member State governments unanimously decide so. Thus, where trade policy and foreign policy interact, this is the amalgam: exclusive Community competence, undefined EU powers, and national competence with strong sovereignty overtones.

The interaction between trade policy and foreign policy was a factor in a number of cases before the Court of Justice, and in several of those Francis Jacobs was the Advocate General. The first case (1991) was *Richardt and 'Les Accessoires Scientifiques'*, concerning the seizure by Luxembourg authorities of certain computer equipment, in transit from France to the Soviet Union.[11] The seizure was based on external security grounds, and the question was whether it could be reconciled with the common commercial policy, which includes a rule of free exportation. Advocate General Jacobs identified some of the core principles which would guide the case law in this area. He unreservedly accepted that the seizure was covered by the common commercial policy legislation, thereby safeguarding the scope and exclusive nature of the Community's competence. However, he also considered that the seizure could be justified on the basis of the public security exception which the relevant EC legislation contains, provided the principle of proportionality was complied with. The concept of public security was broad enough to embrace restrictions on the transfer of goods or technology of strategic importance to countries which were thought to pose a military threat. He thus struck a balance between Community exclusive competence and legislation, on the one hand, and Member States' competence in the domain of foreign policy, on the other.

The *Werner* and *Leifer* cases, concerning exports of dual-use goods from Germany to respectively Libya and Iraq, confirmed this approach.[12] The Court, following the opinion of Advocate General Jacobs, considered that the Treaty provisions providing for a common commercial policy based on uniform principles required a non-restrictive interpretation. Export control measures whose effect was to prevent or restrict the export of certain products could not be treated as falling outside the scope of the common commercial policy on the grounds that they had foreign policy and security objectives. The specific subject matter of

[9] Case 41/76 *Donckerwolcke v Procureur de la République* [1976] ECR 1921.
[10] See Art I-11 CT.
[11] Case C-367/89 *Richardt and 'Les Accessoires Scientifiques'* [1991] ECR I-4621.
[12] Case C-70/94 *Werner v Germany* [1995] ECR I-3189; Case C-83/94 *Leifer and Others* [1995] ECR I-3231. See also the contribution by Alan Dashwood in this volume.

commercial policy required that a Member State should not be able to restrict its scope by freely deciding, in the light of its own foreign policy or security requirements, whether a measure was covered by Article 133 EC (common commercial policy). However, the Court also adopted a broad interpretation of the public security exception, admitting that it was difficult to draw a hard-and-fast distinction between foreign policy and security policy considerations. It also highlighted that it was becoming increasingly less possible to look at the security of a state in isolation, linked as it is to the security of the international community in general, and of its various components. The Court therefore accepted the export controls.

The ruling in *Centro-Com* was based on the same principles, but had a different outcome, arguably because the EC (not yet the EU) had itself become more involved in the policy concerned.[13] The case concerned a UN trade embargo, implemented by the Community, against the Federal Republic of Yugoslavia (Serbia and Montenegro) at the time of the break-up of Yugoslavia. The relevant EC regulations exempted certain exports for medical purposes and of foodstuffs, and organized an authorization procedure. Centro-Com had exported under those arrangements, having received authorizations from the UN Sanctions Committee and from the Italian authorities. When it sought payment through a London bank account, the UK authorities refused on the basis that, with a view to strengthening the sanctions regime, payments could be realized only for export transactions approved by the UK authorities. The United Kingdom argued that the measures had been taken by virtue of its national competence in the field of foreign and security policy and that performance of its obligations under the UN Charter and Resolutions fell within that competence. The Court accepted that the Member States retained competence in the field of foreign and security policy, but also emphasized that national competences had to be exercised in a manner consistent with Community law. It carefully analysed the various regulations in issue, and ruled that Centro-Com had followed the correct procedures and that the UK authorities were required to respect the authorization decisions by authorities in other Member States. In contrast with the previous cases, Community legislation had occupied the field and therefore needed to be respected.

One question which arises from this evolution in the case law is whether the Court would be willing to take a similar approach in a case where the field has been occupied, not by Community legislation, but by CFSP acts. To what extent could a common foreign policy on a particular matter preclude unilateral decisions by Member States? In his famous opinion in *Commission v Greece*, on that Member State's embargo against the Former Yugoslav Republic of Macedonia, Advocate General Jacobs eloquently defended the national prerogative to take

---

[13] Case C-124/95 *The Queen, ex parte Centro-Com v HM Treasury and Bank of England* [1997] ECR I-81.

such unilateral foreign policy decisions, insofar as justified on the basis of Article 297 EC.[14] He rightly emphasized the, from a nation state perspective, partly subjective character of foreign policy conditions and threats, and considered the issues involved – including a threat of war – to a large degree non-justiciable. As a result of the opinion the Commission abandoned the case. However, one is entitled to ask whether this approach of judicial non-interference would be maintained in a case where there is a common EU policy, albeit under the Second Pillar. The Court, of course, generally lacks jurisdiction over CFSP acts, but the accidents and intricacies of litigation do not exclude that it may one day be faced with the legal consequences of such acts, and may have to deal with them.

In fact, some EU foreign policy acts have already been the subject of litigation. The issue in *Racke*, again a case involving Francis Jacobs as Advocate General, was whether the Community's suspending its cooperation agreement with Yugoslavia, as a sanction and means of pressure to stem the bloodshed engulfing that country, complied with customary international law on the suspension of treaties.[15] The actual act of suspension was a Community act, but it was preceded by – and therefore amounted to implementation of – an EPC decision. The Court steered around this, but did examine the suspension's lawfulness.

In today's EU the interaction between the Second and the First Pillars is gradually expanding. It is played out in the field of anti-terrorism policies, where the Court of First Instance accepted an expansive reading of the Community's powers to adopt economic sanctions as including sanctions against individuals.[16] It did so on the basis of a particular construction of the relationship between the pillars: Community action on the basis of Articles 301 and 60(1) EC is in fact action by the Union, as it is mandated through CFSP decisions. This approach risks excessively subjugating the Community to the CFSP. The CFI attempted to justify such subjugation with reference to the imperative of coherence and consistency in the EU's external policies (Article 3 TEU), but it is difficult to see how those imperatives can lead to an expansion of Community competences. The idea that Community law instruments are simply at the disposal for implementing CFSP decisions which would otherwise be more difficult to implement does not conform to the Treaty conceptions of the relationship between the various EU pillars. It remains to be seen whether the Court of Justice agrees with the CFI, as the judgments are under appeal at the time of writing.

The interaction between the Pillars is also played out in the heavily contested ECOWAS case.[17] The issues here concern the delimitation of the Community's

[14] Case C-120/94 *Commission v Greece* [1996] ECR I-1513.
[15] Case C-162/96 *Racke v Hauptzollamt Mainz* [1998] ECR I-3655.
[16] Case T-306/01 *Yusuf v Council and Commission* [2005] ECR II-3353 and Case T-315/01 *Kadi v Council and Commission* [2005] ECR II-3649.
[17] Case C-91/05 *Commission v Council*, pending; see M Cremona, 'Community report', in FIDE 2006 National Reports, XL Xenopoulos (ed), *External Relations of the EU and the Member States: Competence, Mixed Agreements, International Responsibility and Effects of International Law* (2006) 333–6.

development cooperation policy, which includes fighting the proliferation of small arms and light weapons (SALW) in Africa, and the CFSP. Again the case is *sub iudice* at the time of writing, and it would be hazardous to predict its outcome. One point may be noted, though. The general principle which governs the legal relationship between the Pillars, as interpreted and applied by the Court, is not to be underestimated. Article 47 TEU provides that nothing in the TEU affects the EC Treaty, and this has been read as meaning that Second and Third Pillar acts may not encroach on Community competences.[18] This is a very strong principle, since it applies to all Community competences, be they exclusive or shared. Taken to its logical conclusion the principle means that, by concluding the TEU and agreeing to set up a CFSP, the Member States have lost the capacity to take collective foreign policy decisions which come within the scope of Community competences. This capacity clearly existed before the adoption of the TEU, since the Member States were precluded from acting within the scope of *exclusive* Community competences only. Today, collective action would naturally take the form of a CFSP act, but such an act cannot encroach on any type of Community competence.

This alone shows that the interaction between the Pillars is here to stay. Both the ill-fated Constitutional Treaty and the currently negotiated Reform Treaty remove some of the space between the Pillars, but do not collapse them. The said interaction will continue to be emblematic for the character of the EU as an organization based on a federal-type legal system in areas of neo-functional integration, but without a corresponding level of political integration. In political terms, of course, external economic policies will always ultimately risk being subjected to foreign-policy considerations and decisions, and those decisions are not reached through supranational mechanisms. They emanate from national capitals and are the product of consensus or power politics.

III. Effects of International Law

The direct effect of European Community law is the cornerstone of the new legal order which the Court of Justice identified in *Van Gend en Loos*.[19] In that judgment the Court in fact spoke of a 'new legal order of international law', but the international law qualification was shelved in later case law. It is accepted doctrine that the Court sought to distinguish EC law from international law, in particular as regards the effects which EC law has in the laws of the Member States. EC law is dressed in the constitutional gowns of supremacy and direct effect. These features make it more akin to domestic or municipal law, of a federal kind, than to public international law, notwithstanding the treaty character of the legal instrument on which it is based. All this makes the further question, concerning the effects

---

[18] Case C-176/03 *Commission v Council* [2005] ECR I-7879.
[19] Above n 1.

which international law produces in EC law, so fascinating. How open is the attitude towards international law? To what extent are the EU Courts prepared to recognize the effects of international law, and what precisely are those effects?

In the two decades which are sketched here the basic answers to those questions have remained the same. The Court of Justice easily accepts that an international agreement concluded by the Community may have direct effect, in much the same way as other rules and instruments of Community law. The general approach as set out in the 1987 *Kupferberg* judgment continues to be applied.[20] That approach amounts to what is almost a presumption in favour of direct effect: it is only in certain cases that the nature and structure of the agreement may be such that its direct effect must be ruled out. At the time of *Kupferberg* there was only one such case: that of the GATT. In *International Fruit Company* the Court ruled that, in essence, the GATT was too flexible to have direct effect.[21] That approach of denying direct effect has been maintained for the current WTO,[22] notwithstanding the differences between the WTO Agreement and the GATT of 1947, and notwithstanding intense academic debate often including fierce criticism of the Court's decisions.[23] At the time of writing, the GATT and WTO agreements remain the only international agreements facing an across-the-board denial of direct effect.

From a distance, therefore, this part of the landscape has barely changed over the last 20 years. However, if one looks more closely one notices a number of new features as well as incremental change in the finer detail of the landscape. Let me try to sketch some of the developments.

A closer look first of all reveals that international agreements and other norms of international law may produce a range of different effects which the general concept of direct effect often fails to do justice. Those effects can best be seen where the Court has denied direct effect as such: in the case of WTO law. This denial does not signify that no norm of WTO law can ever be relevant in proceedings before the EU Courts. It is, in essence, confined to cases where a party, be it a private party, a Member State, or, presumably, an EU institution, invokes such a norm to question the legality or validity of a norm of Community law or of national law. This applies in actions for annulment, actions in damages, and preliminary rulings cases. The Court of Justice does not accept that WTO law can be relied upon in such cases of conflict. However, it does not extend this denial of direct effect to enforcement proceedings: the Commission may bring an action against a Member State which has failed to comply with its EC law obligation to implement WTO law.[24] There are, moreover, certain types of cases in which the Court does allow a

---

[20] Case 104/81 *Hauptzollamt Mainz v Kupferberg* [1982] ECR 3641.
[21] Joined Cases 21–24/72 *International Fruit Company v Produktschap voor Groenten en Fruit* [1972] ECR 1219.
[22] Case C-149/96 *Portugal v Council* [1999] ECR I-8395.
[23] e.g. S Griller, 'Judicial enforceability of WTO law in the European Union: annotation to case C-149/96, *Portugal v Council*' 3 JIEL (2000) 441.
[24] Case C-61/94 *Commission v Germany* [1996] ECR I-3989.

party to rely on WTO law. The most straightforward type is where Community law can be interpreted in conformity with WTO law. In such cases there is no strict conflict, and thus no issue of direct effect. Less straightforward are the *FEDIOL* and *Nakajima* type applications of WTO law.[25] The Court consistently holds that, where the Community intended to implement a particular obligation assumed in the context of the WTO or where a Community act expressly refers to WTO law, judicial review on grounds of violation of WTO law is possible. The precise scope of this 'exception' is rather unclear, and recent case law does not adopt a broad interpretation. It is mainly applied in the field of anti-dumping.[26]

The overall picture of the judicial application of WTO law is thus more positive than the mere denial of direct effect. If one compares the EC with other WTO members it is, in fact, doubtful whether there are many other members which provide for such extensive application of these international norms. The lack of direct effect nevertheless constitutes a strict limitation. Advocate General Jacobs never had much opportunity to consider the legal effects of WTO law. He did, however, briefly address the subject in *Netherlands v EP and Council*, a challenge to the directive on the legal protection of biotechnological inventions. The applicant relied on the TRIPS and TBT Agreements (both part of the WTO Agreement). Advocate General Jacobs considered that the case called for the application of the *FEDIOL/Nakajima* principle, and not for direct effect. He did, however, also say, in very general terms:

it might be thought that it is in any event desirable as a matter of policy for the Court to be able to review the legality of Community legislation in the light of treaties binding the Community. There is no other court which is in a position to review Community legislation; thus if this court is denied competence, Member States may be subject to conflicting obligations with no means of resolving them.[27]

He thus clearly stated his preference for direct effect of international norms.

There are some new features in the landscape, too. Both the CFI and the ECJ have had to respond to arguments based on norms of customary international law. *Opel Austria* was a case in which the Council was accused of breaching the principle of good faith as embodied in Article 18 Vienna Convention on the Law of Treaties (VCLT).[28] The Council had adopted a regulation which was clearly

---

[25] Case 70/87 *Fediol v Commission* [1989] ECR 1781; Case C-69/89 *Nakajima v Council* [1991] ECR I-2069.
[26] e.g. Case T-256/97 *BEUC v Commission* [2000] ECR II-101.
[27] Case C-377/98 *Netherlands v European Parliament and Council* [2001] ECR I-7079, para 147 of the opinion.
[28] Case T-115/94 *Opel Austria v Council* [1997] ECR II-39. Article 18 VCLT reads:
A State is obliged to refrain from acts which would defeat the object and purpose of a treaty when:
  (a) it has signed the treaty or has exchanged instruments constituting the treaty subject to ratification, acceptance or approval, until it shall have made its intention clear not to become a party to the treaty; or
  (b) it has expressed its consent to be bound by the treaty, pending the entry into force of the treaty and provided that such entry into force is not unduly delayed.

in breach of the EEA Agreement, literally a couple of days before that agreement entered into force. The regulation could not be directly reviewed in the light of the EEA, because the legality of an act must be assessed at the time if its adoption; the EEA was not yet in force at that time. However, the CFI considered that, in application of Article 18 VCLT, in combination with the Community law principle of legitimate expectations, the Council regulation nevertheless was to be scrutinized. It struck down the regulation for breach of the EEA Agreement as a result of this application of customary international law.

One year later the Court of Justice was confronted with questions concerning the effects of customary international law in *Racke*, referred to above.[29] Racke had imported wines from Kosovo, which normally benefited from duty-free entry in application of the EEC-Yugoslavia cooperation agreement. However, that agreement had been suspended by the Council to put pressure on Serbia to observe a ceasefire when Yugoslavia was breaking up. Racke argued that this act of suspension, not provided for in the agreement itself, was contrary to customary international law rules on the suspension and termination of treaties. The Community, however, invoked *rebus sic stantibus*, a fundamental change of circumstances, as a justification. Advocate General Jacobs considered that it was not obvious to accept that a private party could derive rights from the law of treaties. On the other hand, where such a party had rights under a directly effective agreement concluded by the Community, there should be some measure of protection of that party's legitimate expectations. This idea of protection was further strengthened by the force of *pacta sunt servanda*, the basic principle of treaty law. The Advocate General therefore considered that the Court should review whether there was a manifest violation of the law of treaties to the detriment of the individual. The Court essentially followed this approach. It held that customary international law rules concerning the termination and suspension of treaty relations by reason of a fundamental change of circumstances were binding upon the Community institutions and formed part of the Community legal order. Curiously, however, the Court also stated that Racke was incidentally challenging the validity of the suspension regulation, in order to rely on rights which it derived from the suspended agreement, and the case therefore did not concern the direct effect of customary international law. But what's in a name? In my view the case did involve a direct application of the law of treaties, thereby creating rights for a private party. Racke had to pay customs duties on imports of wine, and in essence argued that this was contrary to the law of treaties. If the Court had accepted the argument (which it did not since it ruled that there had been no manifest breach), Racke would have been able to recover the duties on that basis. That seems to me a fairly direct effect.

What is unremarkable about this case law is that the Courts declare that customary international law on treaties binds the Community. How else could

[29] n 15 above.

the Community be an actor under international law? International treaties are not unique acts; they are born into the general system of public international law.[30] It is much more remarkable that the Courts are willing to apply norms of customary international law in cases where private parties challenge certain Community acts. This shows the openness of Community law towards public international law.

The apex of this openness was reached in the 2005 *Yusuf* and *Kadi* decisions of the CFI.[31] Those cases concern yet another type of international norms: resolutions of the UN Security Council. In issue are Community regulations freezing the assets of suspected supporters of terrorism. The regulations implement CFSP common positions, which in turn implement UN resolutions. The Community was thus simply copying a UN list. Messrs Yusuf and Kadi challenged these regulations as violating their fundamental rights. However, the CFI considered that no review on the basis of fundamental rights as general principles of EC law could be undertaken, because of the UN origin of the listings. This results from the binding and overriding effect of the UN Charter. Even if the Community is not a member of the UN, and even if as a matter of international law the Charter therefore does not bind it, the CFI ruled that as a matter of Community law the Charter must be respected. It considered that review of the terrorism regulations would constitute indirect review of the UN resolutions, which is not permissible. The only type of review which it was willing to undertake was whether the resolutions themselves comply with peremptory norms of international law (*ius cogens*), but its conclusion was that they do.

The judgments are under appeal at the time of writing. They have given rise to an intense academic debate, to which I have attempted to contribute.[32] The CFI judgments are a bridge too far. It is important to realize what they involve. They do not simply declare UN law binding on the Community, a proposition which is definitely arguable. The judgments go further by extending the effects of UN resolutions to the setting aside of the EU's own constitutional norms on the protection of fundamental rights. Those norms, first developed by the Court of Justice, are now expressly confirmed in the Treaties.[33] There is no indication in either the Treaties or the case law that there are any exceptions to the principle

---

[30] See J Pauwelyn, *Conflict of Norms in Public International Law* (2003) *passim*.
[31] n 16 above.
[32] P Eeckhout, 'Community terrorism listings, fundamental rights, and UN Security Council resolutions. In search of the right fit' 3 EUConst (2007) 183–206; C Tomuschat, case note 43 CMLRev (2006) 537–51; RH van Ooik and RA Wessel, 'De Yusuf en Kadi-uitspraken in perspectief. Nieuwe verhoudingen in de interne en externe bevoegdheden van de Europese Unie' 54 SEW (2006) 230–41; P Stangos and G Gryllos, 'Le droit communautaire à l'épreuve des réalités du droit international: leçons tirées de la jurisprudence communautaire récente relevant de la lutte contre le terrorisme international' CDE (2006) 429–81; M Nettesheim, 'UN sanctions against individuals – a challenge to the architecture of European Union governance' 44 CMLRev (2007) 567–600; E Cannizzaro, 'Machiavelli, the UN Security Council and the rule of law', Global Law Working Paper 11/05, Hauser Global Law School program.
[33] Art 6(2) TEU, applicable to the EC as well (see Art 46 TEU).

that all EU and EC acts need to comply with fundamental rights. The CFI, however, has created such an exception in *Yusuf* and *Kadi*. This constitutes excessive deference to the UN Security Council, a deference which at the end of the day does not contribute to respect for international law. International law is not well served by elevating the Security Council to an inscrutable legislature, whose decisions are directly applicable and automatically prevail over constitutional-type norms on fundamental rights protection. International law in general, and the UN Charter in particular, embody respect for fundamental rights. As long as the Security Council does not set up appropriate procedures for the review of terrorism listings, domestic courts should not refrain from scrutinizing implementation measures.

It is significant to contrast the openness and receptiveness in *Yusuf* and *Kadi* with recent case law on the effect of WTO dispute decisions. This case law is a further development in the jurisprudence on the lack of direct effect of WTO law.[34] It could be seen as simply confirming this lack of direct effect, but I would submit that there are substantial differences between the question whether an international agreement has direct effect and the question of how to treat a decision by an international tribunal.

The main rulings are *Chiquita v Commission* and *Van Parys*.[35] Those two cases concerned the question whether the direct effect issue needs to be seen in a different light when there are specific dispute settlement decisions against the EC. Could there be something akin to direct effect of WTO dispute settlement decisions in contrast with the lack of direct effect of WTO law in general?

In 2003 the Court of Justice suddenly seemed to raise this question. In the case of *Biret*, concerning imports of beef treated with hormones, the Court on appeal criticized the Court of First Instance for its failure to examine the argument of complainants that there is direct effect of WTO dispute decisions, at least after the end of the reasonable period for implementation which WTO law grants.[36] That criticism by the Court of Justice was *obiter dictum*, since the facts of the case predated the end of the reasonable period for implementation and the issue therefore did not strictly arise. Indeed, the Court did not annul the CFI's judgment. *Biret* nevertheless invited debate on the legal status of WTO dispute rulings.

Chiquita and *Van Parys* concerned imports of bananas. The facts can shortly be summarized as follows. In 1997 the WTO Dispute Settlement Body (DSB) established a number of violations of WTO law. In 1998 the EC amended the banana regime with a view to reaching compliance with WTO law. However, a 1999 WTO panel ruled that this aim had not been achieved. Chiquita in the one case attempted to base a claim in damages before the CFI on the failure to comply with the original DSB decisions. In *Van Parys* Belgian importers challenged

---

[34] See further M Bronckers, 'The relationship of the EC courts with other international tribunals: non-committal, respectful or submissive?' 44 CMLRev (2007) 610–27.
[35] Case C-377/02 *Van Parys* [2005] ECR I-1465; Case T-19/01 *Chiquita* [2005] ECR II-315.
[36] Case C-94/02 P *Etablissements Biret v Council* [2003] ECR I-10565.

refusals to grant import licenses for bananas on the same grounds, leading to a reference to the Court of Justice. The basic question in both cases was whether the EU Courts were inclined to accept that there is only so much time for EC manoeuvre in the WTO,[37] and to accept that ultimately WTO dispute settlement decisions are binding and can be judicially enforced even at an internal EC level. The answer was negative. Both Courts considered that the negotiating room of the EC institutions in the WTO cannot be interfered with even after the end of the reasonable period for compliance. Both courts emphasized provisions in the WTO Dispute Settlement Understanding (DSU), such as Articles 21.6 and 22.8, which state in essence that the issue of compliance remains on the DSB's agenda as long as there is no agreement about compliance. The Court of First Instance even went so far as to say that the effectiveness of Article 21.6 would be undermined if there was judicial intervention in Luxembourg. It also stated that WTO dispute settlement is not a mechanism for judicial resolution by means of decisions with binding effects, comparable with those of a court's decision in domestic legal systems. The Court of Justice on the other hand emphasized the chain of events after the failed 1998 implementation attempt in bananas up to the 2001 resolution of the bananas dispute. It considered that this whole outcome could be compromised if there was something like direct effect of DSB decisions and that negotiation possibilities were not exhausted at the end of the reasonable period. In the pending *Ikea Wholesale* case, Advocate General Léger delivered an opinion in which he considers that WTO dispute reports are not binding on the Community. He goes so far as to argue that to rule otherwise would put the autonomy of the Community legal order in jeopardy.[38]

This analysis of the DSU is not convincing. There are strong differences between the period before and after the end of the reasonable time for implementation. If one accepts that there is a clear international law obligation to comply with the DSB decisions,[39] then it does matter a great deal whether the reasonable period is exhausted. Nearly all WTO rulings and DSB decisions are prospective, requiring a member to bring its laws and regulations into compliance. There is a reasonable period for doing so. However, once it has expired there seems to me to be a legally perfect and complete obligation at that point in time. Of course the DSU provides that the issue of compliance will remain on the agenda of the DSB as long as there is no consensus on compliance, and of course there are remedies such as suspension of concessions in the event of continued failure to comply. It does not, however, follow that the effectiveness of those DSU provisions would be undermined by a domestic judicial decision which remedies the WTO violations. Such a decision would, in fact, contribute to realizing the DSU's objectives

---

[37] As was one of the main considerations in *Portugal v Council* (n 22 above).
[38] Case C-351/04 *Ikea Wholesale v Commissioners of Customs and Excise*, opinion of 6 April 2006, para 87, judgment pending.
[39] See JH Jackson, 'International law status of WTO dispute settlement reports: obligation to comply or option to "buy out"?' 98 AJIL (2004) 109.

such as a prompt and effective resolution of a dispute and compliance with WTO obligations.

It is interesting to reflect a little further about the nature of the international law obligation to comply with WTO dispute rulings. The panels and the Appellate Body establish authoritatively – pursuant to the authority conferred on them by the DSU – that a WTO member has breached its obligations. The DSB, which is a body representing the WTO members, then confirms this ruling. Thus, if a member does not comply with the ruling, there is more in issue than a violation of substantive norms of WTO law. There is, in addition, a violation of the DSU provisions requiring compliance. There is a failure to respect the decision of the DSB. The obligation to comply with WTO dispute settlement rulings is, at its core, nothing less than a specific manifestation of *pacta sunt servanda*; international treaty obligations are ultimately binding. The obligation to comply with a Geneva ruling is therefore qualitatively different from the obligation generally to comply with all substantive WTO obligations. If the EU courts are not willing to give domestic legal effect to such rulings, one can indeed ask questions about the EC's respect for international law.

There is in any event a contradiction, it seems to me, between the receptiveness of *Yusuf* and *Kadi* and the refusal of *Chiquita* and *Van Parys*. The interpretation and application of public international law are increasingly in the hands of all kinds of international courts and tribunals. Cooperation and coordination are required for the system to work more or less effectively, including in the relations between these international adjudicators and domestic courts. The EU Courts have a crucial role to play here, given the economic and political size of the EU and its professed international role as a soft power promoting the rule of law in international affairs.[40]

IV. Concluding Remarks

This panorama of external relations, although brief and limited, shows the enormous evolution of this area of EU law. It also illustrates how important external relations law is for the overall constitutional (dare one still say it) development of the EU. Issues such as how to treat the corpus of WTO law; how to deal with WTO dispute decisions, and by extension decisions of international courts and tribunals; how to conceive the relationship between the Second Pillar foreign policy and the First Pillar external (trade) policies; what effect to give to UN Security Council resolutions; how to construe the relationship between respect for international law and respect for fundamental rights; are all of genuine constitutional significance.

---

[40] See the relevant provisions in both the Constitutional and the Draft Reform Treaty.

From the perspective of the theme of this volume, it is clear that in external relations law there is much continuity, but also tremendous change. The challenge for lawmakers and the judiciary in the years to come is to maintain such continuity whilst adapting the law to novel questions and developments. The issues are by no means straightforward, and the Court of Justice, in particular, must rise to the challenge of devising appropriate rules and principles, often on matters where the existing law is thin and without clear direction.

It is, however, an exciting challenge. One should also note, in that respect, that many of the external relations cases referred to above are groundbreaking, not just for the EU, but in a wider global context. The Court of Justice is a laboratory of 'external law' which has few rivals (or counterparts). Its case law is increasingly watched also from the outside, and rightly so. Let me conclude by saying that Advocate General Jacobs made a tremendous contribution to raising the level of judicial discourse in the Court of Justice, and thus to its global legal laboratory function.

19

Multilevel Constitutionalism and Judicial Protection of Freedom and Justice in the International Economic Law of the EC

Ernst-Ulrich Petersmann

Advocate General Francis Jacobs has pleaded, in many of his opinions, for judicial interpretation of European Community (EC) law and of the international legal obligations of the EC in conformity with the common constitutional principles of EC member states so as to strengthen individual rights of EC citizens (for example, of access to justice) and international rule of law. In the case *Netherlands v European Parliament and Council*, Jacobs acknowledged – in respect of the Netherlands' complaint of an inconsistency of the EC Directive on legal protection of bio-technological inventions with respect for human dignity – that human dignity is 'perhaps the most fundamental right of all, and is now expressed in Article 1 of the Charter'.[1] The EC Court concurred that 'it is for the Court of Justice, in its review of the compatibility of acts of the institutions with the general principles of Community law, to ensure that the fundamental right to human dignity and integrity is observed'.[2] The modern foundation of the ancient idea of the dignity of man (for example, as being closer to God than any other earthly creature) on the moral and rational freedom of individuals, and on their human capacity to self-development, goes back to Giovanni Pico della Mirandola's *Oration on the Dignity of Man*[3] (1486), presumably elaborated in the library of the same monastery which today houses the European University Institute at Florence. As Francis Jacobs often inspired the law researchers here at our European University Institute by his lectures on European constitutional

---

[1] Opinion of AG Jacobs of 14 June 2001 in Case C-377/98 *Netherlands v Council* [2001] ECR I-7079, para 197.
[2] Case C-377/98 (n 1 above), at para 70.
[3] Reprinted in E Cassirer, O Kristelle and JH Randall (eds), *The Renaissance Philosophy of Man* (1956).

law, this contribution in his honour proceeds from the 'empowering functions' and 'limiting functions' of human dignity and human rights for discussing some of the 'constitutional problems' in the national and international judicial protection of individual freedom and justice in the international relations law of the EC.

I. Respect for Human Dignity and 'Indivisibility' of Human Rights as Empowerment of Individuals and Constitutional Foundation of EC Law

According to Article 1 of the Universal Declaration of Human Rights, '[a]ll human beings are born free and equal in dignity and rights' (paragraph 1); '[t]hey are endowed with reason and conscience and should act towards one another in a spirit of brotherhood' (paragraph 2). Also many other UN human rights instruments focus on 'reason and conscience' as moral justification for inalienable human rights deriving from respect for human dignity and from the need for legal protection of an 'existence worthy of human dignity' (Article 23 UDHR). Even though the legal structures of UN human rights conventions and of most other areas of UN law remain intergovernmental and fragmented, today's worldwide recognition of civil, political, economic, social and cultural rights, and of corresponding obligations of all 192 UN member states, reflect a broad conception of human dignity and of individual self-development to be protected by rule of law and democratic self-governance.

Human dignity is likewise recognized as a constitutional principle in Article 1 of the EU Charter of Fundamental Rights of December 2000, as incorporated into the 2004 Treaty establishing a Constitution for Europe (TCE).[4] By legally protecting specific dignity rights (Articles 61–5 TCE), freedoms (Articles 66–79), equality rights (Articles 80–6), solidarity rights (Articles 87–98), EU citizen rights (Articles 99–106) as well as rights of access to justice (Articles 107–10) that are all 'founded on the indivisible, universal values of human dignity, freedom, equality and solidarity' (preamble to the EU Charter of Fundamental Rights), European constitutional law aims at protecting individual and democratic freedom and self-development of EU citizens in a comprehensive manner based on rule of law across national boundaries. Respect for the 'indivisible' individual liberty to decide which equal freedoms an individual values most justifies also the EC guarantees of *economic* freedoms, such as freedom of profession (Article 75 TCE), freedom to conduct a business in accordance with the rule of law (Article 76), or the right to property (Article 77), which may be of no less existential importance for individual self-development

---

[4] On the controversy over whether Article 1 recognizes a fundamental right to human dignity or merely an objective constitutional principle, see the commentary on Article 1 of the Charter by M Borowsky, in J Meyer (ed), *Die Grundrechtscharta der EU* (2003) 45–66.

than civil and political rights. Also according to the European Court of Human Rights (ECtHR), 'the very essence of the Convention is respect for human dignity and human freedom';[5] like the EC Court, the ECtHR protects complaints by *economic* actors (like companies) and fundamental freedoms not only in the polity but also in the economy. Regardless of whether human dignity is recognized as the most fundamental human right from which all other rights are flowing (such as in German constitutional law), or whether human dignity is legally protected only as an objective constitutional principle: 'human dignity as empowerment' justifies not only the constitutional and judicial protection of individual freedoms and other fundamental rights inside the EC, but also the EC's constitutional commitment (for example, in Articles 300 and 307 EC) to 'strict observance and development of international law, including respect for the principles of the United Nations Charter' (Article I-3 TCE), without which democratic governance of the EC could hardly remain effective.

II. Human Dignity and Fundamental Freedoms Require Multilevel Constitutional Restraints

Respect for human dignity calls for constitutional restraints on abuses of private and public power and for legislation protecting, reconciling and limiting equal constitutional rights. International law in the 21st century is recognized by the recognition (such as that by UN human rights bodies and international courts) of an increasing *ius cogens* core of human rights obligations of states. In view of the inherent tendency of freedom to destroy itself through abuses of power ('paradox of freedom'), almost all UN member states have adopted national constitutions limiting government powers, protecting individual rights and mandating legislative, administrative and judicial protection of constitutional rights. Constitutions inevitably differ depending on the preferences of the people and their social traditions and power structures. Democratic constitutionalism inside the EC is, however, increasingly influenced by the Kantian conception of law as 'the sum total of those conditions within which the will of one person can be reconciled with the will of another in accordance with a universal law of freedom'.[6] Kantian legal theory follows from the moral 'categorical imperative' not only that 'every action which by itself or by its maxim enables the freedom of each individual's will to co-exist with the freedom of everyone else in accordance with a universal law is *right*';[7] it also calls for corresponding national, international and transnational constitutional rights and obligations so as to effectively

---

[5] European Court of Human Rights, *Pretty v United Kingdom*, Rep 2002-III, para 65; *SW v United Kingdom* and *CR v United Kingdom*, Rep 1995, 363, paras 42 and 44.
[6] I Kant, 'The metaphysics of morals', in *Political Writings* (ed H Reiss, 1977), 133.
[7] ibid.

constrain abuses of power in all national, international and transnational human interactions.[8] The constitutional laws of EC member states, their common EC law, the European Convention on Human Rights (ECHR), as well as the EC's international legal obligations as 'integral parts of the Community legal system' with a legal rank above other legal acts of the EC institutions, continue to evolve into a unique European system of multilevel constitutionalism that continues to be strongly shaped by the 'constitutional jurisprudence' of national constitutional courts, the EC Court and the ECtHR. The EC's constitutional and judicial guarantees of economic and political freedoms go far beyond those in UN human rights law which, for historical and political reasons, left the regulation of international economic relations to specialized UN Agencies and other intergovernmental agreements (like the General Agreement on Tariffs and Trade (GATT) 1947).

The more governments cooperate internationally for the collective supply of 'international public goods', the more multilevel governance in international organizations is leading to multilevel legal restraints on national policy powers so as to protect mutually beneficial cooperation among citizens across national frontiers. In a globally-integrated world, national constitutions turn out to be partial constitutions. Since the Constitution (*sic*) Establishing the International Labor Organization (ILO) of 1919, also many other constituent agreements of international organizations – such as the World Health Organization (WHO) and the UN Educational, Scientific and Cultural Organization (UNESCO) – were named 'constitutions' in view of the fact that they:

(1) constitute a new legal order with legal primacy over that of the member states;

(2) create new legal subjects and hierarchically structured institutions with limited governance powers;

(3) provide for institutional checks and balances (for example, among rule-making, administrative and dispute settlement bodies in the WTO);

(4) legally limit the rights of member states (for example, regarding withdrawal, amendment procedures, dispute settlement procedures);

(5) provide for the collective supply of 'public goods' that – as in the case of the above-mentioned treaty constitutions (of the ILO, WHO and UNESCO) – are partly defined in terms of human rights (such as core labour rights, the human rights to health and education); and often

(6) operate as 'living constitutions' whose functions – albeit limited in scope and membership – increasingly evolve in response to changing needs for international cooperation.

---

[8] Cf I Kant, 'Perpetual Peace', *Political Writings* (n 6 above), 98.

International 'treaty constitutions' differ fundamentally from national constitutions by their limited policy functions and less effective constitutional restraints (such as on intergovernmental and national policy powers). State-centred international lawyers therefore prefer to speak of 'international institutional law'. From citizen-oriented economic and constitutional perspectives, however, international organizations are becoming no less necessary for the collective supply of public goods than national organizations. Human rights and their moral value premises (normative individualism) require designing national and international governance as an integrated, multilevel constitutional framework for the protection of citizen rights, democratic self-government and cooperation among free citizens across frontiers.[9] *International constitutionalism* is a functionally limited, but necessary complement to *national constitutionalism* which, only together as interrelated networks based on 'constitutional pluralism', can protect human rights and democratic self-government effectively in a globally interdependent world. Both national constitutions as well as international treaty constitutions reflect dynamic, political equilibria between universal and particular, procedural as well as substantive values, whose empowering functions, limiting functions, legitimizing functions and structural interrelationships may differ from one field (like the constitution of political communities) to the other (like the constitution of international markets).

III. Bottom-up Structures of Multilevel Human Rights Constitutionalism

Human rights tend to be protected most effectively inside constitutional democracies. The ECtHR and UN human rights bodies rightly emphasize that international human rights law prescribes only minimum standards leaving national democracies broad discretion to protect human rights more effectively. Hence, the ECtHR often exercises judicial deference in order to respect the 'margin of appreciation' by national democratic institutions[10] as well as by EC institutions.[11] Like UN human rights bodies, the ECtHR rightly resists to become a 'fourth instance' for the thousands of complaints submitted each year to the Court. The subsidiary logic of international human rights law suggests

---

[9] On the 'constitutional functions' of international organizations as a 'fourth branch of government' see EU Petersmann, 'Constitutionalism and international organizations' (1996) 17 *Northwestern Journal of International Law & Business*, 398, 415 et seq.

[10] For instance, in its judgment of 8 July 2004 in *Case of Vo v France* (Application No 53924/00), the ECtHR explicitly left open the controversial question whether Article 2 of the ECHR (right to life) also protects the human embryo and the foetus's right to life: 'it is neither desirable, nor even possible as matters stand, to answer in the abstract the question whether the unborn child is a person for the purposes of Article 2 of the Convention' (§ 85).

[11] See the ECtHR judgment of 30 June 2005 in the *Bosphorus Case*, Application No 45036/98.

that most of the human rights complaints should be more properly decided by national judicial authorities with due regard to the particular national constitutional context. In view of the backlog of more than 89,000 cases at the ECtHR by the end of 2006, it has been convincingly suggested that the ECtHR should concentrate more on 'constitutional decisions of principle' regarding groups of manifestly well-founded cases that enhance the European 'public order' and the Europe-wide human rights jurisprudence, than on the 'individual relief function' and the 'enforcement functions' of human rights courts (for example, leaving the filtering out of manifestly ill-founded cases to a special division and treating follow-up cases as a problem of execution to be dealt with by the Committee of Ministers).[12] The subsidiary logic of international human rights also justifies the mutual cooperation and reciprocal deference among the EC Court of Justice and the ECtHR as long as the EC Court takes regularly into account the ECHR obligations of EC member states. Yet, as national and European human rights law and constitutional law inside the EC tend to go far beyond the corresponding safeguards in UN law, this 'bottom-up structure' of multilevel human rights constitutionalism argues against the position taken by the Court of First Instance[13] that Article 103 UN Charter prevents European courts from reviewing the consistency of the implementation of UN Security Council Resolutions by EC Regulations with the human rights obligations of EC member states. Similar to the ECtHR decision that national courts are competent to review the actions of international organizations notwithstanding the latter's immunity from jurisdiction,[14] the EC Court should not interpret UN law as preventing UN member states from protecting higher national and regional human rights guarantees and judicial standards of review in their domestic implementation of UN law.

IV. Top-down Structures of Multilevel Economic Constitutionalism

Maximizing national consumer welfare and national 'total welfare' through international division of labour requires international economic liberalization and regulation which most governments – in order to overcome the protectionist pressures from import-competing producers and regulate domestic producer welfare in non-discriminatory ways – tend to accept only in reciprocal international agreements rather than unilaterally. The historical reasons for the incomplete protection of individual liberties in international human rights instruments and

---

[12] cf L Wildhaber, 'A constitutional future for the European Court of Human Rights?' 23, Human Rights Law Journal (2002), 161–5.
[13] cf CFI Case T-306/01 *Yusuf* and CFI Case T-315/01 *Kadi* [2005] ECR (nyr).
[14] See *Waite & Kennedy*, decision of 18 February 1999, [1999] RJD, 393.

for leaving reciprocal economic liberalization to the Bretton-Woods Agreements must not lead to the wrong conclusion that economic liberties (such as freedom of profession) deserve less constitutional protection at national levels and international levels (for example, the economic liberties protected in EC law). The 'human rights functions' of the core labour standards and 'tripartite governance structures' guaranteed by the ILO Constitution are emphasized in the ILO preamble, according to which 'the failure of any nation to adopt humane conditions of labour is an obstacle' to social justice and lasting peace also in other countries. The mutually beneficial, peaceful economic cooperation among billions of producers, investors, traders and consumers on the basis of GATT and WTO rules has enhanced economic welfare, freedom and rule of international law in all 150 WTO member countries beyond what has ever been possible without these international agreements. As international agreements on the reciprocal liberalization and regulation of international movements of goods, services, persons, capital and related payments tend to go far beyond national constitutional guarantees, their international guarantees of economic freedom, non-discrimination and rule of law can serve 'constitutional functions' for correcting 'constitutional failures' at national levels of governance and for extending legal and judicial protection of economic freedoms and of mutually beneficial cooperation among free citizens across discriminatory state frontiers, without limiting the sovereignty of countries to protect human rights and their national conceptions of social justice.[15]

The constitutional protection and judicial enforcement of the EC Treaty's intergovernmental 'market freedoms' as individual 'fundamental freedoms'[16] illustrates the potential 'top-down constitutional functions' of intergovernmental prohibitions of welfare-reducing, national market restrictions for the benefit of citizens. Yet, such judicial enforcement was democratically legitimate only to the extent that the EC Court and national courts ensured that EC economic law remained consistent with the human rights obligations and common constitutional principles of EC member states. By conferring on EC citizens fundamental freedoms which citizens had never enjoyed before, such as free access to employment inside the EC as 'a fundamental right which the Treaty confers individually on each worker in the Community',[17] the EC Court promoted not only a rights-based, decentralized enforcement of EC law by self-interested citizens and courts, but also opted for an individualistic interpretation of the 'principle of liberty' (Article 6 EU Treaty) deriving its legitimacy from the indivisibility of individual freedom and from the 'empowerment function' of respect for human dignity.

---

[15] cf EU Petersmann, *Constitutional Functions and Constitutional Problems of International Economic Law* (1991).
[16] cf Case C-55/94 *Gebhard* [1995] ECR I-4165, para 37.
[17] cf Case 222/86 *Heylens* [1987] ECR 4097, para 14.

V. Different Conceptions of Constitutional Democracy: Constitutional Nationalism v Multilevel Constitutionalism in International Economic Law

The post-war leadership of the United States for a liberal international economic order was based on hegemonic US leadership and national constitutionalism (for example, strong distrust of the US Congress and US courts vis-à-vis international law, congressional insistence on powers to adopt measures in violation of international law). Many Anglo-Saxon lawyers and 'realist' politicians continue to argue against constitutionalization of international relations and claim, for example, 'that the WTO is not constitutionalized, and nor, according to any current meanings of the term, should it be'.[18] Outside the EC, most governments continue to favour 'constitutional nationalism' in view of the power-oriented nature of international relations. Likewise, most international theories of justice (such as those by J Rawls) focus on social justice *inside* constitutional democracies rather than in the anarchic *international* relations. Notably in the US, the European openness to international law is often criticized as being inconsistent with national democracy;[19] influenced by process-based (rather than rights-based) conceptions of parliamentary democracy, many North American lawyers perceive international law as mere 'global administrative law', or as being based on a mere 'conflict of laws approach' (such as the GATT rules allocating regulation of product standards to importing countries, and regulation of production standards to exporting countries), from which the US Congress may legitimately deviate at any time. In the EC's external relations, many EC foreign policy-makers and their legal advocates justify their frequent violations of the EC's WTO obligations (such as those determined in GATT and WTO dispute settlement findings against the EC) by power-oriented arguments and reject judicial enforcement of international trade liberalization commitments as 'politically naive'.[20]

An increasing number of international lawyers in Europe and North America, by contrast, acknowledge the potential 'constitutional functions' of international

---

[18] DZ Cass, *The Constitutionalism of the WTO* (2005). Following seven chapters arguing against constitutionalization of international relations, her Chapter 8 concludes that 'trading democracy, not merely trading constitutionalization, should be the key to WTO constitutionalization in this century' (242). Cass admits at the end that her 'received account' of Anglo-Saxon constitutionalism has, indeed, 'been revealed as neither descriptively adequate nor normatively appealing' (240).
[19] cf J Rubenfeld, 'The two world orders' in G Nolte (ed), *European and US Constitutionalism* (2005), 197–238: the post-war US support for internationalism and multilateralism was 'for the rest of the world, not for us', even though America's commitment to internationalism in economic affairs is recognized as serving US interests.
[20] See e.g. PJ Kuijper, 'WTO law in the European Court of Justice', in *Common Market Law Review* 42 (2005), 1313–41, who criticizes the rule-oriented 'Kupferberg jurisprudence' of the ECJ as politically 'naive' (1320).

law for the collective supply of 'international public goods'. They refer to a 'WTO Constitution' in view of:

(a) the comprehensive rule-making, executive and (quasi-) judicial powers of WTO institutions;[21]

(b) the 'constitutionalization' of WTO law resulting from the jurisprudence of the WTO dispute settlement bodies;[22]

(c) the *domestic* 'constitutional functions' of GATT/WTO rules, for example for protecting constitutional principles (like freedom, non-discrimination, rule of law, proportionality of government restrictions) and domestic democracy (for instance, by limiting the power of protectionist interest groups) for the benefit of transnational cooperation among free citizens;[23]

(d) the *international* 'constitutional functions' of WTO rules, for example, for the promotion of 'international participatory democracy' (such as by holding governments internationally accountable for the 'external effects' of their national trade policies, by enabling countries to participate in the policy-making of other countries)[24] and of the enhancement of 'jurisdictional competition among nation states'[25] and 'the allocation of authority between constitutions';[26]

(e) in view of the necessity of 'constitutional approaches' for a proper understanding of the law of comprehensive international organizations that use constitutional terms, methods and principles for more than 50 years (see, for example, the 'Constitutions' of the ILO, WHO, FAO, EU);[27] or

(f) in view of the need to interface and coordinate different levels of governance on the national and international level.[28]

---

[21] See JH Jackson, *The World Trade Organisation: Constitution and Jurisprudence* (1998).

[22] See DZ Cass, 'The constitutionalization of international trade law: judicial norm-generation as the engine of constitutionalization' *European Journal of International Law* (2001), 39–75.

[23] See JO McGinnis and ML Movsesian, 'The World Trade Constitution' (2000) 114 *Harvard Law Review* 511–605; PM Gerhart, 'The two constitutional visions of the World Trade Organisation', in (2003) 24 *University of Pennsylvania Journal of International Economic Law* 1–75, contrasts the 'inward-looking, economic vision of the WTO' in helping member countries addressing internal political failures with the 'external, participatory vision of the WTO' helping WTO members to address concerns raised by policy decisions in other countries.

[24] See, for example, PM Gerhart, 'The WTO and participatory democracy: the historical evidence' (2004) 37 *Vanderbilt Journal of Transnational Law*, 897–934.

[25] See JO McGinnis, 'The WTO as a structure of liberty' (2004) 28 *Harvard Journal of Law and Public Policy*, 81–8.

[26] J Trachtman, 'The WTO Constitution: toward tertiary rules' *European Journal of International Law* (2006).

[27] See, for example, EU Petersmann (n 9 above); N Walker, 'The EU and the WTO: constitutionalism in a new key', in G de Búrca and J Scott (eds), *The EU and the WTO: Legal and Constitutional Issues* (2001).

[28] T Cottier and M Hertig, 'The prospects of 21st century constitutionalism', 7 *Max Planck Yearbook of United Nations Law* (2003), 261.

VI. From Market Integration to Policy Integration: 'International Market Governance' Must Remain Consistent with Basic Human Rights and 'Constitutional Pluralism'

The increasing move from 'negative' to 'positive' integration in the WTO and in the more than 250 regional trade agreements reflects political pressures to reduce the adjustment costs of market integration and of regulatory competition through policy coordination. International governance – for instance, by rule-making, rule-implementation and adjudication at the international level – raises legitimacy problems and constitutional problems which cannot be solved by transferring the constitutional methods applied inside constitutional democracies to the level of functionally limited intergovernmental organizations. Some organizations – like the World Bank, the OECD and the EU Commission – have committed themselves to 'principles of good governance' (such as transparency, democratic participation, accountability, effectiveness, coherence) so as to legitimize their international governance and integration law. Yet, such bureaucratic justifications cannot effectively protect human rights and constitutional democracy from being undermined through intergovernmental collusion, as illustrated by the secretive taxation of citizens and the intergovernmental redistribution of domestic income by means of 'voluntary export restraints' and power-oriented trade governance under GATT 1947. UN human rights bodies, the ILO and civil society rightly insist on the need for human rights approaches to the interpretation and application of international economic law, taking into account the obligations of all UN member states to respect, protect and promote human rights with due respect for the diversity of constitutional democracies and national conceptions of social justice.[29]

Also, economists since Adam Smith emphasize that economic welfare depends on open markets and rule of law which cannot remain effective over time without respect for justice (*ubi commercium, ibi jus*).[30] Markets and human rights proceed from the same value premise that individual autonomy (human dignity) must be respected; that values can be derived only from the rational consent of the individual (normative individualism); and that economic markets as well as political markets are the most efficient, citizen-driven instruments for realizing individual and democratic self-development. The information, coordination and

---

[29] cf EU Petersmann, 'The "human rights approach" advocated by the UN High Commissioner for human rights and by the ILO: is it relevant for WTO law and policy?' JIEL 7 (2004), 605–28.

[30] The founding father of economics, Adam Smith, justified his 'system of natural liberty' on considerations of both economic welfare and justice: 'Justice is the main pillar that upholds the whole edifice. If it is removed, the immense fabric of human society ... must in a moment crumble into atoms' (A Smith, *The Theory of Moral Sentiments* (1790/1976) 167).

'sanctioning functions' of market mechanisms are ultimately based on decentralized dialogues among citizens about the value, production and distribution of scarce goods and services. An increasing number of empirical studies confirm that the economic welfare of most countries, and the consumer welfare of their citizens, are correlated to their constitutional guarantees of freedom, property rights and of non-discriminatory competition[31]: 'individual rights are a cause of prosperity'.[32] Since economic welfare can be increased by 'successful struggle for rights of which the right to property is the most fundamental',[33] 'almost all of the countries that have enjoyed good economic performance across generations are countries that have stable democratic governments'.[34] Rights-based struggles for democracy, and rights-based struggles for economic welfare, are thus closely interrelated; both are instruments for enabling and promoting individual freedom as the ultimate goal of economic life and the most efficient means of realizing general welfare.[35] Modern theories of justice accordingly define 'basic equal freedoms' as 'first principle of justice', and constitutional 'difference principles' as 'secondary principles of justice' justifying preferential treatment of disadvantaged individuals whose personal self-development requires special, social assistance. The progressive extension of these principles of justice beyond nation states to the EC was strongly influenced by democratic and judicial struggles of EC citizens.[36]

VII. The Role of the European Judge as an Agent of Justice and of Multilevel Economic Constitutionalism inside the EC

In European law, national and European courts increasingly presume that *intergovernmental* legal guarantees of freedom, non-discrimination, rule of law and of human rights create corresponding *individual rights* if the rules are drafted in precise and unconditional terms. Such citizen-oriented, judicial interpretations

---

[31] See e.g. the annual reports on 'Economic Freedom in the World' published by the Fraser Institute in Vancouver, which emphasize the empirical correlation between economic freedom, economic welfare, relatively higher average income of poor people and, with a few exceptions (such as Hong Kong), political freedom. Already Adam Smith's inquiry into the *Nature and Causes of the Wealth of Nations* (1776) concluded that the economic welfare of England was essentially due to its legal guarantees of economic freedom, property rights and legal security for investors, producers, traders and consumers.

[32] M Olson, *Power and Prosperity* (2000) 43.
[33] See R Pipes, *Property and Freedom* (1999) 291.
[34] M Olson (n 32 above), 187.
[35] See A Sen, *Rationality and Freedom* (2002), e.g. chapter 17 on 'markets and freedoms'. Sen conceptualizes freedom similar to the budget of a utility-maximizing individual: the more individual freedom, the larger is individual welfare. Such constitutional definitions of 'Pareto-efficiency' complement the moral and legal Kantian 'categorical imperative' of maximizing equal freedoms of individuals in national, transnational and international relations.
[36] EU Petersmann, *Theories of Justice, Human Rights and the Constitution of International Markets*, Symposium on the Emerging Transnational Constitution, 37 Loyola Law Review (2004) 407–60.

are justified less on grounds of textual interpretation of intergovernmental treaty provisions than on constitutional arguments that citizens are the democratic subjects of European law and the most effective guardians of rule of law. Also the UN Charter was adopted in the name of 'We the Peoples' (preamble) and commits all UN member states to 'universal respect for, and observance of, human rights and fundamental freedoms for all without distinction as to race, sex, language or religion' (Articles 55 and 56). Yet, even though UN human rights law has reinforced the status of individuals as legal subjects of modern international law and as 'democratic owners' of (inter)governmental organizations, the power-oriented approaches prevailing in many UN bodies and UN member states shun the constitutional question of whether intergovernmental and national human rights obligations have evolved into 'general principles of law recognized by civilized nations' (Article 38 Statute of the ICJ) justifying the interpretation of 'intergovernmental' guarantees of freedom and non-discrimination as individual rights. Modern theories of justice challenge authoritarian conceptions of 'international law among states' as being neither legitimate nor effective (for example, in terms of protecting human rights and democratic peace); they increasingly claim that the UN Charter obligations – for instance, 'to bring about by peaceful means, and in conformity with the principles of justice and international law, adjustment or settlement of international disputes' and 'respect for human rights and for fundamental freedoms for all' (Article 1) – require more effective legal and judicial protection of citizens as legal subjects of international law, for instance by means of judicial clarification of procedural and substantive principles of justice with due regard to the human rights obligations of governments.[37]

Constitutional democracies and EC law protect individual and democratic self-governance at constitutional and post-constitutional levels; the higher legal rank of constitutional rules requires legal protection and promotion of constitutional guarantees of fundamental rights by all – legislative, executive and judicial – governance powers so as to progressively extend equal basic rights of citizens vis-à-vis the perennial abuses of public and private power. This constitutionally mandated 'multiple protection' of individual and democratic self-government[38] assigns to independent courts an autonomous, judicial function that is different from democratic and administrative governance functions. Judicial review can be constitutionally justified as being necessary for enforcing the constitutional rules prescribed by the people vis-à-vis the everyday exercises of majoritarian politics

---

[37] cf A Buchanan, *Justice, Legitimacy and Self-Determination. Moral Foundations for International Law* (2004) 27, 86. The author bases his book on a 'natural duty of justice... to help ensure that all persons have access to institutions that protect their basic rights' and rejects the 'realist' perception of international relations as anarchic struggles for power and military dominance (the Hobbesian war of all against all).

[38] For such a 'dualist conception' of democracy as a two-track process, see e.g. B Ackerman, *We the People* vols 1 (1991) and 2 (1998); CL Eisgruber, *Constitutional Self-Government* (2001), who argues that democratic legislatures and elections provide only an incomplete representation of the people, and that the judicial interpretation and application of the Constitution by the courts are integral parts of constitutional self-government.

and governance powers, subject to respect for the constitutional limits of judicial powers *vis-à-vis* democratic governance.[39] From a rights-based constitutional approach to international integration, the constitutional ideal of the 18th century democratic revolutions in the US and France – ie that the rights of men depend on the separation of the judicial power from the legislative and executive ones, and that judges must defend constitutional freedoms against abuses of power – may legitimize judicial interpretations of the intergovernmental EC Treaty and of the ECHR as constitutional guarantees of individual rights, without prejudice to the diverse constitutional traditions inside states and the diverse judicial approaches of national constitutional courts towards 'political questions'.

Inside the EC, public reasoning and democracy approved the judicial conceptions of procedural and substantive justice and consolidated the transformation of the EC Treaty, as well as of the ECHR, into 'constitutionals instruments of European public order'[40] that have enabled more effective protection of fundamental rights and of democratic peace across national frontiers than ever before in European history. The democratic legitimacy of this 'judicial constitutionalization' derived not only from the judicial and legal empowerment of citizens enhancing their individual and democratic self-development inside the EC. The judicial transformation of the EC Treaty provisions on free movements of goods, services, persons, capital and related payments into 'fundamental rights' also set strong incentives for the decentralized enforcement of the EC's common market rules vis-à-vis governmental and private restrictions and discrimination. The common market law and competition law of the EC have become integral parts of EC constitutional law guaranteeing 'an open market economy with free competition' (Articles 4, 98, 105, 157 EC Treaty) based on 'a system ensuring that competition in the internal market is not distorted' (Article 3g). The EC Court protects the EC's common market law and competition law not only as instruments for promoting economic efficiency and consumer welfare, but also as protecting individual freedoms rooted in a constitutional 'principle of freedom' (Article 6 EU).

VIII. Limits of European Constitutionalism: Multilevel Judicial Trade Governance without Justice in the Common Commercial Policy Area of the EC

According to the Vienna Convention on the Law of Treaties (VCLT), 'disputes concerning treaties, like other international disputes, should be settled by peaceful means and in conformity with the principles of justice and international law'

---

[39] On the diverse theories of justification of judicial review, see M Troper, 'The logic of justification of judicial review', *International Journal of Constitutional Law* 1 (2003) 99–121.

[40] This concept continues to be used in many judgments of the European Court of Human Rights since the Court's decision in *Loizidou v Turkey (preliminary objections)*, Series A No 310 (1995) 20 EHRR 99 § 75(2).

(preamble VCLT). The WTO Agreement explicitly recognizes 'basic principles and objectives...underlying this multilateral trading system' (preamble). Some of these principles are specified in WTO provisions, for instance in the GATT (for example, Articles III.2, VII.1, X.3, XIII.5, XX (j), XXIX.6, XXXVI.9) and other WTO agreements on trade in goods (Article 7.1 Agreement on Customs Valuation, Article 9 Agreement on Rules of Origin), services (Article X GATS) and trade-related intellectual property rights (in the Preamble of the TRIPS Agreement, Articles 8 and 62.4). The WTO requirement of interpreting WTO law 'in accordance with customary rules of interpretation of public international law' (Article 3.2 DSU) refers not only to *formal* interpretative principles (such as *lex specialis, lex posterior, lex superior*) aimed at mutually coherent interpretations on the basis of legal presumptions of lawful conduct of states, of the systemic character of international law, and the mutual coherence of international rules and principles. The customary law requirement of interpreting treaties 'in conformity with principles of justice' also calls for clarifying the *substantive principles of justice* underlying WTO law, like freedom, non-discrimination, rule of law, independent third-party adjudication and preferential treatment of LDCs. The basic WTO principle of progressive liberalization and legal protection of liberal trade can be justified by all 'liberal' (that is, liberty-based) theories of justice, such as:

- utilitarian theories defining justice in terms of maximum satisfaction of individual preferences and consumer welfare;
- libertarian theories focusing on protection of individual liberty and property rights;
- egalitarian concepts defining justice more broadly in terms of equal human rights and democratic consent; and
- international theories of justice based on sovereign equality and effective empowerment of states to increase their national welfare through liberal trade.[41]

Hence, the diversity of libertarian, egalitarian or utilitarian value preferences should not affect recognition that the WTO guarantees of freedom, non-discrimination and rule of law – by enhancing individual liberty, non-discriminatory treatment, economic welfare and poverty reduction across frontiers – reflect, albeit imperfectly, basic principles of justice. In terms of the Aristotelian distinction between 'general principles of justice' (like liberty, equality, fair procedures, promotion of general consumer welfare) and particular principles of justice requiring adjustments depending on particular circumstances, WTO rule-making and WTO dispute settlement procedures can also contribute to 'corrective justice' and 'reciprocal justice', just as the special, differential and

---

[41] For overviews of these theories see FJ Garcia, *Trade, Inequality and Justice: Toward a Liberal Theory of Just Trade* (2003); A Beviglia Zampetti, *Fairness in the World Economy. US Perspectives on International Trade Relations* (2006).

non-reciprocal treatment of less-developed WTO Members in numerous WTO provisions may contribute to 'distributive justice'.

WTO law and its Dispute Settlement Understanding (DSU) regulate 'the dispute settlement system of the WTO' (Article 3) as a multilevel system with compulsory jurisdiction for judicial settlement of disputes at intergovernmental and domestic levels. The constitutional functions of this multilevel 'judicial governance'[42] remain, however, contested. Most of the more than 200 legal rulings by WTO dispute settlement bodies in the context of the altogether more than 300 WTO dispute settlement proceedings since 1995 have been regularly adopted and implemented by WTO members subject to rare exceptions when, for example, the EC Council or the US Congress lacked the necessary political majorities for amending domestic legislation. Courts in most WTO member countries accept legal obligations to *interpret* domestic trade rules (such as those on customs valuation, antidumping, intellectual property rights) in conformity with the WTO obligations of the country concerned, yet they rarely do so in their actual judicial practices.[43] Even though WTO law commits all domestic government bodies, trade bureaucracies interested in limiting their judicial accountability often encourage domestic courts to disregard WTO law;[44] only very rarely have they agreed to WTO obligations *requiring* domestic courts to *apply* specifically agreed WTO rules (as provided for in Article XX of the WTO Agreement on Government Procurement) at the request of private plaintiffs.

The commitment of the EU to 'uphold and promote its values and interests' in its 'relations with the wider world', including 'strict observance and the development of international law' (compare with Article I-3 TCE), reflects a constitutional ideal of rule of international law that is far from being realized in the administration of justice by national, European and international courts in the external relations of the EC. The increasing judicial recourse – not only by European courts

---

[42] cf A Stone Sweet, *Governing with Judges. Constitutional Politics in Europe* (2000), according to whom (137) constitutional courts perform four basic functions: (1) they operate as a 'counterweight' to majority rule; (2) they 'pacify' politics; (3) they legitimize public policy; and (4) they protect human rights.

[43] cf J A Restani and I Bloom, 'Interpreting international trade statutes: is the charming Betsy sinking? *24 Fordham Int'l L J 1533*. The European Court of Justice has a long history of ignoring GATT and WTO rules at the request of political EC bodies which have often misinformed the EC Court on the meaning of GATT/WTO rules and dispute settlement reports (e.g. in Case 112/80 *Dürbeck*, ECR 1981, 1095, the Commission misinformed the EC Court on an unpublished GATT dispute settlement finding against the EC, and the Court relied on this information without verifying the obviously wrong information of the Court).

[44] At the request of the political EC institutions (whose legal advocates claim that 'it is difficult to point out one specific moment at which it can be established beyond doubt that WTO rules have been breached, even after a decision of a panel or report of the Appellate Body', and 'that it is rarely or never possible to speak of a sufficiently serious breach of WTO law' by the political EC institutions justifying the EC's non-contractual liability for damages pursuant to Article 288 EC Treaty, cf PJ Kuiper, 'WTO law in the European Court of Justice' 42 Common Market Law Review (2005) 1313, 1334), the EC Court has refrained long since from reviewing the legality of EC acts in the light of the EC's GATT and WTO obligations. In the US, courts are barred by legislation from challenging the WTO-consistency of US federal measures.

but also in the case law of the WTO Appellate Body – to 'principles' and 'balancing' for justifying interpretive choices is in line with modern constitutional theories of adjudication, such as Dworkin's 'adjudicative principle of integrity' which requires judges to regard law as expressing 'a coherent conception of justice and fairness'.[45] Yet, national and international Judges fail to cooperate and support the private struggles for rule of law in the international trade relations of the EC. The lack of effective legal and judicial remedies of EC citizens against the frequent violations by EC institutions and EC member states of their WTO obligations to respect freedom, rule of law and nondiscriminatory treatment of EC citizens in international trade illustrates the political limits of rule of law, of the judiciary and of social justice inside the EC.[46] The Machiavellian justifications by EC trade bureaucrats of their own violations of the rule of law are reminiscent not only of the European monarchical past[47] where courts were expected to serve the political rulers rather than the welfare of their citizens; the legal and judicial incoherencies in the international trade policy area of EC law also recall that 'constitutional justice' cannot be realized without individual access to courts and without judicial enforcement of the rule of law. For more than 20 years, Francis Jacobs has shown not only an exemplary interest in the complex interrelationships between European and international trade law.[48] He has also contributed – more than most other Europeans – to the constitutional achievement that the Court of Justice now 'has a key role in the life and work of the European Community and the European Union',[49] as well as to exploring and testing the political limits of constitutional justice in the international relations law of the EC.

---

[45] cf R Dworkin, *Law's Empire* (1986) 225, 243: 'Law as integrity asks judges to assume, so far as this is possible, that the law is structured by a coherent set of principles about justice and fairness and procedural due process, and it asks them to enforce these in the fresh cases that come before them, so that each person's situation is fair and just according to the same standards'.

[46] On the pursuit of 'order' rather than 'justice' in international political relations, see R Foot, JL Gaddis and A Hurrel (eds), *Order and Justice in International Relations* (2003); J Thomson, *Justice and World Order* (1992).

[47] cf Kuijper (n 20 above), who argues (1332–4) for focusing on the political 'law in action' rather than the WTO 'law in the books'.

[48] cf. M Hilf, F Jacobs and EU Petersmann (eds), *The EC and GATT* (1986).

[49] F Jacobs, Foreword to A Arnull, *The European Union and its Court of Justice* (2006) vii.

20

Dual-use Goods: (Mis)Understanding *Werner* and *Leifer*

Alan Dashwood

I. The Cases

Werner[1] and *Leifer*,[2] and the later *Centro-Com*[3] case, are such familiar authorities that it will be sufficient merely to recall their main features, in so far as these may be relevant for the purposes of this discussion. Francis Jacobs was Advocate General in all three cases, and his analysis of the issues they raised, harking back to an earlier opinion in *Richardt*,[4] was closely followed by the Court of Justice.

Werner and *Leifer* were about the compatibility with European Community law of the system that was applicable at the time in Germany for controlling the exportation of so-called 'dual-use goods', that is, products capable of being used for military as well as for civilian purposes. *Werner* arose out of the refusal of a licence to export a vacuum induction oven to Libya, and *Leifer* out of a criminal prosecution against various individuals for the exportation to Iraq, without the requisite licences, of plant and of certain chemical products.

The main thrust of the reasoning of both the opinion and the judgment is that national measures restricting exports of dual-use goods must be compatible with the rules of the common commercial policy, as implemented by Regulation 2603/69 ('the Export Regulation').[5] A non-restrictive interpretation of the common commercial policy was necessary, the Court said, 'to avoid disturbances in intra-Community trade by reason of the disparities which would then exist in

---

[1] Case C-70/94 *Fritz Werner Industrie-Ausrustingen GmbH v Germany* [1995] ECR I-3189.
[2] Case C-83/94 *Criminal Propceedings against Peter Leifer and Others* [1995] ECR I-3231.
[3] Case C-124/95 *The Queen, ex parte Centro-Com v HM Treasury and Bank of England* [1997] ECR I-81.
[4] Case C-367/89 *Richardt and 'Les Accessoires Scientifiques'* [1991] ECR I-4621. The Advocate General noted, at para 27 of his *Werner* and *Leifer* opinion, that the Court of Justice approached the *Richardt* case from a different perspective (that of the Community rules on transit) to his own.
[5] Council Regulation (EEC) No 2603/69 of 20 December 1969, OJ English Special Edition 1969 (II) 590.

certain sectors of economic relations with non-member countries'.[6] In an often-quoted passage of its *Werner* judgment, the Court went on:

So, a measure such as that described in the national court's question, whose effect is to prevent or restrict the export of certain products, cannot be treated as falling outside the scope of the common commercial policy on the ground that it has foreign policy and security objectives.[7]

It followed that a Member State could not be allowed to restrict the scope of the common commercial policy by freely deciding, in the light of its own foreign policy or security requirements, whether a measure was covered by Article 133 EC.[8] National measures of commercial policy were therefore permissible only if specifically authorized by the Community.[9]

Such authorization was, however, available in the form of Article 11 of the Export Regulation, which establishes a derogation from the basic principle laid down by Article 1 of the Regulation that the exportation of products from the EC 'shall be free'.[10] The grounds on which Article 11 allows export restrictions to be imposed or applied by the Member States correspond to those in Article 30 EC, including public security. The Advocate General and the Court were agreed that, while it was for the respective national courts to decide whether the derogation in Article 11 was applicable on the facts before them, the concept of public security was broad enough, in principle, to cover restrictions on the exportation of dual-use goods, more particularly in view of the fact that it was becoming increasingly less possible for the security of a particular state to be considered in isolation, 'since it is closely linked to the security of the international community at large, and of its various components'.[11] The opinion provides, in addition, a careful and balanced analysis of the considerations going to the application of the principle of proportionality, once it has been accepted that the security of a Member State may be at stake.[12]

A similar approach was adopted by Advocate General Jacobs and by the Court of Justice in the *Centro-Com* case. Here the dispute was about a unilateral measure taken by HM Treasury to reinforce the sanctions regime against Serbia and Montenegro, which had been established, pursuant to Resolution 757

---

[6] *Werner*, para 9; *Leifer*, para 9.
[7] *Werner*, para 10. cf *Leifer*, paras 10 and 11, where a similar point is made less rhetorically.
[8] *Werner*, para 11.
[9] *Werner*, para 12; *Leifer*, para 12. Citing Case 41/76, *Donckerwolcke v Procureur de la Republique* [1976] ECR 1921, para 32; Case 174/84 *Bulk Oil v Sun International* [1986] ECR 559, para 31.
[10] 'Freedom' is defined by the Article in terms of the absence of quantitative restrictions on exports. One of the issues before the Court, which is not directly relevant to this discussion, was whether the reference to quantitative restrictions in Article 1 should be read as extending to measures of equivalent effect, such as a licensing requirement. The Court held that the Article must be so interpreted: *Werner*, paras 16–23.
[11] Opinion, para 46; judgment, para 26.
[12] Paras 54 (quoting paras 28 and 29 of the *Richardt* opinion) and 55.

(1992) of the United Nations Security Council, by Regulation 1432/92.[13] Under the 'humanitarian exception' relating to medicinal products that was provided for by Article 3 of the Regulation, responsibility for ensuring compliance with authorizations given by the Yugoslavia Sanctions Committee fell to the competent authorities of the Member State of export. However, following reports of the abuse of the system of humanitarian exceptions, it was decided by HM Treasury that payments out of funds held by Serbia and Montenegro in United Kingdom banks would be allowed only if the products in question were actually exported from the United Kingdom. Centro-Com came up against that rule, when it sought payment from Barclays Bank for medicines that had been exported to Serbia and Montenegro from Italy.

Recalling the language of its judgment in *Werner*,[14] the Court said that, 'even where measures such as those in issue in the main proceedings have been adopted in the exercise of national competence in matters of foreign and security policy, they must respect the Community rules adopted under the common commercial policy'.[15] The prohibition under the sanctions regime laid down by Regulation 1432/92 against exports to Serbia and Montenegro derogated from the provisions of the Export Regulation; however, exports of medicinal products covered by the humanitarian exception remained subject to the common system provided for by the Regulation, because they fell outside the scope of the derogation.[16] While a measure applying sanctions imposed by the United Nations Security Council would, in principle, be justifiable under Article 11 of the Export Regulation, recourse to that Article ceased to be available, once Community rules were in place to protect the interests in question. Such was the case with respect to the disputed United Kingdom restriction, because measures to guard against abuse of the humanitarian exception had been laid down by Regulation 1432/92.[17]

II. Community Control of Dual-use Exports

In his *Werner* and *Leifer* opinion, Advocate General Jacobs remarked upon the recent adoption by the Council of the Community and CFSP measures that together made up the original regime, at the level of the European Union, for the control of exports of dual-use goods.[18]

[13] Council Regulation (EEC) No 1432/92 of 1 June 1992 prohibiting trade between the European Economic Community and the Republics of Serbia and Montenegro, OJ 1992 L151/4. The Regulation was adopted in accordance with the practice that preceded the establishment of the cross-pillar procedure of Article 301 EC.
[14] Para 26.
[15] Para 30.
[16] Paras 35 and 36.
[17] Paras 46–8. Citing Case 72/83 *Campus Oil and Others v Minister for Industry and Energy* [1984] ECR 2727, para 27, which concerned recourse to Article 30 EC.
[18] Para 24.

The relevant Community measure was Regulation 3381/94, which established the detailed machinery of the control regime.[19] The Regulation was 'complemented'[20] by a CFSP measure taking the form of a joint action adopted pursuant to the then Article J.3 TEU.[21] This performed a threefold function: its Annex I established the list of dual-use products requiring export authorization pursuant to Article 3 (1) of the Regulation; its Annex II identified the very short list of destinations covered by a 'general authorization' (meaning that export operations to the countries concerned would not normally require individual authorization);[22] and its Annex III laid down guidelines to be taken into account by the Member States when deciding whether to grant export authorization in a particular case.

There is not the slightest indication in the opinion that Advocate General Jacobs had any qualms as to the validity of combining a CFSP act with a Community act in this way. Indeed, the language of the opinion strongly suggests the opposite. The Advocate General refers to the new control system, after describing the cross-pillar mechanism for imposing economic sanctions, which had been introduced by the TEU, as a further case 'where decisions adopted in the framework of the common foreign and security policy *may* be accompanied by measures taken pursuant to the EC Treaty'.[23]

Nevertheless, on the occasion of the review of the export control regime established in 1994, which had been provided for by Article 19 (5) of Regulation 3381/94, it was decided that the combined CFSP and EC system of controls should be replaced by one based solely on a Community act. Accordingly, a decision was adopted by the Council repealing the 1994 joint action. This refers explicitly in its second recital to the case law of the Court of Justice, with a footnote citing *Werner*, *Leifer* and *Centro-Com*. The impression is clearly given that the combination of CFSP and commercial policy measures had been shown by those cases to be unlawful. Currently, therefore, there is a single Community text, Regulation 1334/2000 containing the dual-use regime; this includes in Annex I the list of items subject to authorization, and in Annex II the list (amended though not noticeably extended) of destinations benefiting from a Community general export authorization, which were previously part of the 1994 joint action.

---

[19] Council Regulation (EC) No 3381/94 of 19 December 1994 setting up a Community system for the control of exports of dual-use goods, OJ 1994 L 367/1.
[20] The word is used by the Advocate General, at para 24 of his opinion.
[21] Council Decision 94/942/CFSP of 19 December 1994 on the joint action adopted by the Council on the basis of Article J.3 of the Treaty on European Union concerning the control of exports of dual-use goods, OJ 1994 L 367/8.
[22] In other words, this was a list of 'good guys', who could be trusted not to misuse dual-use products. The only countries on the list, other than EFTA countries that have since acceded to the European Union, were Australia, Canada, Japan, Norway, Switzerland and the United States. Drawing up a list of 'bad guys' would have been more controversial.
[23] Para 24 (emphasis added).

III. Wrong and Right Lessons of the Case Law

It seems the institutions of the European Union drew the lesson from *Werner* and *Leifer* and from *Centro-Com* that, because it is a measure for the regulation of trade, control of the exportation of dual-use goods falls under the exclusive competence conferred on the Community by Article 133 EC; and this would be so, in spite of the fact that the objectives of such a measure – namely, strengthening the security of the Union itself, and contributing more generally to the preservation of international peace and security – might be thought to belong squarely within the field of the common foreign and security policy (CFSP).[24] In the writer's contention, that was the wrong lesson, though in drawing it the institutions find themselves in distinguished company.[25]

Just because a Member State requires Community authorization to implement a national regime for the control of exports of dual-use goods, it by no means follows that the Community is fully (and exclusively) competent to establish such a regime itself. On a faithful reading of the judgments in *Werner*, *Leifer* and *Centro-Com*, in particular the famous dictum from paragraph 10 of the *Werner* judgment cited above, it is very clear that they are not about the scope of the Community's commercial policy competence, but about the interplay between that competence and the continuing right of the Member States, explicitly acknowledged by the Court in *Centro-Com*, 'to adopt measures of foreign and security policy in the exercise of their national competence'.[26] To borrow the elegant phraseology of Christophe Hillion, compliance rather than competence was the issue.[27] The judgments provide another instance of the Court's habitual insistence that, when exercising their sovereign powers, the Member States must act in accordance with the rules of Community law. The right lesson to draw was the perhaps unexciting one that, if the Member States wish to employ commercial policy instruments in furtherance of the objectives of their foreign and security policies, the rules defining the nature and scope of the competence conferred by Article 133 EC must be complied with (subject, of course, to derogations provided for by the Treaty, such as in the case of the measures to which Articles 296 and 297 EC apply).

The mistaken reading of the three cases, which led the institutions to restructure the Union's dual-use regime, was due to a failure to recognize the distinction between competence, in the sense of legal authorization for the Community to do things (like legislating or taking executive action), and the scope of application

---

[24] See Article 11 (1), second and third indents TEU.
[25] See P Eeckhout, *External Relations of the European Union: Legal and Constitutional Foundations* (2004) 35–9; P Koutrakos, *EU International Relations Law* (2006), 425–8.
[26] *Centro-Com*, para 27.
[27] C Hillion, '*ERTA, ECHR* and *Open Skies* – laying the grounds of the EU system of external relations' in L Azoulai and M Maduro (eds), *The Past and Future of EU Law – The Classics of EU Law Revisited on the 50th Anniversary of the Rome Treaty* (forthcoming).

of the EC Treaty. The significance of the distinction lies in the fact that the obligations Member States have accepted under the Treaty may impose serious constraints on their powers, even in areas where the Community's competence is limited or non-existent, such as those of foreign and security policy.

IV. Complementary EC and CFSP Competences

In the submission of the writer, the authors of the EU's 1994 dual-use regime correctly analysed the measure they were adopting as one calling for the complementary exercise of the Union's CFSP and the Community's commercial policy competences. A trade measure was being used instrumentally, for the purpose of implementing a logically prior foreign policy decision.

A parallel situation is that of the imposition of economic sanctions on a third country. Since the TEU, a mechanism based on the complementary exercise of First and Second Pillar competences has been provided for this purpose by Articles 301 and 60 EC. However, as Advocate General Jacobs noted in his *Centro-Com* opinion, the new mechanism 'codified a firmly established practice, clearly designed to be further developed, and now given a more specific Treaty basis'.[28] Under that practice, there was a similar combination of a prior foreign policy decision with an implementing Community measure. At a time before the establishment of the CFSP, the decision to adopt coercive economic measures against the third country concerned had to be taken under the Member States' national competences; though the Single European Act made it possible for them to act within the formal framework provided for European Political Cooperation (EPC).[29] That foreign policy decision would be implemented by way of a Community regulation based on the then Article 113 EC. The choice of Article 113 EC as a legal basis was dictated partly by the fact that the economic sanctions imposed would typically involve a trade embargo, and partly by the simplicity of the procedure laid down by the Article (the Council acting by a qualified majority on a proposal by the Commission), because normally there would be a need for urgency; the inclusion, among the economic sanctions imposed, of elements that might be thought to exceed the competence of the Community under Article 113 (for instance, the severing of transport links), would be the subject of a 'without prejudice' declaration. The specific function of such regulations, as acts implementing EPC decisions, was shown on their face, by inverting the contents of the Preamble; the visas mentioning Article 113 and the Commission's proposal would be placed at the end of the Preamble, following a series of recitals setting the act in its political context.[30]

---

[28] Para 42.
[29] Single European Act, Title III.
[30] See e.g. the Preamble to Regulation 1432/92.

A dual-use regime similarly involves employing instruments of commercial policy to implement a CFSP decision; that exports of dual-use goods to certain third countries represent a risk to the security of the European Union, or more generally to international peace and security. There was, therefore, at least one element of the 1994 regime that needed to be determined by a measure adopted under Title V TEU, namely the Annex identifying the destinations found to qualify for a general authorization (and hence, by implication, the third countries for which export authorizations were advisable, owing to a possible security risk). On the other hand, the inclusion in the joint action of the list of dual use products and of the guidelines for deciding on applications for authorization seems more questionable; these are essentially technical matters that may be thought to fall within the scope of trade regulation.

In the result, it is submitted that the current dual-use regime, based entirely on a Community regulation, is technically defective. This is of limited practical importance since, apart from the addition of New Zealand, the only changes to the list of 'good guys' in Annex II relate to countries that have now joined the EU.

However, the ramifications of the misunderstanding of *Werner*, *Leifer* and *Centro-Com* in litigation and in the academic literature, extend far more widely.

21

Direct Effect of Treaties in the US and the EU, the Case of the WTO: Some Perceptions and Proposals

John H Jackson

I. Introductory Remarks: Puzzles and Misconceptions

The subject of how international treaties are treated in the 'municipal' or domestic jurisprudence of a treaty member has a long, complex and somewhat meandering (interweaving?) history. It is also a subject of surprising complexity and articulate controversy. Furthermore, the subject can embrace substantially different approaches in different nation states, which makes careful and thorough scholarly commentary extraordinarily difficult – who can study 192 or more systems of treaty application with any degree of thorough empiricism? What at first often seems to be merely a rather technical 'side-road' subject, designed to stimulate the puzzle-solving urges of observers and commentators, turns out not only to be complex with many layers of meaning as the 'onion is peeled', but actually barges itself into the much broader and profoundly important question of the relationship between nation states and international cooperative institutions. Broad generalizations about how treaties should be handled in nation states or other treaty membership entities (such as the European Union) often prove deceptive, and well establish the adage that 'the devil is in the detail'.

With that indication of hesitation and humility, and recognizing the length limitations appropriately urged on authors invited to contribute to this book, the reader should be forewarned that this short essay will leave a lot of questions frustratingly unanswered. However, my goal here is to suggest some approaches to the questions which might be in the nature of 'thought experiments', possibly with uncertain or small chance of actual implementation, while indicating my own interest (reflected in several past works of mine) as well as my hope to pursue this subject further in other longer works.[1]

---

[1] See J Jackson, 'United States of America' in F Jacobs and S Roberts (eds), *The Effect of Treaties in Domestic Law* (1987) 141 (hereafter 'Jackson, *Treaty Effects*'); please see also J Jackson, 'Status

No person whom I could think of in the context of a book with many participating authors relating to European Union law, and indeed inevitably the broader terrain of international law generally, deserves more to be recognized and honoured with such project than Francis Jacobs. In particular, I feel honoured and privileged to participate and indeed to have known Francis as a close friend for many decades, but also I am happy to note that my association with Francis has as one of its links the subject matter of this essay.[2]

I draw partly upon another work of mine published more recently[3] which explores the broader settling of sovereignty, international law and international economic law, particularly the WTO. Clearly, the EU Court of Justice struggles with the potential application of the GATT (earlier) and now the WTO into EU jurisprudence has been one of the major perplexities for that Court, with resulting opinions and decisions being variously described with approval and disapproval, but in some cases criticism of the reasoning coupled with a view that the result (non-direct effect) is probably correct. Critics use terms such as 'not based on valid legal reasoning'; rulings describe GATT and WTO as an 'ugly blot' on the EU Court's jurisprudence; 'one can ask questions about the EC's respect for international law', 'normative basis remains hazy'; 'AG's legal reasoning is faulty and quite contradictory',[4] and so on.

The jurisprudence of the US approach ('self-executing') has also been the subject of considerable controversy and criticism, although in the US much of the debate is focused on the requirements implied by Article VI of the US Constitution. There are those that argue this text requires treaties to be treated as self-executing in the US; others argue to the contrary, and the actual court decisions are much directed this latter way. Language used to criticize the US jurisprudence includes 'state of disarray' and 'sloppy reasoning'.[5]

---

of treaties in domestic legal systems: a policy analysis' (1992) 86 AJIL 310 (hereafter 'Jackson, *AJIL*, 1992'); see also J Jackson, 'Sovereignty, subsidiarity, and the separation of powers: the high wire balancing act of globalization' in D Kennedy and J Southwick (eds), *The Political Economy of International Trade Law: Essays in Honor of Robert E Hudec* (2002) 13.

[2] See Jackson, *Treaty Effects* (n 1 above).

[3] J Jackson, *Sovereignty, the WTO, and Changing Fundamentals of International Law* (2006) (hereafter 'Jackson, *Sovereignty*, 2006').

[4] See, e.g., works such as P Eeckhout, *External Relations of the European Union, Legal and Constitutional Foundations* (2005) 302 (hereafter 'Eeckhout, 2005'); S Griller, 'Enforcement and implementation of WTO law in the European Union' in F Breuss, S Griller and E Vranes (eds), *The Banana Dispute: An Economic and Legal Analysis* (2003) 288; N Van den Broek, 'Legal persuasion, political realism, and legitimacy: the European Court's recent treatment of the effect of WTO agreements in the EC legal order' (2001) 4 JIEL 413, 434; A Von Bogdandy, 'Legal effects of World Trade Organization decisions within European Union law: a contribution to the theory of the legal acts of international organizations and the action for damages under article 288(2) EC' (2005) 39 J World Trade 51, 54.

[5] Vazquez, in J Jackson, W Davey and A Sykes, *Legal Problems of International Economic Relations: Cases, Materials and Text on the National and International Regulation of Transnational Economic Relations* (4th ed, 2002) 100 (hereafter 'Jackson, Davey and Sykes, 2002').

Needless to say, the matters in both jurisdictions are very complex, and the jurisprudence in each place seems rather unsatisfactory, at least as to the reasoning, if not the actual result. In the remainder of this essay, I will first (in part II) address the complex 'policy landscape' in which the intricate reasons and holdings meander. In this part I will explore the policies, without much relation to what the US or EU courts or governments have been doing. I am addressing the question of what *should* likely be the outcome of the holdings regarding treaties in these two domestic or 'municipal' (non-international) legal systems. In part III, I take up in turn a very brief overview of the US jurisprudence, and then the EU jurisprudence. Finally, in part IV, I will set forth some summary propositions to describe the overall state of play of the treaty application jurisprudence. Then I will follow this with several suggestions which governments might consider, if not to actually implement, then at least to use in the analysis of the legal concepts driving the material of this subject.

Several items of terminology should be mentioned at the outset. The subject relates the 'international legal system' to other legal entities, particularly the nation state, and to the regional legal entity of the European Union. In some contexts, I will use the term 'national or regional governments' or systems, or entities, to embrace both the United States (or other nation states) and the European Union. Also, since the technical legal terminology for the European Union has evolved from other terms, especially the phrase 'European Communities', and for some purposes those other terms have relevance in dealing with certain specific legal and political questions within the EU, I will generally use the term 'European Union' or 'EU' as embracing these other concepts or entities of the EU. I will also sometimes use the term 'EU/EC' for the same purpose.

For similar purposes of brevity, I also refer to the 'WTO Treaty' or the GATT. In the case of the WTO, its 'Charter' is part of a massively broader treaty of 25,000 pages, which is the document referred to by the phrase 'WTO Treaty'.[6]

II. The Policy Landscape for Domestic Treatment of International Treaties

A. Some General Policy Considerations Relating to All Treaties

This section outlines (without much elaboration) many of the various policies which should affect the question of nation state domestic effect of an international treaty. At least some of the policy issues seem to be overlooked or ignored in many discussions about this subject. A substantial number of the points made

---

[6] Marrakesh Agreement Establishing the World Trade Organization, 15 April, 1994, in *World Trade Organization, The Legal Texts: The Results of the Uruguay Round of Multilateral Negotiations* (1999) (hereafter 'WTO Charter').

in this section are drawn from and influenced by various writings and court or other decisions, and also some of this author's prior publications alluded to in section I of this essay.[7]

All readers are probably very familiar with the basic starting point of most analyses. The conceptual divide between monist and dualist countries has been well known for centuries. I will not review that here.[8] Although disparaged by some, this conceptual framework, albeit somewhat oversimplified, is very useful, and is a juridically necessary starting point in many legal discussions of the subject. The simplified concept overlooks a huge number of policy issues outlined in this essay, of course, some of which lead to the need for disaggregating the terms monist and dualist, so that we should think more of an analysis which recognizes 'monistic slices' and 'dualist slices' of institutional structure (this author has also written about the need to 'slice' the concept of sovereignty, which is closely allied to the subject of this article).[9] These two terms also somewhat overlook the additional complexity created by new layers of governance such as that of the European Union, which could lead us to a third term, 'triadist'.[10]

There is also an argument that 'monistic' direct effect of treaties will more likely enhance compliance to the treaty norms by the treaty members. There is little empirical elaboration about this but counterarguments suggest that if the international treaty norms lack democratic legitimation (including adequate public participation) which is sometimes the case, compliance may be more difficult to obtain.[11]

If the norms tend to ignore local problems, they can unnecessarily create hostility to the treaty norms. Part of this picture involves constitutional or political structures in some countries that may bypass democratic participation, or may actually or apparently give too much treaty-making power to small elites in the society, possibly including 'lobbyist' monied pressure groups, which are adept in pursuing their interests in the treaty formulation process.[12] Some of these problems were manifested in the United States' 1994 Congressional process for approving the Uruguay Round treaties, during which US officials felt it was necessary in order to persuade Congress to agree to the treaty, to emphasize that the treaty text itself would not become law in the United States, but would be applied by the statute enacted to approve the treaty with its elaborate clauses authorizing approval and setting forth the changes to be made in US law.[13]

---

[7] See nn 1, 3 and 5 above.
[8] See Jackson et al (n 5 above) 97.
[9] See Jackson, *Sovereignty* (n 3 above).
[10] This is admittedly an invented word.
[11] See Jackson, *Treaty Effects* (n 1 above).
[12] ibid.
[13] D Leebron, 'Implementation of the Uruguay Round results in the United States' in J Jackson and A Sykes Jr (eds), *Implementing the Uruguay Round* (1997) 175.

There is another major constitutional and legitimacy issue in the topic of direct effect when this effect is coupled with the norm (sometimes arguably constitutional) that the directly applicable treaty must be accorded a higher status in the hierarchy of norms of the applying society than any nation state norm, even national norms which are enacted later than the treaty. In such a case, the extraordinarily weighty effect is in a sense to raise the treaty to the status of a constitutional norm.[14]

This result can occur without the normal constitutional procedures for amendment, and without participation or approval of the citizen voters. It also has the result of dramatically constraining what the sovereign nation's government can enact or otherwise legally accomplish within its legal structure. This may be desired for some treaties (such as human rights, or treaties developing a federal structure) but, as discussed below, it can make it exceedingly difficult for nations to regulate in certain areas such as economic matters (including taxation, or consumer protection and environmental measures.)

Some of these considerations may in fact be influencing the way some 'monist' nations directly apply treaties, such that some nations seem to be adept in finding exceptions to a general rule of application, or otherwise use judicial techniques to decline the full 'theoretical' effect of monism. It has even been argued that in fact there is no nation that is fully monist.[15]

In addition, it is often not entirely clear what is meant when officials and observers use the phrase 'direct effect'. There are many effects that treaties can have on domestic jurisprudence, including the important 'consistency' principle of interpreting domestic law so as to conform to international norms. There is some confusion or purposeful ambiguity about these concepts. In other works, this author has found it useful to characterize the more rigorous idea of direct effect (or in the US 'self-executing' effect) as being a 'statute-like' effect.[16] This could in some cases be contrasted with ideas such as 'private right of action', 'invocability', or 'standing'.

Finally, before moving to distinctions among different treaties and the effects of these on treaty application, it should be noted that there is a very important alternative to direct application (and in this author's view, a preferable approach.) This is the use of an 'Act of Transformation', by which the nation state authorities enact (or regulate where applicable administrative power exists) a valid domestic law set of norms which 'apply' the treaty. These acts of transformation can vary greatly. One might simply involve a legislative enactment 'approving and applying the treaty' as the treaty language itself states, perhaps embracing the treaty's full text as part of the statute (or in an annex).[17] Of course, this transformation could be very complex if it is designed to resolve all issues embedded

[14] See Eeckhout (n 4 above) and Jackson, *Treaty Effects* (n 1 above).
[15] See Jackson, *Treaty Effects* (n 1 above).
[16] ibid.
[17] See Frowein, chapter 4 in Jackson, *Treaty Effects* (n 1 above).

in it. Thus it could be that the Act of Transformation approach will not be very popular or often used, if not required under a particular system.

Other acts of transformation are possible, but some are more problematic. The United States (discussed in part III below) has in a number of cases, particularly those involving complex trade and economic treaties, extensively reworded much of the treaty in a statute applying the treaty norms. Other situations might be more ambiguous, such as a statutory provision requiring administrators to conform their regulations to the treaty norms, or to act consistently with the policies set forth in the treaty. These could actually be construed as acts of transformation up to a point. These may carve out specific parts of a treaty for such treatment, leaving other parts to remain as 'state-to-state obligations', rather than applicable in domestic law, especially when that seems to be the intent of some treaty obligations.

In fact, it can be observed that even if a treaty is not directly applicable, it can nevertheless have important effects (such as some in the prior paragraph). A tentative partial list could include:[18]

- requirement to interpret domestic norms 'consistently' with international obligations, whenever possible;
- statutes incorporate treaty language by reference, saying such treaty language 'shall apply in this case';
- statutes require government officials to do their task or duty 'consistent with Treaty X or its article Y';
- the legislative history of a domestic statute or other norm may clearly or impliedly indicate that the purpose of the statute is to implement the nation's international obligations specified in the treaty;
- the treaty language may be deemed to articulate policies which treaty parties have accepted, and those policies may influence the interpretation of domestic law;
- the existence of treaty obligations or policies may be used as evidence or indication of a 'pre-emption' by the national or regional government preventing subordinate bodies (regional member or sub-federal national unit) from taking contrary action, or indeed prevent any sub-federal actions.

The most important of these 'non-monist' effects, however, seems clearly to be the principle of consistency, which in the US jurisprudence is generally known as the 'Charming Betsy' effect due to the original US Supreme Court case embracing this principle.[19] There is, unfortunately, some political attempt in the United States (and maybe elsewhere) to undermine this principle by Congressional enactment.

---

[18] See Jackson, Davey and Sykes, 2002 (n 5 above) 102.
[19] ibid.

The principle has also come into conflict with another troublesome principle of US law known as the 'Chevron case' principle, requiring federal courts to give deference to the administrative agency in some matters of administrative interpretation of statutes. This has led to an argument that the Chevron principle trumps the Charming Betsy consistency principle.

In the opinion of this author, the consistency principle is exceedingly important for the international system, and it can be argued that this principle (unlike the direct effect principles) seems obligatory under customary international law and alternatively (or additively) the Vienna Convention on the Law of Treaties, as part of the 'good faith compliance' obligation of treaty norms. It should be noted that this principle does provide a national domestic law 'margin of discretion' (or 'margin of manoeuvre') depending on the clarity of the statute concerned, but it does not absolve a nation state from the possibly stricter international obligation of the treaty.

It is interesting to explore in certain cases whether these 'non-direct' effects attached to an Act of Transformation may equal or improve on the utility and acceptability of a treaty compared to direct effect.

B. Different Treaties and Different Treatments

It is important next to explore ways that treaties (or portions of treaties) can be, and have been, differentiated regarding monist treatment or dualist treatment (the latter through an Act of Transformation), and some of the policies which can or should affect that process.

Let us begin with the concept of justiciability. The basic idea, if put in broad terms, is that a norm otherwise valid and applicable may not be applied (or will not be applied in the court's judgment) if the court finds itself unable to rule on a question posed, or otherwise believes it inappropriate to rule. A list of such situations contains well-known matters, some of which will be briefly noted here. It may be, however, that in certain cases a hesitation to apply treaties directly is a response to one or more of these problems.[20] It is this author's opinion that these principles can be applied to various parts of a treaty, in different ways, depending on a series of policies (some of which go deeply into the relationship of sovereignty and international institutional power, and the degree of deference or 'standard of review' which might be required of the international process). Furthermore, the principles might operate differently on different parts of the same treaty (a circumstance which might indicate a preference for an Act of Transformation which can more carefully allocate some of the 'effects' of a treaty).

A list of examples:

- The language of the norm may be too imprecise for a court to make an informed juridically justifiable conclusion on its meaning.

[20] See Jackson, *Treaty Effects* (n 1 above).

- The language may expressly or impliedly be 'aspirational' or 'recommending' or otherwise suggest that no concrete norm is intended to obligate the treaty members. Language such as 'as far as possible', 'to the extent found feasible' or 'gradually to be achieved over time' might signal this result.
- The language may be conditioned on the development of certain facts which have not yet been manifested.
- The court may not have the necessary expertise to commit its judgment to the problem; for example, it may involve economic or scientific concepts beyond the expertise available to the court.
- The court may decide that the issue is not appropriately decided by courts since it has been relegated to decision by political, legislative, diplomatic or other modes of decision. This could be called a 'political question' hesitation.
- The court may use a 'judicial economy' reason to avoid deciding when it is not necessary to make a decision on an issue in a case.
- The court may find that the documentation of the treaty norm is irregular or not worthy, so it cannot ascertain the norm.
- The authoritative language of the treaty may differ from the languages available to the court proceeding, rendering the norm to be considered particularly difficult to apply.
- A critical issue arises when the treaty language has significant ambiguities or gaps. In this case, there is a constant tension about the role and authority of a juridical institution to resolve the ambiguity or to 'fill the gap'.[21]

Obviously this list can be enlarged. Some of these issues may lead a court to appropriately hesitate to make a finding in a case. This raises the old issue of *non-liquet*, which can often be a serious tension in the appropriate role of juridical body.[22]

There are some other concepts which intertwine with the policies expressed above, only a few of which can be taken up here. In some cases I have elaborated on some of these concepts elsewhere.[23] Consider:

- invocability (who can invoke the norms of a treaty, private right?);
- reciprocity (effect of disparities between member states regarding direct effect);
- the role of various negotiating possibilities within the treaty context, and the effect on questions of direct effect;

[21] See Jackson, *Sovereignty* (n 3 above).
[22] This author believes juridical institutions should have some leeway in this regard, and is not sympathetic to some of the more absolute versions of this doctrine. Probably, however, most courts will find a way to avoid a decision on which they do not want to opine, without explicitly invoking *non-liquet*.
[23] See Jackson, *Sovereignty* (n 3 above) and Jackson, Davey and Sykes (n 5 above).

- the role of Treaty Dispute Settlement procedures;
- overall institutional structure of the Treaty;
- margin for manoeuvre (political need of member state government entities, margin of discretion, standard of review);
- treaty characteristics: size, members and length of expected duration.

C. Subject Matter of the Treaties: Differential Treatment?

An important consideration may be the subject matter of the treaty, and particularly whether that subject implies or establishes the exceptional importance of direct application to the successful implementation of the treaty norms. By way of contrast, other treaty subjects may be more effective without direct effect (at least when such effect also implies superiority to later national rules).

Consider human rights treaties, for example. Many, indeed probably most, human rights treaties are specifically designed to protect individuals including citizens of a nation against measures of that nation's government. Experience with human rights treaties (mostly since World War II) suggests that when individuals have an effective judicial remedy within their own society they will very likely have better protection against human rights violations. To leave these matters entirely to international institutions (often non-existent) tends to relieve national officials and others from effective responsibility. Since the government involved is the very cause of the difficulty, it often seems appropriate to provide at least the possibility of a remedy within that state, in a form that prevents the conflicting interests of the government officials from preventing redress. Of course, in many cases international intervention or institutional measures will be necessary, but these sometimes operate to induce the nation state to make the necessary redress (the European Convention of Human Rights is the remarkable and most powerful example of these principles).

There is another dimension to these considerations, namely the degree to which a given society has confidence in its own human rights protections. For example, to some extent the difference in viewpoint between the US and Europe on this matter may reflect a difference between broad societal viewpoints regarding how best to protect individual human rights. The US has several centuries of operating experience under a remarkable bill of rights, enhanced by a powerful and relatively independent judiciary (of course, nothing is perfect).

Thus many persons in the US trust that process more than they trust an international treaty system. Whereas in Europe, and particularly Eastern Europe, clearly the failures of nation states to protect human rights, especially before and after World War II, would understandably induce citizens there to strongly desire some powerful legal institution outside of the nation state for the protection of human rights. To some extent the constitutional developments in Europe, including Eastern Europe, seem to confirm these different attitudes. This does not, of course, imply that either system is better, or that there are not areas of endeavour which could benefit from examples of successful protections in other system.

Apart from the potential exceptional desire for direct effect for human rights, one should also point to a special need for direct effect in a developing 'federal' system or other institutional developments implying the need of a special legal regime of rules at the higher government level, which will bind citizens directly, as well as the lower levels of government. Clearly the US history reflects this (although even after several centuries there remains much to argue about in the US regarding how to allocate powers between the federal government and the states). Likewise the European Union, with its currently elaborate 'constitutional' debates about allocation of powers, can easily demonstrate the importance of the internal EU legal jurisprudence leading to direct application (and superiority) of the EU level laws. This early EU jurisprudence is appropriately given much credit for the extraordinary success of the European unification policy goals.

A contrary approach is likely important when it comes to treaties involving complex economic matters among large groups of nations. Here the plea in some national or regional (EU) court opinions for the need for a 'margin of manoeuvre' has special relevance, not because of the specific wording or institutional structure of the treaty, but merely because economic matters (especially in a globalized world) often create relatively rapid change, and governments appropriately need to be able to respond to the needs of their constituents, even in times without short-term crises.

D. Who Decides and How?

Another key question, then, is who should decide how a treaty should apply in a given national or regional government, and how should such a decision be determined and itself applied?

The question of who decides divides into two parts (at least): first, the governmental level of legal source of decision-making authority, and second, within a given government level, where does the authority lie (which branch of government)? Where is the legal source of a direction about direct effect or self-executing treaties? Options include international law in general, the mutual intent of the parties to the treaty (at time of formation), the intent of the nation state officials responsible for drafting the treaty, the conclusions (legal or policy) of the national or regional officials responsible for applying the treaty.

First, as to international law, it is quite clear that traditional international law would leave it to the national or regional government to decide how to implement or apply a treaty norm which is an international obligation. Since nations and regional governments vary enormously in constitutional structure and societal and cultural attributes, this norm seems eminently wise. Certain international law constraints would make it virtually constitutionally impossible for a number of important nations to participate in a treaty.

It is possible to think of a treaty which includes an obligation to require a mode of direct application. This would 'internationalize' the decision, but when proposed it has often been rejected, as with many treaties (economic and human rights). A variation, however, is a treaty clause that requires treaty members to take such action as is necessary under their own constitutions to ensure that the treaty norms are implemented into domestic law. Even this can meet some resistance, of course (compare some of the US and EU jurisprudence). Another variation which seems to find considerable acceptance (but with ambiguities) is a treaty rule that requires each treaty member to 'ensure that its laws conform to the treaty obligation'. The WTO has this clause.[24]

Suppose, then, that the decision (as this author believes) is basically up to the national or regional government (unless made international by agreement). This takes us to the second question: where within such government does the decision-making power lie? The courts? The legislature? The executive? Other entities including sub-federal governments? There are many concepts which could be pursued here.

It becomes reasonably apparent that explicit guidance by appropriate authorities would have considerable advantages. This provides an argument again for the use in applying all treaties through an Act of Transformation. That Act could spell out in detail what the national authority feels is required by the treaty, but also what its own societal and constitutional constraints would permit or suggest. A strong argument can be made that the policy-making authorities (executive or legislative or both) would best provide the direction desired. But that still leaves the question, what if they do not? What is the default rule?

E. The Default Rule

The approach advocated above, favouring an Act of Transformation (for all or part of a treaty, at the time of treaty-making or at a later time), may in some minds be optimal, but it still leaves open the question of what should be the rule regarding treaty effect in the event of the lack of an Act of Transformation or lack even of clear policy guidance by the political and policy-making parts of the government.

One approach would be to opt for a presumption against direct effect. This would certainly make solutions conceptually easier (remembering the potential utility of an Act of Transformation to be achieved at a later time). A variant perhaps more appropriate would be a general rule of non-direct effect in the absence

---

[24] WTO Charter XVI:4, XVI:1.

of policy direction, with certain exceptions carved out such as human rights and 'federal-like structures'.

Next, some developments in the two major national or regional entities which have had experience concerning self-executing (US) or direct effect (EU) will be briefly explored.

III. Treaty Application in the Case of GATT and the WTO as Applied in Two Major Jurisdictions: the US and the EU

A. Introduction

With the policy 'landscape' outlined in the previous parts of this work in mind, we now examine a particularly puzzling and high-profile example of treaty application in the two largest economic entities (the US and the EU) with respect to the most significant and extensive international economic institution, namely the World Trade Organization (WTO) and the GATT (as the WTO predecessor). This practice proves to be exceptionally puzzling and perhaps unsatisfactory. It certainly has caused a large amount of debate, discussion and controversy. In sum, with respect to the vast treaty (25,000 pages) establishing the WTO as an international organization, it appears that neither the United States nor the European Union (or European Economic Community) directly applies or gives self-executing effect to that treaty. Even when there appears to be a general rule of direct application of this treaty (most explicit in the European Union), nevertheless the principal juridical institution has been unwilling to apply that general rule to this treaty. This section will present a brief overview of the practices of these two jurisdictions regarding treaty application in domestic jurisprudence for the WTO.

B. The United States

The history of the United States treaty application begins almost at the start of this nation's independence. The famous early US Supreme Court case examined the concept of domestic treaty application as a question of 'self-execution' of the treaty.[25] The Court established a framework of thinking about this subject which is still vital and utilized in United States domestic jurisprudence. The outlines of this history are reasonably well known to most readers of this essay.[26]

---

[25] The US history of treaty application is excellently presented by Carlos Vazquez in 'Treaty-based rights and remedies of individuals' (1992) 92 Colum L Rev 1082. See also C Bradley, 'The treaty power and American federalism' (1998) 97 Mich L Rev 390; Y Iwasawa, 'The doctrine of self-executing treaties in the United States: a critical analysis' (1986) 26 Va J Int'l L 627; Jackson, *Treaty Effects* (n 1 above).
[26] Jackson, *Treaty Effects* (n 1 above).

To illustrate the main point, if one finds that the treaty language is roughly equivalent to a rule which applies on its own terms to parties within the home based society, such as a clause which reads, 'Citizens of each treaty party shall have the right to x, y and z', then the Court would usually recognize this clause as 'self-executing', to be taken into account by any relevant judge in the United States. On the other hand, if the treaty language (or implication) calls on the treaty parties 'to take such action as is necessary to enable citizens (or other entities) to assert the right to x, y and z', then the US Court would characterize that part of the treaty as non-self-executing. The rationale (partly) is that, if the treaty contemplates some additional action be taken by the government before the rights can be asserted 'directly' in a court of law (or other context), then that treaty cannot be applied directly.

The illustration used is, of course, a relatively simple one to assist readers to grasp the point. But in real application, often matters are not so simple, and there may be considerable ambiguity about the meaning of the treaty language. If the treaty is deemed not to be self-executing, then further government action must occur in order to 'transform' the treaty norm into the domestic legal system of the United States, and of course the action is termed an 'Act of Transformation'. It may be a statute, or possibly executive authority or regulation acting with delegated authority. It is even conceivable that the Act of Transformation could be an action of a judicial institution, depending on the authority of such institution. There is a long history in the United States jurisprudence about treaty application, a history that is complex and has been characterized sometimes as confusing (and confused). For example, if the treaty language itself is not clear on this point, the US courts have sometimes tried to establish the intent of the drafters of the treaty, or at least the intent of those US bodies or officials who were charged and authorized to accept the treaty as a binding international legal obligation on the US.

But when it comes to the major GATT/WTO trade agreements (at least during the last several decades), the matter is simplified, because the US Congress has specified in its statutes regarding those agreements just how the treaty norms should or should not be applied. A landmark example of Congressional intent to explicitly control the question of 'self-executing' application of a trade treaty was first manifested in the Congressional 1979 legislation approving the results of the GATT Tokyo Round negotiation. That legislation included words such as 'No provision of any trade agreement... which is in conflict with any statute... shall be given effect under the laws' of the United States. A major Congressional committee report stated that this language 'makes clear that these agreements are not self-executing'.[27]

In subsequent trade treaty legislative approvals, including those regarding free trade agreements as well as the later major GATT trade round negotiation

---

[27] Trade Agreements Act of 1979, 19 USC 2504, sec 3; Committee on Ways and Means report on the bill, regarding section 3. See also Jackson, Davey and Sykes (n 5 above) 99, 238.

results, this notion of non-self-executing status was continued, sometimes with additional statutory and clarifying language, some of which went further to prevent the treaty language operating directly in US jurisprudence, albeit sometimes with additions of certain details which may have clouded their desired approach.

In the United States there has been much debate about the US constitutional status of treaties, with different approaches to the US constitutional language in Article VI, which states that all treaties, like other US federal law, 'shall be the supreme Law of the Land, and the Judges in every State shall be bound thereby'. There has even been scholarship which argued that the Congress did not have the authority to control this issue, urging that all treaties *must* be self-executing (with a few possible exceptions). However, to the knowledge of this author and many others, no US court has ever taken a position which denied operation of the Congressional mandate as to trade treaties (and perhaps as to other issues similarly addressed by the Congress). For example, 1994 legislation approving the Uruguay Round massive treaty added a newer wrinkle when it provided that: 'No person other than the United States... shall have any cause of action or defense' to challenge US or state laws or administrative actions on the basis of that treaty. Thus it expressly rules against the existence of a 'private right of action' in such cases.[28]

The Congress has utilized its authority (and argued supremacy) over international economic matters to join with the President, often with a special procedure known as the 'fast track',[29] to enact a statute which serves multiple functions of approving the treaty, authorizing the President to accept (ratify) the treaty and to enact such legislation as Congress deemed necessary to amend US law or add to it, so as to provide (they argued) that the US would be in compliance with its international obligations under the treaty. This, of course, is the Act of Transformation. In addition, it has the merit of achieving, in the same enactment, approval, potential ratification and the necessary changes in US law. It also has the merit of clarity as compared with the US jurisprudence in the absence of such Congressional mandate. Likewise, it has the merit of clarity compared to the legal situation in many other nations and jurisdictions in the world, including the EU where the situation has often been characterized as 'muddled'. But that does not mean there are no problems with the US technique. Even though such limits on treaty application seem straightforward, the process of enacting the 'transformation' lends itself to much lobbying and potential influence of special (monied) interests (on the other hand, even in a case of direct application, lobbyists have become astute in lobbying the treaty draftspersons as the text is negotiated).

Furthermore, as pointed out in section II of this essay, even without self-executing (or direct) effect, the treaty has a number of effects ('indirect'?), and

---

[28] Uruguay Round Agreements Act of 1994, sec 102.
[29] See Jackson, Davey and Sykes, 2002 (n 5 above), 86.

in many (or maybe most) situations these can be more effective than direct effect when citizen acceptance and the use of such non-direct status to obtain legislative approval of the treaty are considered. In addition, non-self-executing effect can be considered a new and needed dimension of checks and balances, as well as an appropriate allocation of power in the area of tensions between nation state governments and international legal institutions.

One additional important characteristic of the US treaty implementation system must also be mentioned. The US jurisprudence and practice is quite clear (although criticized in some scholarship) that when a directly applied treaty norm (or Act of Transformation text) is in conflict with later US government legislation or other norms, the later in time will prevail. The argument is that the US Constitution Article VI mentions 'Laws and Treaties' in the same sentence and therefore these should be given equal status, which then leads logically (it is argued) to the latest in time trumping. Obviously, as we later analyse possibly different situations for EU law, this difference can have 'constitutional' importance of a very high order.[30]

C. The European Union, Treaty Application of WTO and GATT, and the Jurisprudence of the European Court of Justice

The full story of the European Union application of treaties (particularly of the GATT and later the WTO treaties) is extraordinarily complex and lengthy and cannot be detailed here. Several outstanding scholars have provided us with extensive and scholarly accounts of this story, perhaps most notably the excellent lengthy account by Professor Piet Eeckhout in his book on *External Relations of the European Union*.[31] For the purposes of this work, however, only a few comments will be made, but the discussion in section II provides additional relevant perceptions about arguments used in the EU jurisprudence.

To begin, it is necessary to note that this brief account deals basically with the application of treaties between the EU and non-members, and is not directed to the EC-EU formation treaties nor treaty relations between the EU member states or any of those states and the EU itself. It seems to be the case, however, that the

---

[30] ibid 96.
[31] P Eeckhout, *External Relations of the European Union, Legal and Constitutional Foundations* (2005) 273. See also G Bermann, R Goebel, W Davey and E Fox (eds), *Cases and Materials on European Union Law* (2nd ed, 2002) 1041; M Bronckers, 'Judicialization: can the European model be exported to other parts of the world?'(2005) 4 Tex Int'l L J 443; C Paul and G de Burca, *European Union Law: Text, Cases and Materials* (3rd ed, 2003) 178; A Emch, 'The European Court of Justice and WTO dispute settlement rulings – the end of the flirt' (2006) 7 JWIT 563; J Prinssen and A Scrauwen (eds), *Direct Effect: Rethinking a Classic of EC Legal Doctrine* (2004); N Van den Broek, 'Legal persuasion, political realism, and legitimacy: the European Court's recent treatment of the effect of WTO Agreements in the EC legal order' (2001) 4 JIEL 441; A Von Bogdandy (n 1 above); A Von Bogdandy, 'Constitutionalism in international law: comment on a proposal from Germany' (2006) Harv Int'l L J 223; G Zonnekyn, 'EC liability for non-implementation of WTO dispute settlement decisions – are the dice cast?' (2004) 7 JIEL 483.

fascinating story of the major constitutional role of the European Court of Justice in fashioning a 'unique legal system' that developed the jurisprudential principles (arguably essential to the later success of the EC and EU) has had a profound role for thinking about international EU treaties with non-members, and the related 'direct effects'.

In addition, readers should be reminded that the term 'direct effect' can have a number of meanings (as can the phrase 'self-executing' used in the United States). Furthermore, although the term 'direct effect' is closely analogous to the phrase 'self-executing', it is not necessarily completely congruent. Both terms cover a variety of situations which have become increasingly disaggregated in scholarly and practitioner analyses over some decades (or for the US, centuries). The sub-topics developed in such analyses are not identical between these two phrases, but both embrace the idea that treaty text can be 'statute like' in operation,[32] which can help avoid some ambiguities. However, there are other elements, such as the question of whether a private individual can base a judicial (or other) action on the treaty text, and if so what are the criteria for eligibility ('standing'?) to do that? Likewise, there is the question of to what remedy an individual is entitled, such as damages for harm caused by a treaty violation.

Also there is the question of 'application', relating to not only a nation state or regional entity, but also to sub-parts of these entities, such as legislative, judicial, executive or other elements. For example, direct application may allow only EU or EC entities (Commission, Council, European Parliament, Court of Justice) to take advantage of the 'direct effect' of treaty text. Likewise, direct application or self-execution can have different roles concerning the national state or regional entity, compared to sub-parts of those (states in the US or Member States of the EU, and even subordinate federal units of some of those). There is also a nuance between two nearly like terms regarding the EU treaty story, namely 'direct effect' compared to 'direct application', but these phrases will be treated as essentially the same concept for purposes of this essay.[33]

Several observations derived from the excellent scholarship and some limited examination of case decisions may suffice to set the framework for some conclusions in the next and last section.

First, the European jurisprudence starting position is to give direct effect status to all third country EU treaties. The history of this approach seems at least partly related to the jurisprudence mentioned above, which provides direct effect to the EU 'internal' treaties. That internal jurisprudence can be easily justified as a matter of policy as quite necessary for the development of the EU (or any similar federal system), because without this effect as well as the supremacy principle, the national or regional legal entity would be a very weak legal system indeed. However, the strong need for this direct effect treatment for internal treaties

---

[32] See Jackson, *Treaty Effects* (n 1 above).
[33] See G Bermann et al (n 31 above).

(or other norms) does not necessarily require the same approach for third-party external treaties. There may be some analogy value, and (as suggested in section II) for certain subjects there is a policy value in external treaties having a direct internal effect, but this may not always be the case. The European jurisprudence, however, seems to highly value this approach for external treaties, perhaps without always having thought through some of the troublesome statecraft and constitutional problems which can come with such approach.

Second, even though the general rule for the EU is supposed to give internal (domestic) direct effect to external treaties, for one particularly prominent set of treaties, namely the GATT and its massive successor treaty the WTO (Uruguay Round Agreement), the EU Court of Justice has quite consistently refused to grant that effect. This is the major conundrum for this jurisprudence.

Third, the evolving jurisprudence of the EU Court has shifted the grounds for its position over time, and has reached for a variety of concepts to try to justify the exception it applies to GATT/WTO. Much of this activity has been strongly criticized in the legal literature as noted in section I above. Recall the concepts of language precision and conditional nature and structure of the treaty institution, reciprocal measures and margin of manoeuvre *inter alia* discussed in section II above. Even the critics of the reasoning, however, in some instances agree with the *result* of non-direct application.[34]

In addition, related to the WTO (and maybe other cases) there has been some other indication of policy preference emanating from other EU institutions (such as the Council or Commission) to deny direct effect. However, the Court has seemed to minimize the importance of such preferences, even while coming to the same conclusion of non-direct effect. It could be suggested that the Court may be trying to preserve the power to rule on this effect to itself, and not yield it to other institutions of the EU, such as the Commission or Council.[35] This clearly raises the question of how this power should be allocated in a national or regional political entity. Should it be a judicial function or not?

On this allocation point, the EU Court has indicated a willingness to give deference in some cases. The commentary suggests that the Court will sometimes begin an analysis of the treaty effect problem, by examining the treaty itself to see if it calls for direct effect or non-direct treatment. The EU Court seems willing to follow such direction in the treaty, if it is clear enough. This surely relates to an allocation of power rationale. Of course, most often a treaty does not give direction; so then the issue becomes who decides, and what should be the default rule? Or what other elements in the treaty (or involved in its context) should guide the judicial institution? Is implied direction to apply or not?

---

[34] This seems to be Professor Eeckhout's position; see Eeckhout (n 4 above) 343.
[35] Eeckhout (n 4 above) 294–6 argues that express clauses urging non-direct effect (preamble and introductory note) in the Council Regulation approving the WTO Treaty were not determinate. See also Van den Broeck (n 4 above) 415, 440.

An additional dimension to the prior paragraph is the concept (embraced by this author) that absent clear international legal obligation by treaty direction, the issue of how to implement a treaty is really not an international question, but is a question of the constitution and law of the national or regional legal system.[36]

Excellent scholarly analysis demonstrates that there are some 'exceptions to the exception' by which the EU Court, in a situation potentially to deny direct application, will nevertheless grant such treatment. One prominent example, applied to part of the WTO treaty text (anti-dumping in particular), is the Nakajima test for evidence that the EU authorities have clearly declared an intent to apply the treaty language in a direct way. As suggested earlier, in a sense this is almost an 'Act of Transformation' by the judiciary.[37] Another circumstance to 'almost directly apply' is noted in the 'consistent interpretation' situation previously discussed, where the national or regional government must interpret its domestic law, when possible, to be consistent with the international obligations.

These several 'exceptions to the exception' segue into the situation mentioned in a prior section of this work, demonstrating that even if an external treaty is not 'directly applied' (or self-executing) there are a number of effects, maybe not so 'direct' but nevertheless giving the treaty a significant role in the domestic national or regional jurisprudence.

All of these considerations also relate to another dimension of some society's use of treaty direct effect, namely the degree of supremacy which should be afforded to the direct effect of treaties. It is extremely important whether the domestic supremacy of the treaty occurs to trump all or some of the other norms (legislative, regulatory and so on), and most particularly whether the applied treaty trumps even later in time legislation and other norms. It is this latter characteristic of trumping later in time norms which can pose very serious and severe problems for a legal and constitutional order.[38]

IV. Some Perceptions and Perspectives: Thought Experiments Only, or Suggested Ways Out of the Chaos?

The United States and the European Union are the two largest and most powerful international actors which have faced in-depth the problems of domestic role of international treaties. The United States has more than two hundred years of history on this subject, with an elaborate background of court cases and jurisprudence. While the European Union struggles with the subject are more recent, they are more complex and more detailed, partly because they involve an additional 'layer' of government between the nation state and the international obligations and institutions. Indeed, the EU jurisprudence has provided the world of

[36] See Jackson, *AJIL* (n 1 above).
[37] See Eeckhout (n 4 above) 316.
[38] See Jackson, *AJIL* (n 1 above).

international practitioners and scholars with insights that shed light on problems very likely to be troublesome in many societies over time, particularly with some so-called 'emerging' societies of great importance with new major roles in international affairs (especially economic affairs), such as China.

The question of domestic treaty application is really a further application of a much broader subject of the tensions and struggles for coherence and power allocation between the modern nation state and regional government on the one hand, and the international law obligations and institutions on the other hand. In other words, treaty application is a 'devilish detail' that is part of the current evolving ideas about 'sovereignty', some of which are outlined in a 2006 book by this author.[39]

With those transition paragraphs as background, I would now like to explore two areas of thought regarding the subject of this work. First, I will present a brief outline of some specific conclusions about the treaty application conundrum, which we can learn from examining both the US and the EU jurisprudence. These conclusions or summary concepts are, of course, controversial, and clearly more serious scholarship and commentary is needed to add to the already-rich literature on the subject.

Second, I will briefly put forth some suggestions about how governments might begin to think about the subject of treaty implementation, recognizing that the political reality of existing habits and practices may not be receptive to actually embracing any of these suggestions, although articulating them here may contribute modestly to further study and perhaps experimentation.

We can depend on existing literature of excellent scholars, both in the US and the EU, whose works have obviously been influential; but we recognize that to some extent thinking has shifted, and will further shift, and the jurisprudential developments in both the US and EU in the last several decades have provided much more detail and many more examples to better analyse and disaggregate the subject for further developments in the future.

Now, to briefly outline a perception of the policy and reality landscape of this subject, here is a set of propositions for further examination:

(1) There seems to be increasing recognition that the issue of treaty domestic application is really a policy issue or set of issues, and not foremost a juridical issue. Attempts to distinguish between various treaties as to language precision or conditionality, or to regard the nature and structure including nature of negotiation possibilities, tend to miss the point of some of the policies which must be considered. In the US there seems to be considerable development of express legal control of treaty domestic application by political institutions (US Congress and Executive), as seen in legislative control concerning many large trade treaties, or alternatively by reports of Senate bodies in the Senate advice and consent process on treaty ratification. In the EU,

---

[39] See Jackson, *Sovereignty* (n 3 above).

there clearly seems to be recognition expressed that if the treaty itself controls the treaty domestic application, the Courts should follow. Only when such express view is absent should the EU Courts step in. This has major implications for the future jurisprudence.

(2) Express policy control (political and legislative) seems to be a trend, but of course many of the issues will still be troubling, because without express (or strongly implied) control set forth, governments (mostly through juridical institutions) will be required to decide, and therefore a default rule or set of rules can become very important.

(3) Direct treaty effect is a broad subject, which has many variations which need to be recognized. Does the treaty provide for individual citizen causes of action? If so, for what remedy? Annulment? Compensation for damages? Does the treaty provide for other government entities (legislative, executive, administrative agencies and so on) to be invoked (relied upon) in domestic proceedings? In federal nations as well as regional, does the treaty apply so that subordinate government institutions can invoke it? What other variations on the degree of domestic application may be relevant?

(4) Direct effect of treaties can complicate and unwisely constrain governmental institutions and diplomacy, particularly if the treaty applied is deemed to be superior to other norms of the society. In some cases this supremacy may be correct policy (as section II of this work outlines), but in other areas, perhaps especially complex and rapidly changing economic circumstances, the supremacy, especially if it trumps even later legislation or norm-making, may be unwise. There is a danger recognized in 'constitutionalizing' treaty text in circumstances not appropriate.[40]

(5) The nature and structure of a treaty and/or international institution can be very relevant indeed, but not necessarily for reasons sometimes given. The question of possible negotiations for settling or altering norms, or the role of a dispute settlement system in the international institution, does not necessarily pose significant problems to government domestic application. However, the nature and structural characteristics of an international institutional system mentioned earlier such as number of members, number of members involved in drafting the treaty, the length of the duration of the institution, the breadth and extent of treaty norm subjects, can have great significance.

Turning now to some suggestions:

(1) First, recognizing the policy (non-judicial) nature of many of the issues of treaty domestic application can be very important. The more this is recognized, the better the jurisprudence is likely to be.

---

[40] This danger is mentioned in several important scholarly works. See Eeckhout (n 4 above) 301; Von Bogdandy (n 31 above) 50.

(2) One excellent way for such policy to be expressed and be controlling is through an 'Act of Transformation', which 'domesticates' the treaty norms. Such an Act is, of course, possible even for a so-called 'monist' legal system, although it becomes much more significant in a dualist or hybrid system. (It could be argued that all systems are hybrid, because of the devilish detailed complexity of various exceptions, which are developing.)

(3) As indicated above, there is a significant problem with direct treaty application when the legal system grants such a treaty supremacy, especially if the treaty will be supreme over later in time domestic norm-making. In such a case, it seems best that there be a default rule against direct application in all cases. It can be recognized that an Act of Transformation can more precisely address the many detailed issues of policy facing the democratic domestic institutions. Such an Act might, as seems to be the case in Germany, often be simple approval legislation which approves the treaty and mandates that it be applied domestically (perhaps incorporating the treaty text, or at least explicitly referencing the definitive text). Such an Act can also distinguish between private right of action and invocability only by certain government institutions, and so on.

Let me finish with a brief hypothetical case that may better illustrate and focus the real reasons why governments are (and should be) apprehensive to apply some treaties with direct effect. I use the WTO case (and thus conclude that it is wiser not to apply that treaty directly), although the principles clearly have broader application.

Suppose an economic treaty (WTO) has well over 100 members, mostly nation states but also some regional international institutions. It was negotiated over 10 years between more than 100 members, so inevitably there are gaps and ambiguities which become necessary in the negotiating process (sometimes to reach closure and to defer controversies to a later day). It has broad impact and the dispute settlement process with mandatory jurisdiction over all members as to treaty-related disputes. The treaty is sort of a 'constitution' which is designed to last decades if not centuries. Because the treaty is difficult to amend or change rules, there is a certain rigidity about it. Nevertheless, in a globalizing world, economic circumstances change very rapidly. Thus the 'constitution' must be able to evolve, and the role of the dispute settlement system will be highly significant in that regard.

When the nation state (or regional government) provides direct effect for a treaty with supremacy in its legal system, the government may find it very difficult to govern efficiently so as to provide for its constituents and provide remedies for stresses caused by world events including economic ones. In some cases, the national government may discover that a treaty norm prevents national regulatory methods unless there is a consensus among 150 members of the organization to change the rule. Any member can object and break a potential consensus. Of course, there may be some chance for the acting government to 'buy off' the consensus hold-out, but that means the richer nations of the system have asymmetrical power over the chagrin of the majority of members who would be classified as poor.

To the extent that the WTO poses these types of problems, and this author certainly thinks it does, I suggest that treaty application only through one or more Acts of Transformation (subject to amendment by the national or regional legislative processes) would be best, always subject to later legislation or other norm creation. Of course, this sometimes raises the question of 'breach' of the international obligation. It must be recognized that such breach is not excused by the domestic law, so the acting nation or region is subject to such remedies as the international legal system provides. However, in some historical cases such action has motivated important and necessary amendments to the international norms. In addition, many cases may involve treaty language that has sufficient ambiguity to give a margin of discretion to the national or regional action.

To some extent, this suggests a paradox for some of the existing thinking about treaty direct effect. It suggests, somewhat contrary to the language in some opinions, that direct effect is better (less dangerous) when it is used for treaties which are short-term, have relatively narrow subject competence, do not have significant institutions of dispute settlement and compliance incentives and have language that is imprecise and conditional. Paradoxes are often fun, and if thought-provoking so much the better.

PART V
GENERAL ISSUES

22

The European Court, the Brussels Convention/Regulation and the Establishment of an Efficient System for International Litigation in Europe

Trevor C Hartley

I. Introduction

The Brussels Convention[1] – now transformed into the Brussels Regulation[2] – is the greatest achievement of the Community in the field of conflict of laws.[3] It is probable that no enacted text on the general rules of jurisdiction and judgments anywhere in the world has attained the level of sophistication of this instrument.[4] The purpose of this essay is not, however, to discuss the Convention/Regulation – this has been done elsewhere[5] – but to consider the way in which the European Court has interpreted it, and to question whether some of its judgments pay sufficient attention to the necessity of establishing an efficient system for international litigation in the Community. Before discussing this, however, a brief word should be said about the general scheme and objectives of the Convention/Regulation.

---

[1] *Convention on Jurisdiction and the Enforcement of Judgments in Civil and Commercial Matters*, opened for signature in Brussels on 27 September 1968. A consolidated text may be found in OJ 1998 C 27, 1. The Report by Paul Jenard on the original Brussels Convention is published in OJ 1979 C 59, 1.

[2] Council Regulation (EC) No 44/2001 of 22 December 2000 on Jurisdiction and the Recognition and Enforcement of Judgments in Civil and Commercial Matters, OJ 2001 L 12, 1.

[3] Continental readers should be aware that in English 'conflict of laws' means the same as 'private international law'; it should not be confused with the French *'conflit de lois'*.

[4] It is for this reason that it was taken as the model for the project undertaken by the Hague Conference on Private International Law, though this ended up with a more modest convention, the Hague Convention on Choice of Court Agreements 2005.

[5] See, for example, A Briggs, *Civil Jurisdiction and Judgments* (4th edn, 2005); H Gaudemet-Tallon, *Compétence et exécution des jugements en Europe* (3rd edn, 2002).

A. General Scheme and Objectives

The main objective of the Brussels Convention/Regulation is to attain the maximum level of recognition of judgments within the Community.[6] In particular, the aim is to eliminate, as far as possible, the need for any jurisdictional test to be applied by the court asked to recognize and enforce a judgment from another Member State. To do this, the Convention/Regulation departs from the model of a traditional judgment-recognition convention. Such conventions are widespread and many existed between Member States prior to the coming into force of the Convention.[7] Most conventions of this kind are based on the principle of indirect jurisdiction. This means that the convention contains a set of jurisdictional rules. These are not, however, binding on the court hearing the original case: it is entitled to take jurisdiction under the provisions of its own law, but if it does not have jurisdiction under the rules laid down in the convention, its judgment will not be recognized or enforced under the convention. Under this system, therefore, the court called upon to recognize the judgment must check whether the court which granted it had jurisdiction according to the principles laid down in the convention.

This is not the system adopted by the Brussels Convention. The Convention/Regulation is based on what is sometimes called the principle of direct jurisdiction. Like the other conventions, the Convention/Regulation contains a list of jurisdictional rules.[8] In contrast to the other conventions, however, these rules are directly binding on the court granting the judgment: if it does not have jurisdiction under them, it cannot hear the case. This is true even if the defendant has assets in the territory of the court which grants the judgment, and the claimant has no interest in enforcing the judgment in another EC State. On the other hand, the court asked to recognize the judgment is, subject to certain exceptions,[9] precluded from considering whether the original court did in fact have jurisdiction. The result is that, subject to these exceptions, there is almost automatic recognition of judgments among the Member States, at least in so far as questions of jurisdiction are concerned.

The decision to adopt a system based on direct jurisdiction shows that, in addition to the efficient recognition and enforcement of judgments, the authors of the Convention/Regulation were also concerned with the protection of defendants. However, they were concerned only with defendants domiciled within the Community; so the jurisdictional rules laid down in the Convention/Regulation apply only to such persons. Where the defendant is from outside the Community, each Member State is free to apply its own jurisdictional rules as before. However, judgments against such defendants must be treated in the same way as judgments

---

[6] See the last indent of Article 293 (ex Article 220) EC.
[7] See the list in Article 55 of the Brussels Convention.
[8] Title II.
[9] See Article 28, para 1 of the Convention; Article 35(1) of the Regulation.

against Community defendants: courts asked to recognize them are not allowed to apply any jurisdictional test, except in the special cases where such a test may be applied to judgments against Community defendants.

These two objectives, though the most important, are not the only ones. There are also a number of other objectives. The first is to protect the interests of Member States in having exclusive jurisdiction over certain matters. These include rights *in rem* in immovable property, the incorporation of companies and the registration of intellectual property rights.[10] The relevant provisions override the normal jurisdictional rules in the Convention/Regulation; they also override the rule that judgments must be recognized without any jurisdictional test.[11] This means that a court asked to recognize a judgment can check for itself whether it was given contrary to the rules on exclusive jurisdiction. If it was, it must refuse to recognize it.

Second, the Convention/Regulation tries to give maximum effect to choice-of-court agreements, a jurisdictional device of great importance in international business. A choice-of-court agreement may be either exclusive or non-exclusive. Under the Regulation, all choice-of-court agreements are presumed to be exclusive unless the parties have agreed otherwise.[12] An exclusive choice-of-court agreement has two aspects: it confers jurisdiction on the court chosen and it deprives all other courts of any jurisdiction that they might otherwise have had. Other jurisdictional rules are, therefore, nullified: if proceedings covered by the agreement are nevertheless brought before another court, it must decline jurisdiction.[13] On the other hand, however, it is not possible to resist recognition of a judgment on the ground that the court of origin took jurisdiction contrary to an exclusive choice-of-court agreement. To this extent the objective of efficient recognition prevails over that of upholding choice-of-court agreements.

Third, the Convention/Regulation seeks to avoid unseemly jurisdictional tussles between different courts. Since there are a number of grounds on which a court may assume jurisdiction, it is possible that the same claim may be brought before the courts of two different Member States. To solve this problem, the Convention/Regulation provides that if the same claim is litigated between the same parties in the courts of two different Member States, the court seised first gets to hear it; the other one must decline jurisdiction (*lis pendens* doctrine).[14] If the jurisdiction of the first court is contested, the second court must stay the proceedings before it, until the jurisdictional issue is resolved. If the first court decides that it has no jurisdiction, the second court is then free to hear the case; if not, the second court must give up the case.

---

[10] Article 16 of the Convention; Article 22 of the Regulation.
[11] Article 28, para 1 of the Convention; Article 35(1) of the Regulation.
[12] Article 23(1) of the Regulation. The Convention was unclear on this point.
[13] Article 17 of the Convention; Article 23 of the Regulation. There are certain exceptions, mainly relating to consumers and employees, but these need not concern us here.
[14] Articles 21–3 of the Convention; Articles 27–30 of the Regulation.

In keeping with the policy of paying attention only to the interests of Member States, however, these rules apply only where the court with exclusive jurisdiction, the court designated in a choice-of-court agreement, or the courts contesting jurisdiction are in an EC State. If they are in the outside world, the relevant provisions do not apply.

Finally, it should be mentioned that the Convention/Regulation has a policy of ensuring that claimants have a reasonable opportunity of finding a forum in which to bring their claim. Where the defendant is from another Member State, this policy has to be balanced against the policy of protecting the defendant from excessive jurisdiction. Where, on the other hand, the defendant is from outside the Community, the latter policy does not apply. This explains the rule set out in Article 4(2)[15] that, as against such a defendant, a person domiciled in a Member State may, whatever his nationality, avail himself of the rules of jurisdiction there in force in the same way as a national of that state. This would allow a British citizen domiciled in France to invoke the provisions of the infamous Article 14 of the French Civil Code, under which French courts have jurisdiction against anyone in the world if the claimant is a French national. This ground of jurisdiction is expressly outlawed where the defendant is domiciled in another EC state, but it continues to apply to defendants domiciled elsewhere. What Article 4(2) does is to extend its use against such defendants to cases where the claimant is a non-national domiciled in France.

II. The Cases

A. The 'Italian Torpedo'

We are now in a position to discuss our first case. The story begins in 1997 when an Italian *avvocato*, Mario Franzosi, published an article in the *European Intellectual Property Review* suggesting that litigants from other Community countries should avail themselves of the benefits of the Italian judicial system.[16] The feature of the Italian system he had in mind was its notorious slowness. As is fairly well known, and as Mr Franzosi confirmed, the Italian courts take an inordinate length of time to decide cases. It can take them eight years just to decide whether they have jurisdiction.[17] So great are the defects of the Italian court system that Italy has on numerous occasions been condemned by the European Court of Human

---

[15] Unless otherwise stated, references to particular Articles are to both the Convention and the Regulation.

[16] M Franzosi, 'Worldwide patent litigation and the Italian Torpedo' [1997] 7 EIPRev 382.

[17] See, for example, Case C-159/97 *Trasporti Castelletti v Hugo Trumpy* [1999] ECR I-1597, a case decided by the European Court on a reference from Italy. The issue was whether a choice-of-court agreement in a bill of lading should be respected, a matter clearly covered by Article 17 of the Brussels Convention. Nevertheless, it took 10 years for a decision to be reached. Eight years were taken up in the Italian court system and the other two years in the European Court.

Rights for infringement of Article 6 of the European Convention on Human Rights, a provision which grants everyone the right to a fair hearing within a reasonable period of time to determine his civil rights and obligations. The (old) European Commission of Human Rights condemned Italy in over 1,400 reports for this, and by 1999 the European Court of Human Rights had given more than 65 judgments against it.[18] There have been further cases since then: in the year 2000, more judgments were given against Italy on this one question than the combined total of all other judgments against all other Contracting States on all other matters put together.

Franzosi's idea was a clever one. He suggested that persons in other Member States who thought that an intellectual property infringement action might be brought against them could protect themselves by bringing a claim in Italy for a declaration of non-liability. They would argue that what they were doing was not an infringement. They might lose in the end; nevertheless, they could keep the proceedings going for many years, and during that time the rules on *lis pendens* in the Convention/Regulation would prevent any infringement action from being brought against them in any other Member State of the Community. According to Franzosi, it would not matter if the Italian courts had no jurisdiction, since it would take many years to establish this. The result would be that legal proceedings in other Member States would move at the speed of the slowest 'ship' in the convoy – Italy. To continue the naval metaphor, the Italian 'torpedo' (Franzosi's term) would sink any such proceedings. It need hardly be said that this would cause immense harm to the Community legal systems. However, it would be a boon for intellectual property infringers and other bad faith litigators.

In 2003, the matter was put to the test. Thanks to the European Court, the 'torpedo' performed brilliantly. The case in question was *Gasser v MISRAT*.[19] This did not concern intellectual property, but choice-of-court agreements. Gasser was an Austrian firm that sold its product to MISRAT, an Italian company. The parties concluded a choice-of-court agreement, under which a court in Austria would have exclusive jurisdiction over any dispute arising out of the sale.[20] When a dispute arose over payment, MISRAT rushed to the Italian courts to obtain a declaration of non-liability. It also asked for damages for Gasser's alleged failure to act in good faith. In view of the choice-of-court agreement, the Italian courts were obliged under the Convention (the case was decided before the Regulation came into force) to cede jurisdiction to the Austrian court specified in the

---

[18] See the judgment of the European Court of Human Rights in *Ferrari v Italy*, 28 July 1999, available at *http:www.echr.coe.int/hudoc*. According to the Human Rights Court, such breaches 'reflect a continuing situation that has not yet been remedied', ibid 5, para 21.

[19] Case C-116/02, 9 December 2003. For a comment, see Mance (2004) 120 LQR 357.

[20] There was some dispute regarding the validity of the choice-of-court agreement, which was not contained in the original contract, but the European Court decided the case on the assumption that it was valid.

choice-of-court agreement. However, we know that it could take years for this to happen, especially if MISRAT took advantage of the opportunities afforded by the Italian procedural system for delaying matters.

Was Gasser stymied? To find out, it brought proceedings before the Austrian court specified in the choice-of-court agreement. MISRAT objected that the Italian courts had been seised first. A reference was made to the European Court. The United Kingdom intervened in the proceedings and argued that the policy of upholding choice-of-court agreements should prevail over the *lis pendens* doctrine: the court chosen in the agreement should be entitled to decide for itself whether the agreement was valid and, if it was, to go ahead with the case without waiting for the other court to decline jurisdiction. The requirements of an efficient system for international litigation demanded this. This argument was rejected by the European Court. It said that these considerations were 'not such as to call into question the interpretation of any provision of the Brussels Convention, as deduced from its wording and purpose'.[21] Efficiency of operation was not, in the eyes of the European Court, to prevail over the system of the Convention.

The United Kingdom also put forward a second argument. It said that, even if in general the chosen court must wait for the court seised first to give up the case, there should be an exception where the proceedings before the latter were brought in bad faith in order to take advantage of its inordinate slowness. As summarized by the European Court, the United Kingdom's argument was as follows:[22]

61. The United Kingdom Government also considers that Article 21 of the Brussels Convention must be interpreted in conformity with Article 6 of the ECHR. It observes in that connection that a potential debtor in a commercial case will often bring, before a court of his choice, an action seeking a judgment exonerating him from all liability, in the knowledge that those proceedings will go on for a particularly long time and with the aim of delaying a judgment against him for several years.

62. The automatic application of Article 21 in such a case would grant the potential debtor a substantial and unfair advantage which would enable him to control the procedure, or indeed dissuade the creditor from enforcing his rights by legal proceedings.

63. In those circumstances, the United Kingdom Government suggests that the Court should recognize an exception to Article 21 whereby the court second seised would be entitled to examine the jurisdiction of the court first seised where

(1) the claimant has brought proceedings in bad faith before a court without jurisdiction for the purpose of blocking proceedings before the courts of another Contracting State which enjoy jurisdiction under the Brussels Convention and
(2) the court first seised has not decided the question of its jurisdiction within a reasonable time.

64. The United Kingdom Government adds that those conditions should be appraised by the national courts, in the light of all the relevant circumstances.

---

[21] Para 53 of the judgment.
[22] The para numbers in the quotations are those of the original judgment.

The European Court rejected these arguments. It ruled:

71. First, the Convention contains no provision under which its articles, and in particular Article 21, cease to apply because of the length of proceedings before the courts of the Contracting State concerned.
72. Second, it must be borne in mind that the Brussels Convention is necessarily based on the trust which the Contracting States accord to each other's legal systems and judicial institutions. It is that mutual trust which has enabled a compulsory system of jurisdiction to be established, which all the courts within the purview of the Convention are required to respect, and as a corollary the waiver by those States of the right to apply their internal rules on recognition and enforcement of foreign judgments in favour of a simplified mechanism for the recognition and enforcement of judgments. It is also common ground that the Convention thereby seeks to ensure legal certainty by allowing individuals to foresee with sufficient certainty which court will have jurisdiction.

This judgment is the first piece of evidence presented to the reader of this essay in support of the contention that the European Court fails to pay sufficient attention to the necessity of establishing an efficient system for international litigation in the Community. The Court regards the essentially *political* objective of not offending other Member States as being more important than the *procedural* objective of ensuring that bad faith litigants should not be allowed to gain any benefit from abusive proceedings.

B. Antisuit Injunctions

Our next case is *Turner v Grovit*.[23] Paul Turner was a young man who qualified as a solicitor in England. He went to work for Harada Ltd, a company incorporated in Ireland but having its central administration in England. The company subsequently fell under the control of a certain Mr Grovit,[24] who ran a group of companies in the foreign exchange business. Turner's contract of employment as group solicitor stated that he would be based in London or 'as you may be directed'. In 1997, he was sent to Madrid to work at the office of the Spanish member of the group, a company called Changepoint SA. The move was intended to be temporary: he was still employed by Harada Ltd, which continued to pay his salary. The Spanish company paid Harada Ltd for his services.

A few months after arriving in Madrid, Turner discovered that the group of companies was involved in a tax fraud. Money deducted for tax from the salaries of employees was being used to pay creditors. Turner was expected to justify and

---

[23] Case C-159/02 *Turner v Grovit* 27 April 2004 [2005] 1 AC 101; also available at http://www.curia.eu.int/en. For a comment, see Briggs (2004) 120 LQR 529.

[24] Mr Grovit is no stranger to proceedings in the European Court. He was also involved in Case C-68/93 *Shevill v Presse Alliance SA* [1995] ECR I-415; [1995] 2 AC 18; [1995] 2 WLR 499; [1995] All ER (EC). It was one of his companies that was alleged to be involved in the laundering of drug money, an allegation that led to proceedings for defamation in the English courts.

defend this. Since he could not do so, he resigned and returned home. He brought proceedings against Harada Ltd before an employment tribunal in England.

Harada Ltd challenged the jurisdiction of the English tribunal. However, it clearly had jurisdiction. Though incorporated in the Republic of Ireland, Harada Ltd had its central management and control in England. This meant that it was domiciled in England for the purpose of the Brussels Convention, the instrument in force at the time.[25] (If it had not been domiciled in England, the tribunal would have had jurisdiction under Article 5(5) of the Convention, which provides that where the claim arises out of the activities of a branch of a company domiciled in another Member State, the courts for the place of the branch have jurisdiction.) In addition, the tribunal had jurisdiction under Article 5(1), which provides that, in employment cases, the courts of the State in which the employee habitually carried out his work have jurisdiction. Turner habitually worked in England: his employment in Spain was only temporary. The tribunal, therefore, held that it had jurisdiction under the Convention. It found for Turner on the merits: it ruled that he had been unfairly and wrongfully dismissed.

Grovit's response showed the kind of man he was. He brought proceedings against Turner in Spain in the name of the Spanish member of the group, Changepoint SA. These were obviously intended to intimidate Turner and force him to give up his claim in England. The first head for which damages were claimed was Turner's 'unjustified departure' from the company's Madrid office. This was intended to get the Spanish court to reconsider the precise issue already decided by the English tribunal: whether Turner was justified in leaving his work. The second head of damages was that Turner had committed a wrong against the Spanish company by bringing a 'baseless' claim against it in England. This too was an attempt to re-litigate the issues already decided by the English tribunal. The sum claimed, some 85 million pesetas (almost £500,000 at the exchange rates prevailing at the time), was ridiculously large.

Turner could not defend this claim without retaining Spanish lawyers to appear before the Spanish court. Since he was not qualified in Spanish law, he could not represent himself. However, he was already running dangerously short of money. He simply did not have the means to fight a long battle in Spain. Grovit probably realized this.

Turner therefore brought proceedings before the English courts for an antisuit injunction. The trial court found against him: it ruled that antisuit injunctions were contrary to the Brussels Convention. Turner appealed. The Court of Appeal found that the Spanish proceedings had been brought in bad faith. Their sole

---

[25] Article 53 of the Brussels Convention provided that the seat of a company was to be treated as its domicile. It then went on to say that the determination of the seat depended on the rules of private international law of the court hearing the case. Under United Kingdom legislation in force at the time, the Civil Jurisdiction and Judgments Act 1982, section 42, a company had its seat in the United Kingdom either if it was incorporated there, or if it had its central management and control there.

purpose was to vex and oppress Turner. They were an abuse of process. It therefore granted the injunction.[26]

Grovit appealed to the House of Lords.[27] At this point Turner ran out of funds, and was unable even to appear on his own behalf. Fortunately for him, the House of Lords appointed an *amicus curiae* to ensure that his case did not go by default. A reference was made to the European Court to decide whether the Brussels Convention precluded the grant of the injunction.

The case came before an eleven-judge court, which was remarkable for not containing a single common lawyer. The question asked by the House of Lords was whether the Convention precluded the grant of an antisuit injunction with regard to proceedings in another Contracting State, where those proceedings were brought in bad faith in order to frustrate existing proceedings in the Contracting State in which the injunction had been requested.

The European Court held that, even in cases of bad faith, an antisuit injunction cannot be granted with regard to proceedings in another Contracting State. An injunction, it said, constitutes an interference with the jurisdiction of the other court, which is incompatible with the system of the Convention.[28] The English courts were, therefore, forced to rescind the injunction. Grovit had obeyed it when it was originally granted and had discontinued the Spanish proceedings. He did not recommence them when it was lifted. So Turner obtained justice,[29] but the decision bodes ill for future litigants in Turner's position. Thanks to the European Court, wealthy litigants will find it is easier to intimidate powerless opponents. This case is the second piece of evidence presented in support of the contention set out above.

C. *Forum non Conveniens*

Our final case is *Owusu v Jackson*.[30] Mr Owusu and Mr Jackson were both domiciled in England. Owusu wanted to take a holiday in Jamaica and he rented a holiday villa there from Jackson. The agreement provided that Owusu would have access to a private beach. When he arrived in Jamaica, Owusu went for a swim from the private beach. He dived into the water and struck a submerged sandbank. He was paralysed for life. After returning to England, Owusu sued Jackson in an English court. He claimed that there was an implied term in the contract that it was safe to swim from the beach. He also sued the Jamaican

---

[26] *Turner v Grovit* [1999] 3 WLR 794 (CA). The defendants were Grovit, Harada Ltd and Changepoint SA.
[27] Leave to appeal was granted on special terms: if the appeal was successful, Turner would not be liable for his opponents' costs; if the appeal failed, Turner could recover his costs.
[28] Para 27 of the judgment.
[29] In view of Grovit's abusive behaviour, the House of Lords did not require Turner to pay Grovit's costs. Since he had not appeared, Turner had no costs of his own.
[30] Case C-281/02, 1 March 2005 [2005] QB 801.

company that owned the beach and the Jamaican company that was responsible for its upkeep. He said that there should have been a sign warning swimmers of the sandbank. The actions against the Jamaican companies were brought in tort. Since Jackson was domiciled in England, the English court had jurisdiction over him by virtue of the Convention. The Jamaican companies were not domiciled in the Community. Consequently, the Convention did not concern itself with jurisdiction over them: this depended on the rules of English law.[31]

These proceedings put Jackson in a difficult situation. He maintained that there was no implied term in his contract with Owusu regarding the safety of the beach. However, if he was liable, he considered that the Jamaican defendants would be obliged to indemnify him. The latter were parties to the proceedings and he could ask the court to rule on the matter. However, there was a problem. The Jamaicans seemed to have no assets in England. Under Jamaican law, a judgment given against them by the English court would not be enforced in Jamaica unless they appeared before the English court and defended the case on the merits. If they simply walked away, an English judgment against them would be worthless. This meant that if the English court held Jackson liable to Owusu, but ordered the Jamaicans to compensate Jackson, the first part of the judgment could be enforced but the second part could not. Jackson would be forced to go to Jamaica and bring new proceedings there, proceedings in which any finding of liability by the English court might not be recognized. In addition, an important issue in the case was likely to be whether the beach was safe for swimming, something that could best be determined by inspecting it. A Jamaican court could do this; an English one could not. In view of these difficulties, Jackson asked the English court to stay the proceedings under the doctrine of *forum non conveniens* and invite Owusu to bring the case in Jamaica. A reference was made to the European Court to ascertain whether this was permitted.

The doctrine of *forum non conveniens* has long been a bone of contention between common lawyers and civil lawyers. The former consider that it promotes justice by ensuring that proceedings are brought before the most appropriate court. The rules of jurisdiction are too crude in themselves to ensure that this occurs in every case because they focus on only a limited number of factors. Civil lawyers, on the other hand, maintain that its very flexibility leads to uncertainty. They say that claimants cannot be sure where to sue, and that time and money can be wasted through litigation to decide where to litigate.

The case was heard by a Grand Chamber of the European Court. Again, none of the judges was from a common-law country. The Court held that where a court of a Contracting State (such as England) has jurisdiction on the basis of the defendant's domicile (as it had with regard to Jackson), it cannot refuse to exercise that jurisdiction in favour of the courts of a non-Contracting State (such as Jamaica) just because the latter state would constitute a more appropriate forum.

---

[31] Owusu claimed that the court had jurisdiction over them as necessary or proper parties under CPR 6.20(3).

In view of its composition, the Court was hardly likely to accept the common-law approach to the matter; nevertheless, it was disappointing that the practical arguments set out above were dismissed with the curt statement that they were 'not such as to call into question the mandatory nature of the fundamental rule of jurisdiction contained in Article 2 of the Brussels Convention'.[32] This again shows the Court's unwillingness to give sufficient weight to the importance of establishing an efficient system of litigation in Europe.

The reasoning of the European Court was far from clear; nevertheless, the following argument seems to have been advanced.[33] Because *forum non conveniens* is not based on clear-cut rules, it inevitably leads to uncertainty as to which court will be able to hear the case. This is harmful to both the defendant and the claimant. As regards the former, the Court's argument was expressed as follows:[34]

The legal protection of persons established in the Community would also be undermined. First, a defendant, who is generally better placed to conduct his defence before the courts of his domicile, would not be able, in circumstances such as those of the main proceedings, reasonably to foresee before which other court he could be sued.

This seems to be based on two contentions. The first is that a defendant would prefer to be sued in the courts of his domicile; the second is that in any event he would want to foresee where he will be sued.[35] The major flaw in both these contentions is that English courts never grant a stay unless asked to do so by the defendant.[36] In *Owusu v Jackson*, it was Jackson who asked for the stay. So it makes no sense to say that, in order to protect him, the stay must be refused.

The second argument was that the interests of the claimant must be protected. Here the Court was on stronger ground. However, this leads into the major issue in the case. The United Kingdom accepted that the Brussels Convention contains an unwritten rule prohibiting *forum non conveniens*. The question was to decide when that rule applied. The European Court accepted that the Convention applied only in an international situation – a situation in which links existed with another country – but it ruled that those links did not have to be with another Community country: links with Jamaica were enough to trigger the application of the Convention.

It was at this point that the Court betrayed its narrow-mindedness. It was perfectly entitled to consider that the arguments against *forum non conveniens* outweighed those in its favour. However, a more open-minded court would have accepted that there were weighty arguments in favour of the doctrine, arguments

---

[32] Para 45 of the judgment.
[33] Paras 41 et seq of the judgment.
[34] Para 42 of the judgment.
[35] This was simply wrong on the facts of the case ('circumstances such as those of the main proceedings') since Jamaica was the only possible alternative. In fact, it will almost always be obvious what the alternative is.
[36] The only exception is in a situation such as that in *Attorney General v Arthur Andersen, The Times*, 13 October 1987. This is very exceptional and would, in any event, raise questions of *lis pendens*.

that have been accepted by distinguished courts around the world. It such a situation, a more generous approach would have been to limit the ban on *forum non conveniens* to those cases where there is a genuine Community interest. Since the only respectable argument against *forum non conveniens* is that it harms the interests of the claimant, the logical thing would have been to say that the ban would apply only where the claimant is domiciled in another Community State. Where he is domiciled in the state of the forum, or in a non-Community country, the English courts should be allowed to go their own way. The Court's failure to accept this shows a disturbing streak of dogmatism that augurs ill for the future. After all, the ban on *forum non conveniens* is not written into the Convention/Regulation. It is something put there by the Court. It was put there because the Court bases its thinking on civil law ideas. In view of this, it was not unreasonable to expect it to compromise to some extent.

III. The Court

The cases discussed above show, it is suggested, that the European Court does not give sufficient weight to the interests of private law litigants. A possible reason for this is that the judges themselves seem, in many cases, to have no experience of private law litigation. Their biographies, helpfully displayed on the Court's website, show that the careers of many of them have lain in other directions. Politics, administration, diplomacy, academia and public law seem to feature more strongly than the private practice of law. In this, they differ sharply from English judges. This may not be a bad thing where the Court has to decide constitutional questions. However, private law is a different matter. Questions of private law – and conflict of laws is just one matter that falls within this area – are best adjudicated upon by judges with experience in it and whose appointments were based solely on their attainments in the area. It would be nice if such cases were one day to be decided by a special court composed of such judges, a court in which reasonable representation was given, not to Member States, but to legal systems or families of legal systems.[37] Such a court might be expected to fuse the common law and the civil law to establish a truly European system of private law in the areas in which the Community has jurisdiction.

IV. Legislative Reform

Part I of this essay contained a brief summary of the advantages of the Convention/Regulation. Part II showed that it also has its drawbacks. Some of these draw-backs

---

[37] Member States should give up the right to appoint 'their' judge and agree to allow appointments to be made by a Judicial Appointments Board composed of suitably-qualified people.

are the inevitable consequence of seeking unity with a group of states that are mainly members of the civil law tradition – in other words, of membership of the Community. In this final Part, we shall see whether the Regulation can be reformed to lessen its defects. If the proposals put forward regarding *forum non conveniens* and antisuit injunctions seem rather modest, the reason is that we cannot realistically expect our Continental partners to give us any more.

A. The 'Italian Torpedo'

Criticism of the *Gasser* decision has not been confined to British lawyers. Continental lawyers, at least those concerned with commercial litigation, have also been shocked by it. For this reason, a complete reversal might be possible. To achieve this, the following provision should be inserted into the text of Article 23(1):

Notwithstanding Articles 27 and 28, a court specified in an exclusive choice of court agreement to which this Article applies shall not decline to exercise jurisdiction on the ground that a court of a different Member was seised first of proceedings involving the same cause of action and between the same parties.

This would bring the Brussels Regulation into line with the Hague Convention on Choice of Court Agreements, under Article 5(2) of which an exclusive choice of court agreement prevails over the *lis pendens* doctrine.[38]

B. Antisuit Injunctions

It is unlikely that our Continental partners would ever agree to allow antisuit injunctions full effect within the Community. Although the injunction is directed against the litigant, not the court, it might nevertheless seem to be an undue interference in that court's activities. However, cases such as *Turner v Grovit* show that antisuit injunctions can play a valuable role in preventing abuse and oppression. The solution is to allow the court with jurisdiction over the original proceedings to grant a purely temporary injunction that will preclude proceedings in the foreign court just until the latter has had the opportunity to consider the matter for itself. The court granting the order must immediately inform the foreign court. The foreign court will not be bound by the order. It will consider the matter *de novo* under its own law. It may decide to do nothing. Or it may grant a remedy, such as a stay of the proceedings, under its own law. Once it takes its decision – whatever it may be – the original injunction will cease to have effect, even in the Member State in which it was granted.

---

[38] See paras 127–34 (especially 123 and 124) of the Explanatory Report on the Convention, available on the website of the Hague Conference on Private International Law at *http://www.hcch.net*.

The following is a possible text that could be inserted into the Regulation:

Article X

(1) In this Article, 'temporary restraining injunction' means an order by a court of a Member State prohibiting a party, on a temporary basis, from bringing proceedings in a court of another Member State or requiring him not to continue any such proceedings.
(2) A temporary restraining injunction may be granted only by a court with jurisdiction under this Regulation over the substantive proceedings; it may be granted only if national law so provides.
(3) A court of a Member State shall not grant a temporary restraining injunction unless it considers that the legal proceedings in question are, or would be, an abuse of process. If granted, such an injunction shall not be binding on the foreign court and shall be enforceable only in the Member State that granted it.
(4) If a court grants a temporary restraining injunction under paragraph (2), it shall immediately inform the foreign court of the order and of the grounds on which it was based. A party, including the party against whom the order was made, may also inform that court.
(5) When the foreign court is informed of the order and the grounds on which it was based, it shall decide whether or not to take any action. Any such action shall be on the basis of its national law. Once it takes such a decision, and irrespective of what that decision is, the injunction shall cease to have effect, even in the Member State that granted it.

A few comments might be in order:

- Since the new remedy is radically different from a traditional antisuit injunction, a new name is needed: 'temporary restraining injunction' seems a good one.
- The court granting the injunction must have jurisdiction under the Brussels I Regulation over the substance: Article 31 cannot be used.
- The new provision does not grant the power to issue injunctions. This depends on national law; all the new provision does is to grant jurisdiction to exercise the power given by national law.
- If the injunction is granted, it can be enforced only under the law of the Member State in which it was granted; it has no effect outside that state.
- The sole purpose of the new measure is to ensure that the foreign court is made aware of the problem and to preclude proceedings until it takes a decision. The foreign court must, therefore, be informed of the injunction and the grounds on which it was based. If the process of informing it through official channels takes too long, the party precluded from bringing proceedings may inform it. That party will have an incentive to do so – and to do so as soon as possible – so that the situation can be resolved.

- Any action taken by the foreign court – such as a stay of proceedings – is taken under its own law. It does not recognize or enforce the injunction. If it decides to take no action, the court that granted the injunction must accept that.

C. *Forum non conveniens*

We cannot ask our partners to accept the doctrine of *forum non conveniens* as part of their law. However, we can ask them to allow us to apply it where their interests are not involved. To do this, we must first insert an express rule into the Regulation banning its use. Then we can limit the application of that rule. The following new provision could be inserted into the Regulation:

Article Y

(1) Where a court of a Member State has jurisdiction under this Regulation, it shall not decline jurisdiction on any ground for which provision is not made in this Regulation; in particular, it shall not decline jurisdiction on the ground that a court of another State is a more appropriate forum (*forum non conveniens*).
(2) Paragraph (1) shall not apply where, under Article 4(1), the court has jurisdiction under national law; nevertheless, in such a case a claimant domiciled in another Member State shall be treated no less favourably than a claimant domiciled in the Member State concerned.
(3) Paragraph (1) shall apply only with regard to a claimant domiciled in a Member State other than that in which the proceedings are brought. National law shall apply where paragraph (1) does not apply.

Paragraph 1 lays down the ban on *forum non conveniens*, but paragraph 3 limits that ban to cases where the claimant is domiciled in another Member State. Paragraph 2 makes clear that the ban on *forum non conveniens* is also inapplicable when the court takes jurisdiction under national law;[39] if national law gives jurisdiction, national law can limit that jurisdiction – especially when, as in the case of current English law, the rules are excessively wide. However, it would be desirable to have a non-discrimination rule: United Kingdom litigants should not be treated more favourably than those from other Member States.

---

[39] This would occur where the defendant is not domiciled in any Member State.

23

About Rules and Principles, Codification and Legislation, Harmonization and Convergence, and Education in the Area of Contract Law

Walter van Gerven

In a contribution to a series of essays on principles of proper conduct for supranational, state and private actors in the EU, Francis Jacobs offered some thoughts that he wanted to be 'radical and perhaps provocative' on the subject of Community and Member State liability. Referring to the wording of Article 288(2) EC that 'the Community shall, in accordance with the general principles common to the laws of the member States, make good any damage caused by its institutions or by its servants in the performance of their duties', he put the following words in the mouth of a provocative critic: '[there might], especially in this field, simply [be] no general principles common to the laws of the Member States. If there are, they exist only at the level of generality so broad as to be of little practical use... there are crucial differences [that] go to the most fundamental aspects of the subjects: for example the element of fault... In practice the Court has had itself to fashion the principles of Community liability'.[1] The statement refers to extra-contractual liability but would apply as well to contractual liability rules if, in the EC Treaty, there had been, regarding contract law, a similar reference to the principles which the laws of the Member States have in common.[2] However, the absence of such a reference has not prevented a group of experts

---

[1] F Jacobs, 'Some remarks on community and Member State liability' in Wouters, J Stuyck and T Kruger (eds), *Principles of Proper Conduct for Supranational, State and Private Actors in the European Union: Towards a ius Commune* (2001) 129, 129–30. These essays were written in honour of the present author. In his essay Francis recalled our friendly association for many years going back much further than being Advocates General together at the ECJ from 1988–94 – actually to a workshop which Francis organized in London in 1975 on the subject of *European Law and the Individual* (ed. F Jacobs 1976).

[2] On this contrast between the treatment of tort law v contract law in the EC Treaty, see my contribution on 'The ECJ case-law as a means of unification of private law' in A Hartkamp et al (eds), *Towards a European Civil Code* (3rd ed, 2004) 101, 113–21.

in contract law from different Member States (the so-called 'Lando group')[3] to draft two volumes of *Principles of European Contract Law*.[4] These 'principles' are drawn from 'rules' contained in the contract laws of the EU Member States but, contrary to the (unformulated) principles referred to in Article 288(2) EC, they are worded in very precise terms, and structured and numbered in the same way as articles are in a 'civil code'.[5]

I. Rules and Principles

The preceding raises the question: what are principles, as distinguished from rules? A convincing answer is given by Ronald Dworkin, who points out that rules should be distinguished from principles, and principles from policies. 'Principles' refer to the whole set of standards other than 'rules'; they include 'policies' which refer to a 'kind of standard that sets out a goal to be reached, generally an improvement in some economic, political, or social feature of the community'.[6] As for principles proper and rules, they are distinguished in the following terms:

Both sets of standards point to particular decisions about legal obligation in particular circumstances, but they differ in the direction they give. Rules are applicable in an all-or-nothing fashion. If the facts a rule stipulates are given, then either the rule is valid, in which case the answer it supplies must be accepted, or it is not, in which case it contributes nothing to the decision.[7]

By contrast, a principle – like 'no man may profit from his own wrong' – states a reason that argues in one direction, but does not necessitate a particular decision:[8]

There may be other principles or policies arguing in the other direction... If so, our principle may not prevail, but that does not mean that it is not a principle of our legal system, because in the next case, when these contravening considerations are absent or less weighty, the principle may be decisive. All that is meant, when we say that a particular principle is a principle of our law, is that the principle is one which officials must take into account, if it is relevant, as consideration inclining in one direction or another.[9]

---

[3] In 1994 the International Institute for the Unification of Private Law (UNIDROIT) had published its own *Principles of International Commercial Contracts* (1994). The 'Lando' group is so called after its chair, Ole Lando.
[4] O Lando and H Beale (eds), *Principles of European Contract Law*, Parts I and II, combined and revised, prepared by the Commission of European Contract Law (2000); Part III, prepared by the same Commission (O Lando, E Clive, A Prüm and R Zimmermann (eds, 2003).
[5] Parts I and II contain nine chapters on general provisions, formation of contracts, authority of agents, validity, interpretation, contents and effects, performance, non-performance and remedies in general, and particular remedies for non-performance. Part III contains eight more chapters on plurality of parties, assignment of claims, substitution of new debtor: transfer of contract, set-off, prescription, illegality, conditions, and capitalization of interest. Each chapter has an own numbering (following the model of the Dutch civil code).
[6] R Dworkin, *Taking Rights Seriously* (1977) 22.
[7] Ibid, 24.   [8] Ibid, 26.   [9] Ibid.

Thus defined, principles are different from rules in many respects: (i) by their origin: rules are laid down in a written text, which constitutes an 'act of recognition' (in HLA Hart's terminology in *The Concept of Law*); principles do not necessarily find their basis in a specific legal document; (ii) by their wording: differently from rules, principles are not necessarily set out in precise, autonomous and, as to their area of application, well-defined standards; (iii) by their binding character: principles are flexible, binding only as a guideline indicating the direction to go; (iv) by their effect: principles can be used to support a rule or to contradict a rule, or another principle.[10] Principles can be embodied in one word, such as equality, proportionality, fairness, or take the form of a maxim, such as '*Nemo auditur suam turpitudinem allegans*' or '*donner et retenir ne vaut*'. They may be intertwined with a goal, such as free competition, democracy, rule of law, or have different meanings, such as distributive and corrective justice. Principles may have a substantive or a (more) procedural content and, as such, operate on a different level. Thus the principle of proportionality, which will often be used to weigh contravening substantive law principles against one another. In European Community law, general principles have been classified in three categories: principles which underlie the constitutional structure of the Community (primacy and subsidiarity, for example), principles which derive from the rule of law (equality and legal certainty, for example), and principles underlying the fundamental Community law freedoms or policies.[11] They are derived by the ECJ primarily from the laws of the Member States and used by it to refine the Treaties.[12]

Whatever degree of binding character principles have, the basis therefore remains controversial; that is, when a principle is not embodied (unlike many fundamental rights or freedoms), or is not referred to (as in Article 288(2) EC), in a written and binding legal document. In the case of an unwritten or un-referred to legal principle, the binding character thereof is to be found in my opinion – and not unlike customary law – in the sub-stratum of 'law' (as opposed to 'legislation', in Hayek's terminology in *Law, Liberty and Legislation*), that is, in societal behaviour, in a democratic society, on the part of officials and citizens that gives rise to expectations of compliance as to future behaviour – expectations which a court of law may in a concrete case deem to be enforceable between citizens and against officials.[13] In that respect a distinction is sometimes made between '*principes du droit*' and '*principes de droit*', the latter referring to principles which are already part of the law, the former referring to (meta-) principles which are not yet part of the law, but help to define the law from the outside – such as ethical, socio-economic, political and cultural principles (and/or, in Dworkin's terminology, 'goals').[14] Rule

---

[10] J Leijten, 'Beginsel en Tegenbeginsel in het Recht' in *Rechtsbeginselen* (1991) 7–13.
[11] T Tridimas, *The General Principles of EC Law* (1999) 3.
[12] Ibid.
[13] W van Gerven, *De taak van de rechter in een West-Europese democratie* (1977) 8–10.
[14] See, for readers familiar with Dutch, the seminal article of J Gijssels, '"Rechtsbeginselen" zijn nog geen recht' in M Van Hoecke (ed.), *Algemene Rechtsbeginselen* (1991) 29, 42–3.

of law ('Rechtsstaat') and particularly respect for human rights and fundamental freedoms democracy are, for instance, 'principes *de* droit'; whilst democracy, essentially a political concept, would still seem to be a 'principe *du* droit' – however, one which is in the process of becoming a 'principe *de* droit' for being turned into a legal principle in Article 6 TEU, and becoming enforceable in circumstances as described in Article 7 TEU.

It will be clear from the foregoing that Francis Jacobs was right to say, as stated above, that European (like other) general principles 'exist only at the level of generality so broad as to be of little practical use', and that 'in practice the Court has had itself to fashion [them]'. An example is the way in which the ECJ has used the principle that 'the protection of [Community] rights does not entail the unjust enrichment of those who enjoy them' and the principle that 'a litigant should not profit from his own unlawful conduct', in combination with the Community 'principles of equivalence and effectiveness'. Those principles were used to allow claims for compensation to be brought, as a matter of Community law, before a national court by a markedly weaker contracting party against the other contracting party for injury caused to it as a result of a violation by both contracting parties of EC competition rules. Abstract principles are thus transformed by the Court into a specific rule that is to be observed and enforced by national courts.[15]

II. Codification and Legislation

The aforementioned *Principles of European Law*, as prepared by the Lando group, are *rules*, not principles. Moreover, taken together they form a fully fledged European *Code* of Contract Law – or, more appropriate, it would seem, a European Contract Law *Act*. The concept of *codification* is a concept that is characteristic of 'civil law' – as distinguished from 'common law'.[16] The different approach of civil and common law towards the phenomenon of codification constitutes one of the basic differences in style of mentality between both legal systems.[17] By codification is meant here legislation that is, or is drafted to be, part of a larger whole covering a thematically sufficiently coherent subject, and which does not focus on the protection of specific interests, such as consumer, worker or competitor interests, but tries to take a global view of all interests involved. Codification is therefore

---

[15] Case C-453/99 *Courage v Crehan* [2001] ECR I-6297, paras 30–1. See further W van Gerven, 'Private enforcement of EC competition rules in the ECJ – *Courage v Crehan* and the way ahead' in J Basedow (ed.), *Private Enforcement of EC Competition Law* (2007) 19, 35–6.

[16] On codification of European private law, see W van Gerven, 'Codifying European private law? Yes, if...!' (2002) ELRev 156.

[17] On these differences see W van Gerven, 'Bringing (private) laws closer to each other at the European level' in F Cafaggi (ed.), *The Institutional Framework of European Private Law* (2006) 37, 40–5.

'comprehensive' in two regards: first, in that it is conceived and structured as a whole which implies that it normally includes, or is intended to include, more than one chapter of, for example, private law; and second, in that it takes a global view aiming to regulate matters in general, for reasons of legal certainty and consistency, which does not preclude rules focusing on the protection of specific interests from being incorporated in the larger whole. In consequence, to unify the general part of contract law and certain specific types of contract only is not codification in the proper sense of the word whilst unifying large parts of 'patrimonial' law, as referred to hereafter, would deserve that denomination.[18]

Codification of (parts of) *private law* at the European level raises several important issues, such as legal basis in Community law, cost benefit analysis and democratic legitimacy of the decision making process. This is not the place to discuss these issues.[19] It may suffice to say that I do not believe that there is a sufficient legal basis in Community law as it now stands; nor do I believe that the enormous task of codification is worth the price in an area which, like contract law, is primarily of a supplementing nature. As for democratic legitimacy, in my view, codification can occur only with the involvement of elected parliaments in the decision making process, that is, of the European Parliament and, in a matter so close to the citizens, of Member State parliaments. Legitimacy also implies that the Member States' expert administrations (the Ministries of Justice) be involved.[20]

The point I want to make here is another one; that is, that even on the national level – let alone on the European level – codification has, in certain areas of the law more than in others, become a very ineffective legal instrument. An example thereof is the issue discussed at a colloquium held in Brussels at the occasion of the Belgian (and French) commercial code's bicentenary of whether a new code should be enacted.[21] During the two centuries of its existence, the original code of 648 articles has been subjected to a process of progressive 'de-codification'.[22] Of the four books, the third and the fourth – the former on bankruptcy and the latter on commercial jurisdictions – have been replaced by a separate law respectively integrated in a new code on judicial law (1967). The second book containing 278 articles on maritime and inland navigation law is still in place but the chapters on maritime law have been completely overhauled by a large

---

[18] Thus e.g. the Swiss 'Code des Obligations' or 'Obligationenrecht'. On the coming into existence of the Swiss civil code in 1907 and of its separate part on the law of obligations, see K Zweigert and H Kötz, *Introduction to Comparative Law* (1998) 168–71. The admiration for the Swiss code was such, also in Germany, that 'voices were raised in favour of the immediate repeal of the BGB and its replacement by the Swiss Civil Code', ibid, 171.

[19] See further on these issues my contribution (n 16 above).

[20] On how public and private stakeholders (parliament, the ministry of justice, courts and legal writers) were involved in the Dutch codification process, see A Hartkamp, 'Interplay between judges, legislators, and academics. The case of the new Civil Code of the Netherlands' in BS Markesinis (ed.), *Law making, Law finding, and Law shaping. The diverse influences* (1997) 91.

[21] J-P Buyle, W Derijcke, J Embrechts and I Verougstraete (eds), *Bicentenaire du Code de commerce – Tweehonderd jaar Wetboek van Koophandel* (2007).

[22] P Van Ommeslaghe, 'Le Bicentenaire du Code commerce de 1807. Rapport introductif' (n 21 above) 1.

number of international treaties, and also the other chapters have been deleted or, worse, have been left in place although being totally irrelevant. In the words of an expert: 'Belgian Maritime Law... [has] become obsolete, mainly dead law, not realistic, law with many gaps and law that is chaotic and questionable'.[23] As for the first book dealing with 'commerce in general', it is even more chaotic: nothing remains of the initial provisions, all of them have been deleted or replaced by separate texts inserted in the code but having nothing in common. As stated by one speaker in conclusion: *'seul un constat de décès s'impose'*.[24]

As to whether a new commercial code should be enacted, most of the reporters, each dealing with a specific subject, answered with a 'no' insofar as a comprehensive codification was meant, but with a 'yes' insofar as separate legislation, outside a general *Code de commerce*, was envisaged. And, indeed, many separate laws have already been enacted, such as the Accountability law of 1975, the Bankruptcy law of 1997, the Financial Institutions law of 1993, the Land Insurance law of 1992, the Competition law of 1999, the Company law of 1999 and so on,[25] all of them dealing with private law aspects (covering civil, commercial and consumer law) and public law aspects (relating to supervisory and protective devices). Obviously, merging private and public law aspects was not characteristic of the *Code de commerce* of 1807 which was conceived exclusively as a special private law for merchants, and has given rise now to what is called 'economic law' – an area which, moreover, is now the object in all EU Member States of internationalization, Europeanization, consumerization and self-regulation. A direct consequence thereof, especially of Europeanization (in federal states going hand in hand with decentralization), is that legislative power is transferred to a higher (or lower) level and redistributed among several legislatures. This has resulted in none of them possessing the inclusive normative power that is needed to codify a vast area of the law in a well-structured and easily accessible way,[26] and not even to enact specific Acts (and decide related policy issues[27]) in matters, such as company and financial services laws, which are at the centre of the European internal market. Not only does this lead to multi-layer legislation (to be enacted and amended in accordance with different constitutional or legislative procedures), but also to multi-faceted judicial compliance and enforcement mechanisms (such as preliminary ruling systems, often in different contexts)[28] and different methods of interpretation (thus, for example, the method of Community conform interpretation of national laws), some of them more purposive (teleological) than others.

---

[23] Thus E Van Hooydonk, quoted by Marc A Huybrechts (n 21 above) 343, 352.
[24] P Van Ommeslaghe (n 22 above) 17.
[25] See on some of these subjects the special reports in n 21 above of P Van Ommeslaghe, A Puttemans, K Geens, A Bruyneel and I Verougstraete.
[26] W van Gerven, 'Koophandel zonder wetboek. Synthese en slotbeschouwingen' (in n 21 above) 367, 383–5.
[27] See K Geens, 'Tweehonderd jaar vennootschapsrecht in vogelvlucht' (in n 21 above) 91.
[28] For example, in Belgium preliminary ruling procedures exist not only in the context of EU law but also in the context of Benelux law and of constitutional law.

As mentioned, the redistribution of the normative (and judicial) function in private law matters goes hand in hand with the merging of private and public law aspects. That is also the case in contractual matters, as with regard to banking, insurance and financial market services, surety instruments, and related consumer law protection. More specifically, in contractual matters this has the consequence that traditional theories of autonomy of will, bargaining and reliance are no longer the sole foundations of contract law, but are conflicting with more recent principles of fairness and regard for weaker parties. These principles are protected by fully- or semi-coercive substantive rules and often also by administrative regulatory devices and supervisory procedures. The result is that in the EU Member States contract law consists of two separate parts: general or ordinary contract law and protective contract law, the latter not being limited to consumer protection but also including the protection of business customers, individual or corporate.[29] This separation between two bodies of contract law creates numerous problems on the national and the European level which can best be solved on both levels by 'a systematization and integration of protective contract law in the "general" contract law rules'.[30] Unfortunately, such systematization and integration has not been attempted by the Lando group (nor are they attempted by the Study group on a European Civil Code referred to below), with the result that 'a discussion on the political, economic and social implications of contract law was almost completely avoided'.[31] In recent codes, like the Dutch civil code, such integration has indeed been effected as far as consumer law is concerned, and it is regrettable that this example has not been followed and possibly extended to other sub-areas of contract law. That would have made the restatement of 'principles' less abstract and would have paid tribute, through the aforementioned principle of fairness and regard for weaker parties, to the social face of civil law. It would also have resulted in European contract law being less focused on the internal market freedoms, which under Community law are the prolongation of the principle of contractual freedom and autonomy of the will.[32]

III. Harmonization and Convergence

In the foregoing I tried to make the points: (i) that provisions as contained in the Lando group's *Principles of Contract Law* are not principles but rules which are formulated and structured in a code-like enactment; (ii) that, even at the national

---

[29] See further the seminal article of B Lurger, 'Contract and the new principle of regard and fairness' (in n 2 above) 273, 291.
[30] Ibid.
[31] Ibid, 292. On the issue of political stakes in the Europeanization of private law, see MW Hesselink, 'The politics of a European Civil Code' (2006) in a book with the same title edited by the same author, 142, 143–56.
[32] W van Gerven (n 16 above) 170.

level, codification is no longer a self-evident harmonization device, certainly not in an area like economic law, which combines private and public law aspects that have become indissolubly connected to one another, and in which the normative function is shared between different levels of governance; and (iii) that codification of civil law, if undertaken, should not be based exclusively on the principle of autonomy of the will but also on that of fairness and due regard and that, accordingly, general and protective contract law should be integrated in one legal enactment.

I now turn to the next subject: harmonization and convergence. In the initial version of the EEC (now EC) Treaty, the term 'harmonize' was used in Article 99 (now 93) only in relation to indirect taxes. In all other matters 'approximation' was used, thus in Article 100 EEC (now 94 EC), as the generic term for 'bringing together' (*'rapprocher'*) by way of 'directives' those Member State 'laws, regulations or administrative provisions' that, in the absence of approximation, would 'directly affect the establishment or functioning of the common market'. Later – with the incorporation, by the 1987 Single European Act, of Article 100a EEC (now 95 EC) – the term 'harmonization' became used as a synonym for 'approximation' (see Article 95(4) and (5) EC), with the latter term still being used in the title of the chapter that now comprises Articles 94–7 EC.[33] In contrast to the aforementioned Article 94 EC, Article 95(1) EC deals with the approximation through 'measures' (instead of 'directives') 'of the provisions laid down by law, regulation or administrative action in the Member States which have as their object the establishment and functioning of the internal market'. Consequently, whilst approximation or harmonization on the basis of Article 94 EC must occur through 'directives' (binding as to result only: Article 249 EC), 'approximation' or 'harmonization' on the basis of Article 95 EC can occur through 'measures' generally – which can be either directives (leading to approximation of national laws) or regulations (fully applicable: Article 249 EC, and therefore leading to unification of national laws).

Harmonization through regulations or directives is part of the traditional Community method based on binding legislation. However, with the extension of the Community's powers to areas in which the Member States do not wish to abandon too many of their sovereign rights, more instances have arisen in which the Community legislature is explicitly prohibited from harmonizing Member State laws. These are areas in which, in the terminology of Article I-17 CT, the Union may carry out *only* 'supporting, coordinating or complementary action'. For these areas, the institutions may adopt binding acts which, however, 'shall not entail harmonization of Member States' laws or regulations' (Article I-12 (5) CT). Currently, prohibitions of this kind are found in Articles 149 (4), 150 (4), 151 (4) and 152 (4) EC, concerning respectively education, vocational

---

[33] In the original text of the EEC Treaty, the term 'harmonize' was consistently used in the four original languages: '*harmonisieren*', '*harmoniser*', '*armonnizzare*' and '*harmoniseren*'. For 'approximation' less consistent terms were used: '*rapprochement*', '*Angleichung*', '*ravvicinamento*' and '*nader tot elkaar brengen*'.

training, culture and public health. Moreover, in areas where policy takes over from law, harmonization of laws is replaced by coordination of policies. In that respect, so-called 'new modes of governance', namely the open method of coordination and voluntary accords with, and by, private actors, have taken over from the traditional modes of governance embodied in the Community method. It is characteristic of such new modes of governance that they are 'guided by (1) the principles of voluntarism – that is, non-binding targets and soft law, without formal sanctions; (2) subsidiarity – that is, measures are decided by member states or private actors; and (3) inclusion – that is, the actors concerned participate in defining the policy goals and the instruments to be applied'.[34]

The new modes of governance relate mainly to social policies of employment, retirement pensions and social inclusion,[35] where convergence of objectives, not harmonization of rules, is at the centre. The most prominent of these new modes is the above-mentioned open method of coordination (OMC) which was further elaborated by the European Council in Lisbon (2000) and defined as a deliberative and bottom-up form of constitutionalism.[36] Pursuing convergence rather than binding harmonization, the method can also be used by analogy in connection with coordination of national private laws. In that respect, the term 'coordination' is used herein as a concept comprising harmonization or approximation – either through legislation (directives or regulations) or through case law – but is not limited to it. It refers, indeed, to the broader phenomenon of convergence, a generic name comprising both approximation (or harmonization, possibly unification) of laws through an institutionalized (legislative or judicial) process *and* growing together of legal systems as a result of voluntary action, or even spontaneous behaviour, on the part of legislatures, regulators, courts or academic writings.[37]

During the last few decades, the second form of not institutionalized convergence – convergence as a result of voluntary action on the part of public or private

---

[34] A Héritier, 'New modes of governance in Europe: increasing political capacity and policy effectiveness?' in TA Börzel and RA Cichowski (eds), *The State of the European Union* (2003) 105, 106.

[35] On the use of the new modes in the area of social exclusion (fighting poverty), see KA Armstrong, 'Tackling social exclusion through OMC: reshaping the boundaries of European governance', in ibid, 170–94.

[36] On the new modes of governance, see G de Búrca, 'The constitutional challenge of new governance in the European Union' (2001) ELRev, 814–39; more particularly on the open method of coordination, at 823–30.

[37] In the United States convergence in the field of constitutional law is sometimes called 'generic constitutional law'. It has been described as follows:

The interconnectedness of federal constitutional law to other bodies of law illustrates a broader phenomenon of constitutional adjudication. To expound a constitution – any constitution – is to draw upon and contribute to a body of principle, practice, and precedent that transcends jurisdictional boundaries. Communalities emerge across jurisdictions because constitutional law develops within a web of reciprocal influences, in response to shared theoretical and practical challenges. These communalities are at points so thick and prominent that the result may fairly be described as *generic constitutional law*.

DS Law, 'Generic constitutional law' (2005) 89 *Minnesota Law Review* 652–742, 659.

actors, and/or of spontaneous actions as a result of living together within the same communities – has often been used in the field of private law, particularly contract law. Rightly so, because, as mentioned above, the device of codification and legislation is not always the most efficient device. Surely, at the European level, many legislative acts, mainly in the form of directives, have been enacted in the area of private law, but – because of the limited transfer of powers by the Member States to the EC/EU institutions – these acts have 'not been guided by a coherent concept of private law codification...as a consequence of the functional orientation of the specific empowerments laid down in the EC Treaty and their piece-by-piece use by the Community'.[38] Certainly, in the views of some civil servants in the EU Commission and an important number of Members of the European Parliament, codification should have occurred, had it not been for recent case law of the ECJ that has signalled the unwillingness of the Court to find, in the text of the Treaties, a broad legal basis for a European Contract Law, let alone a European Code.[39] As a result of that case law, and of other factors, the Commission has now abandoned its original idea of unifying general contract law, and has opted for what it calls a 'common frame of reference' (CFR), leaving it to the ECJ to analyse the potentiality and the limits of the harmonization instrument as a legislative device.[40]

Before making a few remarks on this common frame of reference, I should emphasize that, within the EU, uniformity of laws, or even far reaching harmonization, must *not* be an objective in itself, as it is not of itself a higher good than diversity. The diversity between the legal families within the EU is so huge (not only with regard to content but also, and even more so, with regard to style and mentalities), and the task to achieve unity so daunting and time and resources consuming, that unification and harmonization should occur only when there is good justification for it.[41] Within the framework of EC law, such justification consists mainly in the necessity to create and operate an internal market with a sufficiently levelled playing ground, requiring therefore the elimination of concrete legal impediments in the Member State laws. More particularly, and apart from the requirement to set aside such legal impediments (which must be specific according to the aforementioned ECJ's case law), there is no general justification to harmonize matters which touch closely on national identity or culture, or other matters of national interest for which Member States are not (yet) prepared to adopt common legislation. To bring those matters closer to each other, more appropriate instruments than the traditional

---

[38] P-C Müller-Graff, 'EC directives as a means of private law unification' (n 2 above) 77–100 with a long list of EC Directives in the annex.

[39] See W van Gerven (n 17 above) 39, n 8.

[40] On this case law of the ECJ, see the exhaustive analysis of K Gutman, 'Case law' (2006) *Columbia Journal of European Law*, 147–86.

[41] Compare Article 151 EC where the Community institutions are invited to 'contribute to the flowering of the cultures of the Member States, while respecting their national and regional diversity and at the same time bringing the common cultural heritage to the fore'.

method of binding legislation should be put in place. The common frame of reference is such an instrument.

It is not clear what precisely is meant by such a 'common frame of reference'. It was proposed by the Commission in its Communication of 2003 which itself was a follow-up of an earlier Communication of 2001 in which the Commission had exposed its ideas about the development of a European contract law. The choice for contract law as a priority for harmonization – and not for example tort law – is not an obvious one, especially so because initially only the general part of contract law was envisaged, which consists almost exclusively of supplementing law and thus constitutes less of a hindrance for the internal market than the more coercive parts of the Member States' private laws, such as consumer law provisions. The latter changed with the 2003 Communication which laid more emphasis on the protective part of contract law, and, more specifically, on the need to turn existing consumer law directives (and implementing national laws) into a more coherent and consistent body of law – whence the common frame of reference. However, confronted with criticism from some Member States, mainly France and the UK, the Commission made it clear in a further (third) Communication of 2004 that its intention is not to use the common frame of reference as a disguised Code on Contract. In the Commission's view, the frame is indeed no more than a 'tool box' with three drawers: in the first drawer there will be basic principles, which contract laws have in common; the second drawer will contain the most important legal concepts; and the third will contain more detailed model rules. To achieve all this the Commission has set up expert networks of academics and of practitioners. In the most recent Communication of 2005, containing the first progress report, the Commission has again emphasized the need to make consumer and other protective laws, the so-called *'acquis communautaire contractuel'*, more coherent and consistent and to use this *'acquis'* as a benchmark for the common frame of reference.[42]

For an outsider it is confusing to know what the common frame is really about. Partly, it is a collection of principles but not rules; a frame but not a code; not binding but soft law meant to stimulate convergence. It is made by academics from different backgrounds who may, and probably do, have conflicting views on what the frame purports to be. Practitioners are consulted but do not seem to play an important role. The frame looks rather bureaucratic and abstract in that it focuses on concepts and principles, not solutions, drawn from different and differing legal environments. It is drafted in one working language, later to be translated – a difficult job – in all other EU languages. As such, the frame looks like a legal explanatory dictionary without indication, it would seem, concerning the historic, political, cultural and linguistic roots from which the items are

---

[42] On all this, see W Heusel, 'European Contract Law – towards a European frame of reference' (2006), special issue on European Contract Law, ERA, 4–7; B Fauvarque-Cosson and W van Gerven, 'La convergence des droits en Europe' (2007), no spécial des *Petites Affiches* 1–20.

drawn. It will be up to legislators, judges, professors and practitioners to select the items which may help them to prepare legal documents of their own choice. The most important asset of the project so far is that it has been able to assemble lawyers from different horizons and to give them the occasion to meet, to enter into dialogue and to discuss matters of common interest. In that regard, the project is an integral part of a vast and ongoing series of initiatives reflected in a growing number of text-, source- and casebooks, legal periodicals and research projects in which birth is given to truly European cross-border legal thinking and practice.[43]

Such a cross-border dialogue between individuals and institutions is indeed the essence of the open method of convergence as applied to European private law. As explained and illustrated at another occasion,[44] this implies non-institutionalized voluntary or even spontaneous convergence on the part of public and private actors as a result of: (i) spill-over from one part of national law affected by EU law into another (related but not so affected) part of the same national law, or from one jurisdiction within the EU into another outside the EU; (ii) mutual monitoring (to avoid collision) and learning (to take over appropriate solutions) between supranational and national courts; (iii) spreading good practices between regulators and administrators, for example to achieve convergence and equivalence between the now 27 national implementations of EU law; and (iv) making teachers, students and practising lawyers familiar with styles and mentalities of the other legal systems through classes at the master, postgraduate and permanent learning level, with the help of appropriate teaching materials that can be used throughout the EU Member States.

In order to steer such an open method of convergence and coordinate the action of public and private actors at the national and European level, it may be useful to draw up an action plan to make the convergence process more visible and more systematic. Such a plan would have two parts, one focusing on practitioners of the law, judges in the first place, and the other focusing on educational aspects. As for the first part, the action plan should contain an outline of how to stimulate judicial convergences through mutual learning techniques, identifying a number of subjects and pilot projects and offering sufficient resources to allow judges and administrators to meet regularly in working sessions, to communicate and to exchange decisions in a common working language, and to look for best solutions – the objective being to compare solutions and find similarities notwithstanding conceptual differences. Obviously, academics should be able to participate; but the emphasis would not be on legislation or law making, but rather on solution-finding in a context of European integration. Such a process is already functioning between national regulators in different sectors, such as competition

---

[43] For an overview see R Zimmermann, 'Comparative law and the Europeanization of private law' in M Reimann and R Zimmermann (eds), *The Oxford Handbook of Comparative Law* (2006), 539–78.
[44] W van Gerven (n 17 above); also B Fauvarque-Cosson and W van Gerven (n 42 above).

law and financial markets law.[45] As for the second (educational) part of the action plan, it should seek to promote convergence in the longer term by developing, in the terminology of Article 149 (2) EC, 'the European dimension in education'; building further on the Bologna reforms by re-organizing the curricula of law schools in a less national and a more European perspective;[46] by revising teaching methods to allow more space for the less doctrinal, more solution-oriented approach in countries where that approach has been neglected; and by developing teaching material that can be used in masters and postgraduate programmes throughout the Union and beyond.

Such an action plan should not replace the proposed common frame of reference but complement it by emphasizing that the 'top-down' approach (that is, the concept- and rule-oriented approach) should be supplemented by the 'bottom-up' approach (that is, the case- and solution-oriented approach) and that legal education should pay tribute to the three major legal systems: the Latin civil law rule-oriented approach, the Germanic civil law concept-oriented approach and the common law case-oriented approach.

IV. Education

Overlooking the Communitarization of national laws and the Europeanization of Community law during the last two or three decades in the sector of private law,[47] it is surprising to see how much attention has been given to, and funds invested in, European codification of private law; and – except for (considerable but casual) exchanges of students and teachers, and for the (to many) market-oriented Bologna project – how little attention and funds invested in European education of lawyers at home; that is, in their own law schools, bars and other professional associations. That will be needed, though, in order to make all lawyers familiar with the styles and legal mentalities of their colleagues from other legal systems, and to encourage the emergence of a truly European legal identity.

---

[45] See W van Gerven (n 17 above) 72–3.

[46] In the words of H Coing, 'European common law: historical foundations' in M Cappelletti (ed.), *New Perspectives for a Common Law of Europe* (1978), 31, 44: 'The curricula of our law schools must not be restricted to the study of national law, and not even to national law combined with a certain seasoning of comparative law. What is necessary...is a curriculum where the basic courses present the national law in the context of those legal ideas which are present in the legislation of different nations, that is, against the background of the principle and institutions which the European nations have in common'.

[47] On the distinction, see my contribution 'Comparative law in a texture of communitarization of national laws and Europeanization of community law' in D O'Keeffe (ed.), *Judicial Review in European Union Law*. Liber Amicorum in honour of Lord Slynn of Hadley, 433, 435. Communitarization of national laws refers to the overturning of national laws inconsistent with Community law and therefore substituting Community law for national rules; Europeanization of Community law refers to procuring for Community law a firm foundation in the concepts and principles which legal systems of the EU Member States have in common (ibid).

As if legal texts were more important than lawyers, documents more important than human beings, preconceived rules more important than handcrafted solutions. And yet, no European civil code is going to stick, and none of the existing national codes is going to be abandoned in favour of a European one, if no such identity takes root in solid ground. For the latter to happen, temporary exchanges of students and teachers, and comparative law classes at home or elsewhere, are not sufficient if students will be taught in the host country, as in their own, by means of basically national law-oriented classes and materials. To implement those, truly European comparative law materials are needed that can be used in all law schools within the EU, also by students who will not go to 'other places', and are preferably drafted in different languages – although, as we will have to accept, primarily in the currently main working language: Esperanto English. I know, and my friends know (more particularly Francis Jacobs, who is a member of the steering committee), that I repeat myself, speaking again of the series of casebooks for a common law of Europe.[48]

Allow me once more to clarify the 'bottom-up' approach of the casebook method by quoting (rather than plagiarizing) myself from an earlier article:

[I]n concrete terms, the different stages of that approach can be described as follows, ... First, material, i.e. judgments in the first place, but also statutory rules and excerpts from academic writings, is collected from national legal orders – as many as possible, but at least one for each of the four large families (that is including the Nordic countries) – and adding relevant material from the two supranational and international legal orders. The material is selected by reason of its similarity in the factual and legal context of the concrete situation, and is grouped around 10 or more selected themes (of the branch of law under discussion). Second, the material is placed in the context of the legal system to which it belongs, identifying the procedural, constitutional and political peculiarities of that legal system, and describing the place that the excerpted material takes in the legal system and the contribution it can make to convergence or integration in the wider context of European integration. Third, the role that abstract concepts, general principles and specific rules play in reaching the specific judicial or statutory solution in the excerpted material is examined and defined, and compared with the role these elements play in the other legal systems. Fourth, the impact of meta-legal or meta-judicial considerations, often of an ethical, sociological, economic or political nature, on the (judicial or statutory) decision-making process is analysed in connection with the excerpted material and compared with the impact these considerations may have on material from the other systems.[49]

Producing and using a casebook is not an easy matter; it is more difficult than it looks, but it is worth the effort. Let me quote again:

---

[48] In the series, a casebook on *Contract Law* has been edited by H Beale, A Hartkamp, H Kötz and D Tallon (2002). Other casebooks in the area of Private Law have been edited: W van Gerven, J Lever and P Larouche (eds), *Tort Law* (2000); J Beatson and E Schrage (eds), *Unjustified Enrichment* (2003).
[49] (n 17 above) 73–4.

[W]riting or using a textbook... allows... the author [or reader] to reach a level of understanding which one does not reach when reading a textbook, however well written it is. The reason is that learning the law through cases helps one to see how rules operate in a concrete situation that looks familiar to the reader because, if the cases are chosen from daily life and, by definition, similar daily life cases exist in all legal systems, they are fully recognizable to him or her. Fully to understand the case, the author and reader will have to cope with the peculiarities of the system from which [it] is drawn. Moreover, [author and reader] must try to familiarize themselves with the legal position adopted, and the arguments used, by the litigating parties, and with the legal reasoning and arguments which induced the court and/or legislator to decide the case or adopt the rul[ing] as it did. That is a question of not just understanding the legal reasoning, but also the underlying interests and value judgments which led the court or legislator to choose one solution over another that could have been reached under a different line of reasoning.[50]

Envoy

In his contribution to the *Liber Amicorum* in honour of the much regretted Henry Schermers, Francis Jacobs indicates that he chose the subject of European Community Law and the European Convention on Human Rights because both Henry and he had been similarly involved in those two species of European law.[51] I cannot say the same thing about the present subject but I can say that like Francis I have been enabled to exercise the same professions: barrister, advocate general at the ECJ and professor of law. Thus, we have both been involved in advocating, judging and teaching. As it is one of my (many unproven) convictions that the opinions of people are more influenced by their profession than by their national background, I would hope that Francis agrees with most of what I have said herein. But even if he does not – as I should hope for the sake of argument – it has been a privilege to write in his honour.

---

[50] Ibid 74.
[51] In D Curtin and T Heukels (eds), *Institutional Dynamics of European Integration*, vol II (1994), 561.

24
The Americanization of EU Law Scholarship

Anthony Arnull*

Americans are overreachers; overreaching is the most admirable and most American of the many American excesses.

GF Will, *Statecraft as Soulcraft: What Government Does* (1984) 98.

I. The Demise of the Doctrinal Paradigm

A. Introduction

When Francis Jacobs became an Advocate General at the European Court of Justice in the autumn of 1988, even he is unlikely to have foreseen quite how profoundly Europe would have changed by the time he relinquished office. The following 17 or so years saw the fall of the Berlin Wall, German reunification and the 'end of history',[1] as well as 9/11 and the start (but not the end) of the 'war on terror'. The Maastricht Treaty subsumed the then three existing Communities into the European Union, whose membership grew from 12 to 15 and then 25 Member States, some of whom replaced their national currencies with a common currency, some of whom were former members of the Eastern European communist bloc. The difficult process of ratifying the Maastricht Treaty triggered a prolonged bout of introspection about the need to 'reconnect' the Union with its citizens. One product of this was the ill-fated Constitutional Treaty, which at least initially seemed to make matters worse. In the United Kingdom, Thatcherism was eventually replaced by Blairism, though some claimed not to be able to tell the difference. During roughly the same period as these momentous events, a radical transformation occurred in the nature of scholarship on EU law,

---

* I am grateful to Anne O'Sullivan and Gordon Woodman for their comments on some of the issues discussed in this chapter. The usual disclaimer applies.

[1] See F Fukuyama, *The End of History and the Last Man* (1992).

at least in the English language.[2] It is with that transformation, not without significance for students of EU law, that the present chapter is concerned.

In the 1980s, much of the literature on what was then known as Community law had two essential characteristics: first, it was essentially sympathetic to the integration project; second, it was traditional in character, 'based on the exposition of legal doctrine and the analysis of judicial decisions'.[3] Both characteristics reflected the backgrounds of the leading authors. Many were officials of one of the Community institutions.[4] Of the academics who had been drawn to the study of Community law, many came from a background in public international law. That was a field in which scholars, preoccupied for much of the post-war period with establishing the relevance of international law to the way in which international life was ordered,[5] had tended to resort to 'a kind of positivist doctrinalism, that is a dry, seemingly value-free analysis of international rules, and, conversely, a general distrust of theory'.[6] To academic writers who belonged to this school, Community law showed what treaties could achieve. As Joseph Weiler, then of Harvard Law School and the European University Institute, Florence, explained:

> In some ways, Community law and the European Court were everything an international lawyer could dream about: the Court was creating a new order of international law in which norms were norms, sanctions were sanctions, courts were central and frequently used, and lawyers were important. Community law as transformed by the European Court was an antidote to the international legal malaise.[7]

Nearly all writers, whatever their intellectual background, 'embraced their subject with something approaching a missionary zeal'.[8] Community law was special 'because the European supranational project was an indisputably good cause, a triumph of rationality over the passions, of common interest over national insularity, and...of law over politics'.[9] The absence of a 'powerful critical tradition'[10]

---

[2] This is less parochial than it sounds. As in other areas, English is becoming the dominant medium of academic exchange about EU law. See J Shaw, 'The European Union: discipline building meets polity building' in P Cane and M Tushnet (eds), *The Oxford Handbook of Legal Studies* (2003) (hereafter 'Cane and Tushnet') 325, 333–5.

[3] F Snyder, *New Directions in European Community Law* (1990) 1.

[4] See H Schepel and R Wesseling, 'The legal community: judges, lawyers, officials and clerks in the writing of Europe' (1997) 3 ELJ 165, 173.

[5] For a review of changing approaches to international law scholarship, see A-M Slaughter Burley, 'International law and international relations theory: a dual agenda' (1993) 87 AJIL 205.

[6] See W Twining, W Farnsworth, S Vogenauer and F Tesón, 'The role of academics in the legal system' in Cane and Tushnet 920, 942. Although the International Court of Justice is authorized by Art 38(1)(d) of its Statute to apply 'the teachings of the most highly qualified publicists of the various nations, as subsidiary means for the determination of rules of law', it hardly ever does so.

[7] J Weiler, *The Constitution of Europe: 'Do the New Clothes have an Emperor?' and Other Essays on European Integration* (1999) 205–6.

[8] N Walker, 'Legal theory and the European Union: a 25th anniversary essay' (2005) 25 OJLS 581, 586.

[9] Ibid.

[10] Weiler (n 7 above) 206.

in Europe led such writers to see their main task as describing and analysing the intricacies of this 'new legal order'. Its gathering complexity made it hard for outsiders to challenge the prevailing orthodoxy.

B. The Winds of Change

The then dominance of the doctrinal paradigm was reflected in the leading student texts in the English language as Francis Jacobs took up office in Luxembourg: Trevor Hartley's *The Foundations of European Community Law*,[11] Dominik Lasok and John Bridge's *Law and Institutions of the European Communities*[12] and Derrick Wyatt and Alan Dashwood's *The Substantive Law of the EEC*.[13] These were all doctrinal works of great authority in the classic English textbook tradition. But by then change was afoot. It was to lead to a radically different intellectual landscape by the time Francis Jacobs relinquished office in early 2006.

It is hard to pinpoint the precise origins of the change, although a famous 1981 piece by Eric Stein of the University of Michigan Law School[14] is often cited as one of its harbingers. Also influential was Weiler's well-known article in the first volume of the Yearbook of European Law,[15] then edited by its founder, Francis Jacobs. The movement gathered pace in 1986 with the publication, under the general editorship of Mauro Cappelletti, Monica Seccombe and Weiler, of the multi-volume series *Integration Through Law*. That series was the fruit of a project, based at the European University Institute, which set out 'to examine the role of law in the process of European integration as seen against the American federal experience'.[16]

A further landmark was the appearance in 1990 of *New Directions in European Community Law* by Francis Snyder, then the holder of a Chair in European Economic Law at the European University Institute. It may be significant that Snyder also works in the field of legal anthropology,[17] which often involves studying the laws of pre-literate societies which may lack access to modern technology. Those who spend time examining the customary laws of such societies are perhaps likely to see legal doctrine as less important than other factors in legal

---

[11] 2nd ed, 1988. See now the 6th ed (2007).
[12] 4th ed, 1987. See now the 7th ed (2001), renamed *Law and Institutions of the European Union*, by K Lasok and D Lasok.
[13] 2nd ed, 1987. See now the 5th ed (2006), renamed *European Union Law*, by A Arnull, A Dashwood, M Dougan, M Ross, E Spaventa and D Wyatt.
[14] 'Lawyers, judges, and the making of a transnational constitution' (1981) 75 AJIL 1.
[15] 'The Community system: the dual character of supranationalism' (1981) 1 YEL 267.
[16] Vol 1, book 1, 3. Francis Jacobs was one of the contributors to the series; see F Jacobs and K Karst, 'The "federal" legal order: the USA and Europe compared – a juridical perspective', ibid 169.
[17] See e.g. F Snyder, *Capitalism and Legal Change: An African Transformation* (1981); F Snyder, 'Antidumping law and cross-cultural encounters: toward a legal anthropology of international economic relations' in C Eberhard and G Vernicos (eds), *Quête Anthropologique du Droit: Autour de la Démarche d'Etienne Le Roy* (2006) 59.

development. *New Directions* represented a sort of manifesto based on ideas first put forward by the author elsewhere.[18] The first page boldly declared:

> So far European Community law has been conceived mainly as 'black-letter law'... Now, however, it is time to draw upon perspectives from other social sciences and to move in new directions. We must place European Community law in its social, economic and political context. Only in this way can we achieve the deeper and broader understanding – both practical and theoretical – of European Community law that is required to meet the exciting challenges of our time.[19]

Snyder and Weiler were among the editors of the European Law Journal, launched in 1995. Subtitled 'Review of European Law in Context' and based at the European University Institute, whose Law Department had always sought to foster a contextual approach to the study of European law, the first issue contained an editorial by Snyder. In it, he announced: 'the journal seeks to trace a new path. The European Law Journal aims to represent a new approach to European law. Its main purposes are to express and to develop the study and understanding of European law in its social, cultural, political and economic contexts'.[20] The same year saw the publication of Jo Shaw and Gillian More's *New Legal Dynamics of European Union*, a collection of essays written mainly by younger UK scholars. Shaw's introduction declared that the collection formed 'part of a trend towards broadening the focus of legal scholarship' on European integration. 'A more significant understanding', she went on, 'of the interaction between law/legal norms and processes of integration/disintegration (in the various guises in which these terms can be understood) within all areas of European studies can enrich work on integration by highlighting the particular empirical and normative visions of lawyers'. The year 1995 also witnessed the arrival of the first edition of Paul Craig and Grainne de Búrca's ground-breaking *EC Law: Text, Cases, and Materials*, described by Weiler as 'both a law book and a book about the law'[21] and which went on to become a best-selling student text.

An editorial published in the European Law Review in 2003 attempted to sum up the change in climate:

> Approaches to the study of EC/EU law are much more varied now than they were when the first issue [of the Review] was published in November 1975. The vastly enlarged scope

---

[18] See in particular F Snyder, 'New directions in European Community law' (1987) 14 Journal of Law and Society 167.
[19] See also *New Directions in European Community Law* 30.   [20] (1995) 1 ELJ 1.
[21] See the back cover of the 3rd ed (2003), renamed *EU Law: Text, Cases, and Materials*. In a review article concerning another work, Richard Abel described a law book as 'a work of legal doctrine. It is a study of the rules which legal institutions apply, or which regulate the behaviour of those institutions': see 'Law books and books about law' (1973) 26 Stanford LRev 175. By contrast, a book about law was 'a mode of *reflection* upon the legal system. Neither legal training nor professional competence is adequate qualification to write about the legal system... For this reason, efforts to understand legal action have borrowed the perspectives of other intellectual disciplines; the social sciences and the humanities have all been used to illuminate legal phenomena': ibid 176 (emphasis in the original).

of the Union's activities has required specialists in a range of other areas to familiarize themselves with the essential features of its legal order... At the same time, as some of the momentous challenges facing Europe have seemed to call for more than just technical legal exposition, so the boundaries between the law and other disciplines, notably political science and economics, have become increasingly blurred.[22]

Potential contributors were advised that '[d]octrinal, theoretical, contextual and interdisciplinary material will find an equally warm welcome in these pages'.[23] The following years saw the publication in the Review of several important theoretical and interdisciplinary articles.[24] In an article on legal theory and the European Union published in the Oxford Journal of Legal Studies in 2005, Neil Walker acknowledged 'the recent development of a more theoretical orientation in the *European Law Review*'.[25]

C. The Contribution of Political Scientists

A contributory factor in this growth in contextual and critical scholarship on EU law was the discovery of the Court of Justice by the political science community following the success of the internal market programme.[26] The political science literature on the Court, and particularly the Court's relationship with the national courts of the Member States,[27] offered fresh and revealing insights into its role in making the Community work. An example is the 'inter-court competition' thesis put forward by Karen Alter, a political scientist. The central claim of that thesis, which represented a refinement of the notion of 'judicial empowerment' developed by Weiler,[28] was that 'different courts have different interests vis-à-vis EC law, and that national courts use EC law in bureaucratic struggles between levels of the judiciary and between the judiciary and political bodies, thereby inadvertently facilitating the process of legal integration.'[29] According to Alter, it was the difference between the interests of lower and higher courts which was crucial. She argued that the preliminary rulings procedure enabled

---

[22] A Arnull, 'The future of the European Law Review' (2003) 28 ELRev 1, 1–2.
[23] ibid 2.
[24] Examples include C Joerges, 'What is left of the European economic constitution? A melancholic eulogy' (2005) 30 ELRev 461; D Halberstam, 'The bride of Messina: constitutionalism and democracy in Europe' (2005) 30 ELRev 775; C Harlow and R Rawlings, 'Accountability and law enforcement: the centralized EU infringement procedure' (2006) 31 ELRev 447.
[25] Walker (n 8 above) 586 (n 27).
[26] See K Armstrong, 'Legal integration: theorizing the legal dimension of European integration' (1998) 36 JCMS 155; D Wincott, 'Containing (social) justice? Rights, EU law and the recasting of Europe's "social bargains"' (2003) 28 ELRev 735.
[27] See e.g. A-M Burley and W Mattli, 'Europe before the Court: a political theory of legal integration' (1993) 47(1) International Organization 41; L Conant, *Justice Contained: Law and Politics in the European Union* (2002); A Stone Sweet, *The Judicial Construction of Europe* (2004).
[28] Weiler (n 7 above) 197.
[29] See K Alter, 'Explaining national court acceptance of European Court jurisprudence: a critical evaluation of theories of legal integration' in A-M Slaughter, A Stone Sweet and J Weiler (eds), *The European Court and National Courts – Doctrine and Jurisprudence* (1997) 227, 241.

the former to circumvent the case law of the latter by enlisting the help of the Court of Justice. It might as a corollary threaten the authority and independence of the higher national courts.[30]

Two English decisions provide support for the inter-court competition thesis.[31] In the famous case of *Bulmer v Bollinger*,[32] Lord Denning MR laid down an elaborate set of guidelines for the benefit of English judges called upon to decide points of Community law before giving judgment. The guidelines seemed calculated to encourage English judges to resolve questions of Community law for themselves and only in exceptional circumstances to request preliminary rulings from the Court of Justice. It is not inconceivable that Lord Denning saw in the Court a potential threat to the capacity of the higher English courts to shape the future development of the law. In the more recent case of *Coote v Granada Hospitality Ltd* (No 2),[33] the Employment Appeal Tribunal declined, in the light of case law of the Court of Justice, to follow a decision of the Court of Appeal which might otherwise have been binding on it. Morison J said that the Tribunal saw the force of the criticisms made of the disputed decision, adding: 'we would go further and respectfully say that we disagree with it'.[34] The Tribunal accepted the appellant's argument that 'the supremacy of the ECJ's decisions would be undermined were a lower court to feel obliged to follow a higher court's decision in preference to giving effect to what the European Court of Justice has determined'.[35] In a subsequent case,[36] that conclusion was criticized by a member of the Court of Appeal[37] and then by a member of the House of Lords,[38] although another member of the House of Lords said he was 'very doubtful whether that criticism was justified'.[39] These cases may be seen as part of an ongoing conversation between the higher and the lower English courts. Underlying that conversation is a recognition on all sides of the capacity of Community law and the preliminary rulings procedure to liberate lower national courts from some of the constraints within which they usually have to work and uneasiness on the part of higher courts about the consequences for their own authority.

It was also a political scientist who offered the most convincing explanation for the variation in the number of references from each Member State. A study of 11 of the then 12 Member States (all except Luxembourg) carried out by Jonathan Golub and published in late 1996 came to the startling conclusion that national

---

[30] See K Alter, *Establishing the Supremacy of European Law* (2001) 47–52.
[31] See A Arnull, *The European Union and its Court of Justice* (2nd ed, 2006) 99–100.
[32] [1974] Ch 401.
[33] [1999] 3 CMLR 334.
[34] ibid 341.
[35] ibid 342.
[36] *Rhys-Harper v Relaxion Group*.
[37] Buxton LJ [2001] 2 CMLR 44, para 23.
[38] Lord Scott of Foscote [2003] 2 CMLR 44, para 203.
[39] Lord Rodger of Earlsferry, ibid, para 219.

reference rates could be explained almost entirely by quantifiable economic factors:

transnational economic interaction, as well as transnational movement of people constitute the underlying determinants of national reference rates. Quantifiable variables such as intra-EC trade, intra-EC agricultural trade and EU foreign residents explain cross-national variation in patterns of judicial interaction between the ECJ and the Member States.[40]

Other considerations, such as population levels, national litigiousness, the number of courts and judges in a national system, knowledge of Community law among lawyers and judges and national legal cultures, did not explain the cross-national variation in the frequency of references.[41] Political science literature such as this gave added impetus to the growing interest among lawyers in theoretical and contextual questions by suggesting new lines of enquiry which involved more than the traditional task of analysing legal sources.

II. The American Parallel

The theoretical turn in EU law scholarship follows a path already taken by legal academics in the United States, where the trend is much more advanced. There are various possible explanations for the change in the character of much US legal scholarship.[42] Its origins can be traced to the early decades of the 20th century and the rejection of formalism, the idea that legal reasoning involved nothing more than logical deduction from first principles or general legal concepts.[43] Formalism came under attack from the legal realists, for whom the law was a tool designed to serve policy objectives. The extent to which it achieved those objectives therefore required analysis. The realist approach undermined what is

---

[40] J Golub, 'Modelling judicial dialogue in the European Community: the quantitative basis of preliminary references to the ECJ', EUI Working Paper RSC No 96/58, 23. See also A Stone Sweet (n 27 above) 55–62 and 98–106; G Tridimas and T Tridimas, 'National courts and the European Court of Justice: a public choice analysis of the preliminary reference procedure' (2004) 24 International Rev of Law and Economics 125, 132–3. Cf W Mattli and A-M Slaughter, 'The role of national courts in the process of European integration: accounting for judicial preferences and constraints' in A-M Slaughter, A Stone Sweet and J Weiler (n 29 above) 253.

[41] One Member State which did not follow this pattern was the United Kingdom, where the relationship between the number of references and economic factors was much weaker. Golub sought to explain the historically low reference rate of United Kingdom courts in 'The politics of judicial discretion: rethinking the interaction between national courts and the European Court of Justice' (1996) 19(2) West European Politics 360.

[42] See Twining et al (n 6 above) 930.

[43] B Bix, 'Law as an autonomous discipline' in Cane and Tushnet 975, 979. In continental Europe at around the same time, a literal approach to the interpretation of legal provisions (known in France as *l'école de l'exégèse*) was replaced by a more purposive approach. See J Bell, S Boyron and S Whittaker, *Principles of French Law* (1998) 34–5; M Lasser, *Judicial Deliberations: A Comparative Analysis of Judicial Transparency and Legitimacy* (2004) 45, 170; S Vogenauer, 'An empire of light? II: learning and lawmaking in Germany today' (2006) 26 OJLS 627, 641.

sometimes called the autonomy of law, the notion that legal reasoning is self-sufficient and does not need to be supported by recourse to non-legal sources. If the crucial question was whether or not the law was achieving its policy objectives, then extra-legal considerations would sometimes have to be taken into account.

Until the 1960s, however, it was not widely thought that 'the keys to understanding law were held by disciplines other than law'.[44] All that was required, apart from a knowledge of legal texts and the ability to analyse and interpret them, was the general knowledge possessed by a reasonably well-educated person with a modicum of common sense. In the 1960s, the shattering of the political consensus caused the law to become 'deeply entangled with political questions'.[45] At the same time, there was 'a boom in disciplines that are complementary to law',[46] such as economics and philosophy. This led to the emergence in that decade of a new type of legal scholarship which involved the application to legal problems of perspectives drawn from other disciplines.[47] If doctrinal analysts of the law identified more with the legal than the academic community, the emerging body of contextualists and interdisciplinarians saw themselves as part of the community of scholars rather than that of lawyers.[48]

The trend towards interdisciplinarity seems to have been fuelled by the culture of the American legal academy. Richard Posner, an academic turned judge, suggested that the most imaginative scholars wanted to be 'innovators rather than imitators' and to 'strike out in a new direction'.[49] Traditional legal scholarship began to seem 'work for followers rather than leaders'.[50] That theme was taken up by Neil Duxbury, who underlined both the advantages and the disadvantages of this development:

What is especially noticeable is the extent to which American juristic culture has emphasized originality and counter-intuitiveness, and how, in the quest to exhibit these qualities, American legal academics – much as they often purport to behave otherwise – have tended increasingly to value legal scholarship by how visible and in vogue it happens to be.[51]

Duxbury acknowledged 'the imaginativeness, particularly the capacity for lateral thinking, demonstrated by some American jurists with interdisciplinary leanings'. However, he went on to remark on 'an astonishing amount of cross-disciplinary chutzpah in the American law reviews. American law professors... are remarkably willing and confident to wander into disciplinary domains within which they have no professional training'.[52]

---

[44] R Posner, 'The decline of law as an autonomous discipline: 1962–1987' (1987) 100 Harv LRev 761, 763.
[45] Ibid 767.
[46] Ibid.
[47] Ibid 772.
[48] R Posner, 'The present situation in legal scholarship' (1981) Yale LJ 1113, 1122.
[49] Posner (n 44 above) 772.
[50] Ibid.
[51] N Duxbury, 'A century of legal studies' in Cane and Tushnet 950, 951.
[52] Ibid 957.

The quantity and quality of interdisciplinary literature on the law may have been affected by the prevalence in the United States of law reviews edited by students, perhaps too easily taken in by fashionable scholarship 'complete with the cute title, the epigraphs, the fusion of high theory and popular culture, and so on'.[53] Posner went so far as to suggest that, while student editors were good at dealing with doctrinal scholarship, their failure to make regular use of referees to help in deciding which submissions should be published, or in offering contributors suggestions for improvement, resulted in 'the publication of social scientific papers on law that should not be published at all, in the occasional failure to publish good papers, and in the publication of papers that would have been improved greatly by the publication process characteristic of academic fields other than law'.[54]

Economics may also have influenced the changing character of American legal scholarship. It has been argued that the increasing demand for legal education in the US made American law schools richer and increased the number of law professors able to concentrate on academic work, to the exclusion of any involvement in practice.[55] It has also been suggested that many doctrinal analysts in US law schools were enticed into practice by a growing disparity in salaries and the expectation of greater job satisfaction.[56] Both views help explain the diminishing number of doctrinalists in the American legal academy and a perceived 'low regard for the practice of law'[57] among many US legal scholars.

The increasingly theoretical orientation of much American legal scholarship, and its variable quality, was attacked by Harry Edwards, another judge and former academic, in an article published in 1992.[58] Edwards criticized 'abstract scholarship that has little relevance to concrete issues, or addresses concrete issues in a wholly theoretical manner'. He had formed the impression 'that judges, administrators, legislators, and practitioners have little use for much of the scholarship that is now produced by members of the academy'.[59] He argued that there was no longer a 'healthy balance' between what he called 'impractical' and 'practical' scholars and lamented the 'waning *prestige*' of the latter within the academy.[60] Support for this view was provided by Brian Bix, who commented: 'Doctrinal work is still done [by American legal scholars], but it has been overshadowed (particularly in "high status" law journals) by interdisciplinary and theoretical

---

[53] Ibid 964. Most academics have a penchant for 'cute titles'!
[54] Posner (n 48 above) 1124.
[55] Twining et al (n 6 above, 931).
[56] See Posner (n 48 above) 1117.
[57] H Edwards, 'The growing disjunction between legal education and the legal profession' (1992) 91 Mich LRev 34.
[58] Ibid.
[59] Ibid 35.
[60] Ibid 36 (emphasis in the original). Posner (n 48 above) 1117–19 gives two telling American examples of lack of respect for doctrinal analysis of the traditional kind.

work of various kinds'.⁶¹ Duxbury concurred:

> By the 1980s, if not before then, this tendency of many [American] law professors to wander unselfconsciously into other disciplinary domains was beginning to demoralize many of their doctrinally oriented colleagues, who felt that regular black-letter scholarship was being undervalued: it seemed that law professors had an incentive to neglect that body of knowledge over which they had some expertise and begin professing on matters about which they had little or no expertise.⁶²

It is sometimes suggested that one consequence of this trend was to encourage the best minds to concentrate on theoretical work, with damaging effects on the quality of American doctrinal scholarship. This is perhaps going too far. It is possible to argue that the quality of American doctrinal work is as good as ever, but that it is no longer as highly valued by the academy.⁶³

III. Is Europe Following America's Example?

A. Nuff Respec'?

European scholars of EU law have clearly travelled part of the way down the path followed by the academy on the other side of the Atlantic. The image of the law professor who writes articles at a high level of generality and has no interest in whether his or her work is of value to judges⁶⁴ will strike a chord with European academic lawyers. Moreover, at least in England, the increasing disparity between the salaries of academic and practising lawyers in some fields and the progressive professionalization of the academy appear to have reduced the number of academic lawyers with direct experience of legal practice.

There is also evidence that the dismissive attitude of American theoretical scholars towards doctrinal analysis has sometimes infected EU law scholarship (to which many American academics, or academics based in the US, contribute).⁶⁵ A well-known example is the response of Martin Shapiro, a political scientist and Professor of Law at the University of California, Berkeley, to a paper by Ami Barav, then one of Europe's leading scholars of European Community law. Barav's paper, he said:

> is a careful and systematic exposition of the judicial review provisions of the 'constitution' of the European Economic Community, an exposition that is helpful for a newcomer to these materials. But it represents a stage of constitutional scholarship out of which

---

⁶¹ Bix (n 43 above) 981.
⁶² Duxbury (n 51 above) 957–8.
⁶³ See Twining et al (n 6 above) 920, 932.
⁶⁴ See Edwards (n 57 above) 36; Twining et al (n 6 above) 930–1.
⁶⁵ The antipathy is doubtless to some extent mutual. Posner refers to 'the well-known hostility of scholars to types of scholarship different from their own, a hostility captured in the adage, "what I do not know is not knowledge"' (n 48 above, 1129).

American constitutional law must have passed about seventy years ago (although remnants of it are still to be found). It is constitutional law without politics. Professor Barav presents the Community as a juristic idea; the written constitution as a sacred text; the professional commentary as a legal truth; the case law as the inevitable working out of the correct implications of the constitutional text; and the constitutional court as the disembodied voice of right reason and constitutional teleology.[66]

Shapiro's remarks are dripping with disdain. Barav's paper is of no value to anyone other than 'a newcomer' to the subject. It represents a type of scholarship which has become almost completely outmoded in more advanced (that is, American) academic circles. The premises on which it is based are absurd.

A more recent example of this attitude, albeit expressed more guardedly, is Shaw's introduction to the 1995 co-edited collection mentioned above, where reference is made to 'the traditional doctrinal paradigm beyond which this essay collection seeks to go – and also, implicitly, to critique'.[67] In 1996, Shaw put the point more forcefully in an article in the Oxford Journal of Legal Studies: 'to describe EC lawyers in the United Kingdom simply as a rather unreflective bunch, and to lump them together unhelpfully under the headlines of black letter, doctrinal, uncritical, atheoretical, unidisciplinary, and so on, is, it is suggested, rather to miss the point... There may be some truth in the criticisms, but they are, at least today, now significantly overstated'.[68] Despite her coyness, the reader is left in no doubt what Shaw thinks of 'EC lawyers in the United Kingdom'.

There are traces of the same mindset in a review published in 2006 of Michael Dougan's 2004 book, *National Remedies Before the Court of Justice: Issues of Harmonisation and Differentiation*. The reviewer describes the work as 'a fine book...wonderfully researched and carefully argued'.[69] However, he goes on to say that the author:

> treats EU law as a legal science which can be deduced from first principles, and which can be filled in with meticulous detail and elaborate analysis. The result is a dense, intellectually worthwhile book, but it is a book in which EU law is stripped of context and history, and any account of such a seminal part of EU law would surely have to take more account of these.[70]

This is like criticizing an apple for not being an orange. The inclusion of sufficient contextual and historical material to satisfy the reviewer would doubtless have made the book unfeasibly large. In any event, many contextual and theoretical accounts of EU law are 'stripped of' doctrinal analysis – indeed, they often stand on the shoulders of doctrinal writers.

---

[66] M Shapiro, 'Comparative law and comparative politics' (1980) 53 Southern California LRev 537, 538.
[67] J Shaw and G More (eds), *New Legal Dynamics of European Union* (1995) 8.
[68] J Shaw, 'European Union legal studies in crisis? Towards a new dynamic' (1996) 16 OJLS 231, 237.
[69] [2006] PL 650, 651. The reviewer was Damian Chalmers.
[70] Ibid 651–2.

Weiler regularly performs this manoeuvre. In his book, *The Constitution of Europe*, he says in the context of the protection of human rights in the Community legal order:

the story of *Stauder* and *Nold* and all the rest has been told so many times as to obviate the necessity of recapitulation. Likewise, of equal tedium is the investigation into the legal basis and formal constitutional legitimacy of this act of so-called judicial activism by the European Court whereby the Court put in place, or discovered, an unwritten Bill of Rights against which to check the legality of Community measures.[71]

Similarly, in his chapter on the free movement of goods in Craig and de Búrca's 1999 collection, *The Evolution of EU Law*, Weiler announces: 'I will present snapshots of some of the most significant cases in the area of free movement of goods, cases so well known as to obviate the necessity of any detailed description'.[72]

This approach is only possible because other writers have conducted the necessary doctrinal analysis. But it absolves theoretical and contextual writers of the need to set out the premises on which their claims are based and thereby makes it more difficult for readers to take issue with them. Readers who are unfamiliar with the doctrinal analysis, or who lack the training necessary to engage with the primary sources, may consequently form an inaccurate view of the law and the way in which legal uncertainty has been confronted. Where such readers are scholars from other disciplines, the result may be to undermine their own work. Consider that of Alec Stone Sweet, a political scientist, on the 'underlying dynamic'[73] of the process by which the Court of Justice developed the Community rules on equal treatment for men and women. Stone Sweet divides that process into three phases. In the first, the principles of equal pay and equal treatment became constitutionalized, thereby encouraging private litigants, mostly women, to bring legal proceedings to secure the replacement of discriminatory national rules with more favourable supranational ones. In the second phase, the Court responded by developing 'a rights-oriented interpretation of the Treaty (and of relevant secondary legislation), which further empowered women, vis-à-vis national governments, within processes government could not directly control'.[74] This led to the consolidation of supranational governance and the erosion of the capacity of

---

[71] Weiler (n 7 above) 108. The reader is referred to another author's work for an account of the doctrinal background. Weiler's use of the word 'tedium' is telling.

[72] J Weiler, 'The constitution of the common market place: text and context in the evolution of the free movement of goods' in P Craig and G de Búrca (eds), *The Evolution of EU Law* (1999) 349, 350. Weiler himself acknowledges the value of doctrinal scholarship. In the first footnote to this paper, he acknowledges his intellectual debt to what he calls a 'Pentateuch' of 'masters', at least two of which are classic works of doctrinal analysis.

[73] See Stone Sweet (n 27 above) 148. Cf *Democracy in Europe* (2000) by Larry Siedentop, a political philosopher. This wide-ranging and otherwise erudite study of Europe's political health was marred by the author's sketchy knowledge of the Union's institutional architecture and failure to appreciate that some of the few concrete proposals he advanced were already being implemented. See further A Arnull, 'Democracy in Europe' (2000) 25 ELRev 465.

[74] Stone Sweet, ibid.

national governments to resist change. There is much of value in this analysis, but a doctrinalist might say that it underestimates the ability of national governments to influence the development of the case law through taking part in proceedings before the Court, particularly references from national courts.[75] Moreover, it perhaps devotes insufficient attention to the capacity of the Community rules, as interpreted by the Court, to achieve substantive policy outcomes.[76]

B. Europe's Distinguishing Features

The Union's diversity and current state of development perhaps make it unlikely that EU law scholarship will travel quite as far down the same path as American legal scholarship. Of particular importance is the range of legal families represented in the European Union, especially the influence of the civil law systems. In Member States belonging to the civil law tradition, the role of academic lawyers is quite different to their role in countries belonging to the common law tradition.[77] In the civil law systems, legal writing (*la doctrine*) is accorded considerable significance by the courts, whose law-making function is not openly acknowledged. Writing about Germany, Stefan Vogenauer remarks: 'This leaves room for academics to criticize and even disregard judicial dicta in putting forward their account of what the law is or ought to be'.[78] Thus, important judgments are the subject of academic commentary which will be taken into account by the courts in the future. In the absence of a doctrine of binding precedent, a critical academic consensus against a judgment may result it its being revisited by the courts.

Legal writing also helps to systematize fields of law, particularly those which have never, or only recently, been codified. As Twining et al explain,[79] when a new code is introduced commentaries will soon appear. These shape analysis of the code before the courts have had a chance to pronounce on specific provisions. Even in areas which have been codified for some time, practitioners routinely turn to textbooks and commentaries for a concise account of the applicable rules and their place within the legal system as a whole.

---

[75] All references are notified to the Member States, which are entitled to submit observations to the Court: see the Court's Statute, Art 23. Member States may also intervene in other cases before both the Court and the Court of First Instance (CFI) (Statute, Arts 40 and 53) and bring appeals against decisions of the CFI, sometimes even if they did not take part in the proceedings before the CFI (Statute, Art 56). See further M-P Granger, 'When governments go to Luxembourg...: the influence of governments on the Court of Justice' (2004) 29 ELRev 3.

[76] The persistence of disadvantage suffered by women led some writers to take a less rosy view of the Community rules on equal treatment and the approach of the Court, sometimes influenced by national governments, to their interpretation and application. See e.g. S Fredman, 'European Community discrimination law: a critique' (1992) 21 ILJ 119.

[77] See e.g. Vogenauer (n 43 above); A Braun, 'Professors and judges in Italy: it takes two to tango' (2006) 26 OJLS 665.

[78] n 43 above, 655.

[79] n 6 above, 937. See also Vogenauer (n 43 above) 630.

In civil law countries, prevailing academic opinion may therefore be regarded 'as a "de facto" or "indirect" source of law with strong persuasive authority'.[80] Moreover, collective judgments and the absence of dissenting opinions mean that individual judges rarely enjoy the same prominence within the national legal community as their common law counterparts. 'Contrast this to the prestigious position of law professors whose names are associated with legal innovations, whose views are widely debated, and who, especially in Italy and France, have close connections to the political sphere and often get elected to the highest offices'.[81] Writing about France, John Bell, Sophie Boyron and Simon Whittaker even go so far as to refer to 'an integrated community between judges and the academic world'.[82] One result is that much civil law scholarship remains largely doctrinal in character[83] and there has been less movement in the direction travelled by American legal academics.

That is not to say that there has been no such movement,[84] particularly in the field of EU law, where the dominance of English has brought civil law scholars into competition with common law scholars for contracts with the top publishers and space in the leading journals. But the gatekeepers of European scholarly law journals are generally academics themselves who will reject fanciful contributions or suggest ways in which they might be improved. More fundamentally, there is perhaps something inherent in the European project that makes it unlikely that doctrinal work in its broadest sense will ever be eclipsed. So much of EU law involves the application of common rules within a variety of national legal frameworks, the replacement of divergent national rules in particular areas with common European standards, the adoption at the level of the Union of principles and values derived from the national systems. These exercises raise issues of enormous doctrinal complexity which call out for scholarly analysis. Reinhard Zimmermann looks forward to the emergence of an 'organically progressive' legal science transcending national boundaries and supplying 'a common legal 'grammar' for discussing general legal questions and evaluating possible solutions'.[85] This is surely more a task for doctrinalists than for contextualists and interdisciplinarians.

The description of the French legal community as 'integrated' is one that might also be applied to the community of EU law specialists throughout the Union, regardless of the legal tradition in which they were trained. Many present and former members of the Court of Justice (including of course Francis Jacobs) held academic posts before taking office in Luxembourg and there has

---

[80] Twining et al (n 6 above) 937. See also Vogenauer (n 43 above) 651–3; Braun (n 77 above) 677–8.
[81] Twining et al (n 6 above) 939. See also Vogenauer (n 43 above) 656.
[82] n 43 above, 36.
[83] See Vogenauer (n 43 above) 657, 660.
[84] See Twining et al (n 6 above) 940; Bix (n 43 above) 981; Vogenauer (n 43 above) 661.
[85] See R Zimmermann, 'Savigny's legacy: legal history, comparative law, and the emergence of a European legal science' (1996) 112 LQR 576, 605; Vogenauer (n 43 above) 662.

been a good deal of movement between the institutions and the academy in both directions at other levels.[86] Moreover, Community officials are regular contributors to the academic literature. Writing in 1997, Harm Schepel and Rein Wesseling, both then working at the European University Institute, observed: 'In comparison to both national public law and national economic law journals, European legal doctrine has been written to a relatively large degree by the staff of administrative and judicial institutions and to a smaller extent by academics'.[87] They speak of 'the dense fabric of linkages between these institutions and the academic community'.[88]

This phenomenon is also noted by Anne-Marie Burley and Walter Mattli in seeking to explain the success of the preliminary rulings procedure.[89] That procedure, they argue, not only served the interests of the Court of Justice, of many national courts and of those seeking to rely on Community law. The empowerment of the Court of Justice through the preliminary rulings procedure simultaneously empowered those who made their living from analysing its case law: 'Here community law professors and their many assistants join with members of the community bar to form a communitywide network of individuals with a strong stake in bolstering the Court's prestige'. The increasing importance of Community law led to growing demand for academics and practitioners specialized in the subject. Such specialists might in due course become members of the Court of Justice and the national courts themselves, some of them returning to academic posts when their judicial terms expired. Burley and Mattli describe this network as 'a neofunctionalist interest group par excellence'.[90]

It is perhaps paradoxical that this degree of integration has occurred in a continent where most law students are undergraduates and the law degree is (still) seen as forming part of a general university education. Although European students are increasingly choosing to study law for vocational reasons, European law schools have not traditionally seen it as the main part of their function to prepare students for the legal profession. One might therefore expect theoretical work by legal scholars to sit more comfortably within the European tradition of higher education. By contrast, American law students are graduates with strong vocational aspirations. As a result, American law schools have traditionally sought to maintain a close relationship with the legal profession.[91] This may help to explain

---

[86] The editors of this volume, all now academics, served at different times as legal secretaries in the chambers of Francis Jacobs at the Court of Justice.
[87] n 4 above, 173.
[88] Ibid 171.
[89] n 27 above, 65. The importance of this factor is acknowledged by Weiler (n 7 above) 196.
[90] Ibid.
[91] See J Bell, 'Legal education' in Cane and Tushnet 901, 902. There are, of course, important differences between Member States of the EU. Bell (ibid 905) points out that, in continental European systems, university curricula are set by universities and sanctioned by the competent minister. By contrast, in common law legal systems, such as England and Wales, university law schools tend to tailor their programmes to the requirements of the professional bodies. This sometimes produces tension as law schools seek to defend their academic credentials.

the hostile reaction in some quarters to the increasingly theoretical nature of much US legal scholarship.

IV. Reasons to be Cheerful

It would be an exaggeration to say that, if America is united politically and polarized academically, at least in the legal field, the reverse is true of the European Union. Nonetheless, while the objective of 'ever closer union'[92] was abandoned by the authors of the Constitutional Treaty,[93] the European legal academy seems more willing than its counterpart across the Atlantic to embrace a range of different perspectives. As a matter of principle, such diversity is widely regarded as desirable. Duxbury, contrasting legal scholarship in the United States and England, crisply observes: 'To put the point crudely, the English have preferred the microscope to the telescope, the Americans vice versa; both preferences can be commended, and both can be criticized'.[94] Bix argues that 'there is now some risk that scholars will underestimate the autonomy of law – not give enough attention to what is specific to law and to legal reasoning. It remains valuable to focus on what is distinctive to law'.[95] There is, he says, 'a measure of autonomy not only in legal reasoning generally, but also some autonomy in the reasoning of each individual legal system'.[96] The multiple legal autonomies represented in the EU are perhaps one of the features that make its law such a rich subject for doctrinal study.

The need for balance is also recognised in the documentation relating to the 2008 Research Assessment Exercise. The Law Unit-of-Assessment is described as including 'all doctrinal, theoretical, empirical, comparative or other studies of law and legal phenomena'.[97] The Law sub-panel announced that it would assess the significance of the research outputs submitted to it 'in a way that takes into account the diversity of academic research in law'.[98] Some of the leading American protagonists in the debate would approve. Edwards, perhaps the harshest critic of the theoretical turn in US legal scholarship, was at pains to emphasize that he did 'not doubt for a moment the importance of theory in legal scholarship'[99] and that 'it is undoubtedly valuable for law students to learn

---

[92] See the preambles to the EC Treaty and the Treaty on European Union, as well as Art 1 of the latter.
[93] The preamble to the Constitutional Treaty referred instead to the peoples of Europe as 'united ever more closely'. Curiously, the preamble to the Charter of Fundamental Rights, in the version included as Part II of the Constitutional Treaty, continued to refer to the creation of 'an ever closer union' among the peoples of Europe.
[94] Duxbury (n 51 above) 972.
[95] Bix (n 43 above) 976.
[96] Ibid 984.
[97] RAE 01/2006 (J) 23, para 4.
[98] Ibid 24, para 18.
[99] n 57 above, 35.

economics or moral theory'.[100] His main point, he said, was that 'pure theory should not wholly displace the production of treatises or articles that, *inter alia*, focus on legal doctrine'.[101] This meant that the law school 'must make itself...a place where scholars of different approaches and ideologies accord each other the mutual respect they deserve'.[102]

Essentially the same view is held by Posner, an economic analyst of law[103] described by Edwards as 'a pioneer of "law and" scholarship'.[104] Posner maintains that '[d]isinterested legal-doctrinal analysis of the traditional kind remains the indispensable core of legal thought'.[105] Indeed, in the early 1980s he advocated action by law schools 'to attract and retain lawyers who will do doctrinal research, a form of legal scholarship whose importance has not been diminished by the growth of other forms'.[106]

The need for catholicity in approaches to EU law is also recognized by prominent theoretical scholars of the subject. Snyder, for example, acknowledges that teaching and research in European Community law should continue 'certain established lines of enquiry. This includes the tradition of highly sophisticated scholarship concerning legal doctrine'.[107] Contextual and interdisciplinary study, he thought, would partly build on this work. Kenneth Armstrong cautions against political science accounts of the Court of Justice 'without law'.[108] Shaw concedes that some of the European studies literature on EU law 'could itself be strengthened by a greater sensitivity to the specificities of the law and of legal norms'.[109]

EU law scholarship in the early part of the 21st century is therefore in rude health. To the established tradition of sophisticated doctrinal analysis have been added the insights afforded by theoretical, contextual and interdisciplinary work. The path traced by American legal scholarship offers European scholars of EU law some salutary lessons. Its boldness and inventiveness are much to be admired; less so its self-indulgence, susceptibility to faddishness[110] and tendency to disparage scholarship for the time being considered unfashionable. If the European legal academy can nurture, and perhaps even integrate, the various scholarly perspectives on EU law, it can make a major contribution to our understanding of the polity which is affecting so profoundly the political and legal shape of Europe.

[100] Ibid 39.
[101] Ibid 57.
[102] Ibid 51.
[103] See Posner (n 48 above) 1115.
[104] n 57 above, 36.
[105] n 44 above, 777.
[106] n 48 above, 1129.
[107] n 3 above, 14.
[108] n 26 above, 158.
[109] Shaw and More (n 67 above) 10. Cf Walker (n 8 above) 588–9.
[110] Duxbury (n 51 above, 964); Posner (n 44 above) 777.

25
The Effect of EU Law on the Italian Courts

Giuseppe Tesauro

I. Introduction

The specificity of the European Community legal system, and consequently that of the European Union, is evident. The object was not only that of pursuing certain common aims together and adapting various legal systems to facilitate the realization of those aims, along with the possibility, consciously accepted by the Member States, of limiting their autonomy. Member States, rather, wanted to make these systems live alongside one another according to rules which could be applied in substitution for contrasting national ones, limiting the full exercise of the sovereign powers of the states through a complex supranational decision-making process. The 1957 Treaty of Rome – as the Court of Justice declared in 1963,[1] and the judgment was never contested – was an agreement which not only created mutual obligations between the contracting states, but realized a legal system of a new kind, in favour of which the states had limited their sovereign powers in limited areas: what is more, the system recognized as subjects not only the Member States but also their nationals.

The heterogeneity of the rules which make up the EC legal system considered as a whole – international rules, Community rules, national rules – required a mechanism which was also new and different in order to manage adequately the relationship between and the cohabitation of those rules, so that it would not give rise to an endless and purely dialectic exercise and to great practical problems, as traditionally happens with the relationship between international law and national law. In addition, there is another characteristic that is peculiar to the Community legal system. Its regulatory acts are applied and made to be applied particularly by the administrations and by the judges of the Member States. This means that the effectiveness and the effect of the Community rules depend to a large extent on the way those rules are applied in the Member States. As a

---

[1] Case 26/62 *Van Gend en Loos v Administratie der Belastingen* [1963] ECR 1.

consequence, the contribution of national authorities and judges in the development and consolidation of the EC legal system has since the beginning been a decisive element in the integration process as a whole.

The result has been that the most important characteristic of the Community legal system does not lie so much in the relationship between rules of different origin as in the mechanism of legal review, which has been created to manage that relationship. The system for providing such review, founded on the continuing intense link between Community judge and national judge, has proved to be the real general instrument for rendering effective and efficacious the Community legal system as a whole. It is not by chance that, when one analyses the relationship between the EC system and the systems of the Member States, one intercepts an important passage in the dialogue between the Community judge and the national one, in particular – where one exists – the constitutional judge. This makes for more stimulating intellectual reflection, to the extent that it allows for a continuous comparison with concrete problems, in the sense that they actually arise, and to test in the field the validity or even just the utility and the reasonableness of certain hypotheses; and to leave at the level of pure academic discussion – erudite, just as stimulating, but sterile – that which does not find a secure anchor in dynamic and real legal phenomena.

The theme, then, of the relationship between the Community judge and the judges of the Member States is not abstract, nor are the roles of the former and the latter regarding the application of Community law confined exclusively to a dialogue at a distance. One thing is certain: the national judge settles the disputes put to him directly, autonomously applying Community law, using the instruments of interpretation which Community case law has to offer him. It is the national judge (or ordinary judge, if one prefers) of Community law who is called on to interpret and to apply the rules, formed outside his legal system. Conversely, precisely along the lines of these Community rules, as interpreted by the Court of Justice, the national judge must interpret and apply, as far as possible, the national rules: this is the principle of conformity, the traditional criterion of application of foreign rules in private international law and which finds its application in Community law with the *Marleasing* case law.[2]

Finally, the precise application of Community law is already expected and at the same time guaranteed by the obligation of loyal cooperation and by the need to respect the rules of living together, as also expressly provided by the EC Treaty in Article 10. In his turn the Community judge cannot help but be inspired in his work of interpreting Community rules by the legal experiences of the Member States. In fact, an automatic mechanism of reciprocal influence of legal experiences may be said to operate, if only because of the composition of the Court, where different cultures come together, thereby contributing to and qualifying the decision-making process.

---

[2] Case C-106/89 *Marleasing SA v La Comercial Internacional de Alimentación SA* [1990] ECR I-4135.

The effectiveness of Community law is also guaranteed by the formal mechanism of collaboration and synergy between Community judge and national judge, namely the preliminary rulings procedure. It is through that procedure that the national judge, following the judgments of the Community judge which he himself requests in order to decide in a just manner the dispute put before him, applies Community rules even in place of national ones, when the former prevail over incompatible national rules according to the interpretation given by the Community judge.

So the role of the national judge during the course of this last half century of Community experience has certainly proved itself decisive. Such a role has inevitably undergone a significant change over the years, accompanying the growth and evolution of the Community legal system. The perceptible increase recorded in the course of the last few years in terms of information and knowledge of Community law, the growing awareness of the Community dimension of the case in point and of the discipline applicable to it, could not but have an influence not only on the solution to the case and therefore on the social impact of law-making but also on the quality and incisiveness of the process of integration taken as a whole. In all Member States, and not only in the ones which have belonged to the Community for a long time, both in quantitative and in qualitative terms, the contribution of the national judge has noticeably grown, assuming an increasingly conscious and active dimension in regard to the process of integration. This is the case particularly when that process has inevitable moments for pause and reflection.

The instrument of cooperation as stated in Article 234 of the EC Treaty remains, then, irreplaceable even in its more flexible applications introduced in regard to the Third Pillar and the now almost 'communitarized' field of Schengen. It stands up to use and to changes in the Treaties. On the contrary, the contemporary quality of the system emerges more and more evidently, if one considers it in terms of *ante litteram* subsidiarity emerging in some cases which are important from more than a purely economic point of view.

The Italian legal system presents features not dissimilar to the majority of Member States, as far as the relationship with the Community legal system is concerned, including the relationship between the national judge and the Community judge. The differences which have existed and exist on the formal level in fact end up nowadays by having no visible importance and by allowing complex results and practices equivalent to other Member States. The presence of a Constitutional Court, with the role of reviewing conformity of the laws to the rules of the Constitution, including the provisions concerning the relationship with other legal systems, guarantees adequate harmony with the Community system.

Besides, if nowadays the level of conformity of national law to Community law is without doubt satisfying, the way this result was achieved was anything but short and today still presents some critical points. It has been a path marked by an uninterrupted dialogue and by answers, even if not in agreement on the theoretical level, at least satisfactory at the level of practical effects. And so it is to some stages in that dialogue that the following reflections are dedicated.

II. The Relationship between Community Law and Domestic Law

A. The Early Cases

In the beginning the relationship between Community law and domestic law was considered in purely dualistic terms and, consequently, in terms of separation between the two legal systems concerned. In this context, the simple ordinary statute which introduced the Treaty into the national legal system and the ensuing secondary Community law was subject to the application of the *lex posterior derogat priori* principle. It was during this time that an ordinary judge from Milan asked himself whether the guarantee of neutrality between public and private property ratified by the Treaty of Rome permitted the nationalization of the body responsible for distributing electricity under a later Italian law. So he asked for a preliminary ruling from both the Constitutional Court and the Court of Justice.

The former gave a reply in the way we have just mentioned, giving precedence to the later Italian law: the violation of the Treaty entailed the responsibility of the state on the international level, but did not deprive the conflicting law of full effectiveness. Essentially, this meant that the state had to fulfil the promises it had made, but within the national legal system the Treaty had the effect which the implementing law gave it. And since the authority of later laws must remain firm, according to the principles of the succession of laws over time, the result was that any conflict between the former and the latter could not give rise to questions of constitutionality.[3]

The Court of Justice, on the contrary, insisted that the Treaty had set up its own legal system, integrated with the national systems, and Member States could not apply inconsistent later domestic laws without breaking the necessary uniformity and effectiveness of Community law in the entire Community, so that a national regulation incompatible with Community law was unable to take effect even if it was later in time.[4] The perspective of the Court, as is well known, was (and more or less remains so today) that Community law prevails over national law by virtue of its own force. This may be considered a monist perspective.

---

[3] Corte Costituzionale 7 March 1964 n 14 *Costa v ENEL*; Corte Costituzionale 27 December 1965 n 98 *Acciaierie San Michele*.
[4] Case 6/64 *Costa v Enel* [1964] ECR 585.

B. Adapting to the Case Law of the Court of Justice

The contrast between the Court of Justice and the Italian Constitutional Court was therefore evident, both on the theoretical and the practical level. But starting from the *Costa* case, the Italian Constitutional Court has given due attention to the issues outlined by the Court of Justice. A fundamental principle of general international law, founded on a solid, ancient basis, forbids the contracting States to an agreement from relying on an incompatible provision of national law, even if it is a constitutional one, as a justification for non-fulfilment of the agreement.[5] The evolution was remarkable. It was brought about in the mid-1970s where, in *Frontini*[6] and *Industrie Chimiche*,[7] the case law of the Constitutional Court began to take account of the importance of the position of the Court of Justice on the unitary nature of the legal system, at least as regards some of its concrete consequences, even at the cost of introducing a measure of flexibility from a dogmatic point of view and despite the inevitable risk of creating some contradictions. For example, the idea of supremacy based on the simple criterion of chronology has been abandoned as a consequence of the adoption of an approach inspired by the division of competence between the Community and its Member States. Indeed, the Constitutional Court maintained its previous position as far as the separation between the two systems was concerned, but expressly arrived at coordination through a division of areas of competence. In *Frontini* in 1973, the Court pointed to Article 11 of the Constitution as the 'solid basis' for the ordinary law which had introduced the Community Treaty and the subsequent binding acts into the system, recognizing the direct effect of the rules. In the later *Industrie Chimiche* case of 1975, the Constitutional Court drew the consequences of the position reached in regard to the relationship between the Treaty and subsequent national laws, stating that the possible conflict became a question of constitutionality with regard to Article 11 of the Constitution which was for the Court to resolve.

The dialogue continued at a distance. At the end of the 1970s, another Italian judge raised a preliminary question, asking whether the obligation to obtain a prior ruling from the Constitutional Court, in order to apply common law in place of the incompatible Italian law, was in its turn inconsistent with the duty to give immediate, uniform application to the Community rules in all Member States. Indeed, on the basis of constitutional case law as previously mentioned, the Italian system did not allow the judge to apply the Community rule in place of the incompatible Italian one, requiring prior examination by the Constitutional Court.

---

[5] Permanent Court of International Justice, Treatment of Polish Citizens in Danzig, 4 February 1932 Ser A/B n 44 p 24.

[6] Corte Costituzionale, *Frontini* 27 December 1973 n 183.

[7] Corte Costituzionale, *ICIC* 30 October 1975 n 232.

The Court of Justice, as is well known, gave a very clear reply in *Simmenthal*.[8] In the first place, the direct effect and the supremacy of Community law require immediate application of the law and deprive subsequent inconsistent national laws of validity. In the second place, the effectiveness of the system of jurisdictional control and the protection of rights would be reduced if the ordinary judge did not have the power to apply Community law immediately and had to wait for a judgment on constitutionality or the repeal of the inconsistent national law. Finally, the Community judge invited the Italian Constitutional Court to reconsider its decisions in *Frontini* and *Industrie Chimiche*, so as better to guarantee the uniformity and the immediate application of Community rules with direct effect.

The reply of the Italian Constitutional Court to *Simmenthal* came five years later with the *Granital*[9] judgment. That judgment represented the full ripening of the awareness of the above-mentioned need. On that occasion, the Court conceived two different paths, and though this allowed for much room for discussion, it was a real turning point in the evolution of the constitutional case law and made a considerable contribution to the development of a problem-solving approach.

As to the first path, the Court, on the consolidated premise that the systems were coordinated though separated, constructed the relationship between national provisions and directly applicable Community provisions as one which lacked any national regulatory diaphragm and was subject to review for Community compatibility by all judicial bodies. That is, the approach taken hitherto in these circumstances, that of examining Community compatibility as a question of constitutional legitimacy, was abandoned. This examination has become, instead, the task of the ordinary courts which may be performed with the assistance of the Court of Justice through the mechanism of the reference for preliminary rulings. The reference to the Constitutional Court by the ordinary courts in order to assess the conformity of the national law with Community law is no longer possible (such references are 'inadmissible'), where EC rules with direct effect are concerned. The only control maintained by the Constitutional Court, confirming an old and well-established reservation (*Acciaierie San Michele*,[10] a sort of Italian *Solange ante litteram*), concerns an important area, defined by legal literature as that of '*controlimiti*' (counter limits): respect for human rights and the fundamental principles of the constitutional order of the State.[11] In this

---

[8] Case 106/77 *Amministrazione Finanze dello Stato v Simmenthal* [1978] ECR 629.
[9] Corte Costituzionale, *Granital* 8 June 1984 n 170.
[10] Corte Costituzionale, *Acciaierie San Michele* 27 December 1965 n 98.
[11] Corte Costituzionale, n 183/1973 (n 6 above):

under Article 11 of the Constitution, limitations of sovereignty are only allowed in order to achieve the objectives specified therein; hence, such limitations, as are clearly set out in the Treaty of Rome, may not entail unacceptable powers on the part of EEC bodies to violate the fundamental principles of our constitutional order or fundamental human rights. Should Article 189 ever happen to

connection, the relationship between national provisions and Community provisions again becomes a problem of constitutionality and falls, therefore, within the exclusive jurisdiction of the Constitutional Court.[12]

The second path still involves the theory of the control of Community compatibility as a problem of constitutionality. This path concerns, above all, the relationship between national provisions and Community provisions without direct effect.[13] It also relates to all cases of direct access to the Constitutional Court, when the Court has to decide cases like any other court, for instance in cases of conflict between the regions and central government.

On the whole, some significant and now well-established points of principle may be identified. These include: a) the separation between Community law and national law, expressing a quite clear intention not to nationalize Community law, considering also the fact that its origin and context has been identified by the Court of Justice and never denied as international law;[14] b) recognition of the specific nature of Community law and of its most distinctive special characteristics, such as the direct effect of many provisions of the Treaties or Community acts and their primacy in case of conflict with national provisions; c) the need to maintain constitutional review in relation to respect for fundamental rights and the basic principles of the national constitutional order. The theoretical dichotomy between dualism and monism seems today to be less important and without significant consequences on the practical level.

C. The Use of the Preliminary Rulings Procedure by the Constitutional Court

In the Constitutional Court case law there is an unresolved problem concerning the use by the Court of the preliminary rulings procedure under Article 234 of the EC Treaty. In general, the academic literature is for the most part favourable, considering it a very useful instrument for dialogue. In the past[15] the Court had not excluded the possibility of a reference for a preliminary

---

be given such an erroneous interpretation, this Court would still be empowered to assess the compatibility between the Treaty and the fundamental principles referred to above.

Corte Costituzionale 170/1984 (n 9 above); Corte Costituzionale, *Fragd* 21 April 1989 n 232/1989; Corte Costituzionale, *Messaggero Servizi* 15 December 1995 n 536.

[12] Corte Costituzionale n 170/1984 (n 9 above); Corte Costituzionale, 27 December 2006 Order n 454:

national courts may refer the question of compatibility with Community law to this Court in respect of such provisions as are aimed at preventing or jeopardizing compliance on a continuing basis with the Treaty (*viz* with the system or with its core principles) in two cases: i) when consistent interpretation is not possible, or ii) when non-application of domestic provisions entails a conflict – which the Constitutional Court alone can establish – with the fundamental principles of our Constitutional order or with fundamental human rights.

[13] Corte Costituzionale 170/1984 (n 9 above).
[14] Case 26/62 (n 1 above) 12: 'the Community constitutes a new legal order of international law'.
[15] Corte Costituzionale, *Giampaoli* 18 April 1991 n 168.

ruling pursuant to Article 234, although this task was sometimes remitted to the referring court. Subsequently the Court excluded this possibility, specifying that, contrary to what had been suggested in a very old judgment (which had nothing to do with EC law), the Constitutional Court cannot refer to the Court of Justice, as the former 'in essence exercises a power of constitutional review and constitutes the ultimate guarantee of compliance with the Constitution of the Republic on the part of the state and regional bodies provided for in the Constitution'.[16]

The Constitutional Court bases its negative approach on a internal notion of 'court or tribunal' to exclude itself from the corresponding notion in Article 234 of the Treaty, thereby depriving itself of the power to make references to the Court of Justice. However, it has always been clear that the notion of 'court or tribunal' is a Community notion, to be defined on the basis of the interpretation of Article 234, which incontrovertibly is the concern of the Court of Justice. And on the basis of the case law of the Court of Justice, there is no doubt that the Italian Constitutional Court has all the subjective prerequisites for preliminary references. Therefore, where a question of constitutionality is referred to the Constitutional Court by an ordinary judge, one could reasonably maintain that the Constitutional Court does not 'give judgment' on the principal case, this being the responsibility of the ordinary judge, who has the power (or the obligation) to make a reference to the Court of Justice. However, this is less convincing where there is a direct appeal to the Constitutional Court, for example in conflicts between the state and the regions. In this situation, the Constitutional Court is the sole judge and decides the dispute alone and consequently has the obligation to refer the case to Luxembourg for interpretation or examination of the validity of a Community rule.

There still remains a desire not to be part of a relationship which rightly or wrongly is considered to be in substance a hierarchical subordination to the Court of Justice. This really seems to be the greater obstacle – psychological rather than legal – to the use of a mechanism of cooperation which has had so much success for the purposes of the development of the Community legal system. The problem is naturally misconceived, insofar as the relationship with the Court of Justice has never been, for any judge of a Member State, a hierarchical one, rather one of simple, honest cooperation, respecting the division of competence defined by the Treaty. On the other hand, the Constitutional Court is depriving itself in this way of the possibility of contributing to the interpretation of the Community rules in the light of its own reading of those rules, thus rendering the values of its own legal system less important. This is particularly true in the field of fundamental rights, which form such an important part of the case law of both the Constitutional Courts of Member States and the Community judges.

[16] Corte Costituzionale, *Messaggero Servizi* (n 11 above).

D. An Assessment

The overall trend of the case law of the Constitutional Court has remained substantially unchanged during the course of the last 20 years, with just a few further small refinements.[17] The consolidation and the stability of the case law of the constitutional judges has also influenced the case law of ordinary judges who have, generally speaking, followed that case law promptly. On the other hand, the same mechanism of preliminary referral, confirming its function of guaranteeing uniformity in the application of Community law, is contributing to the widespread adaptation of the national legal system to the legal system of the Community. If, then, there is criticism in some passages of the case law of Italian judges, any deviations are really exceptional individual oversights or historical curiosities; in any case they are destined sooner or later to be absorbed.[18] So the fact that Italian judges have contributed significantly to the development and the consolidation of the Community legal system through many preliminary references to the Court of Justice is self-evident: one only has to think of fundamental developments in the case law of the Court, from *Costa*[19] to *Simmenthal*,[20] from *Francovich*[21] to *Fratelli Costanzo*,[22] from *Consorzio Industrie Fiammiferi*[23] to *Traghetti Mediterraneo*.[24]

---

[17] Corte Costituzionale, no 454/06 (n 12 above). On this occasion, the Constitutional Court held, in a sort of abstract of its case law, that the question of compatibility between Italian rules and directly effective Community rules has a logical and legal priority over the review of constitutionality; that, pursuant to Article 11 of the Constitution, national courts must give full and immediate effect to directly effective Community provisions and must not apply, in whole or in part, such national provisions as are incompatible with the latter, if necessary following a reference for a preliminary ruling to the Court of Justice under Article 234 of the EC Treaty; that national courts may refer the question of compatibility with Community law to this Court in respect of such provisions as are aimed at preventing or jeopardizing compliance on a continuing basis with the Treaty (viz. with the system or with its core principles) in two cases: i) when consistent interpretation is not possible, or ii) when non-application of a domestic provision entails a conflict – which the Constitutional Court alone can establish – with the fundamental principles of our Constitutional order or with fundamental rights. More recently Corte Costituzionale, 13 July 2007 n 284.

[18] The Council of State, V Sect 8 August 2005 n 4207, which had in general demonstrated an adequate knowledge of the problems and an evident willingness to enter into a dialogue with the Court of Justice, fell into error, too clamorous to give rise to serious concern regarding the case law of the leaders of administrative justice. The judgment in question even denied direct effect to rules which without any doubt possessed that quality, such as the provisions of the Treaty on the ban on discrimination based on nationality, the right to settle and the free movement of workers. What is more, it has used the category of constitutional counter limits to justify a breach of Community rules, as such control is within the exclusive jurisdiction of the Constitutional Court. There has been a strong critical reaction on the part of more knowledgeable commentators: A Barone, 'On the Federfarma Judgment: between Community and constitutional protection of fundamental rights the Consiglio di Stato lost its way' (2006) Il diritto dell'Unione Europea 201.

[19] n 4 above.

[20] n 8 above.

[21] Joined Cases C-6/90 and C-9/90 *Francovich and Bonifaci v Italy* [1991] ECR I-5537.

[22] Case 103/88 *Fratelli Costanzo v Comune di Milano* [1989] ECR 1839.

[23] Case C-198/01 *Consorzio Industrie Fiammiferi v Autorità Garante Concorrenza e Mercato* [2003] ECR I-8055.

[24] Case C-173/03 *Traghetti del Mediterraneo* [2006] ECR I-5177.

III. Substantive and Procedural Law

A. Competition

The sector which has most rapidly adapted to the case law of the Court of Justice is competition. There are two elements which have contributed to the necessary synthesizing of national and Community practice relevant to competition. The first is that until 1990 national rules specific to competition did not exist; and the Civil Code rules on unfair competition were clearly unsuitable. The only competition law in existence was Community law – Articles 81, 82, and 86 of the EC Treaty, as well as the 1989 Merger Regulation – so it was self-evident that the Community case law would be utilized and followed by the Italian judges. The harmony with the case law of the Court of Justice was, in other words, natural, much more so because EC rules were, for the most part, of direct effect. There were many difficulties since the culture of the free market in Italy, as in other Member States, was not widely established and the structure of the country's economy was characterized by a strong state presence, not only as regulator, but as an actor as well, with many and various exclusive rights.

The second element was law 287 (1990), which introduced an organic discipline of competition. It was actually nothing more than a photocopy of the Treaty provisions and the Merger Regulation. Moreover, to strengthen the connection with the Community rules, the law expressly spelled out the obligation of the administrative authority and the judge to apply its provisions in conformity with the practice of the Commission and the Court of Justice. So the *Marleasing* principle was ratified formally in the law, a kind of a specific application of the loyal cooperation principle that one finds in Article 10 of the Treaty.

The two elements just mentioned concerned the Antitrust Authority created by the law and the Administrative Judge (Tribunale Amministrativo del Lazio and Consiglio di Stato), which was given the power to review decisions of the Authority. So the case law of the Commission and the Court of Justice is copiously recalled in the administrative measures, as well as in the judgments. And even where there was an initial difference in approach, in a short time it was nullified. It seems useful to give some examples of this marked evolution, which also concerns the instrumental notions of the Treaty and of the Italian law, such as undertaking, agreement and abuse of dominant position.

(i) *Undertakings*

It quickly became evident that the notion of an undertaking subject to competition rules would have to be a specific one, not necessarily corresponding to that dictated by the Civil Code. In fact, according to the case law of the Luxembourg Courts, in the context of competition law, the notion of undertaking includes any entity which is engaged in some economic activity, irrespective of its legal status and the source of its funding; the circumstances in which activities are entrusted to public bodies does not prevent such activities from being considered economic in nature.

When the Italian antitrust legislation was first applied, this approach, which was not in tune with the Italian legal tradition, became established following numerous proceedings carried out by the Antitrust Authority relevant to individuals categorized as 'undertakings' precisely because of the economic nature of the activity carried out and the corresponding Community notions. This approach was confirmed by the administrative tribunal and the Council of State. The Authority, supported by the administrative judges, therefore treats even lawyers and other independent professionals as subject to competition law.[25]

(ii) Agreements

Another significant example concerns the notion of agreement. Initially, the administrative judge took a very formal civil law approach, in the sense that one could not take into consideration an agreement between companies when the respective agents did not present a specific authorisation to act, signed by legal representatives of the companies involved.[26] Subsequently, the Council of State affirmed, following the case law of the Court of Justice, that an anti-competitive agreement may well be a simple meeting of minds, however manifested, provided that one could implicitly infer such an agreement from the conduct of the parties on the market.[27]

(iii) Abuse of a Dominant Position

The same consistency has also been achieved in relation to abuse of a dominant position, sanctioned by the Italian law in the same terms as Article 82 of the EC Treaty, as well as for state measures which, linked to the conduct of undertakings, endorse, facilitate or impose conduct which violates the antitrust laws. It is again significant to note the evolution of the Council of State's case law, which initially tolerated violation of the cartels prohibition when the political or governmental context facilitated the undertaking's anticompetitive conduct.[28] More recently, the Council of State has aligned its approach with that of the Court of Justice and the Court of First Instance, affirming the inapplicability of the rules on cartels and abuse of dominant position only when the national law or measure imposes specific anti-competitive conduct, and making it clear that those rules

---

[25] Case C-35/96 *Commission v Italy* [1998] ECR I-3851; TAR Lazio, Section I, 27 March 1996 n 476.
[26] Council of State, Section VI 1996 n 1793.
[27] Council of State, Section VI 2001 n 1189; Case C-1/92 *Hercules Chemicals v Commission* [1999] ECR I-4235.
[28] Council of State, Section VI 2001 n 2053.

remain applicable when the law or measure leaves a margin of autonomy to the companies.[29]

B. Establishment and Services

In recent years, another issue between the Court of Justice and the Italian Court of Cassation has been the limitations Member States are permitted to impose on the right of establishment and the free circulation of services in gaming and betting. In a series of cases the Court of Justice has affirmed that national laws which prohibit collections, acceptances, reservations and transmissions of proposed bets on sporting events in the absence of prior awards or authorizations issued by the Member State concerned constitute illegal restrictions on the right of establishment and the right to provide services, except when such restrictions are justified. It is equally well established that the restrictions must respond to several criteria laid down by the Court, such as the prevention of possible delinquency and infiltration by organized crime and the like, which is to be verified by the national judge. The legality or illegality of the activity depends on the outcome of the review conducted by the national judge following the guidance, often detailed, of the Court of Justice.

For several years, Italian judges insisted on the illegality of the activity of organizing gaming and betting exercised by, or in connection with, foreign companies authorized in their country of origin, even after repeated holdings by the Court of Justice.[30] Eventually the latter intervened with a somewhat severe but very clear judgment,[31] so that the Italian Court of Cassation, with the very clear 'help' of the Constitutional Court,[32] was at last able to align its case law with that of Luxembourg.

C. Remedies

There has even been an adaptation of the Italian case law to that of Luxembourg with regard to remedies. The first area is that of state responsibility for violations of Community law on the part of the legislature, the object of a conspicuous jurisprudence of the Court of Justice starting with *Francovich*[33] and *Brasserie du Pêcheur*.[34] The first judgment specifically considered an Italian failure to transpose a directive, thereby exposing the employees of a failed company to the risk of being without guaranteed minimum economic protection.

---

[29] Council of State, Section VI 2003 n 7243; Case C-198/01 (n 23 above).
[30] Case C-243/01 *Gambelli* [2003] ECR I-13031; Court of Cassation, United Criminal Sections 26 April 2004 n 23271.
[31] Cases C-388, 359 and 36/04 *Placanica and others*, judgment of 6 March 2007.
[32] Corte Costituzionale 2006 n 454 (n 12 above) and 13 July 2007 n 284.
[33] n 21 above.
[34] Joined Cases C-46/93 and C-48/93 *Brasserie du Pêcheur/Factortame III* [1996] ECR I-1029.

Following the *Francovich* judgment, the Italian legislature intervened to implement the financial requirements imposed by the decision, applying it to a pre-existing mechanism of workers' guarantees run by the public social security body (INPS). So the burden of paying damages was borne by INPS and generically defined as an 'indemnity': both the Constitutional Court and the Court of Cassation ruled in this sense. The argument used by the Court of Cassation led to a satisfactory practical result in the case in point, namely compensation of the individual as a result of the behaviour of the State and its legislature.[35] Having underlined that the definition of the individual's subjective position was the task of national law, the Court of Cassation stressed that exercise of the legislative function was outside judicial control and that 'in the face of the exercise of political power subjective protected situations for the individual are not conceivable'. The result was that it was impossible to qualify the violation of the Treaty as an illicit action or to characterize the right of the individual to compensation for the legislature's activity or inactivity as anything more than a right to receive an indemnity for a reduction in assets suffered as the result of the exercise of a power that courts could not review.

The opinion has been much criticized and the idea that the exercise of the legislative function, as an 'expression of political power', is never subject to judicial control seems unacceptable. When the legislature is no longer free but is under a precise obligation to legislate in one way rather than another and does not respect that obligation, it is difficult to understand why its behaviour should not be subject to control. This review already exists vis-à-vis constitutional requirements and, in substance and procedure, is not unlike the review carried out vis-à-vis Community requirements. It is simply a question of admitting that the State must assume the obligation of compensating individuals who suffered damage to their assets due to the effect of a violation by the State itself of a precise EC law obligation. In fact, the most recent case law of the Court of Cassation has taken a different approach, which is now the majority approach, on the payment of damages by the author of illegal acts under Article 2043 of the Civil Code.[36]

This reflects another new approach under which responsibility for injuries to so-called 'legitimate interests' has finally been accepted.[37] This has also been a result of the case law of the Court of Justice, traditionally indifferent to national classifications but careful that subjective positions determined by Community law, however they are defined, receive equal and adequate judicial protection.

IV. Conclusion

This is a brief description of the present state of the dialogue between Italian judges and EC judges. Dialogue with the ordinary judge, who usually interprets

---

[35] Court of Cassation, Labour Section 11 October 1995 n 10617.
[36] Court of Cassation, Labour Section 11 June 1998 n 5846.
[37] Court of Cassation, United Sections 22 July 1999 n 500.

and applies Community law, is enriched by the preliminary ruling mechanism, which builds on the synergy between the Community judge and the national judge to create the very richness of the Community legal system and the fundamental reason for its success. Dialogue with the Constitutional Court, useful and rich as well, remains a dialogue at a distance. If this was appropriate in a less crowded Europe, it is no longer so. But that is another issue, one which concerns the entire EU legal system.

26

The Effect of European Community Law on Irish Law and the Irish Constitution

Nial Fennelly

Membership of the European Communities demanded that Ireland subordinate to Community law the legal and political sovereignty it had won so dearly in 1922. Be that as it may, the Irish courts have embraced the law of the European Community with little hesitation. They applied *Factortame* before *Factortame* and *Francovich* before *Francovich*.

I. A Transcendent Constitution

Ireland became a sovereign independent state in 1922. According to a contemporaneous declaration of the President of the Executive Council: 'nothing is more prized among our newly-won liberties than the liberty to construct a system of judiciary and an administration of law and justice according to the dictates of our own needs and after a pattern of our own designing'.[1] A deep attachment to national sovereignty and independence pervades the present Constitution adopted in 1937. Article 5 states that: 'Ireland is a sovereign, independent, democratic state'. Article 6, in particular, states:

(1) All powers of government, legislative, executive and judicial, derive, under God, from the people...
(2) These powers of government are exercisable only by or on the authority of the organs of State established by this Constitution.

The Oireachtas (Parliament) enjoys 'the sole and exclusive power of making laws for the State' (Article 15.1.2). 'The executive power of the State shall...be exercised by or on the authority of the Government' (Article 28). Article 34 provides

---

[1] Letter dated 29 January 1923 from President of Executive Council (head of government) to each member of Glenavy Committee asking it to report on the establishment of a new courts system.

that: 'Justice shall be administered in Courts established by law by judges appointed in the manner provided by this Constitution'.

Ireland could join the European Economic Community, as it did on 1 January 1973, provided only that the Constitution underwent most drastic amendment.[2] A very direct obstacle was presented by the dualist approach to international agreements entrenched in Article 29.6 of the Constitution: 'No international agreement shall be part of the domestic law of the State save as may be determined by the Oireachtas'.

In the case of *In re O'Laighléis*,[3] the Supreme Court rejected the applicant's argument that his detention without trial pursuant to special powers contained in legislation and based on an opinion of a Minister that he was engaged in activities 'prejudicial to the security of the State' infringed Article 5 of the European Convention on Human Rights. Maguire CJ spoke for the Court: 'No argument can prevail against the express command of section 6 of Article 29 of the Constitution before judges whose declared duty it is to uphold the Constitution and the laws'.[4]

The same Article played a role in the majority decision of the Supreme Court[5] in 1987 where it was held that the Government did not have the power to ratify Part III of the Single European Act. Walsh J, writing for that majority, considered that Part III would commit the State and all future governments to action which would impinge on the freedom of action of the State in foreign policy and within international organisations such as the United Nations. Amongst these was the requirement to endeavour to implement a common European foreign policy and to co-ordinate foreign policy with that of other Member States so as to ensure that common principles and objectives were gradually developed and defined.

One final provision of the Constitution is of major legal importance in this regard. Article 34.3.2 empowers the High Court to decide on 'the question of the validity of any law having regard to the provisions of this Constitution'. This provision is mirrored by Article 15.4.1 which provides that the Oireachtas 'shall not enact any law which is in any respect repugnant to this Constitution or any provision thereof'. This judicial power is regularly invoked in litigation before

---

[2] The Constitution of the Irish Free State (Saorstát Eireann) Act, 1922 adopted the Constitution of the Irish Free State in order to implement the Treaty between Great Britain and Ireland on 6 December 1921. That Constitution was abrogated in its entirety upon the adoption in 1937 of the present Constitution. 'The name of the State is Eire or, in the English language, Ireland' (Article 4). Pending the realization of the aspiration 'that a united Ireland will be brought about only by peaceful means and with the consent of a majority of the people, peacefully expressed, in both jurisdictions of Ireland', laws enacted under the Constitution do not extend to Northern Ireland (see Article 3.1).
[3] *In re Gearóid O'Laighléis and in the matter of the Constitution* [1960] IR 93. The applicant's case (*Lawless v Ireland*, App No 332/57, Series A, No 3) was the subject of the first individual petition heard by the European Court of Human Rights. In its judgment of 1 July 1961, the ECHR found that Ireland was not in breach of its obligations.
[4] n 3 above, 125, per Maguire CJ.
[5] *Crotty v An Taoiseach* [1987] IR 713.

the High Court and before the Supreme Court on appeal. It has encouraged a widely-respected and jealously-guarded culture of judicial independence, accompanied by strong protection of individual rights. Most materially, it means that the Irish courts have long been familiar with the exercise of the power to declare laws invalid as being incompatible with entrenched constitutional provisions.

Henchy J of the Supreme Court wrote extra-judicially in 1977[6] on the effect on the Constitution generally of accession to the Community. He recognized that it was 'necessarily inherent in the scheme of the EEC that Community law shall have primacy over national law', commenting that 'Member States merge their national identities in a new common law'. He continued: 'It is as if the people of Ireland had adopted Community law as a second but transcendent Constitution'.

II. Constitutional Amendment

Thus, the Constitution had to be amended. A proposal for the necessary amendments was placed, as the Constitution requires, before the people in June 1972. It was passed by a majority of 82.4 per cent of the votes cast. The constitutional amendments comprise three elements:

(1) The State was empowered to join the three Communities then existing.[7] The Constitution has been amended, following referendum, on four subsequent occasions to provide for ratification respectively of the Single European Act, and the Treaties of Maastricht (authorizing membership of the European Union), Amsterdam and Nice.[8]

(2) A separate and crucial provision, Article 29.4.10, stipulated that no provision of the Constitution may be invoked to invalidate 'laws enacted, acts done or measures adopted by the State which are *necessitated* by the obligations of membership of the European Union or of the Communities' (emphasis added). This wide-ranging immunity was indispensable in view of the power of the High Court, already mentioned, to declare laws invalid by reason of repugnancy to the Constitution. It accordingly removes entirely from the purview of the Constitution any and all of the mentioned measures, subject to the much-debated proviso that they be 'necessitated' by the obligations of membership.

(3) Article 29.4.7 also provides that no provision of the Constitution 'prevents laws enacted, acts done or measures adopted by the European Union or by the

---

[6] 'The Irish Constitution and the EEC' (1977) DULJ 20.
[7] The European Economic Community, the European Coal and Steel Community and the European Atomic Energy Community.
[8] The constitutional numbering has been confusingly changed following each subsequent amendment. The enabling provisions are now to be found in Arts 29.4.3 to 29.4.7 of the Constitution.

Communities or by institutions thereof, or by bodies competent under the Treaties establishing the Communities, from having the force of law in the State.' This is an enabling provision. Legislation was required to provide that Community laws and acts should have actual legal effect. The purpose of the provision, like that mentioned in the preceding paragraph was to exempt any and all such measures from constitutional scrutiny.

The phrase 'necessitated by the obligations of membership' was substituted for an earlier version proposed by the government, namely 'consequent on the obligations of membership'. This arose from opposition concerns[9] that the original expression would confer immunity from constitutional scrutiny on too broad a range of measures and would amount to a 'carte blanche' for the Community.[10] The provision should be confined to what was strictly necessary.

The constitutional package confers power on the State to join the Communities (later the Union) but, more crucially, exempts Community and national laws and acts from constitutional review. This latter aspect has been described as 'an astonishingly wide immunity clause'.[11] It undoubtedly has the effect that the Constitution simply has no application or relevance whatever to Community laws or acts or necessary Irish implementing measures.

The implementing legislation required to avail of the constitutional amendment took the form of the European Communities Act, 1972. Section 2 of that Act gave the force of law in the State to the Treaties 'and the existing and future acts adopted by the institutions of those Communities'. Section 3 confers power on any Minister to make regulations, subject to the possibility of parliamentary annulment within one year,[12] for the purpose of giving effect to section 2. In addition, such regulations may contain 'provisions repealing, amending or applying, with or without modification, other law'. The reference to 'other law' imports a power to amend statutes, an invasion of what would otherwise be the exclusive domain of the Oireachtas. The Supreme Court has recently decided to prohibit prosecutions under regulations invalidly adopted under this legislation.[13] Furthermore, regulations are to have 'statutory effect' (section 4). There is one important proviso: regulations under the Act may 'not create an indictable offence'. Much of the litigation concerning the effects of Irish membership of the European Community has concerned the exercise of these regulatory powers and, in particular, whether particular regulations are 'necessitated' by the obligations of membership.

---

[9] Debates of Dáil Eireann, vol 258, 25 January 1972.
[10] Language by Mr TF O'Higgins TD, later Chief Justice of Ireland and a Judge of the Court of Justice.
[11] G Hogan and A Whelan, *Ireland and the European Union: Constitutional and Statutory Texts* (1995) 7.
[12] European Communities (Amendment) Act, 1973, section 4.
[13] *Quinn v Ireland and AG and anor, Tector v Ireland and AG and anor, Quinn v Ireland and AG and anor* (No 2), 30 March 2007.

III. The Effect of Membership of the Communities

The passing of the Single European Act (SEA) in 1986 led to the most deep-rooted challenge to the constitutional effects of the constitutional amendment passed in 1972. The Oireachtas enacted legislation intended to give effect to the SEA by inserting its provisions (other than Part III) by amendment into the European Communities Act, 1972 and making them part of the domestic law of the State. Mr Crotty, a citizen, challenged the power of the State to ratify any amendment of the Treaties without further constitutional amendment. The Supreme Court[14] interpreted the constitutional amendment passed in 1972 as amounting to 'an authorisation given to the State not only to join the Communities as they stood in 1973, but also to join in amendments of the Treaties so long as such amendments do not alter the essential scope or objectives of the Communities'. The Court then needed to consider whether the SEA was in fact within 'the essential scope or objectives of the Communities'. The Court observed[15] that: 'The Community was thus a developing organism with diverse and changing methods for making decisions and an inbuilt and clearly expressed objective of expansion and progress, both in terms of the number of its Member States and in terms of the mechanics to be used in the achievement of its agreed objectives'. It proceeded thus to hold that:

Having regard to these considerations, it is the opinion of the Court that neither the proposed changes from unanimity to qualified majority, nor the identification of topics which while now separately stated, are within the original aims and objectives of the EEC, bring these proposed amendments outside the scope of the authorisation contained in Article 29, s. 4, sub-s. 3 of the Constitution.

The Court thus held that the amending Act of 1986 was not unconstitutional. Following on this very clear ruling and, in spite of the Court's expressly-stated reservation that not all other decisions of the Council could be moved to majority voting without amendment of the Constitution in Ireland, it might have been thought that further treaty ratifications would have taken place by means of ordinary legislation and without a constitutional referendum. That, however, is not what has happened.

By reason of the contemporaneous ruling by a majority of the Court that the State did not have the power to ratify Part III of the SEA concerning political co-operation, it became necessary to hold a referendum on that topic. The entire Single European Act was included in the referendum proposal (and was passed). As a political rather than a legal consequence, the Maastricht, Amsterdam and

---

[14] *Crotty v An Taoiseach and others* [1987] IR 713. The Court, as required by the Constitution in cases of the constitutionality of a law, delivered a single judgment, pronounced by Finlay CJ.
[15] Page 770 of the report.

Nice Treaties have each been submitted to referendum and passed.[16] The Courts have not subsequently been asked to consider the limits to the power to amend the Treaties without referendum.

IV. Status of European Law in Irish Courts

Having regard to the virtual carte blanche conferred by the constitutional amendments, Irish courts have readily accepted the general concepts of direct effect and supremacy. In *Pigs and Bacon Commission v McCarren*,[17] Costello J held that Community law 'takes effect in the Irish legal system in the manner in which it itself provides'.

In the course of its judgment in *Crotty v An Taoiseach*, the Supreme Court had no difficulty in acknowledging that:

- decisions of the Court of Justice 'take precedence, in case of conflict, over the domestic law and the decisions of national courts of Member States';
- decisions of the Council 'have primacy over domestic law'; and
- the Council's capacity 'to take decisions with legislative effect is a diminution of the sovereignty of Member States, including Ireland'.[18]

It is tempting to contrast this position with that in Member States which have simply given effect to the Treaties by means of the enactment of ordinary law. In Italy, for example, as pointed out by Advocate General Lagrange in his Opinion in *Costa v ENEL*,[19] the Treaty had been 'ratified by an ordinary law not having the character of a constitutional law and as such not having the power of derogating from either the rules or the principles of the [Italian] Constitution'. The Treaty did not, therefore, enjoy any special status in the Italian constitutional system, a matter which led the Court of Justice to declare (in the case of *Costa v ENEL*) the principle of supremacy of Community law.

A most striking example of the implicit application of the principle of direct effect is to be found in the decision of the Supreme Court in *Pesca Valentia v Minister for Fisheries and others*.[20] The plaintiff was the registered owner in Ireland of sea-fishing vessels, formerly registered in Spain and largely crewed by Spanish nationals (this was prior to Spanish accession to the Community). Its fishing licences, granted by the defendant Minister, contained conditions inserted pursuant to statute regarding the nationality of crew. The plaintiff complained that

---

[16] It will be recalled that a second referendum had to be held in respect of the Nice Treaty.
[17] High Court (unreported, 30 June 1978). For the decision of the Court of Justice on the questions referred, see Case 177/78 *Pigs and Bacon Commission v McCarren & Company* [1979] ECR 2161.
[18] Page 769 of the report.
[19] Case 6/64 *Costa v ENEL* [1964] ECR 585.
[20] [1985] IR 193.

the conditions were contrary to Community law and sought an interlocutory injunction, pending the hearing of its action, restraining the Attorney General from enforcing the condition by conducting prosecutions of the plaintiff. The State argued that an injunction could not, as a matter of principle or precedent, be granted so as to prevent the State from prosecuting for a criminal offence created by statute. Finlay CJ held that there was no such general principle. The power to grant an injunction 'must exist in an appropriate case'. The matter should be considered in accordance with ordinary principles. There being a fair case to be tried, the case justified the grant of an injunction.[21]

The case bears comparison with the celebrated *Factortame* case, where the House of Lords held that it had no power to suspend the operation of an act of parliament and therefore could not grant interim relief in similar circumstances, even though it accepted that the claim of the plaintiffs that they would suffer irreparable harm if relief were not granted was well founded. The Court of Justice held that: 'a national court which, in a case before it concerning Community law, considers that the sole obstacle which precludes it from granting interim relief is a rule of national law must set aside that rule'.[22]

The contrasting positions adopted by the Irish Supreme Court and the House of Lords arise, in the first instance, from a differing view as to whether there existed a rule of law preventing the grant of an injunction against the State or the Crown respectively, so as to suspend the operation of a statute by restraining the taking of prosecutions. Finlay CJ explained the Irish context as follows:

It is, as has been so frequently stated, the duty of the courts to protect persons against the invasion of their constitutional rights or against unconstitutional action. It would seem wholly inconsistent with that duty if the Court were to be without power in an appropriate case to restrain by injunction an action against a person which found its authority in a statutory provision which might eventually be held to be invalid having regard to the Constitution.[23]

It is reasonable to infer that the absence of the power of judicial review of validity of statutes constitutes the principal explanation for the difference of approach. It is interesting to note, however, that McCarthy J, in his concurring judgment, suggested that the constitutional presumption upon which States relied was irrelevant since it was not contested that there was a fair question to be tried on the basis of Community law and: 'the Constitution itself envisages at least some freedom from constitutional scrutiny of "laws enacted, acts done or measures adopted by the Communities, or institutions thereof", as to having the force of law in the State (Article 29.4.3)'.[24] The Irish courts have consistently applied Community

---

[21] In the event the plaintiffs' case was rejected by the Court of Justice: Case 223/86 *Pesca Valentia* [1988] ECR 83.
[22] Case C-213/89 *The Queen v Secretary of State for Transport, ex parte Factortame Ltd* [1990] ECR I-2433.
[23] Page 201 of the report.
[24] Page 204 of the report.

law as required in the many fields in which they have progressively been required to do so, with little evidence of deviation from the jurisprudence of the Court of Justice.[25]

In the sequel to Case 177/78 *Pigs and Bacon Commission v McCarren & Company,* already mentioned, the Irish courts had to determine the extent of the right of the plaintiff, a statutory body, to recover statutory levies it had imposed on the production of bacon. The Court of Justice had determined that part of the purposes to which the levies were applied (payment of bounties on sale of bacon) infringed the articles of the Treaty and regulations concerning the common organisation of the market in pigmeat. However, it left it to the national court to determine the extent of recoverability of levies and repayment of levy already paid.[26]

Costello J held that the plaintiff Commission could recover sums due under levy orders but only insofar as the proceeds were not applied to purposes declared impermissible by the Court of Justice. The Supreme Court, on the other hand, held that the orders imposing levies were *ultra vires,* insofar as their purposes infringed Community law. Applying domestic law principles, they were, therefore, 'null and void, and incapable of severance'.[27] Neither court considered the matter in the context of the notion of 'inapplicability' of the levies. The Supreme Court, in particular applied the more familiar concept of invalidity. In each case, the Court arguably went further than was required by Community law.

The longest-running saga of competition litigation originating in the Irish courts was that between the respective Irish subsidiaries of Mars (Masterfoods) and Unilever (HB Ice Cream Ltd).[28] The Irish courts demonstrated that a noted reluctance to accept competition law could be used to challenge the exclusivity clause imposed by the dominant undertaking (HB Ice Cream) so as to prevent retailers from stocking their competitors' products in freezer cabinets provided by them free of charge. Keane J thought that the right claimed by the plaintiff 'constitute[d] an infringement of HB's rights of property in the cabinets which is so radical in nature as to violate Article 222 of the Treaty'. The parallel Commission investigation and decision of the Court of First Instance (upholding the Commission decision)[29] and Order of the Court of Justice of 28 September 2006[30] led to a quite opposite conclusion. In particular the Court of First Instance explained that HB's property rights in its freezers were not infringed.

---

[25] An example from the field of environmental law is *McBride v Galway Corporation* [1998] 1 IR 485 and from public procurement law *SIAC v Mayo County Council* [2002] 3 IR 148.
[26] Case 177/78 *Pigs and Bacon Commission v McCarren & Company* [1979] ECR 2161, 2192.
[27] Page 470 of the report.
[28] *HB Ice Cream Ltd v Masterfoods* [1990] 2 IR 463; *Masterfoods v HB Ice Cream Ltd* [1993] ILRM 145.
[29] Case T-65/98 *Van den Bergh Foods formerly HB Ice Cream Ltd v Commission* [2003] ECR II-4653.
[30] Case C-552/03 P *Unilever Bestfoods (Ireland) Ltd, formerly Van den Bergh Foods Ltd v Commission* [2006] ECR I-9091.

Over time, competition law has taken its place as a standard and regular subject of litigation. Articles 81 and 82 have been incorporated into Irish competition law so as to affect purely domestic circumstances. In fact, Masterfoods' claim for damages is now, some 17 years after the commencement of the litigation, pending in the High Court.

The Irish courts have referred questions of interpretation to the Court of Justice at a rate, approximately two per annum, which could be described as regular though hardly frequent. In recent years, there has been a noted reluctance on the part of any courts other than the Supreme Court to make references.[31]

A striking decision of the Supreme Court was that in *Campus Oil v Minister for Energy*.[32] The High Court had decided to refer questions to the Court of Justice. The defendants appealed against the order to make the reference. The Supreme Court decided that it had no jurisdiction to set aside the High Court order on the interesting ground that Article 177 (now 234) of the Treaty had become part of Irish law and that interlocutory orders of that type could not be disturbed on appeal.[33]

V. State Liability: Damages

The notion of State liability for damages for the commission of a civil wrong presented no principled objection for the Irish courts. The Supreme Court had decided in 1971[34] that the former prerogative of State immunity from suit (based on the maxim: 'the King can do no wrong') had not existed in Ireland after 1922. The State, as a juristic person, is liable vicariously for the tortious act of a servant of the State. The Court later held that a claim for damages lay generally at the suit of an individual for breach of constitutional rights.[35] Thus, the notion of the liability of the State for damages was not essentially novel. As a consequence, Irish courts have awarded damages against the State in respect both of directly applicable Community regulations and the direct effect of unimplemented directives.

In *Emerald Meats v Minister for Agriculture,* the plaintiff company complained that the Minister had deprived him of the right to meat import quotas contrary

---

[31] See E Fahey, 'An analysis of trends and patterns in the Irish Courts of practice and procedure in 30 years of Article 234 preliminary references' (2004) 11 IJEL 408; N Fennelly, 'Preliminary reference procedure: a factual and legal review' (2006) 13 IJEL 55.
[32] *Campus Oil v Minister for Industry* [1983] IR 82.
[33] For a critique of this decision, describing it as 'questionable,' see GW Hogan and GF White, *JM Kelly's Irish Constitution* (2004), para 5.3.61. The *Campus Oil* case is of some personal interest. This writer represented the Irish government and one Francis Jacobs that of the United Kingdom. Mr Jacobs, as he then was, played no small part in persuading the Court to interpret the notion of 'public security' in Article 36 (now Article 30) of the Treaty as possibly encompassing the restrictions on trade adopted by the Irish government.
[34] *Byrne v Ireland* [1972] IR 241.
[35] *Crowley v Ireland* [1980] IR 102; *Conway v INTO* [1991] 2 IR 305.

to Article 1(1) of Commission Regulation No 4024/89.[36] In a judgment delivered on 9 July 1991 (that is, more than four months prior to the judgment of the Court of Justice in *Francovich*[37]), Costello J, in the High Court, awarded damages for the specific loss of these quotas to the plaintiff for the breach by the Minister of his duties under the Regulation. He did not award general damages. However, the Supreme Court, on appeal, applying *Francovich*, which had been decided in the interim, upheld the High Court award and held, in addition, that the plaintiff was entitled to general damages.[38] The Supreme Court declined to refer the matter to the Court of Justice, considering that the law had been 'clearly settled' by *Francovich*.

The case of *Tate v Minister for Social Welfare*[39] represented the culmination of a saga of litigation in the Irish courts,[40] followed by several references to Luxembourg over a period of more than 10 years, all related to the failure of Ireland to implement the Council Directive[41] on equal treatment in matters of social security. The High Court (Carroll J) ultimately awarded damages to a number of married women against the State. Carroll J held that the plaintiffs' rights arose under the direct effect of the Directive. She described that right as follows:

In my opinion, the wrong committed by the State in continuing the discrimination by failing to fully implement the Directive is a wrong arising from Community law which has domestic effect. It is not a breach of constitutional rights; it is not a breach of statutory duty and it is not a breach of the duty of care. It is a breach of duty to implement the Directive and it approximates to a breach of constitutional duty. Every type of action which would be available in the national domestic law to ensure the observance of national law is available to ensure observance of the Directive once it took on the mantle of direct effect.[42]

The designation of the wrong committed by the State as 'approximating to a breach of constitutional duty' did not prevent Carroll J from applying the statutory limitation period appropriate under Irish law to actions based on tort.

In *Maxwell v Minister for Agriculture*,[43] the High Court (McCracken J) awarded damages against the State for breach of Article 40(3) of the EC Treaty,

---

[36] Commission Regulation (EEC) No 4024/89 of 21 December 1989 laying down detailed rules for the application of the import arrangements provided for in Council Regulation (EEC) No 3889/89 for frozen meat of bovine animals, [1989] OJ L378/16.
[37] Joined Cases C-6/90 and C-9/90 *Francovich v Italy* [1991] ECR 1-5357.
[38] *Emerald Meats v Minister for Agriculture* [1997] 1 IR 1.
[39] [1995] 1 IR 418.
[40] Case 286/85 *McDermott and Cotter v Minister for Social Welfare* [1987] ECR 1453; Case C-377/89 *Cotter and McDermott v Minister for Social Welfare* [1991] ECR I-1155; Case C-208/90 *Emmott v Minister for Social Welfare* [1991] ECR I-4269.
[41] Council Directive 79/7/EEC of 19 December 1978 on the progressive implementation of the principle of equal treatment for men and women in matters of social security, [1979] OJ L6/24.
[42] Page 438 of the report.
[43] [1999] 2 IR 474.

based on discrimination in applying a scheme of payments to producers suffering from the effects of the BSE crisis, between beef producers who exported animals live and those who sold them for slaughter within the State. Applying *Brasserie du Pêcheur* and *Factortame*,[44] McCracken J held that the breach was sufficiently serious because the scheme had been applied retrospectively.

VI. The 'Necessitated' Debate

The word 'necessitated' is the hinge on the door which opens up or shuts out constitutional scrutiny of national implementing measures. Necessitated measures are rendered immune from the normal need to meet constitutional standards of respect for fundamental rights, such as, to give the most relevant example, property rights.

The word 'necessitated' appeared, as already explained, in the amendment adopted in 1972 as the result of earnest parliamentary intervention of some opposition politicians who were concerned to place limits on the removal of constitutional protection which would follow membership. It was not then (1972) as clear as it has since become that individuals were entitled to protection of their fundamental human rights under Community law.

It is not surprising that the scope of this particular exception from constitutional scrutiny has been subject to the greatest legal controversy. The notion of being 'necessitated' was debatable. Was a national implementing measure necessary only in the strict sense that there was no possible alternative? Should the word 'necessitated' be interpreted more broadly in the sense of what was expedient? The drafters of the 1972 amendment had not anticipated the practical issues. Community measures, whether regulations or directives, frequently permit Member States to exercise choices as to how to give effect to Community law. Is the choice of one option in preference to the other 'necessitated' by the obligations of membership? These problems came to be addressed in a number of cases mainly in an agricultural setting. The courts have, on the whole, opted for an expansive and purposive rather than a literal interpretation of the constitutional amendment. Some decisions have attracted controversy. The courts have not been immune from – mainly academic – criticism.

In 1990 the High Court (Murphy J) held against a complaint that the Irish government had infringed a landowner's property rights by deciding to give retroactive effect to milk quota regulations.[45] He decided that the word 'necessitated' must be extended to 'acts or measures which are *consequent upon* membership of the Community and in general fulfilment of the obligations of such membership,

---

[44] Joined Cases C-46/93 and C-48/93 [1996] ECR 1–1029.
[45] *Lawlor v Minister for Agriculture* [1990] 1 IR 356, which involved Commission Regulation (EEC) No 1371/84, [1984] OJ L132/11, implemented by the European Communities (Milk Levy) Regulations 1985.

and even where there may be a choice or degree of discretion vested in the State as to the particular manner in which it would meet the general spirit of its obligations of membership' (emphasis added). This decision has been criticized for its 'unusually broad' interpretation of the term 'necessitated'.[46] In effect, 'necessitated' has been replaced by 'consequent upon', which was the term originally proposed by the government in 1972.

Clearly, the standard of being consequent on membership confers immunity on a much broader range of measures than if the word necessitated were strictly construed. In addition, it is a less exact criterion when it comes to interpretation. This point is illustrated by the judgment of the same judge in a later case. He thought that 'laws enacted, acts done and measures adopted by the State' were 'necessitated' 'even where the particular actions of the State involve a measure of choice, selection or discretion'. He proceeded, nonetheless, to recognize that 'there must be a point at which the discretion exercised by the State or the national party is so far-reaching or so detached from the result to be achieved... that it cannot be said to have been "necessitated" by it'.[47]

The most far-reaching attempt to rely on the limits imposed by the need for a measure to be necessitated, in that case a law, came in the case of *Meagher*.[48] The subject matter was the power conferred by section 3 of the European Communities Act, 1972 to make regulations amending 'other law', thus extending to the amendment of statutes by order. The case concerned the implementation of a directive. The High Court (Johnson J) held that this power was not necessitated by the obligations. He declared the section to be unconstitutional. The State appealed.

It is clear that Community law does not require that Community measures be implemented by any particular method. A directive is binding only 'as to the result to be achieved' (Article 249 EC). The Supreme Court took a pragmatic view. It looked at the matter from a practical point of view. It explained:

The Court is satisfied that, having regard to the number of Community laws, acts done and measures adopted which either have to be facilitated in their direct application to the law of the State or have to be implemented by appropriate action into the law of the State, the obligation of membership would necessitate facilitating of these activities, in some instances, at least, and possibly in a great majority of instances, by the making of ministerial regulation rather than legislation of the Oireachtas.

The Court is accordingly satisfied that the power to make regulations in the form in which it is contained in s. 3, sub-s. 2 of the Act of 1972 is necessitated by the obligations of membership by the State of the Communities and now of the Union and is therefore by virtue of Article 29, s. 4, sub-ss. 3, 4 and 5 immune from constitutional challenge.[49]

---

[46] GW Hogan and GF White (n 33 above) 522. See also C Costello, 'European Community judicial review in the Irish Courts' in MC Lucey and C Keville (eds), *Irish Perspectives on EC Law* (2003) 24.
[47] *Greene v Minister for Agriculture* [1990] 2 IR 17.
[48] *Meagher v Minister for Agriculture, Ireland and the Attorney General* [1994] 1 IR 329.
[49] Per Finlay CJ, delivering the judgment of the Court at page 352.

The relationship between European Community law and the constitutional prerogative of the Oireachtas as the sole law-making authority for the State was further considered in the confusingly similarly named case of *Maher v Minister for Agriculture and Rural Development*[50] concerning changes to the milk quota regime effected in 2000.[51] The changes adversely affected a number of farmers who had leased their lands and/or quotas. They complained of infringement of their property rights and that the Irish implementing regulations were ultra vires and unconstitutional. The Constitution reserves to the Oireachtas the exclusive right to pass laws. Legislation by ministerial order is permissible only to give effect to 'principles and policies' set out in a parent statute.[52] The Supreme Court delivered a number of very lengthy judgments. The key question was whether implementation by statutory instrument was valid under Irish public law. It was held that as the Council Regulations were part of Irish law they could be regarded in the same way as an enabling statute of the Oireachtas, so that the regulations could be considered to be adopted to give effect to 'principles and policies' found in the Council Regulation.

VII. Future Shock: Conflict and its Resolution

It is not surprising that the areas of possible conflict concern fundamental rights. Two cases spring to mind as exemplifying the possibilities.

SPUC v Grogan[53] concerned the extremely sensitive issue of protection of the right to life of the unborn under the amendment of the Constitution adopted in 1983. A student society provided a pregnancy advisory service to students including non-directive information concerning the availability of abortion services in the United Kingdom. The plaintiff, a pro-life organization, applied to the High Court for orders restraining these activities. The students claimed that their right to receive information in relation to services provided outside the State gave a corresponding right to impart such information. The High Court referred questions of interpretation to the Court of Justice concerning the status of UK abortion services as services for the purposes of the EC Treaty and refused to grant the injunction sought.

On appeal by the plaintiffs, the Supreme Court granted an injunction. Finlay CJ stated:

If and when a decision of the Court of Justice of the European Communities rules that some aspect of European Community law affects the activities of the defendants impugned in this case, the consequence of that decision on these constitutionally

[50] [2001] 2 IR 139.
[51] The case concerned the implementation in Ireland (by the European Communities (Milk Quota) Regulations, 2000) of Council Regulation 1256/1999 amending Regulation 3950/92 establishing an additional levy in the milk and milk products sector, [1999] OJ L 160/73.
[52] *Cityview Press Ltd v An Comhairle Oiliúna and others* [1980] 1 IR 381.
[53] *The Society for the Protection of Unborn Children (Ireland) Limited v Grogan* [1989] IR 753.

guaranteed rights and their protection by the courts will then fall to be considered by these courts.

Walsh J, in a concurring judgment,[54] said that the 'Constitution forecloses any attempt to argue that life does not exist before birth', and that an earlier decision of the Court had 'given an interpretation to the [relevant provision] which is not open to question in any court in this State or in any other state or in any international court'.

It is apparent on the face of these judgments that there existed a real possibility of direct conflict between the Irish courts and Community law. The decision of the Court of Justice avoided that outcome.[55] Advocate General Van Gerven advised the Court[56] that medical operations for the termination of pregnancy did indeed constitute services for the purposes of the Treaty, but applied a proportionality analysis to the Irish law. He advised that the Treaty provisions did not 'prevent a Member State where the protection of unborn life is recognised in the Constitution and its legislation as a fundamental principle from imposing a general prohibition... on the provision of assistance to pregnant women... specifically through the distribution of information as to the identity... of clinics located in another Member State'. The Court agreed on the services issue, but held that the information-giving activities of the students were not commercial and did not benefit from the protection of the Treaty.

Thus direct conflict between the Treaty (and the Court) and a deeply entrenched provision of the Irish Constitution was avoided. Possible future conflict in this area has almost certainly been eliminated by later amendments to the Constitution, which, while retaining the protection of the right to life, provide that it is not to be interpreted as affecting freedom to travel (in reality to the UK) or the right to provide information 'relating to services lawfully available in another state'.[57]

The *Bosphorus* saga of litigation provides another object lesson. An aircraft, owned by a Yugoslav company (the subject of UN sanctions related to the war in Bosnia), was leased to an entirely unconnected and innocent Turkish air charter company. The plane was seized while in Dublin for the purpose of maintenance,

---

[54] Page 766 of the report.
[55] Case C-159/90 *Society for the Protection of Unborn Children (Ireland) Limited v Grogan and others* [1991] ECR I-4685.
[56] Pages 4731 and 4732.
[57] As this essay was being written, the High Court decided (on 9 May 2007) a case of *D v Health Service Executive*. A pregnant girl of 17, in care of the health authority (HSE), discovered that her unborn child was anencephalic, meaning that it would survive birth by a matter of days at most. She wished to travel to England to have an abortion. The HSE said it could not permit this. The girl was not suicidal, as had been the case in *Attorney General v X* [1992] 1 IR 1. The High Court decided that she was free to travel. McKechnie J ruled that there was 'no statutory or constitutional impediment against allowing her to leave the country for an abortion'.

based on the UN sanctions against the Federal Republic of Yugoslavia as implemented by Council Regulation[58] and in turn by Irish statutory regulation.

In a challenge to the decision of the Irish government to seize and impound the aircraft, the Irish High Court[59] interpreted the Regulations as not being applicable to the (innocent) Turkish company. Subsequently, the Court of Justice,[60] on reference from the Irish Supreme Court, reached the contrary conclusion. The decision turned on the interpretation of Article 8 of the Council Regulation, namely whether a 'majority or controlling interest in' the aircraft was held by an 'undertaking in or operating from The Federal Republic of Yugoslavia'. The Irish High Court (Murphy J) adopted a teleological interpretation of the Council Regulation, aimed at achieving its purpose while avoiding injustice. Murphy J thought that the controlling interest must be held by a person or entity in a position to 'exercise a decision-making function on a day to day basis of the asset in question'.[61]

Advocate General Jacobs carefully analysed the High Court judgment but came to a different conclusion, one which was followed by the Court. He thought that the High Court had taken too narrow a view of the intent of the United Nations. He preferred a literal interpretation of the Council Regulation. While acknowledging that the fundamental rights of Bosphorus were severely restricted, he identified a strong public interest in enforcing an embargo imposed by the UN Security Council. He thought it 'difficult to think of any stronger type of public interest than that of stopping a civil war as devastating as the one which engulfed the former Yugoslavia'.

This case illustrates the possibility that different results may be reached by means of detailed analysis of the purpose and object of one legal instrument. It illustrates the wider point that future instances of conflict cannot be excluded. The Irish Constitution is a living instrument, embodying much of the beliefs, principles and aspirations of the Irish people. Interplay between the Constitution and international instruments has yet to be fully explored. The Court of Justice took radically different views of the proportionality of imposing punitive sanctions on innocent persons.

VIII. Conclusion

The experience of the Irish courts in the application of Community law has, on the whole, been positive. Irish courts have generously embraced and applied

---

[58] Council Regulation 990/93/EEC concerning trade between the European Economic Community and the Federal Republic of Yugoslavia (Serbia and Montenegro), [1993] OJ L102/14.
[59] *Bosphorus Hava Yollari Turuzm v Minister for Transport, Energy and Communications* [1994] ILRM 551.
[60] Case C-84/95 *Bosphorus Hava Yollari Turuzm v Minister for Transport* [1996] ECR I-3953, following the advice of Advocate General Jacobs.
[61] [1994] ILRM 551, 559.

Community law, its subject matter and its principles. Direct conflict has, happily, been avoided.

The decisions of the Supreme Court in *Meagher* and in *Maher* demonstrate a willingness to abstain from constitutional scrutiny of measures necessitated by the obligations of membership, by application of a flexible test.

Nonetheless, direct conflict cannot be ruled out in all future circumstances. It is not simply a question of different views of the same set of facts, such as occurred in *Bosphorus*. Different views of rights may be held in different legal systems.

Index

abuse of rights
  doctrine of
    agriculture, in field of 207, 223
    description of 205
    development in Community law 206–8
    origin 206
    status of 206
    VAT cases 207, 212–13, 223
  freedom of establishment, in context of *see* freedom of establishment
access to justice
  essential element of 78
  right to 168
administration
  good, right to 168–71, 174
administrative justice
  constituent parts 175–6
  Constitutions incorporating 173–4
  democratic necessity 173–6
  judicial review *see* **judicial review**
  justification, towards culture of 185–6
  progressive and incremental articulation of 175
  rule of law, justification by 175
  substantive and/or procedural protections 174–6
administrative law
  Community law, influence of 66–7
advocate
  boundaries, crossing 54
  case law, impact on 63–6
  Court of Justice, before, pleading techniques 48–9
  European, role in national courts 66–8
  litigating before ECJ, challenge of 68–9
  new point of law, finding 69
  role of 48
  working methods of Court, effect on role of 54–7
Advocates General
  allocation of 56
  CFI judgments, decision on exceptional review of 24–5
  choosing 13–14
  continued need for 31–3
  contribution to cases 27
  Court, assisting 20
  double scrutiny by 28
  draft orders, review of 29
  early days of 21–2
  EFTA case law, reliance on 98–101
  EFTA Court
    dialogue policy 118–20
    functions of dialogue 120–2
    moral support to 121
    references to opinions by 115–18
    role in 97
    substantive discussion with 111–15
  European Union Charter of Fundamental Rights, reference to 134
  function of 70
  increase in number 31
  independence 12–13
  internal importance of 22
  Jacobs, Advocate General, views of 22–3
  jurists acting as 20
  Opinions
    CFI appeals, in case of 26
    Court asking for 14
    decision as to need for 28
    default value 26
    delivery, timing 16–18
    dispensing with 24
    European Union Charter of Fundamental Rights, influence on case law of 163–4
    first 20
    general questions on EC law, on 26
    judicial panels, on appeals from 26–7
    public, made 30
    published, transparency 23
    request for 26
    research 30
    role of 22–3
  preliminary rulings, references for 29
  quasi-judicial contribution of 33
  ratio to judges 25–6, 28
  role of
    change in 23–4
    continuation of 30–1
    Court, assisting 20
    redefined 27–30
  term of office 12–13
annulment action
  private applicants, accessibility 75
antisuit injunctions
  Brussels Convention/Regulation, cases under 391–3, 397–9
biotechnological inventions
  legal protection of 338

Brussels Convention/Regulation
  antisuit injunctions 391–3, 397–9
  choice-of-court agreements, maximum effect given to 387
  conflict of laws, achievement in field of 385
  direct jurisdiction, principle of 386
  forum for bringing claim, opportunity for 388
  forum non conveniens 393–6, 399
  general scheme and objectives 386–8
  interests of Member States, protection of 387
  Italian Torpedo case 388–91, 397
  jurisdictional tussles, avoiding 387
  legislative reform 396–7

Chancery Division
  Europoints in 67
choice of law
  cross-border activity, as to 262–4
  institutions, as to 264–5
  private law sphere, in 262
  single market, accommodating
    Distance Marketing Directive 276–81
    see also **Distance Marketing Directive**
    EC Treaty 266–7
    Electronic Commerce Directive 270–6
    see also **Electronic Commerce Directive**
    general directives 267–8
    Rome Convention 265–6
civil law
  academic opinions 428
  codification 403–4
commercial law
  de-codification 404–5
Common Foreign and Security Policy
  common positions, regulations implementing 333
  complementary competences 359–60
  development of 324
  nucleus of 323
  other external policies, institutional separation from 325
  subjugation of Community to 328
common law
  Europe, of 413
community institutions
  agents of 51–2
  damage by, right to compensation 169
community law
  abuse of rights, doctrine of *see* **abuse of rights**
  authorities 417
  catholicity in approaches to 431
  common frame of reference 410–11
  developed system, operation of 68

direct effect 126, 329
Directives, use of 267–8
doctrinal analysis 426
domestic law, relationship with
  early cases 435
  ECJ case law, adapting to 436–8
domestic rules, interaction with 261
effectiveness 434
fundamental rights, inclusion of 125–7
harmonization
  common rules, agreement on 261
  convergence 408–9
  coordination of policies, and 408
  means of 407
  measures of 260
  Member States' laws, of 260
  radical use of 261
  techniques of 261
  use of term 407
heterogeneity of rules 432
Ireland, in *see* **Ireland**
Italy, in *see* **Italy**
judicial interpretation, plea for 338
law, influence of 66–7
legal review, mechanism of 433
legal science, 425
legal system, development of 228
literature on 416
multiple legal systems, addressing problems of 260
national courts, enforcement in 32
national judges, interpretation by 433–4
new directions 417
new legal order 329
open method of co-ordination 408
precise application of 433
primacy 126
regulatory acts, application of 432
review of 418
scholarship
  American parallel 421–4
  economics, influence on 423
  English, dominance of 428
  Europe's distinguishing features 427–30
  European scholars 424–30
  integrated community of 428–9
  interdisciplinarity 422–3
  political scientists, contribution of 419–21
  Research Assessment Exercise 430
  respect for 424–7
  systematization 427
  transformation in 415–16
  winds of change 417–19
special nature of 416
specificity of system 432
State responsibility for violations of 443

Index

supremacy 329
treaties, achievement of objectives of 416
uniformity of 409
Community Patent Court
    proposal for 45
competition
    abuse of dominant position 442
    agreements 442
    Court of First Instance, expertise of 44
    ECJ case law, adaptation to 441
    Ireland, litigation in 453–4
    undertakings 441–2
conflict of laws
    antisuit injunctions 391–3, 397–9
    Brussels Regulation, achievement of objectives of 385
constitutionalism
    democracy, views of 345–6
    European, limits of 350–3
    multilevel
        EC, within 348–50
        economic, top-down structures 343–4
        human rights, bottom-up structures 342–3
        international economic law, in 345–6
        restraints 340–2
contract law
    codification and legislation 403–6
    common frame of reference 410–11
    Community liability 400
    convergence 408–9
    foundations of 406
    group of experts 400–1
    harmonization and convergence 406–12
    open method of co-ordination 408
    Principles of European Contract Law
        preparation of 401
        rules, as 403, 406
    Rome Convention 265–6
    rules and principles of 401–3
Court of First Instance
    actions against acts of Community
        institutions, transfer of 41
    appeal court, as 40
    appeals from 43
        opinion in case of 26
    beginnings of 36–7
    case load 41–2
    competition cases, expertise in 44
    complexity of cases 42
    creation of 4
    decision creating 36
    development, direction of 37
    European Union Charter of Fundamental
        Rights, influence on case law of 162–3
    exceptional review of decisions 40
    future of 44–7

judgments, exceptional review of 24–5
judicial tasks, allocation of 38–9
maturity, reaching 41–4
review of operation 38
role, re-definition of 39
specialized courts attached to 40, 46
transfer of direct actions to 38–9

democracy
    constitutional, views of 345–6
Distance Marketing Directive
    application of protections, disagreement as to 278
    consumer protection measures 277
    country of origin 279–80
    enforcement of requirements 279–80
    financial services regulators, duties of 278
    imposition of rules 279
    maximum harmonization measure, as 276–7
    transitional measures 279
    UK law 280–1
dual-use goods
    authorities 354
    export of
        case law, lessons of 358
        CFSP decisions, implementing 360
        community control 356–7
        defective, regime being 360
        German law on controlling 354
        national regime, implementation of 358
        review of regime 357
        trade and foreign policy 326
        Werner and *Leifer* cases 354
    sanctions, reinforcement of 355–6

Economic and Monetary Union
    capital movements 301–2
    convergence criteria 304, 314
    counterfeiting, protection against 306
    Delors Committee Report 297–8
    differentiated integration 302–8, 319
    economic policy coordination 306
    economic union
        coordination and enforcement 314–19
        discretionary machinery 317
        excessive deficits procedure 314–16
        sanctions 318
    ECU, replacement by euro 308–10
    Euro Group, Protocol 306–7
    European Central Bank
        establishment of 299, 307
        fundamental monetary function 311
        Governing Council 313
        independence 312–13
        note, issue of 311

Index

Economic and Monetary Union (*cont.*)
   role of 311–14
   sanctions, imposition of 307
  European System of Central Banks
   creation of 299, 307
   exclusion of Member State from 307
   governors, term of office 313
  form of 297
  institutional structure, establishment of 300
  mechanisms for achieving 299
  monetary policy
   ECU, replacement by euro 308–10
   European Central Bank, role of 311–14
   exclusivity and independence 308–14
   national currencies, replacement by euro 310–11
  participating States 297
  public budgets, deciding 298
  single currency, introduction of 300
  single financial area, establishment of 299–300
  Stability and Growth Pact 317–19
  Sweden, treatment of 303
  Target 305
  UK and Denmark, special treatment 302–5
  Werner Committee 298–9
economic law
  internationalization 405
education
  lawyers, of 412–14
EFTA Court
  Advocates General
   dialogue policy 118–20
   functions of dialogue 120–2
   moral support from 121
   references to opinions 115–18
   role of 97–101
   substantive discussion with 111–15
  case law 91
  case load 90
  Community judiciary, dialogue with
   Advocates General, role of 97–101
   alcoholic beverages, private imports of 114
   case law, reference in ECJ 92–101 *see also* European Court of Justice
   clarification of case law in light of 109–11
   free movement of capital, as to 104–5
   functions of 120–2
   matter of course, as 122
   Motor Vehicle Insurance Directives, scope of 108–9
   mutual references 103–6
   policy of ECJ 118–20
   precautionary principle, definition and scope of 106–8
   reasons, differing 119
   reconsideration of jurisprudence in light of 106–9
   set-off arrangements 111
   state liability, as to 106
   tax credits, denial to shareholders in EEA countries 113
   trade mark cases 109–10
   withholding tax exemption for intercompany dividend payments 110–11
  ECJ rulings, taking account of 91
  EEA Agreement, interpretation of 91
  judges of 90
  model for 90
  potential competition, creation of 91
  seat 90
EFTA States
  internal market, extension to 90
  obligations of 90
EFTA Surveillance Authority
  obligations of EFTA States, monitoring 90
elections
  Gibraltar, in 142–3
Electronic Commerce Directive
  co-ordinated field 270
  country of destination 271, 273–4
  country of origin 271, 273
  freedom to provide services, reinforcement 272
  home or host state, no mention of 271
  internal market clause 270–5
  jurisdiction of courts, no impact on rules 275
  multiple legal systems, tackling problems of 276
  regulatory competence, interference with 275
EU Staff Tribunal
  creation of 34, 41
European Central Bank
  establishment of 299, 307
  fundamental monetary function 311
  Governing Council 313
  independence 312–13
  notes, issue of 311
  role of 311–14
  sanctions, imposition of 307
European Union Charter of Fundamental Rights
  binding force, lack of 157–8
  Constitutional Treaty, inclusion in 148
  ECJ judgments, in 134–5
  enforcement 133
  establishment of 132

EU constitutional law, as part of 168
European case law, influence on
  Advocates General, opinions of 163–4
  Court of First Instance, of 162–3
  ECJ, of 164–8
future legal status 158
good administration, right to 168–71, 174
growing interest in 134
imperative, as 133
influential effect of 158–68
institutional practice 162–3
inter-institutional case, reference in 148
interinstitutional agreement, as
  formal publication as 159
  institutional practice 162–3
  legislative practice 160–2
legislative practice 160–2
means of referring to 160
new rights enshrined in 170
Ombudsman, reference to 171
opinions, use in 134
proclamation of 147
scope of 147
social directive, lack of references in 161
status 133
test of compatibility with 159
treaties, inclusion in 157–9
European Code of Good Administrative Behaviour
aim of 133–4
European Community
English legal system, impact of 64–6
European Convention on Human Rights
adoption of 126
Communities not party to 139
European system, foundation of 155
European Union, accession by
  arguments against 150
  arguments for 149
  Charter, impact of 147–8
  current position 146
  effect on Court 153–4, 156
  key issues arising 151–2
  lack of competence 146–7
  scrutiny of activities of Union 155
  status quo, living with 152
France, ratification by 128
identification of fundamental rights, source for 128
jurisprudence, reconsideration of 129
legal space of Contracting States, operation in 140
states, application to 139
transferred powers, violations arising from 141
European Court of Human Rights
concerns of 139

effect of EU accession to ECHR 153–4
state's responsibilities, broad view of 139
system of protection 137
European Court of Justice
advocacy
  common law style 63–4
  impact of 61, 63–6
Advocates General *see* **Advocates General**
allocation of cases 55
antisuit injunction case in 393
appeals as to questions of law 50
appearing before, opportunities 49
authority and integrity, acceptance of 35
balance, alteration of 23
British Institute of International and Comparative Law, report of 39
busy administrator of justice, as 60
case law
  advocacy, impact of 63–6
  generations of 228
case load 229
CFI, appeals from 43
chambers, allocation to 55
changes, making 18–19
confidence in 35
consideration of case, stages of 16
direct actions 50
EFTA Court case law, reference to
  additional argument, reference as 101–3
  alcoholic beverages, private imports of 114
  ban on marketing of fortified foodstuffs, justification of 94–5, 107
  BSE protection measures, as to 95–6
  clarification of case law in light of 109–11
  development of border zone, German law on 97
  ethyl alcohol, import of 97
  free movement of capital, as to 96, 104–5
  functions of 120–2
  generically modified maize, case on release of 95
  matter of course, as 122
  Motor Vehicle Insurance Directives, scope of 108–9
  mutual references 103–6
  pharmaceuticals, repackaging 97
  policy of 118–20
  precautionary principle, definition and scope of 106–8
  reasons, differing 119
  reconsideration of jurisprudence in light of 106–9
  set-off arrangements 111
  state liability as part of EEA law 101–2
  state liability, as to 106

468 Index

European Court of Justice (*cont.*)
  succession of contracts, as to 92–3
  tax credits, denial to shareholders in EEA countries 113
  trade mark cases 109–10
  transfer of undertakings, as to 93
  withholding tax exemption for intercompany dividend payments 110–11
European Union Charter of Fundamental Rights, influence on case law of 164–8
evolution 47
exceptional review of CFI decisions 40
external relations law, as laboratory of 337
forms of proceedings 50–1
forum non conveniens case in 394–6
fundamental rights, protection of *see* **fundamental rights**
GATT/WTO treaty jurisprudence 375–8
internal organization 54
interventions by Member States 4–5
issues raised by 62
judges
  agent of justice, as 348–50
  choosing 13
  communications with 9
  consideration of case, stages of 16
  each Member State, for 11–12
  French, knowledge of 10
  independence 12–13
  oral discussion between 9
  private law litigation, experience of 396
  recruitment 10
  term of office 12–13
judgments
  improving 4
  quality and acceptability, increase in 6
  single 9
  technical excellence, aim of 4
  urgent cases, in 29–30
judicial tasks 34
  allocation of 38–9
jurisdiction
  expansion 33
  forms of proceedings 50–1
languages
  English, possible change to 19
  external dealings, of 5–7
  French, use of 10
  judicial deliberations, of 9
  oral hearing, of 7–8
  pleadings, of 57–8
  regime 6, 8–11, 56
legal traditions 56–7
litigants 51–4
litigating before
  challenge of 68–9
  UK courts compared 49
location of 35
locus standi see **locus standi**
national administrations and courts, close cooperation with 6
oral hearing
  advocacy, impact of 61, 63–6
  usefulness of 60–1
oral procedure 60–3
original judicial structure, inadequacy of 36–7
pattern of work 42
pending cases, drop in 38
pleadings 8
  access to 15
  contents of 15
  language of 57–8
  lodging, time limits 54
  subject matter of 55
  written 59
preliminary fact-finding by 55
preliminary rulings
  disadvantages of 74–5
  freedom, security and justice, in area of 25
  Italian Constitutional Court, use of procedure by 438–9
  judicial review, as alternative means of 74
  references 51
  success of procedure 429
  time taken for 29–30
  transfer of competence 45
  urgent procedure 29
  wait for, unrealistic 35
prepared speeches in 62
present challenge for 36
previous judgments, citing in 65
private law litigants, weight given to interests of 396
Procedural Committee 4
relationship of courts 46
Report for Hearing 58
Rules of Procedure
  alterations 4
  approval of Court for 15
  discretion as to 16, 19
  interpretation 15–16
  scope of 15
skeleton arguments 59
submissions
  impact of 62–3
  structure, content and delivery of 61
success of 35
suggestions from 58
translators and interpreters 6

users of jurisprudence 32
workload 4
written procedure 57–60
European Economic Area Agreement
aim of 90
interpretation of 91
regulation in breach of 331–2
European Monetary System
exchange rate mechanism 304
Mark II 304–5, 317
European Parliament
right to take part in elections to in Gibraltar 142–3
European System of Central Banks
creation of 299, 307
exclusion of Member State from 307
governors, term of office 313
European Union
common commercial policy 325–7
multilevel judicial trade governance in area of 350–3
restriction of scope 355
community of law 34
enlargement 3, 23
European Convention on Human Rights, accession to
arguments against 150
arguments for 149
Charter, impact of 147–8
current position 146
effect on Court 153–4, 156
key issues arising 151–2
lack of competence 146–7
scrutiny of activities of Union 155
status quo, living with 152
growth in 415
international agreements, conclusion of 323, 330
international human rights instruments, accession to 155
international organizations, membership of 323
judicial functions, allocation of 40
judicial restructuring 34–6
law *see* **community law**
legal order or 3
legislative and administrative competencies, use of 3
liability of 400
new judicial architecture 39–41
Nice Treaty 39–41
political tensions within 3
scope of 3
specialized courts 40, 46
treaties
EU institutions, policy preference of 377
external, internal direct effect 377

GATT/WTO trade agreements 375–8
implementation 378
third country, direct effect 376
external relations law
adaptation of 323
common commercial policy 325–7
multilevel judicial trade governance in area of 350–3
restriction of scope 355
Common Foreign and Security Policy
common positions, regulations implementing 333
complementary competences 359–60
development of 324
nucleus of 323
other external policies, institutional separation from 325
subjugation of Community to 328
continuity and change 324, 337
Court of Justice as laboratory of 337
development cooperation policy, delimitation of 329
development of 323
evolution of 336
foreign policy coordination 323
growth in 323
international agreements, conclusion of 323, 330
international law, effects of 329–36
trade and foreign policy
dual-use goods, export of 326
embargos 327
external policy 324–9
interaction 326
litigation as to 328
parallel development 325
Pillars, interaction between 328–9
unilateral decisions, and 327–8

financial services
authorization and prudential supervision 281–2
choice of law
cross-border activity, as to 262–4
Distance Marketing Directive 276–81
see also **Distance Marketing Directive**
EC Treaty 266–7
Electronic Commerce Directive 270–6
see also **Electronic Commerce Directive**
general directives 267–8
institutions, as to 264–5
private law sphere, in 262
Rome Convention 265–6
single market directives 268–70
traditional methods, rethinking 281

financial services (*cont.*)
  home country control 281
  private and public law, firms having regard to 262–3
  single market directives 268–70
  single market, accommodating
    Distance Marketing Directive 276–81
      see also **Distance Marketing Directive**
    EC Treaty 266–7
    Electronic Commerce Directive 270–6
      see also **Electronic Commerce Directive**
    general directives 267–8
    Rome Convention 265–6
    single market directives 268–70
forum non conveniens
  Brussels Convention/Regulation, cases under 393–6, 399
  common and civil lawyers, bone of contention between 394
  ECJ, decision of 394–6
free movement of goods
  foundation and consolidation of case law 230–3
  outer limit of case law 237
  political responsibility generation 233
  selling arrangements 237
  trailblazer, as 253–4
free movement of services
  abortion 250–1
  abuse of rights 206
  advertising case law 237–8, 250
  Article 49, judicial retuning 236–41
  balancing approach 232
  case law, generations of 228–9
  cold calling 255
  construction contracts 249
  continuity 259
  country of origin principle 258
  development of law 244
  establishment, and 245
  expansion of sector 229
  foundation and consolidation of law 230–3
  indirect taxation cases 239–40
  inherent restriction test 239
  internal market, place in map of 253–9
  Italy, in 443
  jurisprudential outer limit 241
  Keck, application of 238
  lawyers 232
  market access, principle of 255–6
  mixed activities 249–50
  moderation 232
  nationality or habitual residence, prohibition of restrictions based on 230
  other freedoms, relationship with 248–51
  patent agents 230–1
  provision, of 245
  public health requirements 232
  receipt of 252–3
  recurring cycles 241–2
  remoteness, concept of 256–7
  remuneration criterion 251–2
  repositioning in case of 240
  restrictive effect, relevance of 231
  skilled worker, of 258
  sporting events, selection rules for 239
  temporary 230
  temporary and permanent establishment 249
  Treaty provisions 244–6
freedom of establishment
  abuse of rights
    additional conditions, imposition of 211–12
    analysis of 227
    artifice to avoid tax, establishment as 214
    Danish legislation, avoidance of 210–11
    development of 207–8
    evolving scope of 213
    fraudulent conduct 217
    illegal 209
    imperative requirement, justification by reference to 213
    level of justification, analysis at 215
    motive, relevance of 221–4
    national company law requirements, avoidance of 210–11, 216
    pre-emption or justification 208–15
    presumptions 224–6
    proportionality 224–6
    right which is abused 215–20
    sickness insurance benefit scheme 210
    tax cases 212–15, 226
    tax regime, escaping 217
    Treaty rule, purpose of 215
  entitlement to restrict 226
  formal requirements, exercise in accordance with 223
  founders of company, of 218
  genuine economic activity, lack of 218
  Italy, in 443
  no economic integration, leading to 219–20
  restrictions, justification 225
  subsidiary, setting up 217–19
  tax-driven 221–2
fundamental rights
  Agency, creation of 162
  Charter see **European Union Charter of Fundamental Rights**
  Community law, construction of inclusion in 125–7
  Constitutional Treaty, impact of 136

domestic regimes, differentiation
    between 130
early lack of protection, effect of 126–7
elections, right to vote in 142–3
equivalent protection doctrine 140, 145
    European Court of Justice
    body of rights, discovering 129
    continued protection by 138
    Charter, reference to 134–5
    extension of jurisdiction 131–2
    protection, intervention in 125
fair hearing, right to 141
    Italian courts, cases against 388–9
future prospects 133–9
general principle of Community law,
    inclusion in 127
good administration, right to 168–71, 174
human dignity, to *see* **human dignity**
identification, source for 128
integral part of Community legal order,
    as 127
Joint Declaration as to 131
judicial Bill of Rights 127–30
Maastricht Treaty, provisions of 131
Masters of the Treaty 131–3
multilevel constitutional restraints,
    requirement of 340–2
national level, at 137
national measures of protection 129–30
reasonable time, judgment in 141
recent trends 133–9
supervision, Bosphorus Airways
    Case 143–6
Treaty of Amsterdam, provisions of 131
Treaty of Nice, provisions of 131
widening of scope of protection 129

Gibraltar
European Parliament, right to take part in
    elections to 142–3
governance
good, right to 168–71
modes of 408

human dignity
constitutional principle of 339
fundamental right, as 338
multilevel constitutional restraints,
    requirement of 340–2
respect for 339–40
human rights
case law, development of 152
Community legal order, protection in 426
constitutionalism, bottom-up
    structures 342–3
European judge as agent of justice
    348–50

founding Treaties, no reference in 126
good administration, right to 168–71, 174
guarantees for 154
human dignity, to *see* **human dignity**
individuals, empowerment of 339–40
indivisibility of 339–40
international market governance,
    consistency of 347–8
multilevel economic constitutionalism,
    top-down structures 343–4
treaties
    confidence in 369
    violations, protection against 369

insurance
Motor Vehicle Insurance Directives, scope
    of 108–9
intellectual property
infringement, cases in Italian courts 389
internal market
general approach 255
legal infrastructure 254
services, place of 253–9
international law
customary, norms of 331–2
status of individuals as legal subjects
    of 349
international organizations
constitutions 341
equivalent protection doctrine 140
European Union as member of 323
personality of 139
international public goods
collective supply of 341, 346
Ireland
Community law
    application of 460–1
    conflicts with 458–60
    courts, status in 451–4
    direct effect, acceptance of 451
    subordination to 446
    supremacy, acceptance of 451
competition litigation 453–4
conflict, resolution of 458
constitution 446–8
constitutional amendment 448–9
EEC, joining 447
EU membership, effect of 450
national implementing measures,
    constitutional scrutiny of 456–8
Single European Act, ratification of 447
sovereign independent state,
    becoming 446
State immunity 454
state liability, damages for 454–6
statutory levies, recovery of 453
unborn, right to life of 458–9

Italian Constitutional Court
   case law, assessment 440
   Community law and domestic law, relationship of
      early cases 435
      ECJ case law, adapting to 436–8
      preliminary rulings procedure, use of 438–9
      negative approach, basis of 439
Italian courts
   fair hearing, right to 388–9
   legal system 434
   rate of progress in 388–91, 397
Italian legal system
   Community legal system, relationship with 434
Italy
   Antitrust Authority 441
   competition law
      abuse of dominant position 442
      agreements 442
      laws 441
      undertakings 441–2
   establishment and services law 443
   judges, dialogue with EC judges 444–5
   remedies, adaptation of case law 443–4

judicial review
   constitutional justification 349–50
   intensity of 180–5
   justification, burden of 180–5
   preliminary reference procedure as alternative means of 74
   proportionality
      meanings of 176
      penalties 177–8
      rationality, and 177–80
      relevant considerations, manifest imbalance of 178–9
      rights or duties, infringements of 177–8
      situations in which employed 180–1
   rationality
      decision, of 179–80
      proportionality, and 177–80
      relevant considerations, manifest imbalance of 178–9
      situations in which employed 180–1
   reasonableness review, intensity of
      abuse of power 183
      anxious scrutiny 182
      constitutional right, identification of 182–3
      institutional capacity, lack of 184–5
      no latitude 183
      reformulation 181–3
   substantive
      preliminary questions 172
      single test for 172
      standards of 176–85
      unreasonableness test, abandonment of 186
      Wednesbury unreasonableness test 172, 181

languages
   Community, right to correspond in 169
   European Court of Justice, of *see* **European Court of Justice**
   European Union, of 3
   external dealings of Court, of 5–7
   official, growth in number of 5
   regional, authorization of use 161
legal profession
   specialized practice 53–4
   United Kingdom, in 53
litigants in person
   ECJ, before 52
locus standi
   individuals, of
      annulment action, for 75
      closed-category test 71
      comparison of tests 79–81
      concern, establishing 73
      consistent disagreement between ECJ and CFI 82
      customs classification regulation, annulment of 86
      EC Constitutional Treaty 83
      ECJ judgment in *Jégo-Quéré* 81–4
      economic reality, and 74
      effective protection, strict approach denying 73–4
      effective remedy, burden of providing 82
      identification 74
      individual concern, redefinition 74, 79, 81
      Jacobs, Advocate General, contribution of 71
      legislative measure, contesting 73
      liberalization, acceptance of 83
      narrow reading of individual concern 85, 89
      national courts, challenge in 75
      new test of 75–6
      post-*UPA* developments 84–6
      pre-*UPA* case law 71–4
      state aid proceedings 87–9
      strict approach, departure from 72
      test in *Jégo-Quéré* 77–9, 136
      UPA decision 74–7, 135–6
      validity of act being decision, contesting 72

Index

maritime law
  Belgian, de-codification 404–5
marriage
  Church, modernity of 167
measures having equivalent effect to quantitative restrictions
  Dassonville, applying basic principle in 192–204
  de minimis approach 201–2
  definition
    debate on 189
    early approaches 191–2
    Keck case 195–8
    path to *Keck* 192–5
    post-*Keck* 198–202
  dynamism of Community law 204
  examples of 194
  factual analysis 201
  imported goods, legislation fixing, 209
  justifications
    case law based 192–3
    mandatory requirements, under 190
    public policy grounds, on 194
    Treaty-based 190–1
  local-grab measures 201
  range of 203
  selling arrangement, concept of 198–200, 237
  trade between Member States, not regulating 200–1
Member States
  individual legal systems 260

national courts
  challenge to community measures in 75
  clarification of ECJ case law in light of EFTA jurisprudence 109–11
  community rights, protection in 76

patents
  Community 45
  Community Patent Court, proposal for 45
private law
  choice of law
    cross-border activity, as to 262–4
    Distance Marketing Directive 276–81
      see also **Distance Marketing Directive**
    EC Treaty 266–7
    Electronic Commerce Directive 270–6
      see also **Electronic Commerce Directive**
    general directives 267–8
    institutions, as to 264–5
    Rome Convention 265–6
  codification 404
  education in 412–14
  jurisdictional and choice of law problems, resolving 262

normative and judicial functions, redistribution of 406
open method of co-ordination 408
public law
  community law, influence of 66–7

Rome Convention
  choice of law under 265–6

self-governance
  protection of 349
services
  corporate activities, regulation of 258
  economic and financial 257
  economic importance 245
  education 251–2
  free movement *see* **free movement of services**
  growth and diversification of sector 246
  import and export of 248
  internal market, place in map of 253–9
  meaning 243
  persons, relationship with 257
  receipt of 252–3
  remuneration for 251–2
  right claimed, link with 252–3
  scope of
    factual 248–51
    personal 246–7
    private 247–8
    residual 246
    Treaty provisions 244–6
  Services Directive
    economic activities, change in 243
    excluded activities, list of 235, 241
    strange case of 233–6
  technological developments 243
state aid
  proceedings
    locus standi 87–9
    party concerned, status of 88
state liability
  EEA law, as part of 101–2, 106
Strasbourg Court *see* **European Court of Human Rights**

trademarks
  community 45
  dedicated court 44–5
  distinctiveness, assessment of 289
  EFTA Court case law 109–10
  equal treatment, principle of
    alternative approach 288–90
    borderline cases 294
    circumscribed powers, doctrine of 284–6
    comparison of slogans 293

trademarks *(cont.)*
  correct approach to 295–6
  decisions on 289
  descriptiveness, rejection on ground of 283
  grey area 294
  non-discrimination 285–6
  similar case, favourable decision in 291
  unlawful act, another applicant benefiting from 291–3
  examiners, discretion of 290–1
  international exhaustion of rights 112
  legal formalism 286–8, 295
  registration
    consistency of decision-making 296
    equal treatment, principle of *see* equal treatment, principle of above
    erroneous decisions, by 292
    lottery, as 295–6
    subjective element 287
  unequal treatment, instances of 285
treaties
  constitutions 342
  customary international law binding Community 332–3
  direct effect 376
  disputes 350
  domestic treatment
    Act of Transformation, use of 365–7, 371
    Chevron case principle 367
    deciding on 370–1
    default rule 371
    different treaties, for 367–9
    direct effect 365
    federal system, in 370
    general policy considerations 363–7
    local problems, norms ignoring 364
    means of 378–82
    monist and dualist countries 364
    non-monist effects 366
    policy and reality landscape 379–80
    policy landscape 363–72
    solutions 380–1
    status of norms 365
  subject matter, differential treatment of 368–9
  US and EU, problems faced by 378
  justiciability, concept of 367–8
  municipal or domestic jurisprudence, treatment in 361
  private party deriving rights from 332
  self-executing, jurisprudence 362–3
  United States, application in
    conflict with legislation 375
    constitutional status 374
    GATT/WTO trade agreements 373–5
    history of 372–3
    self-executing 373

United Nations
  Security Council
    excessive deference to 334
    resolutions, nature of 333

World Trade Organization
  Agreement 351
  Appellate Body, case law of 353
  Constitution 346
  dispute decisions 334–6, 351
  Dispute Settlement Understanding 335–6, 352
  EU jurisprudence, potential application in 362
  guarantees 351
  law
    direct effect, denial of 330
    judicial application 331
    reliance on 330–1
  move from negative to positive integration 347
  treaty
    Act of Transformation, use of 382
    constitution, as 381
    EU, application in 375–8
    European Court of Justice jurisprudence 375–8
    members 381
    size of 372
    United States, application in 372–5